by Candie Zenon

My Precious Wedding Gift by Candie Zenon
Published by Creation House
A Strang Company
600 Rinehart Road
Lake Mary, Florida 32746
www.creationhouse.com

Cover design by Mark Labbe

Library of Congress Control Number: 2006936888
International Standard Book Number: 978-1-59979-091-6

First Edition

08 09 10 11 12 — 9 8 7 6 5 4 3 2 1
Printed in the United States of America

CONTENTS

Dedication

To my daughters Eladria, Ashanti, and Imani, thank you for being the motivation that makes me persevere, "I press on toward the goal to win the prize for which God has called me heavenward in Christ Jesus" (Phil. 3:14).

Introduction

THE GREATEST LOVE story ever told was in John 3:16 (NKJV), "For God so loved the world that He gave His only begotten Son, that whoever believes in Him should not perish but have everlasting life." The greatest gift ever given was when Christ gave Himself on the cross for us. God went through great depths to preserve you for Him. On the cross Christ died for our spiritual, physical, and emotional well-being. He has dressed us in the finest of His Word for daily living.

Somehow we allow the words of others to detour us from our path of righteousness. We allow the pressures of the naysayers of the world, as well as our own unbridled will, to hinder our virtuous walk. Some of us set out to keep our bodies preserved for our vowed mates, while others of us did not know to do so. Thank God for the words of wisdom shared that, yes, testing times do come, but God's grace is sufficient. We can know that those who oppose our morals and standards are indeed our adversaries and we must immediately rebuke them!

A single woman's greatest prophecy is, "The Lord will bless you with a husband." But, what if He doesn't? Can you handle living for God wholeheartedly? Can you withstand the testing, trying times? Will you allow your flesh to fulfill its lustful desires?

In the thoughts of many, God turns His head when you sin—but He doesn't. This is why He says that everyone saying, "Lord, Lord," will not make it into heaven. (See Matthew 7:21.) Do not think you can just plan a wedding for safety's sake, for the first man that comes along. That is not playing safe; that is just playing "god." You place him in a tux and hurriedly give him the time and directions to the church, thinking you will soon have a husband. You might wind up with a husband, but not a God-sent mate. Besides, God knows your heart, so why go through that drama?

God knew of the testing times ahead for you. That is why He gave us an owner's manual—the Bible. The owner's manual instructs you on how to handle singleness, worries, anger, gossip, friends, family, spouse, parents, work, prayer, faith, and so much more. The Lord has seen your trial and He will send you a word of wisdom either through His voice, obedient servants, or His written Word. He has sent me to share my life's experiences and revelations with you.

We all share our "I wish I knew then what I know now" stories with our closest confidants. I wish I would have known how precious my virginity was, not only to me, but also to God. I now know that my body is truly the Lord's temple. When God says He is coming back for the church, He will not come to Earth to gather up a bunch of brownstones. He is coming for His people—those who are called by His name. (See 2 Chronicles 7:14.)

In 2 Samuel 6:6, the holy ark of God was being carried to its new home. Prior to David building a permanent home, Uzzah carried the ark of God on a cart pulled by oxen. For some reason, the oxen stumbled and Uzzah reached out his hand to keep the ark from falling. Right then God struck him dead. Six books prior, in Numbers 4:15, God gave Moses and Aaron clear instructions that only the sons of Kohath, from among the children of the Levites, had the authority to touch the ark. God said your body is His temple. He gave you clear instructions about the one who will have permission to touch you. Set your mind to preserving and protecting your body, the Lord's temple.

One

The Seeking

IT WAS EIGHT o'clock in the evening when I rushed to the mall to get an outfit. I arrived home about quarter after nine, hurrying to match accessories. Finally, I was ready: hair set, body set—get ready, here I go.

I walked into the club with a strut and found a seat close to the lights. I was determined to find my knight in shining armor. Instead, let me tell you what I did find: Mr. Pretty Boy, Mr. Ugly-&-Rich, and Mr. Cheap-&-Handsome. Mr. Pretty Boy approached me requesting a dance. I accepted because I already decided that tonight was not the night for chair dancing. We danced for a couple of songs, had a brief conversation, and then exchanged numbers. I knew by his sweater he was not "the one."

Soon after he left, the waitress came to me and said, "The gentlemen over there would like to know what you are drinking." I replied, "Blue Hawaiian." A few seconds later another waitress came over with some roses from the gentleman sitting by the dance floor. I could not believe it when two more bouquets from two more guys arrived, with more drinks and requests. I felt good when a guy in a black and blue suit walked by. I thought to myself, *I can't let this one go.* He was tall, dark, and had a face his momma and I could love. I gave myself a brief coaching session: *Candie, brace yourself—this could be your knight in shining armor.* Before I knew it, I stopped him and asked, "Excuse me, would you care to dance?" I was surprised when he replied with astonishment, "Why yes, I would love to dance."

That is the beginning of the story with Mr. Cheap-&-Handsome, but first let me tell you about Mr. Rich-&-Ugly. This was the brother who would go to the gift booth and buy all the vendor's gross little gifts just to let a woman know he has money. I danced two fast songs with him and thanked him. Then Mr. Rich-&-Ugly started talking fast, telling me what he could do for me…blah, blah, blah. Like the saying goes, "All that shines ain't gold." I politely excused myself from him and went to the ladies room. By this time, the club was going to be closing in forty-five minutes, and I knew I had to find the man in blue. Finally we met up and exchanged phone numbers, and at the same time, I gave a prayer to God in hopes that the man in blue (Mr. Cheap-&-Handsome) would call me bright and early the next day.

As I started to walk away, Mr. Rich-&-Ugly reappeared, begging for a breakfast date. Since I was hungry, I went ahead and accepted. We drove our own cars and met up at a nearby restaurant. The conversation was good, and his heart seemed to be in the right place, but it was time to call it a night.

The Morning After

At eight o'clock the next morning the telephone rang. I answered half awake, head hurting, voice a little bit hoarse, but just wanted to know who was calling.

"Hello, may I speak to Candie?" That was all I needed to hear. My smile went from ear to ear.

"This is she," I answered.

"Good morning, this is Pretty Boy. I was calling to see if you have any plans for today. Maybe we can get together before you leave for Dallas." Now this invitation was tempting, but I had a tight schedule. I was only visiting Houston for the holidays. I was residing in Dallas and had to return home for work on Monday. Yet, even so, this guy whom I called Pretty Boy would have made a nice date; I think considering the time he would not have been the right date. We talked for a while and I decided to call him back.

About an hour later the phone rang again. Finally, it was a date I could live with, the man in blue from last night. We decided to visit a local restaurant and then the mall. (This was where he received the name Mr. Cheap-&-Handsome). After we left the mall, we headed to a show for which he had purchased tickets earlier that morning. The show was nice and we did not want to call it a night, so we took the date to this very romantic park that had streams, waterfalls, and carriage rides. We just walked and talked like we had been friends forever. At the time, I had been debating whether I should move to Houston. Sitting there with him made me think I could probably get used to living in Houston.

Changing Over

One day Mr. Cheap-&-Handsome came over to my apartment. I explained to him that I would be having a couple over for dinner and movies. He told me, "I tell you what, I'll go half on the movies with you."

I said, "They're my guests; it's no big deal. Let's just go to the movie rental place."

We picked out our movies, and when the cashier told us how much it cost, Mr. Cheap-&-Handsome gave her a deer-in-the-headlights stare, so I paid with my own money. When we got outside Mr. Cheap-&-Handsome handed me one dollar, insisting that he was paying half. I looked down, thinking he must have dropped some money. He said, "Baby doll, what are you looking for? I only gave you a dollar." I just laughed and thought *He can't be serious.*

I had some business that needed to be attended to in Dallas, and since Mr. Cheap-&-Handsome and I had been dating for a while, we decided to use the drive as our first road trip together. I showed him the hot spots in Dallas and introduced him to my former roommates. Later we went shopping, and still he just window-shopped. Afterward, he treated me to dinner at a popular spot.

We found a nice hotel to settle in for the night. He paid all the expenses. (This worried me.) This was the first time we had spent the night together. I had never been in a situation like this before. I mean, I dated, but I never really understood what a physical relationship was. Besides, I pictured my first time being more romantic than shopping, dinner, and then a hotel. The sad part in my little master plan was that it did not include the idea of *marriage.*

I was brought up in the church and regularly attended Sunday school, Sunday morning service, Sunday evening service, mid-week service, and vacation Bible school, and I still ended up looking like and making the same mistakes as the unchurched. I didn't know I could actually take God's Word and apply it to daily living. I thought God was to be worshiped at a specific time and place while I took care of the rest of the week myself.

My Mom and I had an open-door relationship, although I have always felt she should have answered questions for me that I did not know to ask. Instead of just saying, "Get on birth control pills before you leave for college," I wish she would have told me the blunt facts about what my first time would be like. Maybe then I would have realized that I could never get back what I so casually gave away—that it was gone forever.

The Trip Home

The ride back to Houston was filled with conversation. After the two-hour drive, we had lunch and went to a movie, then we called it a day. When I walked into my apartment, I rushed to the phone and called my mom. I felt she had some explaining to do. She answered, "Hey baby, is everything OK?"

"Yeah, I'm OK. I just returned from Dallas," I said.

She asked, "Did you drive or did you ride the bus?"

"No," I told her, "I rode with Mr. Cheap-&-Handsome."

She said, "Oh, really."

I told her about what had happened the night before, but her response surprised me, and to this day it still rings clearly in my head. She paused and said, "I don't know whether to laugh or cry. My baby has lost her virginity." I do not even remember the rest of the conversation. I know now that we both should have cried because I was not married. This alone should have told me that the time was not right.

One day I prayed out to God, "Who are You? Who are You to me?" From that moment I started to see God in a whole new light and began to gain revelation from His Word. Those times when I felt strongly that I should go a certain way or follow my gut feeling was actually wisdom crying out.

> Wisdom calls aloud in the street, she raises her voice in the public squares; at the head of the noisy streets she cries out, in the gateways of the city she makes her speech.
>
> —Proverbs 1: 20–21

> Whoever listens to me [wisdom] will live in safety and be at ease, without fear of harm.
>
> —Proverbs 1:33

> And it is the [Holy] Spirit who bears witness, because the [Holy] Spirit is the Truth.
>
> —1 JOHN 5:6, AMP

God allowed me to see that He was there with me on a moment by moment basis, providing me the truth. Ultimately it will be my decision whether I choose His advice or my own will. In choosing my will over His I also choose the consequences of the decision.

> Since they hated knowledge and did not choose to fear the LORD, since they would not accept my advice, and spurned my rebuke, they will eat the fruit of their ways.
>
> —PROVERBS 1:29

It is strange how a relationship that starts in compromise continues to compromise. First it can be your morals, standard of living, upbringing, and then your God. I did not find wedded bliss with the man I like to call "cheap and handsome"; however, I did find a new sense of myself. I realized I did not want to live a life of compromise. Through life's trials, setbacks, and distractions I continue to gain a perspective of who I am. By having a keen insight of who I am, I will alleviate time lost with the wrong someone.

Two

The Meeting

I WAS NOT MARRIED, and I figured I still had several good dating years in me. But, what is a girl to do? At some point, you have to realize that you cannot give yourself to every man you date. The Bible teaches us to save ourselves for our avowed mate. If you start your marriage off right with God—the high priest, the Husband, with yourself as the helpmate—you will have a fighting chance.

The *Webster's Dictionary* definition of the word *monogamy* describes the practice of marrying only once during a lifetime.[1] Monogamy does not mean only sleeping with the person you are dating at any one time. Nor does the Bible teach you to only sleep with the person you are dating. It teaches you to only make love with your spouse. Proverbs 5:15–17 says, "Drink water from your own cistern, running water from your own well. Should your springs overflow in the streets, your streams of water in the public squares? Let them be yours alone, never to be shared with strangers." Anything outside of that is fornication. You are compromising your health and your eternal future. Ask yourself if his love is worth hell?

You cannot continue the cycle of collecting spirits. Each time you lay down with a man, your souls are bound together. In God's eyes, you are now man and wife, but in your eyes, he was just there for the night because you needed to be with someone.

Even though physically he may leave in the morning, his spirit will remain with you. You will take his spirit to your next physical dalliance, as well as the next and the next one after that. After he is gone, you find yourself in spiritual turmoil. Why? Because now, in the eyes of God, you are spiritually joined as one, and your half is longing to be with the other half.

You can win this spiritual battle with repentance! The only way to win is to repent of your sins, never to repeat the act of fornication again. Ask the Lord to purge you of yesterday's mistakes, to mend broken hearts and heal old wounds. Ask Him to create in you a new heart and mind of God.

With This Ring I Thee Wed

In the beginning, God stated, "It is not good for the man to be alone. I will make a helper suitable for him" (Gen. 2:18). God believes in marriage and in unity. When we read this verse we can see many views. First, we see that God desires a mate for each of us. Second, He will put them together, as described in the passage. Third, He desires that they be "suitable" for one another. And fourth, we see that it was not several mates that were made for Adam to choose from, but one specifically, because when God's hand is present, there is no need for man to intervene.

> Marriage should be honored by all, and the marriage bed kept pure, for God will judge the adulterer and all the sexually immoral.
>
> —Hebrews 13:4

Do not follow the common path and its "men are from Mars" mentality. Stay on the narrow path of the Lord, knowing that He brought all of creation into being. Just as He knows the number of hairs on your head, He also knows what you desire in your mate. Know that, "the reason you don't have what you want is that you don't ask God for it" (James 4:2, TLB). I suggest you pray for your mate, but when you pray, make sure you pray for the inner as well as the outer. Pray that he is a God-fearing man who will love you "just as Christ loved the church" (Eph. 5:25).

- If he loves you as Christ loved the church, he will respect you.
- If he loves you as Christ loved the church, he will pay his tithes.
- If he loves you as Christ loved the church, your bosom will satisfy him only.
- If he loves you as Christ loved the church, he will accept you for who you are.
- If you have kids, he will love your kids for being a part of you.

Pray that your mate walks in the authority God gave him, having dominion over all things on Earth and the ability to petition God in His ways. He will be a distinguished gentleman who is ready for any task placed in his family's way, and will be able to deal with life's trials with the strength of God.

> My grace is sufficient for you, for my power is made perfect in weakness.
>
> —2 Corinthians 12:9

Let's look at the Book of Exodus. In Exodus, we meet Moses who was called to do a mighty big task—deliver His people from Egypt. Exodus speaks of the mumbling and gripes and complaints he had to hear from the people when things did not happen as quickly or as smoothly as the Hebrews had hoped. Moses had to go home to his wife after a long day's work of petitioning Pharaoh. His wife Zipporah had to be a praying woman; a woman after God's own heart. She had to be prepared to pray for her man to encourage him and exhort him.

Learn to give what you expect to be given to you. Learn to listen when he needs you to listen and advise when he needs you to advise. Sow into him the love that you expect to reap.

Trusting the Relationship

We all go through that period of vacillation when we want to be saved, but do not know "how saved" we want to be. You know what I am talking about. We hope that God will allow us the occasional "club moment." But trust me, you will not find your God-sent mate in a bar. Besides, when the Lord is ready to send you someone, He will not need your help. God is God all by Himself. When you find someone on your own, you just end up interfering with God's plan for you. You cause Him to be unable to advance you in His Word because you are trapped in a relationship that hinders your spiritual growth and blinds you to the gift He has for you—your destined mate.

Sometimes we allow relationships to trap us in a land of confusion. The Book of Genesis explains that God wanted to bring Abram to the Promised Land. During the journey from Ur to Canaan, Abram's father became tired and weak in health, so they set up camp in Haran, even though Haran was not the Promised Land.

I realized I was stuck in a Haran of my own with Mr. Cheap-&-Handsome, and unless I did what the Bible told me, I would never reach my Canaan. When a relationship requires you to lower your standards or throw away your morals, it is not of God! In the natural world, we are taught that two is company and three is a crowd, but in the spiritual realm, three is company—the Father, the Son, and the Holy Spirit.

Before you involve yourself with anyone, ask yourself if it seems like God can be a part of that relationship. If you feel in your spirit that the answer would be no, you will need to cut ties as quickly as you can. Notice in Genesis when God told Abram to pack and go, he did not know where he was going, but he did take familiar people with him. That included his cousin Lot. They set off together, but they eventually had to agree to go their separate ways, because there was confusion between Abram's people and Lot's people.

It is always good practice to *let go and let God*. In order to get where God needs you to be, you should evaluate your surroundings. If it takes cutting ties with those who do not respect you or your beliefs, let them go. There will always be people around you who are unwilling to grow up with you. That is when you have to trust God to place positive people in your path.

> Cursed is the one who trusts in man, who depends on flesh for his strength and whose heart turns away from the LORD.
>
> —JEREMIAH 17:5

If He Makes You Happy, Why Are You So Sad?

We have all read the scripture about not being unequally yoked. In order to plow the fields back in biblical times, two oxen of the same strength were placed on one yoke. In order to get the field plowed, both oxen needed to work in the same direction. Thus, if you are going in one direction and your mate in another, you perpetually will be at odds. Being equally yoked does not simply mean that he goes to church or that he is the same religion as you. It means his relationship with Christ is rock solid:

> But that you may live in a right way in undivided devotion to the Lord.
>
> —1 Corinthians 7:35

Being equally yoked is being like-minded and having the same desires and wants of life. If you desire to be an entrepreneur but your prospective mate desires to work at one job the rest of his life, or if you love the outdoors but end up with someone who loves the indoors, one of those desires will overpower and lead, and someone will be left unhappy.

We all stand on the shore waiting for the best ship to come in. We think it carries the precious cargo of compliments, love, peace, income, and the answer to loneliness. Let me tell you something, if you do not have an intrinsic sense of self, you will never be happy. You cannot look for a man to make you complete. You have to be complete for a man to look for you. Our Bible teaches us, "He who finds a wife finds what is good" (Prov. 18:22). Pay yourself a few compliments; know your strengths and weaknesses. You do not need a man to point them out to you.

When David went to Saul, he went with a goat and a bottle of fine wine. He knew not to go to a king empty-handed. Stop worrying about what your mate might be bringing to the table, and start talking about what you are presenting to your lord. I say *lord* because in Song of Solomon the woman referred to Solomon, her mate-to-be, as her lord. You cannot go to your lord empty-handed. Bless your lord with gifts, not with burdens.

Never fall into the trap of cohabitation. If he is worth living with, marry him. Every girl wants the fairy tale of love, marriage, and the baby carriage—who is he not to want that for you? Cohabitating is nothing but a high cost for low living. If it is taking you a long time to marry him, maybe he is Mr. Available, and not Mr. Right.

Three

Learning About Him

It has been said that life is 10 percent what happens to you, and 90 percent how you choose to respond. Your responses can cost you a lifetime of either pain or happiness. Maybe you are divorced or, like me, you lost your virginity before you were married. You now have to reclaim your virginity—thank God we serve a God of second chances!

Your flesh desires what it knows, but you can repent and ask God to cleanse you. In your moment of weakness, His strength is made perfect in you. That is why He says, "Greater is he that is in you, than he that is in the world" (1 John 4:4, KJV). It is not by your own strength that you will achieve what you set out to do, but by His. Discipline and obedience are spirits we have to pray for because we were born into sin and shaped in iniquities. Pray for discipline and obedience to God's will. Do not place yourself in a position that would trip you up.

If a prospective mate invites you to the movies, make sure it is at the theater and not a DVD at his place. Speak up! Let a guy know where you are coming from and where you are not willing to go. Your body is your temple and the Holy Spirit can't dwell in an unclean temple. You have to guard your gates. The enemy will try to storm your temple through any unguarded gate. Your gates are your five senses, taste, touch, sight, smell, and sound.

> Then God said, "Let us make man in our image, in our likeness, and let them rule over the fish of the sea and the birds of the air, over the livestock, over all the earth, and over all the creatures that move along the ground."
>
> —Genesis 1:26

> The Lord God formed the man…from the dust of the ground and breathed into his nostrils the breath of life, and the man became a living being.
>
> —Genesis 2:7

God states that we shall have dominion over all the earth. You have the power to speak to your urges and they have to obey and subside. That is your God-given power. "Resist the devil, and he will flee" (James 4:7). Why, you ask, will the devil flee? He will flee because he was cast to the earth from heaven and now creeps around the earth. God said that you have dominion over every creeping thing on the earth!

My mother told me a long time ago that life is a long, crooked road where we sometimes fall when the curves get too sharp. Yet there is always a way to get back up, even if it's just to benefit someone who loves you. There will be times when you won't love yourself. You just have to keep the faith, no matter what. There are a lot of devils in this world that will lead you in the wrong direction. So, please, be strong and do what is right, even if it means standing alone. Remember—you are never alone when God is in your heart.

Dress for Success

If you are not yet dressed for where you are going, change your garments. Ruth 3:3 says, "Wash and perfume yourself, and put on your best clothes." Your best is God's very best. Romans 13:14

says, "But put on the Lord Jesus Christ, and make no provision for the flesh, to fulfill its lusts" (NKJV).

Let it be known that you are what you attract. If you still attract what you once were, then that spirit still lingers around you and has found a comfort zone in you. You need to cleanse yourself of it. Pray to God for anything that is not of Him or is not pleasing to Him to be taken out, and let Him shape and mold you into His image.

I was thinking recently that maybe our iniquities have a lot to do with us being made from dirt. What I mean is, when you think of dirt, you think of something as "dirty." God responded to my thoughts, telling me that nothing made from dirt has anything to do with my iniquities. He said He chose that material to create us because it was easy to shape and mold. Now I understand better what pastors mean when they say we are clay in the Potter's hands. When we put on the Lord Jesus, God will reconstruct us from the inside out. We will no longer have that profane speck, and even our walk will be brand new.

I have lived in an apartment most of my adult life. Each time I leased an apartment, the manager would tell me the "make-ready crew" had to come and steam clean the carpet and paint the walls before I could move in. That reminds me of how God says He will not leave us alone, but will send us a comforter. The Holy Spirit is sent to dwell in you to prepare you for eternity, similar to the "make-ready crew's" preparations. God's Spirit is there to counsel you, convict you, purify you, and purge you of yesterday's fears, pains, habits, insecurities, and desires. Now your desire is to please the new Tenant.

Identify with your singleness and get yourself emotionally healed. Now that you know Christ, edify yourself with His Word. That is simply reading and meditating on what you have read. Jesus told a woman caught in the act of adultery, "Go and sin no more" (John 8:11, NKJV), meaning this day is a new beginning; your past can no longer hold you accountable. The slate was wiped clean, so a renewing of the mind has taken place as we have learned that all old things have passed away.

> Do not conform any longer to the pattern of this world, but be transformed by the renewing of your mind.
>
> —Romans 12:2

You've Got Mail

With the renewing of your mind, you should now be about kingdom business. First Corinthians 7:34 says, "An unmarried woman or virgin is concerned about the Lord's affairs: Her aim is to be devoted to the Lord in both body and spirit." Start by finding out what your spiritual gifts are. By using your spiritual gifts, the body of Christ can be edified to serve at its fullest potential. Pray and ask God where He would have you serve. It is normally right there in front of you, but sometimes we need a little help. It is usually the passion or desire you have, but the enemy tells you that you cannot do it, that you will fail, or that the saints will laugh at you. Where the enemy fights you the most is the thing at which you will be the greatest.

Do not sit around using all your "single" time praying for a mate. There is too much work to be done. Stop searching for the perfect mate on the Internet. God did not tell you to hit the search button for love—love is not something you download! God will meet your deepest need, filling the void of loneliness. He created you and He knows what is inside you. God knows you and is in every way capable of giving you what you need. But, to whom much is given much is required. (See Luke 12:48.)

Take care of yourself—you cannot ask for a muscle-bound man when the only iron you see is a fork. Have a sense of self-worth, self-love, and self-value. Do not be self-centered, but be self-knowing while centered on God's love. Know your worth in God. He loved you so much He came here, died, and rose for you. Proverbs 31:10 says that your value is worth far more than rubies. Hear the Proverbs 31 woman say, "She is clothed with strength and dignity; she can laugh at the days to come" (Prov. 31:25).

I know it is now hard to face the reality that no man on a white stallion or driving up in a Bentley is going to take you to your "once upon a time" fairy tale. For so long, we as girls have been taught that Prince Charming will come to save the day. But ladies, I have good news. Our day was saved by the King of kings and the Lord of lords. The price was paid and everything we need is in Christ Jesus.

First Peter 5:7 says, "Cast all your anxiety on him because he cares for you." Psalm 37:25 says, "I have never seen the righteous forsaken or their children begging bread." Know that the Lord will provide for the assignment that is on your life. If you say you need a car, the Lord will provide. Even if He has not given you a car yet, He has probably provided a ride for you in the form of bus tokens or healthy legs to walk. The job you have may not be a dream job, but you are not in the unemployment line. You might say, "Every time I get the check, it's spent before I can deposit it." This only means that you have thirty more days with lights, thirty more days with a phone, or thirty more days that you are not homeless. The Lord is providing, so thank Him.

Sure, your Boaz may come, but if he comes now you may not be able to handle him. The Lord wants to make sure you are first conditioned to know that your help comes from Him, the Lord. If you still think marriage has at best a fifty-fifty chance to succeed, you will only present yourself as half of 100 percent.

Then, when you get in the marriage with your needy spirit, the man might soon realize the only thing he needs to conquer with you is a begging, borrowing, pleading, needy person who can be satiated by casting you a few dollars. Then soon the realization will hit that you are not a challenge but a servant.

What happens at a restaurant if you cannot pay your bill? You wash dishes to pay your debt; and you were not able to enjoy the meal presented to you.

> The rich rule over the poor, and the borrower is servant to the lender.
>
> —Proverbs 22:7

Four

ENGAGEMENT

A person's a person, no matter how small.[1]

—DR. SEUSS

UNFORTUNATELY IT IS after the fact that we recognize the voice of wisdom that forewarned us, and we wonder how different things would have been if we had listened. That time has passed, and we cannot torment ourselves with yesterday's decisions, but we can make the best of today. If your decision has left you in a single-parent situation, know that God placed each baby on Earth for a reason. Each life has a purpose. Just think, if Mary the mother of Jesus had decided she could not have her baby because of what people might think, today she would have a veritable buffet of options from which to choose to end her pregnancy. Cold, clinical medical terms such as embryo, zygote, and fetus can make the choice in favor of an abortion artificially easier. But, being taught that it is merely tissue and not yet human does nothing but attempt to remove the truth from the decision.

Even though today you can get rid of a baby in a matter of seconds, it will be the emotional torment that lingers forever. That emotional healing is a lifetime process. The tormented second-guessing is a side effect left unmentioned by the physicians, nurses, politicians, and the radical elements that influenced the Supreme Court to define an abortion as nothing more than a "choice." Our Lord knew the dark side of that rainbow painted by the world. He told you to save yourself for marriage, and to not be unequally yoked. He said that not to hurt you, but because He knows what lies ahead.

> Train a child in the way he should go, and when he is old he will not turn from it.
>
> —Proverbs 22:6

You have an assignment to nurture your child's emotional, physical, and spiritual well-being. You have to be an intercessor and pray on your child's behalf that all generational curses are reversed from his or her life. Your baby is observing you. He or she is waiting to be held and loved by you. That child is longing to have a conversation with you. You should be the first example of what love is. You should be the first in line to nurse the wounds and kiss them to make it all better. You should be the one to wipe their tears, not place them there.

Spend time with your kids. Sometimes we think if we cannot get the tickets to the coolest shows or purchase the newest computer game we have somehow failed our kids. Kids do not even remember the hottest game, but they do remember Momma tickling them, singing to them, or playing games with them. My favorite pastime was being lifted up and down with my mom's legs. She gained muscle and I had a blast. Sometimes it takes just rolling on the floor with your kids or asking them how their day was. That question will give you quite an earful.

Being a full-time parent is not easy. Joint custody or single parenting is a further strain. Whatever the situation is, do not belittle the child's father. Do the best you can do as a mother.

If the child's father is not active in the child's life, seek mentor programs for your children such as Big Brothers Big Sisters of America, the Boys & Girls Clubs of America, or seek out church organizations that offer alternatives.

When dealing with the financial aspect, it can be disappointing when child support arrives late or does not come at all. But that child cannot take on adult problems nor give answers to the lack of responsibility of the absent parent. I believe you should never tell the child what is going on behind the scenes. That child might grow up and tell you what is going on better than you can explain it. Children observe. They recognize the struggles, but they do not always put things into grown-up words, such as "I appreciate what you do." Each time they bring home a good report card, clean their room, or tie their own shoes, they are trying to tell you, "Hey, I see what you do," and, "Let me help, this is the only way I know how."

Because the Bible teaches you that you will have to give an account for every idle word that departs from your lips, you must speak life over your child. They will be better off because of it, and there will be fewer idle words departing from your lips that you will be held accountable for.

> Praise the LORD. Blessed is the man who fears the LORD, who finds great delight in his commands. His children will be mighty in the land; the generation of the upright will be blessed. Wealth and riches are in his house, and his righteousness endures forever.
>
> —PSALM 112:1–3

Know that seeds planted will take root and bare good fruit in harvest if good seeds were planted. God has willed that a righteous person's seed will be blessed generation to generation. They will be strong and wealthy. That is why Satan tries so hard to attack the seed. If he can attack the seed of the righteous, he can damage several generations to come. Your decision now, can affect a generation later.

The Interviewing Process

A company has a position available. You think it could be your dream job so you request an interview. You know that you are skilled and educated and could be the best candidate for the job. You wonder if that job is the best thing for you, so you arm yourself with questions for the interviewer. What duties are required for this position? What are the hours? What are the benefits? Is there a 401(k) plan?

> The LORD said to Satan, "Where have you come from?" Satan answered the LORD, "From roaming through the earth and going back and forth in it."
>
> —JOB 1:7

The devil is going back and forth looking for unguarded gates through which to gain entry. There is no time for religion, but there is always time for a relationship with Christ. Plant His Word in you, let it sprout roots, and allow its branches to produce wisdom, knowledge, and discernment in you.

When a man shows up in his church suit, carrying his Bible on Sunday morning, but then on Sunday night he asks to spend the night, you can take him for who he really is. He will turn out to be nothing but a delay in your blessings from God. Do not excuse his behavior as just him "being a man." These days there are men telling women, "I'm not going to hell for you," and if they are not going to place themselves in a situation that will trip them up, you should not either.

God will always send someone who is headed in the same

direction as you. You just have to be patient and wait on the Lord.

> Do not be anxious about anything, but in everything, by prayer and petition, with thanksgiving, present your requests to God.
>
> —PHILIPPIANS 4:6

If you spend time improving yourself, studying, working out, getting your hair styled, and having a manicure and pedicure every week so you can look good and "catch a man," then why in the world would you allow someone to present themselves to you half done? Why would you ever accept the man who has no job? Or a man who is "going" through a divorce but never actually gets the divorce, is behind in his child support, and has a car that is so old it is not even listed in the *Kelly Blue Book*? Why would you allow any man to present himself to you who says, "We can take care of each other," when that is just code for, "Can you give me a place to stay, and something to eat, and possibly let me drive your car so I can go hang out with the fellas?"

The day you confessed that Jesus Christ was your Lord was the day you gave God permission to perform His plan for your life. Know that God has a plan for your life. (See Jeremiah 29:11.) Do you really think in the Creator's plan He would leave out a mate for you when He was the One who said it is not good for man to be alone? (See Genesis 2:18.) Ezekiel 40:6 says God's plan for your life is so precise it can be measured.

> For you created my inmost being; you knit me together in my mother's womb. I praise you because I am fearfully and wonderfully made; your works are wonderful, I know that full well. My frame was not hidden from you when I was made in the secret place. When I was woven together

> in the depths of the earth, your eyes saw my unformed body. All the days ordained for e were written in your book before one of them came to be. How precious to me are your thoughts, O God!
>
> —Psalm 139:13–17

You are God's *precious gift*. He carefully knitted you in your mother's womb and placed a plan for you before the foundations of the Earth. He desired above all things that you prosper and be in good health (3 John 2), whether it is spiritual, relational, or financial. Your well-being is His concern. On the day of your wedding your husband will receive this precious gift—*you*—a woman who knows who she is, where she came from, and where she is going.

We Louisiana folks have our own interviewing process. We ask, "Who's your peoples?" We get that out of the way first, because if we know you are coming from a certain clan, then we already know things will not work out. As we say in Louisiana, "When you take the man, you take the clan." A man's family background says a lot about him, such as which generational curses you might face or what is socially acceptable to his family and him. When we go to family functions, we work that family get-together like we are campaigning for an election seat. Then, inevitably, we run into the cousin who has been waiting to talk to us all evening so he can tell all the family stories. At a later date, we deliver a sweet potato pie to his mom and pops to see how they act without their holiday happy faces.

Through these chores like ours in Louisiana, you will be able to discern if your prospective mate is truly saved, sanctified, and set apart. Remember, the choice will be left up to you. You cried too many tears. You stayed slain at the altar for too many Sundays to start over. Remember that God allowed you to confess and believe that He is Lord, and that He gave you the power.

> Then the LORD said to Moses, "Why are you crying out to me?... Raise your staff and stretch out your hand over the sea to divide the water."
>
> —EXODUS 14:15–16

Take up your staff and separate the good from the bad. Ask yourself if you have another two, five, or ten years to give to a relationship in which you are trying to change your mate. A man is raised. Do not be deceived, because what you see is what you get. His parents sent him out all grown up by now, so he should be prepared to handle the responsibility of a job and a family. Who are you to think that you will change him? Are you saying that you are greater than his Creator, the Lord God? If your future spouse does not line up with the Word of God let him know that his application is denied, and the position remains posted. You do not have to go looking for your mate. Just be in a position to be found. The Lord will send the right applicant on his way.

No More Fairy Tales

The damsel in distress is better left to the movies. Thank God for His Word, that in it we not only learn daily living, but we also learn how to greet, meet, and marry our Boaz! We love the story of Ruth meeting this great kinsman redeemer, but somehow we missed the part when Ruth asked for his hand in marriage. Ruth was a woman of noble character who gained a spirit of wisdom from the mother of her deceased husband. She attached herself to Naomi, learning from her who God was and is to Naomi and her people. Ruth wanted to follow that God: the God of the Israelites, the God of power, the God of Abraham, Isaac, and Jacob.

One day, Naomi asked if she needed to help her find a home. Ruth listened to the wise woman. For, when we hear with a listening ear, we can apply all that is good. Simply living life does not compare to learning from the life that has been lived. We can all benefit from someone who has been there, without rejecting teachings because we have a know-it-all attitude. With that sort of attitude, you will miss the mark and have to start over all due to missed or ignored teachings.

Ruth of the Moabites knew who she was, where she came from, where she was going, and what she wanted. When she applied all she was taught by Naomi, she left prepared. With the right acquired knowledge, we can go after that desired college, job, or dream house. The application of knowledge will work for you. In Ruth's case, she was going after her desired mate, Boaz.

Ruth was told to wash and perfume herself and put on her best garments. Then she went to get her Boaz. She already knew who he was, what he was, and where he would be, because she consulted with wisdom (Naomi).

> "Who are you?" he asked. "I am your servant Ruth," she said. "Spread the corner of your garment over me, since you are a kinsman-redeemer." "The LORD bless you, my daughter," he replied.
>
> —RUTH 3:9–10

He went on to tell her that he would do all that she asked, which meant that he had accepted her proposal. The Book of Deuteronomy says that a kinsman can marry a deceased kinsman's wife to provide an heir. That is why Ruth referred to Boaz as the kinsman's redeemer.

To signify covering and protection in the Hebrew custom, a man will place a corner of his shawl over a lady as a show of a vowed commitment.

> He who finds a wife finds what is good and receives favor from the LORD.
>
> —PROVERBS 18:22

This is not a license to women to play hide-and-seek with their destined mate. God may place in your heart a person of interest. Just as Ruth washed, allow God to take your black soul and wash it in his red blood to make your soul white, and cleansed of your past. Next, perfume yourself. This is asking the Holy Spirit to fall fresh on you, guide you, direct you, and counsel you. Always listen to the counsel and the convictions of the Holy Spirit. Then, put on your best garments. Your best garments are God's very best, as we learned in the Book of Romans, "put on the Lord Jesus Christ, and make no provision for the flesh, to fulfill its lusts" (Rom. 13:14, NKJV).

Let your petitions be known to God. He will show you the person He has ordained for you. As Ruth found favor in Boaz's sight long before she noticed him as "the one," so God will set the stage for favor. Your ordained mate may know long before you that you are "the one," but may not feel the timing is right and may refrain from approaching you. This is similar to Boaz having known that Ruth had recently been widowed. Since he honored and respected the fact that she cared for her mother-in-law, he wanted to make sure he took care of her, too. He allowed her to get the good grain of the harvest and not the leftovers that were reserved for the less fortunate.

> Who can find a virtuous wife? For her worth is far above rubies. The heart of her husband safely trusts her; So he will have no lack or gain.
>
> —PROVERBS 31:10–11, NKJV

A wife should be a model of excellence to a man. That word *virtue* does not just refer to martial fidelity. It refers to her being honorable and noble—a woman of wisdom. A married woman carries her husband's name. Her character should mirror his. In Proverbs 31, King Lemuel's mother speaks of a married man being praised by the community because of his wife, and the confidence he has knowing that she brings him good and no harm. Boaz knew that Ruth's worth was far more than rubies. Boaz's outward demonstration of favor was a representation of the greater act yet to be demonstrated by God himself. God had shown favor on Ruth. She was soon to play a part in the messianic ancestry. Boaz and Ruth bore a baby that became the ancestor to King David, and then to the promised Messiah.

Five

WEDDING BELLS

Oh, what a tangled web we weave, when first we practice to deceive.[1]

—SIR WALTER SCOTT

A gossip betrays a confidence; so avoid a man who talks too much.

—PROVERBS 20:19

DO YOU REALLY and truly know the power your tongue possesses? The Lord says you can speak blessing or curses. Everything in existence happened by His spoken word. God spoke light into darkness, fish into the sea, beasts onto the earth, and water to separate from the sky. If you are speaking to a person or situation, you are speaking life or death.

You can be aborting and killing your blessings with the words of your mouth. Sometimes, you can get to talking for too long and you start lying. Then, when you run out of lies, you start telling secrets entrusted to you. So shut your mouth! Try to find some type of outlet to vent. Tell God in a prayer or in a letter. Sometimes when I do not have the words to say, or do not want to say the words I have, I just start humming like Big Mama used to. In the old-school church, Big Mama used to just hum.

Nobody knew what was on her mind, but everyone could relate, because tears would start welling up in her eyes and roll down her cheeks. The women of the church would start screaming, and then say, "Thank you Lord. Thank you Lord." It was as if the Holy Spirit had spoken to their souls and told them, "It's OK. While you were over there humming, I was over there translating. And God told me to inform you, it has already been worked out."

Tangled Webs Woven in the Family

I know that when the subject is family, you think because you are kin it is OK to talk about another person's trials, tribulations, and setbacks. An elder, or someone who has experienced what those other family members are going through, should call that kinsman and share with them their similar experience. If you know a stove is hot, will you allow your child to touch it? Of course not, and you are similarly responsible for your other relatives. If you are made aware of their situation, it is not for your entertainment, but for you to have the opportunity to give God glory. He will get the glory! In everything that has happened to you, God had more than you in mind.

> Do not spread false reports. Do not help a wicked man by being a malicious witness.
>
> —Exodus 23:1

He knew that one day the conversation of so-and-so was going to come to you. Now you can gladly share what happened to you and how the Lord brought you out. You will be able to share that, though the other person may walk through the valley of the shadow of death, they do not have to fear evil. (See Psalm 23:4.) If you are walking through, that at least means that you are still alive and are headed to the other side. For every valley low there is a mountain high, and the appearance of the shadow is larger than the actual circumstances.

Maybe there is a problem between two relatives. One calls you to vent, but you cannot take one side over the other when there are two people involved. To every question there is an answer, and who better to answer the question than the accused. Inform that person that you are willing to listen only as a mediator between the two. In the Old Testament, the accuser had to go to the accused in the presence of two elders. Thus, once the issue is resolved, be sure to leave it there. Do not call the rest of the family to tell them what they missed. Just let sleeping dogs lie.

What if you are the one being accused? Handle it the same way: confront your accuser in the presence of two trustworthy persons of wisdom. If your accuser lies, speaks negative words against you, and slanders your character behind your back, just listen to the Word of the Lord, saying "No weapon formed against you shall prosper," (Isa. 54:17, NKJV), and "Touch not mine anointed, and do my prophets no harm" (Ps. 105:15, KJV). You do not have to answer or justify their lies. You cannot change anyone. Just know that the Creator will deal with His creation.

Tangled Webs Woven in Friendships

What about those so-called friends? First and foremost, know who your friends are. Everyone smiling and grinning and having conversations with you are not necessarily your friends. Some are waiting to covet what you have. Some are waiting to find out what they can find out about you so they can go back and report to other depressed, miserable women. Some are trying to get close to you to imitate and duplicate you because they have not yet defined who they are.

> But mark this: There will be terrible times in the last days. People will be lovers of themselves, lovers of money, boastful, proud, abusive, disobedient to their parents, ungrateful, unholy, without love, unforgiving, slanderous, without self-control, brutal, not lovers of the good, treacherous, rash, conceited, lovers of pleasure rather than lovers of God—having a form of godliness but denying its power. Have nothing to do with them. They are the kind who worm their way into homes and gain control over weak-willed women, who are loaded down with sins and are swayed by all kinds of evil desires, always learning but never able to acknowledge the truth.
>
> —2 TIMOTHY 3:1–7

Be careful with whom you spend your time, because you are identified by the company you keep. Your surroundings are your habitat and your habitat dictates your behavior. If miserable people are around you, you will be miserable. It is very true that misery loves company. Ask God to reveal the hearts of your company. You can be certain that not everyone is praying you up. Some ladies will swear they are the best friend you will ever have, but if you check those daggers in your back for fingerprints, you will be able to identify them as belonging to your "friend." Some of them might be the ones who were supposed to be your prayer partners, but each time you pray together you end up hearing your prayer from someone that was not even in the room. God already knew they were coming. That is why He said, "and such you should stay away from" (2 Tim. 3:1–7). They mean you no good.

The King James Version of the Bible refers to that type of women as "silly women," which means they have not yet learned, and that they are too full of sin, which makes them wicked. We learn in Proverbs 1:7 that the wicked despise knowledge. *Webster's*

Dictionary defines the word *silly* as lacking in common sense and judgment, foolishness.[2] If you are taught to seek wise counsel, you must recognize that a silly woman will give you the opposite. She wants you to give up heaven for the world. She wants you to give up your dreams, your desires, your ideas, and your enthusiasm.

Because she cannot find her way in the world, she keeps stumbling and falling. That is why every time you speak with her in faith and sharing your long-term goals, she tells you, "You may want to think that one through." Why? Because she sat and thought about her life, and she came to the conclusion that, "This is the way it is, and this is the way it will always be." But she does not want to be alone. Her agenda leads her to attack your dreams in the hope that she can force you to sit back and be left behind like her.

If you cannot let go of a taunting friendship, chances are you are trying to be defined by that relationship. Stop trying to be defined by other people.

> Do you not know that the wicked will not inherit the kingdom of God? Do not be deceived: Neither the sexually immoral nor idolaters nor adulterers nor male prostitutes nor homosexual offenders nor thieves nor the greedy nor drunkards nor slanderers nor swindlers will inherit the kingdom of God.
>
> —1 CORINTHIANS 6:9–10

Christ has already defined you. He tells you that He has adopted you into His family. He said that He has made all things known to you. He said that He has given power to you, and whatever you ask in His name will be given to you because He will go to the Father on your behalf. Seek the Lord's definition of you in the Bible. Stop trying to define yourself by who you are—instead of whose you are.

Tangled Webs Woven in the Workplace

> Put on the full armor of God so that you can take your stand against the devil's schemes. For our struggle is not against flesh and blood, but against the rulers, against the authorities, against the powers of this dark world and against the spiritual forces of evil in the heavenly realms. Therefore put on the full armor of God, so that when the day of evil comes, you may be able to stand your ground, and after you have done everything, to stand. Stand firm then, with the belt of truth buckled around your waist, with the breastplate of righteousness in place, and with your feet fitted with the readiness that comes from the gospel of peace. In addition to all this, take up the shield of faith, with which you can extinguish all the flaming arrows of the evil one. Take the helmet of salvation and the sword of the Spirit, which is the word of God.
>
> —EPHESIANS 6:11–17

Add these necessary items to your wardrobe: belt, breastplate, boots, shield, and a helmet. Get it? *War'd* robe? With these accessories added to your company uniform, you will be less likely to get mad enough at someone to make you walk off your job. You might not get fired for insubordination. You will not decide to get up and cuss everyone out because they made you mad.

You know the assignment that is on your life. You know you have bills that need to be paid and children that need to be fed. When you dress yourself in the spiritual armor, you know that the armor protects you from the enemy's fiery darts. Remember that merit raise you should have received? Or that bonus check you were promised, and the promotion you were due for, but it got overlooked? Know that what is for you is for you, and your Father in heaven will open doors that no man can close and close doors that no man can open. So, do not fret over these things. Hold on to God's Word, "Don't allow your faith to be in man's wisdom but in God's power" (Jer. 17:5).

Now you are fully dressed for the job. Being a voice of reason, sharing new ideas, speaking clarity into chaos, or just by rendering to Caesar what is due, you can make a difference at your place of employment. You were hired for a service. Whatever that service is, do it and do it well. Do not complain about your duties or added assignments. Just know that when people add to your workload, they had you in mind. They could have contracted your assignments out somewhere else. You glorify Christ each time you do your job with a smile and without gripes or complaints.

I call those complaints "coffee talk," when everyone is in the break room talking about what they think should happen, or what needs to happen. I make it a policy to avoid the "coffee talk." Tell your coworkers to take up their murmurs with the proper chain of command. Each company has grievance polices. No one can get their point across better than them. You think a coworker will get your point across better than you? When they see you are not complaining or engaging in their conversation, you will get labeled, but simply inform them that you have a God to tell your complaints to. Tell them you are simply a relay from the source of need to the Source of power, and that your God is no respecter of persons. The same God that answers your prayers will answer theirs. Imagine if every coworker prayed to God in one accord.

I know all of your coworkers will not be easy to get along with, but remember that you have to work with them, so it is worth it to try to figure out a way to get along with them. If there is an issue between you and your coworker let that person know. Talk amongst yourselves; most grievance policies call this a one-on-one. Everyone in the office does not need to know the details of your meeting. Point out the area of grievance. Maybe it is just a simple oversight. Give constructive criticism and allow the other person involved to do the same. Maybe you need to respectfully apologize for your offense. If the two of you cannot resolve the situation, you should call in a mediator. Whatever the case may be, the final results do not have to end up being coffee talk or lunchtime gossip.

Six

Happily Ever After

> For you, O God, tested us; you refined us like silver. You brought us into prison and laid burdens on our backs. You let men ride over our heads; we went through fire and water, but you brought us to a place of abundance.
> —Psalm 66:10–12

O, daughters of Zion, know that God knows just how much you need to refine your faith. Just as muscle is developed under strain, so is your faith. With tests, trials, and tribulations, you, too, can see how much you have grown or how much you need to grow. When you know that your help comes from the Lord, you will have arrived at your place of abundance! Work your job diligently, but know that your help comes from the Lord. Manage your checking account intelligently, but know that your help comes from the Lord. Have a savings account with which to be prepared—famine is only famine when you are not prepared—but know that your help comes from the Lord. God can use any avenue to bless you. Your source of income is simply an "avenue" of the Lord. Do not get caught up in the pavement, but in the One who paved the way.

You cannot allow life's circumstances to dictate your joy, peace, and happiness. As long as you know the One in the control room, you can go straight to the Controller in prayer because we have the Holy Spirit interceding on our behalf. Allow your faith to rest, rule, and reside in God. The day you can speak to your winds and they subdue, the Lord will tell you "Well done my good and faithful servant" (Matt. 25:23).

In Exodus 3:14, God said to Moses, "I am who I am." God is your peace in the storm, your clarity in the chaos, your comfort in loneliness, your joy in your sorrow, and your strength in weakness. He did not promise you joy without pain or sunshine without rain. He gave you those things to arrive to your place of abundance. Just as Canaan, a land flowing with milk and honey, was promised to Abram's descendants, you have to fight the good fight of faith daily. Pick up your cross each day. Continue in God's strength. When He tells you, "Don't add tomorrow's trials with today's" (Matt. 6:34) learn how to take it day by day. Cast your cares upon Him. Resist the devil, and dress in the armor. Be slow to speak, but quick to listen. Take up God's easy yoke today and lighten your burdens. Surround yourself with wise people who can add the things of God to your life. Oppose the silly, wicked people who subtract from your life, and leave you drained, dismayed, and confused.

The Fire of Desire

> Now faith is the substance of things hoped for, the evidence of things not seen.
>
> —HEBREWS 11:1, NKJV

Read that verse again. Did you catch that word *hope*? It means to desire with expectancy; to expect with confidence. Hope is a good thing. That desire in your heart is there because,

"Yet when you were in your mother's womb" (Jer. 1:5) God knew you. He placed in you a purpose to fulfill. When you are roaming around trying to find yourself, what you are really saying is, "I need a way to birth this desire." That is why we go through the tests, trials, and tribulations. Some are by fiery darts from the enemy, and some result from the unbridled will of man.

> These have come so that your faith—of greater worth than gold, which perishes even though refined by fire—may be proved genuine and may result in praise, glory and honor when Jesus Christ is revealed.
>
> —1 PETER 1:7

Once you yield to the desire, you have to know the substance, which is *faith*. Without faith it is impossible to please God. Faith is simply the fire of the desire. You have to ignite that desire. Faith is the vehicle that will take your desire from your needs to the Lord. You have to have faith in God, unwavering in your knowledge that what God has placed inside of you will come to pass. Even though the road will get crooked, and you might sometimes fall, it will be OK because God talked about that, too. He said it is OK to fall. Just do not fall like there is no hope, because you serve a God who is all knowing and all powerful. Even though crying is purifying and purging, wipe those tears and know that God has overcome this world and the prince of this world. If He said it, it will be.

You just have to keep believing and faint not, because in due season, which is God's timing, it will be added unto you. As I mentioned earlier, make sure you keep your armor on. When those friends tell you, "Girl, you can't do that," you will be able to block those fiery darts with your shield of faith. When your family tells you, "Well, you know, Uncle Ray tried that and he failed," swing that sword, the Lord's Word, "Greater is he that is in me than he that is in the world" (1 John 4:4). You are not trying to accomplish anything with your life only in Uncle Ray's strength, however you will accomplish everything in God's strength.

When the self says, "I'm just crazy. No one will invest in my desire," you must put on the helmet of salvation to protect yourself in the battle. The greatest battle you will ever have to fight is in the arena of your mind. Make sure you keep your boots on. We can wear our cute shoes to the celebration, but for now keep on the "boots of readiness" (Eph. 6:11).

God knew you were going to have to walk through some rough terrain on your journey. That is why He said boots of preparation. Hope is the evidence of things not seen—if you will allow me to add—*yet*. (See Hebrews 11:1.) We know that Daniel went in the lion's den and came out. We know that the three Hebrew boys went into the furnace and came out. We know that Lazarus went into the tomb and came out.

> So they took away the stone. Then Jesus looked up and said, "Father, I thank you that you have heard me. I knew that you always hear me, but I said this for the benefit of the people standing here, that they may believe that you sent me." When he had said this, Jesus called in a loud voice, "Lazarus, come out!"
>
> —John 11:41–43

God says His grace is sufficient. In the beginning of John 11:41–43, the Lord said, "Father, I thank you." So, go ahead and thank God for what is to come.

> "We have here only five loaves of bread and two fish," they answered. "Bring them here to me," he said. And he directed the people to sit down on the grass. Taking the

> five loaves and the two fish and looking up to heaven, he gave thanks and broke the loaves.
>
> —MATTHEW 14:17–19

Jesus saw with His natural eye that there were five thousand to feed. But, He believed in that which was not seen. He gave thanks for what was to come. He did not look to the multitude and the naysayers; He looked to God! He knew five thousand had not been fed yet, but the evidence of their provision was yet to be seen.

Go ahead and thank God, right now, for that desire being made tangible in you today. Thank God for that husband He will send you. Thank God for that new car, the increase in business, that invention or new idea, that new design, song, art, or dance, and whatever else He has given you. Thank Him right now for that desire He has made in you. Jesus gave thanks to God for what He was about to do. He knew in His heart of hearts that whatsoever he desired was going to come to pass. That was faith.

The Power of Praise

> ***Lord I worship You for who You are and continue to be to me, and for what You have done for me. You said on the cross that it is accomplished. Everything I can think of, desire, hope, or imagine, has already come to pass.***

The power of increase is in your praise. I am not talking about the mere cosmetics of worship during church service: stand, clap, wave your hand, repeat. I mean your private time with God. Do not allow your method to shape your communion. Simply allow the communion to shape the method by getting up early enough to sing praise unto to the Lord.[1]

> Worship the LORD with gladness; come before him with joyful songs.
>
> —Psalm 100:2

Let us rejoice and be glad in the day the Lord has made. We have made it through yesterday and have arrived at today. God has breathed His breath into you, graciously giving you another day to encourage, advise, lead the lost, tell the untold, and reach the unreached. Praise Him! This day was surely not given in vain. It comes with purpose and substance. Before your feet touch the floor in the morning, shout out unto the Lord, *Thank You Lord, for waking me up this morning in my right mind, body, health, and soul.*

> This, then, is how you should pray: "Our Father in heaven, hallowed be your name, your kingdom come, your will be done on earth as it is in heaven. Give us today our daily bread. Forgive us our debts, as we also have forgiven our debtors. And lead us not into temptation, but deliver us from the evil one." For if you forgive men when they sin against you, your heavenly Father will also forgive you. But if you do not forgive men their sins, your Father will not forgive your sins.
>
> —Matthew 6:9–15

Our Father in heaven

In the opening of the Lord's Prayer, you are acknowledging God being your God who is not of this earth.

Hallowed be Your name

There is no other name above the name of the Lord.

Your will be done on earth as it is in heaven

You are submitting to God's will to be fulfilled through you because obedience is better than sacrifice.

Give us today our daily bread

You are asking God to feed you with His Word, His peace, His honor, and His strength to carry out your day.

Forgive us our debts, as we also have forgiven our debtors

You are petitioning God to forgive you of your sins, and you are stating that you have held no grudges against those who have sinned against you.

And lead us not into temptation, but deliver us from the evil one.

You are saying to the Lord, "God, please allow Your Word to be a lamp unto my feet on the pathway to righteousness, not allowing me to give way to the devil's taunts, schemes, and lies."

God is a spiritual being who deals with us in a physical as well as spiritual way. We *see* evidence of prayer, we *feel* God's presence, and we *hear* His voice. In order to keep the line of communication open, we have to continue our good A.C.T.S.:[2]

- **A**doration—"Through Jesus, therefore, let us continually offer to God a sacrifice of praise—the fruit of lips that confess his name" (Heb. 13:15).
- **C**onfession is restoration of intimacy. Sin keeps us from worshiping wholeheartedly. A feeling of distance lingers when we are not honest with God and ourselves. Take the time to confess your sins and ask for discipline so that the sin is not repeated. "If we confess our sins, he is faithful and just and will forgive us our sins and purify us from all unrighteousness" (1 John 1:9).

- **T**hanksgiving is not just a holiday! Thanksgiving is a daily attitude of gratitude. Knowing that all that was accomplished was not through our strength but through our continued dependency on God. "Give thanks in all circumstances, for this is God's will for you in Christ Jesus" (1 Thess. 5:18).
- **S**upplication is the personal request for specific needs for yourself and others. This is the part when I prostrate myself before God on the threshing floor. A football player has his stadium and a surgeon has his operating room. A praying woman has her threshing floor. On the threshing floor loved ones are saved, sick ones are healed, children on crooked paths go straight, and all wicked plots, schemes, and plans are cancelled. No's becomes yes's, denials become approvals, blessing and increase are given, pressed down, and shaken together in good measure. When praise goes up blessing comes down!

The communion starts when you allow God to talk back to you. After worshiping, praying, and making your requests known to God, listen for His answer. It can be direct, with Him speaking to you, or it can be through your pastor, teacher, leader, friend, or even a foe. God hears your calls and He responds. Your first step to hearing is allowing yourself to. "In your quietness and confidence shall be your strength" (Isa. 30:15). In your quietness you will hear His still voice giving you guidance and answers. Do not think God does not talk to you—He is talking, you just need to listen. Close your eyes and hear His words.

Rise Up, Daughters of Zion

We rise knowing that we serve a living God. Knowing that the Lord will supply each and every need, we pray that the Lord will wash us in His blood, perfume us in His Holy Spirit, and place on us His garments of praise. We pray that the Lord will bless us with the strength, dignity, and endurance to carry out God's assignments for today's journey. We are like tools from the toolbox. The pew is the toolbox and you are the tool. Just as certain jobs are best suited for a hammer or a wrench, there are specific jobs assigned to you. What is in you that God can use to get the job done?

> "I am the Lord's servant," Mary answered. "May it be to me as you have said." Then the angel left her.
>
> —LUKE 1:38

Look at each and every creation as your equal. We are all created in God's image. We all possess something different to help one another. If your advice can comfort a sister, give her advice. If your knowledge can teach your sister, give her instruction.

If your constructive criticism can correct your sister, then offer that criticism. What is in your closet that can clothe your sister? What is in your refrigerator that can feed your sister? Can you offer her a ride before your sister asks? Give her a shoulder to cry on. Rejoice in her blessings, and grieve in her pain. Touch and agree to get a prayer through. Sometimes we need a piggyback ride on another's prayer when we cannot pray for ourselves or just do not know how to pray. Whenever she confides in you or confesses to you, let it stay with you. When you profess that you are a Christian you are saying you are Christlike. All siblings resemble one another, and all children have characteristics and traits of their father. You should resemble your big Brother, Jesus, and walk and talk like your daddy, God.

Afterword

THE MOST PERFECT gift that can be given to your husband is yourself, coming to your spouse wholeheartedly, and without a moment of doubt or regret.

Precious Wedding Gift

Your body made in such a perfect way
The most uniquely designed out of all of mankind
So allow your body to be God's temple
By living your life as an example
Letting the contents of your character exemplify Christ
After all, He is the One that paid the price
Save yourself for your avowed mate
No, the Lord is not being mean
He just knows if you don't, He would have to come to the scene
With healing for the broken heart
Joy for the pain and a kind word to dry the tears from your face
To live an unblemished life will require God's strength and
An abundance of grace
Get full on God's love and affection
He will keep you from temptation with His protection
And remember He who findeth a wife findeth a good thing
Sealed with love and a kiss and a wedding ring.

—CANDIE ZENON

I know a lot of reference has been made to Christians and saints. If you have not yet accepted Christ into your life, I invite you to do so at this time. You need Christ to live. You need His Word to survive. You cannot hope your way through life. He said, "Without faith, it is impossible to please God" (Heb. 11:6). You need more than an optimistic attitude. You need to know of a word that is true and unwavering. No job, relative, man, or friend can give you that. Only the Word of God can.

> Heaven and earth will disappear, but my words remain forever.
>
> —MATTHEW 24:35, TLB

Pray this prayer:

Father God, I thank You this day that it was not by accident that I read this book, but by Your creative design. You have predestined me to be in Your family and I confess with my mouth that Jesus is Lord and I believe in my heart that You raised Him from the dead so that I may have eternal life with You. In Your precious Son Christ Jesus' name, Amen.

Welcome new saint! I must tell you, God is not a genie in a bottle. You do not rub the Bible and make three wishes, with the third wish being for more wishes. God has adopted you into His family, and as a member of His family you now have a claim to the Father's kingdom. You have to fight the good fight of faith. No matter how hard it may look, do not give up. Find a church home that will feed your spirit, so that you may grow and be used as a tool in God's ministry to win souls to Christ. Continue to be a good steward of what God has entrusted to you. Know that He is the Owner and you are the manager.

Afterword

The Proverbs 31 women were praised for working diligently. They were entrepreneurs, caregivers, volunteers, mothers, and wives who were praised by their community, their husbands, children, and by the Lord. You can be who you are—just be it in Christ Jesus, *Amen!*

Notes

Two
The Meeting

1. *Merriam-Webster's Collegiate Dictionary*, 11th ed., s.v. "Monogamy."

Four
Engagement

1. Quote available online at www.quotationspage.com/quote/34275.html.

Five
Wedding Bells

1 Web site: www.quotationspage.com/quote/27150.html (accessed October 4, 2006).

2. *Merriam-Webster's Collegiate Dictionary*, 11th ed., s.v. "Silly."

Six
Happily Ever After

1. Notes from Dr. Ralph D. West's Brookhollow discipleship class.

2. Ibid.

MUSICAL NUMBERS

ACT TWO

21. "Our Lady of the Underground" (An entr'acte) .... Persephone & Hermes
22. "Way Down Hadestown Reprise" .... Fates, Eurydice, Workers, Hermes
23. "Flowers" .... Eurydice
24. "Come Home with Me Reprise" .... Orpheus & Eurydice
25. "Papers Intro" .... Hades, Hermes, Orpheus, Persephone, Eurydice
26. "Papers Instrumental" .... Instrumental
27. "Nothing Changes" .... Fates
28. "If It's True" .... Orpheus, Workers, Hermes
29. "How Long?" .... Persephone & Hades
30. "Chant Reprise" .... Company
31. "Epic III" .... Orpheus & Company
32. "Epic III Instrumental" .... Hermes & Orpheus
33. "Promises" .... Eurydice & Orpheus
34. "Word to the Wise" .... Fates
35. "His Kiss, the Riot" .... Hades
36. "Wait for Me Reprise Intro" .... Hermes, Orpheus, Eurydice
37. "Wait for Me Reprise" .... Company
38. "Doubt Comes In" .... Fates, Orpheus, Eurydice, Workers
39. "Road to Hell Reprise" .... Hermes & Company
40. "We Raise Our Cups" (An encore) .... Persephone, Eurydice, Company

Neither Red Nor Dead

Coming of Age in Former Yugoslavia During and After World War II

By

Stevo Julius

Published by Medvista
Medivista POB 3053
Ann Arbor, MI 48106-3053
www.medvistaa.com

Publisher's Cataloging-in-Publication
(Provided by Quality Books, Inc.)

Julius, Stevo.
Neither red nor dead : coming of age in former Yugoslavia during and after World War II / by Stevo Julius.
p. cm.

ISBN 0-9729511-1-3 (paper)
ISBN 0-9729511-0-5 (cloth)

1. Julius, Stevo. 2. Croatian Americans—Biography. 3. Croatia—History—1918–1945. 4. Croatia—History—1945–1990. 5. Yugoslavia—History—1918–1945. 6. Yugoslavia—History—1945–1980. 7. Communism—Yugoslavia. 8. World War, 1939–1945—Croatia. 9. World War, 1939–1945—Underground movements—Balkan Peninsula—Biography. I. Title.

DR1598.J855A3 2003 949.702′2′092
QBI33-1306

To Nicholas and Natasha,
and to Susan,
who raised them while I pursued a scientific career.

About the Author

Since 1964 the author has resided in Ann Arbor, Michigan where he is Professor of Medicine, Physiology, and Frederick G.L. Huetwell Professor of Hypertension at the University of Michigan. He is internationally recognized as one of the leading scientists in the field of hypertension.

Contents

CONTENTS

Preface

The events described in this book happened on the territory of former Yugoslavia—the Land of South Slavs. ("*Yug*" means "South" and "*slavia*" stands for "Slavs.") The human side of my story can be understood without reference to the general background. However a few readers of the early versions of the manuscript were bewildered by complex conflicts that forced the Julius family to seek survival in the mountains and forest of Yugoslavia. It was hard for them to understand the passions, which could transform apparently normal people into cruel executioners. They were baffled by vicious politics of the region in which I grew up. For them I have appended a chapter entitled: "Souths Slavs. A historical primer."

Acknowledgements

My thanks to Michael Weber, Norman Kaplan, Bert Pitt, Robben Fleming, Tony Schork, Dennis Jensen, and Professor Thomas Trautmann for their encouragement.

Thanks are due to my daughter Natasha Julius for the first thorough review of the manuscript, her advice about the form and her help in removing my annoyingly consistent grammatical errors. The second major review by Mrs. Sands Hall was very useful. She taught me how to rearrange the content into a more attractive format and for that I thank her most sincerely. I also owe a debt of gratitude to Benjamin Stolz Emeritus Professor of Slavic Languages at the University of Michigan who, pencil-in-hand, thoroughly reviewed the manuscript. His positive assessment of the content gave me courage to complete yet another full revision of the manuscript.

I wish to express my thanks to the Perry Castaneda Library Map Collection, University of Texas. All maps in this book were downloaded from public electronic files of the Library: (www.lib.utexas.edu/maps).

Pronounciation Guide

Both the Croat and Serbian languages use the phonetic principle: "write as you hear, read as written." Each letter stands only for one sound regardless where it appears in the word or what other letters are around it. There are no "silent letters," each letter is always pronounced. To accomplish this, four extra letters have been added to the alphabet. However the letters q, y, and w are not used. The four letters unique to the Croat alphabet have their special symbols but in this book they are represented with two combined letters: ch, zh, sh, and dj.

Another peculiarity of the Croat and Serb languages is that a strongly pronounced letter r can be a vowel. Thus what we call "Serb" is actually spelled and read as "Srb" Finally, the accent is almost invariably on the first syllable of the word. My city is not Zagreb but Zagreb. Sarajevo (contrary to what American television personalities reported during the Bosnian war) is not Sarajevo but Sarajevo.

Here is the alphabet:

A as in "aha!"
B as in "boy"
C as in "cent"
CH as in "chair"
D as in "darling"
DJ as in 'judge"
E as in "egg"
F as in "fly"
G as in "grapes"
H as in "hello"

I as in "in"
J as in "yes"
K as in "coca cola"
L as in "less"
M as in "me"
N as in "no"
O as in "over"
P as in "pro"
R as in "riot"
S as in "so"
SH as in "show"
T as in "tip"
U as in " moo" or "true"
V as in "we"
Z as in "zest"
ZH as in "Zhazha" (Gabor)

Now that you know how, for the fun of it, try to pronounce "crkva" (church) or "Brckovljani" (a village near Zagreb). Here are the syllables: BRC-KOV-LJANI and remember, every single letter is pronounced.

Vrapche

(1941–1942)

FORMER YUGOSLAVIA

MAP OF CROATIA

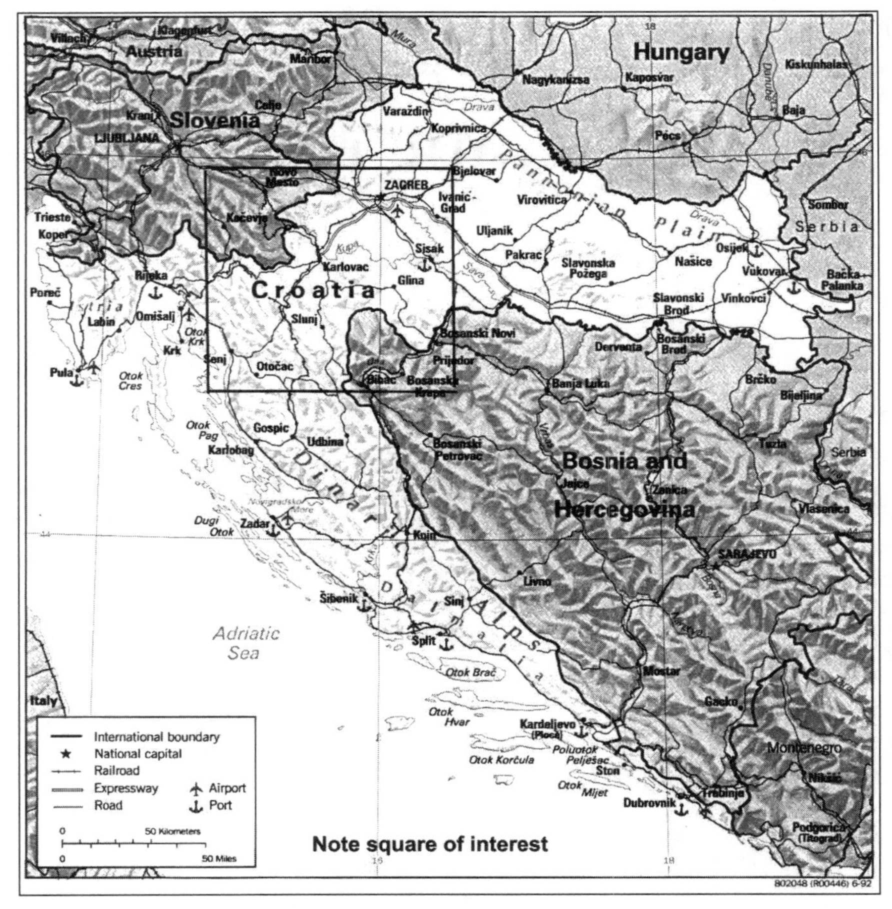

Highlighted is the area in which most of events described in this book took place.

Like so many of our friends we did not recognize the signals. Surely, there were occasional muted unfriendly references about Jews, and a few itinerant refugees from Austria or Czechoslovakia spoke about horrors, but all that was somewhere in the distance. Then, in late May, two days after Hitler first bombed Belgrade and later declared war, a single plane appeared over Zagreb and the ground defense opened fire. Nobody felt threatened by the high-flying airplane and, instead of taking shelter, we watched the

little puffs of antiaircraft ammunition decorating the skies. The children had fun guessing which battery on which hill had a Serb or a Croat crew. The Croats hated the King of Yugoslavia and had no intention of fighting the Germans. The single battery, which consistently shot miles away from the airplane, must have been Croat. It felt more like a carnival than a war.

Reality rode in the next day on the wheels of German motorcycles. Our hospital was in the village of Vrapche on the western outskirts of Zagreb, the capital city of Croatia. A small group of German motorcycles took the half-mile detour from the main road to the hospital entrance. They were attracted by the hospital's impressive avenue, which had four parallel rows of mature horse chestnut trees. The trees towered over the central asphalt road and over the two pedestrian walkways on either side of the road. The avenue led to the main vehicle gate, flanked on both sides by a wrought-iron-decorated pedestrian entrance. Behind the open gate and its ornate wrought iron arch was a circular turnaround with the obligatory fountain in its middle. The six huge motorcycles came through the gate in a single column and having spotted the roundabout, the motorcycles zoomed around the fountain in an endless circle. They kept the bikes at a perilous incline, all the while holding the sidecars in the air. The noise of powerful engines was deafening. The drivers were frozen in a stiff posture while the sidecar men performed a precisely choreographed exercise with their submachine guns. It was designed to impress and impress it did. The damn Master-race!

Standing next to me, my brother Djuka was obviously impressed. He loved motorcycles and for a moment had forgotten who was on them. Eventually he snapped out of it and in a conspiratorial whisper, as if the Germans could hear him, ordered me to go home.

I could not stand his constant bossing. Who in the world did he think he was?

"Why should I go home and not you," I yelled at the top of my lungs.

For once I won. Djuka turned in disgust and left.

When I returned home, he let me have it. "You stupid fool, had we both left at the same time the Germans might have considered this as an ostentatious protest."

A recent picture of the entrance to Vrapche Hospital. The wrought iron gate continues to defy time. The fountain behind it had been removed.

Again, as he did so many times in the past, Djuka implied he had better, and more mature judgment than I. Such a provocation required a response.

"You are wasting words. Every fool is stupid and all stupid persons are fools."

Not a bad approach. Djuka was livid and ready to hit me. Holding the door handle, just before sprinting away, I delivered the punch: "And the Germans were too darn busy trying not to fall off their bikes to notice whether two boys were watching them or not."

That was a great line. Djuka was four years older and by reducing him to just another boy, I insulted him beyond description.

Among adults a four-year difference does not count that much but the gap between Djuka at sixteen and me at twelve years of age was immense. I was playing marbles while Djuka already chased girls, an avocation, which he pursued throughout his life. I did not much care about his friends. To put it simply, they were bores. Puffed up they discussed arts, philosophy and politics and never laughed. I could occasionally play with real grownups but not with Djukas' gang of self-centered would-be-adults. I ignored them to show that I did not care, but I could not disregard Djuka. He had a short temper and always had to be right. Somewhat taller than I, he was heavy-set, tense, and had an overbearing physical presence. I handled him with astute verbal arrogance and a rabbit-like alertness; I knew which but-

A picture of Djuka and me taken in October 1940, six months before the German invasion. Note: the privilege of wearing long pants was afforded only to my older brother.

ton to push to get a response and knew well enough when to escape. Once in a while, when Djuka gave serious chase, I paid for my indiscretions but I never showed the bruises to our parents. It was between him and me and deep down I knew I was guilty.

During family dinners Djuka and I would suspend our warfare. There were good practical reasons for this truce, not to disturb

Father, but mostly to cope with Mother's demands. Mother got it into her head that Djuka was eating too much and I too little. My plate was regularly loaded with goodies, while Djuka got meager portions. We found an imaginative solution to the problem, but it required superb precision. Somewhere in the middle of dinner, when Mother looked away, and Father pretended not to see, we would quickly switch the plates. As soon as the dinner was over, we were back to our little wars.

At the dinner after the German motorcycle show, true to form, Djuka did not raise the issue. But to my surprise, Father, who was usually quiet, started to talk.

"Hard times are ahead of us," he said. "You simply cannot continue with your spats. You will very soon find out what a precious commodity it is to have a brother. I wish I had one to call on."

I was not impressed and Djuka gave me that special leer reserved for a sworn enemy.

"So what else is new? Everybody knows hard times are around the corner," I mumbled to myself.

But I had no idea how hard the hard times could be and how quickly they would come. Leaving the dinner, we had no intention of obeying Father's dictate of brotherly love, but the fact is, that we never again had a major fight. There was no time for it.

We came to Vrapche in 1936 from the village of Kovin in Serbia, a rural commune of about five thousand Serbs, Romanians, and ethnic Germans. Three wide parallel roads traversed the village. The roads were flanked on both sides by lush mulberry trees and widely spaced houses, each with its courtyard, behind which lurked stables, sties and chicken coops. These "lanes," the Serbian, the German, and the Romanian protected the village from ethnic problems. A citizen of Kovin tended to associate with ethnic friends from his lane and communications between the "lanes" were rather sparse.

By the end of the eighteenth century, Kovin evolved into an important military outpost on the southeast edges of the Austro-Hungarian Empire. Situated near the north shore of the river Dan-

ube, and controlling the roads to the rich plains to its north, Kovin had a choice strategic position. In the battle of Belgrade in 1717 the Austro-Hungarian troops defeated the Turks and pushed them back to the south shores of the Danube. Subsequently the military command in Vienna erected a complex of stockades for a large garrison in Kovin. The garrison had little to do and was sitting there just to remind the Turks they had better stay put on the other side of the Danube.

After the First World War, the Austro-Hungarian Empire ceased to exist and Kovin lost its strategic significance. The old Empire had been divided into a number of smaller states and Kovin became just another village in the newly formed Kingdom of Yugoslavia. However the authorities in the capital of new Yugoslavia, Belgrade, soon found out they had to pay an unusual price for the independence. The old Austro-Hungarian Empire had a network of large chronic psychiatric hospitals and many newly formed small countries inherited large psychiatric hospitals. Predictably, these new states had neither the money nor the interest to take care of mental patients and thus started a massive deportation of patients to their countries of origin. Unexpectedly, the Kingdom of Yugoslavia became a net "winner" in this unforeseen exchange of lunatics. Yugoslavia was poorly equipped to cope with such a large influx of mental patients, many of whom could no longer speak the native tongue. Somebody in Belgrade remembered the empty stockades in Kovin and designated them to become a new psychiatric hospital. But the new country of Yugoslavia had just a few psychiatrists. Good jobs in large cities were plentiful and none of the psychiatrists volunteered to maroon themselves in a small village. None until my Father returned to his homeland.

Father was born in 1880 in Panchevo, near Belgrade. After finishing high school in Temesvar (in present-day Romania), he was admitted to the medical school in Vienna but in 1914, when the First World War broke out, he found himself on the eastern front in Russia. In 1918 when the war ended, he resumed studies in Budapest and later moved to Prague where he obtained an MD degree from the famous Charles' University of Prague. Thereafter, Father completed specialization in psychiatry in Slovakia, and in 1923 returned to

his home. Unfortunately, during his stay in Budapest Father had acquired a police record and the Hungarian police felt obliged to inform their new colleagues in Belgrade about Father's involvement in Bela Kuhn's Communist revolution in Hungary. Father soon realized that in spite of excellent letters of recommendation, he would not get a decent appointment in Yugoslavia and eventually accepted the job in Kovin. There he supervised the adaptation of stockades into pavilions of the new hospital and after two years, when the construction was completed, Father finally got the chance to practice psychiatry.

I was born in Kovin in April of 1929 when the melting snow from one of the worst winters on record turned the unpaved roads into mush. Mother could not safely reach the obstetric hospital in Belgrade, where four years earlier she had given birth to Djuka. Consequently, I was born on the grounds of the psychiatric hospital in Kovin, a fact which Djuka always evoked to explain my true or imaginary shortcomings.

Father's hard work in Kovin paid off and when I was seven years old, he was transferred to the much more desirable hospital in Vrapche, near Zagreb. The psychiatric hospital in Vrapche was a veritable little city, housing close to thousand patients and some five hundred personnel with their families. Inside a fenced territory of two square miles, hidden from the road by rows of trees and overgrown hedges, there were twelve large pavilions, each with its independently fenced park. Outside of these pavilions, there were many support buildings. In the center of the hospital stood a cluster of larger buildings to accommodate the administration, kitchen, power station, and the central heating. Around this recognizable core, without rhyme or reason, a myriad of smaller buildings spread every which way. Most of the buildings were interconnected by a maze of covered walkways and the rest could be reached by paved sidewalks. In between buildings there were parks, beds of flowers, and grass lawns with ornamental stones on their edges.

Just outside the main fence the hospital had a few villas for physicians. Ours had a few mature fruit trees, a large chicken coop, and a vegetable garden. Across the road from the villas, the hospital maintained another large vegetable garden, a flower nursery, and a number

of greenhouses. The gardens and the large array of workshops inside the hospital gave opportunities for many patients to lead meaningful lives, have a sense of achievement and helped them in breaking the monotony of chronic incarceration. The hospital needed its gardens and most of its workshops, but a few of them also catered to the outside market. The wicker works made in Vrapche became very popular and commanded a good price in Zagreb.

The hospital had its social life. A few times a week there were evening movies. A paid music teacher resided on the premises and prepared the employee chorus for occasional evening performances. Even the hallucinating patients enjoyed these events. They may not have known what was really going on but the reassuring presence of others, the novelty of the music, and the overall pleasant atmosphere somehow got through to them.

In the weird community of Vrapche, eccentricities were tolerated and sane people freely socialized with lunatics. In spite of delusions and bizarre behavior, psychiatric patients were considered neither ridiculous nor pitiful. The employees' children were taught that behind the zany facade there was a person to whom one ought to relate the same way as with normal people. Some insane people were nice, some were nasty and it was up to you to find that out. There were among chronic patients a "bishop," an "admiral," a "friar," and an "earl." Particularly sad was "Admiral Von Spisasich" in tattered clothes with his pretend-navy cap tucked under his arm and with a stick for an "admiral's baton" in his hand. The contrast between his claimed rank and the reality could not have been larger. Nevertheless, we stood at attention, not to tease, but out of a wish to communicate. I enjoyed many a patient's company. Some were pleasant pets, from others one could learn a lot. I remember well the ceremonial blessings by Blazh, the friar. If it had come from a true friar, I would have most likely ignored it but Blazh was sincere. He performed benediction because he liked me. At the end of the ceremony, when the protocol so required, I kissed his hand and I meant it.

The hospital personnel were attentive and the nuns positively adored us. Most of the hospital physicians had no children and they became a part of our extended family. Djuka and I called them "uncles" and their wives "aunts." Though apparently normal and

capable people, the psychiatrists in Vrapche were an odd collection of eccentrics. There was Uncle Slavko Zhupich who believed in anthroposophy. He studied the works of Rudolph Steiner who, incidentally, was born in Croatia but developed his philosophy in Germany and Switzerland. Uncle Slavko tried to teach me anthroposophic principles but I could not understand a word of it. It did not escape me, however, that outside of traditional religions, he sought to find a spiritual and ethical lifestyle. His medical concepts were truly obscure as he wished to establish some unity of the body and soul in confused mental patients. He spent hours working with them—with no obvious results.

Another physician, Dr Koshec, was so obsessed by theories of homeopathy that he barely noticed anybody. I did not like this quirky, egocentric and short-tempered man. Once, by chance, I ventured into his office while he was preparing one of his homeopathic potions. I asked what he was doing, upon which he theatrically threw the test tube into the garbage and started to scream. How did I dare, he wanted to know, to interrupt him in the middle of the most important phase. He had just started to work on the sixth solution when I crashed into the room. In this phase, he had to mix the solution while holding the test tube strictly in an east-west direction. Because of my crass interruption, he suggested, a poor patient would be left without the remedy for that day. For those who do not know homeopathy, let me explain that the sixth solution meant that he took a drop of the first solution and put it into a large distilled water-filled test tube, than took a drop from that tube—and so on, six times over. There probably were no more than two molecules of the original "active ingredient" left in the sixth tube but Dr Koshec had to align them in sync with the magnetic field of the earth! I was eight years old, but even a child could recognize the nonsense. I stopped calling him uncle and never again entered his office.

Other doctors did not harbor esoteric philosophical or therapeutic ideas but most of them, one way or other, deviated from the norm. Three of them were unmarried, which at that time was most unusual. One, whose name I've forgotten, was agoraphobic and never left the hospital premises. Who knows what horrible problems

lay behind the facade of a well-mannered and polite man who voluntarily incarcerated himself in a psychiatric hospital?

Uncle Branko Gostl, on the other hand, was an outgoing, witty charmer whose entire bachelor's life evolved around classical music. This small, balding and physically unattractive man would immediately establish his intellectual superiority and take over the conversation. But he was not self-centered. He knew he was smart, appreciated those who were equal or better than him but had no tolerance for what he openly called the "minor brains." Teaching me to appreciate classical music became Uncle Branko's pet project. I already loved Beethoven, Mozart, Vivaldi and Tchaikowsky but he decided I must be exposed to more "serious" music. It was a gallant,losing, effort. I was visibly uncomfortable when he made me concentrate on the heavy stuff, which mercilessly rolled from his gramophone. But Uncle Branko was forcefully optimistic.

"All right," he would say," you might not like it right away but one day you will learn what great music is all about." And like Cicero commenting on Carthage, he'd end each session with "Bruckner is the genius. Musically speaking, nobody is a grown up until he starts to love Bruckner."

It did not work. I am still, to this day, stuck on my childhood favorites. Admittedly I did add Mahler from Uncle Branko's list to my repertoire and I still keep trying. Remembering Dr. Gostl, every year or so when I am preparing for a long drive, I stick a Bruckner into my CD player. So far, the effort has done nothing for my cultural growth and, in fact, this exercise in self-improvement occasionally endangered public safety. Typically, a Bruckner symphony slowly builds up to a loud crescendo, but its lengthy reiterations have a way of putting me to sleep.

Our parents also did their level best to educate and entertain us. Mother was in charge of culture. Every two or three weeks she would take Djuka and me to a concert or a theater performance in Zagreb. Father was responsible for "male" entertainment. He would take me to the Central City Square in Zagreb to buy some coffee in Shulhoff's store. Mr. Shulhoff had his own suppliers and according to my father, no other store, including the famous Julius Meinel chain,

could come close to Shulhoff. Shulhoff's was a magical, aroma-laden place where they roasted selected coffee beans to Father's taste and, upon his approval, ground them up in shining machines right before our eyes. From Shulhoff's Father and I would proceed to a few well-stocked delicatessens from which we brought home a weeks supply of cheese, ham and sausages.

In his college years Father had been an accomplished varsity short-distance runner, and in keeping with his athletic tradition, he took us to track events or soccer games. In summer, Father organized various trips. We went mountain hiking in Slovenia, explored caves in the nearby hills and visited the beautiful lakes in the national Park of Plitvice. But most exciting were our elaborate weekend bathing expeditions to the banks of the Sava River. Father's favorite spot was the beach near the bridge at the southern entrance to Zagreb. The frenzy usually started a day in advance as Mother and the maids began to pack bags full of towels, swim wear, blankets, sandwiches, drinks and the like. Next morning the overstuffed bags were somehow fitted into the trunk, Mother completed the final crosscheck and after each of us asserted his right to cause a last minute delay, we were on our way for the twenty-kilometer ride to the river. The Sava was not particularly suitable for bathing. The uneven banks with small spots of grass between long stretches of rough gravel were quite inhospitable. Behind the embankment lay many stale ponds for the pleasure of frogs and mosquitoes and under the dike, what passed for a beach was just a narrow irregular strip of gravel. Swimming in the cold, murky waters of the swift and treacherous river was not the main attraction. A day on the Sava was a pleasurable social event. There was plenty to do and everybody could enjoy himself in his own way. The elders in comfortable reclining chairs read books, played cards or just lay there soaking up the sun. The children were at liberty to enter into ever-changing alliances. Soccer teams were formed and dismantled in a hurry, parties assembled for hide and seek in the bushes, stone-skipping contests were organized and if all else failed one could always take a stab at fishing. Usually unproductive, but lots of fun, the fishing was a great way to pass time as was digging for worms, chasing after grasshoppers, casting the bait into just the right pool and then guessing whether the bobbing of the

cork was a bite or only a snag at the bottom. At the end of the day, pleasantly exhausted, our family would gather on the terrace of the famous Repush restaurant for a taste of the excellent local cuisine.

In the fall of 1940, my personal routines changed a great deal as I started to commute by train to high school in Zagreb. The railway station in Vrapche consisted of a small house from which the stationmaster operated the level crossing gate over the main road, managed the railway traffic signals, received telegraphic information about incoming trains, and sold passenger tickets. The station in Vrapche did not have cement platforms from which to board the trains. Instead, about two hundred yards east and west from the station, the ground had been leveled on one side of the track. This short and narrow strip of flat ground could not comfortably handle more than a few passengers stepping in or out of the trains.

We could choose from two trains, both of which made only a short, almost perfunctory, stop in Vrapche. The "Slovenian" coming from the west had a huge steam locomotive with a characteristic yellow ring around its chimney. The other train coming from the Hungarian border to our north, the "Zagorac," was pulled by a smaller engine, which had a steel collar behind the chimney. The trains were rarely on time and it was important to correctly guess which one was approaching. The one from Slovenia was long and a few of its coaches regularly overshot the level ground of the station. There were disadvantages and advantages to getting aboard such a distant coach. The steep grade of stones on the side of the track made it difficult to enter and we had to pull ourselves upward to reach the first rung of the stairs. However, this bit of acrobatics was well worth doing as other passengers rarely attempted to enter the train the hard way. Djuka was expert at placing us at the railway track in a good position to quickly jump into the train. One wagon in each train was reserved for the commuting students, but amid the trains' steam and the crowd congestion, it was hard to tell where the students' coach was. We often spent the biggest part of the twenty-five-minutes ride to the town in trying to reach the students' coach. We would work

our way through the crowded corridors and as we navigated around baskets of farm products and hopped over pairs of tied live chickens, we constantly argued with passengers. The students were not at all popular with regular passengers. If an adult as much as peeked into the less crowded student coach, he was immediately met by loud protestations. The sassy youngsters didn't mince words to assert their rights to the reserved space.

Naturally, travelers in general and particularly those over whose baskets we were forced to jump had no sympathy for Djuka and me. Nobody was in a hurry to let us through. Once we reached the coach, Djuka gravitated to his peers and I was left to my own devices. Zagreb, with its ten high schools, attracted students from a radius of about eighty miles. Many of the regulars in the student coach were of my age. We played chess, solved crosswords, exchanged stories and formed little groups to walk to school. The composition of walking groups changed every day depending on whether the train was late or on time. If the train was very late, knowing we had already missed early classes we'd all leisurely walk to our destinations. If the train was on time some students were in a hurry whereas others, hoping to miss a class or two, took their sweet time to reach the school. Depending on priorities one could join the group that got off at the Zagreb West station, or proceed to the Main Station. Closer to my school, the West Station was a drab edifice and the way from there went through boring neighborhoods. Walking from the Main Station in Zagreb was much more fun. The spacious station had all sorts of shops and the route to the school passed through lovely tree-lined avenues. The main station also increased the scope of our bartering. Mother dutifully prepared for me luxurious sandwiches and I frequently traded them with ever-ready-to-deal gourmets. In return, the happy recipient of Mother's culinary delights owed me a favor. One student had a stack of blank, pre-stamped, stationmasters' forms. A sandwich could buy me three empty forms attesting that a train was late. I could use the forms at my convenience, but this was a fairly risky proposition. If caught, I could have easily been expelled from the school. I used the form chiefly to avoid long lines at the stationmaster's office when a train was truly late. Of course if it suited me, I could add a few minutes to the form.

I could also swap sandwiches for items the other student would buy for me at the station. On the top of my list were candies and "dog bomblets." The bomblets resembled a candy in a wrapper. The contraption had a body and a twisted paper tail, akin to Hersheys' Chocolate Kisses but the body in the wrapper was oval and somewhat weighty. One grabbed the bomblet by its tail and hurled it towards a person where, on impact, the contraption exploded with a loud bang. The "dog bomblets" were surprisingly safe. We carried them in our pockets and none ever accidentally exploded. When thrown at a target, even if it exploded at a person's head, the bomblet never caused injury.

Truth be told we, the railway kids, were little monsters. I was a bit shy ("I did not inhale!"), but I could easily be persuaded to join in the mischief. We frequently aimed the bomblets at women from Zagorje who were on their way to the market. Clad in colorful national costumes of long white pleated skirts and ornate embroidered red jackets, these women carried produce to the town in an extraordinary fashion. They used their heads in the most literary sense of that phrase. Women from Zagorje would stuff huge round baskets with all sorts of farm produce, put a wreath made of linen on her head, hoist the heavy basket atop the wreath and walk away as if it were nothing. It was amazing to see them balance the basket on their heads as they navigated in the traffic, accelerating or slowing as the need required, squeezing in between other pedestrians and all the while moving their hips just the right amount to keep the basket in perfect balance. This peculiar technique left their arms free to either carry additional bags or, more frequently, to fight their way through the crowd.

Throwing bomblets at these caryatids was a mean trick, but luckily, we never quite succeeded to score a direct hit. The women would hop and scream, but none of them ever dropped a basket. However, another conspiracy to do harm succeeded beyond my wildest dreams.

My high school was in one of the most impressive edifices of the town. Three stories high, the building was a city block wide and had two wings, each turning at a right angle into its own city street. My school, the Fourth Male High School of Zagreb, occupied the south wing and behind the ornate doors, it had a palatial stairway. The very wide central stairway went up to a midway landing whence the stairs

split into two narrower stairways, which led to the next floor. The landings on each floor had nice balconies from which one could look downward over the elegant stairs. Unfortunately, in addition to its beautiful architectural view, the balcony offered a great position to launch bomblets. One could easily float a bomblet right to the feet of a person climbing up the wide middle stairway. Before he retreated down the corridor or into the nearby toilet, the bombardier could for a few seconds safely enjoy the fruits of his mischief. Somehow the dangerous game never caused a major disaster but it could have. We were too young to worry about whether somebody would break a bone or worse.

I took part in one of the most vicious bombardments. For some reason we chose as the target our lady teacher of French. We did not particularly dislike her but she happened to be an ideal target. Every teacher in our school carried to the classroom a large, folio-sized logbook to make notes about the topic of the day, to read the class roster, to grade students' responses to questions, and to make notes about class behavior. The unfortunate teacher of French had two bad habits. She used to come to class well after the bell and she always used the logbook as a platform to carry ink and pens up the stairs. To be precise, she carried two inkwells, the red to enter interim grades and the blue ink for other notes. I leave it to the reader's imagination to visualize what happened when the bomblet landed at her feet and the inkwells took off in opposite directions.

As an immediate response and to our horror, the director of the school showed up in the class. He kept us in dead silence throughout the time allotted for the class and through the next recess. He knew that a lengthy investigation would yield no results. Instead of wasting time, he chose to show his contempt for the entire class. The director was a mountain of a man and simply by staring at the class in a dramatic dead silence, he sent shivers up everybody's spine. Thereafter, we were on our best behavior during French classes.

~

The very next day after the German motorbikes showed up at the entrance to our hospital, everything changed. All high schools were

closed "until further notice" and we stopped commuting to Zagreb. This forced both Djuka and me to interact more with friends in the hospital, but our previously homogenous extended hospital family started to fracture along the anti-Semitic line. Some people came to assure us of their support, others coldly turned their backs including a few people whom Djuka and I used to call "uncle." In a way, this was not so bad. The disappointments were by and large balanced by a surprising number of supporters. The real problem was with the majority, which had not yet altered its behavior. There is no neutrality in a war. Down the road, these people would have to make choices. We had seen the extremes, but the real question was whether the middle would hold.

Father knew he could not shield us from the reality and openly discussed good and bad news at the dinner table. He treated me as an equal and this, more than anything else, helped to stop fights between Djuka and me.

After a few months, the German occupation started to show its teeth. The Gestapo began to arrest people or incarcerate entire families in concentration camps. Distressing as such news was, more devastating was the lack of reason. Even in the madness of occupation, there were some ground rules. Do not violate the curfew, do not listen to the radio, do not irritate the Germans lodging in your house and things may work out. But these reoccurring random arrests of prominent Jews made no sense. Why did they take Mr. Cohn and Dr. Stein? To contemplate the possible reason was even worse. Which neighbor, acquaintance, former or present employee did them in? Did somebody covet someone's apartment, someone's wife or someone's business?

My world changed. Before, I had been accountable to my family and the school. Now I had to watch every step. I learned to control rage, to walk away from an argument and to constantly evaluate a relationship. It was not any more with whom you want to play, but who would agree to play with you and why. As former friends openly turned their backs or surreptitiously faded away I suffered the rejection without showing it. And I had to learn additional new skills. Some children were offering friendship because their parents ordered them to do so and others were sincere. I had to figure out

who was who. Thus started a long schooling in interpersonal relationships, enriched in the resistance movement, fine-tuned during the postwar Communist oppression and superbly polished during my services as a county physician in Gorazhde.

As if the occupation by itself were not bad enough things got even worse when in late 1941 the Germans dissolved the Kingdom of Yugoslavia and created a puppet "Independent State of Croatia."

The German generals needed more troops for the Eastern front in Russia. Never mind that Hitler considered Slavs to be vastly inferior to the Aryan master-race. According to Hitler's book, *Mein Kampf,* after they had won, the Nazis would establish a "new order" in which Slavs would not be permitted to have higher education and could be employed only as manual laborers. The generals needed new cannon fodder and they knew the local history well enough to trust their Croat allies. All police responsibilities were transferred to the Croat nationalists, the Ustashe.

Historically, the South Slavs, long subjugated by other nations, always dreamed about independence and national identity. In the Middle Ages, Serbia succeeded in establishing a kingdom, but after a few royal generations everything was lost to Turkey. The Croats had similar luck. Their short-lived kingdom fell to the Hungarian conqueror. Even the Bosnians had their own rulers for a few generations.

The defeat of the Austro-Hungarian Empire in the First World War gave the Serbs, Croats and Slovenes a glimmer of hope to reassert their independence. The victorious allies had decided to once and forever carve up the old Empire into smaller units. Though insignificant in size, the Kingdom of Serbia had a strong standing, since it fought against Austria alongside the allies. In December of 1918 the Allies endorsed the formation of the "Kingdom of Serbs, Croats and Slovenes." The Serbian king became the head of the state and proceeded to consolidate his power in no uncertain terms. He soon enacted a Constitution, which gave him absolute powers and changed the name of the State into Kingdom of Yugoslavia.

The new country had very little chance of success. Nobody in his right mind would put money on a state formed from people of the same stock who have for centuries been at each other's throats and whose new borders abutted on seven unfriendly neighbors. The

acronym of the countries surrounding the newly formed Yugoslavia spells "BRIGAMA" (Bulgaria, Romania, Italy, Greece, Albania, Magyarorszag /Hungary/, Austria) which, in the languages of all South Slavs translates into "with worries." As the saying went: "Yugoslavia, surrounded by worries, is a country formed of three nations (Croats, Serbs and Slovenes), divided by three religions (Catholic, Orthodox and Moslem) and sharply split by one common language (Serbo-Croatian)."

Serbian repression against Croat nationalists was quite brutal. In 1928 during the plenary session of the Yugoslav Parliament, three Croat deputies were shot to death. As far as the Croats were concerned, nothing had really changed. They had just acquired a new ruler and the state of Yugoslavia was equally as bad as Austria-Hungary. There is no right or wrong in these matters. Perceptions count. The hatred between the Serbs and Croats became palpable. Not having other enemies at hand, the South Slavs turned one against the other. In due course, Croat nationalists killed the king of Yugoslavia on his visit to France.

No wonder then that after the Germans invited them, the Croat nationalists jumped at the opportunity of having their own state. Nothing good can be said about these nationalists turned fascists, the Ustashe. Full of incredible hatred they instantly turned to brutal prosecution of Serbs and, for good measure, Jews. More was to follow. Ustashe's free-floating hostility kept finding new outlets. As the average Croat citizen woke up to the ugly reality and started to express some civilized concern, the Ustashe began to terrorize their own people. A special military court replaced the civilian legal system. The early tensions created by arbitrary arrests of Jews gave way to the true horror of a country gone mad. The whole system was entirely out of control. Now even regular citizens faced the longer, but very real odds of sudden arrest as hostages. As the resistance movement started to shoot at the invaders and their collaborators, groups of hostages were executed; ten for each German soldier killed, twenty for an officer. Long lists of names, ages and professions of executed hostages started to appear with painful regularity. These lists were the epitome of arbitrary power. Occasionally they got rid of some undesirable people, but many of the names made no sense whatsoever. A merchant, a

peasant, a teacher, a student and so on. Why? Presumably to instill a feeling of terror and somehow make the population angry at the "cause" of the trouble: the resistance movement. Of course it had just the opposite effect. If the friends and family of an innocent victim were apolitical, the barbaric execution left them no choice but to seek revenge. And the grotesque pictures of hanged people, instead of spreading fear, caused universal revulsion.

The Ustashe were not burdened by formal bounds of civility. In Glina, the local Serbs were brought to their Orthodox Church for conversion to the Catholic faith. The area was sealed off and after an execution of around 300 souls, the church was dynamited into a massive grave.

The Jews did not fare any better. By the end of the first year of the new regime, all male Jewish high school students in Zagreb born in the years 1923 and 1924 were rounded up and sent to a reeducation camp in the village of Jadovno in the province of Lika. It was a camp all right, but not for their reeducation. The Ustashe used the camp to teach some important skills to the elite new members among their ranks. The apprentices had to learn some finer points before they could be entrusted with the complex job of mass murder. They were given large knives and the Jewish boys in camp Jadovno served as training material. None of the prisoners ever returned from this place of incredible horrors.

The new regime found fervent support in the village of Vrapche. A decidedly pro-fascist Village Council had been quickly installed. It was only a matter of time before these outside forces would establish themselves in the hospital and, of course, removing Jewish physicians would be the first thing on their agenda.

Immediately after the German occupation, all schools were closed, but after it established itself, the new Croat regime decided to credit the previous school year, which had been two months shorter, as a full one. In due course, I received by mail the "Commemorative Diploma" in honor of the Independent State of Croatia. The back of the diploma indicated I had been enrolled into the next year's class. It was not "chic" to love school but I was bored. I missed train rides, my classmates and, horror of horrors, even some teachers. It seemed

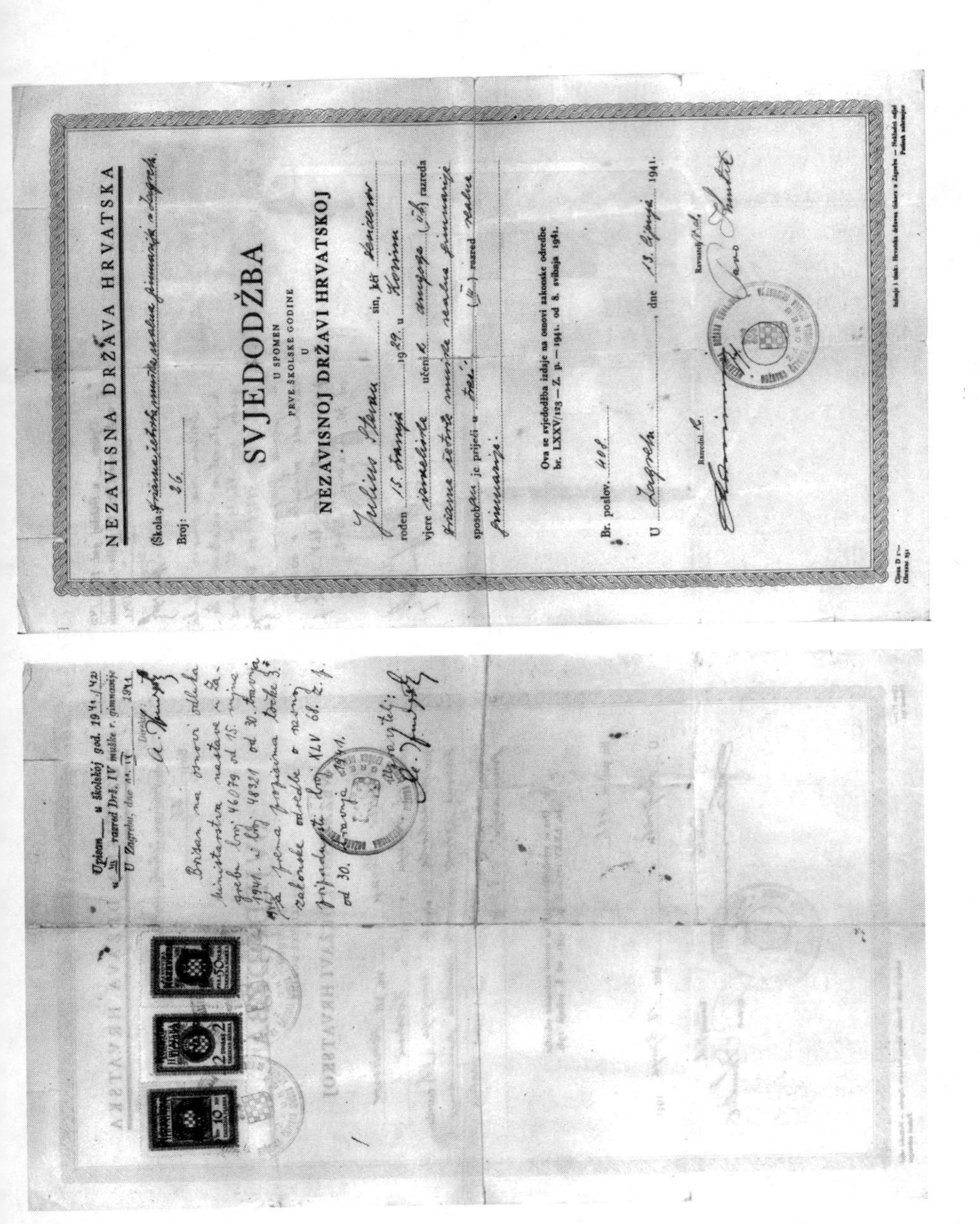
NEZAVISNA DRŽAVA HRVATSKA

Škola:

Broj: 26

SVJEDODŽBA

U SPOMEN

PRVE ŠKOLSKE GODINE

U

NEZAVISNOJ DRŽAVI HRVATSKOJ

Julius Stern sin, kći

rođen 15. travnja 1929. u Kovinu

vjere izraelske učenik razreda

sposoban je prijeći u treći (III.) razred

Ova se svjedodžba izdaje na osnovi zakonske odredbe br. LXXV/123 – Z. p. – 1941. od 8. svibnja 1941.

Br. poslov. 408

U Zagrebu, dne 13. lipnja 1941.

Razrednik

Ravnatelj

Upisan u školskoj god. 1941./42

The high school diploma of 1941. On the back, the stamp on the top indicates states I've been enrolled in the 1941/42 class, and the handwritten part states "Eraased . . . based on the laws of racial origin."

a lesser evil to wear the large yellow medallion with the Star of David every school day than to stay put in the nuthouse.[1]

When I reported to register for the new class, a clerk handed me the last year's diploma and without a word pointed to its backside. Under the official rubber stamp of my School, the Director of the school wrote in pedantic calligraphy the following words: "Based on the rules of the Ministry of Education and reflecting the Basic Law of racial origin, not eligible for enrollment into the High School." That was it!

I would not recommend to others this particular way of building family unity, but the occupation brought me much closer to Djuka and to our parents.

My Father was short, probably only five feet two inches tall, but nobody ever noticed it. He was well proportioned, slim and elegant, both in body and mind. Father was at peace with himself and, unlike so many other short people, his stature did not bother him a bit. He was kind, deliberate, rational and calm. Father was very busy with patients and even when he had time for me, I perceived him more as a very pleasant but somewhat distant teacher, than a father figure. His brain operated on a higher plane than that of other adults and he never showed an emotion, that was Mother's department.

By all standards, Mother was a beautiful woman. An inch taller than Father, she had gorgeous black hair and blue eyes. She was very outgoing and loved to be the center of attention in every company. That apparent lack of shyness was at the root of her romance with Father. She was born and grew up in Budapest, and eventually enrolled in the Medical School of Budapest. One day Father, who was three years ahead in medical studies, came to her class and delivered

1 The Germans made sure that every Jew carried insignia of his race. How could you avoid or ridicule the Jews if you did not know who they were? The medallion was, in fact, an improvement—earlier we had to pin on two 4 × 6 inch pieces of yellow cloth: one hung over the chest and the other over the back.

an oration about the ongoing Bela Kuhn's Communist revolution in Hungary. Mother did not care whether Hungary would become another Soviet Republic or not, but she was attracted to the speaker. Being a person of action, she walked to the dais, took Father's glass of water, drank it, and calmly returned to her bench. Father, revolutionary as he might have been, was not blind. They started to date. Soon thereafter Admiral Horty staged a counter-revolution and Father was arrested. Mother pulled some strings through her family's connections, got Father released from the jail on the condition that he should every day report to the prosecutor's offices. A few days later accompanied by his fiancée, Father escaped to Prague and continued with medical studies. Apparently he was not as progressive as he pretended and made it quite clear, that if they were to get married, he would expect Mother to be the head of the Julius household and not a practicing physician. They got married in Koshice in Slovakia where she had an aunt and where Father took up a specialization in psychiatry. Mother deeply regretted that she gave up medicine and when they came to Yugoslavia, she felt her loss even more acutely.

Having left family and many good friends behind, Mother moved to a country whose language she did not speak. Admittedly there was a substantial colony of Hungarians in Kovin but they were not the kind of city folks Mother was accustomed communicating with. She eventually learned to speak Serbian quite fluently but with a heavy accent. I now realize that much of Mother's attention-seeking behavior and her tendency to dominate others was rooted in her personal discomfort and insecurity.

Mother's movements were quick and she never could relax. Her seductive deep alto voice eventually cracked from smoking and from abuse as she always spoke in loud, excited tones. Extremely critical of others, Mother was proud of her ability to dish it out and "tell it like it is" straight to everybody's face. Her assessment of what constituted "it," that is to say her version of truth, was highly subjective. She loved hyperbole. Middle categories did not exist for her. The conductor had either "brought her to tears" or he was "horrible" and the orchestra was either "out of this world" or a bunch of tone deaf clods. Our neighbors were "superb" or "impossible" and, of course, only a few qualified for the high distinction. I was occasion-

ally embarrassed by her confrontations but generally I did not mind. Unfortunately, Mother had the irritating habit of expecting everybody to partake in her excitement and that was where I drew the line.

I was eleven years old when she took me on a long tour of churches and museums in Florence. At that age I loved classical music in a most platonic way but my real passion was reserved for soccer. Mother decided to change this. The trip to Florence would instantly convert me into a fervent connoisseur of visual arts. Needless to say, I was bored stiff. Nevertheless I dutifully followed Mother on her lengthy and tiring peripatetic treks. Mother would stop in front of many a picture or sculpture, where she'd first hyperventilate and then let off a stream of loud superlatives. Just as Johan Sebastian Bach could write endless variations on the same fugue, Mother could incessantly alternate adjectives on the theme of beauty. In public places every eleven-year-old boy has a need to assert that he is not hiding under mother's skirt. He will discretely float away pretending he had come alone. I was not better than my peers but I stayed close for fear that, had I ever left, she would fetch me and hold my hand throughout the tour. So I bravely stood by her but that was not enough. After she completed her adoration of a picture, Mother would turn around to ask for "my opinion!" Saying something like "Yeah, this was nice," would not do. I was supposed to express my opinion with Mother's intensity. I could not and would not. I did not like the darn pictures and I had not taken acting classes.

It was a disaster. Back in the hotel Mother was all over me; my behavior was very disappointing. The family had spent all that money to teach me beauty and I behaved as a thankless brat.

A good diagnosis! I certainly did not feel like offering thanks for something I hated and an eleven-year-old boy is, by definition, a brat. It took me a good forty years to heal the Florence wounds. Eventually I forced myself to visit museums and I even enjoyed some of them. But not for long! After an hour or so, I am beset by the irrational urge to run away. I wonder whether I would have had more joy discovering beauty as an adult had I not been dragged through Florence as a child.

Being as emotional as she was, Mother was warm and loved to hug me. Unfortunately, her warmth turned to fire if she felt I had to

be disciplined. Back then corporal punishment was considered a normal part of parenting. The theory had it that the reasons for the punishment must be explained without anger and the penalty ought to be inflicted in cold blood. Not so with Mother, who would hit first and explain later. Or never! You were supposed to know!

Mother's punishment had next to no effect. She disciplined me so frequently that I forgot what it was for. However I do remember very well the one and only punishment I got from Father. He caught me making faces at some beggars in front of our door. With a typical child cruelty I started to imitate the beggars' miserable stance and their stereotypical wailing. Father pulled me by the ears into the house, took my pants off, delivered a few painful blows and quietly asked whether I knew what that was all about.

"I do, I do," I asserted through tears.

"Good," said Father leaving the room. And that was the end of it.

During the occupation, my perception of my parent's behavior changed. I drew a great deal of comfort from Father's calmness. He inspired confidence and seemed to have a solution for every problem. I never had any doubts he would steer us to safety.

Mother continued to be herself. Before the war, she constantly felt slighted by something or somebody and the occupation gave her more reasons to complain. She lost sight of the larger conflict and somehow viewed everything around us as a personal affront. Before the Germans came, Mother's antics did not bother me but during the occupation her attitude started to weigh on me. The times were bad enough and I needed neither her pessimism, nor her "poor us" attitude. During the day I took refuge in the carpentry shop, staying as much as I could out of her sight.

The dinners with Father were quite a relief. He did not hide difficulties but he neither wrung his hands nor attempted to fake optimism. He was looking for solutions. Father's active realism, his let's-see-what-we-can-do approach and his willingness to share the truth with us were very reassuring. I felt protected.

One evening Father had a bit of good news to report: "As you know, Dr. Suchich is well connected. His uncle is the Deputy Head of the State of Croatia."

Father took a pause, cleared his throat and looking into his soup, continued to talk in a deliberate voice. "Before I continue with the rest of the story, let me remind you that Suchich is a good man and that all of us, including his uncle, are in a big mess."

"How can you tell that?" I protested. "With all those connections, Uncle Suchich is doing just fine and what could be the problem for his uncle? Isn't he the big chief? His Excellency must have the time of his life."

"Well, Dr. Suchich had to call on his uncle and ask him for a favor. If you ask for something and the favor has been rejected, your relationship with that person will sour. And if he does you a favor, you have less of a right to ask him again. There is a reason why in all fables only three wishes are granted. And as they say in the village: 'if you go too often to the same well it will run dry.' "

Somehow it didn't sound right. Something was amiss. Father looked around the table and seeing we were attentive, he continued.

"Anyhow, Uncle Zvonko intervened on our behalf and you ought to know that this was by no means a small deed. Asking his uncle to help a Jew was brave. Helping a Jew these days is considered a high crime. And as to Stevo's question why everybody, including his Excellency is involved in the mess, the answer is that the uncle had been presented with the unpalatable choice of refusing his nephew or risking the wrath of his peers. Rough as he might be, Suchich's uncle probably cares about his brother and would hate to refuse his son."

"Oh sure. My heart is bleeding for the poor Deputy Head of the State," I intoned. Just as I was about to say more, Djuka interrupted.

"Come on Dad. You seem to walk around the house looking for the back door." Djuka used the Serb version of 'beating around the bush.'

It struck me Djuka was right. Father still did not say what was the result of Dr. Suchich's intervention.

"Right, I should come to the point. Let me start with the good news first," Father said. "I will be permitted to keep my appointment as a state employee. This implies we will have the same legal rights as others."

"That is absolutely fantastic," emoted Mother in her inimitable style. She was about to jump and hug everybody around the table.

"Let's be fair, Lilly," Father said, "It does mean a lot, but under the present circumstances, everybody's rights are limited. I would say that the new situation means only that somebody who wanted to harm us would have much easier targets than our family. My being a state employee does not provide us with a perfect shield. We still ought to be rather careful and diplomatic."

The last sentence had been clearly addressed to Mother. Father did not want her to resume her in-your-face, tell-them-like-it-is, style.

"Oh, you have to always spoil everything," complained Mother. "Can you not permit us to have just a minute of joy?"

"I am just realistic."

"But this is nevertheless a major achievement." Djuka jumped into the conversation, "It beats the state guidelines. How did Suchich succeed in securing a state employment for a Jew?"

"He didn't," said Father, "and that is the bad part of the story. In three days, this Sunday, we will be converted to the Catholic faith. Suchich arranged it all. And, mind you, this was not simple either. He had to convince the village priest to obtain permission directly from the Archbishop in Zagreb."

After Father announced our pending conversion to Catholicism all eyes around the dinner table focused on plates in front of them and, save for the occasional clinking of knifes and forks, the dining room fell dead silent. Everybody needed some private time to process the news.

I could not understand why Father had to hesitate so long. He should have known that the news would not bother us all that much. Our parents were not religious. Father was, in fact, an outright atheist. For him being Jewish was an ethnic, cultural, and not a religious bond. We were always reminded that we were Jewish and should be proud of it. We went to the synagogue to learn from the Rabbi about the culture and history of Jews. But in Father's opinion, one could be Jewish without being religious.

Father, who could always read my thoughts, broke the short pause. "You might think this is not a big deal and in many ways it is

not," he said "but it bothers me that we had to capitulate. Throughout centuries of hatred, persecution, and forced migration, Jews refused to assimilate and disappear in the sea of people around them. They never lost their identity and neither should we. We are Jews, albeit not religious ones, and we had better remember that. I have seen a few Jews who changed their last names and pretended they never were Jewish. They became real pariahs, despised by their brethren and never truly accepted by gentiles. After a while, realizing they did not belong anywhere, they became heartbroken shadows of themselves. Denial is a bad strategy in life; it eventually comes back to haunt you."

Even in these hard times Father was first and foremost a psychiatrist, but he did not throw at us a psychoanalytic slogan, he had a message. "It would be horrible if any one of us started to feel different from other Jews," he said in a voice I never heard before. Father was quite emotional and had dewy eyes.

"Don't do it! It would be wrong and, anyhow, it would not work. For the Germans and the Ustashe, you will remain Jews, no matter what you do."

Realizing how upset our old man was, Djuka and I remained respectfully quiet. Mother ran out of the room to have a cry.

Three days later, in the parish church of Vrapche, we were converted to the Catholic religion. I was oblivious to the solemn ceremony in the same way as I used to ignore proceedings in the synagogue. However the darkness of the Church and the smell of incense made me very uncomfortable. The local priest delivered a nice sermon about the continuity of the old and new Testaments but I could not breathe. I grabbed the pew with both hands and my tense legs were poised to jump. As soon as I heard the last *amen*, I was out of there.

The religious conversion had one big advantage. We were no longer obliged to wear the yellow emblem with the Star of David. That was a great relief. Other hospital children had gone back to school but after they returned I could again join them for various sporting outings. But throughout the main part of the day I had no routines.

Father again came to our rescue. He found some jobs for Djuka and me. This was a very progressive move, as at that time the chil-

dren of intellectuals were not supposed to engage in manual labor. I went to work for the local flower growers and Djuka landed a job in an auto mechanics workshop on the periphery of Zagreb. I loved working among endless rows of flowers, cutting them and preparing bouquets for the market. I don't think I learned much about gardening techniques, but those few months in the flower nursery left a lasting impression. As an adult I became a dedicated gardener.

Everything seemed more or less back to normal. I learned to keep my distance from unfamiliar adults just in case some of them expressed anti-Semitic sentiments. My garden work was interesting, Djuka seemed similarly engrossed in what he was doing and we both were quite content not having to rub elbows with each other. But in

the middle of a large external storm, our idyllic lives could not last too long.

The Ustashe leadership of the Vrapche Village Council resented the fact that personnel decisions were made in the hospital without their consent. A tug of war broke out between the more moderate hospital leadership, including Dr. Suchich and the Council. They seemed particularly irritated by our family's religious conversion, which they viewed for what it really was, a protective shield erected by higher authorities. As a rule, lower administrative units, regardless of the prevailing political system, hate challenges to their supremacy and diligently work to assert their leadership. The Vrapche Village Council was out to get us and in the long run they would succeed. Our friends were looking for ways to defuse the situation. Eventually they found a solution.

Father got an offer to organize a new psychiatric hospital for children in the small village of Stanchich about 30 miles to the east of Zagreb.

There, out of sight, and still remaining a state employee, Father could practice his craft in a much safer overall atmosphere. Again, as in Kovin, Father would take on transforming old buildings into a new hospital. Only this time instead of stockades he was to supervise the renovation of two huge stables.

There was something unusual about Father's new task. Why would the crass and ruthless Ustashe, who had put many a child to death, all of a sudden want to erect a hospital for mentally ill children? As it turned out, they did not see such a need but were persuaded by the Croatian novelist Slavko Kolar. By profession an agronomist, Kolar wrote novels in his spare time. The German occupation found him in the position of the director of the state-owned demonstration project in Bozhjakovina. Since the state of Yugoslavia became such a bitter disappointment the Croatian intellectuals were immensely proud of all literature written in a "proper" Croat language. With his bittersweet stories about village life, Kolar gained admirers on both ends of the Croatian political spectrum. He knew

many luminaries of the new "Independent State of Croatia" and soon had to put his connections to good use.

After they took over, the Ustashe established a large-scale concentration camp in Jasenovac, near Zagreb. Many Jews, Serbs and Gypsies died in this harrowing place. Jasenovac was a low-tech workshop of massive slaughter where the sledgehammer be-came a favored tool of execution. People were brought to a ramp over the Sava River, their heads smashed and the bodies thrown into the river. Days later, grotesquely swollen corpses would resurface downstream, a terrible reminder that a nation had taken leave of its senses.

One of the first detainees in Jasenovac was Dr. Rudi Rosner, a Jewish neurologist from Zagreb and a friend of Slavko Kolar. As soon as Kolar learned about Rosner's arrest, he went on a campaign to save him. In those dangerous days he could not go straight to the police. As there was no obvious reason for the arrest, one could not argue guilt or innocence. Nor could Kolar challenge the detention. Protestations about Rosner's good character were irrelevant. The only way out was to argue for release on the grounds of "need" and Slavko Kolar immersed himself in creating a pretext for such a need. He enlisted the help of Dr. Petrich, a fellow Croatian armchair nationalist who had just become the Minister of Health in the new Croatian Government.

First, the Ministry of Health prepared a position paper about the need for a new children's psychiatric hospital. In parallel Kolar submitted a report asking the agricultural authorities to relieve the enterprise in Bozhjakovina of the useless buildings in Stanchich. Kolar's request was steered to the Ministry of Health where Petrich professed interest in acquiring the buildings. A budget was drawn for conversion of the stables into a hospital. Everything was ready to go as soon as a head physician could be found. None of the Croat physicians volunteered to set up offices in an abandoned horse farm. Consequently, a ministry report suggested that a Jewish physician be forced to abandon private practice in Zagreb and be ordered to run the new hospital in Stanchich. It came to pass that Rudi Rosner might be ideal for the job.

With all these preparations in place Kolar was ready to face Ante Pavelich, the supreme leader of the Croatian fascist movement. Years

of exile turned Pavelich into a savage brute but he maintained a careful facade. His regime was among the worst ever visited upon a nation. Nevertheless, this dangerous man viewed himself as the caretaker of "thousand of years of Croatian culture." Well aware of Kolar's contributions to Croatian literature, he was pleased to grant him an audience.

The interview went quite well. Pavelich placed a call to the chief of security police, a certain Dido Kvaternik. To his surprise, the man on the other end of the line was quite obstinate. Pavelich grew visibly irritated. Finally, in the icy voice of a boss talking to an underling, he ordered Kvaternik to immediately receive Kolar and make arrangements for Dr. Rosner's release. That did it. Kvaternik gave Kolar a polite reception, provided him with papers and sent him with an escort to Jasenovac. When Kolar reached Jasenovac, the head of the concentration camp, ever so polite, was sad to report that Dr. Rosner had died just that very morning. And no, the body could not be recovered. This was a clear indication that Kvaternik had decided to teach Pavelich a lesson as to who was the real boss. While formally in compliance with the supreme leader's orders, he phoned his trusted lieutenants to arrange a preemptive sledgehammer execution.

The idea of a new hospital in Stanchich could not be abandoned lest it became obvious that the plan was tailored for Rosner's sake. By and by Kolar started to search for another Jewish physician for the job in Stanchich. Father's friends got wind of it and suggested he'd be the ideal candidate. Under the circumstances, this was the best possible move.

As we prepared ourselves for the move to Stanchich I felt an eerie air of finality around us. The new quarters would be much smaller than in Vrapche and we had to dispose of many of our possessions. Selling them on the market was out of question. Some of our belongings were quietly given away; some stored for safekeeping and some simply left behind. I still vividly remember those surrealistic days. It was a continuous feast of sorts. We ate the best chicken from the pen. The

kitchen help was busy transforming flour and sugar reserves into marvelous cakes. Friends came in droves for farewell dinners. But under this almost festive atmosphere lurked a deep sorrow.

It was also a rude awakening. In hard times you learn the truth about people. As a rule those professing a great friendship disappear from sight. The help comes from utterly unexpected quarters as dramatic events shake some previously nondescript individuals into action. They might go different distances— from limited help to self-sacrifice. Unfortunately, in difficult times each such helper will be matched by a citizen ready to throw away the appearance of civility in order to appease personal greed. The shades go from simple bargain hunters to outright robbers. A good example was Aunt Marica, the wife of Dr Suchich, the decent and brave man who protected us. When we started packing our belongings, she took regular walks through our household. She would suggest what items we may not need in our new circumstances and offered to buy them at bargain prices. That included our best china and silverware.

Mrs. Suchich was a virtuoso of self-deception. It occurred to me as a child, but not to her, what kind of hopeless finality was packed in those ominous suggestions. As far as she was concerned, she was just stating the obvious, just trying to help. And help she did, with packing, providing boxes, moving things and the like. That sort of ambivalent bondage was particularly despicable. She helped to alleviate her guilt feelings and to satisfy her curiosity. And there was nothing we could do about it.

Stanchich

(1942–1943)

In November 1941, a few months before the final move to Stanchich, we took the hospital's old Dodge and went to inspect our future residence.

East of Zagreb the scenery abruptly changes from a busy city to open fields and scattered villages. The edges of the large mountain behind Zagreb descend into small hills and they gradually dissolve into the plains. At the lowest ring of hills where the forest yields space to small vineyards, the color changes from solid green to patches of gray. Snuggled under the hills, protected from the wind, close both to the vineyards and the arable land are the hamlets. The small wooden houses blend so well into the terrain that they are barely visible from a distance. Here and there in the fields, an occasional hill, having somehow lost its contact with the Mother mountain, points skyward and interrupts the monotony of the plains. On these domineering hillocks one is sure to find a church, a school, a grocery store and an occasional larger administrative building.

In this general topographic order, Stanchich did not make much sense. It had no particular geographic advantage, just a bunch of huge buildings among a few lonely oak trees. From afar the conglomerate was quite impressive: two large horse stables built of cement, stretched in parallel for a good one hundred yards each. Next to them were three large buildings. When you got closer the impression of grandeur gave way to a shabby reality. The stables

were overgrown by grass, not an animal inside. The washings hanging from windows bore witness to some life inside other buildings, but the crumbling plaster warned against undue optimism. The horse farm in Stanchich was dilapidated and only a few former hands lived on the premises. It did not at all look promising.

On the return to Zagreb, we stopped in Bozjakovina to pay respects to Slavko Kolar. He discouraged any thanks. After all, he'd done nothing but give up a bunch of useless buildings for the benefit of sick Croatian children. He said this with a straight face and a twinkle in the eye. I will never forget this clever, witty and kind man. At first sight one might have mistaken him for a country snob. He wore knee high shiny boots over riding breeches, a hunter's leather jacket and a Bavarian hat. Mother remained behind to chat with Mrs. Kolar while Slavko Kolar took Father, Djuka and me for a short visit to various remote buildings. We squeezed into his elegant carriage which, pulled by a pair of beautiful Lipitsaner horses and guided by an uniformed coachman, gave the image of a nineteenth century aristocrat on a visit to the countryside. This was his official pose but in private Kolar was relaxed and devoid of any pomp. After we settled in Stanchich, Kolar alone or in the company of his wife frequently took his elegant coach for the six-mile long ride to visit my parents in Stanchich. Since my parents had no other peers to talk with, Kolar's visits were very much appreciated. His trips to Stanchich were also a political statement to others that a Croat patriot need not be an antisemite.

Slavko Kolar was an extraordinary human being whose conscience did not permit him to stay on the sidelines. After a few other risky moves, including an open debate with some powerful Croatian nationalists, his situation became very difficult. In 1994 Kolar "went into the forest" to join the Partizan guerrilla movement.

~

When we came to Stanchich the builders and the core personnel for the future hospital had already moved in. The place teemed with life.

Unfortunately there were no children to associate with. The more talented ones commuted to faraway high schools and the rest worked

on the land. Djuka struck up a friendship with some younger farmers but I could not find anybody of my age. By and by, I became the pet of various young adults in the vicinity of Stanchich. I was treated as almost an equal but they knew where to draw the line. Whereas Djuka got an unlimited ticket, I was never drawn into the other dimension of my mentors' lives, that of sexual fantasies and exploits. These adults were excellent teachers within their area of competence. I learned how to distill brandy, diagnose veterinary problems, when to shoe horses, and how to tell different kinds of trees. Most of my companions were hunters and they taught me how to handle a gun. They understood animal behavior, knew what the animals ate, where they would likely be, and which way they would run or fly. The hunters of Stanchich were not the greedy city dwellers out for the once-a-week quick shot. They refrained from long shots that were more likely to wound than kill. When they reached their self-imposed one-animal-per-hunter limit, they emptied the guns and headed home, though some of them bagged quite a few animals, whereas others left empty-handed. Nobody ever complained. Everybody understood that hunting was only a game and that today's loser might tomorrow be the winner. There is a great therapeutic value in the single-minded patience and concentration during the hunt. All bad thoughts were left behind and one was in good company.

At the center of village life were the three Selec brothers and Jozha Meashich, their brother-in law. All four of them were strong, healthy and dynamic. The oldest Selec, Mato, would permit me to join him in his job as *pudar*, the caretaker and the single patrolman of the vineyards in the remote hills. During certain periods the vineyards were abuzz with activities; cutting back the vines, turning the earth between rows, spraying with copper sulfate and, of course, when the time came, harvesting the grapes. In between these spasms of activity the vineyards were deserted. It was the *pudar's* responsibility to watch the property during those low periods. As a matter of convenience every vineyard, no matter how small, had its "*kljet*," a utility house usually consisting of one room atop a walk-in cellar. Situated on the highest points, invariably offering a pleasant view, loaded with food and useful tools, the *kljets* could easily attract unwanted visitors.

Checking on all the vineyard houses was not a simple matter. The next kljet might be within a hundred yards, but to avoid ups and downs, the road followed the terrain and meandered for miles before it got there. Mato cut a great figure patrolling the vineyards with the shotgun on his shoulder, the semiofficial green felt coat, a pheasant's feather in his hat and the ammunition belt around his waist. The high visibility served as a deterrent and was part of the job. I do not remember us ever catching anybody, but we did a lot of useful small things. Mato was a good observer. If a fresh horse carriage track led where it should not have gone, he'd investigate and inform the owner about the unwanted visit. After the rain we frequently stopped to fill larger potholes in the road with the last year's vine cuttings mixed with wet clay. When the road dried out, that provided a firm dust free base and prevented accumulation of water during rains.

Even when there was nothing to do I enjoyed strolling through the vineyards. Often we would sidestep into the forest to pick mushrooms or observe the wildlife. The theory had it that crows and magpies were feeding on pheasants' eggs or snatching young rabbits and every hunter had to shoot at least one crow a week. This gave Mato an ideal opportunity to teach me how to handle the gun. The instruction had very little to do with marksmanship, that would have to come from practice. Rather, Mato kept explaining how to load and unload a gun, when to unlock the safety, which way to point the barrel when one has to sneak through the bushes, and what is an effective shooting distance. Most of his teaching was dedicated to safety: never point the barrel toward yourself or others even when the gun is presumed empty, do not lean a loaded gun against a tree, and unload the gun when it's not in use. Mato taught me not to shoot unless I knew where other hunters were and to make sure nobody else gets inadvertently into the line of fire.

By and by as I gained his confidence, Mato let me carry his very heavy gun. It was a high honor for me, and a good riddance for him. I would get the gun at the final stretch of our peripatetic journey as we neared Shtakorovac, a small village about two miles from Stanchich by road and a good ten miles through the vineyards. The name loosely translates into "Ratville." I've no idea how it got its name. The small village grew next to an impressive two story-eighteenth century aris-

tocratic country house. The building had its back against the forest and, perched on a small hill, it offered a beautiful view of the plains around and beyond the river Lonja. One could make out the bushes and willows on both sides of the river, which meandered like a snake through the patchwork of yellow corn, green grass and bluish cabbage fields. That must have been the view that some hundred years ago intrigued a local aristocrat, the Count Drashkovich, to build a hunting lodge in Shtakorovac. Drashkovich had no heirs and the property eventually passed on to the state, which incorporated it into the agricultural enterprise in Bozhjakovina. Slavko Kolar, in turn, made it a part of the land deal of the new hospital. The plans called for the buildings and the land around them to eventually become the core of a large-scale vegetable garden for the hospital.

Stanchich and Shtakorovac were quite different. Bustling with renovation, Stanchich had its inner core. The large whitewashed buildings dominated village life. All notable events started in them and from there imposed themselves upon the village. On the contrary, the center of Shtakorovac was dead, a sleeping giant of a house only occasionally brought to life by activities on its periphery. Sparsely inhabited by unemployed former stable hands, the large building was of no interest to Mato or me. We would routinely pass it by and go straight ahead to the Meashich house at the other edge of the village. The big yard of the house teemed with cats, dogs, pigs, chickens, geese, even a few Cornish hens, peacefully coexisting with larger domestic animals. It was well worth navigating through that zoo towards the Meashich house. The hosts always rolled out some ham, sausages, cheese, and a loaf of hot fresh bread. I loved their smoked cheese. Depending on how old the cheese was, how long it was kept in the smoky attic and what kind of wood was burned it tasted different each time. Sometimes both generations had time to sit down with us—the parents in their sixties and Jozha with his wife in their thirties. The younger couple did not seem to fit together. Jozha's wife was Mato's sister, a stocky village girl at loss for words, constantly embarrassed about something. Jozha was six feet tall, slender, with an intelligent oval face, well spoken, lively and sure of himself. He was the pride of the village, an unquestioned leader of men. There was a special air about him.

My father was intrigued with Jozha's elegant long fine hands and his spiritual face dominated by deep-set observant eyes.

"After all, aristocracy was not necessarily opposed to bedroom populism and, who knows, maybe the Count Drashkovich did have an heir," he once said only half-joking.

Jozha's graceful appearance was matched by an inquisitive mind. Though he spoke with the same slang as anybody else, the sentences were complex and reflected a deeper level of functioning. Jozha was an excellent judge of humans. It did not interest him what so and so did, but why he did it. He was decisive and for him right and wrong were not academic categories. If something was wrong, Jozha would to do his level best to make it right. When the time came, these personal characteristics made Jozha into one of the most respected leaders in the guerrilla movement.

~

In the fall of 1942 a string of festivities replaced most individual activities in Stanchich. Some of the autumn celebrations in the village reflected economic necessities. Grapes ripen late and must be picked before the first frost. It was too large a job for a single farmer and his family. Neighbors, friends, even town folks, were invited to help. The host would do his best to reward the crew for the hard work. The best grapes were eaten, the sweet freshly pressed grape juice flowed abundantly and each intermission was a small feast. The "*kljet*" had been stocked with sausages, cheese, smoked ham and other goodies. After a few exhausting hours one worked up a ravenous appetite and it was great to savor good food in pleasant company.

Since Roman times, harvesting the grapes has remained a joyous affair, but not because of the wine. Though it is freely available, very little old wine is consumed; the freshly pressed 'must' is the drink of the moment. Somehow the fresh air, the good weather, the beautiful fall foliage and positive expectations combine to guarantee a success. I do not recall any disappointing grape harvests. People were on their best behavior, ready to sing, chitchat, and celebrate. It all came by itself and the host did not have to worry.

Once the grapes were processed the time came for "baking" the famous shlivovica. Not too many plums in Croatia got a chance to become prunes. They were picked and squashed into big barrels and left to ferment for weeks. Some stray plums would fall to the ground and as the fermentation in and out of the barrel advanced, a sweet smell engulfed the village. Geese loved to eat plums off the ground and did not care whether they were still fresh or had already fermented. After they had eaten fermented plums, the geese would get grotesquely drunk. The aimlessly wandering and obviously tipsy geese were only the harbingers of things to come. At the height of the distilling season the whole village would get into high spirits. The primitive stills leaked, alcohol vapors were in the air and anybody who spent some time in the distillery, even if he did not taste the brandy, would become unreasonably happy. During the distilling season the villagers cheerfully beckoned passing strangers to taste the newest brew. Opinions were sincerely sought. Did the brandy have the right aroma, was it strong enough or should it be "baked" again? By baking it again, distilling the brandy twice, the farmer could produce a much stronger liquor. However this was a time consuming and risky enterprise as the new product might lose its aroma. I dislike shlivovica but this strong and aromatic brew is widely popular. The joke had it that the only reason for Germany's invasion of the unimportant and poor Yugoslavia was to get hold of some shlivovica.

The fall was also the pig slaughter season which, of necessity was rather short. Wine making and brandy baking had to be completed first, lest the grapes froze and the plum mush deteriorated. That left only a few weeks from mid November till Christmas for pig slaughter. The smelly procedure required plenty of open space. After Christmas it was too cold to suspend the huge pigs head-down, pour boiling water over them to remove the bristles, and with frozen hands it was impossible to remove the innards. A large portion of the pig could be preserved as ham, smoked sausages, lard, and roasted meat but some of the by-products were perishable. What might have started as a necessity, to get help with dressing the pig and to share the perishable foods, continued as a festive tradition even after refrigeration became commonplace. Sending the pig to a butcher and get-

ting back the finished products was out of question. It would spoil all the fun! Villagers usually fed three large pigs, two for themselves, the third for the festivity. Everybody had his little secret and exchanging recipes added spice not only to the sausages, but also to village life in general.

In contrast to fall, none of the winter activities were urgent. Everything was indoors, the winter was long, and nobody was in any particular hurry. People were in a hibernating mood, the weather turned ugly and one had to have a darn good reason to venture outside his homestead. The farmers learned to beat winter's monotony with a string of parties. Contrary to the joys of fall, these winter parties had to be prepared well, or nobody would have shown up.

Most popular of all winter events was husking of the corn from the cob. Friends would gather around a large heap of cobs to pry loose as many kernels as was possible. To attract visitors, the host would secure attendance of a few good voices and some pretty faces. Songs were sung, pretty girls were wooed, but nothing matched a good evening of stories. No matter how old the story was, a good narrator could grab the audience by his intonation, with beautiful sentences, or by the smallest twist in the plot. Like opera lovers, the villagers savored every little nuance. After the guests had absorbed a string of heroic tales and were about ready to leave, the host would invariably unleash his grand finale. A ghost story! These terrifying tales did not follow a fixed scenario. Would the ghost appear as an eerie sound, a screaming cat, a knock on the door, or a mirage? Young listeners first feigned surprise, but after a few oohs and aahs, true fear would set in. Driven by a primordial herding instinct, the bodies drew closer to extract one from another some measure of comfort. There is safety in numbers and nobody was in the mood to leave, just in case a real ghost waited in the dark! A good story, properly timed, could produce many extra bushels of corn!

~

By the fall of 1942, Mother had learned the ways of the village and carefully scheduled our own pig slaughter not to coincide with other gatherings. She hired the best butcher and set the date at the end of

the season, just before the winter snows. This was a strategic but risky decision since the event could not be postponed. If the weather turned bad we would have had to brave the elements and complete the outdoors portion under umbrellas. Technically, with a great deal of strain, and if it was absolutely necessary, the outdoor slaughter could be completed. However, bad weather would reduce the number of guests. And without guests, instead of a festive event, a pig slaughter could turn into a tiresome routine. For taking her chances, Mother was rewarded by a beautiful cool, clear December day. By four o'clock in the afternoon, with plenty of outside help, all three pigs were dressed. This relatively early finish left enough time for such indoor fun as processing meat, rending the lard, filling the sausages and savoring new products.

Making the sausages unleashes collective creativity. The recipes are never the same; nothing is precisely measured. You add a tad of this, a dash of that, and taste the raw meat on the way. It is a tricky business as one has to make allowance for the final taste of the cooked, roasted, or smoked sausage. When everybody is satisfied with the taste, the actual production starts. Big syringes are filled with the seasoned ground meat and the gut is attached to the nozzle. As one pushes the piston the amorphous pile of casing springs to life as if a big angry snake were attached to the syringe. I was fascinated with the process and used to go from one slaughter to another just to watch. The sausage-making left childhood memories that I can neither explain, nor understand. Had Sigmund Freud lived in Stanchich instead of Vienna, he would have written about it. The emerging wiggling shape obviously must have stood for who knows what suspicious, deeply repressed experience. Whatever it might have been, I had a bad case of it.

During our own pig slaughter, however, I felt strangely detached and did not volunteer to taste the sausages. By five o'clock I had a splitting headache, and started to shake. I had an obvious fever and felt so weak that Father had to carry me to bed. I had just started a month-long battle with typhoid fever.

Typhoid starts with high fever and a feeling of hopeless exhaustion. For a week the fever oscillates, and the next two weeks, it is steadily in the 103 to 105 range. Confusion, delirium and hallucina-

tions soon supersede that overwhelming feeling of tiredness. In the fourth week the fever starts decreasing, but there is still the danger of a sudden perforation of the gut with dire consequences. As diseases go, typhoid is not so bad; the mortality is in the 15% range. The feeble and the elderly are at highest risk, but death could claim even the strongest person.

Because of a low white cell count, typhoid was suspected on the second day of my fever. There are only a few febrile diseases with such a blood cell response. Somewhere in the second week the diagnosis was confirmed by a serologic test. To shield me from fear, Father had invented a substitute diagnosis. I was told I had Brucellosis, an equally long fever with a low white cell count. Even at thirteen years of age, I had considerable interest in medicine and presenting me with a plausible, but exotic diagnosis of a less dangerous disease, was supposed to put me at ease. That is how medicine was practiced in those days. The patient was not permitted to know the gravity of the situation and it was the doctor's duty to keep him happy.

Father acted with his usual confidence and calmness. Nevertheless I knew something was very wrong. All around me were serious faces, people tiptoed through the room and visitors, pretending they were not concerned, kept glancing at me from the corners of their eyes. And then there was the *consilium*! The institution of a consilium was invented for the benefit of the rich and Father frequently made jokes of his participation in various consiliums. The primary physician would summon two or three top experts to a patient's home where they heard the medical history, examined the patient and asked additional questions. Eventually the experts and the doctor withdrew to a suitable room to discuss the case. Occasionally these sessions came up with new ideas but as a rule, the consilium endorsed the primary physician's approach. Yet a short session would not do and the secluded physicians routinely sat through the requisite half hour, talking about private matters or exchanging jokes.

My *consilum*, however, was serious business. Father was not comfortable in the dual role of a physician to his family and a psychiatrist-turned-general-practitioner. Three top doctors came from

Zagreb. At thirteen, I had fallen into a habit of calling attention to myself through all sorts of imaginary symptoms. As a confirmed hypochondriac, ordinarily, I would have enjoyed the attention but the doctors in the consilium got to me. Two of them kept a patently false facade of cheerful optimism. Surely they had not traveled the distance just to give me a patronizing pat on the head! The third doctor, a thin, ascetic, gray-haired gentleman, gave me a thorough exam. There was an aura of concern, competence, and decisiveness about him. Others treated him with deference and he was the obvious leader of the pack. This austere specialist gave me a great deal of confidence. He was the top specialist for infectious diseases in the country. How could he possibly be wrong? Well, he was. His uncanny ability to make accurate diagnoses was beyond reproach, but when it came to the treatment, he almost did me in. Back in 1942 there was nothing physicians could do about typhoid fever but this did not stop them from trying. They used all sorts of remedies based on their 'internal logic.' If scientific reasoning suggested something *ought* to work, then a physician accepted that it *did* work, particularly if a top Professor said so! Unfortunately, the austere professor from Zagreb concluded I should be given daily injections of *Omnadin*, a hard-to-get German medication for stimulation of 'the non-specific defenses' of the body. Aroused by *Omnadin*, my body was supposed to mobilize its hidden potential and better fight the typhoid bacillus!

Omnadin injections immediately caused a terrific reaction. After each painful shot I started to feel extremely weak and the fever climbed a few notches up. Mother had on standby a bathtub full of sheets submerged in tepid water. As soon as the fever reached the predetermined danger point, I was stripped naked and packed into wet sheets. To a feverish person the tepid water feels extremely cold. After *Omnadin* I would invariably trade the sleepy confusion of a pre-delirious state with the even worse sensation of shaking chills. As soon as I got half-comfortable, my benevolent torturers would find the linen too warm and embalmed me again into a new set of tepid sheets. In the 1940s, failing to admit its limitations, and instead of just standing by, 'modern' medicine consoled itself with useless activities. It is hard to understand how Father, who was such a rational man could, on blind faith, accept this nonsense. For one month he

suspended scientific judgment and became just another concerned parent grabbing at every straw of hope. Needless to say, *Omnadin* or not, the disease ran through its classic four-week course.

During these rituals and generally throughout my disease, I noticed a great deal of change in Mother's behavior. She stopped complaining about everybody and everything and she did not engage in one of her habitual "poor us" laments. A focused style replaced her previously hyper-excitable manner. The change was enormous. At that time I did not understand why Mother changed so much, but I now realize that my disease reconnected her with things she missed in her life. Medicine was her true love and my illness gave her a chance to practice the forbidden craft. Mother became as organized and purposeful as she had been thirty years earlier during the Hungarian revolution when she smuggled her fiancée out of Budapest. Attending me in Stanchich, Mother embarked on a road to personal happiness. The coming three years, by all standards the hardest she ever faced, were also her best ones. She became useful to others and the war gave her a chance to spring out of the mold of a bourgeois housewife. But about that later.

There is a silver lining to every cloud. In the third week, as the fever slowly melted away, the torture by tepid water-soaked sheets ceased. Instead, marvelous things started to happen thanks to yet another unproven medical practice. The physicians viewed red wine as an excellent remedy for convalescence from infectious diseases. In the 1940s the status of red wine had been upgraded from the mistaken theory that it was helpful because of its similarity in color to blood, to its newly exalted status as a reliable source of iron. Be this as it may, my regimen changed from the brutal fever-inducing followed by cold packing ritual, to a compulsory two small glasses of red wine per day. And not just any red wine. Everybody in the village offered his best bottle for my benefit.

The undisputed winner was the Burgundy from the church vineyards in Brckovljani. High on the hill, overlooking Stanchich, the church was surrounded by vineyards and the priest, Mato Kralj, had

The church and the hill of Brckovljani in 2002.

turned one side into a demonstration project. With the help of agronomists from Bozhjakovina the vines were trained onto long wires stretched between cement poles. Each mile long row was planted with another variety of grapes and if they liked the grapes, the villagers could order saplings for next year's grafting. In 1941 the Burgundy row yielded about three hectoliters of grape juice which by the winter of 1942 had turned into delicious, smooth sweet red wine. Ivo Kralj, the priest's nephew, had just graduated from medical school and unexpectedly turned up to live in Uncle's manse on the hill. He introduced himself, placed two demijohns of the precious fluid under our nondenominational, sparsely adorned, Christmas tree and suggested that "the wine will replace the candles by glowing from the inside."

Every evening there was a small ritual—a glass of wine at the ready, to be drunk only if I had consumed the requisite dinner. The first effect of the smooth, oily, sweet wine, was a pleasant warmth in

the stomach followed by giddiness and relaxation. The dose was too small to make me drunk. The memory of the priest's Burgundy is stronger than anything I remember from those days. In fact, six decades later I still compare each new bottle of red wine to the elusive childhood standard. Some French Burgundies have come close by their warmth, by smell, or by taste but none of them had all those qualities at once. None! And the original is gone forever. The priest got old, gave up the experiment, and after the war the vineyard was plowed over.

For a good two months, the whole microcosm of Stanchich revolved around my bed. While I had fever, my parents were permanently at the bedside, and the convalescence was not about to change their routine. What went on then would nowadays be called "bonding" but it was more than that. We formed a small cozy world of family and selected villagers to keep at some distance the ugly reality of the brutal German occupation around us. Every evening Father, Mother, Djuka and I would huddle around the short-wave radio to listen to the BBC. Listening to the BBC's Croatian broadcast became a pleasant family ritual. It was our connection with a better world and an invisible pipeline to a hopeful future. Occasionally the regular broadcast was peppered with cryptic messages and we frequently wondered what, if anything, they meant. It was both mysterious and irritating. Some exciting report from the Eastern front could be suddenly interrupted with a nonsensical sentence:

"To George, the sun will rise again."

"To my children, how is the weather?"

"Peter, the fat lady will not sing." Or some similar gibberish.

Why did they do it? For sure the Allies could have had a better and more direct contact with the operatives behind the enemy lines. The cryptic messages were, we reasoned, just a part of the propaganda game. To leave an impression, even if it were not true, that London was coordinating a network of resistance movements in various countries. Upon reflection, the use of a public broadcasting facility to send messages was a clever device. It might have had some propaganda value and could have possibly sent the Germans on a wild goose chase, but it also obviated the need for direct radio contact. The Germans were quite skillful in using goniometers to locate

illegal transmitters. A fleet of conspicuous cars with globe shaped antennas kept crisscrossing the territories under German occupation. They could within minutes localize the general area and given more time, pinpoint the illegal radio station to a single house. To avoid capture, the operators constantly changed the band frequency and the location of the transmission. As the operator moved from one safe place to another, the contacts with numerous confidants greatly increased the likelihood of detection. One gullible person or one house under surveillance could put an end to the enterprise.

Our conspiratorial and highly illegal listening to the BBC was the best part of the evening. It was absolutely crucial to be well-informed but regardless of the content, these daily reminders of a large war effort against Germany were tremendous morale boosters. Equally enchanting and heart-warming was our physical and emotional closeness during those broadcasts. However, my family did its best to provide me also with good entertainment during the day. When the word got out that I was no longer infectious to others, my bedroom became the center of all activities. As visitors came by, a new world started to develop in front of my eyes. My previous knowledge about the resistance movement amounted to a string of unrelated anecdotes, small vignettes without a common thread. Now with everything more or less openly discussed in my presence, I started to comprehend the scope of the emerging conspiracy. Under the leadership of Jozha Meashich and the Selec brothers, many hospital employees had joined the resistance movement cell in the nearby villages. In and around Stanchich the resistance movement was organized and led by the Communist Party of Yugoslavia.

Illegal and persecuted by police, the Communist Party of Yugoslavia systematically prepared itself for a confrontation with the invading Germans. Their resistance to Germans was in part ideological. Hitler proclaimed himself violently opposed to the "worldwide Communist-Jewish-Masonic conspiracy," a term nobody quite understood but in practical terms it meant that exterminating Communists was at the top of Hitler's priority list. The other reason for Communist

resistance to the Germans was political. The Communists speculated that if Hitler were defeated by the Allies, the Communists participation in the resistance against the Germans would give the Party legitimacy and power. The Yugoslav Communists quickly transformed their extensive network of illegal cells into a well-organized military infrastructure. First they started to collect arms from the disintegrating Yugoslav Army. Soon thereafter, the Communists organized fighting units and initiated guerrilla actions. The emerging Communist-led "Partizans" ignored all ethnic or religious differences. Prospective fighters, be they Serbs, Croats, Slovenes or Jews were equally welcomed. The strategy of inclusiveness worked well. Within a year the Partizans became an effective fighting force. Eventually they successfully tied up numerous German divisions in a war of attrition.

Elegant, polite and blessed with natural wisdom Jozha caught the eye of the guerrilla movement recruiters. They appealed to his sense of patriotism and his feelings against social injustice. The latter point did not require elaboration; the whole village was on the receiving end. Jozha joined the movement and swiftly rose through the ranks to become the head of a "*veza.*" The "*Veza*" (meaning "the connection") was an intricate secret organization that connected the enemy controlled territory with the guerrilla movement. The sector of "*veza*" under Jozha's command, was an important thirty-kilometer channel through which volunteers from Zagreb joined the resistance movement. Jozha was responsible for three sections, each covering as long a distance as one could reach in an all-night walk. At the end of each section the volunteers were led to basements or haylofts of safe houses to hide during the day. Next night they'd resume walking towards the new safe haven. After three days, Jozha's confidants passed the volunteers on to the next sector of the *veza*, which, depending on the chosen direction and circumstances, would in two to six days bring them to the free territory.

Jozha's task required much more than having steady nerves and knowing no fear. He had to select guides from distant villages so that one guide knew only the alias but not the true identity of his contact person. The guide would walk during the day towards the meeting point from which, during the night, he'd take his charges back to the safe houses. Jozha organized for each segment of his *veza* multiple

sets of guides and safe houses. That way he'd have replacements in case of need but he was also careful not to engage the same person too frequently. Small villages have well-established routines and on a given day everybody pretty much knows what the others are doing. Someone's repetitive and unusual behavior could have become suspicious to others. On a higher level, Jozha chose a few go-betweens to contact guides on both ends, organize the meeting point, and give guides some specific information. An incoming group could be larger or smaller, or instead of humans, the guides would sometimes pass on supplies for the guerrilla.

Jozha was successful in his work chiefly because he knew how to judge people. He chose guides who were self-reliant, capable of making decisions and hopefully brave enough not to be caught alive by the enemy. Jozha's guides were keen observers and they carefully studied the deployment of enemy forces. If one of the elite SS units were on patrol, the guide would call off all activities for that night. The Ustashe were equally dangerous but because they spoke the same language, sometimes they left plenty of information in local watering holes. If the guide thought the information was solid enough, he could gamble and attempt to squeeze through the Ustashe lines. The situation with Wermacht, the regular German Army, could vary from easy to extremely difficult, depending on the makeup of a given unit. The majority of units sent to maintain the occupation of Yugoslavia had either been decimated on the Eastern Front, or were not yet in full battle shape. The local *veza* guide had to find out whether the unit in his area was eager to fight or whether it preferred to avoid trouble. The intent of a Wermacht unit could be best judged from its relationship with the local population. The more stops at local pubs, the more contact with village children, the more rests at the roadside, the less likely were they to venture into the darkness or to set up a daytime raid. The easiest to deal with were the conscripts into the Croatian National Army, the Domobrani ("the home guard"). All adult males in Croatia were subject to military draft. Children of the rich, well-educated or well-connected people found ways to avoid service, and the rabid Nationalists volunteered to serve in elite Ustashe units. Consequently the Domobrani were a ragtag, poorly armed, ill-trained army of uneducated and unmotivated peo-

ple whose only interest was to survive the war. Invariably the guide knew among the Domobrans enough local boys to arrange that at the right time, everybody looked the other way.

Besides enrolling the right guides Jozha had to line up safe places for overnight stays. This was a very delicate task. He had to convince the host to provide a sanctuary and risk possible destruction of his household. Because of his instinctive understanding of people Jozha was eminently successful. Only once, and through no fault of his own, did Jozha run into trouble.

A highly recommended person came down to the *veza* and Jozha decided to meet him personally. As soon as he set his eyes on the volunteer, Jozha became uncomfortable. To dislike Germans was reasonable. However, this man's exaggerated hatred and the steady stream of anti-Nazi curses were unusual. People hiding in a basement were usually nervous and preoccupied with thoughts of uncertain future. Not this guy. He was boastful and unconcerned as if he were going to a picnic. Equally worrisome was his request that he be led directly to regular units. On the spot Jozha decided not to lead him anywhere, not until he could assess him better. The rest of the group went with the regular guide and Jozha took the guy by himself. As the twosome wandered through the night, the stranger tried to strike up a conversation, but Jozha insisted on silence. He led him in a circle and to make sure that the man got the message, Jozha chose to rest twice under the same statue of crucifixion in the vineyards.

"I haven't the foggiest idea why I did it. Probably to show I did not trust him. If he had an ambush lined up, we sure were way off course," explained Jozha later.

Perfect intuition! In the middle of the third merry-go-around circle, Jozha felt a dull pain in the back. The stranger had stabbed him. Jozha grabbed the hand behind him not allowing another strike. As they wrestled, the man let go of the knife and went after Jozha's submachine gun. Starting to feel more pain and getting dizzy, Jozha summoned all his strength, pushed the attacker off, and shot him dead.

Jozha dragged himself to the house of Mato Selec who took him to a *kljet* in the vineyard where my father took care of Jozha's wound. He was weak and for a few days ran a high fever which

responded well to sulphonamides. By and by he improved and in two months was back to work. The incident did not change him a bit. Just like a race driver, undeterred by the accident, he was ready to give it his best again. Brave people don't turn into cowards overnight. Jozha made just one adjustment. He permanently cut off the tentacle of the *veza* from where the traitor came. He never reported the case to his superiors, just in case a traitor was sitting somewhere higher up in the *veza*.

It turned out that none of the newcomers came to Stanchich by chance. The innocuous Dr. Kralj, a man of great warmth and quiet humor, was rather mysterious. He was slim, tall, and did not look a bit as if he were of the same stock as his uncle, the priest in Brckovljani. Uncle Mato's yellowish face was leathery and unkempt, whereas Ivo Kralj had the pale complexion of a city dweller whose face had not been exposed to sun. Even when one took into account differences in lifestyle the two faces bore no resemblance. Ivo Kralj never denied his general dislike of the German, but steadfastly refused to have any contact with the local guerrilla organizers. To the extent that he could, Dr. Ivo Kralj kept out of everybody's sight. He did level with my father in an indirect way—by asking that Father secretly inject him with vaccines against tetanus and typhus. The fact that he obtained the vaccine against typhus spoke volumes about him. He must have been very well connected. Ricketsia Prowazecky, a microorganism by size on the border between bacteria and viruses, thrives only in living tissues. German scientists had just figured out how to grow the Ricketsia on chicken embryos to produce a weakened microorganism suitable for vaccination. However, the production was very limited. The vaccine could be obtained only by stealing or by directly trading with German officers. Why would Dr. Kralj wish to be vaccinated against the exotic danger of typhus? Typhoid, as my own case proved, did sporadically occur in and around Zagreb, but typhus, which is transmitted only by body lice, was nonexistent.

We logically concluded that Ivo Kralj was about to join the Partizans "in the forest" where, due to poor personal hygiene, typhus

fever was rampant. The priest's nephew was whimsical. He was willing to discuss the military situation in Europe to the same degree as any other anti-fascist sympathizer, but never spoke about his personal plans. He admitted to suspecting that we might be acquainted with the local network of guerrilla organizers but insisted, rather forcefully, that he did not want any contact with them. "Not my cup of tea," he would insist, leaving the distinction rather moot as to whether he was uninterested in the guerrilla movement or whether he did not trust the local guys. Once when Mother pressed him in her usual nosy ways, he neither denied nor confirmed but shrugged his shoulders muttering something to the effect that these days one does what one has to do.

Another person out of place in Stanchich was the foreman of the hospital construction crew. I've forgotten his name. He stood out from the other workers. Well-spoken, intelligent and knowledgeable, he let it be known that he was good at playing "Preference." That was a bit surprising. This complex card game, once the exclusive province of the Austrian aristocracy and its officer corps, between the two World Wars became the favorite pastime of the middle classes. Had the habit reached the working classes or was the foreman just pretending to be a worker? In due course, Mother invited the foreman to come for a round of Preference and it turned out he was a very good player. He was even more circumspect than Ivo Kralj. The first evening he immediately drew the line; he liked the card game but hated political discussions. And he stuck to his guns. All attempts to find out where he stood in regard to the outside world failed. When one evening Ivo Kralj came for his vaccine shot, Mother invited him for dinner and a round of cards. She also invited the foreman to the card game and when the two men met they grew visibly uneasy. Silent throughout the game, peering over his hand of cards, each would catch a glimpse of the other and instantly turn his head away. Towards the end of that uncomfortable evening, it became clear that the men did not wish to leave together. Mother rose to the occasion, inviting Ivo Kralj to stay for the night. He accepted but half an hour later, after the other man had left, suddenly remembered he had to complete some important chores for his uncle early in the morning.

"Not exactly an average foreman," said my father.

"Not at all," replied Ivo, "I met him sometime ago at a place we both would just as soon forget. No idea how he breathes these days."

"Well he seems rather apolitical," explained Father.

"Good, at least he is not acting as a typical information-seeking agent-provocateur. Wonder whether he is with the movement or hiding."

With these words, Dr. Kralj exited the house and never came back. In a week or so, he left for good. At about the same time the foreman also disappeared. Was he Kralj's contact and had they left together? Ivo Kralj became an important organizer of the Partizans' health services and quickly advanced to the rank of general. I lost track of the foreman and never got around to asking Dr. Kralj about him. I suspect both of them followed the prescribed routine. If your cover is blown take no risk. Unless the other guy presents you with current credentials you had better break off all relationships and leave as soon as you can.

The two unusual visitors at our house, the doctor and the foreman, were a small part of a complex, paranoiac world of the resistance movement. The basic organizational principle of the movement was its multi-layered structure. Kralj sensed we had our contacts but he kept in touch only with his guys. The old-time Communists were trained to ask and know as little as possible. In case they got caught and could not withstand the torture, the less they knew, the less harm they could do.

The behavior of our own group was much more relaxed than that of the secretive Communist types. We were amateurs who had never experienced torture or betrayal. Luckily it worked out but, in retrospect, I would not have trusted a thirteen year-old boy as my comrades trusted me.

We broke the basic rules and loved to gossip. What was Branko Sruk doing in Tashler's grocery store? He was another person out of place. We heard he was a medical student or something like that. Came from town and quietly latched onto Marica Tashler, the widow, who must have been at least ten years older. Good-looking, energetic and more than able to account for herself, she really did not need a man to run her store and the adjacent pub. Her large enter-

prise was strategically placed on the intersection of the local road to Stanchich, the main road from Dugo Selo to Vrbovec and the arrow-straight road up the hill to Brckovljani. One could choose the shorter but steeper path to Brckovljani or take the main road detour around the hill. In any case, the crossroad was the right place to take a break.

The Tashler pub had all the attributes of a place where one would rather take an extended break than a short pause. The numerous tables under the huge horse chestnut trees could accommodate a busload of people. If the weather was not nice or if a traveler wanted to mix with the locals, he could step into the cavernous, musty dining room. Next to the dining room was the grocery store. And then there was the bowling alley, a unique facility found nowhere else along the road.

In addition to the profitable pub and grocery store, Marica Tashler owned substantial lands and had one of the largest vineyards in the area. Unfazed by her husband's death, she ran the business with an iron hand and a foul mouth, all the time continuing to rake in the money. Everybody accepted her as a no-nonsense entrepreneur, a person equal to the best of men. Not too much was known about her love life and it was a sign of her total acceptance as an equal that nobody even tried to endear himself. There were rumors about her brother-in-law, a butcher who lived in the house, but if she had any relationship with him, it was surely on her terms. In public she spoke to him only to issue orders.

Now in the middle of this routine comes Branko, presumably a distant relative, who knew nothing about the business or farming. What promised to be a short visit, became eventually a way of living. Branko was going nowhere. One could see why Marica would have him, young and good-looking as he was. But why would a medical student move to the countryside? He just was not the village type. Finally everybody concluded that Branko was lazy, that he did not wish to study, and that as far as he was concerned, being Marica's common law husband was much better than working.

Marica was apolitical but Branko let it be known that he did not like Germans. Everybody took this as a statement of principles, a platonic declaration of an armchair spectator. We were wrong. Branko never blew his cover but after the war it became known he had been

running the regional counter-intelligence for the Partizans. The strategic position of the Tashler house on the crossroads was ideal for assessment of troop movements and the pub gave Branko a superb listening post. In 1945, when the Party came into power and started handing out lucrative posts, Branko did not cash in on his achievements. Instead of becoming an important functionary he stayed in the village, married Marica, helped raise her children, and continued his low-key existence in the shadow of the dragon lady.

~

By the spring of 1943 the old "everybody to himself rule," and the use of *noms de guerre* became a problem. Thanks to the brutality of the occupiers the number of volunteers dramatically increased. Poorly trained and not coordinated by a central authority, various local cells embarked on all kinds of ill conceived and poorly executed actions. Stanchich was the worst of all places. Everybody seemed involved in the resistance but nobody knew what the others were doing.

The proliferation of uncoordinated guerilla activities in our territory finally backfired. Literally overnight, a poorly conceived local raid changed the entire situation in Stanchich. Djuka and the boys from Stanchich got it into their heads to blow up the electrical transformer station near Bozhjakovina, where a high mesh wire fence surrounded a maze of various transformers, directly connected to huge power lines. The fence was generously adorned with skulls and crossbones, bolts of lighting, and with written warnings of danger. Maybe the authorities thought the warnings by themselves were a sufficient deterrent, or more likely they had just overlooked the place. In any case, unguarded and sitting in the middle of a field, the transformer station presented an inviting target for sabotage. Though they knew how to rig an explosive, the would-be saboteurs had no idea about the art of demolition. They cut through the fence, quickly placed charges at various points, lit the fuses, and "withdrew" in a hurry. The pitiful explosion caused little damage to the transformer but the bang was loud enough to provoke immediate countermeasures. Before the incident the enemy did not have a permanent outpost in

the territory around Stanchich and Bozhjakovina. Within days, a troop of Ustashe took up residence in Bozhjakovina at the crossing between the road to the transformer and the main Dugo Selo-Vrbovec road. The garrison provided guards for the transformer, but from their new post Ustashe also began sending small reconnaissance parties in all directions.

Things were getting quite difficult. Instead of coming and going as they wished, the Partizan movement now faced an alert enemy. A detachment of Ustashe could appear at any time, mount a checkpoint, or suddenly burst into anybody's house. Because of the new situation the Partizans had to reroute the illegal traffic in people and supplies to lengthy back roads. Furthermore the Ustashe established contact with some local people and began to receive valuable information. Everything had to change. Gone were the days when a large group could meet in someone's house to plan further action. There was a real possibility, though to my knowledge it never happened, that someone could report the suspicious meeting. It would take the enemy a very short time to show up in force.

Most disconcerting was the Ustashe's ever-increasing focus on the hospital in Stanchich. Their quarters were a good five miles away, but members of the Bozhjakovina garrison kept showing up in Stanchich with increasing regularity. Sometimes a few officers on motorcycles would drop in "for a chat." On other occasions a small unit on patrol would take a rest on hospital premises. However a few times the enemy showed up in full force and with obvious ill intentions. They descended from the Brckovljani Hill in a wide single row, each soldier twenty to thirty feet from the other, guns at the ready. They combed the fields and unmistakably moved towards the hospital. When they finally arrived, the soldiers deployed in a circle around the hospital and remained there for a good two hours. The Ustashe said nothing, nor did they send anybody into the hospital proper. The natural instinct was to walk over and ask the soldiers what was on their mind. Instead, the hospital personnel affected normalcy, as if they had not noted the menacing intruders. Eventually the Ustashe arranged themselves into one column, hung the guns over their shoulders and took off for a leisurely walk via the main road back to their headquarters.

The second time the maneuver was even more menacing. First a group arrived by truck and ordered everybody, patients and personnel alike, out off the yard into the buildings. Instantly the hospital became a ghost town. Soon the soldiers set up three machine gun emplacements to face the hill in Brckovljani. They also positioned a sentry in front of the administration building and another one at the hospital's power station. Then, as before, in the distance on top of the hill, there appeared a chain of soldiers. Only this time, they moved much faster and soon the hospital teemed with soldiers. Saying nothing, they kept everybody bottled up inside the buildings for the rest of the day. At evening, just as suddenly as they'd come, without a single comment, the soldiers left.

The Ustashe did nothing one could complain about and yet these were clear messages of ill will. The second deployment was much more than a simple military training exercise. Apparently the Ustashe acted on information and expected to catch somebody inbetween the descending chain and the waiting machine gun nests. Had they been successful, the final battle would have been fought on the hospital grounds, a fact that was not lost on anybody.

Ustashe obviously knew that the hospital was a hotbed of resistance activities, and decided to show us some force. Father was getting quite concerned. At any moment the Ustashe could detain our family and that would have been the end of us. Theoretically we were under the protection of the Ministry of Health but nobody had illusions about that.

The troop detachment in Bozhjakovina was hard to read. Slavko Kolar had his contacts with the top leadership in Zagreb and could develop general clues as to what the future may hold, but the guys in the field made friends with nobody. There was a new element in the equation: an independent, proactive and enigmatic enemy. The situation was too dangerous. Any further procrastination could be fatal. In the fall of 1943, Father sent the word that we were ready to join the movement and that he had accumulated enough medical supplies to outfit a Partizan field hospital. A preliminary date was set and confirmed two days before the Partizans came to pick us up.

The Night Walkers

(September 1943)

The line shows the 220 kilometers, one-week-long, trek to the free territory.

As scheduled, at dusk a ragtag group of about fifty Partizans descended upon the hospital. Some wore civilian clothes; others were clad in an assortment of military uniforms—mostly those of the old Yugoslav Army, a substantial number of Croatian Domobran outfits, and an occasional German or Italian uniform. Their weapons were even more picturesque, as if they had acquired them at some international bazaar. They ranged from very short Italian carbines to the clumsy and extremely long Austrian, three-shot World War I infantry rifles. About half of the platoon carried the very reliable and precise standard nine millimeter caliber gun of the Yugoslav Army. A few soldiers brandished with pride their semiautomatic guns. The group had two machine guns, each assigned to two fighters, one to carry the gun and the other the ammunition. The machine guns were quickly deployed at the two entrances to the hospital. The formidable looking and probably more effective full-sized World War I issue Maxim dominated the driveway; the other, a light German model, controlled the pedestrian access downhill from Brckovljani.

The guerrillas carried out their work in remarkable silence. They rarely said a word and when they had to, they spoke in a low, close-to-whisper volume. It was unnecessary in Stanchich, but the guerrillas could not shake their conspiratorial habit. In a forest camp, sneaking through the enemy lines, hidden in a basement or just going from place to place, a guerrilla had better be quiet not to be heard and more importantly, to hear who is approaching.

Within an hour, the quiet Partizans emptied the hospital pharmacy into waiting horse wagons. They relieved the supply magazine of blankets, canned food, flour, dry beans and all other nonperishable food. The loaded wagons took off. Mission accomplished, the Partizans busied themselves leaving propaganda messages on the walls while the commander played out the prearranged charade which was supposed to provide us with a cover in case the enemy intercepted us. The commander assembled the employees and asked them to join the guerrilla movement. Nobody volunteered. He then

"in the name of the people" informed Father he was mobilized to serve as a physician in the People's Liberation Army.

"You have got half an hour to prepare yourself," said the commander in an unusually loud voice. "Dress the best you can for adverse conditions. You are likely to march for days on end and sleep outdoors. You may as well forget the comforts of the civilian life. We treat doctors very well. However our own life is hard." The scene might have been choreographed but the message was sincere.

"Where are we going?" asked Father.

"You would not expect me to reveal a military secret," said the commander. Again he was sincere. Had Father pulled him to the side and discretely asked for information the answer would have been identical. The less people knew, the better it was.

Father protested. He could not leave the family behind and he could not possibly pack up all four of us in half an hour.

The commander responded in kind. Yes, Father could take the family along and yes, an extension of one hour could be granted. "But not a minute longer," said the commander sternly.

Of course, everybody but Father was already fully dressed and eager to leave. As far as I was concerned we were heading towards a big adventure, an exciting trip into the abstract darkness, a heroic march of the brave Julius family to fight the Germans. I do not recall having any fears. Back in 1943, the feeling of invulnerability and willingness to take stupid risks, so typical of teenagers, served me very well.

Right away everything turned out differently than I had expected. For one thing, our fearless comrades were not that fearless. They were very cautious and at every turn stopped to assess the situation. Small advance groups went ahead while we sat in dead silence flanked by the machine guns. Our escort was a detachment of the famous, battle-tested, *Zagrebachki Odred* and I expected to meet a bunch of loose, extremely brave, "damn the torpedoes" types. Instead, we shared the night with tense, circumspect and almost pathologically careful individuals. And of course that is what a good guer-

rilla fighter should be. Alertness is the currency of the deadly serious business of war. Before an open conflict, even the bravest soldiers quietly maneuver themselves into advantageous positions; to surprise and not be surprised. Once the battle starts, a hero will disregard the danger and take incredible risks. But it would be plain stupid to act with abandon before the conflict.

There were too few fighters in the *Zagrebachki Odred* to cause any serious trouble to the enemy. But the two hundred or so Partizans of the *Odred* succeeded in establishing a credible guerilla presence at the outskirts of Zagreb, right in the enemy's backyard. They were hit-and-run specialists to let the enemy know things were not entirely safe in the occupied lands. Besides the small provocations, an attack on an outpost here, a roadblock there, the careful Partizans of the *Zagrebachki Odred* had other important duties. One of them was to organize the shipment of large-bulk supplies from the occupied to the free territory. This difficult task routinely broke the golden rule of guerrilla warfare. Instead of just a few well-informed persons, a wide range of people had to be involved. Our case was particularly complex. The three wagons of hospital supplies took separate routes. While we traveled under cover of the night, the wagons took their chances in broad daylight. In a village everybody goes to bed early and the night is quiet as a grave. At night the clatter of the wagons with hospital supplies would inevitably attract attention.

The horse and wagon are a very important part of village life. A man becomes a real man only after he has earned enough to buy his own set. The owners proudly strive to distinguish themselves from others in the way the wagon is kept, in the horse's appearance or by some special touch on the harness. It was nearly impossible to surreptitiously move these well-marked vehicles away from the village of origin, not to mention trying to pass them through unfamiliar places. In distant villages everybody had two chances to recognize the strange vehicle; when it went full and when it returned empty. The absence of horses from the village of origin, the suspicious traffic through distant fields, the highly irregular goings-on during the off-loading could at any moment trip up the entire scheme. The suc-

cessful passage of supplies depended on the willingness of many villages to turn a deaf ear and play stupid. It all functioned amazingly well.[1]

~

The very first night our escort gave us a splendid demonstration of the Partizan network. The guerrillas led us away from the hospital, through the familiar trail over the vineyards. We expected to take a straight northward course to the distant mountain of Kalnik; the first Partizan-controlled free territory in the Croatian Zagorje. Instead of going north, we descended on the same side of the hills and proceeded to closely follow the dividing line between the vineyards and the fields. After two hours of meandering around the foothills, the commander called for a rest. We sat down on the edge of the road, using the roadside as a stool to dangle our legs into the ditch. It was a relief for a while but soon the new position became quite uncomfortable. However the Partizans did not appear bothered at all. The machine gunners took up positions on both ends of the column and the rest, about forty people, positioned themselves at a discrete distance from our small family group. Some of them lay down in the middle of the road—apparently to stargaze. The others sat in an embryonic position with knees drawn towards the chest, some paced the road, but all were visibly enjoying the chance to take the heavy guns off their shoulders. Nevertheless, they kept their guns within easy reach.

---

1 When in the early 1990s the tensions between Yugoslav ethnic groups boiled over into an civil war it suited the nationalistic leaders to rewrite history. Mr. Miloshevich's propaganda from Belgrade depicted Croats as collaborators of Germans during World War II. This is simply not true. The Ustashe controlled larger cities and had some genuine popular support only in provinces of Lika and Herzegovina. In the territory around Zagreb the warriors of the *Zagrebachki Odred*, almost all of them Croats, developed an ever-growing network of safe villages. Two years into the German occupation the Ustashe regime hung on to only a few enclaves in an otherwise safe, Partizan-dominated, territory around Zagreb.

In Stanchich Father taught me some elementary lessons in astronomy. As we sat idly under the clear sky, he could not resist the opportunity.

"Look up."

"Yes, the stars are beautiful, *Tata*," I responded, expecting another lecture in astronomy. I usually loved to watch the sky with him but under our exciting circumstances, another lecture seemed just a bit out of place.

"Sure they are, Stevo, but that is not the issue. Can you tell where we are going?"

I spotted Ursa Major, extended its last two "wheels" four times, located the North Star, positioned myself towards it and concluded we were heading west.

"Right," said Father. "And what is west of us?"

"Zagreb."

"Right again. The commander is a clever fellow. He is leading us in the least likely direction. But at some point he will have to change the course or else, by the morning, we will be marching through the city streets."

Just then the commander came by and said, "Comrades, it is time to move."

"Where to?" whispered Father.

"To a friendly village. I just spoke to the man from the *Veza*. Everything has been arranged."

I chimed in, "How long will we have to walk?"

"Two more hours,"

"Towards Zagreb?" asked Father.

"So you noticed! Yup. Toward Zagreb, and we had better start right away," responded our leader.

The commander had broad shoulders and a small beer belly, well in harmony with his mid-size stature. Two long ammunition belts hung diagonally from both shoulders, and crossing over his impressive stomach, they projected an image of higher rank and superior authority. He spoke with a local accent in short to-the-point sentences and wasted neither words nor movements. He never gesticulated and his face was frozen in an alert but relaxed stance.

The road went through a number of villages. Only once were we forced on a long detour through the fields. In all other instances, a local connection was waiting at the entrance to the village greeting us with an informal half salute. But our local hosts had no control over the village dogs that went mad as soon as they sensed our presence. Nobody could possibly sleep through such a loud cacophony but not a person ever came out to check. Maybe the whole village was well briefed. Or, more likely, the villagers would just as soon not know what was going on.

Six hours after departing Stanchich, leaving a string of barking dogs behind us, we arrived at the destination. The village was indeed very close to Zagreb; at the horizon we could see the brilliant red aura of the city. The village church stood at the end of what one would call a village square had there been any other houses around and had the space in front of the church been paved. Instead, two tree-lined roads converged onto the church, delineating between them a field of grass large enough to accommodate a booming county fair. The commander ordered his soldiers to wait at the edge of the field until the local *veza* came to take them to sleep in a bunch of haylofts in the village. He turned to us.

"I will take you to the church," he said, "and, by the way, we are in the village of Cerje. You may as well know where you are. The local priest is a good guy."

The commander knocked on the door of the priest's manse.

"Who is it?"

"The Peoples' Liberation Army!"

"Well I am the peoples' priest. Come in," responded the priest cheerfully. He was young and very hospitable. Did we wish anything to eat? Nobody was hungry. He directed us to the large attic replete with religious paraphernalia. In the corner leaning against the wall, arched between its posts, was a moth-eaten "sky," a canopy, which villagers proudly carried over the priest's head during religious processions. Next to it were somewhat better preserved long poles to display the picture of the right saint for the right occasion. The priest pointed to a huge chimney. Behind it, the attic extended into another comfortable space not readily visible from the top of the stairs.

Hams, sausages, garlands of onions and branches with half-dried grapes hung from the beams. In one of the distant corners of this extended attic was yet another opening to a very low space directly under the roof. Conveniently the floor was covered with hay.

"God chooses for some of us to walk during the day and the others must wander through the night. He made you night walkers and only He knows why. But every one of us must sleep at some time. Have a good rest. Nobody will bother you. Should you get thirsty there are a few bottles of wine and mineral water on the other side of the attic," said the priest. And then he discretely pointed out the bedpan in the corner. Obviously this was not the first time he'd hid somebody in his attic.

"Feel free to feast on the sausages. But please walk very lightly. You never know who may be visiting downstairs and I would not want the mortar from the ceiling to fall on the wrong head."

We felt safe and as soon as each of us found a good place in the hay, we fell asleep. We must have slept a good ten hours. When I awoke Father and Mother were already chatting and Djuka stood upright trying to get rid of the hay on his pants.

From my space I could see the top of the stairs to the attic. The priest's head and shoulders popped into the larger room. "Ah, finally you are up and about," said the pleasant torso, "for the last four hours every half an hour or so, I checked on you and you were out cold. A good sign of clear conscience." With these words the priest invited us down for a dinner.

"But isn't it dangerous?" wondered Mother. "It is still daytime. I can see some light coming thorough the cracks."

"Not exactly. You slept right through the day and in an hour it will be dark again. You need to eat and furthermore this is an unusually safe day."

"What do you mean by that?" inquired Mother.

"Come down, the dinner is ready and you can see it for yourselves."

The "people's priest" had prepared a veritable banquet and as we sat down to eat, the commander came to fetch us. Contrary to the previous night, when he was so reserved, he had a big smile on his

face. "We will have ourselves a party," he said, "but I will wait until you finish the dinner. Father priest's hospitality cannot be refused."

"The commander will show you something rather interesting which you ought to see while there is still some daylight," said the priest. "Eat quickly—otherwise you will spoil his day."

It was a big surprise indeed. The huge field in front of the church teemed with soldiers. Cerje was famous for its fairs but this time, instead of accommodating the merry-go-around and vendors, the village was hosting the entire *Zagrebachki Odred*. We had a prearranged rendezvous with the rest of the Partizans in a village which was less than fifteen miles away from the powerful enemy garrison in Zagreb! Their guns neatly stacked in small pyramids, the relaxed two hundred odd Partizans walked around or rested on the ground as if they had not a single concern on their minds. A large pig on the spit was ready and the soldiers were lining up for dinner. Of course, the *Odred* implemented the necessary precautionary measures. Nobody was permitted to leave the village and substantial forces had been deployed around its perimeter. Nevertheless it was an incredible display. There must have been a good reason for this unusual bravado. Most likely it was just a move in the propaganda battle for the countryside. By the time the soldiers completed the dinner it was pitch dark. The *Odred* gave us an escort group of about twenty men to see us through to the next destination. After 15 minutes we came upon the main road from Zagreb to Dugo Selo. Incredible! Not only were we close to the City, but we were having a Partizan bazaar next to the only asphalt road to Zagreb. At any moment, the enemy could have brought in truckloads of soldiers.

The terrain around Zagreb was almost always irregular. A little patch of corn, then a patch of wheat, a small grove of trees, a field for grazing, all in perfect disorder reflecting the multiple divisions of the land among numerous owners. However the path to the road followed the margin between a large field and a tall forest. The border of the forest descended in a straight line to the edge of the main paved road and provided exceptional cover. Even if somebody had chosen to comb the area with a floodlight, he would not have seen us against the background of tall trees. When we reached the road, the man in

charge was not in a hurry to cross the road. Instead of a quick run to the other side we were told to sit down and wait. After about half an hour, intensive gunfire broke out to our left towards Dugo Selo, followed almost immediately by a veritable pandemonium to the right in the direction of Sesvete. With both garrisons on our flanks engaged by the rest of the *Zagrebachki Odred,* we leisurely walked across the road.

On the other side of the road, the commander of the escort group arranged everybody into a single column with our family in the middle. With battles raging behind us the enemy was not likely to send out a patrol but our leader was not about to let his guard down. Instead of taking us on a straight line walk across open fields, he chose the tortuous trail along hedges or next to the tall cornfields. In dead silence we went through the middle of every forest, no matter how small it was, and when we came upon a creek, we followed its meandering willow-covered banks. The man in charge was a seasoned practitioner of the art of camouflage. He was so successful that I remember him only as a slightly forward-bent silhouette. That evening the danger may have been small, but as a matter of principle, we availed ourselves of every bit of natural cover around us. The progress was slow. After an hour we had covered a lot of ground but were, as the crow flies, only about a mile from the main road. The commander considered the distance safe enough to sit us down under a large willow tree and explain what was ahead.

"Our orders are to escort you south to the Sava River. From there you will proceed eastward to Oborovo. There is one bridge to pass on the way but that will not be difficult; we have friends there. Our real problem is just about a kilometer ahead. We must first pass over the railroad, and as you know, these particular tracks are the main supply routes to the German troops in Greece. The Germans are heavily patrolling the line and they make particularly frequent rounds during the night. Earlier they used to deploy permanent units at all bridges and from these small garrisons they'd only occasionally send patrols on special railroad-compatible trucks. This strategy was so predictable that our comrades kept placing mines almost at will. The Germans learned the lesson and presently they are sending out very well-armed infantry patrols. These are seasoned units, itching to

fight and they are too strong for us. But we have one advantage. On a night like this, in spite of their efforts to be quiet, you can hear the Germans from a fair distance. So we will move close to the tracks and spend some time listening."

Our leader had a superb technique. He was half-whispering and whereas we understood him quite well, his voice could not possibly be heard from more than a few yards. He came closer to the four of us."I want to congratulate you on keeping quiet so far. It's second nature to us but you may forget yourselves. Under no circumstances are you to speak out loudly. Even if you get lost, do not call for help. Just sit down and wait. I am checking all the time. If somebody is missing, we will go back and find him."

"And there is yet another thing," he continued after a short pause. "We will be crossing a bog under the railway tracks. You must watch every step carefully. We do not want any loud splashes from missteps. And of course you could also break your leg."

The area around the Sava and Lonja rivers has patches of a peculiar terrain. What from afar looks like a smooth grass field, at closer inspection proves to be a series of dry islets protruding from deep irregular water-filled channels. Diabolically, the islets are not larger than half a yard and the ankle-deep channels are just wide enough to trap a foot and break an ankle. Even if a person's bones did not snap, as soon as his foot fell into the trap, the water would soak his feet and if he also picked up a leech, his boots would fill up with blood. Walking over these obstacles is hard enough during the day. At night it was downright dangerous. But our leader was clever to choose that particular spot. Walking high on the embankment, the Germans would not realize we were underneath them and if they somehow spotted us, they could not pursue us across the bog.

Walking through the bog was demanding and painful. After half an hour my back was sore and my knees started to hurt. It was a quiet night. The frog concert was winding down to just a few persevering solo performers; there was no wind in the air to rattle the willows and the murmur of the creek behind us provided an idyllic steady background. We would occasionally stop to listen but did not detect any strange noises. When we came directly under the railway tracks, a Partizan volunteered to climb up the embankment. Sud-

denly I realized what it would have sounded like if the Germans were up there. I could clearly hear each of the volunteer's steps. Soon, careful not to make noises, we climbed over the track. On the other side we waded another half an hour through the bog. When we finally reached better ground our leader eased up a bit. While still quiet, he led us in a straight line to the road towards the bridge. At the edge of the road about five hundred yards from bridge, the commander ordered us to rest and went ahead to assess the situation. He returned a different person. Fully relaxed, he spoke in a normal loud voice.

"Everything is ready, comrades. Our friends at the bridge will be delighted to let you pass. On the other side of the bridge you will meet a guide to take you to Oborovo. From now on you do not need a military escort. In Oborovo, comrades, you are in the free territory."

It was hard to fathom that only twenty miles from Zagreb, as large a village as Oborovo would be free. But at that particular point in time it was. We shook hands with the escort group and proceeded towards the bridge. The military outpost at the bridge was well lit. Though they were nominally our enemies, two soldiers of "*Domobrani*" ("Home defenders") of the Croatian National Army lifted the ramp and stood at attention. An officer came closer to wish us a good journey. "And don't worry about the theater," he said.

"What in the world is he talking about?" I asked Djuka.

"Wait and you will see."

I was steaming.

"You chose just the right moment to show me your superiority. As we are entering the free territory, I should be reminded I have a wise older brother who knows more than me but is not ready to share his hard-acquired wisdom."

"I really do not know but I suspect that . . ." Djuka could not finish his sentence. All of a sudden the *Domobrani* opened fire. Bullets were flying all over the night sky. We took cover but, miraculously, none of the bullets came in our direction.

"This is what I thought would happen." said Djuka, "I was told that after they let the Partizans through, the *Domobrani* usually open

fire to make it look as if they fought a battle against us.

"No need to lie in the ditch. I am sorry I did not warn you in advance," said our new guide to Oborovo. He was a village boy in his early twenties and he had only good things to say about the *Domobrani* on the bridge.

"They are helping us much more right where they are than if they were to join us. Let's hope it lasts. One of these days somebody will ask why they never killed anyone or took a prisoner in those 'battles' and that will be the end of the nice arrangement."

On the same northern side of the big Sava River as Zagreb and less than an hour distance from the city center, Oborovo for all intents and purposes was a free village. Uniformed Partizans walked around in broad daylight and they were brazen enough to openly display symbols of their presence. A sign on the local school indicated it had been turned into the Headquarters of the Regional Command. Another larger building, believe it or not, had been converted into a guerrilla hospital. How in the world could the Partizans feel safe enough to deploy a hospital so close to the capital of Croatia? The guerrillas did not have larger units to protect the approaches to Oborovo. In essence, Oborovo was a fluke, an insane illusion. The village was "free" only because the enemy kept looking the other way. But the situation must have bothered the regime in Zagreb. In other areas around Zagreb, the day belonged to the Ustashe and the night to the Partizans but in Oborovo the guerrillas refused to play by the usual rules. If an Ustasha ventured alone into Oborovo, he would be shot on the spot. Apparently everybody understood the situation and not once did a Nazi inadvertently put himself into harm's way. To individuals Oborovo was off-limits, but if the Quisling regime of the Independent State of Croatia had ever wanted, it could have easily sent a larger force to assert itself. And militarily speaking, Oborovo was a bad spot. Had the enemy mounted an offensive, the defender's backs would have been pinned against the wide and treacherous Sava River.

Nobody in Oborovo seemed concerned in the least by the precarious military situation. As far as the happy Partizans were concerned, the one-hour's distance from Zagreb might as well have taken a whole year. It is hard to explain this collective bravado. How much the guerrillas divorced themselves from reality was particularly evident in the Oborovo "hospital." Jasha, a first-year medical student who openly admitted not having the faintest idea about the art of healing was in charge of the outfit. Somebody found out he was a medical student and saddled him with a task which he neither liked, nor knew how to execute. He was twenty-four years old, short and on the verge of becoming overweight. Cheerful by nature, Jasha could not resist the opportunity to give us a royal banquet. His hospital was the happy beneficiary of charity from surrounding villages and its stores were bursting at the seams. Jasha was particularly nice to me. "Just ask," he said. "Uncle Jasha will find any food your heart might desire." After the feast Jasha asked Father to inspect the hospital. Only one person was truly sick; the rest came to take a well-deserved rest in the hospital.

The only real patient suffered a nervous breakdown after he'd survived an attempted execution. In retaliation for the slaying of a high officer the Germans took twenty hostages out of the jail in Zagreb, transported them to the suburb of Dubrava and lined them up against upright poles for execution by garroting. Technically a form of hanging, garroting is terribly brutal. With regular hanging the weight of the body frequently breaks the person's neck, a fatal injury that renders him instantly unconscious. Garroting works slowly. A tight loop of rope is placed around the victim's neck and from behind the pole, the executioner tightens the choke by turning a lever inside the noose. It is a horrible death. The victim loses more air with each painful turn of the lever. The death is slow in coming and all the while the choking body desperately fights for a breath. The end result is a repulsive corpse with a swollen blue head, protruding eyes and a blood-tinged, grotesquely distended, hanging tongue. To inflict terror on the populace the Germans staged the garroting at nightfall in an open field next to the main road. The next morning posters listing the names, the time and the location of the

execution appeared all over the town. Anybody wanting to gawk was welcome to come and see it for himself.

My father later reconstructed the man's story. The Germans were coldly correct with placid victims but they became incredibly brutal with anybody offering resistance. The patient recalled the pain and the terrible choking but soon thereafter lost consciousness. He woke up in a field about five hundreds yards from the main road. Somebody had taken him off the pole! It probably was not a local person—the Germans must have had sentries around the field. Was it a German soldier who did not have the stomach to finish him off? Or did somebody wish to embarrass the officer in charge? The ways of charity in a cruel war can be rather convoluted; your life could be saved just to spite somebody else. Whoever saved the patient from Oborovo did not stick his own neck too far out. He just dragged the victim away from other dead bodies and left him unattended in an open field. Under certain circumstances there is only so much someone is willing or can do for a fellow human being.

The victim knew the terrain. Shivering and suppressing cough, he turned through the fields in the direction of the River Sava. He found his way over the railway tracks, continued southward and somehow dragged himself to the edge of a slightly familiar village where he knocked on the first door. When the door opened, the poor man broke down and could not utter a word. But his visible distress and the horrible circular bruise around the neck spoke for themselves. The people in the house took him right away to Oborovo.

When we met him he had been about ten days in the hospital. Physically he was doing quite well but he had fallen into an anxious depression. For hours on end he sat on the edge of the bed unable to communicate and afraid of others. If somebody came close he started to shiver or sob. The other patients were wise enough to leave the man alone. Father spent about two hours talking to him. I have no idea what transpired during that first interview but in the end the patient agreed to join us on our trek to the interior of the country. We had gotten ourselves a new traveling companion.

"Well, you took away the only serious patient I had" Jasha said. "The rest could go back to fight tomorrow. Do you think having a hospital in Oborovo makes any sense?" inquired Jasha.

"Not very much," responded Father.

Next morning all "patients" agreed to return to their units. Jasha and Father wrote a report that the only serious patient had been evacuated and that, having no more patients, they closed the hospital. These were the marvelous times of the early guerrilla flexibility. Nobody ever asked on whose authority did the two of them close the hospital. Jasha had freed himself to become an active fighter and political organizer, which was why he had joined the guerrillas in the first place. After the war he gave up medicine, completed studies in economics, became a leading theoretician and eventually was elected president of the prestigious Yugoslav Academy of Sciences in Zagreb. "All thanks to your father who convinced me in Oborovo, without as much as saying a direct word, that I really did not have what it takes to become a doctor," said Jasha many years later. He was only half joking.

The next evening three wagons with hidden hospital supplies from Stanchich arrived in Oborovo. The other side of the Sava River was reasonably safe as long as we kept our distance from the Ustashe garrison in Velika Gorica. The true free territory, defended by larger military units was only a few day's of walk away. Consequently the Command in Oborovo consolidated the goods into one openly loaded wagon, gave us horses and a driver, and without a military escort sent us towards the free territory.

"As normal people do, you will once again sleep at night and travel during the day," said Jasha. "Everything is organized. You will hit the road tomorrow morning. There will be three rest stops, the first of them in the village of Kravarsko, which you should reach by nightfall. Next morning they will give you fresh horses, a new driver and further directions. You are traveling towards Vrginmost, which is the site of the Territorial Command for the region of Kordun. We expect you to reach Vrginmost in about three days."

"And what about you?" I wondered, "What will you do?"

"I will see whether I can reach the Kalnik Mountain and join the *Kalnichki Odred*. This is where I was supposed to be in the first

place, before somebody decided to maroon me in this fake oasis. Believe it or not, I do want to fight the Nazis!"

We believed him.

Next morning at dawn we came to the ferryboat landing. One could hear the river but it was still too dark to see what was ahead. After a while, as the sun rose, the outline of things around us started to show. We were sitting at the low end of the bank and higher up on the levy was a solid pole from which hung the robust guide-wire for the ferry. But the ferry was nowhere in sight. Our driver went to the higher bank and came back with the good news. From tugs and vibrations he was quite sure that the ferryman was on his way. For some reason the ferry remained overnight on the other side and was about to return back. Instinctively, we withdrew towards the willow trees on higher ground, just in case. We'd learned the guerrilla logic in a hurry. The ferryman was supposed to wait for us. Why had he stayed on the other side? And how could we be sure the ferry was in friendly hands? As it turned out, everything was just fine, but the questions asked and the precautionary measures taken were appropriate for the circumstances.

The ferry was a clumsy catamaran of two larger boats connected by a flat platform. The contraption could accommodate up to twenty people, two horses and a wagon but the boatman was not in the mood to wait for other regular passengers. He pushed us off the shore and with the long oar aligned the ferry diagonally to the flow of the river. Soon the ferry's wire to the cable tensed up and the pulley on its end started to roll in the desired direction. We were on our way to the free territory and to untold adventures. Normally such a prospect would trigger all sorts of teenage fantasies in my head. But that morning aboard the quiet ferryboat we were overwhelmed by the beauty of the moment. Above us, the early morning sun decorated the sky with orange flames. A low mist was rising in streaks from pools of quiet water near to the shore and the surface resembled a gigantic steam bath. Father and Mother were looking up and Djuka, who would never admit to such sentimentalities, quietly lay on his back with his eyes trained on the sky. But Father's new patient was oblivious to the morning glory. Against the rising sun, with his head resting on the knees, he cut a lonely, sad silhouette. As

I watched him, a poem by Dobrisha Cesarich came to mind. I love the works of Dobrisha Cesarich and to this day, when I am in the right mood, I will recite some of his poems to myself. His simple melodic lines often hide a deep meaning and the more one recites them, the better he understands the poet. That morning I wanted to recite the poem half aloud, so the man could hear it but I knew I shouldn't bother him. Instead I kept reciting the poem in my thoughts. I translated this and all others poems in this book from memory.

Over the city in the sky
not heeded by the crowd
There floated up and high
a pretty little cloud

In reddish evening skies
it began to glow
But people set their eyes
on things below

They hurried bound by duty
to get who knows where and why.
And the cloud, bleeding with beauty
just basked in the evening sky

Ever higher up and away
the cloud shot as a dart
With high winds it began to play,
the high winds took it apart

After the poem I felt even more sympathy for the patient. He did not ignore the beauty in the same mindless ways as the citizens in the poem. Overtaken by his internal turmoil the man was unable to register anything from the outside world.

Everybody in the ferry was quiet, even the horses. I had plenty of time to think. What did the last few lines mean? Did Cesarich simply

end up with a nice figure of speech or did he have other things in mind? Were those lines a warning against excessive ambition on the ground- a reiteration of the Icarus story that those who aim too high, close to the gods, risk destruction? Did he feel pity for the plebeians, the simple busy crowd which had no time for beauty?

Or was his poem an elitist diatribe saying: 'See, I the poet, can see better and understand deeper than most of you will ever grasp?'

Engrossed in thoughts I almost forgot where we were. Then the ferry hit the South bank of the river.

The ten hours walk to the first destination on the south side of Sava was fairly monotonous. Father walked all the way alongside his patient. Mother, Djuka and I took turns sitting next to the driver, who himself occasionally dismounted to walk alongside the wagon. I alternated between walking and sitting on the wagon and never quite learned what was worse: pain in the legs from the long walk or pain in the back from the rough wagon ride. And so it went.

Throughout the first day Father and the patient walked a few paces behind us. They did not seem to be talking or otherwise communicating, but they were making progress. At each rest stop they sat just a bit closer to the rest of us. By the end of the day, the patient was comfortable enough to sit together with everybody. But Father still kept shielding him; the ban against direct talking with him was still in force.

The first day of our voyage was quite smooth. Only once, near Velika Gorica, did we have to take a detour through the fields. The danger was minimal and when we reemerged on the main road, Kravarsko was pretty much a straight shot ahead. Everything appeared peaceful. The farmers were working in the fields as if there weren't a war around them and we had the road all to ourselves.

Towards the evening, we arrived at the safe house in Kravarsko. Our hosts gave us a good dinner and sent us to sleep in the hay of their very comfortable barn. Next day we got fresh horses and a new driver to take us for another ten hour-long lap to a small village past Pokupsko. There the "People's Committee" distributed us to different houses for food and lodging. The patient did not seem to mind sleeping alone. Father's psychiatric expertise had a lot to do with his

amazing progress. Apparently the two of them had been chatting the whole previous day.

Next morning, reinforced by a new pair of horses and a new driver we embarked on the third leg of the journey. After three hours' the driver stopped the wagon next to a small forest.

He jumped off the wagon calling out loud "Let's have a rest!"

As we started looking where to sit down, the driver, a typical local farmer to whom God gave a booming voice turned toward us. "Come on," he said. "Do not sit at the edge of the road. Get yourself into the forest."

"Why shouldn't we sit right here? It is not hot; the sun is behind the clouds, no enemy in sight. Why bother getting into the forest?" I wanted to know.

"When you become real Partizans, you will understand. Each tree will be your best friend. The forest will hide you, protect you against bad weather and you will use it for shortcuts. There will be days when you will pray to God to find a forest. You had better start loving trees right now! And by the way, there are no snakes in that one!"

I was offended and about to tell the guide off. Admittedly we were townspeople, but that didn't mean we knew nothing about nature. Why did this farmer treat us as incompetent and naïve weaklings? But before I could say much, I felt a tap on my shoulder.

"Let's go to the forest," Father said loudly. He turned towards me and started to whisper. "This is a nice man. You looked as if you did not get it. This was supposed to be a joke of sorts. No reason to get offended. Come to think of it, it is quite a good idea to take a rest in Mother forest."

The forest of oaks and beech trees was well thinned-out. There were plenty of stumps to sit on. We found a nice glen, entirely covered by a carpet of yellow flowers. A pleasant smell of a forest after rain permeated the glen. The shiny smooth pale-gray bark of slim but tall beech trees contrasted with the rough crust on the wider trunks of impressive oaks. The type of trees and the wetness after the rain were ideal for mushrooming. I did then and still do passionately love picking mushrooms. But that time around, I had other things on my mind.

Whereas the Julius clan sat together, the driver and the patient took their separate places at a reasonable distance from us and from one another.

"Tata, your patient changed a great deal for the better. How did you succeed? What did you do for him?" I inquired.

"Nothing, literally nothing." said Father, "I was just there to let him know somebody cared. He needed old-fashioned compassion. I guess he was not so much scared from the event as he was deeply confused by the random brutality. Our normal system of punishment and reward, besides enforcing compliance with societal standards, serves also as an important guide in a person's life. After a normal day passes people usually take a tally. There is no reason to worry if one has done nothing wrong. Imagine the terrible shock when somebody who's played by the rules suddenly realizes he is being punished for something he did not do. It is the old "why me" syndrome. Why was he chosen and why did the Germans not see he was a decent person? Rational people can not accept random events. There has to be a reason for everything. In the absence of information, quite frequently a victim starts to blame himself. There must have been something wrong with him to have attracted this terrible fate."

By nature Father was not talkative, but this time without prodding he continued the little lecture. "His withdrawal into a corner and abject fear of all people was not cowardice. It was confusion. People around him had stopped abiding by the usual standards. Once they attacked you without provocation it might happen again. So how was he to know who was a friend and who a foe? I suspect the irrationality of the German fury and the uncompromising Partizan violence against the invaders is what got to him. Both sides were mad and he could not sort it out. May as well withdraw into a corner and lock out the raging madness of the outside world."

Father stopped to take a breath. From somewhere deeper in the forest I heard the cackle of a male pheasant. Normally I would jump up to explore and try to sneak closer. Frequently the pheasant would fly away cackling and making a loud noise with his wings. On rare occasions, I came near enough to enjoy the beauty of the regal bird

sitting on a branch. But this time I was preoccupied with Father's lecture.

"Some people will withdraw into a full catatonic depression," Father continued, "but the majority slowly work their way out of the corner. Our friend took the first step on the road to recovery, but he is far from normal. It is a long process. He will probably be able to get rid of his fears but whether he will ever learn to trust anybody is a very different question. I had a few patients who could not trust anyone. They are sad enough. But people who are always suspicious, who constantly think it necessary to defend themselves, who cannot for a second drop their guard, are truly miserable. . . . And they are also despicable," added Father after a short pause. His face was unusually animated and he uttered the last words with a scornful grimace. He always taught us to respect psychiatric patients. Never before or later did I hear him speak of patients with a modicum of dislike. Just for a moment, in the relaxed atmosphere of the forest, did Father let down his guard. I realized that there was more to psychiatry than he would have us believe. It must have been difficult for him to sit with equanimity in front of some truly miserable human beings.

As we left the forest and proceeded down the road, things started to change. First we met a small group of partizan soldiers in full uniform looking more like a party of hunters than a fighting unit. Their guns pointed in all possible directions—to the sky, forward, or to the ground. Loud and cheerful, greeting everybody as a long-lost friend, they were a huge contrast to the careful ways of the *Zagrebachki Odred*. Gone was the excessive caution. These boys had no reasons to hide; they owned the road. Next we encountered a checkpoint. In contrast to the group on the road, these Partizans were not at all friendly. While a larger armed group watched from a safe distance, the small bunch on the barricade displayed the classical rigidity of people in charge. They were the bosses and we had to explain who we were, where were we going, and what was our business. In my dreams I had expected a warm welcome to the free territory. Not from these guys. They just waved us through. Welcoming new freedom fighters was not in their job description.

As soon as we passed the checkpoint, almost magically, the entire scene changed. Earlier we met only an occasional pedestrian or a horse wagon, now the road teemed with bikes, motorcycles and trucks. And then, behind the curve, there stood two tanks! In military terms, those two small Italian tanks meant nothing, but they were a great morale-booster. We had our own armor and could give the enemy the taste of his own medicine! Full of excitement, Djuka and I jumped off the wagon to take a good look at the tanks. The man in charge was an approachable young soldier from Dalmatia. He was delighted to show the inside of a tank to an audience that was just a bit younger than him. As he explained to us the finer details of various instruments of death, all three of us lost contact with the outer world. The visit to the tank turned from a straightforward demonstration into simple unadulterated play. The three of us cooped up in the small cockpit of the brutal war machine play-acted war, just as we used to do a few years before, complete with "ta ta ta tas" and "bam-bams." For a short moment we were what the outside world would not permit us to be; playful children. I can precisely pin-point the loss of my childhood to that day on the road to Vrginmost. Never later could I drop the pretense of being more serious, wiser and more mature than my age. The Second World War propelled me from childhood to adulthood. Not once after the episode in the tank was I given a chance to play.

Our excitement in Vrginmost was understandable but, in reality, the Partizans had no use for the tanks. On the few occasions when they gave up the hit-and-run tactics and deployed the tanks, they suffered bad losses. A few months later I ran into two destroyed tanks on the road to the town of Glina. The Partizans had attempted to mount a "lightning" attack on the bridge leading into the town. Alerted by the loud clatter, the defending Ustashe took an antitank cannon to the middle of the bridge and lay in wait. As soon as the Partizan tanks appeared behind the curve, they were in the straight line of fire. It took the defenders only one shot per tank to score direct hits and transform the tanks into fiery infernos.

When I saw charred tank remnants near Glina, I convinced myself that these could not possibly be the same tanks we had inspected

in Vrginmost. The thought that the young Dalmatian who befriended us in Vrginmost may have lost his life in Glina was unbearable. The crew of the seared tanks must have died horrible deaths.

Vrginmost, the center of Kordun[2] was only a few miles away from the tanks. For the largest part Vrginmost consisted of a single row of houses on each side of the main road. Eventually we got to something that might be called the center, a few larger buildings and an orthodox church. We had instructions to report to the Territorial Command located in one of the more substantial buildings.

The large room of the commander of the territory was practically empty. The commander's desk was in the middle of the room; on the side were two stools, one with a field telephone and the other with a telegraph. The only other furniture were two chairs in the corner of the room diagonally across from the desk. They served no other purpose but to carry the commander's overcoat. Standing in front of his desk, the commander greeted us with a stiff military salute. He was in his early fifties, had a huge dark moustache, and stood perfectly straight like a monument cut out of stone. The man wore a clean, closely fitted and freshly pressed old Yugoslav Army uniform. He had golden stripes with two stars on each sleeve, indicating he was a Lieutenant Colonel. We had just met one of the rare professional Yugoslav Army officers who volunteered to join the Partizans.

Father's old Austro-Hungarian military instincts prevailed and he too stood at attention. It was slightly entertaining to see these two adults acting out a silly old-fashioned military protocol, but I did not

2 The name Kordun—comes from "cordon" a buffer zone of Serbian people whom the Austrian authorities had resettled to parts of Croatia, bordering on the Turkish Empire. The well -trained and traditionally anti-Moslem Serbs of Kordun provided a preliminary shield against the Turks. The fierce military tradition of Kordun continued into the twentieth century. When we arrived to Vrginmost, most of the local Serbs in Kordun and in the adjacent Banija joined the Partizans and both provinces were free of Germans.

dare to crack a joke. Just as well that I didn't! I soon learned that nothing whatsoever was funny in that room in Vrginmost.

Father reported he had with him a victim of an attempted hanging and requested that the patient stay with us so Father could continue to help him.

"Yes, I can understand he is still sick and that is exactly why we have hospitals," the commander said. "We will send him deep into the forest. You can drop a note to your colleagues about his case, but I won't let him tag along with you."

Father insisted but to no avail. Eventually the commander felt compelled to disclose his true reasons.

"Comrade Doctor," he said, "we are not discussing this in somebody's living room in Zagreb. This is a war and there are different rules to go by. First is the question of a personal physician. Even Comrade Tito does not have one. Furthermore if the word got out that you took a patient with you, soon you'd be inundated by requests. Imagine yourself walking around with an entourage of madmen. Second is your new job description. We need doctors, not psychiatrists. The sooner you understand this, the better you will be able to adjust."

There was considerable frost in his voice. Sensing he might have overdone it, the commander proceeded to argue in a more congenial tone. "Third, nobody can guarantee that people will stay together a day, not to mention a month. If you promise him a month of togetherness and tomorrow the circumstances force you to separate, he will be worse off. In your patient's case, I prefer to go by the rules. After all, Comrade Doctor, I already had to break the rules on your behalf. A good friend of yours requested that we permit you to stay together with your family. I went along but this is as much as I am willing to do and nothing more."

We had just entered a rough new life with strange rules. The commander did us a favor because Ivo Kralj intervened. But the Partizan rule that families cannot stay together would be eventually enforced. And once you realize the inevitable, you make your adjustments.

The Command in Vrginmost catalogued the supplies we brought along and took responsibility for their shipment to various hospitals

in the region. We were sent to travel to Otochac in the province of Lika, about ninety miles away. There the offices of the Chief of the Staff for Croatia would hand out our assignments. For the first leg of our trip to Otochac, the Command in Vrginmost found us a place on a truck for a thirty-five miles ride to Slunj.

The road from Vrginmost joins the main road from Karlovac to Lake Plitvice and once we reached the Karlovac road, we were on familiar territory. The National Park around the Plitvice Lakes had been our favorite summer vacation spot. Any time we went to Plitvice, we would stop at the bridge in Slunj. The bridge spanned high across the Korana River and one could take a bird's eye look at village houses on the shores of the fast-flowing, cascading, river. Before the war, a few excellent restaurants next to the bridge offered lamb on the spit and freshly caught trout.

In 1943, in spite of the war, Slunj still managed to keep some of its attractions. The bridge was intact and the restaurants were still open, but now they offered only beer and no fresh food. The war did not entirely eliminate the local trade in Slunj. Women on the road-side offered wool products, cornbread, and fresh double-baked polenta. But they were not interested in paper money and one could purchase their products only by bartering or paying in solid silver.

Each of us had our own pouch with silver coins. I was quite proud of this wealth since I had a major role in its acquisition. A few months before we left Stanchich, Father made me the family's silver coin purchasing agent. The merchants in bars and grocery stores routinely pulled silver coins out of circulation to keep them for "black days." It was my responsibility to scoot on my bike and look for coins in a thirty-mile radius around Stanchich. In Slunj, I could not resist putting some of my treasure trove into action. Finally I found a pair of gloves and paid for them royally. This was probably a mistake. I made no attempt to hide my coin pouch. Nobody told me so.

Low under the bridge, the local Command in Slunj put us up for the night and intended to send us the next morning by a truck to Otochac. By noon the truck did not show up and late in the afternoon, the Command found a horse and wagon to take us to Vrhovine. We would arrive to Vrhovine, the first town past Lake

"SASTAVCI" FALLS; THE LOWEST LEVEL OF 7 PLITVICE LAKES

Plitvice, late at night. Ever since we passed from Oborovo to the south side of the Sava River, we traveled by day. Remembering our night adventures on the north side of the river, it seemed just a small challenge to undertake yet another night trip. In retrospect, we should have not agreed. The territory around Lake Plitvice was not firmly in the Partizan's hands.

Normally, the National Park around Plitvice Lakes was a great place to visit. The edge of the large virgin forest where the park starts is ten miles away from even the smallest village and it takes another good twenty miles to come out of the forest on the other side of the park. In the midst of the trees surrounded by mountains are seven terraces, one above the other, each containing a lake of incredible beauty. Every lake has its own unique hue ranging from vivid green to sky blue. The high calcium content of the water petrifies the fallen trees whose distorted, surrealistic, grayish shapes lurk in the water. Protected from the winds the quiet surface of the lakes mirror an ever-changing panorama of inverted hilly forests. As each lake drains into the lower one, there are hundreds of waterfalls in Plitvice. All are loud, but each is different. Some falls are broad, shallow and multi-layered; some rush past tree-studded

islets, whereas at other locations the upper lake drains into the lower one in a single powerful column of water. It all ends up in the final dazzling display at the lowest lake. There the huge amount of water from the lake forms a massive hundred feet deep and sixty feet wide fall. Its magnificence is reinforced from the flank by a whole river which, high above, has lost its way and precipitously falls three hundred feet down into the boiling pool. Out of the pool, there flows the magnificent, newly formed, Korana River.

However, what was beautiful during peace turned dangerous during the war. In fact, Plitvice's main attraction, the long winding road through the forest, became a huge trap. Nobody could ever be sure who was in the forest and a roadblock could be waiting behind the next curve.

We reached the Sastavci Falls at Plitvice just before dusk. From there on, for about twenty miles, the road went through dense forest. Our driver, in his early thirties, was a particularly sour, rough character, and spoke only if spoken to. In response to a direct question, he'd first spit at the road and then mumble something that barely could pass as an answer. We could not figure out whether this odd fellow was bored, unhappy with the assignment, or hostile. Eventually the weird man managed to create tension between us. When I asked him to stop at Sastavci so we could take a look, he lashed the horses into a fast trot and with a dogged determination continued, straight down the road. The breach between the driver and us kept increasing. The more I insisted, the faster he drove the horse. When Father asked him why he did not reply, he just shrugged his shoulders.

Eventually our trip through Plitvice turned from discomfort into a nightmare. As night fell, we all sat at the back of the wagon as far away from the weird guy as we could. Soon it became pitch dark. I had never been in Plitvice at night. It would have been scary even under the best of circumstances, but our crazy driver made it into a harrowing experience. The road had so many loops through the forest that after a while we lost any sense of progress. The disorienting noise of the waterfalls drowned out all other sounds and we could not tell whether somebody was coming or going on the road.

And the wagon just kept going on and on. There was not a single traveler on the road. We hoped to find the site of the old hotel further on. The hotel had been burned at the beginning of the war but there was a chance that somebody, a military patrol or a truck driver, was taking shelter among the ruins. Every once in a while, one of us succumbed to wishful illusions, proclaiming he recognized some marker and suggesting the hotel was just around the corner. When we finally got there, the place was so thoroughly burned that it offered no advantage to anybody.

Totally silent and oblivious to our distress, the driver just kept pushing ahead. We did not know exactly what, but something was deeply wrong. Finally a weak light started to appear and disappear between the trees. It was hard to tell how far away it was, but after a few minutes it became clear that the road would lead us directly to the light. We asked the driver to stop when we reached the light. Instead, he whipped the horses into a near gallop. We came to a fork in the road. By now the house was clearly visible to our right but, predictably, the driver went to the left. There was no time to waste. Djuka pulled out his big hunting knife, put it to the guy's back, and ordered him to drive towards the light. Still saying nothing, the driver turned the horses around. When we came close enough, we jumped off the wagon and ran towards the house. Djuka yelled at the driver to wait on the road.

A sentry positioned straight ahead ordered us to stop. Soon other soldiers joined from the side and from behind. We were well covered. They heard the wagon coming and were ready. People in Slunj had given Father the password for the night and after we properly identified ourselves, they let us into the house. The Partizans, who now resided in the house of the former chief forester, were not particularly excited by our story. Two soldiers went down to the road in a leisurely way to investigate. The wagon was gone.

In one fell swoop we had lost everything but the clothing stashed in our rucksacks! But nobody complained. We already learned the cardinal rule of guerilla warfare: In hard times, private belongings are more likely to be an impediment than help. One might carry too many possessions with him, only to drop them somewhere in the

middle of a long march. And in hard times when everybody lacks just about everything, it feels downright immoral to have more than the others.

Pointing to the area where we were to sleep on some straw, the lieutenant in charge promised to find us some transportation to Vrhovine in the morning. Our host was not as incommunicative as the driver, but he certainly wasn't talkative. After some prodding, warmed up by brandy, he matter-of-factly explained that the fork in the road would have eventually lead us to Vaganac, a village in the hands of local Chetniks.[3] We would have very likely come to a bad end—particularly if we had any valuables on us!

The lieutenant showed no emotion or empathy—none whatsoever. In the daily parade of horrors, our little adventure was quite insignificant. We were alive and that was all that counted. I fought off the temptation to ask why they did not cover the dangerous fork in the road or why didn't they give chase after the driver. I actually knew the answer. Sometimes in the business of war, it is more important to have good a rest than to look for conflicts. Our comrade's duty was to patrol the road during the day and we should have known better than to venture into the Plitvice forest at night. Furthermore, the road to Vaganac was outside their jurisdiction. Later, many people confirmed that Vaganac was an extremely dangerous village. Anybody who got there was stripped of all his possessions and could count himself exceptionally lucky if he was let out alive.

I cannot help thinking that I might had provoked the whole incident by the stupid display of silver coins in Slunj, that the truck was delayed on purpose and that we were deliberately sent to an almost sure death. When we arrived in Otochac, we reported our suspicions to authorities, but nobody appeared particularly concerned. First on the list of many things that are rationed during a war are expressions

3 Reminder: The Chetniks were Serbian guerrillas loyal to the King of Yugoslavia. By 1943, they turned from resisting the Germans to fighting against Tito's Partizans.

of emotions and compassion. But infiltration into the network was serious business, and I am sure appropriate measures were taken.

~

After he had a good night's sleep, the lieutenant became downright pleasant.

"Good morning, it's time to get up!" he said, "So yesterday you had a hard day or, to be more precise, a hard evening. Let me see whether I can make it up to you. How about a good breakfast? We've got some chicory coffee, fresh sheep cheese and whatever fish my comrades may have caught in the lakes." The lieutenant's colleagues were lucky indeed; each of us got a nice broiled rainbow trout.

As we sat around the table, the lieutenant stood up and leaned out of the window. "Well, good for you. What I heard was not a mirage," he said, "Let's see whether we can catch you the real big fish. I can hear a truck making his way up the road." Djuka accompanied the lieutenant to the road and after a while they returned together with the driver.

"No problem—I'll take you to Otochac," said the driver. "Three of you can easily fit in the cab, but the fourth one will have to sit in the truck's bed. I can stop every half an hour and you can rotate positions."

"That is fantastic," professed Mother with a great deal of enthusiasm. Father was not sure. We were supposed to go to Vrhovine first and from there proceed to Otochac. He asked the driver to stop "just a moment" at the town Command in Vrhovine to let them know we were on our way to Otochac.

"No way! If I stop they will realize the truck is empty and 'in the name of the people,' they will order me to drive somewhere else. In fact, I will step on the gas in Vrhovine. The truck can go pretty fast, which is the only way not to acquire unwanted passengers. If it is really so important for you to stop there, I can offload you a kilometer before the entry to the village and you can walk to the Command."

Father still hesitated. The lieutenant joined the conversation.

"Doctor," he used a more informal term than 'comrade,' "this is an unique opportunity. The next truck may come in an hour or in a week and even if it came, it could be fully loaded or driven by an uncooperative chauffeur. This guy wants to step on it in Vrhovine-the other guy may do that to us. What could we do? Shoot his tires up?"

Seeing that Father was not yet quite convinced, the lieutenant resumed talking. "Just think about it. You are obeying orders of people who gave you a dangerous driver and sent you on a road of no return. It might have been an accident or somebody might have set you up. In both instance, they will not be particularly happy if you spill the beans in Vrhovine. Just go to Otochac and ask them to inform Vrhovine you have arrived."

This bit of straight talk was helpful. Father shook off his attack of Austro-Hungarian military habits and decided we ought to go directly to Otochac. Everybody shook hands with the lieutenant. Both Djuka and I volunteered to sit outside. We jumped on the huge Italian-made "OM" truck and started the nonstop ride to Otochac.

A few months after we should have stopped in Vrhovine, we learned that Ivo Kralj, the priest's nephew from Brckovljani was waiting there to greet us. It would have been nice to see him and, more importantly, he could have briefed us about our immediate future. A week later, Colonel Kralj got transferred and we lost further contact with him.

However, under those specific circumstances in Lake Plitvice, Father made the right decision. In 1943 a healthy dose of suspicion and a bit of subordination was the modus operandi of every successful Partizan.

Otochac

(September–October 1943)

It was quite uncomfortable sitting in the bed of the truck. Djuka and I tucked ourselves behind the driver's cab. Somewhat protected against the wind, we sat on our rucksacks but they were not soft enough to compensate for what seemed to be a total absence of shock absorbers. The road was full of potholes and we shook, veered, and twisted. I firmly hung onto the edge of the cab as long as I could. When my hand got numb I'd exchange "seats" with Djuka. That way we could both use a "fresh" hand to hold onto the truck. Nevertheless, Djuka and I enjoyed the ride. The dense and wild forest around Plitvice was different from the thinned-out woodlands near Zagreb. In the national park of Plitvice, the trees were never cut for lumber and even when a tree fell under its own weight, it was left at the spot where it came down. Only when a trunk fell on the road did the management of the Park reach for a saw. They would remove only the part that obstructed the traffic, leaving untouched the remnants of the tree on both sides of the road. The territory around Plitvice was just on the right elevation to have a mixture of evergreen and deciduous trees, and their shade was so dense that it prevented the growth of underbrush. The administration of the National Park did not permit the building of bridges for shortcuts; the road meandered endlessly through the hilly terrain. The driver could never see more than one hudred yards of the road in front of him. This and multiple sharp-angled curves in the narrow road limited us to crawl-

ing at a speed of twenty-five miles an hour or less. We had ample opportunity to enjoy nature. Unfortunately the slow ride also gave me plenty of time to think.

What if somebody decided to attack the truck? The thoroughfare in the thick forest could not possibly be defended. Even if one were to deploy thousands of soldiers on the road, a resourceful enemy could pick and choose his spot for a quick attack. Realizing they could not secure the road, the Partizans limited themselves to placing reasonably strong detachments of troops on both ends. From there, they'd occasionally send a patrol to walk along the road or to pitch a tent somewhere near the road for a day or two. The natural beauty, which we enjoyed so much, provided an ideal cover for ambush. A potential attacker could hear the truck coming and might have enough time to roll a few hidden logs onto the road. We'd have to stop. The driver could not possibly turn the truck around and we'd become sitting ducks. The steep upward slope of the terrain on the left side of the road gave the intruder a superb vantage point from which to take a well-aimed shot at the target below him. If attacked, we would have to roll down the other side of the road and hope for the best. But if the enemy wanted to pursue, he could drive us to the edge of the lake, pin us down there, and make a short job of it.

After about an hour, having scared myself silly, I started to shiver—only in part because it was cold. Luckily we soon broke out of the forest. The driver halted the truck on the side of the road and cheerfully explained how much he hated to drive through the Plitvice Forest.

"Anyhow, we made it this time around. No reason to fret about it," he said, "From now on, we do not look to the sides of the road but to the sky. The Germans love to send an occasional airplane to bother us. Nothing to it! You boys keep eyes on the sky and bang on the cabin if you see something. As soon as the truck comes to a stop, we all jump straight into the ditch! First time around the airplane is only taking its bearings and always misses the target. But second time around-watch out! However, it takes the pilot about five minutes to turn the plane around and if you keep your cool, you can run far enough away to enjoy the show."

The driver turned toward me and continued with his traveler's education course. "Now Boy, you know what a crow looks like? Remember, a crow is not an airplane and when you see one, don't bang on the cabin. If we were to stop each time you see a crow, we'd never make it to Otochac."

He could see I did not take his joke in stride. "Do not look so offended, Buddy, I had to stop many a time on account of a crow. But most of the passengers were adults. I know a young fellow like you would know better. Sorry I even brought it up," he added reassuringly.

The man had a sense of humor! As he warned us back in Plitvice, when we reached Vrhovine, he stepped on the gas and raced through the village. It was easy; Vrhovine was only a thousand yards long, had no crossing roads, and nothing in the village resembled a center or a square. An hour later, we arrived in Otochac. The driver stopped at his garage and pointed towards the center of the city.

"You can see the church spire from here. It is about a fifteen-minute walk. Good luck to you all." But he would not step out of the cabin to shake hands. When Father attempted to thank him in the name of the family, he shrugged it off. "It is all in the line of duty. It was a pleasure to help you, but there are times when I must refuse a ride. If I get down, we will all grow dewy eyed and I can't afford that," he said and drove the truck into the depot.

The center of Otochac consisted of a park lined with old horse chestnut trees, a Catholic Church, and a few multi-story buildings. The small city of about ten thousand people grew at the base of the mountains, at the western end of a round mountain plane of about 30 kilometers in diameter. Nearby, the capricious Gacka River, prone to disappear into the karst and then resurface under another name, decided to put on a solid show. Crystal clear, the river ambles through the plain for about 30 kilometers before it sinks into the ground to finally, about sixty kilometers to the southwest, drain into the Adriatic, deep under its surface.

Otochac was one of those logically situated places where one only had to look around to understand why the town developed where it did and not, let's say, ten kilometers to the left or right. On the rim of the plain, at the beginning of the natural passage down to the sea, blessed with good water and somewhat protected from the winds, Otochac was a logical resting place before or after the long trip to the seaside. The road from Otochac leads to Senj, a secluded little harbor on the seaside. Once a traveler committed himself to the long tortuous road, there was nothing in between the two points—only howling wind, no water, no trees, and not even a flat place to take a rest.

As we'd been instructed in Slunj, we went to report to the City Command. The City Command of Otochac was a large building in the center of the town. The duty officer somehow knew of our pending arrival. As a temporary solution, he reserved two bedrooms in the local hospital and by the next afternoon he hoped to have our final lodging ready.

Mother, always ready to criticize others, started to complain. "Captain, if you can do it tomorrow and if you knew we were coming, why don't you give us our quarters right away?"

"Comrade, I am doing exactly what I was told to do."

"But why? It does not make sense!"

"Many things in the war, actually most of them, do not make sense." responded the captain with a chill in his voice.

For a moment, Mother was at loss for words. Seeing her first approach didn't work, she tried another angle. "I apologize, but this is our eighth day on the road. We are tired, have not had a decent wash for a week and we were so much looking forward to finally get some decent rest in Otochac. As a Mother I am concerned about my children."

"You know, your older son is not much younger than I," said the captain. He waited just for a second for the message to sink in and then added, "I think we are treating you quite nicely. You can wash better up in the hospital than anywhere in town. Furthermore, we still consider you as a family which is highly unusual. I got my orders, but if you must know the real reasons, let me give it to you straight. Each of you will be given an individual assignment tomorrow. This

is a big country. What if they give a different assignment to one, two, or all of you? For how many people do I have to prepare the quarters tomorrow? So go and enjoy your togetherness while it lasts. Rest and get ready for tomorrow."

With that, the captain handed one envelope each to Father, Mother and Djuka. Djuka was to report to the Central Committee of the Communist Youth Organization of Croatia, Father to the Chiefs of Staff of Croatia and Mother to the commander of the Hospital in Otochac.

As the brutal truth hit her, Mother was on the verge of tears. The captain also looked sad and politely took us to the door. "Enjoy the family unity and relax," he said again.

The rooms in the hospital were clean. There was plenty of hot water and in the morning we felt quite refreshed. Without discussing it, everybody accepted the inevitable reality. Somebody, somewhere, carefully planned a breakup of the Julius family. We had run afoul of a long-standing Partizan policy. The Partizans discouraged any expressions of sexuality. Men and women were supposed to postpone all personal feelings until the end of the war. Keeping a husband and wife together was out of question.

I frequently wonder about the Partizan's anti-family policy. Certainly it would have logistically been very difficult to keep families together. But the policy went beyond that. The rule not only forbade a husband and wife to stay together, the same was true for brothers and sisters. Most of this policy reflected hard-line Communism. Akin to many other hierarchical, disciplined organizations, the Communists requested of individuals to fully devote themselves to the larger cause. Celibacy in the Catholic Church, Party devotion among Communists and corporate loyalty all are a part of the same phenomenon. Dogmatism does not tolerate outside influences. Failing to go to the same extremes as the Vatican, the Communists nevertheless resented any encroachment on their final authority. It is not by chance that one never heard about the private lives of communist leaders. They were not supposed to have any. The war gave a good, if temporary, excuse to the Yugoslav Communist to push the family aside and take a firm grip on everybody.

In reality, the Partizan policy against families and against sex did not work. Following the dictates of human nature, the resistance soldiers found creative ways around these artificial barriers. And the policy became the butt of many jokes. One of the better ones was about the attempt to recruit a Gypsy into the guerrilla movement.

"If you join us in the sacred battle against fascism, you will have to leave your home," intoned the recruiter.

"No problem, I don't have a home," said the Gypsy.

"And you might have to stay hungry for days."

"Not a problem, I am always hungry."

"When the Party calls, you will march for hours on end."

"No problem, I am accustomed to long walks."

"And you will not be permitted to have sex!"

"What?"

"No sex!"

"Hmmm? Fine! No sex, no problem, if you say so."

"And finally if the Fatherland calls, you must sacrifice your life!"

"No problem. Who'd care for such a life?"

The dispersion of our family started already on the second day of our stay in Otochac. Djuka received orders to go back to Vrhovine. There he would join a select group of youth organizers attending a political course. However, it was, made clear that Djuka would not be enrolled in the course. He had to stay in Vrhovine until further orders.

Mother became the head nurse of the Otochac Hospital and Father its staff physician, but as with Djuka, Father's was an interim assignment "pending further orders."

When we again visited the captain in the City Command, Mother had not yet come to terms with the new situation. She could not bear the thought of losing the sight of her first born. She was downtrodden and her eyes were red from crying. The captain was polite but aloof.

"I understand I am to provide you with quarters for three persons," he said. For a second he hesitated and I wondered whether he was looking for words to console Mother. However, he soon returned to business as usual.

Otochac (September–October 1943)

"I think I found you the best possible lodging in Otochac. You will stay with the local dentist who has a large free-standing house and we ordered him to let you use two of his rooms."

This was a bit surprising. In other places the Partizans considered themselves as guests and worked through local volunteer 'housing committees,' but in Otochac they behaved differently. Before the war, Otochac harbored a few Ustashe cells and they constantly agitated against the Kingdom of Yugoslavia and the Serbian suppression of Croats. Their message stuck. Inasmuch as the Partizans stood for united Yugoslavia, nobody in Otochac volunteered to provide lodgings for the soldiers. Under these circumstances, the City Command in Otochac acted like any other occupying force and confiscated space in private houses for military use.

"I must remind you," said the captain, "that the dentist did not volunteer his room and he will be sore. This man will never change his mind. You should not try to appease him or, for that matter, his family. They are all the same. And you should not apologize. This is a war and that is how things are during a war." The captain took a pause to see whether we were listening. We were, and he continued with the sermon.

"Remember, you did not take their room, we, the military, took it. Had we not sent you, it would have been somebody else. And by the way, I am sending a messenger telling the dentist you will move in tonight!" he said.

Within a few hours we knocked at the dentist's door. He was in his forties. His hair had already been reduced to a narrow, salt-and-pepper-colored, horseshoe-shaped strip, which separated his colossal ears from his shiny skull. Hiding behind the spectacles the mousy eyes of this smallish person seemed lost between his ears and his oily forehead. He was polite and calmly asked his wife to show us the rooms. She took us to the rooms barely saying a word. The dentist was the boss in his house, and his wife had been reduced to the role of family cook. The couple had two daughters, one in her early teens and the other seven years old.

Mother was extremely uncomfortable. At the onset of the German occupation, when we were not yet forced to wear Jewish in-

signia, two German officers were sent to live in our house. They were civilized and unassuming but it was nevertheless very difficult to have strangers in the house. Realizing we were now the intruders, Mother tried to soften the blow. Contrary to the captain's instructions, she started to apologize. The more she spoke, the more aloof became the dentist. The more aloof was the dentist, the more Mother felt she hadn't sufficiently explained her honest intentions. When Mother got excited, she'd lose control over her pronunciation and for good measure, she'd mix a few Hungarian words into her Serbo-Croat sentences. The dentist's poor mute wife could not fathom what to do with this storm of barely comprehensible words.

As Mother continued talking at an ever-increasing speed and pitch, it occurred to me and I am sure also to the dentist, that her lament was out of place. If she really felt so bad about staying in the dentist's house, she should have simply left. There are some times when one should either put up or shut up and this was one of them. The relationship between the two sides, the dentist's and ours, had been predefined by the circumstances and nothing could change that.

After a few days we learned how to circumnavigate around one another. Eventually a few weeks later, both families settled into an uneasy, rather formal, *modus vivendi.* On the surface the arrangement seemed to work admirably. After a while we even had occasional dinners together. The dentist supplied fresh produce whereas we provided canned food, flour and various other staples from military stores. During these meals, the dentist came to know my parents and decided they were soft liberals. Realizing they'd never inform the police, he started to discuss politics. First Mother and Father politely disagreed with him, but later the discussion became quite heated. One evening, after he consumed more than a few glasses of wine and after he had just learned from Mother we were Jewish, the dentist lost control.

"Tell me Doctor, why are you using our hospital in Otochac only to handle local patients? Why don't you fill up the hospital with Partizans? There are plenty where the previous ones came from."

We knew what he meant by 'previous' patients. In spite of being reasonably close to the center of the town, the hospital in Otochac stood alone in an unpopulated area. A single dead-end road led from

the town to the turnaround in front of the hospital. The closest house in the direction of the town was about four hundred yards away and on the other side of the hospital there was a deep ravine of a dry riverbed. About a month before we came to Otochac, a troop of Ustashe sneaked out of the garrison in Gospich, the capital city of Lika. They took a truck to the perimeter of the territory under their control and from there, under the cover of night, went on foot through the river-bed. After three hours in the ravine they reached the back of the hospital in Otochac. Then the Ustashe overwhelmed the guard and methodically cut the throats of every wounded Partizan in sight. They did not fire a single gunshot and undetected, with the mission accomplished, silently withdrew back to Gospich.

"You did not respond, Doctor," said the dentist, "Why don't you again start admitting wounded Partizans into our town hospital?"

Father said something to the tune that for tactical reasons it is considered better to have the military hospitals closer to the fighting units.

"Oh no, my dear doctor. It is for fear that our boys might repeat their splendid performance. Your comrades are afraid that a company of Ustashe may slip out of Gospich again and wreak havoc on the patients. Doctor, you came too late. Had you come here earlier and walked through the blood-soaked corridors, you'd understand why your superiors had lost the taste for bringing more wounded Partizans into Otochac. It is fear, shear fear. Your commanders got the message. The count was thirty-five. The boys put thirty-five wounded Partizans out of their misery. And there was no mercy, no exceptions."

All of a sudden, from underneath the veneer of a balding, polite petit bourgeois sprung out a cruel, vicious, sub-human being. The dentist gloated as he trained his small eyes on us and continued, "No exceptions, you understand. Inherent laziness and a lack of true commitment saved your doctors. Had they slept in the hospital, as they should have, our boys would not have shown them any mercy either."

Mother was shocked. "How can you as a medical person speak with such nonchalance about other people's death. It really does not matter who is killed—a loss of human life is a loss for everybody. On

graduation from the dental school you must have taken the Hippocratic oath to help suffering humanity. How can you condone such an action?"

"First of all. I did not personally do it. And second, this is a war, my lady. It's us, or them. Civilian morality gets you nowhere during a war. I strive to preserve some semblance of normality in my house. This is why we can talk about such things. Here we behave by peacetime standards. And if the boys were to knock on the door just now, I would feel obliged to protect you—just as you feel the obligation not to tell the police about me."

"That is how it is in my house." He turned to speak directly to Father, "But if we ever meet as opponents, I advise you, Sir, to stay away from me."

I was not prepared for this cold display of ill will. I heard about the horribly brutal camps in Jasenovac and Jadovno; I read posters announcing executions of hostages', I'd seen pictures of people executed by hanging but I had never before directly faced a true enemy. I was petrified and begun to shiver from fear. The menacing face across the table made me realize I was not such a hero as I had hoped to be.

This exchange taught me more about war than anything. Here was a bigoted hateful person who could barely wait for the signal to discard the shackles of civility and with pleasure let loose his pent-up violence. And there were thousands like him waiting for the moment to suddenly turn from polite civilians into unthinking, bestial instruments of hate. Their hatred is generic, against everybody and everything. An ill-defined feeling of paying back the other side for centuries of perceived injustice. This unfocused hatred permits them to act with utmost violence. When somebody settles an individual score, the fault of the other person is rarely large enough to contemplate murder. But everything is simple when a person starts to settle untold scores from the past and if he acts in the name of the collective "us" against all of "them." To a war criminal, the individuals in front of him are not persons; they are the smallest definable part of a larger group. By getting one of "them," he is not killing a person—he is only diminishing the size of the other group. He participates in a totally depersonalized, even-handed, process. No mercy, no exemption! For, if such a brutalized person were to make even one

exception, he would have to accept individual responsibility. A war criminal prefers to remain an instrument of collective retribution and does not dare to become a thinking human being again.

Never mind the subtle dichotomy that the dentist separated his household from the general events. This did not make him any better than the others around him. He just followed a common old Slavic ritual; anybody admitted to your house for any reason is your guest. Honor requires that you guarantee his safety. But that does not make the host any less cruel. Next time around, he would without mercy cut your throat. "On the street, Sir, stay away from me"[1]

~

The morning after the incident we went to the City Command to request new lodgings. Father complained to the captain that his chronic migraine headache had become quite intolerable most likely because he developed an allergy to something in the dentist's house.

The captain was in good mood. "If you are allergic to the dog, we could easily shoot the beast," he smiled, "but if you are allergic to the dentist, that is an entirely different matter."

"Are you, or is anybody in the family allergic to the dentist?"

Mother fell for the joke. " I think allergies to a person's hair have been reported but they are extremely rare."

"Come on, you know what I mean. Maybe you people cannot tolerate the dentist? How about that?" the captain laughed heartily.

"No sweat," he continued. "You do not have to tell me anything; I know enough as it is. I could arrest the bastard tomorrow, but we have reasons not to. Anyhow, back to your request! Why don't you people wait an hour or so? I need to talk to some comrades." Father decided we ought to return to the hospital and the captain promised he'd phone as soon as he resolved the situation.

---

1 People are astonished by the recent bloodshed in former Yugoslavia. When I think of the dentist in Otochac, I fully understand the situation. All it took was for somebody to give the signal. Once the war had been declared, a vile minority, probably not more than one in ten thousand people, got the opportunity to show its worst, draw the first blood, and pull everybody into the endless spiral of dehumanization.

On the road to the hospital, as we passed by the dentist's house, I remembered the captain's unusual comments and decided that the dentist must be under surveillance. His house was the last building on the road to the hospital and he knew quite a lot about the massacre. If Ustashe needed a local contact, he'd be in an ideal position to help.

I asked Father what he thought about my idea. "I don't know," he said. "Frequently when push comes to shove the tough-talking people turn out to be cowards. However your thought is logical. Let's call it a good hypothesis but it could also be a coincidence. We do not have to pursue this further. Obviously the dentist is under some kind of surveillance and that is good enough for me. If the captain gave him the benefit of the doubt, so should we."

I did not agree. "He did not give him the benefit of the doubt. They are waiting to catch him in the act or until they figure out who else is involved."

"Same thing," said Father. "In both instances it is none of our business. The captain will figure it out and when he needs our advice, he will ask. Have you noticed that he did not want to hear any details from us."

I did notice.

Somewhat later, the telephone rang. The captain from the City Command made some inquiries and had decided we ought to move out of the dentist's house that very evening. The captain succeeded in outfitting an empty room in the City Command with three beds and some basic furniture. We'd stay overnight there and the next day the captain would make final arrangements.

This time Mother, who a few weeks ago protested against a temporary solution, did not object. She grew to understand the typical Partizan "*snadji se druzhe*" ("improvise comrade") style of operations. A Partizan was never to assume that something was impossible and he was trained to come up with the best solution under the circumstances. By the same token, others had to accept less than the perfect solution. Besides, we were eager to get out of the dentist's house at any cost.

As we were leaving his house, the dentist franticly apologized for his "childish and drunken outburst." Of course he regretted the loss

of human lives. He hated to lose his "best possible and kindest" tenants. And how would his family survive without the canned food, kerosene and medical supplies, which his guests so kindly provided?

I expected Father to let him have it, but nothing of the kind happened. Instead, Father fell back on the allergy explanation and reassured the dentist that he was entitled to his opinions.

"I told you that regardless of my sympathies, I would never personally do such a loathsome thing, didn't I?" said the dentist.

He did not, the bastard!

The moment I caught Father alone, I accused him of caving in and being too conciliatory.

"Two things," said Father. "First, do not forget we were intruders in his house. Had we not gone there, the situation would never have arisen. And second, if people were punished for thoughts and not for actual deeds, the jails would be overflowing with innocent people."

"But I am sure we had a potential killer in front of us," I complained.

"So we have a difference of opinion. But nothing ought to be done until it is proven he did a criminal act. Let's just hope we never find out who was right or wrong. Do not forget he has two daughters. If ever proven guilty he would leave two orphans behind him. And there are plenty of orphans around as it is."

Father's equanimity, objectiveness and willingness to examine both sides of an issue were admirable in peace, but during the war these traits were irritating. Luckily, Mother had enough anger and black-and-whiteness for both of them. Only when we finally fell asleep did she stop cursing the dentist for what he said and for the fact that in our new quarters, we had to walk to a distant toilet.

When we woke up I found an envelope under the door. It was a letter from Djuka. The letter, dated 10.3.1943, started with "My Darling Dears," and ended with "Loves you all and many, many kisses and love." Unusually soft, redundant words for a "tough guy." Djuka was quite homesick. He was in the village of Rudopolje together with other youth leaders who attended the political seminar. Their house was clean, "no louse in sight," and Djuka, who had never been in Mother's kitchen, now "cooked for them all!" He was

awaiting new orders but hoped he'd be permitted to attend the political course in Vrhovine. Djuka heard that Dr. Ivo Kralj was in the vicinity but, try as he could, he failed in finding him.

Mother was optimistic and predicted that as soon as Djuka finds Ivo Kralj, he'd for old times sake arrange for Djuka to attend the political course and thereby keep away from the front line.

Father said nothing but his face was grim. In this case, at 14 years of age, I understood the circumstances much better than my parents. Not hindered by wishful thinking, I simply *knew* that what Djuka described in his letter was bad news. If Djuka knew Kralj was in the vicinity, the converse was also true. Kralj must have known Djuka had arrived to Vrhovine but he chose not show up, and that meant there was nothing he could do about Djuka's situation.

An orderly knocked on the door with an envelope for Mother and Father. Both were to report to the Medical Department of the Chiefs of Staff of Croatia.

I wanted to come along but Father objected.

"Stevo," he said, "going with us to the City Command to discuss our lodgings was perfectly normal. But this is the high military Command and they are about to give us our permanent assignments. You do not belong there. Rest assured that whatever the Command decides to do with us, they will also take you into account."

Again I understood the situation and could predict what would happen. In line with the standing policy, the Command would eventually have to separate Mother and Father. I reasoned that our conflict with the dentist gave the Command a good reason to act right away. Rather than searching for a new semi-permanent accommodation, the Command would send Mother and Father on their way to new permanent posts.

I was dead right! Father had been ordered to go to the province of Banija where he would be the chief sanitary officer in charge of military and civilian health affairs of the province. Mother would stay in Lika to work in a hospital under the direction of the legendary surgeon, Dr. Jozha Kajfesh. There she would assist during operations, prepare the surgical theater and learn methods of physical rehabilitation for wounded patients. The medical officer in the High Command of Croatia delineated a curriculum for Mother. Major

hospitals were overcrowded and the sanitary service decided to develop a new tier of hospitals for "lightly wounded patients." Instead of physicians, nurses would run such hospitals and if Mother succeeded in acquiring sufficient skills, she'd become director of a new hospital. The medical officer let my parents decide whether I should join Mother in the hospital or remain in Otochac to attend school. Should it be decided that I stay in Otochac I would be registered with the City Command and they would take care of my lodging, provisions, and safety. If the Partizans had to withdraw from Otochac, I would be on the high priority evacuation list and they would send me to join Mother's hospital.

My parents decided I should stay to enjoy the near-normal civilian life in Otochac. I was a typical independence-craving teenager and the news of becoming my own boss filled me with joy. No more little Stevo! Soon I would become a real Partizan, an independent participant in exciting adventures of World War II. Not for a moment did I stop to think what my staying alone in Otochac would mean to my parents. Teenagers do not only feel invulnerable; they are also brutal. All arrangements notwithstanding, my parents knew there was a good chance that they'd never see me again. They must have been shocked to see my joy with the dissolution of our family but to their credit, they were calm and supportive.

Poor Father! Not only was his son delighted to fly the coop, his wife also did not care to hide her delight with the impending separation. She loved Father dearly, but she looked forward to her chance to practice medicine, a craft that thirty years earlier she was forced to give up. Never happy with her petit bourgeois role as the dutiful wife of an eminent physician, Mother cherished the prospect of becoming useful in her own right.

The Chief of Staff's office indicated we would stay together in Otochac for a few days longer until they secured transportation to distant Banija. Mother would share the truck with Father and get off in Vrhovine. From there, the local authorities would direct her to the secret location of Dr. Kajfesh's hospital. Mother was enthusiastic. She could walk from Vrhovine to Rudopolje and have a visit with Djuka!

Again, I had a bad premonition and, sure enough, a truck driver delivered a message from Djuka that he had been assigned to the

Third Brigade of the Sixth Division of the People's Liberation Army, known also as the Lika Division. The Lika Division was one of the toughest, most venerated Partizan units, and it had all the characteristics of the province for which it was named. The province of Lika nested behind the steep northern Adriatic coastline had shallow arable land only in a few plateaus and the rest was either forest or naked karst stone. Only two towns in the region, Gospich and Otochac, exceeded ten thousand people. The rest of Lika's populace lived in small villages and worked very hard to eke out a meager living. Bad weather, cold winters, isolation, and coping with hunger were facts of life in Lika. Lika's people were as tough as their land was. A man in Lika was born with a gun in the cradle; to defend his herd from predators, take care of himself and to partake in adventures. In the last five centuries Lika had been wedged between the Venetian, Austrian and the Ottoman Empires. Living in the shadowy territory between major powers, the people of Lika willingly involved themselves in smuggling and military skirmishes. During the Second World War, half populated by Serbs and half by Croats, Lika provided both sides in the conflict with the fiercest and most reliable fighters.

Djuka was slated to join the superstars in the third Udarna Brigade. *Udarna*, which literarily translates into "Striker," synonymous with 'shock troops,' was a special distinction given only to the most successful units. The Third brigade was known for its ferocity and the more famous it got, the tougher were its assignments. Its latest orders were to prepare for a march to Bosnia.

At the beginning of the winter in 1943, thinking that the war was coming to an end, Tito decided to establish a permanent free territory in Bosnia and turn it into a training ground for the development of institutions of the future, post-war, state of Yugoslavia. In the Bosnian town of Jajce, Tito convened a mini Constitutional Assembly of the "Anti-fascist Peoples Council of Yugoslavia." They declared that future Yugoslavia would be a Republic and a Federation of States of Croatia, Serbia, Slovenia, Bosnia, Montenegro, and Macedonia. To keep the embryo of the future state of Yugoslavia secure, Tito decided to consolidate elite troops in Bosnia. As Djuka's

Third Brigade readied itself for the long march to Bosnia, we realized he would face hard times. But nothing we could imagine came even close to what was ahead for him.

While we waited for the inevitable separation in Otochac, nobody quite knew what to do and how to behave. We were concerned about Djuka, but nobody wanted to talk about it. Everybody pretended nothing had happened but underneath the surface the atmosphere was heavy and almost funereal. Knowing the inevitable goodbye was just around the corner, I became tense and occasionally felt that it would be better if we were to 'get it over with' right away. In the next second I was deeply ashamed of such thoughts. Father appeared to be reading but I could see he couldn't concentrate. How do you face the dissolution of a family? We already said we would keep in touch, that we would write, we repeatedly stated how much we would miss each another-what else was there to do?

Mother threw herself into making arrangements for my stay but realistically there was little she could do to help. The captain in the City Command who previously handled our affairs joined a fighting unit but his replacement, also a captain, was equally effective. By the accent we could tell that this short chubby fellow in his fifties was from Zagreb. He arranged everything. I would get a room in the hospital; he would give me new coupons for the military mess every week and most importantly, I would get a military uniform.

"There were plenty of smallish Italian soldiers and I bet somewhere in the storehouse, there is perfect uniform waiting for you," he said to me and then turned to Mother. "Why don't you go with him and if adjustment need be made, let me know? We have a workshop for alterations."

It was nice of him to give Mother a chance to once again act as a mother. I was not so pleased with the idea but chose not to complain. I had other things on my mind.

"Won't you also issue me a gun?"

"Why should he?" objected Father, "You are staying in Otochac to attend school and you are not a regular soldier."

"I disagree! He is a regular soldier and I am his direct commander," said the captain but proceeded to talk like a true diplomat.

"However, you are right Comrade Doctor. For the time being he does not need a gun." After a short pause the captain looked straight at me. "Comrade Julius Junior you will obey all my orders and you are to report to me every Wednesday at fifteen hours sharp. Right now your orders are to go to school, but I might in the future change that. Because I am responsible for your evacuation, you must sleep in the hospital at night and if after nightfall for some reason you are not there, I need to know where you are. During the day keep your eyes open and if you think our troops are moving, come right over to me. Got it?"

"Yes, Comrade!" I stood at attention.

The Italian uniform fitted just fine. When we came back, a big military truck was standing in front of the City Command. The Sanitary Command found a vehicle earlier than expected and gave my parents one hour to get ready. There was no time for a nice farewell. We hugged, kissed and, as good soldiers were supposed to, hid our emotions. It was all too quick and too impersonal but it was probably better that way. Even my usually emotional Mother kept her cool, but I am sure she cried in the cabin.

Just for a second I felt a terrible pang and wondered whether I would ever see them again. But in another second I forgot it all. It was great to be young!

~

As soon as I settled into my new room in the hospital I decided to get myself a gun. I had in my pocket written identification papers attesting to my appointment as a courier to the City Command in Otochac. The captain said I did not need a gun but on the other hand, he didn't order me not to get one. I went to the storehouse to request a gun and the guy in charge didn't ask for additional papers. I was in uniform and for him that was good enough. He was sitting on a mountain of undesirable Italian Army guns and he was delighted to get rid of one. There is fashion in arms. Soldiers went around showing their hardware and, akin to a car in peacetime, certain models were highly appreciated. The desirability of a gun had a vague connection to its availability and performance, but much of it

was in the style. The mean-looking bare barrel and the curved handgrip propelled the German Luger to the top of the pistol line closely followed by the compact, elegant and reliable Italian Berretta. Among rifles, the standard issue Italian gun was at the bottom of the heap. Unimpressive with a very short barrel, the gun had a ridiculous built-in bayonet. The bayonet ran parallel underneath the barrel as if it were some kind of structural support for the whole flimsy contraption. Furthermore it was not a real bayonet but a dull triangular pin, which when pivoted around the hinge, protruded in front of the small gun like a glorified knitting needle. Because of its short barrel the gun was not precise. All other European armies used the standard nine millimeters sharp bullet ammunition but the Italian was a long, stubby-nosed, seven and a half millimeter bullet atop of overcharged shell. The magazine for the rounds inelegantly protruded in front of the trigger, which, if you pulled it, made an incredible bang, and gave you a hell of a kick. At night, the short barrel and the generous amount of explosive in the shell let off a huge ball of flame and in no uncertain terms telegraphed your position to the enemy. No wonder that nobody liked the Italian rifle.

Having learned the basics in Stanchich I had no difficulties handling the gun. Almost every day I stood on the edge of the ravine behind the hospital and took shots at stones beneath me. There was nothing wrong with the gun. The rifle never jammed, it was reasonably accurate and I soon learned to cope with the kick. Later the gun, "Piccolino," became a great source of comfort during many of my lonely marches.

Theoretically I was supposed to attend high school classes, but in the exalted state of an anti-fascist fighter, I felt considerably above the mere local children. To my teacher's horror, bent on underscoring my special status, I always brought my gun along. Needless to say, the gun was entirely out of place in the high school classroom in Otochac and later in Glina. Unfortunately, nobody had the guts to set me straight. In Otochac the teachers did not even insist that I unload the gun. Crazy, crazy, dangerous war times!

Knowing that the Germans were around the corner nobody in Otochac, including the captain in the City Command, took my school attendance seriously. Why bother with the education of a youngster

who would soon be gone. This, combined with my attitude of superiority, was not very conducive to learning. There were plenty of other things to do in the town. Thanks to its road to the seaside, Otochac became a huge storage area and a seemingly rich oasis of normalcy in the midst of a ravaged country. On the seaside, south of Rijeka, a two hundred kilometer-long stretch of steep, forbidding mountains separates the Adriatic coast from its hinterland. Along the seacoast, there is barely enough flat land to build a few houses and the shore cannot support meaningful agriculture. The Adriatic coast had a longstanding maritime tradition and benefited from its contacts with the commerce and culture of the world. But culture does not feed the belly. For that and for the trade, the coast entirely depended on its hinterland. Consequently the towns on the seaside developed only in a few spots that offered both a natural harbor and a path to the hinterland. Senj, a fierce windswept little pirate cove, was one of these towns. For centuries before Austria built a modern road, smugglers used the footpath across the mountain from Senj to Otochac for their own purposes. Food and tobacco came down, and up the mountain went products from various far-away places. Senj was the home base of the Adriatic version of pirates' called *Uskoci*, and some loads making their way inland were definitely ill-gotten.

History has a way of repeating itself. What in the fall of 1943 went up the mountain from Senj to Otochac was also loot, but somewhat less illegal. Italy had just capitulated and having confiscated all their military belongings, the Partizans sent tons of supplies up to Otochac. But the roads from Otochac onwards were treacherous, the gasoline reserves were limited and it was difficult to pass the goods deeper into the country. Otochac was knee-deep in excess supplies.

A few months after Italy capitulated the Germans had to secure the north Adriatic coast against a possible invasion by American and British troops from Italy. Eventually they took back Senj and soon a precarious balance developed between them and the Partizans. Loathing to test whether a gunman waited behind piles of rock and aware that a few strategic explosions in the road to Otochac could easily cut off an armored column, the Germans seemed happy to stay on the coast. But had they changed their minds they could have easily taken Otochac.

Otochac (September–October 1943)

Because of the developments on the coast Otochac also accommodated a large number of refugees. As the Germans advanced down the coast, the road from Senj to Otochac became the only available escape route for Jews from the north Adriatic coast. The refugees that flocked to Otochac in 1943 were the "*creme de la creme,*" a selection of activists among traditionally passive Jews. When the war broke out in 1941, the more energetic Jews left all their real estate behind them and moved to the Adriatic coast, which was under Italian occupation. After the end of the First World War the historically Croat lands of Istria and around Zadar became legal Italian territories. Mussolini planned to extend this hold and annex the entire Dalmatian coast to Italy after the Second World War. Contrary to the Germans who transferred all administrative responsibilities to the puppet "Independent State of Croatia," the Italians governed the occupied territories by themselves. The Jews on the coast became a bone of contention. The fiercely anti-Semitic Ustashe complained to Germans about the excessive Italian "kindness" towards Jews and eventually forced the Italians to take some action. By the end 1942, the Italians moved most of the coastal Jews to a concentration camp on the island of Rab, but by and large, they did not mistreat them. After Italy capitulated most of the prisoners took small boats from Rab across the straits to Senj and from there traveled to Otochac.

In Otochac the refugees had access to food and if they were good negotiators, they could get limited supplies from military stores. The refugees could also purchase goods on the market but to this day I do not understand how they paid for things. They were more than two years on the run and during that period gold and silver were the only accepted currencies. How could a family carry enough of the bulky, heavy metal to last for over two years? Where was it hidden, how was it protected against soldiers, officials and other robbers? Amazingly, most of the refugees seemed to thrive in Otochac and some even managed to open businesses. I remember particularly well the bakery, which produced an expensive imitation of the *Petit Beurre* cookies. What a luxury in time of war!

Otochac was bursting its seams from the influx of Partizans and refugees. The Partizan Command made a tactical decision not to hold on to the town if the Germans were to attack. Consequently,

local officials were extremely generous with supplies, particularly certain types of supplies. They sent as much canned and dry foods as was possible for storage in the forest, but the rest was fair game. Anybody who wore uniform and knew the right places could take whatever he wanted. I became a regular visitor to the depot of stored Italian cheese and sausages until the day when some wise guy decided to put things into order. The last three weeks I spent in Otochac all Italian food was declared off limits. However the Partizans had confiscated hundreds of huge barrels of salted sardines, garfish and mackerel from a cannery on the coast and we could get as much salted fish as we wanted. One could make the fish more palatable by dunking it into the River Gacka to wash off some salt but even after a most meticulous desalination, the fish remained salty and kept its rotten odor. After a few days of a diet of salted fish I could not bring myself to look at the barrels. Nevertheless we continued to force ourselves to swallow the fish and preserve personal supplies of canned food for black days.

The salted fish made everybody permanently thirsty. However, every cloud has a silver lining: The Otochac brewery was in full working order. Every person in a uniform was entitled to free beer. I was not necessarily drunk but washing everything down with beer made eating the fish, and life in general, more bearable.

The fish-beer routine was only one of the strange aspects of life in Otochac. In those days, almost everything was weirdly surrealistic. There was General Ljubichich riding his white horse as if he were preparing for a peacetime parade. Local markets were reasonably well stocked, shops were open, and coffee houses did a brisk business. And no paper money changed hands. To purchase something one had to either barter the goods or pay in precious metal coins. I still had some silver coins for finer things, for the rest I bartered supplies from military stores. Winter was coming and I stocked up on warm clothing.

All of this was quite entertaining but instead of spending time in coffee houses I preferred to hang out around the Agitprop (agitation and propaganda!) department of the ZAVNOH. The cumbersome acronym stood for the "Assembly of Antifascist Councils of People's Defense of Croatia," a precursor of the formal civilian government. In

the Communist nomenclature the words agitation and propaganda acquired a double meaning—good in the cause of justice and devious when it came from the likes of Goebels. We were told that plain propaganda and dirty propaganda were two very different things. The Agitprop teemed with artists who were quite happy to support the propaganda effort against the Germans. I loved to rub elbows with them. Eventually I got written permission from the captain in the City Command to take on "additional responsibilities which might be useful to the movement and which would not interfere with my schooling." After that I was accepted as a regular in the Agitprop. There I learned a little bit about printing techniques—setting type, running pages off matrixes, and linotyping. But they mostly wanted me in the drama and music departments. Utilizing the old format of a village get-together, the Communists skillfully used the national oral tradition for their own purposes. Good political commissars knew that "political education" lectures did not work and preferred to assemble their troops around campfires for evenings of songs and poems. The artists around ZAVNOH kept providing an ever-ready supply of politically correct material. And when a village was liberated the soldiers routinely entertained the populace. Prompted by an almost instinctive habit for collective entertainment and regardless of their basic political orientation, the villagers invariably came to the show and a good portion of them bought the message.

The news kept spreading with incredible speed through these oral channels. In early 1945 within weeks of the Yalta Conference, a catchy tune celebrated the Black Sea encounter between Churchill, Roosevelt and Stalin. In parallel, the political education arm informed everybody about the contents of the meeting. It is not known how Tito got the news, but the Partizans were superbly informed about the relevant aspects of the meeting. Soon the commissars started to explain how west and east had agreed to share their political influence in Yugoslavia. Not quite understanding what they were doing, these political operatives were laying the groundwork for the independence of Tito's Communist Party from the Soviet Central Committee. Tragically, many of them were planting the seeds of their own destruction. While talking about the mixture of Soviet and western influence in future Yugoslavia they continued

to sing the praises of the big Communist motherland, Russia. Only a few understood that, if the West and East were to have an equal influence, post-war Yugoslavia could not possibly be the same as the Soviet Union. After the war, when Tito finally openly broke with Stalin, many of these old hands were at best bitterly disappointed and at worst ended in concentration camps.

The parroting act of the semiliterate commissars, who conveyed a message without fully understanding its meaning, occasionally had humorous results. Somebody higher up who explained the Party line to the Party apparatus, must have been an English-speaking intellectual. To underscore the meaning of the deal in Yalta, he used the English phrase "fifty-fifty." The melodious phrase stuck, got corrupted for easier pronunciation and the commissars happily kept exclaiming "fiffy-fiffy" as if they were trying to summon a French poodle.

The propaganda effort of our little group in ZAVNOH was a bit more sophisticated. We were preparing a full evening show. Winter, the best season for village performances, had already shown its teeth. If our program were good, we'd become an official traveling company. Whereas we all hoped to put on a good performance, our success was vitally important to a few talented refugee Jews working with us. If they were accepted into the official ZAVNOH troop for "cultural education" they would have the right to withdraw together with the Partizan political machine. To them this would make all the difference in the world.

Undoubtedly the Partizans also genuinely fought for a better future of all people but the truth is that during an acute conflict, the civilians became a burden to them. During a war high altruistic principles are promoted through self-centered behavior. The Partizan soldiers had special privileges. If food was in short supply, the Partizans ate first, and if there were only a few trucks, the soldiers rode on them. In times of danger the Army pulled out and left the civilians behind. Most likely this is how it had to be or the Partizans would have ceased functioning as an effective war machine. Such is the logic of war. Take care of yourself; let somebody else worry about others. During a formal withdrawal the Partizans gave the refugees general information but exactly where to move and how to get there was not the responsibility of the military. And once the refugees were on the road, the sol-

diers generally pretended not to see them. Only occasionally would some soldiers stop at a distance to shout warnings of dangers or give advice about water, food and shelter. But that was all.

~

Our program was coming along quite well. The opening number was a choral rendition of the Pan-Slavic hymn "*Hej Slaveni.*"("Oh you Slavs"). Composed in the middle of the nineteenth century on the occasion of the first Pan-Slavic congress in Prague, this century-old song survived as the only remnant of the ineffective movement for unification of all Slavs. Sung in the tempo of a slow march with crescendos the song permitted the chorus to sing their collective hearts out. The tune, as well as the simple words about the common heritage, and the Slavic "spirit" was easy to remember. The song served the Partizan's purposes well. The Germans had already occupied the Slav countries of Czechoslovakia, Poland, Bulgaria, Yugoslavia, and in the Russian plains, they were fighting to occupy the last Slavic country. Hitler was the common enemy of all Slavs.

Next was a skit about captured Russian children taken by German soldiers to a concentration camp. At the last moment, almost at the door of the extermination camp, a troop of Russian Partizans saves their lives. I played the brave Partizan's leader who operated behind the German lines in Russia. At the end I rendered a heartwarming speech extolling Comrade Stalin.

After that came a string of songs ending with the popular piece "*Comrade Tito You are a White Violet.*" Written in the style of a typical Yugoslav folksong, the words of the catchy tune proclaimed the love of the youth for their unique and fearless leader. After the songs the first segment of the program ended with the recitation of a poem about the brotherhood and unity of all Slavs within the borders of Yugoslavia.

The main message of this heavy propaganda was that the Yugoslav Partizans were not alone. They were fighting alongside millions of other Slavs and together with mighty Russia they will eventually win. And when they prevailed, the Partizans would forever erase nationalistic divisions within former Yugoslavia.

The middle of the program was a lighthearted part devoted to children. There was a melodic poem by the widely popular humorist Branko Chopich assuring the children that the adults would protect them during the night. It described the old "Uncle Bora" who, fighting his own fear of night, bravely patrolled the village and kept an eye on the sleeping children.

Next came a one-act propaganda masterpiece. The author was witty and he wrote the piece to appeal to the peasant's age-old rough sense of humor. In the eighteenth century the writers from the Dalmatian coast produced a number of comedies under the influence of the Italian master Goldoni. Some of these plays focused on the naïve peasant who came to town and became the object of a number of practical jokes. This kind of crude humor was the staple of the prewar dilettante theaters. The author of our skit used the same technique to portray the German prisoners of war as the butt of practical jokes. But the play had had an unusual humanistic line, which the author of this heavy propaganda piece must have written to save his own soul. The main character in the skit was a single Partizan in charge of ten German prisoners. The Partizan played all sorts of demeaning practical jokes on the Germans. Needless to say the German prisoners went along with the silly ways of the man with the gun in his hands. After a while the Partizan got carried away with his power over the former enemy and began to force the prisoners to repeatedly sit, stand up, lie on the ground, and roll over in the snow. The audience at first laughed but soon became uncomfortable with the senseless tyranny. Just at that moment in the play the author inserted a brilliant counterpoint. Recognizing his own inhumanity the Partizan in charge offers the prisoners a decent rest and then, just before the curtain falls down, he turns to the audience to deliver a monologue about his shame of having acted as such a brute. "After all," he says, "they might be Germans but they too have mothers, wives and children."

I do not know about our audience but I will forever remember this expression of human values amidst the cruelty of a war.

One evening in the middle of our final dress rehearsal the director was called out of the room and soon returned to interrupt the proceeding with one dramatic word; *Pokret*! "*Pokret*" (movement)

was the single word for the absolutely unique experience of a guerilla evacuation. The Partizans liked to keep a semblance of normalcy until the last moment. Even when everybody knew the enemy was advancing, the Partizans went about their routines as if they had no other concerns on their mind. But when somebody in the City Command ordered a general evacuation everything changed in an instant. Magically trucks and horse-drawn wagons would show up at predetermined places and a frantic loading would ensue. What was an hour earlier a studied nonchalance would turn into an open frenzy. Frenzy, but not panic, since everybody was executing standing orders. The degree of advance organization was quite impressive. I went through five "*pokret*s," one in Otochac and four in Glina, and each time they functioned very well. I never heard of anybody being left behind even though two of my "*pokret*s" in Glina came in the middle of the night. In Otochac I got an instant offer to join our performing group but my standing orders were to report to the captain in the City Command. He did not even for a second consider a change of plans.

"You are to report to the third mobile hospital in Vrhovine. If they have already left, the Village Command will help you find them. Have you already picked up all your belongings?" asked the captain.

"Yes I am ready and fully prepared," I said with a bit of theatrical redundancy.

"Well that is a problem," smiled the captain. "I have a few trucks for the ready soldiers and another one for prepared comrades. But the ready and prepared guys like you are so rare, that I have no specific transportation for them. Why don't you hop on this truck full of ready guys and join them? Off you go to Vrhovine and God be with you!"

God be with me? Such an open religious weakness from the mouth of an officer would not be normally tolerated but all rules changed during a "*pokret*." From our previous interactions I would not have guessed that the captain had a sense of humor. He chose the right time to show it. I jumped into the truck laughing at myself and unconcerned about what lay ahead, I was indeed ready for my first *pokret*.

Trnavac

(November 1943–February 1944)

Our evacuation from Otochac turned out to be quite difficult. At first there were just a few snowflakes but they became a heavy storm of the kind I have seen only in Lika. Normally an invisible curtain separates the weather between the seaside and Lika. I recall swimming on my back in the Adriatic and looking at the clouds over the Velebit Mountain. First a few small clouds took a discreet peek at the seaside, soon many others joined, and gradually the cheerful fraternity of playful shapes built up into an ominous and angry-looking front. But it was all a show. A magic hand always kept the clouds at the edge of the mountain. All hell broke loose over the mountain; lightning hit the barren limestone of the Dinaric Alps, thunder echoed from the sea, curtains of rain were seen over the cliffs, but not a drop ever fell on the sunny shores. And on infrequent occasions when southern winds picked up humidity from the sea and drenched the shores with sheets of rain, the reverse was true. A lovely sliver of crystal-clear blue sky appeared at the edge of the mountains letting everybody know that the high grounds in Lika had been spared from the nastiness below.

But in the winter, the warmer wind from the coast occasionally succeeds in breaking through, picks up moisture from the sea and, all the while howling and whirling, drops a huge amount of snow on Lika. The sheer amount of snow doesn't really matter; it is its distribution that takes the toll. At some spots, after they descend though narrow mountain-passes upon the valleys of Lika, the violent gales from the sea start to spin around and whip up huge snowdrifts.

On our way from Otochac to Vrhovine the wind quickly created huge, almost impenetrable, snowdrifts in quite a few spots. Each time one half of the truck's passengers picked up shovels to open a narrow pass and, laboring from the back, the other half strained to push the truck through. Instead of an hour, it took us half a day to get to Vrhovine. The village teemed with withdrawing Partizans. There was not enough time for bonding on the truck and with not as much as a handshake everybody scrambled in different directions. I found the hospital, which had just started withdrawing from Vrhovine, and was greatly embarrassed by my tearful, hugging mother. What a spectacle! Under the onslaught of impending maturity, a garden-variety teen-

ager is ashamed of showing emotions. Now imagine the embarrassment to a gun-toting, fourteen-year-old, budding hero!

But there was no time for rancor. I reported to the commander of the hospital's escort unit who, to my disgust, ordered me to stay next to Mother.

The entire hospital couldn't be evacuated during the day. The Germans kept sending spotter planes to check out the roads and against the background of snow, they could easily detect the caravan. Consequently only small widely scattered groups of personnel and supplies made their way during the day. Hauled by wagons or carried on stretchers, the patients started their journey at night.

Our group consisted of one oxen-pulled wagon, a platoon of ten soldiers and a group of about ten hospital workers. Five soldiers walked a good two hundred yards ahead of the wagon. Closely behind the wagon were the hospital personnel including Mother and me. Behind us, for no known reason or no reason at all, the soldiers in the rear guard deployed themselves in a long, staggered single file. We started around noon. The winds had calmed down, the clouds lifted, and reflecting from the snow, the blinding winter sun made everybody squint. The snow had been somewhat packed down on the road but walking was still difficult. The bumpy surface was particularly hard on my ankles. Each time my eyes misjudged or coordination failed, my foot slipped sideways and the cumulative effect of the repeated stress began to take its toll. I had woolly socks and comfortable boots but to no avail. Slowly my toes turned into painfully frozen icicles and my hands did not fare any better. I was cold to the core.

Mother seemed to be doing quite well. She was excited about the task at hand and continuously spoke to others about all sorts of organizational and logistical issues. From time to time she asked how I was doing and I pretended to be fine but the false bravado did not make me feel any better. Finally, just about when I was ready to admit how miserable I really was, we reached the top of a hill and all of a sudden, in a perfectly round mountain plain, there lay the village of Trnavac. At the perimeter a loop of houses precisely followed the sharp dividing line between the hills and the flat field. Mountain planes are frequent in the limestone terrain, but this one in Trnavac

was unusually small, no more than two miles across. In the middle of the field was an eerie Orthodox cemetery with its tall, elaborate crosses. With the mountain at its back every house faced the field. Anybody looking through a window could not avoid seeing the cemetery. The villagers were not given to philosophy, but during those long winters, hopelessly stuck inside the houses, it must have occurred to them how depressing their life really was. Work hard, plow the land and eventually you'll end up under one of those crosses. We all must die one day, but nobody wishes to be reminded.

We came to the village with about eighty wounded, a staff of seven physicians, a few nurses and quite a large group of other personnel. Somebody had done a good advance job. We were very well received. Patients were farmed out to various houses and the largest one was converted into a surgical theater. The thirty or so days before the village elders requested us to leave, were downright pleasant. We had a marvelous respite in the midst of an ugly war. Deep in free territory, the village was friendly, the enemy airplanes rarely flew in our direction, and the hospital had a large store of necessary supplies. Urged by Winston Churchill, the Allies finally recognized the Partizan movement as the only effective anti-German fighting force in the region. Churchill had set aside his anti-Communist sentiments for the sake of the larger good and in the winter of 1943 the British began to parachute supplies. I never saw an actual drop, but they must have been somewhere close. Not only did the hospital get cans, chocolates and bandages but, to everybody's delight, actual pieces of parachute also came our way. Catching a good swath of the shining silk and turning it into some part of personal clothing, or just carrying the smooth material around was the pinnacle of happiness. The parachute ropes were particularly intriguing. They were shiny, braided and incredibly strong. I do not recall putting them to any good use, but my pockets were always full of rope. It was simply a good thing to have around. A toy of sorts.

Our only serious problem was infestation with lice. Nobody really knows where they hide under normal circumstances but give them a massive concentration of people, lower the standards of personal hygiene, and within a few months the lice are all over the place. And for the Partizans lice were not just pests. In our territory they

carried the Ricketsia germ, which caused devastating epidemics of Typhus. The microorganism—larger than viruses—but smaller than bacteria, is not infectious on its own. The disease can be spread only through lice. I am sure somebody knows everything about the life cycle of the Ricketsia, but to me the typhus epidemic is a big enigma. There are no cases of typhus during peace but the disease does not disappear. The bug seems to have struck some sort of deal with the local population, and just sits there opportunistically waiting for the next war to show what it can do.

The guerrilla's sanitary service mounted a huge effort to control lice but in spite of it, we were all infested. At the head of the unsuccessful effort was Dr. Rasuhin, a Russian emigrant trained in epidemiology, and an optimistic, resourceful person. He developed the prototype of the "Partizan's barrel," a simple and easily manufactured equipment for fighting lice. Its basic elements were huge barrels that drivers used to discard on the side of the road as soon as they emptied them of gasoline. Rasuhin tapped into that supply and turned the barrels into steam chambers for delousing. His construction plan was simple. Build a raised wooden floor with large holes inside the barrel, pour water into the lower half, put the underwear and shirts into the upper half, cover the barrel with a lid and light a fire underneath the contraption. Eventually enough steam develops to kill the lice while leaving the underwear only slightly moist. If needed, the clothing could be used right away. The other cornerstone of Rasuhin's efforts, were elaborate dry chambers he had built on all-important crossroads. These contraptions had a huge capacity and were much more effective. Since thermometers were not available, Rasuhin grappled with the problem and eventually found an admirably simple solution. He got hold of sufficient amounts of naphthalene, a white powder used to keep moths away from stored clothing. Naphthalene had the correct melting point. Small packages were inserted into each load. If the powder melted into a crystallized mass, the heat was sufficient to kill the parasites and their eggs. Rasuhin went around happily building dry chambers, giving lectures and fighting the bugs. He was a true eccentric- an elderly man with a great head of white hair protruding in all directions, a French beret atop his hair and, where others had ammunition belts, draped across his chest, he carried a large

garland of onions. "My personal reserve of vitamin C." he'd proudly announce. His enthusiasm was infectious and everybody willingly cooperated, but the problem was overwhelming.

Every evening in Trnavac, physicians, nurses and the administrative personnel got together in one house to "read the book"—a euphemism for fighting lice. We would sit next to a lamp, take off our shirts and start looking for lice. They hide in the folds of the clothing. You hold your shirt between your hands, just like a book, and slowly screen the seams for lice. The procedure is disgusting. When squashed between the nails, the creatures pop with a characteristic crack. But the reward for a job well done, a quiet night, was well worth it.

The hospital staff was a lot of fun. Not exactly a MASH unit, but a group of nice and serious people, some of them on the eccentric side. Like Dr. Dora Filipovich, a middle-aged, thin-faced bacteriologist, who carried on a private war with the village dogs. Weighed down by pockets fuls of assorted stones, she could barely move through the village. In the evenings, Dora used to give a hilarious account of her latest exploits and muse about her unreasonable fear of dogs. Cila Albahari, a good-looking woman who had just graduated from medical school, entertained the group with true or contrived stories. Like the one about the illiterate nurse's aide who fancied he learned Latin. As new patients arrived he would cry out loudly "diagnosis sinistrosis" if the wound was on the left side and "diagnosis dextrosis" for the right side. Soon came a patient with multiple wounds and our Latin expert was at loss for words. "What's the next one like?" inquired the physician. "Like Swiss cheese," came the laconic answer.

I do not remember who came up with the idea, but one evening the company took an inventory of books I had read and then proceeded to tell me about the ones I had not had a chance to read. The fact that I was the only youngster around and that for two years I did not go to regular school must have brought out the best in these marvelous people. From memory they put on night-long performances complementing each other, interrupting to highlight their favorite plots, correcting verses. It sounds melodramatic, but the truth of the matter is that we were holed up in a small space, the wind was

whistling around the house and yes, you could hear the wolves howling. But all this "*Hound of the Baskervilles*" atmosphere did not register and we were cozy and happy. In the absence of kerosene, the potato lamp provided yet another visual and olfactory enhancement to this unreal atmosphere. One manufactured the lamp from a large raw potato by digging out a hole in the middle, stuffing it with a wick and topping it with soft lard. After some perseverance a smelly flickering light engulfed the room.

All my cognitive processes are abstract and completely non-pictorial. I recognize a person or a place when I see them but in their absence the image is gone. However the picture of the circle of torsos growing out of the packed dirt floor, that peculiar darkness barely broken by the weak yellow light in the middle of the circle, and those tired serious faces lit from below, is an image forever etched in my memory. Pictorially the scene had an intensely Dutch master's quality. Had one of the talented painters who joined the Partizans, and there were many of them, attempted to capture these moments it would have told more about the war than a dozen heroic battle scenes. I also remember that particular image because of its smell. What I lack by way of visual memory I do make up for with crisp recollections of odors. I have never forgotten the mixed aromas of the potato lamp, fireplace smoke, body odor, and the stench of dried mutton that hung beneath the thatched roof. And the verbal accompaniment is forever with me. Memories of poems recited around the potato lamp are so strong that I never bothered to go back to the text in books.

The poems have a peculiar non-transferable meaning to me. Particularly, the repetitive, monotonous, but deeply meaningful poem "On the Lipari" by the Serbian poet Aleksa Shantich. It became my personal mantra, a soothing music to keep unpleasant thoughts at bay. As I walked alone through the night at age of fourteen years, I was able to keep the fear away thanks to Shantich. Here is my translation of the magical song:

The ocean is deep
asleep
descends the coolish dark.

Behind the cliff there play,
the gray
and the sun's last spark.

Sad is the bell's song
among
the doleful evening sounds.
Tired to the core,
once more
people kneel on the grounds.

Seeking relief they face,
with grace,
an icon of endless pains.
But there on the cross
at loss
silent the martyr remains.

One evening somebody realized I had not yet read all the poems of my favorite Croat poet Dobrisha Cesarich. My mentors decided to immediately redress the situation and the evening turned into an uninterrupted stream of "remember this one?" recitations of Cesarich. It was magic. Cesarich was capable of coining haunting, melodious and unforgettable little poems. They ranged from socially conscious works about the poor to little reminders about daily beauty, which we all tend to ignore. And then there were poems expressing his anthroposophic philosophy. Akin to oriental religions, Cesarich believed in the eternal soul that constantly transfigures, but in his system, the spirit could take any form. One poem, short and succinct, entitled "When I Turn into Grass" celebrated the simplicity of his imagined future life. "My only burden will be the dew and my single concern the scythe," proclaimed the poet. But to me the top poem of the evening was "Who Knows," a beautiful anthroposophic poem about love. I cannot do it justice but that will not stop me from trying.

Who knows? Nobody, nobody knows
Brittle the knowledge seems.

Did I stumble on a shard of truth
Or are these dreams?

Maybe love could happen to us
Happen I say
But I do not know do I wish it
to stay or go away

In the Ocean of life that boils
And never stops
By chance there could meet
Again the same two drops.

Unknowingly, darling, my desire
might not be in vain
If two old lips were to meet
in the same kiss again?

The reader may not quite appreciate how subversive this was. All idealistic philosophies were anathema to the Communists, and anybody practicing them was considered an enemy. Daring to assume that there may be some mystical, spiritual principles was diametrically opposed to the "can do" core of the Communist philosophy. And yet in Trnavac, in the presence of many old-time Communists, we were enjoying a good infusion of spiritualism without fear of consequence. We had formed an inner circle and nobody reported to the higher-ups about this deviation from the doctrine. Those who understood would not tell and those who would tell did not understand.

In Trnavac, I also learned the truth about the Soviet Union. Ervin Shinko, an old-time revolutionary, poet and philosopher had been attached to the hospital as a "cultural worker." Not a very pleasant chap. He was a moody, conspiratorial, careful and painfully indecisive. His unnaturally large head was full of facts. A living encyclopedia and a superb educator, he gave me a crash course in the history of philosophy.

Somehow the atmosphere got to this careful philosopher. One evening somebody felt inspired to talk about the big socialist motherland and Stalin's genius. That was too much for Shinko. For two full hours he spoke about the massacre of the leadership, including

almost all Yugoslav immigrants to the USSR, Stalin's brutality, his collusion with the Germans and the horrifying internal oppression. Above all Shinko took exception to the primitive and false outline of the Marxist philosophy given in the official bible: *The History of the Soviet Communist Party.*

The Spanish Civil War had been an eye opener to this old revolutionary. As he volunteered to fight alongside the Spaniards, he realized that fighters came from all over the world, except from the Soviet Union. "So don't look in the sky for Russian parachutes, just take what Churchill is sending. The Russians would never help. They see themselves as the center of the world. Everybody should be ready to die for them—after all, they are the first Communist Country in the world." At that point Shinko got quite aggravated. "Communists, my foot—just a bunch of impostors! That is not what Marx had in mind."

I never got a chance to ask Shinko what were Marx's real thoughts since from the next day on, realizing he had been too candid, he was running scared. He buttonholed us all and extracted solemn promises of secrecy. It was sad to realize that this one-night brave man was a full-time coward. In all likelihood, he started as a selfless idealist but was ground up by the system into a shadow of himself- too far gone to defect, too much aware of the dangers from his comrades, bitter and probably loath to look in the mirror. For he must have seen how little was left of the idealistic youth who only a decade before, was ready to sacrifice his life in Spain.

One evening when we again sat down for a session of collective delousing-cum-entertainment, the approaching Christmas became the main topic of conversation. The Communists understood that Christmas was a deeply entrenched festivity. Before the war every household, be they Christian, Jewish or atheist, had a major celebration around Christmas. Understanding that they could not possibly abolish these celebrations, the Partizan leaders decided to subvert them for their own purposes. In a way they were repeating history. Remembering how the Christians cleverly converted the pagan cele-

bration of winter solstice into a Christmas celebration, the Communists decided they would celebrate "Father Winter," a Partizan replica of St. Nicholas. We planned how to bring down a few fresh evergreen trees and cut a large number of five pointed red stars. For the program we organized singing of Partizan songs and recitation of patriotic poems. Whereas the rest of us were excited, Mother became visibly sad and after a while withdrew into a far corner. I went to check and found her crying. She had just received two letters from Djuka. We had not heard from him since the beginning of October.

"Why are you crying? What happened to him? Is he in trouble?" I wanted to know.

"Not in any more trouble than the others. Read this and you will understand," said Mother.

"Fine, but you should join the company so I can quietly peruse the letter. If the others get wind of the letter, they might want me to read them aloud. I am sure you would not like that."

"I don't care," she said. Mother was truly upset. Normally she would care!

I took a potato lamp to the corner and began reading.

Near Mazin 9.XI.1943.

My own beloved and dearest,

Constantly marching. Ten hours of march and 14 hours of rest and so all the time. Now the whole Division is aiming towards Srb near Lapac where we are to join some other Divisions. The Kom. of the Brigade Shijan told us in a speech that we would deploy in the direction Bihach-Donji Lapac-Knin. Where would we actually go, he himself does not know but we are going far away and to the East.

My feet are still in order but I do not know how they will hold out in the future. The only thing that really bothers me is the absence of your letters. When will I see you again? Dear Dad try through Ivica[1] *to have them assign me somewhere closer to you.*

Otherwise everything is excellent. The camaraderie is of the highest degree.

---

1 Refers to Dr Ivo Kralj

Do not upset yourselves if I do not write for a while but I truly do not know when there would be another opportunity.

Are my letters arriving regularly? This is already the fifth letter. My address is The Third Company, Third Battalion the Third Udarna Brigade of the Sixth Division.

Write !

With love, Djuka

Missing his family and under miserable conditions Djuka managed to write five letters. That two of them had arrived was a little miracle. A civilian mail service did not exist. Couriers carried letters along certain general routes to vague destinations. People were on the move and the addresses had to be vague. Mother's and my address was "On position in Lika", Father's "Medical Services of Banija" and letters to Djuka were marked "Direction of Bosnia." This is no better a description than addressing a letter to John Doe, Rhode Island. Nevertheless the mail kept flowing in the right direction. Information gathering and sheer gossip were the favored guerrilla pastimes and it was not that difficult to find out who was where. Nobody was in charge of a formal postal organization but nevertheless, following the tortuous path of gossip, the mail eventually found its target.

The next letter was actually written only a day after the first one. When I read it I understood why mother cried.

For Dr. Dez. Julius!

Srb,10.XI.1943

My dearest and only ones!

I endured the worst Calvary you could think of. Imagine an uninterrupted 13 hours march in icy winter and thunderstorms. From five in the afternoon to six in the morning without a rest. Through the mountains and forests. Thickets without trails, let alone roads. Old Partizans, already two and half years in the battle, tell me they have not experienced anything harder than this. Eight Comrades froze and were left dead in the mountain.

Srb is a scraggly little place in the middle of a quadrangle Bihach-D. Lapac-Grachac-Udbina. I spoke with the Politcom of the Division and he told me that we would travel 5–6 days more until we

reach the destination. Ergo, we are going far away, the whole Division, even the hospital, is going. My flat feet are hurting badly. I will have to report for the medical.

I need not explain to you my beloved Parents and particularly emphasize to you Stevica[2] *that I am going so far away that possibly I might not see you for a long time. So help me God the battle and the effort are not as hard on me as the fact that I am missing you terribly.*

Otherwise I am healthy and cheerful. I hope you have situated yourselves well. Why are you not writing?

Kisses, hugs, respect and love until the grave. Yours

Djuka

Addendum on the vertical margin of the letter; *From now on I will write less frequently, have no time.*

P.S. III. Comp, III Bat., III Ud. Brig, VI Div.

Djuka's letter made me cry too. The war had changed him. For the first time he expressed brotherly love. There was true love in those letters and Djuka expressed much more emotion than I ever thought he was capable of. Two phrases in his final salutations got to me: "respect" and "until the grave." After so many years of obstinacy and pretense of being tough, Djuka found a way to show respect to his parents. And his reference to 'grave' was not a figure of speech. Djuka just had a brush with death and wanted to express his feeling while he had a chance.

After those letters I spent much more time with Mother. I was supposed to carry messages or supplies from one point to another but in Trnavac people were content to walk across the field and do the job themselves. Not having too much to do, I drifted between two favored stopovers; the kitchen and the general store. Rajko, who before the war served as chef on one of the Adriatic liners, ran the

2 Diminutive for Stevo

kitchen. His improvised kitchen was always tidy and clean. He was delighted to teach me a few tricks including making pancakes for the whole hospital. It was a special show entirely for my entertainment. He really had no business even thinking of such an extravagance. Making pancakes for 150 people is not a small job even with a superb kitchen. And he was going to do it in an open field, all by himself. We dug a long pit outside the house. On one side I kept the fire and pushed the hot coals towards the other end. Over the hot coals we placed some iron rods, spaced just right to accommodate 4 pans. Rajko was walking in a circle seemingly always with two pans in his hands. A pan progressed in an orderly way from the left to the right, always moving one space, until it reached the right end where the finished pancakes were stacked up. Then Rajko would pour the dough into the empty pan and form the pancake while walking to the left. He'd lift the pan on the left, flip the pancake in the air, simultaneously putting the pan with the new pancake over the coals. Than he'd pick up the right pan, flip the pancake and so forth. Quite a show! There was constant motion and seemingly at any moment a pancake was turning in the air. In the midst of an ugly war Rajko had done his peace-time best. Magnificent! And to think that I was the only audience! However I did spread the word and when we sat for the dinner, Rajko got an enthusiastic round of applause.

The hospital had a large stock of supplies, acquired by Partizans either after Italy capitulated or from goods parachuted to us by the British. Dragec, a peacetime grocer, managed the store with gusto. He somehow made a bunch of shelves, and erected a semblance of a counter in front of them. The goods were arranged as if they were for some exclusive window display. There were pyramids of Italian, German and English cans, all labels turned in exactly the same direction. Stacked boxes formed clean geometric pictures and from the ceiling sausages hung in orderly fashion- the thin ones bunched in bouquets, the thicker ones arranged by size and length.

We were always half hungry. It was tantalizing to look and not touch that display of prosperity. The showpiece of the store was the Eiffel tower of round cheeses piled one upon the other. At the bottom was the largest cheese I ever saw. In Dragec's mind that truck tire sized

monster was the last reserve for black days. Nobody could persuade him to cut it up. The cheese became the last symbolic connection to his former orderly civilian life and the living proof that things were not yet at their worst. Of course he was a sitting duck for teasing. People would ask him to cut up the cheese just to see him recoil in horror. Even Dr. Joza Kajfesh got carried away. As the commanding officer he sternly ordered that the "moon" be cut up. As Dragec approached the cheese, hesitant, and visibly upset, Joza withdrew the order and entrusted the "*moon*" to the grocer's discretion. It would be up to him to decide when to cut the cheese up. "But use your judgment. The thing is big and hard to move around," Kajfesh said.

A few weeks later, just as the Italians before us, we lost the cheese. Orders came to move in a hurry. The cheese was too heavy. Our grocer kept postponing and hoping that more transportation would become available. Finally it was too late to cut up the monster and put a decent chunk of cheese in everybody's pocket. We left the *moon* behind us and I wonder whether anybody ever ate that cheese.

Those idyllic days when everybody behaved as if it were peace ended with a bizarre incident. Dr. Joza Kajfesh had organized a good surgical suite capable of major interventions, but he never gave a thought to the disposal of amputated limbs. Previously those things were automatically taken care of. Not in Trnavac! On the fatal day, the village dogs got hold of an amputated leg and dragged the badly disfigured limb through the village. The villagers had seen just about everything in their lifetime. They had learned to ignore brutalities, but this disrespect for a human body was more than they could tolerate. Instantly a stern delegation let it be known that the hospital had outstayed its welcome. There was nothing Dr. Kajfesh could do but to apologize and pack up the hospital.

On the face of it, Dr. Kajfesh's willingness to honor the request and evacuate the hospital seems to have been guided by the highest ethical principles. Armed as we were, we could have easily imposed our will. However, he was simply executing standing orders against locating a hospital in an unfriendly village. Unfriendly villagers could have easily summoned the enemy who'd be more than happy to help the village rid itself of unwanted guests. Admittedly we had only

Trnavac in 2002. The village had disappeared, only a few people live there. Trees and bushes grew over the arable field.

offended their sensitivities, but nobody dared to wait and see whether the villagers would change their minds. Kajfesh promised to get us out of Trnavac in a week.

A few months later, in another village, the people were not so forthright. Under the cover of night somebody whisked in the Chetniks. They executed all patients and slit Joza Kajfesh's throat. The legend has the butcher screaming, "You can cut, so can we!" True? Who knows, but it could have easily happened that way. It was a dehumanizing, brutal, fratricidal war.

The decision to evacuate the hospital thoroughly changed my life. In the new situation I had to live up to my job description as a messenger. My first task was to personally carry the request for relocation of the Trnavac hospital to the Territorial Command in Vrhovine. It was the first of numerous trips up and down the winding, snow-covered road to Vrhovine. I was delighted. Finally I would

have an independent role in the great adventure of war! Fearless as only a stupid teenager can be, I was concerned merely about the physical problems; the long walk, how to keep myself warm, what was the right pace to arrive before dark, and physical markers I'd use not to get lost. I did not give any thought to possible danger. The road was barren and if anybody cared to set up an ambush, there was nothing in his way. Not that anybody was particularly interested in me as a person, but anybody could easily guess that a lone and armed youngster must be a courier. Had I fallen into enemy's hands I'd be in for less than civilized interrogation.

Mother must have been petrified at the thought of me walking alone to Vrhovine but if she showed as much as an inkling of resisting the orders, the hospital's commissar would have had an excuse to reassign me to another unit. The commissars were high priests of Communist morality bent on enforcing political purity at any cost. Accepting the inevitable Mother and other women in the hospital managed to put a good face on the whole thing. Within a few hours they transformed me into a superbly dressed and well-supplied traveler. The centerpiece of my newly acquired elegance was the khaki British Army trench coat; warm, water repellent and indestructible. Underneath I had a brand new British military jacket, a marvelously casual piece resembling much more a skier's wind jacket than a military uniform. I had also gotten new military boots, but the group decided I'd do much better if I wore a few layers of thick woolen socks and put on a pair of *opancy* over them. The opancy, crafted from tanned cowhide with the hairy surface on the outside made you look like a cumbersome hoofed animal. Particularly when the cow was multicolored and when, as mine did, the Moccasins reach up to the knees. But the opancy worked very well.

In the morning I reported to the commander and the political commissar of the hospital.

"Comrade Julius," the commander said," you will carry messages to the Village Command in Vrhovine and they will forward them to the nearby Headquarters of Medical Operations."

The commander, a local Serb from Lika, stopped for a moment to collect his thoughts but seeing from the corner of his eye that the commissar was about to say his piece, he continued to talk.

"Now, this is a strenuous road but it should not take you longer than three hours to reach Vrhovine. When you get to the Village Command work your way close to the stove and stay put. Under no circumstances, and this is an order, should you take the message any further."

I looked askance.

"You see," the commander continued, "in a war everybody tries to preserve his resources. I am dead sure that instead of doing their job, they'd generously offer to let you take the letter a few extra miles. And I do not want that. You are to take a good rest before you return."

I was about to say something to the effect that walking a few miles more could not hurt, but the commander would not let me talk.

"I told you that this is all about resources. Got it? And do not imagine, Sonny, that this has anything to do with you as a person. You are my resource and I need you, excuse my honesty, as I would a fresh horse after a long ride. Don't even think about unnecessary heroics. This darn war is full of heroes and what we need right now is a reliable horse."

A nice way to summarize the situation! One could not argue about the logic and anyhow, it was an order. "Yes, Comrade," I said. He left me no space for any other response.

"You must leave Vrhovine by 13 hours sharp (1 p.m.) If the return response does not reach you in time you must stay overnight and come up to Trnavac early in the morning. Here are the orders to that effect and don't let anybody tell you otherwise. Just show them the papers."

All the while the commissar, a well-educated city dweller and a stalwart old-line Communist, was itching to join the conversation. Finally it was his turn.

"Comrade Julius we trust you," he said, "but I would like to talk to you about the rare, in fact, distant possibility that. . . ."

"Oh come on now! You are not going to give him that shit about the code of behavior!" yelled the commander. "This kid will not get caught, period. I would not send him on the way if it were not reasonably safe."

The sophisticated commissar was shocked with the commander's crude, tell-it-like-it-is, profanity-laden sentences. The commissar might have been offended but the commander was boiling mad and before the commissar could recover, turning to me, he continued to yell.

"In short, the commissar wanted to remind you of our code of conduct if you were caught by the enemy. And I am telling you that first of all there is little if any chance that you might get caught, and second, should you somehow get caught—sing, Brother, sing. They will find the letter anyhow and you might as well tell it up front."

This was heretical beyond belief. The commissar was speechless.

The commander now spoke directly to the commissar's face. "Right, I should not tell the youngster the real truth. What would you Comrade Commissar, want the kid to do? Stall, get the nails torn from his fingers until he coughs up the secret? It would buy us about half an hour. It is not worth it."

"If you were caught, you'd probably resist. I respect your revolutionary background," continued the commander, "and you'd likely withstand the pressure. For myself, I do not know. But for God's sake, this is a child. Cut out the crap and let the kid go."

"Julius, you are dismissed. Move on!"

These two guys deeply disliked one another, but they were stuck together. The commander was a local hero, a minority Serb who instead of joining the Chetniks joined the Partizans, whereas the commissar had impeccable Communist credentials. I had no doubt which one was my friend.

All of a sudden, the commander changed his mind. "Come back," he ordered, "We got carried away and did not give you some details of the trip."

He proceeded to describe various markers on the way to Vrhovine, where to find shelter, how to hide from a spotter airplane and what supplies to take with me. His instructions were very useful. The commissar had nothing practical to offer and just sat there looking miserable.

"Now let's talk about the wolves," said the commander. "You are more likely to hear than see them. However if they are very hun-

gry, they might follow you from a safe distance. As long as you move they will not attack. Don't get frightened, just keep going ahead and don't slow down. If they keep their distance, do not waste ammunition. You won't scare them away and you don't need to advertise you are on the road."

"And what if they come really close?" I wanted to know.

"Shoot to kill a few. That might slow them down. Sometimes they feast on their brethren."

"Really?"

"So they tell me. I never tested the theory but I know that the wolves stand a chance only if you are scared. I have heard of scared people trying to run away until they get exhausted or climb up a tree in panic. The wolves will patiently circle around the tree. Remember they can take the cold weather and you can't. Eventually you'd fall off the tree like a ripe fruit."

Finally the commissar found something to talk about. "I would like to remind you that you are now a soldier and that you ought not to mix with the civilians. Do not stop to help, do not discuss your mission. Just push ahead, time is the essence."

"You mean I ought to ignore them like the wolves?"

"Well not exactly, but excessive compassion will not do them any good. You are carrying enough supplies only for yourself. If you share them with others, somewhere down the line you might be sorry. You never know."

It sounded callous but to my surprise the commander was in full agreement. "He is telling you the right thing and yes, you ought to treat them exactly as you would the wolves. That is the truth!"

The commander had a way of cutting a discussion short.

I had no problems following the snow-covered path and after two lonely hours I had reached the point where the path from Trnavac merged in a "T" fashion with the main road to Vrhovine. There at the bottom of the Trnavac trail I met my first *zbjeg* of about two hundred hundred people. To my best knowledge "*zbjeg*" is a relatively new word in the Croatian language. I certainly learned it dur-

ing the war. Roughly translated the word is a contraction of elements of "together" and "run." "*Izbjeglica*" is a refugee and *zbjeg* is a group of refugees. *Zbjeg's* were alliances of convenience, among people looking for safety on the back roads of the war. Groups of refugees would amble from place to place not knowing exactly what they were doing, desperately trying to avoid the physical threat of the war, and hoping against hope to find a safe haven. If there has been only one direction, the group would have grown larger but at the first opportunity, when there was a choice, the groups would fall apart. Without words, good wishes or handshakes, the former companions would head in different directions to pursue the same elusive goal. Decisions were made on hunches. A steep road versus a flat one, aiming at a more or less friendly village, or betting that the chosen road might be out of the enemy's way. Each *zbjeg* was a mixture of adults and children, villagers from the area, refugees from distant cities and orphans from who knows where. In times of trouble religious differences were set aside and Jews, Catholics, or Orthodox would cluster together in the same *zbjeg*. These agglomerates of dead-tired, poorly dressed, disoriented humanity in search of a shelter were one of the saddest sights of the war.

I could see the *zbjeg* from the top of the hill. In spite of strict orders to avoid civilians, I decided to check whether there was anything I could do for the poor people on the road.

But I was not prepared for the loss of dignity that goes with being in a *zbjeg*. Some of the hungry refugees asked loudly for food and soon I was surrounded by a small mob which, pushing and shoving, kept getting closer to me. When someone tried to pull the gun off my shoulder I got quite scared. Fear will either paralyze you or give you immense strength. I pushed the people away and let off a shot in the air. It worked! All of a sudden, I was alone in the middle of a quickly widening circle and as soon as it was clear which way I wanted to go, a respectful corridor opened up. Just then I noted on the side of the road the elderly man who used to make the *Petit Beurre* cookies in Otochac. I wanted to apologize and give him some of my supplies.

"Run as fast as you can and don't give me any of your stuff," he said. "If I accept something, they will take me apart. Right now you

are the least popular person on this road. Just go, for God's sake! Let me get out of this mess on my own!"

"Don't go to Trnavac. Trust me. That is the wrong way." I said. I could not help him but at least I gave him good advice.

~

My other trips from Trnavac to Vrhovine were generally uneventful. I do not remember being scared or concerned on the road and after a while, I convinced myself that there were no enemies along my path. A few times I saw an occasional single wolf but never a pack. At a distance a wolf looked as innocent as a village dog.

On my last trip from Vrhovine, I brought the final orders to Trnavac—the hospital would be relocated to the Lika village of Turjanski. Mother was reassigned to Banija where she'd first take a course in hospital organization and then become the director of a rehabilitation hospital. Excellent news. Finally Mother would be geographically closer to Father who already worked in Banija. Everybody urged us to leave as soon as possible. Another German offensive was in full swing and the connection with Banija could be interrupted any moment.

Next morning, together with a group of well-armed Partizans, we took a truck from Vrhovine to Slunj, past the Lake Plitvice area. The visibility in the leafless winter forest was excellent. I was not a bit nervous. What a difference compared to last time, when in the middle of the night, the scary wagon driver attempted to deliver us to the enemy in Vaganac! From Slunj, another truck took as for the long ride to the weird and unreal world of Topusko. Topusko, a peacetime spa, was practically intact and every Partizan residing there participated in a big show of nonchalance.

Whereas in other towns we'd first go to the local Command and ask them to assign us some lodging, in Topusko we went directly to the spa's main building and asked for rooms. No problem! Mother and I got separate rooms with full bathing privileges. The attendant inquired whether we were infested with lice. If we had lice, it would not bother him. He had just obtained a full barrel of the magic British powder called DDT. It instantly kills the bugs and it is easy to use.

Physician's Congress in Topusko. My mother and I are seen in the right top corner.

He offered all guests a temporary robe while he sent their belongings around the corner for delousing in the dry chamber. And for good measure he spread DDT over the sheets of every bed. As a result, his spa was lice-free. We gladly accepted the offer and clad in bathrobes, enthusiastically availed ourselves of the spa's services. In the main building the individual tubs and the swimming pool were overflowing with hot water. The peacetime spa attendants busily prepared baths, gave massages and generally behaved as if we were their paying guests. We had all fallen into a delusion. It must have been equally refreshing to the personnel of the spa as it was to us, to act as if everything was just fine and normal.

Next morning, refreshed by the spa and dressed in our fully deloused uniforms Mother and I walked in a leisurely way towards the City Command. In Topusko, in the middle of an enemy offensive,

oblivious to reality, everybody play-acted peace. In an exaggerated slow tempo people took walks under the tree-lined main alley, greeting each other, stopping to chat and generally behaving as tourists.

Somebody was waving at us from afar. I could not believe my eyes! Coming our way was the trio of hospital physicians from Trnavac—Dora Filipovich, Vera Sharich and Cila Albahari!

After hugs and kisses, it turned out that soon after we left, they too got the orders to report to Topusko. The hospital in Turjanski was reorganized and downsized. Jozha Kajfesh and his group would continue to perform surgeries, but as soon as the patients were reasonably stable, they would be transferred for further care to special postoperative care hospitals. This would free the surgeons to perform more operations. In the meantime, the three of them were sent to attend the congress in Topusko.

Detail from the picture on page 143.

Congress? What congress?

"Oh, you did not know?" said Cila Albahari, "They told us we will be attending a course in hospital management but what is cooking, is a full-fledged congress of Partizan physicians of Croatia to discuss modernization of our health services. About sixty people, if not more, will attend."

"But I understand that the enemy is about to start an offensive," said Mother. "This does not seem to be the right time to call a big meeting."

"Right," said Vera, "but you are not in charge and stupid as it seems, this is exactly what will happen. Go to the City Command, pick up you orders and than let's have dinner together." Vera was a straightforward person.

The City Command had clear instructions for both of us. Mother was to attend the congress and after that she'd be asked to organize a hospital in the village of Buzeta. I was assigned to Glina where I

would act as the youth organizer in the local high school. However I could postpone going to Glina until the end of the medical congress.

That was fantastic news. Father's headquarters was in the village of Klasnich and the new orders had situated us in an easy triangle. Glina, Klasnich and Buzeta were within an easy two hours walk from one another. Somebody was trying to help the family but to this day I do not know who it was. Our former protector, Dr. Kralj, had long ago been transferred to Bosnia.

Within a few days, medical personnel from far and wide, including my father, converged on Topusko. I did not partake in the sessions but stood in for the collective picture- one of the two preserved wartime photographs which are reproduced in this book. The person with the French beret is a Major Rogers, a British physician. He had been parachuted to provide care for Allied pilots who frequently limped with their damaged airplanes to bail out over our territory. He also introduced modern traumatological techniques to the Partizan's sanitary services. Little did we know that a few moths later, he would play an important role in our family affairs.

The evolving military situation prevented immediate implementation of the plan to place my parents and me within a reasonable distance from one another. The Germans were pushing and Glina was about to be evacuated. As soon as the congress finished, Father got the orders to return to Klasnich, Mother was assigned to a hospital that was withdrawing from Banija in the direction of Lika and I was to report to the regional chief of medical services to serve as his personal courier.

Before I tried to locate the regional director of medical services, I decided to take a look at the American Flying Fortress, which had crash-landed in the middle of a field near Topusko. Most of the airplane was well preserved. I had never before seen an airplane on the ground and with a great deal of excitement started to inspect the instruments in the cockpit, the twisted wires and the undamaged large-caliber machine guns. All of a sudden I heard the sounds of German dive-bombers, "*Stukas*." I pretty much knew they would not attack a destroyed airplane but the menacing sound of these war machines nevertheless sent shivers up my spine. The *Stukas* were in

the middle of an attack on an old factory just a few miles from Topusko.

The German *Luftwafe* built the *Stukas* for two purposes-to enable pinpoint precise dive-bombings and to terrorize people under attack. As they sped down from high altitude towards the target and before they ascended again to complete the diving loop, the *Stukas* would in the last moment slow themselves down by letting the airflow through loud sirens. The deafening noise of attacking *Stukas* added terror to the horror of bombing.

After they dropped the first bombs on the factory, the airplanes returned to the sky just above the downed American airplane. There they regrouped into a single staggered file for another round of dive-bombing the factory. In spite of knowing that the airplanes were busy hitting their target, I was scared out of my wits. Any time a plane roared over me I winced, stuck a finger in each ear and assumed a fetal position. During the war I got somewhat inured to the sound of various explosions but the horrifying noise of sirens was unbearable. I could not even imagine what it would have been like sitting in some basement, listening to the crescendo of Stuka sirens, and waiting for a direct hit.

The bombing ended in about fifteen minutes and somewhat shaken, I went back to the Command in Topusko to locate my new boss—the regional commander of the health service. I was sent to the village of Perna to report to a certain Dr. K. who held the rank of a colonel.

Colonel K. was quite eccentric and very likely mad. I found him and two of his aides lying on blankets under a hedge at the outside perimeter of the village. From afar, flat on their backs, screaming at the top of their lungs right into the air, they acted like a bunch of lunatics. At closer range I spotted the field telephone and grasped at least a part of the commotion. Colonel K. kept trying to connect with various parts of his operation. While the operator frantically turned the little handle to ring the other party, the colonel busily cursed the primitive telephones. On those rare occasions when he established an actual contact, Colonel K. screamed even more to overcome the poor transmission. I wonder whether he ever got anything done. Eventually, he took note of my presence and stood up. He was in his early

forties, had broad shoulders and a pair of large very dense sunglasses dominated his face. The man was extremely nervous. He constantly moved along a straight trajectory a few meters long. Having made the four steps to the end of the route, he'd turn on his heels and start pacing in the opposite direction. His motions were wild and his whole being emanated incredible impatience. He did not have to hide behind the dark glasses, his jerky motions prevented any eye contact. In fact, through half of his agitated conversation he had his back turned to me.

"Oh, you are the young Julius," said Colonel K. "So, I hear you will be my personal messenger. Lucky you. Congratulations! I am giving you an important and highly responsible assignment right away. You will carry my personal message to Dr. Franz Kleinhapel in the forest hospital inside the Petrova Gora, and you will bring me back his written reply."

Unable to wind down from his role of a wild telephone operator, colonel K. kept yelling at me.

"No sweat going up; you will join a small group heading in that direction. But keep your eyes open, since on your way back you will be all alone. Better come down during the day so you don't get lost. It is simple! Downhill, and to the north. In the morning keep the sun to your right and in the afternoon to the left. And don't go the other way unless you wish to have a conversation with Hushka's people.[3] Ha ha ha." Colonel K. laughed out loud as if he had just told the best joke of his life. It was not funny at all.

I was petrified. Not so much because I might get lost. I had more than the usual share of the invincible teenager syndrome. Somehow I would eventually find my way back, but the thought of straying into the Hushka territory was genuinely scary. Hushka had assembled a cruel group of Moslem privateers beholden to no one. Looking for quick profit, constantly shifting alliances and true only to their own self-interests, they'd shoot you for a pair of shoes.

---

3 Hushka was a much feared local "neutral" Moslem leader whose fiefdom extended over the roads on the other, southern, side of Petrova Gora.

What was on Colonel K.'s mind? How come he could not figure out what his misplaced sense of humor would do to me?

"Any problem?" he asked.

"No, Comrade Colonel. No problem."

"I have it all ready for you. This fellow here will take you to the meeting point with the rest of the group. The comrade in charge of your group is very reliable. He has been up the mountain many times but, as I said before, on the way down you are on your own. Have a good time!" said Colonel K. and turned his back for good.

Soon we were on our way to the stationary "forest hospital" in Petrova Gora. The mountain of Petrova Gora was fully covered by virgin forest. From its highest peak of only 2500 feet the mountain cascaded downwards in a widespread and apparently endless succession of hills and valleys. The Germans knew that somewhere deep in the forest there was a hospital but the territory was too large and too inaccessible for them to mount a systematic search.

The path through the forest was quite good and I made sure to remember every fork in the road. No problem, I could return without trouble. But after about three hours the road suddenly ended at what appeared to be an old lumber camp.

"Confused?" smiled the leader. "That is where we leave the wagons and unload everything."

"How will you carry all that heavy load up the mountain? Will people come from the hospital to help?" I asked.

"Not at all, the hospital is much closer than you think."

Try as I might, I could not see any further trails. The leader pointed out a tall tree on the other side of the valley and ordered each of us to enter the forest at different, widely separated points. When we reassembled under the tree, the leader arranged us into a single file column.

"Follow me. And by the way, as the crow flies, we are only five hundred meters from one of the first hospital wards. They are empty right now. See whether you can spot them."

Each member of the small party carried a heavy load of supplies on his back. After a while it was time for rest. We sat down. Somebody pulled out a piece of smoked cheese; another person had a bottle of wine on him. It was a nice break.

"So nobody found the hospital yet!" said the leader after a while. "I would not wish to depend on your powers of observation. Keep looking. You should be able to see it from where you are now." Everybody looked around, some even got up, but no luck.

"Oh you fools. You are sitting on it!"

Finally, one of us spotted a leaf-covered heap of earth that somehow looked slightly out of place. Having seen the first one, we soon made out a few similar mounds scattered throughout the area. In the middle of each mound, covered by a leaf-filled net, was a short five-inch-wide pipe that served as the vent for the underground facility. We were sitting on a "*zemunica.*"

*Zemunica*s (loosely translated as *under-grounders*) were the last resort to protect gravely wounded soldiers. In most instances the hospital would pack up and evacuate on foot. If the next destination was too far away to carry patients on stretchers, the most gravely wounded ones were left behind in *zemunicas*. The underground chambers were about 5 feet high, support beams ran through their middle and on each side there was a longitudinal row of hay-covered wooden platforms. On one end the hole became deeper, permitting a normal-sized person to stand upright. These "rooms" served as nursing station, storage facility and toilettes. The camouflage around *zemunicas* was superb. Somehow the builders were capable of digging deep ditches in the forest in spite of the tree roots and succeeded in not disturbing the undergrowth. They then had to hide the earth and cover up the underground structure to appear perfectly natural. But the life inside the wet, stench-filled chambers must have been sheer hell. The Partizans left the *zemunicas* open as long as was possible. At the last moment the guard on the surface would drag the prepared cover over the entrance, pile some leaves over it and slip away. Generally, the patients were left in *zemunicas* for only a few days as the Germans had little taste for long sojourns into the forest. As soon as the Germans left, the Partizans returned to spirit out the survivors to safer places. However it did not always work. In one instance, in Banija, the enemy came upon a *zemunica* and, the Geneva Convention notwithstanding, made short work of everybody.

After the rest atop the *zemunica* we made our way to the hospital proper. It consisted of four log cabins cleverly hidden at the bot-

tom of a deep ravine. The forest around was so thick and the ravine so deep that the buildings could not be spotted from the air.

I was looking forward to delivering the message to the legendary Dr. Franz Kleinhapel. He was an exception in the Partizan health services. He did not volunteer and, in fact, the Partizans kidnapped him from a Bosnian town where his devotion to the community, hard work and competence had become a legend. In spite of his German extraction Dr. Kleinhapel was an anti-fascist, but his primary commitment was to the local community. Being the only surgeon in a large territory, he did not feel he could walk out on his civilian patients. Once he was with the Partizans, kidnapped or not, Kleinhapel worked with his characteristic ardor and competence. On one occasion his hospital had been quickly evacuated, and having lost contact, he turned back in the direction of his old house. However the Partizans intercepted him and sent him back to the field hospital. What he had done would for anybody else be considered high treason. But in the case of this superb surgeon the issue was never brought up. Everybody accepted him for what he was-a non-ideological, hard-working physician fully devoted to the welfare of his patients, whoever they might be. His work was recognized after the war and Dr Kleinhapel retired in the rank of general.

Dr. Kleinhapel was a very kind person. A slim gentleman in his early sixties, he did not behave like a run-of-the-mill surgeon. Typically, surgeons are quick and decisive, but after I handed him the letterhe walked slowly to the chair, took out his glasses and carefully perused the message. Though Colonel K. expected me to return to Perna alone, Kleinhapel would not permit it. Next day he assigned a guard to accompany me back to Perna, where I found Colonel.K. lying under the same hedge. I handed him Dr. Kleinhapel's letter. Having read it, the mad colonel jumped up to pace back and forth along his usual short route.

"Good job," he yelled. "Your mother has joined a hospital on the move towards Slunj but on the other side of the mountain. They have an armed escort, so we sent them through the Hushka territory. Hushka does not attack larger units-not his style. I guess you should join her. So back you go through Petrova Gora, my boy, in the oppo-

site direction. But this time you will have company. I am sending a platoon to take over the guard duty once the hospital settles in its final destination. These are local boys, so do not worry. They know their way. And if they march too fast let them know. They will either slow down or carry you on their backs." And then he turned to a man next to him "Got that, comrade commander? This is just a kid and you must be considerate."

Quite a change in tone! Dr. Kleinhapel must have put some strong words of disapproval into the return letter. All of a sudden Colonel K. became a model of concern. Who knows? Maybe he realized on his own that it was reckless asking a teenager to return alone from the mountain.

Our little group easily crossed Petrova Gora and on its edge, close to the main road, made an overnight camp. It was too dangerous to light a campfire. Those asleep bunched together to keep warm and the two soldiers on duty walked circles around the camp. Early in the morning we woke up to the loud clatter of two tanks on the road. We were well hidden inside the forest and parading at a distance of three hundred yards the tanks were no danger to us. But their psychological impact was overwhelming. One feels naked in the face of the impenetrable armor. We were prostrated on the ground barely daring to make a move. I was as scared as I never had been before. My heart was racing and, to my shame, I was visibly shaking. Luckily others were too preoccupied to notice.

Eventually curiosity prevailed over fear and we dragged ourselves to the edge of the forest to take a better look. The two solitary medium-sized tanks carrying the Ustashe insignia were slowly moving away. They made no sense. Usually tanks on a hostile reconnaissance mission are flanked by platoons of soldiers but these tanks leisurely moved on the road as if they were on a Sunday stroll. This was Hushka's territory and the Ustashe commander in Petrinja may have decided to show Hushka that Ustashe could come and go as they pleased. Or Hushka, who permanently changed alliances, sent the word that larger Partizan units were crisscrossing his territory. A few tanks would serve his purpose well. Without logistical support, the tanks could not be permanently deployed but for a while they'd

keep larger Partizan units off the road. Hushka was nobody's friend. His goal was to keep all military units away from his territory or if they ever ventured through his land, Hushka made sure that they thought it over twice before they tried to return. Hushka's vicious active neutrality could not have lasted endlessly. He eventually formally joined the Partizan movement and, predictably, soon thereafter, I read a Partizan obituary about the brave Colonel Hushka who died under mysterious circumstances.

After the tanks left, our group proceeded on the road to Slunj. It was an eerie experience. The peasants in the fields turned their heads in the opposite direction and pretending they were terribly busy somehow managed to ignore us. Hamlets on the road appeared deserted. We did not see a person or an animal. Even the dogs did not bark. But somewhere behind the closed shutters we were carefully watched and a wrong move would have cost us our lives.[4] When we finally arrived in Slunj, Mother's hospital was already there. Content to be on the safe side I stayed with her as long as it was possible. Finally we made the full circle back to Topusko. There we enjoyed the spa for a whole day and the next morning we went our separate ways—she to Buzeta to start her new hospital—I to my permanent post in Glina.

---

4 The cumulative effect of passing through Hushka's little Moslem oasis in Croatia bestowed on me a permanent ability to sense danger. I cannot explain, but it is a fact that I developed a sixth sense for hostility. Years later in the middle of a visit to Teheran, I started to feel the same way as I felt in Hushka's territory. I could see how people, while ostensibly ignoring us, kept casting furtive hostile looks our way. As we passed through the half-empty hotel, all conversation and all normal activities seemed to stop. There was thick suspense in the air, so thick that you could cut it with a knife. It was the Hushka experience all over again. My American colleagues felt nothing of the sort. As far as they were concerned, the visit went just fine. I left Tehran with the next airplane. A few days later my colleagues returned without problems. But they were cutting it close. A week later the brutal Iranian revolution was in full swing. The experience on the back roads of the Hushka territory cured me forever of attempting to be a peace-time hero.

Glina

(February to July 1944)

Note. While we felt reasonably safe, the air distance between the " free" town of Glina and the occupied Croat capital Zagreb, was only 50 kilometers (32 miles). By road, the distance was about 55 miles.

About a year after each of us was sent in different directions out of Otochac, Father, Mother and I found ourselves in reasonable proximity. Father's headquarter in Klasnic and Mother's hospital in Buzeta, were only about 10 kilometers removed one from another and both were within an easy walking distance from Glina.

I formally reported to the Command in Glina somewhere in early February of 1944. The commander was the youngest of the three legendary Djurovich brothers from a nearby Serb village. The economic reality of their village permitted only one of them to graduate as an agronomist from the University of Zagreb but all the brothers completed the high school in Glina. This was highly unusual; most of the boys in their village remained functionally illiterate. When the war broke out, the brothers joined the Partizan movement and all of them quickly rose through the ranks. The one assigned to the City Command in Glina, Ratko, had already earned high marks as a commander of a brigade and because of his knowledge of the town, he had been delegated to run the civilian and military affairs of "liberated" Glina. I was thrilled by the opportunity of meeting the famous man. Nothing but his penetrating eyes distinguished Ratko from other run-of the-mill middle-aged local people. He spoke in the local dialect and like other Banijans did not gesticulate while talking. This outside appearance of a detached calmness gave a special emphasis to his words. He looked straight into my eyes and without any signs of emotion, as if I were in front of legal clerk reading a decree, delivered a string of orders. There was no doubt that this man meant what he said and that I must obey his orders.

"You are a soldier assigned to the high school and therefore you must be the first to arrive and the last to leave. Your orders are to study and that is what you will do. Furthermore, as a youth leader of the school you must set an example to others," he said.

"And what exactly are my responsibilities?" I inquired.

"First of all you must be there. If we need you, we will let you know. In the meantime talk to your colleagues about the movement and study hard."

Most likely because in the past he struggled to get educated, the commander took my schooling very seriously. As much as I would

like to think that he was a nice guy helping a youngster during the war, a later experience unmasked him as a true martinet. He did not care about me. It was a matter of military discipline. If I was sent for a duty, whatever it might be, including studying, I was to execute the orders.

"That will be all," Djurovich said." You should now report to the *intendant's* office. He will take care of all other arrangements. If you really need me call on me."

When I reached the door, Ratko change his mind.

"Wait a moment, I almost forgot to give you your evacuation orders," he said. "Of course we do not intend to cede Glina to the enemy but sometimes the military situation requires that we withdraw for a while. In that case you are at the top of the evacuation list and I will be personally responsible for your safety. I will assume that at evening you will be in the hotel and during the day in the high school. Anyhow, this is a relatively small place and we will find you. But you can not leave the town without my permission. If the situation is 'gusto' I will not let you go." Ratko used the Serb word *gusto* meaning *dense* but in the Partizan jargon, the expression referred to a tense and murky situations. "I must know where you are at all times," he continued," Even if you are out of town, you remain my responsibility."

I apparently did not act as if I were paying attention. He trained his eyes on me and continued to talk:

"Now listen to me! I will evacuate you out of town but I probably will not be able to deliver you to your final destination—your mother's hospital in Buzeta. You should think twice before you go in that direction. Very likely the hospital will also be on the move. Keep in touch with the medical command line and somebody will eventually send you in the right direction."

"Got all of that?" he asked rhetorically, "And as soon as the *pokret* is over, you are to return to my command and to the school."

"Got that too?"

"Yes Comrade, I did!"

"Good! And now you are truly dismissed."

As ordered, I went to see the *intendant*—a foreign word that the Partizans used for people in charge of supplies and logistics. The

intendant issued me coupons for meals in the Glina hospital and gave me a letter to the owner of the local hotel. In the hotel, I got a one-bed room for permanent use in exchange for a regular monthly supply of flour, kerosene and canned food from military stores. The deal must have been quite favorable to the owner and throughout my stay he treated me as an honored guest. The supply officer also gave me some cash in the currency issued by the Independent State of Croatia. People in Lika would not even take a look at that paper money, but Glina had a reasonable amount of black market commerce with the Ustashe-held territories. Because they were Serbs, the peasants did not dare to take produce to the markets in occupied Croatia. This gave the opportunity to all sorts of intermediaries to astutely identify shortages on both sides of the border and, at an incredibly high profit, barter the goods. It is a universal law that during a war most people suffer but a few individuals reap enormous benefits.

Up from Glina went pork fat, ham, rye, salt and cigarettes and back came coffee, sugar, textiles, medicine, and metal ware. Therefore the paper money had some value in Glina. I used my weekly allowance to pay for laundry, buy chestnuts for roasting and occasionally purchase something from the excellent local pastry shop. But I also saved money for special occasions. At that time I had a passion for a special type of hard salami produced in Petrinja by the Gavrilovich factory. The recipe, which the owner kept locked in a safe, had been passed through three generations of the Gavrilovich family. The owner or the foreman would add two barrels of secret ingredients to each batch of meat. Nobody quite knew what was in the barrels. People speculated that the casks contained more than spices. Why else would the volume of additives be so large? Some swore that the barrels contained horse meat, others spoke about addition of sinew and skin to enhance the firmness of the salami, and yet another camp believed that the secret was in a wheat-based thickening agent. The end-result well justified the secrecy surrounding the production. Covered by a dry whitish skin, the rock-hard salami was very different from other meat products. Cut cross-wise, the salami had dark brown firm meat interspersed by very fine, rice-kernel-sized specks of fat. But it was its taste that distinguished the Gavrilovich from mere

imitations. One's taste is a subjective quality, which one can neither explain nor justify, so let me simply say that for me, a Gavrilovich winter salami was and still is by far the best and most desirable dry meat product. A gustatory pinnacle and something that today, even when the doctor forbids it, I cannot resist.

Immediately after the war broke out, the salami disappeared from stores and the word got out that the owner had escaped together with the recipe. Imagine then my surprise when the hotel owner in Glina offered me a slice. Apparently the Gavrilovich factory owner decided to return and started producing his superb delicacy from memory. I was in seventh heaven. The salami tasted every bit as good as before the war and I badly wanted to get some. Eventually I saved enough money to order a whole salami, three pounds of it, from Petrinja. Every evening I'd cut a few thin slices and savor them. The salami lasted me for a good four months.

Having satisfied my salami fancy, I began to save money for a gift of coffee to Father. During the German occupation coffee was very hard to come by but he could barely live without it. Though he was generous by nature Father never shared his personal coffee cache with anybody. When we left Stanchich he took with him a kilogram and only once in Otochac was he able to replenish his "iron reserve." Every morning he pulled out his copper brewing pot, carefully measured the right amount of ingredients, and made himself a small cup of Turkish coffee and for a few minutes quietly enjoy the experience. Both the coffee and the brewing ritual were important to him; the first for the taste and the second because the orderly routine reminded him of the peacetime. I knew Father's coffee reserves were coming to an end. The hotel owner in Glina had good connections with black marketeers and could order me coffee at an exorbitant price. After three months I saved enough money for the purchase. I took possession of the precious sack of coffee beans in March and gave it for delivery to a classmate who lived next to Father's headquarters. My friend delivered the parcel the same evening and the next day I got Father's nice thank-you note. Rarely did giving a present provide me with so much pleasure as that one. I knew Father would enjoy the coffee and he knew how much pain it took to arrange the present.

But, happy as he was, Father's letter ended with what became the closing sentence of all our letters.

"Have you heard anything about Djuka?"

It was about four months that nobody got a single note from him. We consoled ourselves with rumors of sightings of him or of his brigade. Mother, Father and I regularly exchanged letters and while each of us affected nonchalance, deep down, we were very concerned. What was going on? Where was he? His last letter described the horrors of a winter march through Bosnian mountains; did something bad happen to Djuka?

Then one day, only a few weeks after he had written it, I got a letter from Djuka. It had been addressed to Mother but it somehow got delivered to me.

Bosnia 9.III.44.

*My dearest Mama (*Mum*) and Stevo!*

What's with you? Why don't you write? Your last letter arrived exactly a month ago, it was dated 27.I. I am not nervous but nevertheless I don't like that you have not sent a message for such long time. Besides, take into consideration that Tata (Dad*) did not send me a single word, nor do I know whether you heard from him, and then judge my state of mind. I am firmly convinced that you and Tata are alive but it still means a lot to me when you write. A letter is a mental, but for me also a real, connection with my dearest and besides it gives me a great morale boost.*

I am in the Escort Company, working hard and striving to conscientiously fulfill my responsibilities. My work is in the political field. The camaraderie here is good and I feel very well. From the comrade deputy politcomissar, who is an intellectual, I have a chance to learn a great deal and I sure utilize this to the full extent. Physically I am healthy and perky which greatly affects my overall situation.

How are you living? Is Tata writing and how is he? If you can and if it is safe, try to send me 2 underpants, 1 shirt, 1000 K (Kuna, the currency of the Croatian Independent State*), envelopes, "streptazol" and "aspirin." I for sure need these things, so send them if it can be done.*

Soon the whole brigade will be completely dressed in English (uniforms*)! I think the day of our reunion is near and therefore I am happy and content and hope so are you and Tata.*

Kisses thousand times, Djuka

Dj. J. Escort Company III.Ud Brig. I Pro.l Korp.

This letter was particularly interesting. Djuka wrote on the clean side of a legal document from the recorder of deeds in Glamoch, Bosnia. The document was dated April 1 1907, and describes the disposition of a claim of debt against the property of a certain Shime Danich in favor of brothers Jankovich. The court clerk visited the plaintiff to impound the property but the issue was settled when he received a cash sum of fifty-one kroners and eighty hellers. (See picture)

By then Djuka had to play by military rules and could give his address only as *Bosnia*. He cleverly used the old paper to let us know he was somewhere around Glamoch, another one hundred kilometers away from his last destination.

I was enthusiastic. Finally Djuka reached the deep heartland. The Germans did not penetrate there, and he had only the Chetniks to worry about. The Chetniks had no heavy equipment and generally were on the defensive. Furthermore Djuka's talent had been recognized and he was assigned to the Escort Company of the Brigade's headquarters. An escort Company was considered a deep reserve and would be sent into battle only under exceptional circumstances. Good news!

Next morning I dropped out of the school and took the letter to Mother's hospital in Buzeta. The distance from Glina to Buzeta or to Klasnich was about the same but I chose to deliver the letter to Mother not only because it was addressed to her, but also because I pretty much knew how she would react. When I gave her the letter, Mother yelled and jumped from joy.

Totally overwhelmed with emotions, she laughed and cried at the same time. And she once again forgot to speak Serbo-Croatian. She waved the letter and gave anybody willing to listen a report about Djuka in a mixture of Hungarian and German. It must have been confusing but everybody understood and nobody minded.

Bosna, 9.III.44

Najdraži moji Mama i Stevo!

Što je to s Vama? Zašto mi ne pišete? Zadnje Vaše pismo koje sam primio pred točno mjesec dana, datirano je sa 22.I. Nisam nervozan, ali mi ipak nije drago da se tako dugo ne javljate. – Uzmite pored toga u obzir da mi se Tata još uopće nije javio, niti znam da li se Vama javio, pa onda sudite kako mi je pri duši! Ja sam čvrsto uvjeren da ste i Vi i Tata živi i zdravi, ali mi ipak mnogo znači kada mi pišete jer pismo mi je neka duševna i jedina stvarna veza sa mojim najmilijim, i pored toga daje mi veliki moralni podstrek!

U Pratećoj četi puno radim i trudim se da što savjesnije ispunim svoje dužnosti. Radim na političkom polju. – Drugarstvo je ovdje dobro, pa se odlično osjećam. Od drugog zamjenika politkomesara, koji je intelektualac, imam prilike da mnogo naučim, i to u punoj mjeri iskorištavam. Tjelesno sam zdrav i čio, pa i to puno utiče na opće moje stanje. –

Kako Vi živite? Piše li Tata, i kako on? Ako možete, i ako je sigurno, pokušajte mi poslati: 2 gaće, 1 košulju, 1 [illegible], kuverti, „Sepazola" i „Aspirina"! Ove stvari bi mi potrebne bile pa ih pošaljite ukoliko se to može!

Uskoro će se [illegible] naša Brigada [illegible] kompletno u [illegible]! Mislim da je blizu dan našeg sastanka pa sam stoga i zadovoljan, a nadam se i Vi i Tata. Ljubi Vas bezbroj puta

B.J. – Prateća četa III. ud. Brig. I. prol. korp. Duka

Zapisnik — Записник

od / од 1 Aprila 1907

sastavljen u ime kotarskog ureda kao suda u / састављен у име котарског уреда као суда у Glamoču na licu mjesta / на лицу мјеста

u / у Glamoču

Predmet — Предмет

je obava ovršne pljenidbe pokretnina / је обава овршне пљенидбе покретнина Simre Damića

iz / из St...

zbog tražbine / због тражбине Braće Janković

iz / из Glamoča iznosom od / износом од 45 K / K . h s pp. uslijed naloga / х с пп. услијед налога

od / од 27/11 1906, broj / број 2457 gr. / гр.

Prisutni: — Присутни:

od strane suda: — од стране суда: od stranaka: — од странака:

V. Gemović

kao sudski izaslanik — као судски изасланик.

Potpisani sudski izaslanik uputi se u stan ovršenika i .... našavši istoga kod
Потписани судски изасланик упути се у стан овршеника и .... нашавши истога код

kuće, uruči ovršnu odluku .... (§ 272. g. p. p.), pak mu
куће, уручи овршну одлуку .... (§ 272. г. п. п.), пак му

priopći, da ima obaviti ovršnu pljenidbu pokretnina za gore navedenu tražbinu s pp.
приопћи, да има обавити овршну пљенидбу покретнина за горе наведену тражбину с пп.

Ovršenik položio je na to u ruke sudskog izaslanika u gotovom za isplatu
Овршеник положио је на то у руке судског изасланика у готовом за исплату

glavnice / главнице	45	K / K .	h / х
... % kamata od / камата од ... 1 do danas / до данас		K / K	h / х
parničnih troškova / парничних трошкова		K / K 80	h / х
ovršnih troškova / овршних трошкова pljenidb. i dražb. pristojbe	6	K / K .	h / х
ukupno / укупно	51	K / K 80	h / х
svotu od / своту од Pedeset i jedna		K / K 80	h / х

Sudski izaslanik izdao je ovršeniku potvrdu o primitku gornje svote, te odustao od provedenja ovrhe,
Судски изасланик издао је овршенику потврду о примитку горње своте, те одустао од проведења оврхе,

pak se ta svota od 51 K / K 80 h / х sa ovim zapisnikom predlaže sudu — ~~sa popisom uručuje~~
пак се та свота од ... са овим записником предлаже суду — ~~са пописом уручује~~

~~muhtaru — мухтару~~ — ~~upravitelju ispostave, — koji primitak svojim muhurom — potpisom — potvrgjuje.~~
~~knezu — кнезу~~ — ~~управитељу испоставе, — који примитак својим мухуром — потписом — потврђује.~~

Zaključeno i potpisano. — Закључено и потписано.

SUDSKI GLASNIK — СУДСКИ ГЛАСНИК

Golubović

Relation des Gerichtsabgeordneten über erfolgte Zahlung (Mobilar). Bj. 426/03. Kleinconcept Lager-Nr. 2449.

When the dust settled, I offered to take the letter to Father in Klasnich. I'd walk over the hill, descend to Klasnich, and return with the other road back to Glina.

"I don't want you to go," said Mother. "I will send the letter to Father with a courier right away. You should rest here and return to Glina tomorrow morning. I can fetch a horse carriage early in the morning in time for you to attend school."

I was amazed.

"You are not telling me that it would make any difference if I were to miss yet another class of school. We both know that I will never complete a year in that school. Sooner or later the Germans will push us out of Glina."

"You may or you may not complete a year but what you learn will be yours for the rest of your life. Enjoy the opportunity."

That was all I needed; Mother lecturing me on the virtues of learning.

"Well let me tell you that the school is not that hot. I doubt I am learning a single thing. In fact, it is all a bit boring." I said.

I expected Mother to continue lecturing about learning. In the past she never missed the opportunity to reiterate an important message. But Mother had changed.

"Oh come on," she said, "Rest and relax. Yes, I think one of these days the enemy will kick the Partizans out of Glina, but the later the better. It is the end of March and winter is not yet giving up. As long as you attend the school we can justify your stay in Glina. We have a good arrangement. So do not rock the boat. I am glad you got permission to bring me the letter."

Permission, what permission? I never gave it a thought.

"Sure, Ratko would love me to report to him every little move I make. I consider this visit as a leisurely stroll rather than a real trip. Why should I ask for permission?" I wondered, "I am a free man."

"No, you are not. You eat military food, your lodging is paid, you have a salary of sorts and you have a political responsibility in the school. No, Stevo, you are a soldier and you cannot have it both ways. You should report early tomorrow morning to Ratko Djurovich and apologize. And you had better be humble."

"So what could happen to me?"

"For one thing he could send you as a courier to some active military unit. If he wanted to make a fuss, which I do not think he would, he could discipline you."

"You mean put me in the clink?"

"If he felt so-yes, he could. But let me repeat again that he probably would not want to do that. However you breached the discipline and he could portray you as somebody setting a bad example to others. Next thing you know we'd be in big trouble. Just listen to me and do what you were told."

I was surprised. Earlier Mother would have tried to make me feel guilty and explain how thankless I was. This time around she gave it to me straight. She was concise, summed up the argument well, and in essence issued me another military order.

Next morning, I asked the driver to take me straight to the school. That was a mistake. Though I had every intention to apologize, Comrade Djurovich was not in mood to wait. He summoned me from the school, gave me a dressing down and sent me back to school.

"Comrade Julius, you will never do that again!" he said. "Never ever again! Got it?"

Well, I did not get it. Not entirely! Three months later I got into a similar conflict with commander Djurovich. But on that occasion, I broke the rules on purpose and for a good reason.

~

Both my first and second wartime residences, Otochac and Glina, were in many regards similar but I felt much more comfortable in Glina. Both places had just enough population to deserve a larger dot on the geographic map and to call themselves towns. Both had a nice little center with a few larger buildings nested around a park of shady old trees. They both drew sustenance from out-of-towners but with a substantial difference. Otochac did not cater to surrounding villages. It sat there all by itself, a solitary in the middle of a small agricultural plane—a place for offloading cargo and restocking supplies before or after passing over the mountain. Glina, on the other hand, was entirely dependent on the network of villages in its vicinity. A myriad of

little stores and workshops catered to every need of local farmers. Even during the war both towns managed to keep their identities. The stores in Otochac remained reasonably well-stocked with heavy merchandise and the town teemed with long-range vehicles brought in for maintenance or storage. In Otochac you may not have been able to find little knick-knacks for daily living, but you rode in or out of the town on a truck. In Glina you could buy a candle or resole your shoes, but if you had to move, you were sure to walk. However the major difference between the two towns was in their population. Most people in Otochac were either detached or openly pro-Ustashe and the mostly Serb population of Glina was solidly anti-fascist. In Glina I felt welcomed and I made many friends. Almost all students came from villages that repeatedly changed hands. Being the anointed youth leader, I still acted in a somewhat officious manner but I realized that the high school students in Glina were not much different from me. They had endured hardships and since most of them were Serbs, if Ustashe took Glina, their education, too, would be interrupted.

The Partizans had a much harder time keeping a semblance of normalcy in Glina then in Otochac. A long and steep road over a high mountain distanced Otochac from the enemy on the seaside. In contrast, only fifteen odd miles of a straight road over a flat terrain separated the Partizan defenders of Glina from the Ustashe garrison in Petrinja. The commander in Petrinja kept himself busy with all sorts of raids. Just as he sent a surprise column of tanks to patrol Huska's backlands, he would occasionally organize forays to attack villages in the Partizan-held territory. Generally these raids were small, a house burned here, an official killed there, just a nuisance to remind the population to watch its steps. However, occasionally independent units would depart Petrinja in ostensibly different directions, only to later, under cover of night, converge on the same target for a larger attack. As if these night raids did not keep the defenders of Glina on their toes, the troops in Petrinja frequently gathered in large numbers on the road to Glina, walked a few miles, and then returned to the safety of their barracks. But sometimes the columns continued moving towards Glina. This constant fluidity kept the Partizan brigades guarding Glina guessing.

The military stance of the garrison in Petrinja was quite effective. It caused constant interruptions and repeatedly demonstrated to the population that when they wished, the Croat Nazis could assert control over the Serbian area in and around Glina. It was also an effective psychological warfare tool. Twice we were evacuated from Glina only to find out that the enemy was bluffing. One felt rather stupid for running away from the mere shadow of danger. Not very heroic!

To his credit, Ratko Djurovich, the commander, was well organized. Two evacuations were at night and had his coworkers neglected to wake me up, the next morning could have been the end of me. However, both times a messenger came to the hotel ordering me to report to the local hospital. There I would join others and serve as a courier to the withdrawing party. According to standing orders, at some later point during the evacuation, when I saw fit, I would leave the group, locate Mother's hospital and join them as their courier.

Being a courier during an evacuation was serious business. Often I went alone looking for shortcuts in order to bring back a message or give advanced notice of our arrival. Ready for adventure, stupidly fearless, and eternally optimistic, I loved to explore the beaten paths around the moving front line. The possibility of getting lost or the chance that the enemy might drive a wedge across my path never crossed my mind. Happy to play a part in the heroics, the Italian gun swinging from my shoulder, I confidently ambled ahead. But during the second withdrawal I got into trouble.

At dawn on a bitterly cold February day, I took a shortcut through knee-deep snow to Buzeta. The path followed the terrain between two converging hills, and under the snow one could easily make out the flat surface of the road. Eventually I came upon the wide creek at the spot where the farmers usually drove their wagons through the ford. I thought the creek was frozen solid, but it wasn't. To boot, I also failed to choose the shallow part! A few meters from the bank the ice gave way. The shock of the cold water up to my waist was overwhelming but I had to contend with more urgent matters. In the morning mist it was hard to make out the other side. Should I go forwards and risk deeper water or turn back? Just then I heard the crowing of a rooster, a sure sign that the village was within

reach. I pushed the gun on the ice and it slid a few meters towards the other bank. Sure it was important to keep the gun dry, but it was a stupid move. To reach the gun I now had to crack the ice with my bare hands. After the initial shock the water under my waist did not feel all that cold but my wet hands became two painful, useless, heavy logs. Luckily the creek did not get much deeper. Eventually I recovered the gun and used its butt to make my way through the ice towards the other side. Having climbed on to the main road, I started running to keep myself warm.

By now, loud and clear, as if they were just around the corner, the roosters were in full concert. Morning sounds can be deceptive. The village was much farther than I thought. I could not run all the way. When I finally reached the first house my pants were covered with ice, my feet were numb and I was shivering. Luckily the house of the *veza* I had to contact was on the near side of the village and right across from it was the Martich household. The son was a classmate in Glina and I had been in their house once before. They were incredibly good to me. They sat me in front of the stove, gave me dry clothes and fed me royally. The delicious reheated bean soup, spiked with chunks of smoked ham, pleasantly settled in my stomach and its warmth slowly engulfed my body. This was not a simple meal; it was a symbolic reaffirmation of life's pleasures after fording an icy creek. To the Martich family, I was essentially a stranger, their son's casual acquaintance, but they willingly shared meager and dwindling resources with me. In those hard times when at one point a household may have had a bit of excess but soon could find itself starving, it was natural to become selfish. But for the Martich family and many Banija Serbs, the Slavic tradition of hospitality prevailed over self-interest.

Serbs like the Martich family were the backbone of the Partizan movement in Banija. In early 1942, the villages around Glina solidly aligned themselves with Partizans as a matter of self-preservation against Ustashe. Well-to-do farmers like the Martich family were a rarity in Banija. If a farmer had a daughter in rural Yugoslavia he had

to give away a part of his land as dowry when she grew up. If he was lucky enough to have a boy, some land could come back to the family. The end result of this tradition was a permanently changing shape and size of individual farms. In the present-day vernacular, what went on in the villages of Yugoslavia was a zero-gain proposition. Nobody could advance. And during the war only the rare well-to-do farmer had reserves to share with others. Nevertheless, after the war, guided by Stalin's drive against private property, the Communists turned against people who fed them during the struggle against the Germans. The land was taken from larger farmers and redistributed to other families. Not only was the-post war agrarian reform ruthless, it was also senseless. The Communists had set the limit of land a family could have to such a low level that it practically guaranteed the continuation of inefficient and unproductive small farms. Life can be incredibly unfair.

I wish I could say I did something to repay the Martich's kindness, but I did not. Not that I forgot them. I could not; ever since the Buzeta episode any time my feet are exposed to a bit of lower temperature they get inordinately cold and start hurting. Thanks to American air conditioning, particularly in airplanes, I have had plenty of opportunities to remember my benefactors from Buzeta. But life has its ways. The memory-driven good intentions do not necessarily translate into action. Call it the "one-day-I-must-write-to-old-Joe" syndrome. And now it is too late.[1]

Thanks to the Martich's hospitality I reached Mother's hopital in time to embark with them on the longest trek of my guerilla career. In Buzeta we formed a lengthy queue of about 150 people. Most of

1 Recently people of Banija were involved in a horrible, senseless fratricidal war. I would like to think that the gentle Martich clan, and in particular my classmate, were above it all. But I doubt it very much. If they did not perish in the conflict, the victorious Croats very likely evicted them from their home and along with other Serbs, forced them to take refuge in Serbia proper.

the patients were able to walk but the long procession of people with bandages, the amputees on crutches, and the feeble recovering from fever was a sorry sight. The organizers on purpose scattered the few precious wagons throughout the entire line to give the most needy patients a short ride. Nobody had a reserved seat. The patients willingly and fairly rotated on and off the wagons. Because of German airplanes we avoided main roads. The progress was very slow.

The Buzeta hospital had a detachment of about sixty soldiers who normally served as sentries. During our withdrawal half of the detachment walked in front of the hospital caravan and the other half walked as a rear guard. The soldiers provided armed protection on the road and when we entered the forest they carried the most exhausted patients on stretchers. We reached the bottom of Petrova Gora in two days. Our supplies were offloaded to a truck and went ahead to wait for the hospital in Slunj and we were sent though the naked forests of Petrova Gora. It is not clear to me why the Command had not chosen to send the patients to Slunj with the trucks. Maybe the risk of air attacks was too large or possibly it was a matter of habit. The Partizans loved the forest and felt safest in the middle of it. After two days we reemerged on the Kordun side of the mountain. A day later we had reached the town of Slunj but by that time the enemy offensive was over.

Mother's hospital was scheduled to rest a few weeks before it again returned to Buzeta. I knew commander Djurovich would kick up a fuss had I not returned in time for my youth leader's post in the Glina high school. Furthermore I started to miss my classmates. When I told Mother I'd like to return back to Glina, she did not complain. Somehow Djurovich and Mother worked on the same wavelength; the school was important and I ought to enjoy the civilian life in Glina as much as was possible. Instead of complaining, Mother found me a truck driver to take me on the eighty miles ride to Banija.

It almost came to naught. In the morning the driver could not start the engine. In the winter the big Italian diesel OM trucks were nearly useless. The low temperature would turn the fuel into viscous glue that made it impossible to crank up the huge start-up inertia wheel. We built a fire under the truck to thaw the engine. Or at least that was what the driver believed should be done. The small pyre of

dry wood under the high front wheels of the truck soon evolved into an impressive bonfire. After a while another soldier and I volunteered to turn the inertia wheel. The technique is quite different from the one-turn-of-the-handle cranking up of a gasoline engine. For these giant diesels we had to set in motion the lheavyinside inertia wheel at an ever-increasing speed of cranking until the wheel gave off a high-pitched whirling noise. The driver then injected the fuel into the engine, hoping that the inertia of the huge wheel would be sufficient to compress the fuel to the point of ignition. After a lot of huffing and puffing, at the third trial, the engine gave off the first sign of life-a few loud growls and an impressive plume from the exhaust. Finally after the fifth trial we had a successful ignition.

The driver opted to drive through Huska's territory on the south side of the Petrova Gora. He figured that this lesser road might be safer for a daytime ride. He was wrong. After a few hours on the road somebody screamed, *Roda, Roda*. The truck came to a full stop and we scrambled to the ditches. *Roda*, the *Stork* (Fieseler Storch) was the main German spotter plane. The old-fashioned two-seater plane with an open cabin and a long wing atop the body appeared clumsy and innocuous. But not when it was right above you firing its machine gun at will. The plane was designed for low-speed flying. The slowly approaching *Stork* looked as if it were ready to stop right above you. It certainly did hover long enough for the pilot to choose and pick his target. The stork was also very maneuverable; it could turn a sharp corner and be back in a minute.

It was terrible to be pinned down under the imposing, slow airplane. An uncontrollable fear took me over. The guy up there, safely out of the range of small arms ground fire, transformed me into a scared shivering mess, and I felt like a huge fixed target. Every two minutes or so I could clearly make out the crew; the co-pilot at the back was leaning over the side to let off bursts of machine gun fire or lob a hand grenade. I lay on the ground, face down, curled in a fetal position, like a guilty dog awaiting punishment.

Hiding from airplanes never became comfortable but in later encounters I dared to look up and had enough control to run for a better bush between the attacks. But first time around on the side of the road near Petrova Gora I acted like the proverbial Gypsy-turned-

Partizan. A commissar spotted him in the heat of the battle with his head firmly planted at the bottom of the trench. Next evening, during the obligatory self-criticism session, he had to explain his behavior.

"I am more of an anti-fascist than all of you" he responded. "I hate the enemy so much I cannot even look at him."

The stork must have flown over us at least twenty times before it finally left. The co-pilot had succeeded in puncturing two tires. The driver decided to walk back to Slunj to find some spare tires. Rather than join the two passengers who headed for Cetingrad, which was well out of my way, I decided to transverse Petrova Gora and get to the main road in Kordun. The traffic on that road was much heavier and the population was friendlier than the moody, reserved Moslem inhabitants of Hushka's territory. Having passed through it three times I was confident I knew the mountain well enough. That was a gross miscalculation. When night fell I was still climbing uphill but had gone too far to turn around. I had to walk right through the night or risk freezing. Nowadays you would just unroll your sleeping bag, find a shelter and retire.[2]

I kept walking through the night chanting the relaxing "On the Lipary" poem by Aleksa Shantich. Everything blended, the poem, my steps, monotonous trees, and as I had done many times before, I fell asleep. Some things are not described in medical literature, but there is no doubt in my mind that you can fall asleep while walking: For those who had not had the experience, the closest analogy is the trance they may have fallen into during a long railway trip years ago, when each fifty yards or so, the tracks used to be separated by a small gap. The monotonous "click-clack" of the wheels, the exhaustion from the journey, the boredom of it all eventually leads to a trance. People's words come and go as if they are hiding and reemerging from an ill-defined pit somewhere in front of your eyes. You may even carry on a pseudo-conversation and provide perfunctory responses to the few words that have penetrated. Hours later

2 I do not know why the Partizans did not have sleeping bags. They would have been ideally suited for their kind of warfare. Most likely, because other armies from whom they drew supplies did not carry them as standard issue.

you do not remember a thing and realize that, sitting upright and with open eyes, you were actually sleeping. Dobrisha Cesarich caught the scene beautifully. It will be hard to reproduce the poem's onomatopoeic quality, its words evoking the exact double-short-one-long metallic sound of wheels passing over the gaps between the tracks. But I must try:

> "Telegraph post, telegraph post,
> the shadow flies
> A face of a ghost, whose soul is lost
> behind empty eyes"

I continued to amble from tree to tree, alert enough not to run into them but sufficiently asleep not to notice a thing. Fortunately I had enough will power to keep walking. Had I lain down and fallen asleep, by and by my body would have passed from deep sleep into irreversible coma and sure death. Apparently the urge to sleep prevails above everything else. During the war I ran into one frozen body. There was a trace of smile on his serene, relaxed face. A comfortable death, but nevertheless a death.

When the day broke and the fog lifted I could finally see the top of the mountain. With the help of the morning sun I took a rough northeast aim over the first ridge. After first, there was second and third ridge with no end in sight. Where I'd chosen to cross it, Petrova Gora was not the familiar single gently sloping mountain, but a bunch of hillocks, a succession of small waves emanating from the large epicenter. Steadily descending, with the mountain behind my back, I was never quite lost but the progress was very slow. It took almost another whole day. By the afternoon the hills started getting smaller and an hour later I spotted a few magpies. They are never far away from villages or vineyards. Soon I saw the first arable lot and by the evening I had reached a small village still a good six miles from the main road. The Kordun side of the mountain was solidly in our hands and well organized. I located the president of the village People's Council and he assigned me to a household. When the hostess found out that her young guest had not eaten for thirty six hours, she set out a gala dinner: flour soup, polenta, and from her secret jar the

piece de resistance—honey. The term polenta applies to a whole range of products made from roughly milled corn. It can be an amorphous, mashed potato-like mass. If further cooked, it transforms into solid lumps. Sometimes the cooked polenta is further baked in the oven, which produces a rock hard substance with two advantages; it will not spoil and it will absorb anything you wish to dunk it in. After the Petrova Gora experience I used to carry lumps of polenta in my pocket, just in case.

Let the reader be advised. If you have not eaten for a few days do not load up on polenta with honey. To speak physiologically it induced an osmotic overload of the gastro-intestinal tract. In simpler terms, I got a terrible case of diarrhea. Thanks to my hostess' best intentions, I had a second sleepless night. Next morning, feeling thoroughly miserable, I had barely enough energy to walk down to the road.

A friendly trucker took me to Topusko. Young bodies are amazing. I slept a whole night and the best part of the next day in the comfortable bed in the spa, woke up for dinner, slept again and the next morning took a few long hot tub baths. In the afternoon I was ready for a leisurely stroll under the chestnut trees and next morning I headed back to Glina and to my go-to-school, eat-in-the-hospital, sleep-in-the-hotel, routine. But above all, back to my leftover Gavrilovich salami which, safely locked in the hotel owner's pantry, awaited my return!

Each time I returned from an evacuation to Glina, I felt as if I were coming home. In Trnavac and many other friendly villages the primitive conditions and lack of privacy prevented the enjoyment of otherwise genuine hospitality. But in Glina I was my own boss, an almost-paying guest in the hotel, free to come and go. Every week I handed the owner the coupons from the military Command. They must have had some commercial value to him since he was quite keen to get them. I think he turned them in for military supplies and later sold the supplies on the black market.

For me, life in Glina was comfortable. Three months passed without a single evacuation. I started to study in earnest and generally had a good time. On the 25th of May at five in the morning, a

courier woke me up and accompanied me to Commander Djurovich's office. He first congratulated me on the good work in school but soon came to the point.

"Comrade Julius," he said, "my brother Pero is taking a rest in Topusko." He stopped just for a moment and then continued. "May as well tell you. He is actually sick, but that is a military secret."

His brother was sick and that was supposed to be a military secret? I looked incredulous.

"Why are you so stunned?"

Ratko was a perceptive man.

"I guess I have to tell you something about life in these parts of the world," Ratko continued. "My brother is the commander of the 3d Brigade and a veritable national hero. The enemy has great respect for his bravery and military skills. Should the enemy get the idea that he is out of commission, they may think the brigade is in disarray and attempt some premature action."

This did not sound right either, but it was plausible. More likely Pero Djurovich did not want to admit to his staff how sick he was. In the military, as in any other organization there are ambitions, envies, and it is never in the interest of the top guy to show his weaknesses.

Seeing I bought his story, Ratko became his old self. He was concise, deliberate and had no time for nonsense. "You love to walk about and I am sure you would not mind taking some medicine to him in Topusko. I finally got the tablets yesterday from Petrinja and he needs them badly."

"Who is his doctor?" I asked reflexively.

"None of your business. Do what you were told and be on your way. I will notify the school. And, by the way, you should return by the evening. Right?"

"Right!" I responded.

I took off directly from the City Command over the Glina River Bridge to the road to Topusko. The road was empty, everything was quiet and the sunrise presaged a crystal clear day. The weather was just right: neither too hot nor too cold. Field flowers were in bloom and I had plenty of time to enjoy nature.

In about half an hour I detected a distant boom, which progressively became louder. There was no doubt—a large group of airplanes was coming from the north. I scrambled to the hedge on the side of the road. The noise was unusual. Too loud for the allied flotillas which, passing high in the skies, used to fill the ground with a dull deep rumble. It had to be Germans. I could easily tell a Stork from a Stuka or a Messerschmidt, but this sound was different. The first group of aircrafts came into sight and hiding under the bush I curiously watched the unusual parade. First was a wave of old biplanes, forty–fifty of them, each pulling a sleek long-winged glider. Just as the biplanes disappeared behind the horizon, another wave arrived. The next formation consisted of ten huge three-engine Junkers. I had never seen anything like that before. Not knowing it, I was admiring the flotilla that in less than an hour was set to attack Drvar in Bosnia.

I proceeded to Topusko and throughout the entire walk could not get the unusual air squadron off my mind. Around ten in the morning I delivered the package of pills to comrade Pero Djurovich. He was pleased.

"I hope this works." he said, "The damned amoebas. You brought me some *enterovioform*. It will not kill all amoebas but it will slow them. In a few days I am supposed to start feeling better. Tell my brother I thank him very much for finding the pills."

Djurovich senior gave me a good lunch and after some chit-chat, sent me on my way back. The return trip was uneventful but I just could not forget the airplanes. Something about them bothered me but I did not know what.

~

Come June, I really started to enjoy Glina. For one thing, I again discovered the love of learning. I had a very good memory and learning came easily. The adventures in Stanchich and the exciting events after we joined the Partizans left me no time to think about school. But now in Glina I was again getting into it. Furthermore I slowly became a citizen of Glina. I knew my neighbors, I greeted people on the streets and as a regular in the hospital's cafeteria I had steady

company at a reserved table. In the evening I would chat with the hotel guests and generally, I developed a comfortable daily routine. And then one afternoon late in June, Ratko Djurovich summoned me to the City Command. I was in for a surprise!

"You are to pack all your belongings and tomorrow morning head for Topusko. Must be there by afternoon. From Topusko you will be evacuated to Sicily," said the commander.

"To Sicily?"

"Yes to Sicily-Italy. The Runjevac High School will be evacuated by plane and your orders are to join them."

I had heard about the Runjevac high school. The commander of one of the brigades in Banija took responsibility for some of the homeless children in his territory. A High School was organized in the safe village of Runjevac and the brigade took responsibility for its security and supplies. This must have left the political leadership rather ambivalent. It was a nice gesture as well as a great opportunity to correctly educate the *creme de la creme* of village children. Nevertheless, the higher leadership had to balance this rare opportunity for indoctrination of the elite youth against the obvious parochial slant of the whole arrangement- a school for local children sponsored by a local brigade.

Early in 1944 Tito started reorganizing the Partizan movement into a regular army with no territorial ties. Only a few brigades could keep their geographic name, but they were sent far away from their home bases quite on purpose. To the authorities the close identification of a local brigade with a local school in Banija was not all that welcome. No surprise then that as soon as the Partizans established ties with the British Air Force, the children from Runjevac were slated for evacuation.

I was deeply offended. How could they treat me the same way as those children in Runjevac? They were noncombatant students. And I was a volunteer anti-fascist fighter on duty in the Glina High School!

What a certified selfish and stupid brat! Instead of thanking the person who tried to save my life, I pressed the commander to let me know who it was so I could appeal the decision. If I had to be evacuated, I insisted, it should be by a separate order unrelated to those

children. I would go to Italy only as a military person sent to military duty.

"But we do not have an Army in Italy. At best you may be able to get a position in one of the military hospitals. They may need couriers. Of course this is none of my business. Try for a reassignment when you get there. But go you must," said the commander.

Stupidly I kept pressing for the source of the order. The more I asked the more he got irritated. I wish I had been more reasonable. Because of my intransigence I never learned who did me the favor. However my teenage prepotence and lack of communications skills had a more immediate and unpleasant consequence.

Finally realizing that I must obey the order, I decided to say goodbye to Father in Klasnich, about ten kilometers away. The distance was not a problem. I could easily reach Klasnich before midnight and next morning Father could provide me with transportation back to Glina. In the worst case, if Father had no transportation to offer, the visit would add three more hours to the four hours distance between Glina and Topusko. A perfectly doable feat!

But Ratko was irritated to the core and would not hear of it. In no uncertain terms he ordered me to stay in the hotel: "First of all, I do not trust you and second, the trip may be too arduous. I will not risk you missing the flight."

"You know my father well. It is not unreasonable to say goodbye to him. Let me worry about getting tired. You have my word I will be in Topusko on time," I insisted.

Ratko never had to deal with insubordination. It was up to him to give orders and to others to execute them. He was getting mad. His eyes were fixed on me and there was murder in them. He spoke even a bit slower than usual and, to properly underscore what he said, Djurovich took a pause after each single word.

"I do not think it is safe for you to walk alone through the night and I have no personnel to accompany you," he said. "Better stay where you are. Tomorrow morning I will send a message to Comrade Doctor Julius telling him I prevented you from visiting him. I am sure he will approve of my action. Safety first. These are not times for sentimentalities."

Maybe he was truly concerned about me. If I had not irritated him with my childish protestations, he would have eventually agreed. Instead we were at an impasse.

"How can you stop me from sneaking out at night and returning in the morning before anybody knows a thing? Are you about to put a sentry in front of the room?"

"I do not have to do that." he replied with a mean grin. "I simply will not give you the password."

In the heat of the moment I forgot that I needed a password. Of course he had me under control.

A dark road during the war was not the place for a decent person. The night provided cover for all sorts of illegitimate activities: surprise attacks, sneaking behind front lines, desertion, and smuggling. To sift out false from legitimate, friend from foe, the Partizans had a new password for each night. Upon hearing somebody approach, the sentries would put themselves into an advantageous position and shout out the opening part of the age-long, well-established ritual.

"Stop!"

"I stopped!"

"Who is coming?"

At that point you had to state whether you were a soldier or civilian and what your business was.

"Password?"

Time for you to recite the first part of the formula.

"Gun," you might say.

"Pistol," might be the reply.

If both parts of the formula matched, you were in the clear. If the answer was incorrect, you had better beat a fast retreat before the other guy opened fire.

Sounds somewhat operatic but the system worked quite well. It was unthinkable to walk at night without the password. A trigger-happy sentry had no time for explanations or negotiations.

Totally out of control, in spite of all the dangers, the lack of a password notwithstanding, I set out to walk to Klasnich. Certainly not from filial devotion. I respected Father but as a proper teenager

I was not aware of any strong emotional bond to him. Most likely I just felt guilty for getting an easy way out and wanted his official blessing. It was a stupid formality, but I wanted my Father to tell me to leave. What else could Father do but be happy that one member of our family would escape the war and wish me all the best?

Anyhow, stubborn and fearless, I was on my way to Klasnich. That is to say, fearless for the few first miles. Sneaking out of the town was relatively easy. I knew the guard post on the edge of the town and took a long loop through the fields around it. Soon the night got the better of me. With every passing yard I became tenser. To get to Klasnich in time, the pace had to be brisk and I could not possibly tiptoe throughout the night. I tried all sorts of tricks. First I quietly walked in the ditch, but after a few minutes of stumbling had to get back on the road. Then I thought it would be better to walk on one side of the road. Or maybe on the other one? In the middle? Nothing worked. Somewhere out there was an ill-defined danger. It could be waiting for me around the bend, behind the fence of the dark lonely house, or laying in ambush under the oddly shaped pile of stones in front of me. Under murky moonlight one sees just enough to suffer from anthropomorphic delusions. A tree, a rock, a road sign transfigure into threatening images. Walking through the night one feels like a gigantic moving target. A person at war with the unknown surroundings.

I finally settled on a routine. After a few minutes of marching loudly and fast I'd quickly lie down or sink into the ditch to carefully listen for suspicious noises. The maneuver, a good mix of daring and carefulness gave me a good feeling that I was in charge. But my routine became itself the cause of more fear. After a while I did not listen for whether an enemy was out there; I knew he was there. Otherwise why would I be doing all those maneuvers? I had thoroughly scared myself. First the gun hung from my shoulder, then it was in my hands and finally, with the bayonet pivoted, arms fully extended, I stabbed through the darkness in front of me. That evening on the road, drained of all bravado and scared to the core, Stevo Julius, the young cousin of Don Quixote fought mirages. I am usually bent on making fun of past experiences, but even today I cannot help but feel

sorry for that poor teenager. The adventure on the road to Klasnich forever defined my adult behavior. Decades later my own children dared me to try a difficult amusement park ride. Gladly accepting the label of a coward, I refused. Around the corner on the road to Klasnich there lurked enough danger to last me a lifetime.

In all the misery I also had some luck. Apparently nobody else took to the road that night. Exhausted from my maneuvers, and within the reach of Klasnich, I took a long rest to contemplate my next step. There would certainly be a checkpoint at the edge of the village. There had to be. Without the password how would I placate a trigger-happy sentry? No brighter idea came to mind than to shout my name as loudly as I could and ask for Father. I would lie in the middle of the road as long as it took them to fetch my old man.

It was not necessary. The sentries were quite calm. They pinned me down to the earth just long enough to surround me, took me into custody and called for the man in charge. It was easy to see I was who I claimed to be. Not that many city-boys-turned-soldier walked on the back roads of Banija. The officer took the bullets out my gun, gave me an escort and in a few minutes we woke up Father. He was pleased. Yes, I had to go and no, I did not have to report back to the commander in Glina. He would send him a messenger in the morning expressing appreciation for the commanders concern and explain that I was on my way to Topusko.

But Father appeared unusually subdued. Habitually he was always quiet and calm but this time there was more to it than that. He seemed joyless, almost depressed.

"Sorry I had to wake you up but there was no other way. Your sentries are pretty strict. Are you tired? You do not look all that good," I said.

"I know," he replied. "Don't misunderstand me. It is great to hear that you will be evacuated. At least one of us will be safe. But as much as I enjoy your good luck, I am saddened by what happened to Djuka. Read this letter. I got it a few hours ago."

"Is he alive?"

"Yes."

"Is he OK?"

"No!"

Father withdrew into a corner to watch me reading the letter. He was very calm, but very sad and for the first and last time in my life I saw him shedding a tear. I could have missed it but the light fell on his left cheek, and like a solitary diamond reflecting the rays, I spotted a big drop.

The Surgical Hospital of the V th Korpus

13.VI.44 On the Position.

Dear Old ones and Stipe, my dearest.

(Stipe = a Lika version of my name, I did not like it and it did not stick.)

*After a long time here is my first opportunity to let you know that I am alive. Unfortunately with a heavy heart I must let you know that during the parachutist attack on Drvar I was wounded in the left shoulder. You should not excite yourselves, the wound is, thank God, improving, and about the wound proper, from a medical standpoint, there would be a letter from Dr Tatlich, an excellent surgeon and comrade who is treating me with outmost care and who personally knows Tatek! (*Daddy*). Now I shall describe how I got wounded. As I already stated in my two previous letters the Staff of the Brigade appointed me the Secretary of the Intendatura (*supply department*) of the III.rd Proleterian Brigade (*the Brigade had been again promoted, the title "Proletarian" was the highest distinction a Unit could earn*) and naturally I was in Drvar which was the site of the Intendantura. On the 25.V. in the morning about 7 o clock, first there was a bombardment of Drvar, and immediately thereafter parachutists descended and gliders landed with SS troops. I found myself surrounded from all sides by Germans, all in a circle of 25 to 250 meters. I took up position and opened fire with my Russian smajser on the Krauts who were possibly only 20 meters away. However from 4* Sharac's (Partizan nickname for the German light belt-fed machine gun*) and 2 smajsers they returned such a horrible fire that I threw my smajser into a basement and started to run toward Kamenik. They aimed a hellish fire at me but luckily they missed. So I ran into a hedge where others noticed me and opened fire, but as if I were protected by magic, they also did not hit me and, all happy I finally*

*managed to reach the road from Drvar to Kamenica. No sooner had I jumped on the road than I saw 6 Krauts in front and they screamed: "Halt." I turned around in a hurry and jumped over a fence but they were so close that a bullet got me just as I had jumped. The bullet from the Sharac went through the armpit and exploded as it exited on the top of the left shoulder. Of course I fell immediately but did manage to throw the beret and the belt into bushes. Tree Germans came to me yelling "Da liegt er ja. Na wie shutzen die SS Maner?" (*There he lies though. So, how do the SS men shoot?*") But I had my wits and responded "Bitte nicht toten, ich bin ein Volksdeutscher aus Banat und bin aus 44tem Sturm Battalion der 2ter panzierarmee und ich bin by Srb von Partizanen gefangengenomen" (*"Please do not kill, I am a Volksdeutscher [German national] from Banat [a province in Serbia] and out of the 44th attack battalion of the Second armored Army I got taken prisoner by Partizans near Srb*") I knew that there was such a battalion because during the battle of Srb we did take a Kraut prisoner from that Unit. "Was, du bist Deutsher?" (*What, you are a German?*") "Jawohl"(*"Yessir*")

The German looked and looked at me and then all of a sudden turned around and yells at the medic "Hallo da verbienden!" ("Hello, bandaging needed here*") and left. The Medic came and asked me where I was wounded. In the pocket of my shirt he found an English bandage, threw it on the ground and screamed "Wer dir dieses Verband gegeben hat soll dich auch verbinded"* ("He who gave you this bandage should also bandage you") *and he was gone. I lost consciousness and as soon as I regained it dragged myself uphill to the last few houses toward Kamenica. There at around 14 hours two comrades and a nurse came upon me, she bandaged me, a nightfall some youths carried me to Kamenica to Dr. Kremzir of the Surgical Team of the VI.th Division. They gave me a Tetanus injection and bandaged me again. Next day they carried me far away into the forest into the hospital of the Englishman Dr. Rogers.*[3] *As soon as I*

3 Several months earlier, during the physicians Congress in Topusko Mother, Father and I met Dr. Rogers. See picture in the chapter "Trnavac." Dr Rogers is on the left side and carries a French beret.

told him who I was he remembered Tata and dressed my wound with great care. In the meantime they carried us even deeper into the forest where I was temporarily in the Hospital of the First Corpus, Dr. Kishik, and later they took me even further away into this hospitaly, for the time being my final destination.

*They are taking great care of me—and if there were a possibility they would have already sent me to Italy. Lets hope that I may soon be healthy enough to get a medical leave and visit you. Mentally I feel very well, particularly after the opening of the Second Front (*the D Day invasion*) and even physically I am in reasonable shape. The doctor will give you the details of my "Status praesens".*

Please don't be despondent, be brave as I am, for it all could have been much, much sadder.

Write me through Captain Tatlich Surgeon of the V Corpus of the N.O.V.J.

With unmeasurable love Yours
Djuka

"But Father, he is OK!" I said after reading the letter. "As he said it could have been much worse."

"I know, but it is horrible nevertheless. Can you imagine what he went through! Horrible. He is still suffering and there is nothing we can do about it. Nothing!"

"And the wound is very bad," Father said after a short pause," His left shoulder is completely destroyed. The head of his long arm bone was shattered into hundreds of small fragments. His arm hangs solely on the muscles and skin. The wound and probably the bone marrow in the long bone are infected. It will take a long, long time for all of this to heal. He might lose the use of that arm. It will fill his sleeve as a useless appendage."

Father then got out of his corner, forcefully grabbed me by the shoulders, shook me back and forth, looked into my eyes, and quietly, but very forcefully said. "Please leave for Italy. Go! Do not look back! That way at least one of us will make it for sure. The two of you are all I have. It will be a great comfort to know you are protected."

"But Dad, we will all make it. The war is coming to an end."

"Yes, I think we will make it. But you have a better chance than the rest of us and you must go."

Father was back to being the rational, practical, old himself.

"Let's catch some sleep and tomorrow you go," he said.

I twisted in the bed but could not fall asleep. I again remembered the airplane formation I saw on May 25th. So that was why the unusual flotilla kept coming back to my mind! I sensed there was something unusual about these airplanes, I had a premonition. Up in one of the gliders I watched, a German soldier was destined to shoot my brother!

Wide-awake, I kept thinking about Djuka and the attack on Drvar. How foolish we were to think that Djuka was safe deep in Bosnia! I heard earlier about the attack on Drvar but did not for a moment think Djuka could be involved. Last time we heard from him, he was in Glamoch a good hundred miles away from Drvar.

The bizarre happenings in Drvar were a direct result of a change in Tito's tactics. In a number of previous offensives, akin to what sheep dogs do with herds, the Germans attacked from all sides and forced the scattered Partizan units to retreat in one general direction. Once they had them bottled up in a "kettle" the Partizans would have to fight on German terms. However the Partizan tactic was to withdraw deep into the Bosnian mountains and forests. The closer the Germans got to encircling the Partizans, the less passable the roads were, the tougher became the German logistic problems, and the smaller were the German's chances of deploying heavy equipment. Eventually the Partizans would find a crack and slip out of encirclement.

But by early 1944 Tito decided to concentrate most of his troops in central Bosnia. He started to reorganize the Partizans into a regular army; corpuses, divisions, brigades, all of them streamlined into a rigid hierarchical structure. Gone was the freedom of territorial units to strike and disappear. This large concentration of troops gave the Germans a good target for attack. But Tito reckoned, correctly, that the Germans would not pursue the Partizans with the same vigor as they did in the previous seven offensives. In 1944 they did not anymore have sufficient manpower to organize a large offensive and

were quite happy to just protect vital supply lines in the Pannonian Plains. Had Tito miscalculated, it would have been a great mistake, as he was now voluntarily doing what the German officers wanted to achieve during previous offensives.

Tito was right and wrong at the same time. Whereas the Germans could not organize yet another major offensive, by deciding to settle in Drvar, Tito presented himself as a good target. Admittedly he was cautious enough to place his headquarters in a natural cave near Drvar. Protected against air bombardment, surrounded by a large number of troops, in the middle of a fairly large free territory, the cave in Drvar seemed the safest place in the world. But the Germans had excellent intelligence. Realizing that Tito was now permanently anchored in one place they decided to go after him. The German command assembled a special taskforce, and trained them for the specific landing. Their task was to catch Tito dead or alive, and thereafter quickly move in the direction of an advancing German armored column. The task force consisted both of selected SS veterans and a bunch of desperados who got a new lease on life. If they survived, whether they were a demoted officer or a jailed soldier, they would be reinstated to their previous status. The planning for the mission was excellent, down to choosing to attack on Tito's birthday on the theory that he might have invited important friends to celebrate in his cave. The German surprise attack almost worked out as planned. However the Escort Unit of the Chief of Staff deployed and held off the attackers long enough for Tito and his entourage to slip away.

Djuka did not escape, but he was lucky enough. The German parachutist had been given unusual latitude. Taking prisoners in Drvar was out of question and the individual German soldiers had to make their own decisions. To the paratroopers who came upon him, Djuka's story that he was a German taken prisoner by the Partizans must have sounded fishy. But funny things do happen in a war and there was no time for interrogation. Under pressure, two German soldiers, the one who shot him and the medic, independently chose not to dirty their hands. Apparently Djuka ran into two desperadoes who were in Drvar to redeem themselves but whose hearts were not

in the fight. Had Djuka run into the hardcore SS veterans, that would have been the end of it.

What fantastic presence of mind Djuka had! How horrible it must have been to look up the barrel of a German gun. And how brave Djuka was to remain so optimistic. He was not complaining and he did the best he could to reassure us in his letter. I could not stop thinking about him and did not sleep at all that night.

The next morning my farewell to Father was rather subdued. We both understood what was at stake. I might make it, and the rest of the family might not. We might never meet again. My mother would not have missed the opportunity for a tearful mini-drama. She would have exhorted me to never forget her and somewhere along the line insert a barb to make me feel guilty. Something like, "When you are over there sitting at a full table, do not forget us hungry folks who are not so lucky and who will continue to love you," which would have made me miserable. Father was supportive, optimistic and saw no need to reiterate the obvious. In the morning he found a wagon back to Glina. The messenger went to the City Command and I proceeded through the town, over the bridge, and started the familiar walk to Topusko. Most of the time I kept thinking of Djuka. How clever and brave he was, how much he had changed and how frequently he inquired about his younger brother. And how much I loved him!

Off to Italy

(July 1944–March 1945)

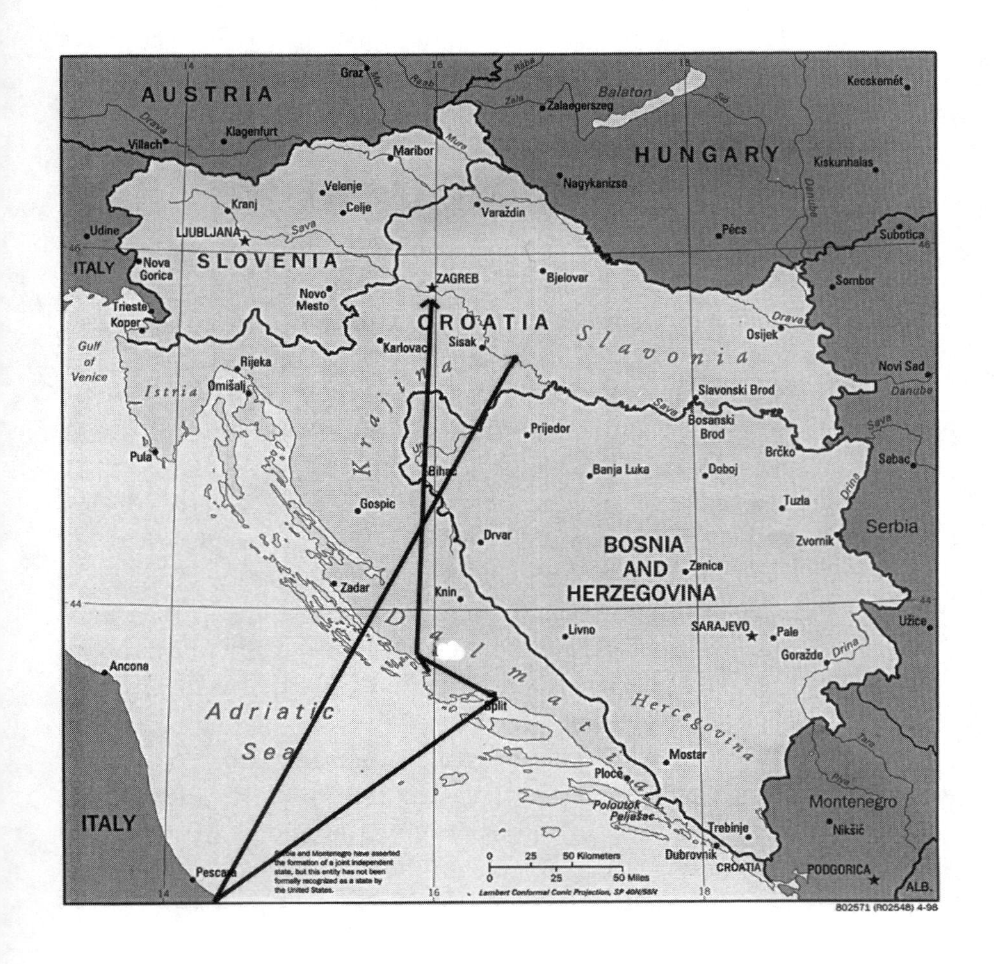

I reached Topusko in good time and went to pick up further orders in City Command. They directed me to register with the British Command in a nearby village whose name I have forgotten. The thought of meeting British officers sprung all sorts of fantasies. Even today I am given to daydreaming. A few hours before some important meeting you can find me gazing at a distant point, or even worse, talking half-aloud to a nonexistent audience. As a teenager, on the road to the makeshift airport, I was busy play-acting the anticipated encounter with English officers. I visualized an extremely busy place with orders flying left and right, translators loudly passing on urgent commands, and British officers hunkered down with their secret equipment out of reach. Yet I had to somehow get through to them and make them understand the important distinction between other children and me. I planned to stand in front of the officer and make myself a nuisance until he was forced to summon a translator. Then I would do my explaining. And of course the officer, never before having seen a teenage soldier, would treat me with the greatest respect.

Instead of the expected turmoil, the room was church quiet. In the dark corner three British officers and two translators huddled over a radio. The familiar BBC's three short-one long drumbeat emulating the opening notes of Beethoven's Fifth Symphony came clearly through. Motionless, relaxed, seeming to have no other cares in the world, the officers continued to listen to the radio. Suddenly, as if some strange power pulled them all at once by the scruff of their necks, the five figures jumped up. Thereafter the three foreign officers went about their business, each connected with an earphone to his little black box. I got it right away. The officers were waiting for a coded message during the regular BBC broadcast. Back in Stanchich we used to argue whether cryptic messages during BBC broadcasts were a propaganda ploy or whether London in fact had a network of agents in Yugoslavia to whom it sent messages. On that day I learned the truth. A predetermined nonsensical message over the public broadcast, such as, "Peter, our friend Paul feels fine," meant nothing to others but it told the officers that come evening, the airplanes would be on their way. The officers on the ground had enough time

for preparation and at the right moment, they were ready to send short intermittent radio signals for the pilot's direction. Signals short enough to avoid detection.

The danger of detection was high and the Partizans were masters at countermeasures. Not too many villages in the vicinity had enough flat land for a smooth landing. The Germans flying in Storks over the territory constantly looked for physical signs of a makeshift airport or for unusual movements. Too many people at one spot could trigger the red light. It was very important to project a picture of normalcy in the village; only essential personnel were permitted to walk in daylight. Every evacuee had to stay indoors until nightfall. To my chagrin soon after they took note of me and before I could talk to them, the British officers unceremonially kicked me out of the command center. I was to sit in the designated house and wait for further orders. No chance to explain myself.

By nightfall we were finally permitted to move around. Everybody was to keep with his group and each group was assigned to an area around the field. Of course I immediately broke the rule. Why should I sit with those kids? Gun over my shoulder I walked to the group of soldiers in charge of preparations. Could I help them?

"Sure," said the man in charge, "right after you turn in your gun to the storage room."

He was slim and tall, in his forties, and though he spoke with the local accent, all sentences were grammatically correct. Obviously he was a local but educated man. I knew right away he was not a Communist organizer. He had no military insignia and generally he did not care to look as a person in authority. He stuck his military cap under the shoulder strap, his jacket was unbuttoned, and behind his ear, the man carried a pencil. He was relaxed and found time to listen to what I had to say.

I tried Mother's technique. "Why would you take my gun away? I bet you don't do this to other soldiers. You should not mistreat me just because I am young."

"Oh, come on now," said the amused Partizan, "British orders. They will not take anybody with arms on the airplane. I let an old buddy of mine hide his pistol. They disarmed him on the other side

and I got a hell of a thrashing here, right in front of the British officers. Let me put it another way. Would you rather have your gun confiscated by them or leave it behind for other comrades to use?"

"You mean in spite of us being Allies, they will search us on the other side?"

"And how! Just wait and see."

I could not take issue with his impeccable logic and went for a last little concession. I explained how I wanted the officers to know I was a soldier, and that I should be separated from the school children. Could he leave me the gun until the last moment? It might serve as my passport to talk with the officers.

The pleasant man must have had children of his own. "OK. Empty the magazine and you can carry the darn thing until we ignite the fires. But it won't do you any good. When the first fire goes on you are to dash back to me or I will get into really big trouble. Ever read *The Golden Calf*?

Now that was a surprise. The man read books and yet he did not look that much different from the locals!

"No, I did no, but somebody told me all about the book."

"Fine. Then remember you are not my Oscar Bender, and I will not be your Sitting President."

I had to laugh. The story of Oscar Bender had been often retold during those evening delousing sessions in Trnavac. I read the book *Golden Calf* after the war and it remains my favorite. Written by the Soviet team of Ilf and Petrov the book was a thoroughly irreverent account about the first decade after the Russian revolution, when Lenin tried to revive the economy and permitted some degree of private enterprise. The central character is an unscrupulous wheeler-dealer looking for a quick profit. Anywhere he goes, Oscar opens a new enterprise and appoints as its pro-forma president, a stupid local Party member. He explains to the candidate that he will be well paid for doing nothing. As the "Sitting President" of the firm, he only has to be in the office and pass all inquiries on to Oscar, who is doing all the work. Of course "sitting president" was exactly the right term, as Oscar invariably escaped with the ill-begotten profit in his pockets and the local fool ended up sitting in jail.

I was surprised to find on the edges of a field in a small Banijan village another devotee of Ilf and Petrov. Who was this clever man? Why was he given such a minor job?

"Let's go, *Ucho*" (Teacher) somebody said. That explained it. A local teacher, a noncommunist fellow traveler, who could organize complex tasks but could not be entrusted with a more serious command!

Teacher was a genius. Everything functioned like clockwork and his predictions were right on target. The gun notwithstanding I could not get closer to the officers. Teacher had by now lined up small haystacks doused with gasoline to mark both sides of the landing strip. I was curious how he could avoid being detected during the day. After all, the burned out haystack would leave lasting marks.

"It is not easy. Of course we have other haystacks to move over the burned ones and then some more to disguise the pattern. The real trick is not to be too long in one place. After a while we plow the field over and move to another location," he explained.

Just then came the signal for general assembly. "Sonny, I will do you a last favor," teacher said, "You will not be on the same airplane with the Rujevac School."

Just a little favor to a youngster. He must have known it would not make any difference. With the list in his hands somebody on the other end would soon find out where I belonged.

"Now listen to me. The guys on the other end are very rigid. There are a few unpleasant steps to go through and some soldiers tried to rebel. It did not help them. You should play along. Be a clever man and keep your eyes open. Timing is everything. Do not jump from a running train, but when the right opportunity presents itself, do not hesitate. May God help you." And with these words, the nice man gave me a big hug, the only one I got from any man during the war.

~

All the haystacks burst in flames almost simultaneously. We had all been sitting for hours in total darkness and for a while, blinded by the sudden burst of light, I could not make out anything beyond the

nearest flaming haystack. Then the pattern became clear. Eight large fires clearly delineated a wide landing strip in the middle of the field. On the edges of the field, behind the fires, one could spot small groups of people, their heads turned towards the dark sky. We heard the sounds of circling airplanes but it was impossible to see them. As is usually the case when strained senses and vivid imagination combine, some people reported spotting the planes. One guy next to me loudly explained how large and beautiful the airplanes were. Eager to leave the war behind him, but afraid of flying, the poor fellow had seen what he wanted to see—big safe airplanes!

Then the noise intensified. Spaced no further than 3 minutes from one another, three airplanes landed. I had not seen a large airplane on the ground before. In the nineteen forties, Zagreb had no regular airline connections. Now I could marvel at the DC-3, which was waiting in front of the fire for its turn to taxi to the dark loading area. Even today the DC-3 is a decent-sized airplane but then it seemed enormous. The DC-3 were arguably the best planes ever designed. They could land and take off from just about anywhere.

It took a good airplane and capable pilots to fly through the night with no guidance until the last few miles, when an intermittent radio signal might have provided general directions but was not precise enough to land an airplane. Anybody in that unarmed airplane flying through enemy territory to land on a makeshift airport in an unknown country must have been incredibly brave. The pilots knew how precarious the situation was. Had the German intelligence gotten wind of the landing, they would drop illuminating flares over the airport and turn everybody into a sitting duck. On the ground, however, surrounded by excited strange people, the crew was incredibly calm.

That night in the field near Topusko there was none of the "hurry up" tense atmosphere to which I'd become accustomed during previous evacuations. The Allied soldier at the door patiently pointed out the airplanes stairs to all comers. Had he been a Yugoslav, he would have urged me to speed up and given me a good shove on the back while nervously urging the others to get on with it. Not because he was a coward trying to get out as fast as he could! That was not the point. The Slavs are accustomed to expressing their emotions. So much so, that a simple statement of fact is not sufficient. A calm

demeanor will not move others to immediate action, just as a flat statement may not be convincing. In fact in Yugoslavia one could, and I presume still can, make a profession out of expressing emotions. In some parts of the country one could hire *narikacha* for funerals, a wailer to loudly bemoan the death of the dear one. These women were true artists. Intermixed with loud screams of pain, they would tell everything that was important about the deceased. The wailing, not unlike our obituaries, described the achievements of the deceased, enumerated the surviving family members and vividly described the loss to family and friends. If a narikacha brought everybody to tears she had succeeded in her task.

The goal-oriented and calm behavior of these foreign heroes had a profound effect on me. I realized I was in a new world, with its own rules of behavior. An impressive, but strange world. It is fair to say that after more than three decades in the USA, I still haven't made a full adjustment to this new world. Occasionally, but only for an irrational second, I feel ready to trade the blandness and discipline of the new world for a good, old-fashioned Yugoslav melodrama. Only for a second do I wish somebody would hug me when I get an award, bemoan with me the injustice of a rejected paper, and above all, I wish I had an occasional audience for bragging. Only for a second! Then I wake up. The same old passionate Yugoslav ways are at the root of the murderous hatred which has overtaken the country. And over there, even in peacetime the superficial joviality, envy, jealousy, or friendship, are the engines that drive people to form essential, but frequently dubious, alliances. In the country I came from, almost nothing is assessed on its merit. It is with whom you are associated and who your family is that gets you the promotion. And the loss of time is incredible. Hours are spent in plotting. You may not attempt even the simplest task until you have assessed all its personal and political ramifications. No, thank you very much, I'd rather have the fair, if somewhat bland, American ways.

~

Teacher kept his promise. I boarded the last airplane along with a group of women and little children. In my mind, I faced a terrible

dilemma. Feeling almost naked without my gun, how could I convey to the soldier in the cabin that I was a military person? The man in charge soon realized I did not want to sit with others and permitted me to move closer to the front of the plane. That was a mistake. Sitting in close proximity—I now badly wanted to strike up a conversation. There was only one little problem. I did not speak English. Of course that did not stop me and for a while, I entertained the soldier with a pantomime. He was bemused to see me pointing at the imaginary gun on my shoulder, saluting, acting out battles, all in an effort to explain that I was an active resistance soldier. "Partizan, Partizan," I intoned while thumping my chest with open palms. That should have been sufficient to convince anybody about my military pedigree. And it was. The soldier nodded consent and shut off his flashlight. Now there was a problem. How do you communicate to a foreigner in the dark? I tried my German. It did not work. With a great effort I put together the best English sentence I could.

"British good," I said. A flashlight went on pointing to the soldier's shoulder.

"I am not British, I am from New Zealand," he said, pointing to the insignia.

That should have stopped me but instead, I tried to redeem myself by showing my knowledge of geography to the soldier. Unfortunately I got that wrong too. Somehow I mixed up New Zealand with New Guinea and, recalling from geographic maps how Guinea was divided by contrasting colors into two parts, I hurried to inform the soldier that I was aware of this important fact. He must have been perplexed watching me delineating with my hands a roughly oval shape, which I'd then with a stern move cut in half. Not surprisingly, the poor fellow did not understand a thing. On my second try he had had enough, found a piece of chocolate in his pocket, removed the wrapping, shoved the delicacy into my mouth and turned off the flashlight. Even a persistent teenager could understand that this was the end of the conversation.

The flight must have lasted about two hours and just as we landed the day broke out. Ratko Djukich, the commander in Glina, was wrong; we did not fly to Sicily. The DC-3 descended on the large military airport in Fogia in southern Italy. From there, the Serbo-

Croatian-speaking people on the ground explained we would be transported to a camp in the Carbonara region near Bari. But not before we were properly deloused!

I soon understood why Teacher suggested one should not resist the few unpleasant things at the beginning. Women were screaming as the reception committee mercilessly cut off their hair before forcing them through showers. In Yugoslavia, people just do not parade naked in front of one another. Nor was taking showers a normal practice. Certainly not in the morning. It is a common belief in the old Country that a wet human body is susceptible to diseases. If you are not dry and catch a draft, the next day you will get pneumonia. Protestation about their sure deaths and the orphans that they would leave behind did not help a bit. But that was not the end of the humiliation. Everybody was stripped of personal belongings. Gone were all the esthetic expressions, those individual touches, which required so much effort during the war. Courtesy of the Red Cross, the relief workers on the ground replaced the old personal clothing with ill-fitting second-hand outfits.

I was adapting fast. "Don't fuss. Keep your eyes open!" Teacher said. A woman in charge of taking temperatures had a hard time of it, since it had to be done the British way. Back home the temperature was measured with a large thermometer in the armpit. Here the order was to stick the little rod under your tongue, a procedure which many of the newcomers found repugnant and unhygienic. The line in front of the gentle lady grew longer, threatening to become a serious bottleneck. I saw my chance and went down the line to explain with a great deal of authority that the thermometers had been disinfected with alcohol, that they were safe, and that it was important to have the temperature taken. At the end of my little sermon I came up with a special touch. "If you fuss, they will not be able to separate typhoid suspects and will keep all of us in quarantine for at least three weeks right here at the airport." It was an effective half-lie.

The line shortened considerably and I positioned myself next to the nurse as if I were some sort of an official. I explained to her my "predicament" and she listened with considerable sympathy. No, she had no authority to co-opt me into the reception team. Everybody

first had to go to the camp in Carbonara. However the nurse promised to try to get me a clean new military uniform instead of the civilian clothing she routinely distributed to others. She had access to a store from which, according to the agreement with the Allies, she and her colleagues could issue uniforms to the arriving fighting men. Everybody agreed that I ought to be treated as a soldier and I got British military clothing: a jacket, long pants, long-sleeved undershirt, underpants and a pair of boots. They even found a matching khaki-colored Partizan beret adorned with the obligatory red star. I had won a great victory. The uniform would give me access to military personnel and it would be only a matter of time before I recouped my lost military stature.

The uniform was ill-suited for the hot Italian summer but I never complained. Later, in the hospital in Bari after my military status had been officially confirmed, they offered me shorts but I wouldn't have them. After all I was Partizan. I was not about to adopt the ridiculous English habit of showing your naked knees. Furthermore, in Britain the adults might sport shorts but in Yugoslavia only children wore them. I grew attached to the British uniform. It became a status symbol, the substitute for my lost gun.

The camp in Carbonara was large enough to accommodate close to hundred huge tents, each sheltering about fifty people. The tents were arranged in a geometric fashion along rectangular intersecting avenues. In the center, a few oversized tents contained the kitchen and the administrative offices. The administration of the camp was quite complex. There were persons from the Red Cross, British nurses, and a few British officers. Amongst them, with characteristic communist intransigence, the Partizan personnel made every effort to be heard. The British Army organized the camp. They gave us the food and shelter, they provided the logistic support; theirs was the occupied Italian territory and their airplanes brought us over. Nevertheless the Yugoslavs insisted that they should be in charge. The camp in Carbonara was to be a little piece of Yugoslavia on foreign soil.

And from the first moment the Communists started to project their trademark image. Get anything you can get, ask for more, and never be satisfied. You deserve what you are getting and you do not owe thanks to the donor. It is the moral obligation of the haves to give to the have-nots. Sure they are giving you something but they could do much better. Just look at their soldiers' rations and their own level of comfort. Everything is given grudgingly in recognition of your superb war efforts and if you did not push, they would give you practically nothing. "Who do they think we are? A bunch of primitive tribesmen?" So went the Party line. For once, they were close to the truth!

The Party systematically and constantly maintained a barrage of counter propaganda. The help was coming form the "historical enemy," the rotten British imperialists who could not possibly have a speck of real humanity in them. Winston Churchill's help did not come as a result of sincere appreciation of the Partizans. He had to do it; it was a necessity in order to assist the Allied war effort.

However the same Communists did not for a moment stop to ask why Stalin never offered any help. Not a word of encouragement, not a single bullet made its way from the Soviet Union to Yugoslavia. Instead of questioning the inactivity of mother Soviet Union, the Yugo-Commies busily parroted the selfishness of their mentors. Just as the Soviet Union constantly wailed about the needs of the "first socialist country in the world" and because of its "historic significance" expected everybody to help, so did the Yugoslavs jealously corner for themselves the anti- German resistance market in the Balkans. As active anti-Fascists they deserved the help. It was coming to them.

The language problem, the Partizan's intransigent attitude and the complicated governance of the camp made everything quite difficult. The day-to-day logistic operation was in the hands of the British who gladly delegated its major portion to the Red Cross. The Yugoslavs had the right to be consulted in matters of disposition of the population in the camp. The British could say that half of the people ought to be moved to the huge camp in El Shat in Egypt: the Yugoslavs decided which 50% would go. The supreme Yugoslav au-

thority lay in the military delegation of the People's Liberation Army in Bari, a small Partizan embassy of sorts. The leaders of the Carbonara camp were a particularly unimaginative bunch. They would not agree even to the smallest change without a prior consultation with the delegation.

Generally speaking, in spite of tensions, things functioned reasonably well but occasionally both frustrated sides worked into a stalemate. I had been in Carbonara about a week, carefully staying away from the Rujevac children, when the Yugoslavs and the British got themselves into a shouting match about a pregnant woman who was scheduled for evacuation to another camp. She rightly argued that a trip at her advanced stage of pregnancy might be too risky. The British commander could not swallow this insubordination. This was the last straw and he decided once and forever to cut the Gordian knot. If the woman did not wish to go, that was her privilege, but he had already taken her off the Carbonara camp rolls. She could not stay in the Camp, but he was sure that in its wisdom, the Yugoslav Delegation in Bari would find a solution to her problems.

Recognizing the Commander played hardball, the Yugoslavs quickly shifted gears, but to no avail. Frustrated and fed up, the Commander didn't yield an inch. He conceded that his trucks went to town often, but the regulations permitted them to take aboard only residents of the camp and the woman had already been signed out of the camp. This unfortunately, precluded him from permitting her to use any of the trucks.

Downtown Bari was about ten miles from the camp. The Yugoslav leadership decided that the woman should be escorted to the delegation quarters in Bari, and they would somehow take care of her. Nobody volunteered for escort duty. The big shots were too important for such a minor role and the rank and file members of the Carbonara staff were not quite sure if they could find their way. Somebody suggested I'd be ideally suited for the job; my uniform would help me hitchhike a ride in a military vehicle and, anyhow, escorting others duty was usually a courier's duty. I was excited at the prospect of getting in touch with the delegation and pleading my case. No doubt they would have a job for me.

Somebody who had been there before gave me general directions. The road from the camp passed through the village and then connected with the main thoroughfare around Bari. And off we went!

My companion was a very, very pregnant woman. She had a huge belly. Her legs could barely service the combined weight of her natural obesity and of the gigantic womb in which-so it seemed-a big baby was swimming in a veritable lake of amniotic fluid. The only way the poor soul could walk was to move her legs sideways and then bring them in a semicircle forwards.

She was a youngish village woman, probably in her early twenties. Totally overwhelmed by the ill-timed pregnancy far from home, she didn't have a clue what was happening. I couldn't talk to her; no matter what I said, she'd burst into tears. Our progress was painfully slow.

Finally, after two hours we reached the main road. The traffic on the road was heavy and I hoped to catch a ride to the port of Bari. The delegation was on the waterfront right across from the port. Just then the poor woman started to complain of cramps. Soon she was in full labor. Something had to be done in a hurry. Between her cramps we somehow managed to get ourselves to the curbside opposite an MP directing traffic. I walked up to the MP and from the middle of the road kept pointing towards the woman on the curbside. After a superb pantomime in which I played out a bulging stomach, groaned and generally suggested extreme distress, the soldier got the message. He stopped an ambulance to take us to the nearest military hospital. Honor required that I stay with the woman inside the ambulance. Unfortunately, military ambulances have no side windows. At the beginning, this did not strike me as a problem but as I got accustomed to the woman's distress, between her labor pains I started to look through the little window into the driver's cabin. Peeking over the driver's shoulder I hoped to get a feel for the general direction of our ride. It did not help. By the time we got to the British hospital, I had no idea where we were.

Our arrival created a major commotion. In typical unrestricted Dalmatian fashion, the mother-to-be was yelling at the top of her lungs. This was quite a shock for the personnel, who in the disci-

plined British world had never been exposed to such screaming. The British military hospital was not exactly set to handle births. Finally a surgeon ready to take the responsibility showed up. As they wheeled away my unhappy companion, it dawned on me that I was in real trouble. How was I supposed to find my way back? Nobody in the hospital had ever heard of the military delegation in Bari. Finally I drew a sketch of the peripheral road around Bari and with an arrow pointed to an area I had adorned with cranes to symbolize the harbor. The sergeant at the admission desk got my message but he indicated that all hospital traffic went in the opposite direction from the harbor. He could get me to the main road but no further. "Fine, just get me there. I will find my way," I thought and not knowing how else to express my gratitude, I bowed. The man must have served in the Orient. He bowed even deeper than I did and with a pleasant smile showed me to the ambulance.

The driver dropped me off at the crossing with the main road. From there it was relatively easy to find transportation to the harbor. After I located the delegation, the duty officer was utterly uninterested in the pregnant woman story. He perfunctorily took down her name but I could tell he was not about to act. The woman had become a British problem. Why should he worry? Eventually the hospital would call and if they did not, that was just as well. Somebody else would take care of her. The officer also did not care about my glorious military past and me. Lowering his voice to a conspiratorial "for your ears only" tone, he suggested that the situation between the British and the delegation had become rather tense. There'd be all sorts of complications if I did not return to the camp.

It was impossible to move this defensive man. Unwilling to cope with anything out of the ordinary he had insulated himself from the world by a studied facade of indifference. He was a superb practitioner of the art of 'no.' No, other officers were not available to talk with me. No, he could not keep me overnight, had no authority for such a move. No, he had no transportation back to the camp. And then hit me with the Partizan's favorite noncommittal expression, *"Snadji se druzhe,"* which roughly translates into *Improvise, Comrade*. The only "yes" this indolent man managed to say was in response to my incredulous question, "Do you expect me to leave

right away?" It was stupid of me to even try Mother's technique. This man would never feel guilty about anything. To the contrary, I gave him a good opening.

"Yes, Comrade, you had better leave right now. Soon they will stop working in the port and you may miss catching a truck."

When I realized the finality of the situation and was about to leave, the officer showed a modicum of humanity.

"I have some freshly baked pastry. Take a few with you."

His were not ordinary pastries; they were veritable replicas of my pre-war favorite tortes—an offer I could not refuse. I tried a piece of *creme schnitte*, the Viennese kind, and it was superb. Seeing my delight the man loaded six pieces into a bag and handed them to me. But that was it. After a soft moment he was back to his surly uncompromising behavior.

I stopped a truck driver who was on his way to Brindisi, which meant he had to get to the circular highway on the periphery of Bari. In sign language we agreed I would let him know where to stop. Unfortunately, there were no distinguishing buildings along the road. Every once in a while, a larger road branched away from the town, wiggling its way into distant provinces. Finally we came to something that looked vaguely familiar and I got off the truck. None of the few people on the road had heard of Carbonara. Convinced I was on the right track, I proceeded to walk away from the town. All roads leaving Bari were quite similar: asphalted, with endless olive groves on both sides and here and there, secluded behind the oldest trees, stood an occasional flat-roofed stucco house. The sunburned peeling yellow paint turned every facade into an irregular geographic map. This and the uniformly shut wooden Venetian blinds robbed the houses of any individuality. If there were any people behind those closed blinds, they had insulated themselves, both from the afternoon sun and from visitors. These austere houses were so uninviting that I did not even think of knocking on a single door.

Unlike the road to Carbonara, which went uphill, this one was flat and if anything, veered slightly downhill. When evergreens replaced the olive trees and the simple neglected houses gave way to large well-kept villas, it was clear I was lost. Somehow I had ambled into a rich district. Not knowing what else to do, I continued. The

houses got closer to one another and after a while I found myself in something that before the war might have been the main street of a resort town. In the middle of the village stood a strategically placed British MP checkpoint. I wore a military uniform but had no documents. I mumbled something about the camp in Carbonara, which did not elicit a visible reaction from the stoic and stern soldiers. In no uncertain terms, they pointed to a spot on a stone fence where I was to sit. There on the fence I reached into the pastry bag and in short order polished off three pieces. The other half I preserved for future use. Just in case. After the long walk in the hot sun, the leftover cakes were in a sad state, sticking to one another, each attached to its own ugly circular fat spot on the bag.

It was getting dark. Finally a duty officer came by. He took me to the gate in a high stone-built wall surrounding a large villa. Behind the wall lay an unexpected surprise. I had run into a full-fledged gala party. Everything inside the villa was in sharp contrast to the outside wartime austerity: the line of parked cars, the waiters offering drinks and, on the balcony, a group of formally dressed guests engaged in animated pre-dinner conversation. What was this party about? Some of the guests were British officers, but who were the men in tuxedos and the ladies in glamorous evening dresses? The question remained unanswered. The contrast between this unexplained oasis of prewar formality and the outside world could not have been larger. All of a sudden, I became self-conscious—a dirty youngster in the midst of an elite world. Inside the villa the splendor was even more overwhelming. Until then I did not realize what the war had done to our evenings. Three years of candles, petroleum light and forty-Watt light bulbs had turned everybody I knew into a somnolent, low-key, introvert, and the dimmed lights served only as an overture to the main evening activity—sleeping. But inside this strange Italian villa, the blinding luxurious light from high chandeliers, side-wall light fixtures and table lamps did what it was meant to do, provide a background for a lively social interchange. Everybody was pleasantly cheerful, or so it seemed.

The officer left for a moment. Beset by an acute feeling of inferiority, I withdrew to a corner. After a while the officer returned in the company of a man in a well-fitting tuxedo, hard collar, bow tie,

waistcoat, cummerbund, the whole works. He spoke perfect Serbian. Who was I and how could he help me?

I should have been happy to finally have somebody to communicate with, but the Partizan indoctrination and my acute feeling of insecurity prevailed. Facing the unknown, I fell back on standard communist clichés. I decided the man in front of me must be an "imperialist lackey" in some suspicious British service. Just as we had a delegation with the British, the Serbian Chetniks very likely had their own official representatives. The man was either a spymaster or a true enemy. The mere thought drove my imagination into high gear. Soon the suspicion turned into conviction. I was certain that the man was a Yugoslav King's Army officer who, while everybody else was fighting the Nazis, danced with beautiful ladies, all the while plotting how to damage the Partizan movement. I should not cooperate with such a traitor.

The poor man must have been frustrated. Here he was trying to help a lost countryman and the youngster refused to cooperate. He did offer me food but I proudly held out the dirty bag with the homogenized pastries. No sir, I do not need favors from the class enemy. The offer of a drink met with the same answer. By then I had worked myself into a paranoiac frenzy. "Sure," I told myself, "he will slip some chemical in the drink to crack my will and make me spill all the secrets." There is no logic in paranoia. Not for a moment did I stop to think why somebody would want to drug a teenager and what secrets I could possibly betray. Nor did I remember that this gentleman did not seek me out, I came upon his place. He continued to be pleasant, even offering to let me stay overnight so they could escort me to the camp the next day. There was not a hint of threat in his behavior. But I had lost all judgment and, triggered by extraordinary events around me, my fantasy ran wild. Had I just managed to ask the man who he was and what the party was about, he would have given me satisfactory answers. Instead I treated my potential benefactor to a display of teenage stupidity.

Besides giving my name and the position of the camp, I refused to answer any other questions.

"Which part of Yugoslavia did you come from?"

"Sorry, that is a military secret."

The man must have had a big chuckle.

"Here we have a lot of people from various parts of Yugoslavia. If I were to know which town you are from, I might find somebody to whom you'd relate better."

The man tried his best.

"I am a soldier of the National Liberation Army, have no permanent residence and where I lived before the war is not relevant."

What was the guy to do with me? He said something to the officer and left. The officer took me back to the street—back from the blinding light into the dark evening, from the island of luxury into the drab reality. I was made to sit on the same stonewall across from the checkpoint.

Eventually a jeep with two British soldiers showed up. To those who did not grow up in Communist-dominated Eastern Europe this would be hard to understand, but I was absolutely convinced that the two Tomy's would take me to a jail or worse. Whatever little hope I may have had instantly disappeared after they refused to share my pastry. It never entered my mind that they were well fed and that the mushy, unappetizing pastry was not their type of sweet to start with. The soldiers were predictably surly as anybody would be whose evening had been interrupted by a nonsensical order. They had to drop whatever they were doing to drive a lost youngster back to his destination. Of course the soldiers had no evil intention. Unless you count the neck-breaking speed with which they delivered me to Carbonara! I must have interrupted some important activity to which they wished to return in a great hurry.

After the jeep delivered me to the camp, I was sent to the tent of the Runjevac School. Early next morning we were on our way to the school's new permanent location. The Allies had found a building in the south of Italy in Santa Maria di Leuca on the Gulf of Taranto. I had always kept my distance from the Runjevac School but this seemed to be the end of the road. As of tomorrow I would become a regular student in that school and lose my independent status of a Partizan soldier. Had I listened to the nice gentleman and stayed overnight in the villa, I would have missed the Runjevac convoy.

Luckily, even as a youngster I had the propensity to analyze my, and other people's behavior. Next morning on the truck to our new

home, I laughed at myself. How could I have been so stupid as to exaggerate my own importance and make such nonsensical assumptions? It served me right, I thought.

~

The incident in the villa was not one of those defining moments everyone speaks about. I understood the irrationality of yesterday's actions but did not instantly change my behavior. However the incident in Bari taught me a great deal and, to my credit, nowadays I am pretty much free of Eastern European pathologic suspicions.

By the time we came to Santa Maria di Leuca I had drawn the right conclusion; my behavior was inexcusable and I had made a big fool out of myself. However in regards to the mysterious villa near Bari, I could have been partially right. The villa possibly was the headquarters of the King's diplomatic mission to the Allies. But I was too embarrassed to ever inquire.

Santa Maria de Leuca turned out to be a seaside resort at the heel of the Italian boot. We were given rather nice facilities, the food was good and the school was just getting organized. The period of a few weeks before the start of formal classes turned into a nice vacation. I had my own room in the hotel, which housed the entire school. From the hotel high up on a cliff, I had a gorgeous view of beaches and the open sea. I decided to make myself a swimming suit from a pair of parachute-silk pants I had acquired in Bari. It was a disaster. The product covered every part of my body but the one it was supposed to. Another project of mine, creating a fishing hook from a sewing needle also failed. It was all quite entertaining and I started to warm up to the place. Nevertheless, the idea of eventually returning to military duty was always on the back of my mind. I would have probably escaped right away had I known where to go.

The opportunity came when I got a letter from Mother who had been flown into Fogia and was assigned to the military hospital in Grumo near Bari. That was all I needed to know. Next day I volunteered for duty on the school truck to fetch some supplies from Lecce. From there I stood a good chance of catching a long distance truck going up north. The main road from Lecce to Bari, via Brindisi, was

always busy. There were four of us on the truck; the driver and three students to help him loading supplies. We arrived in Lecce in the middle of a torrential storm. While everybody was looking for cover, I slipped away and when the storm subsided, found an American truck to Brindisi. Youth is reckless. Not for a moment did I wonder what happened to the poor driver when he realized he had lost a child.

The American driver dropped me off at the periphery of Brindisi and from there on, it was very easy to reach Bari. Teeming with traffic, the main road between the two Adriatic harbor towns resembled a modern-day American highway. Americans had introduced the previously unknown practice of hitchhiking. People quickly learned to stand at the roadside and raise their thumbs. Everybody did it—soldiers, civilians and many pretty girls of questionable intentions. Within a minute I got a ride to Bari from where I took off on foot to nearby Grumo and its military hospital. I sneaked in and succeeded in surprising Mother who was changing the dressing on a patient's wound. She jumped with joy, hugged me, dropped everything she was doing and took me to her quarters. There she showered on me many presents she had been collecting for our reunion. The *piece de resistance* was a thick bar of British military chocolate. When I say thick, I mean thick! It was a massive bar the size of a paperback and one inch thick. We spent the rest of the day reminiscing and trading information about Djuka and Father. I had little to offer, but Mother had gotten a letter from Dr. Tatlich describing Djuka's wound. As Father predicted in Klasnich, Djuka's wound was quite bad.

Dr. Tatlich undertook the first "revision" of the wound, carefully removing bone fragments and placing drains to prevent accumulation of the pus deep inside the wound. The outer surface of the wound was regularly washed with hydrogen peroxide and potassium hypermanganate. Slowly, Djuka's fever decreased and the surface of the wound began to show healthy granular tissue. There was no question of stitching the wound together; it had to remain open to heal gradually. Eventually, suggested Dr. Tatlich, the huge cavity would fill from the inside with scar tissue, over which the skin would grow from the sides to the center. However Dr. Tatlich also predicted that the wound would remain "active" and would have to be

drained from time to time "until all bone fragments work their way to the surface or get totally encased in the fibrous tissue." Dr Tatlich also reported that in order to reduce the pain and foster the healing of the wound, he had immobilized Djuka's arm in a cast.

"I bet you they fixed him with an 'airplane'," Mother said.

Poor Djuka! Dr. Tatlich outfitted him with a contraption that could be only described as a portable torture chamber. The purpose of the cumbersome cast was to hold the arm extended sidewise at a ninety-degree angle to the chest. The arm was kept in the desired position by a support truss connecting the basis, a firm circular cast around the whole chest, with the extended arm. The designation of "airplane" was very apt; with the upper arm stretched sidewise and the lower arm angled forwards the patient resembled a winged creature about to soar in the air. I have seen many a patient with the cast and many could barely take it. The unnatural contraption made it impossible to sleep, the pain was frequently excruciating. Skin under the cast around the chest repeatedly broke out in uncomfortable blisters, but a constant itching was worst of all. The patients would itch from the heat, from their own sweat and often from louse bites. Itching and not being able to scratch is one of the worst afflictions that can befall a person. And the lice would crawl under the cast, and where nobody could reach them, they had a feast. Hopefully Djuka learned a few tricks to make the predicament more tolerable—talk the nurses into opening little ventilation windows, scratch under the cast with a pin crafted from thick wire, and how to take just the right position for sleeping.

From Italy to Home

(April-July 1945)

We heard no news about Father but were not too concerned. Slowly but surely, the Partizans were moving all hospitals to Italy and many physicians were evacuated with them. The elderly physicians and specialists in non-surgical fields that could not be sent to the front line were at the top of the evacuation list. We knew it was only a matter of time before Father would show up in Italy.

Mother and I were similarly optimistic about Djuka's chances to arrive in Italy. His wound seems to have stabilized, but his "airplane" prevented him from taking long walks. Eventually he would be too much of a logistic problem to the authorities and, furthermore, Djuka needed specialty surgical and orthopedic care. In my imagination I could see him sitting somewhere in Bosnia next to a row of burning haystacks and, as I did in Banija, enjoying the bravery and skills of the descending British pilots.

The chances were good that in the near future the whole Julius family might be reunited in Italy. Our general analysis was correct but it did not work out exactly as we expected. As they say in Yugoslavia; "People dream but God decides."

Mother secured for me a formal appointment as a courier in the Grumo military hospital. I had full access to military stores and if I wanted, I could eat in the hospital's club for British Officers. But I made little use of the club. For one thing, there was porridge. It was

hard to fathom how they could enjoy the semi-solid amorphous mass, which reminded me of the leftover mush which our farmers fed to pigs. And when I finally tried porridge, it tasted as bad as I thought it would. I did not fare any better with kippers, the other British breakfast delicacy. They vividly reminded me of the salted fish in Otochac. Occasionally I'd enjoy ham and bacon but then I missed the bread. The snow white, squashy and porous, precut squares that went for bread in the Officer's Club had nothing to do with the solid, dark aromatic slices we ate in Yugoslavia. No wonder the officers toasted each slice before they ate it. That was fine, but toast is toast and bread is bread, they cannot replace one another.

Truth be told I had very little to do in the Grumo hospital. I carried biochemical samples from tents to the lab and occasionally distributed documents from the administration to various subunits of the hospital. But that was the extent of it. I had plenty of time on my hands and decided to learn English, using a picture book the British distributed to foreign soldiers. I presume the booklet was somebody's brilliant attempt to teach English without translation. That way, the British Army did not have to translate the booklets into scores of funny foreign languages. I vaguely remember somebody explaining that the booklet had been based on "natural learning," the same way the children learn words. Well, dear reader, if you have to learn a foreign language and if you do not have a good sense of humor, avoid the picture book method. The book was excruciatingly silly.

The first two pictures were of a dog and of a table.

The text proudly announced: "This is a dog. This is a table."

Good! I got that!

Next was: "No, this is not a table, this is a dog!"

A great, profound, comparison!

After that came a combined picture of the dog and the table. The text underneath the illustration explained: "The dog is under the table. The table is above the dog."

And that is how I was supposed to learn the language of William Shakespeare!

Surprisingly the booklet worked, but not the way the author intended it. I loved the text for its absurdity. The silly stuff tickled my

funny bone and I quickly learned the words. Imitating the senseless comparisons, I went around the hospital making up absurd sentences such as: "No this is not a bus, this is my grandmother." Or, "Peter, why did you eat the dog?" And, "Why did you eat this and not that dog?" Maybe that was what the writer wanted to achieve. Unconsciously, I adopted the method and kept not only learning more words, but also how to use them in some context.

Next I got a text called *Basic English*. Its author chose the most frequently used English words and translated them into German. The foreword suggested that by acquiring the 3000 selected words the reader would have sufficient tools for every day communication in English.

I mastered quite a number of words and in doing so became attracted to English. What a great language! In English, unlike the Serbo-Croat or German language, if you know the words, you do not need to bother that much with the grammar. Compare this with Croatian. After thirty years in Yugoslavia, my mother knew most of the words, but their gender remained a mystery to her. Yes, in Croatian, even inanimate objects have a gender and to complicate things the Croats invented a neuter gender to add to the female and male. A child has a neutral gender until it grows up—physiologically correct, but linguistically, a torture. With each gender comes a choice of a few gender-specific, seven tenses declension and not to be outdone, all verbs must be conjugated.

English? Nothing to it! William Shakespeare, here I come!

Of course I was dead wrong, but in Grumo I thought I'd be speaking English in a few months. Youth is eternally optimistic! It took me ten years to become fluent in daily conversations, another forty years—and counting—to master idioms, and some English rules I will never learn.

~

About a month after I joined Mother in Grumo, we learned that another hospital in nearby Andria had begun to receive patients from Bosnia. On a hunch that somebody may have seen Djuka, we set out to Andria, where to our surprise and joy, we found him in person.

The meeting was very emotional. Everybody cried. After eighteen months of separation, three-fourths of our family had been reunited!

Djuka did not look all that good. He was skinny, pale, in obvious pain, and as Mother predicted, he wore an "airplane cast." Djuka's wound was still troublesome. After a period of apparent normalcy, he'd first get pain and then fever. His arm would swell, a sure sign that scar tissue had overgrown the wound and underneath it trapped some pockets of infection. The infection usually started around a bone segment and another surgeon would have to lance the puss, remove bone splinters and "revise" the wound. Djuka had already had two such surgeries and he knew a third was coming.

The pus had worked its way through Djuka's cast and above the wound, on the top of the "airplane," there was a huge yellowish-brown area. Unfortunately Djuka's wound was infected with some putrid bacteria and a terrible stench emanated from his cast. In various Partizan hospitals, I learned to cope with wound odors, but I could not handle the situation with Djuka. Back came memories of horrible wounds, the stinking ones and the ones infested with fly larvae. To think what might be under that cast was more than I could take. I had to leave the room to compose myself. Upon returning, I realized that Mother was also barely able to cope. Nobody quite knew what to do. I forced myself not to look at the cast. Mother chit-chatted in an unnatural fashion and Djuka pretended to be comfortable when in fact he was in pain. The atmosphere was patently false and play-acting replaced the initial spontaneity.

And then Mother broke down. She cried and loudly lamented the horrors of the war—Hitler, her beautiful son, the horrible wound and the forthcoming surgery. For the first time in my life I found Mother's emotionality useful. When she was done, everything we didn't dare to say had been said and her catharsis cleared the air. We could again relate in a normal fashion.

After she got everything off her chest Mother, full of energy, started to make plans. She'd ask that Djuka be transferred to Grumo, where she'd personally take care of him. She knew how get to him a new uniform in Grumo and she'd frequently change the cast. Once again after such a long separation, we would live together.

But Djuka had matured and got tougher. The wound, political indoctrination, and rough people around him took their toll. Whereas his previous letters expressed a deep longing for his family, Djuka did not jump on the opportunity to join us in Grumo. To the contrary, he preferred to stay with his comrades in arms in Andria. They were as important to him, he said clumsily, as the family. It did not take me long to realize that Djuka had become uncompromisingly doctrinaire. He had bought into the belief that until the end of the war, the allegiance to the Party and to the battle against fascism ought to be the top priority. Everything else could wait.

Mothers always have difficulties handling a child's emerging independence but this abrupt change in Djuka's attitudes must have been particularly difficult for her. But our Mother had also changed. She said nothing and took it straight on the chin. I was proud of her.

Even on our return to Grumo Mother did not complain. Djuka did his part. Every week he wrote at least one letter to inform us about his health and when he had a chance he'd send small presents. In the beginning we went a few times to visit him but Mother realized how much Djuka cherished his independence and we left him alone.

The next day after our first visit, a highly skilled Slovenian surgeon completed the third operation and Djuka was again outfitted with an "airplane." Eager to return to Yugoslavia Djuka never complained. After two months in Italy, still in the cast, he sweet-talked his way onto a ship for Split. After he landed there, he wrote us a letter with some interesting news. He learned that Father had been reassigned from his post in Banija to the Adriatic island of Vis, close to Italy, where Tito established his new headquarters.

Tito's strategy to first secure the south Dalmatian coast and move his Command post to Vis was a good one. The Germans had had to shorten the lines in Yugoslavia according to the events on the Italian side of the Adriatic. When in Italy the Allies advanced northward past Rome, the Germans simultaneously withdrew from most of the Dalmatian coast.

The road was now open for Djuka's Eighth Corps to push north and liberate Lika, the North Adriatic coast (Primorje) and the Istrian peninsula. Djuka was about to complete a long circle from Lika to Bosnia, then to Italy, back to the Dalmatian Coast and onwards to Lika from where his corpus advanced to the north towards the Yugoslav-Italian border.

In the fall of 1944, brisk military traffic shook out of lethargy the inhabitants of the small coastal town of Karlobag. The place was crowded. All public houses—the school, the township hall and buildings in the port had been confiscated for military purposes. The few local pubs overflowed with soldiers and many a private house had to cope with temporary lodgers. Karlobag had become a beehive of activity. Whereas Djuka's units were moving up the tortuous pass, Father together with a group of Allied pilots, worked his way down the pass to the seaside.

Many Allied pilots that flew from Italy to Central Europe faced heavy antiaircraft defenses. If their airplane was damaged the pilots did their best to limp towards guerrilla-held territory and bail out. The Partizans developed a sophisticated network for recovery of parachuted pilots. These rescues were so effective that Britain sent Randolph Churchill to coordinate the evacuations. Space permitting the British would evacuate an occasional guerrilla officer along with the pilots. Father carried with him a letter from the Chief of Sanitary Operations for Croatia asking that he be evacuated to Italy from where he was to sail to Vis. In spite of his reputation and a strong smell of whisky, Randolph Churchill was pleasant and accepted Father for evacuation. However when the group reached the seaside, the submarine was smaller than anticipated. The pilots squeezed into the vessel and with a polite but firm apology, Father was left stranded in Karlobag. After a few days he found his way to Vis via Split.

In one of those ironies of war, Father and Djuka lingered in Karlobag for three overlapping days but they never met!

About a month later Father was reassigned to Italy. Once again—three fourths of our family was reunited but only Mother and I had seen everybody. Father was unhappy not to have seen Djuka. Uncharacteristically for him, Father worried a great deal about Djuka. Admittedly Djuka was not on the front line but he was not

entirely out of danger. Bombs also fell on soldiers behind the front line. More importantly the entire country had been studded with land mines. As Djuka followed his troops into new territories, the chance that he might step on one of these horrible instruments of war increased. One could, though I never understood why, glorify the bravery of a direct confrontation with the enemy, but there is nothing else one could say about the mines but that they the worst and lowest form of warfare, aimed which indiscriminately at causing personal injury.

Father was sent from Vis to Italy to urgently address the epidemics of the embarrassing "Kozara" disease. A form of massive hysteria, Kozara disease broke out in the Grumo hospital. A classical attack would usually start with the patient warning others that he "felt it coming." With everybody's attention properly focused on him, the man would roll his eyes, appear confused, and soon slide into a full-fledged attack. There was always an element of theatrics in these fits as the maniac reenacted war scenes, frantically chasing the mirage of the enemy, throwing imaginary bombs at him, mowing him down with a nonexistent machine gun and occasionally bemoaning the loss of a fallen comrade. Eventually it all evolved into sheer lunacy; uncontrolled over-activity, foaming at the mouth, hyperventilation and at the end, from the hyperventilation, convulsive seizures. Finally, totally exhausted, the patient would fall into a sleep from which he awoke with total amnesia. There was no organic cause to this new disease. It was mass hysteria, pure and simple. But the condition was as infectious as any bacterial disease. If one soldier in a tent got the attack, within a day that tent became a madhouse; ten others were on the floor busily acting out their war experiences. It was not so much a conscious faking as a loss of restraint and an empathy with the other soldiers. Unfortunately, the "disease" turned into the worst possible one-upsmanship about whose experience in the war was more dramatic.

In Grumo, Father took a straightforward position. The disease was mass hysteria, similar to the outbreaks described by Charcot during the French Revolution. There ought to be two components to the treatment; sympathy and firmness. Sympathy, since these people were not malingerers. They had nightmares in the middle of the day

and were reaching out for sympathy. Firmness was needed, for if such immature reactions were condoned, the conditions might spread like a fire. There was something besides sympathy to gain with these attacks—one was not sent back to the front.

First Father gave a series of lectures explaining that every Partizan had troubling experiences, but the mature ones, the real fighters, were able to control their emotions. By acting out, the soldiers exposed their weakness and greatly damaged the reputation of Partizans as a group. Invariably, offended by the mere thought that the disease may be emotional, somebody would immediately get an attack in the middle of the lecture. But Father was well prepared. Unfazed, he'd calmly continue to point out how demeaning and sad it was to be in this state. The Kozara disease was not a medical condition, he would insist. It was just an immature attempt to get people's attention. The personnel had been instructed to stay out of it. Let the man convulse—no one had yet hurt himself during such attacks. This worked quite well. The number of convulsions first leveled off and then started to decrease. After a month only core of about fifty patients continued to have attacks. Father decided to evacuate them back to Yugoslavia.

Some wounded Partizans in the Grumo hospital were professional seamen. They'd hitch a ride to Bari and for old time's sake take a stroll through the busy harbor. A group of them spotted a boat resembling *Ljubljana* of the Adriatic line. The painted over ship had an Italian name, but that did not deter the seamen. Convinced it was *Ljubljana,* they boarded the ship, confirmed their suspicion, threw out the astonished Italian crew, hoisted a Yugoslav flag, and proclaimed the ship property of the People's Republic of Yugoslavia. Facing a band of wounded soldiers who swore not to leave without a fight and expecting the ship would never put out to the sea, the British military administration gave in. To keep the ship from leaving, the British Navy did not disclose the plans of the mine-fields outside the port of Bari. But nothing could stop the Yugoslav sailors. One day the Captain closely trailed an Allied ship leaving the harbor. After a while the *Ljubljana* turned east, and fervently hoping the Allied airplanes would not mistake it for a German ship, sailed towards the Dalmatian port of Split.

Ljubljana had established the precedent. Soon the idle seamen from Grumo commandeered another ship, the *Sitnica. Sitnica* operated under similar rules as *Ljubljana* and Father was offered space for his patients on the ship's maiden voyage to Split. The ship dropped anchor off the docks in the Bari harbor. All patients with Kozara disease were brought aboard. They thought of it as an out-of-sight floating hospital and calmed down. Next morning, *Sitnica* trailed a tanker and took off towards the Dalmatian coast. There was quite a ruckus, but the crew stood its ground. Many patients fell ill on the high seas and upon arrival in Split all were docile and cooperative. After a fast triage in Split, the older ones were discharged from the military service, the salvageable young ones enrolled into a special rehabilitation program, and the very bad ones were incarcerated in the psychiatric wing of the Shibenik hospital.

⁂

By the winter of 1944 the medical services on the mainland improved and the Partizans ceased to evacuate their sick and wounded to Italy. A few months after Father left, the hospital in Grumo had shrunk to half of its original size. Eventually Mother, with me in tow, returned to Dalmatia where she accepted a new appointment in the Shibenik hospital.

Ljubljana had just returned to Bari from its third journey to the Dalmatian coast. However, the British command decided to act on two formal complaints; one from the Italians and the other from the Yugoslav pre-war owners of the ship. After it had confiscated the liner, the Italian government sold it for cash to an Italian shipping company. The Italian shipping line suggested that if the Yugoslavs had any issues to settle, they had better talk with the Italian Government. In the meantime the company requested that the *Ljubljana* be returned to them as the ship' s "legitimate" owners. At the same time the original owner of the ship who had immigrated to London also petitioned the British Command for the return of his ship. The British were in a bind. They took no official position as to who was right or wrong but, as the legitimate occupying authority, they had to do something. Eventually they told the captain that he and the

crew could stay on the ship but until further notice, the ship should not leave the harbor.

Earlier the British simply ignored the ship while permitting it to sail away on its own recognizance. Now the ship would not only sail at its own risk but also against specific orders. And orders from the British Navy could not be taken lightly. When in 1941 France made its own tenuous peace with the Germans and formed the "free" Government in Vichy, the French Navy found itself in a difficult situation. The peace agreement called for neutralization of these ships but everybody knew that eventually the Germans would try to take over the fleet. A few major French ships sailed off to an African port to put some distance between themselves and the Germans. But having accepted the terms of capitulation, the French Navy was not interested in further battles against Germans. As soon as the French arrived in Africa, the British lined up an awesome flotilla outside of the port and gave their former allies an ultimatum—either to join the British or scuttle their ships. When the French refused both difficult choices, the British Navy in cold blood opened fire and sunk the French battleships.

The captain of "*Ljubljana*" was not a great scholar of naval history but as a practical man he knew the British would eventually evict him from the ship. It was now or never. In addition to my mother and me, *Ljubljana* had already accepted aboard about hundred former patients eager to return home. More had been scheduled to arrive from various other hospitals in Italy. The captain asked the British to intercept these transports and send them back. Instead of bothering to meet them on route, the British waited until trucks arrived in the port and then turned them back. This created all sorts of conflicts. Having their hands full, the British gladly accepted the Captain's proposal to let those who already were aboard stay on the ship until next morning. At about midnight the Captain called a general assembly. He had memorized the position of the minefields, would have no difficulties getting out of the harbor and was perfectly willing to take the risk. In fact he and the crew would sail back no matter what. Those willing to join were welcomed, and those who'd rather stay in Italy would be off-loaded at the last moment. As I recall, nobody jumped the ship.

Around three in the morning "*Ljubljana*" quietly sneaked out of the harbor and started its perilous journey. At dawn we successfully cleared the minefields and were about twenty miles from the coast. The next few hours were as tense as they could possibly be. Large groups of bombers repeatedly flew at very low altitude directly over our ship. We found ourselves underneath the meeting point of a huge air fleet. Once it was assembled, the invincible flotilla would fly towards industrial targets in Central Europe. The fact that we were not their primary target did not help that much. If the British commander was so inclined—it would have taken just a radio call and one of those monsters could have easily spared a few bombs to dispose of us. Facing an airplane on the ground is bad enough, but coping with it on a ship is much worse. There are no bushes to hide behind, no ditches to take cover in. Those minutes when the airplanes kept buzzing over and around the ship felt like long hours. It was a terror that affected me much more than I knew.

Four years after the war I went to watch one of those Hollywood apotheoses of wartime heroism. This one included some real footage of a convoy's antiaircraft combat. Shaking, I had to leave the theater and naval warfare was added to the growing list of movies I would never see again. I carefully avoid movies about war, oppression, hopelessness, and injustice. Only twice in my entire life did I experience short bouts of depression. The first was after viewing "The Seventh Cross" a horrifying movie about the escape from a Nazi camp. A good ten years later somebody tricked me into seeing *The Garden of the Finzi Continis*. Watching the plight of Jewish teenagers who were growing up in the oppressive isolation sent me again into a depression. And after seeing *Dr. Zhivago* with all its wandering, lost and miserable people, I pretty much decided that for the rest of my life I'd stay out of movies which I cannot bear. No, thank you, I do not need soul-wrenching spectacles. Forget the films with what the Supreme Court calls "redeeming social value!" I have seen enough misery to serve me a lifetime.

The rest of the trip on the *Ljubljana* was uneventful. We landed in Split and joined Father in Shibenik. The war was winding down. In May 1945 soon after it had been liberated, my parents returned to Zagreb, but I stayed on to complete the fourth grade of the high

school in Shibenik. Given the rigidity of the school system in old Yugoslavia this was a good move. Nobody could craft his own curriculum and unless they failed a year, all students were expected to progress in a similar manner. There was no use pleading with teachers to let me go at a faster pace. It simply was not done. Instead I pretended to be a year older and claimed I had completed the third, not the second, grade in 1941. Sorry, I neither had the diploma nor the birth certificate on me. The principal enrolled me in the fourth grade in the middle of the term but made it abundantly clear that a failure to catch up with others would cost me the year.

In Shibenik I finally gave up my "freedom fighter" mentality. It dawned on me that I had lost four years of high school. The thought of finishing school at twenty-two instead of eighteen years of age was equally painful, as was the prospect of sitting the next six years in classes with much younger children. I worked very hard in Shibenik, enjoyed learning new things, and eventually I returned to Zagreb with the fourth year diploma in my pocket. Nobody later asked for the third year certificate. Nevertheless I was still well behind the normal pace; there were four more classes to finish before I could graduate.

The town of Shibenik goes back to Roman times. It grew around a remarkable natural harbor at the mouth of the River Krka. The river carved out a small and deep inland bay from which it drains through a fjord into the Adriatic Sea. Before it reaches the sea, the deep fjord meanders about two miles between high cliffs, that fall straight into the water and leave no room for a foothold. Once a boat starts a journey through the Shibenik channel, it had better finish it. The channel protects the inner bay from winds and on the seaside of the fjord, eight little islands act as natural wave breakers. The town proper is located about eight hundred yards directly across from the fjord and the inner bay in front of it is so calm, that the city's entire four miles-long waterfront serves as a harbor. The town evolved around a narrow strip of land at the base of a hill that is probably no more than five hundred feet high, but was nevertheless deemed ideal for a fortress. The fortress of Saint Ann has a commanding view of

the fjord and of the road descending on the town from mountains. On the sea end of the fjord another large fort, the fortress of San Nicholas, arises straight from the sea. Its 150-foot high walls dotted with artillery emplacements and observation posts fully control the entrance to the fjord. The position of Shibenik was important enough to cause the king of Naples, the king of Hungary and the Republic of Venice to fight over it. But its fortifications were so formidable that Venice, which ruled the Adriatic Sea, could not take it by force. It took a popular revolt against the feudal lords in Shibenik, followed by a ruthless suppression in the name of the Hungarian king, to destabilize the situation. Eventually the citizens of Shibenik petitioned Venice to become a Venetian protectorate.

During the renaissance Shibenik developed remarkable architecture and a vivid cultural life. Adorned by sculptures, carved doors and numerous ornamental windows, the Shibenik cathedral built by Jure the Dalmatian was as beautiful as it was impressive in scope. The city had one of the older Dalmatian theater houses, nicely decorated in gold and red brocade, but with no more than two hundred seats. When I landed in Shibenik, many old buildings were badly neglected but among them one could easily find reminders of past glory. Long deserted by their former noble owners, badly treated by weather and by their more recent plebeian inhabitants, many dilapidated buildings still featured beautiful details of their grand old facades.

To me the beauty of Shibenik was in its narrow streets, in its remarkable open waterfront, its people and in its perpetual holiday atmosphere. The whole town had less than fifty thousand inhabitants—there was no space for more. The citizens kept the old city reasonably clean. They had to. The well-polished centuries-old paving stones in the narrow streets would instantly expose any unwanted piece of dirt. Between the hills and the inner bay, Shibenik had very little space to develop, which accounted for the lack of linearity in the old town. The narrow streets meandered in every direction and were full of surprises. Behind each corner there was a new vista but, more importantly, behind every bend one could in a second be flattened by carelessly running youth.

Centuries ago Shibenik must have had some clever city planners, as the town never encroached upon its shores. The entire city had

been separated from the inner bay by a long flat walkway. I suspect most of the wide seafront had been artificially reclaimed from the bay and the fairly straight, palm-dotted thoroughfare provided a great contrast to the old city. One could walk with ease on the seafront but as far as citizens were concerned, the old city was the place to be.

The Dalmatians are sociable people and also creatures of habit. As all other seaside cities, Shibenik maintained the traditional institution of *Corso*. In Shibenik well-dressed young people would converge at sundown on a specific area, where for the next two to three hours, they'd walk back and forth. Constantly pacing across the limited space they'd chat among themselves, exchange greetings with others and only occasionally would they interrupt the perpetual motion long enough to hear the newest gossip. One walked to see and be seen. Boys and girls would form separate small groups. Boys frequently engaged in elaborate plans to intercept girls. This was by no means easy. The girls routinely walked arm in arm and the beauties in the center were invariably flanked on the sides by the less fortunate girls. There was safety and justice in the *Corso* rules. To divert his flame from the prescribed path towards a coffee house or to poorly lit benches along the shores, the suitor had to invite the whole group, including the homely girls. Nobody fooled anybody. As soon as a group disappeared out of sight, spies were sent to check on the progress and report back. And if next evening a boy and a girl did not show up for the walk one could easily put two and two together. A deal had been struck the previous evening and somewhere a twosome was taking a private look at the stars.

The *Corso* in Shibenik bordered on silly. In other towns the miles-long path wove its way under the palms next to the sea, but Shibenik had very little space to spare. Somebody with a good sense of humor must have given the name *Cale Larga*, the "wide street," to the main walking strip of Shibenik. The street was so narrow that at peak hours it could not accommodate the *Corso* and most of the walking took place on *Poljana* (the Field), a two hundred by one hundred yards paved square in front of the theater. Peopled mulled back and forth on the Poljana and when they reached one end, they'd execute a complex turnaround mxaneuver. The turnaround was particularly elaborate

for girls who paced the *Corso* holding their friends' arms. Of course they could have broken the bond and each turn around on her own axis but that would have been too simple. So with a lot of ooh's and aah's, the girls pivoted around the anchoring person on the side or in the center of the row and fanned out. Following the laws of physics, the girl on the end would spin around at a high speed screaming with joy and feigning surprise. And it was even more fun if the maneuver swept an innocent bystander off his feet.

Corso was also a good place to organize social events. As we walked around we'd discuss politics, school, girls, and of course, also what we should do next. Since stopping another group would be impolite, the exchange had to be short and to the point. I was quite good at it.

"The day after tomorrow, two of us, swimming, afternoon?" I would say.

The answer could be either "Fine," or "Nothing doing," or" We'll see."

The *Corso* system of communication had a few clear advantages. First of all, one could disregard such a fleeting inquiry and nobody would object. And second, the word to one group was also an advertisement to the others.

If the initial answer was "fine," next time around both groups would stop to work out details. But if the original response was "We'll see," something like "Talk to Mandich" might be the next message. If Mandich did not care to swim, our request had been passed to others and more likely than not, somebody from yet another group would express interest.

On the Poljana we arranged to go to movies, theater, dance halls, or concerts. It all looked so innocent and pleasant but the *Corso* also had its dark side. *Corso* was a place for constant evaluation of other people's behavior. I learned the hard way how brutal the passion stemming from the *Corso* could be.

~

Previously when I got into a new town I routinely reported to the City Command but in Shibenik I was told to get in touch with the

Shibenik, 1945. I am offering thanks to citizens for their presents to the hospital

local youth organization. After I introduced myself, the city secretary of the "The League Of Antifascist Youth" asked me, without going into any detail, to come to an evening meeting. There I sat in front of a small group of grim people. I expected to partake in a meeting of the youth organization but some participants in the session looked well over thirty.

"Comrade Julius," said an old-looking fellow, "I am the secretary of the Communist Party in Shibenik and it is my pleasure to welcome you to the city."

He said the right words but he looked everything but pleased. In fact the whole atmosphere was quite funereal. However, I knew how to respond.

"Thank you comrade for telling me who you are. I appreciate your confidence." In 1945, the Communist Party was still a secret organization. It took about five years before the Party gave up its atavistic conspiratorial ways.

I wondered what was on his mind.

"Well comrade, we have decided to promote you to the position of a regular member of the Communist youth organization," said the sullen and deadly serious semi-young man. It never crossed his mind that I might not want to join. Truth be told, in 1945 I was still impressed with the movement and willing to join but the proceedings in Shibenik were typical of the way the Communists handled people. There really was no choice: you were "promoted" whether you liked it or not. Refusing an offer was at best tantamount to giving up a good job or, in my case, not getting the permit to enroll at the university. And in the worst scenario one might end up in jail.

"I am honored and delighted to serve," I intoned, choosing just the right expected words. But the solemn atmosphere got on my nerves and I wanted to get out of the room as soon as possible.

"What do I do next?" I hesitated for a moment and realizing he did not introduce himself by name, I repeated the sentence: " What do I do next, Comrade Secretary?"

"You will meet Comrade Bujas tomorrow and he will take it from there," said the secretary. "We will now have a Party cell session and you are free to leave."

"What a pompous ass!" I thought. Free indeed! As soon as he finished the sentence, I was out of there.

Next day I met Bujas, who in essence told me that joining the Communist youth cell would be a piece of cake. Under his leadership the cell met once a week and the agenda focused either on theoretic issues of Marxism or on practical questions of improving students' grades.

"You know the proverb 'First God made his own bread,' don't you?" Bujas said. "Well, that is how I see our responsibilities. Not all members of the cell are brilliant students. But we cannot lead others

if we ourselves are not top students. I will not rest until all members of the cell take their studies seriously."

That sounded good. I was afraid the Communist youth cell would organize mass meetings, lecture about virtues of socialism, and try to regulate all aspects of young peoples' public life. That suited me just fine.

"Julius, you would not be one of those heroes who sleep on their laurels and expect society to reward them with a high school diploma?" asked Bujas.

"Even if I were, I would not admit it. But luckily I am quite eager to get on with my education."

"I thought so," said Bujas and shook my hand.

Bujas did not lose any high school classes during the war and he was a senior in the Shibenik High School. Though he never "went into the forest," Bujas was widely recognized as an effective organizer of the resistance movement in Shibenik. He was an ascetic, calm and self-effacing person with a knack for philosophy. I was attracted to his abstract and complex way of thinking. We started to meet outside the regular cell sessions to discuss literature, philosophy, or generally shoot the breeze.

I considered him a friend but, unfortunately, our frames of reference were very different. Eventually the local conditions forced us into a serious conflict. Bujas could not forget the hard times during the Italian occupation and was very bitter. I came "out of the forest" with a positive attitude and did not carry any grudges. Our conflict centered on two Lajchich sisters. During the Italian occupation of Shibenik the two teenage daughters of a prominent local physician, fearing to miss their best years, did not shy away from associating with the occupiers. They went to parties and danced with Italian officers. Apparently in Shibenik the *Corso* habit did not die during the war and the Lajchich sisters did not mind stopping at the Poljana for a chat with their foreign friends.

As young people kept retracing the same route over and over again, the infatuation of the sisters with the Italian officers became the talk of the town. Soon the classmates started to ostracize the girls but that only made things worse. Teenagers know no reason. The war was far away and in the girls' opinion, the charming benevolent

Italians were poor suffering souls caught against their will in a foreign country. The girls did not realize that amidst a bloody conflict there was no place for neutrality. You were either with or against the enemy. That was the way the wartime cookie crumbled. Unaware of the wider context, the sisters perceived the classmates' boycott as envy of their good fortune. It was a self-fulfilling prophecy. The sisters were marked as enemy collaborators and having lost the companionship of local peers, there was nothing left for them to do but to associate even more with foreigners.

None of that was forgotten at the war's end. The girls were formally indicted but the judge, finding no specific crime and citing the defendants' youth, refused to mete out a sentence. The sisters were released to their parents' custody. Dalmatians are passionate people and when they hate, they hate passionately. The realization that the objects of their scorn had been released to walk the streets of Shibenik brought the collective blood of the local Communist youth organization to the boiling point. We were called to an emergency session. Nobody spoke reason and the proposals ranged from burning their house to beating up the girls until the group finally settled on cutting off their hair. I did not know the girls but the idea that we would organize a public lynching was too much to bear. In retrospect, I should have known better. There was no chance of me stopping them. Expressions of public scorn in one form or other are a deep, if ugly, tradition in Dalmatia. One had only to hear the roaring approval during the performance of one of those Dalmatian or Italian medieval comedies, which poke fun on the out-of-town peasant, to realize that the habit was old and very much alive. The Dalmatians are particularly attuned to peoples' vanity. Though it had justifiable political overtones, the idea of hair cutting was just another in the series of Dalmatian pranks against vain behavior. Not very much different from the conspiracy that the citizens of Split mounted against a particularly pompous Admiral of the Navy whom they drove off the streets by the simple trick that everybody, whether they knew him or not, loudly greeted him by his first name.

Dissent at a Communist youth meeting was unheard of and when I launched a qualified defense of the girls, everybody was stunned, including myself. By that time I had become an accomplished public

speaker. Thundering about the foolishness of the youth, I realized I had gone too far. After all, deep inside I knew the girls had been wrong. In an elaborate change of tune I acknowledged the girls' mistakes but took exception with the tactics. Instead of the hair-cutting I proposed continuation of the boycott and argued this would mobilize the masses, show the girls the extent of the public disapproval and prevent the comrades from breaking the law.

The reference to not breaking the law produced an absolute fury. The leadership was seething at the relative independence of the courts. The usually mild-mannered Bujas took me on.

"Do you realize that the same judge who freed the girls served also as a justice during the occupation? He could have sentenced any of us for a violation of the curfew. And now he uses the same law to protect two whores!"

These were strong words and I realized I was out of my depth. My father taught me objectivity and always to consider both sides of an argument. I never felt so strongly about anything as Bujas felt about the sisters. And if the moderate and wise secretary felt that way, I could barely imagine what the rest of the cell felt.

If I had any doubts about how offensive I was to others, what happened next provided a visual illustration. We held the meeting in a classroom and, by and by, people started to move away from me. First they moved from my bench and then gradually, they emptied the entire side of benches I was sitting on. At the end I was alone. The entire group sat on the other side and in front of them, sternly looking at me, stood Bujas. I felt horrible but I also felt that unless I offered an abject apology, which anyhow would not have helped, I had to continue.

"Comrades," I said, "ours is a lawful country and we must obey the courts. Anybody who thinks otherwise should remember the special courts the Ustashe appointed. They'd accuse, arrest, convict and execute you all in one hour. That's what happens when you take the law into your hands."

"And what law are you talking about?" said Bujas. "The judge abides by the laws of the King of Yugoslavia and those laws are a carryover from the Austro-Hungarian legal system. Nothing in such laws is relevant to what happens during an occupation. We will have

to write new laws but who can wait for that. There is law and then there is justice! But to satisfy you, Julius, we will dispense some formal justice!"

Having said his piece, the future law student proceeded to organize a kangaroo court. In ten minutes the girls were found guilty and sentenced to hair-cutting. Thereafter, things started to heat up. Invoking the principle of the "democratic centralism" somebody proposed that I be forced to personally cut the girls' hair. The democratic centralism, a classic instance of double talk, was the backbone of the communist political doctrine. Once a decision has been made after a "democratic" discussion, any further democracy was suspended. An individual had no right for further dissent. He had to put aside personal convictions and faithfully execute the dictum of the majority.

Luckily for me, Bujas realized the proceedings had taken a very bad turn. Had he ordered me to take up the scissors, I would have refused and he would have had no choice but to expel me from the Communist Youth League, which he was not willing to do. After all, I sat there in uniform with a newly acquired ribbon of the medal for bravery, which had just been bestowed on me for my services in the Trnavac hospital. The secretary, who had not joined an active fighting unit, was loath to undertake such a serious move. He found a clever way out.

"Yes, the centralism rule would indeed call for Comrade Julius to execute the deed if so ordered," he said, "but why should we entrust this task to somebody who did not grow up in Shibenik, a foreigner, as it were. It is a local matter. We are aggrieved, we witnessed the injustice and we will take our revenge. I will suggest that Comrade Julius does it only if there are no volunteers."

There were plenty of volunteers and the next day, the poor girls' hair was so badly chopped that the local barber had to shave the remnants off their heads.

The incident soured my relationship with Bujas and with the entire Communist youth cell. I missed the next two meetings but the school year was coming to an end and I knew the cell would stop functioning during the summer recess. Both Bujas and I were leaving town, he for law school and I back to further high school studies in

Zagreb. We met only once when he handed me the letter of "characteristics." These letters, which described a person's behavior, were obligatory when a Youth Party member moved from town to town.

"Now look," Bujas said, "what went on in the last meeting was ugly and I would just as soon forget it. Unfortunately everybody knows about it and I cannot ignore the conflict. Yet it is not my intention to hurt you. I made a reference to it in the letter but in a way that should not do you harm. But be ready, you will have to do some explaining."

When we shook hands, Bujas looked quite drained and sad. I knew he wanted to make amends but there was no time. In a week we both left town.

The Catch-up Game

(Zagreb, 1945-1947)

With the certificate of graduation from the fourth grade of high school in my pocket, I caught a military truck to take me from Shibenik to Zagreb.

In spite of four years of war, Zagreb did not look that much different. Our truck had just passed over the Sava Bridge and, as if nothing happened in the meantime, there stood the blue streetcar on its customary short break before it turns back to the city. To our left, Father's favorite restaurant on the bank of the Sava River, the Repush, appeared to be in full working order. I remembered the good meals we had there before the war and our elaborate bathing expeditions from Vrapche to the banks of the Sava in Zagreb.

As the truck worked its way into the town I saw no evidence of war. The traffic was reasonably heavy, people strolled on the sidewalks and not one building had been destroyed. Zagreb had managed to sail almost unscratched through four years of hostilities. But the town, like its people, had aged a bit. Nowadays when a visitor returns to a town after a longer absence he will find signs of rejuvenation: new skyscrapers, reconfigured neon signs, retouched facades and old buildings cleverly rehabilitated for new use. While spared the physical damage of the war, Zagreb stagnated and aged a bit. Every building became a shade grayer, every monument acquired a bit more patina and most dilapidated were the large wooden entrance doors to buildings. Even with good care wood will show its age. Back

in the summer of 1945 the crooked, warped doors with their unkempt handles eloquently reminded the visitor that the town had fallen on hard times.

Sitting in the middle of a large square, devoid of flowerbeds to distract the view, the magnificent National Theater had aged even more than other buildings. Diagonally across on the Roosevelt Square my old high school was in equally bad shape. The park in front of the building had been ruined. The school, one of the largest buildings in the town, remained impressive but a lonely grayness had replaced its previous grandeur.

As a Partizan I used to daydream of my triumphant return to the liberated City. When it finally happened, instead of exhilaration, I was overcome by sadness. At sixteen years of age I got the first taste of the unpleasant sensation so characteristic of later encounters with old friends not seen for a long time. As you search for the remnants of the familiar face and see him going through the same process, you realize the irreparable damage of years. Everybody is getting just a bit closer to the end of the line. Amazing but true; in my teens, standing on the bed of the truck that brought me back to Zagreb I had morbid thoughts about aging and dying. That's what a war will do to you!

The road took us to a narrow street. On the entire right side, as far as the eye could see, stood the long wall of a military compound. Constructed of solid brick, the edifice was tall enough to maintain the delusion of secrecy so characteristic for the military all over the world. All of a sudden, two formidable explosions shook the truck and it came to a full stop. Looking for cover, arms at the ready, we jumped down. As I tried to find out where the fire was coming from somebody yelled, "Look at him." In front of us stood a sentry. The young conscript was trembling and with sheer panic in his eyes, he drew the gun in our direction. As we rolled to the safe side of the truck the driver put an end to the tense confrontation.

"You idiots," he said, "had you never heard an engine backfiring before?"

Well, we did not. At least not from that particular truck. At no point on the long trip had the truck ever backfired. The freak incident in front of the military stockade in Zagreb could have ended in

a tragedy. Luckily the inexperienced soldier had enough civilian mentality to ask the logical question before he shot. Why in the world, five months after the end of hostilities, would somebody mount an attack on his stockade? Had a veteran seen a group of armed people jumping off a truck, he would not have hesitated to open deadly fire. On my first day in Zagreb, I came closer to facing death than at any time during the war.

After the incident I had enough of the truck and proceeded on foot to the Rebro hospital where my parents had set up residence. Father and Mother met me with three pieces of good news. First: I would be officially "demobilized" from the Army with the rank of lieutenant, which entitled me to immediate and extended benefits. Right away I would get a lump sum of "separation" money and in the long term, the war years would count double towards retirement benefits. Second, we'd soon be moving into an apartment in the town. Third, a special high school had been organized for students who had lost time during the war. It would be possible to take two classes in one year.

The significance of early retirement benefits was lost on me but the rest was good news indeed. Paying money to former soldiers to help them return to civilian life was a splendid idea—theoretically speaking. On a practical level it meant very little. There was absolutely nothing to buy; the shops in Zagreb were empty. I itched to somehow put to use this first-ever independently earned money. The City Command also gave me a large amount of the most desirable "R-number-one-forest-worker" food coupons. With these coupons, I could have purchased a decent amount of staple food but the free meals in the hospital were reasonably good and I had no reason to buy more food. Nevertheless, as a child looking for miracles, I kept going from shop to shop. What they offered I needed as much as a hole in the head: candles, wicks for kerosene lamps, chains, axes, and various pots and pans. Commerce was never my strong suit. I should have bought some merchandise, taken it to villages and traded for other goods. Instead I kept looking for the impossible. Eventually my perseverance paid off. I found a merchant who had stashed away some "Kiki" candies. Made by a local factory, these chewable, soft lemon-tasting caramels in their characteristic wax

paper wrapping had once been my favorite sweets. Having paid a huge sum for a bag of candies I sat on a bench under the old plane (*platanus*) trees in front of the Academy of Science and did not get up unitl the bag was empty. The memory of that half-hour with half a kilo of "Kikis" under the shady trees served me well for a long time. Years passed before I could again engage in sheer luxury consumption.

The food supplies were replenished reasonably soon after the war, but it took a long time for the shops to fill up with nonessential merchandise. The process was slow and on purpose discriminatory. It was not that there were no luxuries or that they were too costly. Some shops were full of merchandise. Under the guise of assuring a normal living standard for foreign diplomats, the Party had carved out for itself special stores. These "diplomatic stores," loaded with luxury items, were off-limits to everybody but a selected elite. There were precious few diplomats in the town. Most had their own sources and did not care to use the special stores. Diplomatic stores were created for the benefit of the Party leadership. The Yugoslav Party emulated the hypocritical and corrupt Soviet regime. One of these days—every Yugoslav worker would live in a paradise, but in the meantime it was the holy duty of the leadership to pamper itself. How else could these leaders fulfill the exalted task of guiding the blind masses in their search of a better future?

This notion of amorphous exploited masses, which are essentially stupid and stand not a chance of success, unless the practitioners of Marx's "scientific socialism" lead them, is the single most important cause of all evils and ills of the world-wide Communist movement. If you ever visit a former Communist country and wonder whether they had embarked on a new course, just listen to the speeches. The doctrine is so deeply embedded that it permeates all walks of life and the malaise is so obvious that it can be diagnosed at first glance. Not so long ago I attended a cardiology congress in Beijing. The Deputy Minister of Health greeted the congress and after some general pleasantries, he informed us that heart disease is of great importance to the Party, government and the masses. There it was, the old Communist jargon with its demeaning order: Party first, then the government and finally the masses. Not people but masses.

It was not a government by the people, for the people. Rather it was "them," the masses and "us," the leadership. None of my American colleagues on visit to China took notice and it was difficult to explain to them why a simple sentence could be so offensive to me. It meant that communism is alive, well and deeply entrenched in China. In a subdued form the Chinese health official exuded the same haughty attitude that was unabashedly overt in 1945 in Zagreb. The privilege of shopping in diplomatic stores became a badge of honor. To the ordinary folks the windows of diplomatic stores were a vivid reminder of the new social order and access to those stores became shorthand for "who is who" in post-war Yugoslavia.

For weeks after the Kiki episode I could not find a thing to buy and finally deposited the money in the bank where, due to devaluation, it lost almost all its value. A good three years later, better things started to show up sporadically in shops. Having some money started to make sense again. In fact those times of relative abundance ushered in their uniquely pleasant psychodynamics. Looking for good items and having inside information became an exciting sport. Appreciated for his connections, a well-informed person was in the driver's seat. He could selectively leak the information to assert an old friendship, use the piece of intelligence to build a new relationship or he could choose to flaunt the knowledge just for the fun of it.

To a pessimist those days were a mark of relative austerity—to an optimist a sign of impending abundance. To everybody these were tantalizing times. It is infinitely more pleasant to have plenty of money and little to buy than to have little money and plenty to buy. In those days, finding something after a long search was a pleasure and one was instantly ready to blow the money. Today the lengthy comparison of alternatives and the concern whether the money was wisely spent tends to spoil the joy. In those first few years after the war, one could turn the irritating off-and-on flow of imported goods into an exciting search. Occasionally the results were hilarious. By the end of my first year in the medical school my friends Mijo and Dina Rudar decided to marry. As their best man, I eagerly set out to hunt for a memorable present. I learned from a reliable source about a new shipment of Czechoslovakian glassware to a downtown shop and bought a beautiful crystal pitcher with eight glasses. Next day I

went to the big party in Mijo's village. I came early and the gift was much admired by everybody. Soon the next guest arrived and unveiled an identical crystal set. That present, too, was admired and appreciated. When the next three guests brought the same crystal set, the Rudar's somehow managed to hide their disappointment. After a while everybody realized how ridiculous the whole thing was. In a city of 300,000 people, there was nothing else to buy. The crystal sets became the joke of the evening, each additional one causing a louder roar of laughter. By the end of the evening my friends were stuck with eight identical sets. It was useless to return the merchandise. The shop had nothing else to offer in exchange. But everybody was in a good mood and the crystal sets provided just the right comical background for a joyful wedding party.

~

After a while, Mother, Father and I moved into a spacious, three-room apartment in the center of town. Mother started to visit people with whom she had four years earlier left our belongings for safekeeping.

We left our bedding and finery with the Medvedec family in Vrapche. Throughout the occupation they refused to believe rumors of our deaths and four years later they handed back two huge trunks. Nothing was missing. "I could not sell the contents, they were not mine," said Mr. Medvedec. For him this was a matter of elementary logic. Yet the temptation must have been enormous. As the years of lost contact dragged on, the living conditions in occupied Croatia became quite harsh. Why not use the sweaters when the winter was so cold? Or sell something to buy food? The Medvedec family, a childless couple, he a doorman and she a nurse in the Vrapche hospital, could better afford to be impeccable than some larger families which had put to use some of our stuff. And we understood that. Though the circumstances had forced them to use or sell some of our possessions such families were nevertheless glad to see us and readily returned whatever was left. Mother declined all offers of compensation and expressed our sincere thanks.

Some people, however, either sold our stuff or were unwilling to return it. Take the example of MT, a well-paid administrator of a large commercial enterprise in Zagreb who lived a good life largely untouched by the events. The Germans came to his apartment, he said, and removed all our possessions. None of his and all of ours, including two elegant golden Pelikan fountain pens! Amazing! Somehow the Germans knew exactly what belonged to us and somehow he was able to give them our hidden assets without getting into trouble for abetting Jews. What could Mother do when the man told her such a lie with a straight face? She turned around and walked away. Mother had paid a price for an important practical lesson: next time she would be better equipped to tell a friend from a con man.

But the worst were the virtuosos of self-deception. Those with selective amnesia who could not for the life of them remember that we ever gave them something for safekeeping. And then there was Aunt Marica, the lady who "helped" us pack up to move from Vrapche to Stanchich and who "bought" our "excess" silverware at a bargain price. She shamelessly attempted to resurrect the old "friendship." Marica paid a visit to let us know how glad she was to see us back. But as far as she was concerned, a deal remained a deal. She never offered to return or sell the things back to us. And she convinced herself that she had sincerely helped us in our time of need.

Mother was well-known for her short temper. However, forced to face these major league offenders, this straight-to-your-face lady found herself speechless. She was simply outplayed. Arguing with somebody who'd lost a common sense of morality was like preaching to the deaf. In one instance, however, when the Germans really had taken away our possessions, Mother proved to be her old persistent and resourceful self.

When we joined the guerrillas, the Ustashe confiscated our possessions. All the paintings had been left on the walls but our furniture was distributed among the friends of the new regime. Mother somehow managed to trace our dining room furniture and the piano to a union hall in Dugo Selo. The union had taken over the hall lock, stock and barrel from an Ustashe-sponsored Croatian nationalist organization. The president of the union had no use for the chairs

and the table but he did not want to return the piano. As far as this old Communist was concerned, the contents of the hall were properly confiscated from the enemy and who owned them before the war was none of his business. He deployed all sorts of delaying tactics. How could Mother prove this was her piano? Weren't there many similar ones around? In fact nobody was selling similar pianos in Yugoslavia. The large concert-size piece made in Austria had been purchased as a wedding gift while Mother and Father resided in Prague. But such a fine point could not possibly be explained to the union man. Instead Mother pointed out the idiosyncratic features of the piano, which only someone familiar with the instrument could tell: how the left pedal had been broken, that one leg had a replacement wheel. As a dramatic finale she demonstrated that one solitary key was out of order. No matter how hard you hit it barely produced a sound.

The president could not continue delaying and he finally openly showed what was on his mind. The old time doctrinaire Communist had fallen victim to his own propaganda. For a moment he had forgotten that the victory against the Germans had not yet ushered in Communism in Yugoslavia.

"I do not care to whom these things belonged before the war. They are now peoples' property," he said. "I will let you take the dining room set; it just takes up space, but we need the piano. Music is important to the working class. It's just not right that you should take away an instrument which so many others could enjoy. You people will have to give up some of your petit bourgeois attitudes about property. Technically it may have been yours but between us antifascists such a distinction should be a mute point. The piano is the centerpiece of our educational efforts and I will keep it. Of course you could easily donate the piano to the union. And before you refuse my offer I suggest you had better think it over. Such a selfish attitude would not be in keeping with the rank you are holding in the People's Army. Instead of praise, I would have to write a strong letter of criticism to your Party organization."

There in the nutshell was the whole Communist technique. First you classify somebody as an "anti-fascist"—a term that connotes both praise and condemnation. In the terminology of the Yugoslav

Communist Party, an anti-fascist was a fellow traveler close enough to be called upon in times of need, but definitely not a member of the inner circle. While slightly appreciated, an anti-fascist nevertheless remained a "member of the masses." After the union leader set himself on a higher plane from my mere anti-fascist Mother, he applied the rest of the formula in short order: call on people's higher instincts, shame them into cooperation, praise them a bit and threaten a lot.

Mother was too enraged and the union leader too clumsy for the formula to work. During the war my parents became members of the Communist Party, an honor they could not refuse and a nuisance they could not avoid. The president's threat was by no means trivial. Mother well understood the impact of a letter of condemnation

The Party rigidly enforced attendance at the meetings of its cells—not when the need arose, but regularly as clockwork once a week. The routine was as boring as it was unavoidable. The sessions were divided into "practical" and "theoretical." Generally there was enough content to conduct the practical sessions about the function of the hospital. But the leaders were hard-pressed to organize discussions of the Communist doctrine or to dwell on the finer points of the contemporary political situation. Instead they preferred to replace one of theoretical sessions with a session of self-criticism. During these unbearable sessions members had to stand up and, one by one, say something negative about their recent actions. In the Roman Catholic Church, the confessions are at least secret and there is the guarantee of absolution. These painfully public self-criticism sessions held no promise of absolution. On the contrary, the comrades were only too happy to add insult to the self-inflicted injury. And in a classical *catch 22*: a person could not defend himself lest he be accused of being insufficiently self-critical. If anybody ever doubted that communism is a religion, he should have attended just one of these sessions. Christianity and Communism share the same suspicion of the individual. Nobody can possibly be good enough; people are born selfish and everybody is a sinner. After the war when the tension of the military conflict gave way to the triviality of daily life, the self-criticism sessions turned from demeaning to disgusting and from boring to grotesque, dog-eat-dog exercises.

Mother must have been a rotten-to-the-core petit bourgeois. Unimpressed by the prospect of criticism, she returned to the union hall with a group of loyal patients to take back all our possessions. In a fit of bravado, true to her pugnacious Hungarian heritage, she left behind a terse note acknowledging the "receipt" of the items. Recognizing he had no leg to stand on, the union man did not pursue the matter further. Thanks to Mother's persistence we did acquire enough basics to set up our household in the downtown apartment and to start living again as a family.

Djuka shared the apartment with us for about a year. He came back from the Army six months after me. He had been demobilized with the rank of a captain. His wound was still active. As various bone fragments worked their way out to the surface, Djuka had four major surgeries. Finally in Zagreb he got into the hands of Dr. Riesner, a world-caliber thoughtful neurosurgeon. He explained to Djuka, he would pay respect to Isaac Newton. It occurred to Dr. Riesner that all previous colleagues approached the wound from the top. "We've got to make gravity work in our favor and let the wound drain in its natural way, downward." As a neurosurgeon Riesner was well-suited to do what others did not dare: patiently work his way from the armpit past the brachial nerve and blood vessels and from below reach the core of the infection. It worked like a charm. After the drain closed, Djuka was cured for the rest of his life.

Djuka missed just one grade of high school. He made it up and graduated in half a year. Thereafter he enrolled in the law school in Zagreb but, very much involved in other political work, he gave up studies and moved to Belgrade to work on ideological issues in the Central Committee of the Party. Eventually he became attracted to foreign policy and became a leading political commentator for the Belgrade newspaper *Politika.*

Sadly, the warm words about me in Djuka's letters and my appreciation of his wartime bravery failed to bring the two of us much closer. The four-year age difference now loomed as an even bigger gap than before the war. Djuka had very little time for me. He was consumed by two major passions, politics and chasing girls. He noticed me only when he needed some practical help. In tight situations I used to provide him with an alibi. We had practically identi-

Family reunion, Zagreb, winter 1945

cal voices and sometimes when he was out with another flame, I doubled for him on the phone. In the beginning this was fun and a good joke, but I soon realized what sort of havoc Djuka created in these girls' lives. We had a word or two about it and I ceased to answer the phone for him.

Though I hated the thought of it, after a week in Zagreb I went to present my "characteristics" to the City Committee of the Communist Youth League. During and after the war the secretaries of Party cells kept notes about their comrades. A similar practice was adopted by the Communist youth organization. When a member moved to another place, the secretary had to compose a letter of the person's "characteristics" to introduce him to new comrades. I knew the well-sealed letter in my pocket was not entirely complimentary; Bujas told me so in Shibenik. But I could not weasel my way out. Had I not handed the letter in, the Committee would eventually get the mailed version and somebody would look me up. The Communist organi-

zations took no chances. These letters of "*characteristics*" became an instrument of control. Sitting in front of the secretary, I wondered what my letter said about the conflict over the Lajchich sisters.

"So what was this lack of discipline all about?" inquired the secretary in Zagreb. "The comrades in Shibenik say you are a great guy who occasionally does bad things."

Okay, I thought to myself, Bujas did not go into details.

"So the Shibenik cell sent you one of those 'the-comrade-is-timid-and-slightly-bloodthirsty' letters, didn't they?" I said.

"That is right, one of those letters," replied the secretary with a grin all over his face. He got the inside joke and did not take it badly. The joke referred to the ambivalence and legendary illiteracy of the wartime Commissars in charge of writing letters of *characteristics*. It takes good insight and considerable style to describe another person. Failing on both accounts, the careful commissars frequently produced little pearls of useless ambivalence. For those in the know the phrase "the comrade is quiet, timid and slightly blood-thirsty" was a code for the stupidity of the leadership. I took a heck of a chance but it seemed to pay off.

"Come on", said the secretary. "I know Bujas and he is anything but illiterate. He apparently likes you but there is hint of disappointment in the letter. Tell me what was going on in Shibenik."

That was good. I had a chance to explain myself and I presented to the secretary in Zagreb a heavily edited version of events in Shibenik. I acknowledged the girls' obvious guilt and portrayed the discussion as a conflict about the best means to register the justified anger with the judges' decision. I could not afford to test whether the secretary shared my outrage at the lynching by card-carrying members of the youth organization in Shibenik. Too much was at stake. A wrong move and I may have ended in plenty of trouble. If he wished, the secretary could have further tested my allegiance by giving me one unacceptable task after another until I finally refused. Next, I'd be expelled from the youth organization, which would preclude my enrollment in the medical school. Furthermore, I was still very much obliged to the Party for giving us a chance to survive. Whatever their motives may have been, the fact remains that our family survived only because of the Partizan movement. My separa-

tion from the Communists came later, after I had completed my education and when my slow alienation from former war comrades eventually boiled over into an open conflict.

The secretary in Zagreb was an enlightened person. The usual response to a bad letter of characteristics was to keep it secret, lie in wait for the member's next indiscretion and then throw the book at him. Rarely was the problem brought out in the open. If the problem were discussed in public, the usual resolution was to give the member a hard task through which he could rehabilitate himself. The secretary chose yet a third way. He acknowledged that normally he'd give me a special responsibility and that he could easily use my talents, but he received orders from above to facilitate schooling of Partizans who had lost time during the war.

"The more school you lost, the less we are permitted to enlist you for other activities," he said. "So you are to report to the basic organization in the Marshal Tito high school. But don't be surprised if they have nothing for you to do. After all, the school is overcrowded with all sorts of luminaries. Let them have fun. You had better concentrate on studying." It was a sound bit of advice.

I think, but cannot prove, that the secretary did me a great favor. He must have put something benign but slightly damning into my personal folder in Zagreb. From then on I was entrusted only with minor responsibilities, all of them directly related to student activities. Never again was I asked to partake in a strictly political action. Maybe the secretary described me as a "softy." Whatever he did, helped me a great deal.

~

The Marshal Tito High School" was assembled to serve the special needs of students who'd missed their education during the war. A group of excellent professors developed a condensed curriculum cramming two classes of high school into one year. However, the standards remained high and if a student were not able to cope with the intensive curriculum, he would be advised to try his luck in a regular school.

The "Partizan High School," attracted two types of students.

First was a group of somewhat older people who voluntarily joined the Partizan movement, and the other group was a mixture of Jews, Serbs, orphans, and displaced refugees, who could not go to school during the war. Due to common goals, in spite of different ages and different frames of reference, these two groups got along reasonably well. Everybody was keen to get a diploma in time and most students were genuinely interested in acquiring knowledge. I enrolled into the class slated to complete high school grades five to eight in the academic years of 1945/46 and 1946/47. This ambitious goal was made easier by a select group of superb teachers.

Seating assignments were handed out on the first day. I was directed to the first row. The large first bench accommodated four persons. For the next two years my bench mates were Boris Puks, Milovan Domijan and Vinko Guberina. It turned out that we were quite compatible, something that one could have not predicted from our backgrounds. We all wore uniforms but I was much younger than the others. Boris and I were from larger cities in the interior; the other two came from small places on the coast. Boris and I came from families with higher education; the other two had a working class background. Puks and I had a common interest in arts and letters; Milovan and Vinko were hard working, willing to learn but had little time for poetry, philosophy and similar "intellectual nonsense."

In spite of different backgrounds we became a close-knit group. In retrospect, I realize the other two must have had a great deal of inborn tolerance. Boris was difficult and I was at that time a typical teenage overbearing fuzzy-thinking pseudo-intellectual. There was, of course, an underlying basic thread to hold us together. We were ready to work and learn as much as possible. Initially we wore uniforms to let others know we were bona fide former guerrillas. However we soon got the wartime heroics out of our system and the four of us in the *Banca Prima* were the first to shed the uniforms.

"From now on my dear comrades," Boris said, "we are four ordinary swimmers in the scholastic mainstream."

"Come on! You meant to say we are the best swimmers. Then you remembered we are supposed to be modest." I protested.

"I see no reason why we shouldn't be the best but let's wait until

the grades come in. Julius, you are clever but do you have the sitting-flesh? Will your *glutei* listen to what your brain wants them to do?" And before I could respond, Boris was out of the room.

We were right to get rid of the uniform. How a person handles his past tells a lot about his chances in the future. Unfortunately some veterans in our school could not let bygones be bygones. Permanently moored in the past, they drifted into bitterness about the present. They disliked classmates who'd rather not speak about the war, who were unimpressed with past heroics and who preferred personal pleasure to the joys of building socialism. In the USA, Rodney Dangerfield successfully created his laughable "I get no respect" persona. Back in Zagreb some former soldiers felt they were not sufficiently appreciated. But whereas Rodney Dangerfield was funny, our frustrated warriors were mean and dangerous.

It is to our credit that the entire *Banca Prima* came to the defense of a certain Boris Singer. A Jewish boy from Zagreb, Boris sublimated whatever might have bothered him into an incredible passion for jazz. His enthusiasm bordered on mania. He spent hour upon hour with the short-wave radio, scanning various Allied radio stations. With his homework untouched, he used to come to classes red-eyed and seemingly totally exhausted. But as soon as somebody gave him a chance to talk about last night's music, Boris instantly became animated. He'd pucker up his lips into a trumpet, imitate the drums with the palms of his hands, and measure the beat with his upper torso. The poor fellow was probably tone deaf or alternatively he might have been just a poor performer. In any case he did not convert a single soul to jazz. Standing there and politely acknowledging the rendition, we knew there was much more to it than enthusiasm. With the help of jazz, Boris was suppressing demons from his past. If this was what he needed to keep his sanity-so be it. But the performances did not sit well with the old guard Partizans in the school.

First, they affected great concern about Boris' lack of scholarly progress. Singer's case kept coming up over and over again at the meetings of the Communist youth organization. Boris Puks and I tried to stop the nonsense. Taking turns, we argued that the whole issue was immaterial. We could not force him to study, we said, and

no matter what we said, he would do what he wanted. After all he was the one who lost the years and it was up to him to catch up. The other side was not impressed and skillfully pulled out the perennial "bad example" argument.

"Bad example to whom?" asked Boris Puks rather logically. "Who has fallen into the clutches of jazz? Whose studies have slowed down on account of Singer? Just by looking at uniforms, I assume that a large majority of students in this school are comrades. To assume that Singer might have a negative effect on anybody in this room or on any seasoned comrade would be preposterous."

Puks was clever to speak about "comrades" and not Party members. The Party insisted on secrecy. We were not supposed to know who was a member. However, the implication was clear: how could a youngster listening to jazz be a bad example in a school where the Communists had a heavy majority?

Puks' jab threw the secretary off just for a moment but he soon bounced back. This not particularly smart but crafty man was quite dangerous. He had an uncanny ability to twist things and to frame everything as a matter of principle. And once something had been cast as an issue of principle, the doors were open for the secretary to satisfy his need to hurt other people.

Beware of people who see everything as a matter of moral principle. When morality exceeds normal bounds it becomes a perversion. The zealots who never have any doubts and who "know the truth" will "help" to rearrange your life to fit their ideals. Be this religion, politics or a type of diet, these compulsive meddlers share a disregard for the rights of others. Looking down from the high platform of absolute truth they will "save" you whether you wish it or not. When such zeal to improve others evolves in a mean, mistrusting and paranoiac person, the combination is as ugly as it is dangerous. Jovo the secretary, suffered from the "lack of enemy syndrome." Not being able to vent his anger on Nazis he needed a replacement.

And poor Singer presented him with an ideal target. It was not Boris Singer or how he studied or even whether he listens to jazz, Jovo insisted. It was a test case. Can the Communists, or can they not, lead others? Singer's musical improvisations during the recess were to Jovo a challenge and a constant reminder of leadership's failure.

"If you think, comrades, that he does not know what he is doing, you are mistaken," thundered Jovo. "He knows and enjoys every moment of it. Ask him whether he would sing any of the resistance songs or even folk tunes. The answer, comrades, is no! He is not interested in music. No, my friends, he is using western trash to replace patriotism in arts with modern decadence, to make us forget our glorious artistic creativity in favor of alien subversive tunes. No, Singer does not favor jazz-he uses it to promote a cause! And his cause is to make us ashamed of our cultural heritage, to replace it with what only on the surface appears as nonsense. And when you hear him trumpeting jazz, remember that is not what he cares about; it is his music replacing our music. If you do not believe me, just ask him to sing a patriotic song."

Crafty, sick, bastard! It was a good speech. He succeeded in portraying Singer as a malicious influence. From a jazz aficionado, Singer had been promoted into a monster whose hidden agenda was disconnecting the present generation from its anti-fascist and nationalistic roots. Jovo had finally found his enemy! This had the making of serious business. If that line of reasoning prevailed, Singer would have not only been forbidden to listen to jazz, he would have been ordered to sing nationalistic songs instead. "Ask him to sing a patriotic song," Jovo said, and that was not a figure of speech.

I first started chipping away at the edges. How could the secretary assume that people must equally like all types of music? Was it fair to assume that Singer was equally familiar with Partizan songs as with jazz and that he consciously chose jazz? Or was it possible that not singing patriotic songs, far from being a political statement, was a simple matter of taste. After all, if the secretary's logic were extended, all of us who liked patriotic songs should also love the Croat national opera.

"Might I remind Comrade Jovo that the other day he'd told me how much he hated every moment of the opera performance in the National Theater?"

"Mind you," I continued, "I am not imputing any motives. Jovo, you can like and dislike the music as you please. Personally, I thought the opera was marvelous and its music exquisite."

It was a silly discussion but not a bad line to stall for time. The

opera in question was a particularly dense piece of musical writing, its only claim to fame being that it was one of the first Croat operas. There are very good reasons why nobody has ever heard about *Porin* or *Nikola Shubich Zrinjski* while everybody knows Smetana's *Bartered Bride*, written at about the same time by a composer from an equally small Slavic country. However at that moment it suited me very well to extol the virtues of the Croat opera. Jovo had to swallow some of his medicine in more ways than one. If he disliked the opera as a matter of taste then Singer had the right to his own taste. If it was not a matter of taste, the secretary's patriotism could be questioned.

I was quite pleased with my oratorical performance. "You can twist things around and so can we, my dear fellow. See how you deal with this one," I thought to myself.

Boris Puks got the idea and chimed in. "Yes, the music of the opera was fine but the libretto was horrible," he maintained. "How could anybody enjoy the piece when the story was so stupid and contrived?"

Someone else took the hook and started to argue about the content of the opera. He wondered whether at that point in history it was particularly wise to revive the Croat nationalism. During the war it was fine to call on national anti-fascist feelings but presently, with Marshal Tito continuously stressing the need for brotherhood and unity, such nationalistic themes could prove counterproductive. Maybe our secretary's dislike for the work was not on musical, but on political grounds?

We did well. The discussion was way off target. Instead of debating about Singer, we became deeply involved in a general consideration of art and politics. Jovo finally reined in the discussion and the meeting was adjourned without specific conclusions about the jazz maniac.

We knew Jovo would not give up, particularly since his new enemy appeared to have collaborators from within Jovo's own organization. Our nasty secretary had only one emotional connection to the world: hatred. He needed to fill up the post-war emotional emptiness with a new tension. Like a bloodhound, he was bound to pursue the lead. And then, quite unexpectedly, Jovo's case got a great boost.

Radovan Zogovich, an old-guard Montenegro Communist intellectual had just written an article about western music. I suspect, he too, needed an enemy. Zogovich was an accomplished polemicist, a leftover from the small group of Communists who, before the war, on the fringes of Croatian and Serbian literature, engaged in written debates. Zogovich wrote a masterpiece diatribe about the emerging music of the west in post-war Yugoslavia. The paper ridiculed the decadence of the music and in a number of clever reiterations he kept coming back to the song *Chattanooga Choo-choo*. Why would anybody care about the Chattanooga choo choo? Did the local singers know what it meant? Should Yugoslavs be sentimental about a defunct train in a far-away country when things back home. . . . and so on.

Zogovich was not an idle journalist; he was in charge of cultural affairs in the Central Committee of the Yugoslav Party. The gist of the piece was almost identical to Jovo's thinking. There was an organized onslaught on the national heritage. Zogovich made no bones about his disgust for the youth that so readily accepted the western trash. Overnight, the whole western musical opus had been branded as politically and culturally undesirable.

In a classical miscalculation, the Communists decided to launch a direct assault on the alien culture. Instead of capitalizing on the youth's love of music, as many clever Catholic priests did, the Communists took jazz head-on and failed miserably. For the next two years the music halls in large cities became battlegrounds for guerrilla warfare. The jazz aficionados-the players and the public—did not give up. Thrown out of one dance hall, they moved to another one and the audiences followed. Semi-secret dance sessions were organized and jazz bands kept mushrooming. Having started in all innocence without political goals, the musicians and their entourages soon realized that they indeed had a political issue on their hands. It was called freedom of expression. Many of them got badly beaten up, some instruments were destroyed, but this only hardened their resolve.

After a few years the Party threw in the towel. And, as is so frequently the case, as soon as jazz became commonplace in record stores and on the radio, the interest waned. One after another, the

dance halls started to close. Yugoslav leaders had learned the important lesson—confrontation does not win a cultural war. Only a better and more appealing alternative can attract followers. The only alternative the Yugoslav authorities offered was the police.

Unfortunately for us, back in 1946, the vindicated vicious secretary was ready to extract his pound of flesh. The time had come to look for a compromise.

If this book ever sees the light of day, somebody may accuse me of "relativistic ethics," a dirty phrase connoting a lower form of life without ethical standards. But I am proud of what we repeatedly succeeded in doing in Yugoslavia. By making compromises, we helped good people, prevented some of the egregious excesses and in a small measure introduced some element of accountability for the decision-makers.

To thwart Jovo, we found a compromise and simultaneously launched a preemptive action on Singer's behalf. At the next meeting Puks self-critically admitted how both he and I were wrong in not understanding the depth of the problem. Comrade Jovo was right. It was therefore appropriate that we correct our mistakes by some concrete action. We had solemnly undertaken to work with comrade Singer. We guaranteed that in the future he would not bother other classmates with his renditions of jazz, and expressed our optimism that comrade Singer would improve his scholastic performance.

On the surface we won by taking Singer out of Jovo's hands, but we knew he'd not be satisfied until he had humiliated Singer. Rehabilitation was the least of his concerns. He wanted revenge. That was the Party way—drag the guy through public self-criticism, have him make abject apologies, isolate him like a leper and constantly monitor whether he had changed his ways. However instead of isolating him, we claimed that we would be working with Comrade Singer, which included joining him for evening sessions of jazz. Not because we liked jazz but because we understood that Singer, whose mouth would be soon shut, had a need to share his kind of music. And he truly could have done with some help in his studies.

Having organized everything else, there was one last unfinished piece of business on the way to full rehabilitation of Comrade Boris. He had to offer a public apology. Eventually, just as we were leaving

for recess, Singer got up in front of the class and in a few sentences explained that he had no political intention and was sorry if he caused any trouble. We all understood it was a formality.

Jovo was fuming. How could we, he wanted to know?

How could we what, we wondered? Singer's act was spontaneous and we could not prevent him from doing what he thought was right.

"But it should be done in front of the whole school!" Jovo insisted.

"Well it was," I explained. "We posted the information about his regret on our class bulletin board for everybody to read."

During the next session, Jovo suggested Singer's case was still open. We agreed and indicated we'd be delighted to report back on his progress. Jovo kept going on, not realizing he had lost support. Everybody else was tired of the jazz enthusiast's story. Finally, during the youth cell meeting, somebody got up and suggested Jovo needed to take a self-critical view of his actions. That was the end of it. We had beaten him at his own game and snared him in the nastiest trap of them all. If he protested against self-criticism, the secretary would fail to show proper revolutionary humility and if he said yes, he would open the door for the humiliating procedure of a public self-critique. During a self-criticism session, a person could not simply say he was wrong. At least an hour had to be spent on the case. He'd first have to restate the wrong position, then acknowledge he was utterly and hopelessly in error and propose some remedy. It was a long well choreographed act, false in substance but true in its dehumanizing humiliation of the individual. We did not witness Jovo's *mea culpa* since he was a Party member. But I know it happened. There were enough of his peers among us to bring up the issue and enjoy his pains at the Party cell session.

~

In the second year of the "catch up" high school in Zagreb I learned to cope with the huge workload and found some time for leisure. Once a month I took off a weekend to visit my friends in Stanchich. I'd show up in the village without any advanced arrangements. In the

city this would be considered very impolite and I suspect I might have, to a certain degree, also violated the village etiquette. But my friends in Stanchich had no telephones, and it would have taken an extraordinary effort to notify them in advance. Furthermore, they did not mind some interruption of their weekend routines. Saturday was a working day and if they had to stop working in the fields to entertain me, so be it! And Sunday was a rest-with-the-family but somewhat boring day. An excuse to leave children and women behind in order to entertain "Stevica," the little Stevo, was in most instances welcomed. On rare occasion when I interrupted some important activity the friend would tell me so, and I'd look up someone else.

Whereas Zagreb stagnated after the war, the villages around the city made considerable progress. Electricity first reached houses on the sides of the main road and from there started to spread to more distant households. The electric poles on the side of the road and an occasional newly built brick house amid old log homes altered the quaint village panorama. But that was the price of progress. The network of wires dramatically changed the village for the better, but there was also a downside to electrification. Soon radio receivers made their way into every home and in-house entertainment replaced the traditional winter parties. Gone were the evenings when I could walk from house to house in impenetrable darkness, feeling both strangely alone and fully content. And the quiet of the evening had also disappeared. Earlier only when I came close to the house would the dogs interrupt the silence. Now the loud music emanating from the new insomniac's homes hit my ears well I before the dogs could detect me. And I swear that having to compete with the noise from the house, the dogs gave up on barking.

On the positive side, the electricity brought a new daylight to the village. The old houses had small windows and even during a bright day, their interior was engulfed in semi-darkness. A visitor stepping in from full sun would grope around hoping to adjust to darkness. And even when his eyes had fully accommodated, he'd barely see the distant walls of the room. At night the weak flickering, yellowish light from the kerosene lamp would replace the shady grayness of the

day. People's behavior inside the house matched these shades of darkness. Everybody spoke slowly in a low conspiratorial voice and without gesticulation. The overall sleepy atmosphere was conducive to just that—going to bed early.

The abundance of electric light during the day and at night changed peoples' behavior. Conversations became more animated and the villagers showed more interested in everything around them. In northern Scandinavia people's mood reflects the annual light cycle: during long winter nights they hibernate and during summer's everlasting days, their excited behavior borders on the maniacal. Mood changes in the village were not as dramatic. However more things changed in Stanchich than peoples' behavior. The inside of the house gradually adjusted to match the new circumstances. The walls were first adorned with the ubiquitous portrait of Tito but soon ceramic plates, family photos or, much preferred by my hunter friends, paintings of wildlife found their place next to the national hero. The ladies of the house realized that it mattered what the table covers looked like. Thus started a small revolution inside village households. Earlier the tradition of color and artistry around Stanchich was most evident in women's traditional national costumes, colorfully adorned with geometric patterns or hand-knitted flowers. But after a woman's wedding ceremony, they were taken out of mothballs only on festive occasions.

After the electricity came to Stanchich, women's latent creativity found a new outlet. The insides of houses livened up. It was a chain reaction: if the hostess wanted to display her artistry, the bright light would also shine on the floors, furniture, nooks and crannies which, in turn, called for a thorough cleaning of the premises. Eventually all domestic animals, except the dogs, lost their indoor privileges. It is a fact of life that chicken and other poultry cannot be house-trained. It was simpler to evict them than to clean up their mess.

As much as I appreciated the new indoor splendor of Stanchich, I preferred either to stay outdoors or meet friends in vineyards. The vineyard utility houses, *kljets,* retained their old simplicity. The owner would store tools for the maintenance of the vineyard and for processing of grapes in them. Each kljet also had its wine cellar. In

kljets the villagers wined and dined friends or met with neighbors for a leisurely afternoon. If you were invited to somebody's *kljet*, you knew you'd have good time.

On my first visit I went straight to Jozha's house. For a good year after we left Stanchich, Jozha continued to work as the head of his *veza*. In late 1944, when people could join the Partizans by simply walking a few hours into the countryside, his organization became less important. Jozha joined a Partizan unit, distinguished himself as a brave fighter and after the German capitulation, returned to Stanchich. Jozha was sincerely pleased to see me. After he gave his entire family some time to marvel how much I'd grown, we went to Jozha's *kljet*. He had not changed a bit. He was still elegant, thoughtful, and importantly, still dressed as a farmer. I heard he had gotten a good job in Zagreb.

"Oh, it is not exactly a job," Jozha said. "Buddy, I am a student, just as you are. Comrades offered me a very good job in the Central Committee but I do not want to be a full-time politician."

"You are a leader of men. You could be a good politician if you put your mind to it." I interrupted his train of thought.

"Maybe. But during the war I worked with volunteers. That was easy. Now I would have to light the fire in uninterested people. For that you have to be a good orator. I am good at convincing a small group of people but I doubt I could thunder from a dais day in and day out."

Once again Jozha showed his good judgment. He knew his strengths and weaknesses and did not succumb to the lure of a high position.

After a pause, as an afterthought, Jozha said what really was on his mind.

"You say I am a leader. Sure! But only when I know where I am going. Who knows where this whole thing is moving. It is not as simple as it was during the war and I had better stick with what I know."

This was not idle talk. I realized Jozha had some doubts about the direction the Party was taking. I wondered what motivated him to put some distance between himself and professional politicians. But before I could ask further, Jozha continued to talk.

"Furthermore, I like the village life," he said, "That is how I was born. Farming is in my blood. I can't see myself spending the rest of my life in Zagreb. You have been only two years in Stanchich and yet you love to return. Now imagine me!"

"But you told me you are going to school!" I said. "Why do such a thing if you are about to return to your old life."

"Look at him," Jozha complained. "Young Julius thinks that a simple farmer has nothing to learn. Not true my friend."

Seeing me recoil at his implied critique, Jozha tapped me on the shoulder:

"Oh, you shrinking violet—relax! I know what you mean but I did not say I wanted to be a farmer. I said I would like to return to Stanchich and return I will. With my friend's help I found a job compatible with village life. I am learning bookkeeping and how to run a larger enterprise in an area I am familiar with. Since I know something about domestic animals, I will become the director of a modern chicken farm—or better said, a chicken factory."

I was disappointed. I thought that with his good standing with the Party and a stellar wartime record, Jozha could have done much better for himself. I tried not to show what I felt but Jozha could read people's minds.

"This may look like a small thing to you, but it is not. When I am done, everything relating to chickens will change. You know that to this day, kilogram per kilogram, chicken is the most expensive meat you can put on the table. And eggs are expensive too. All because of ineffective farming! We will change the entire scene and I will not rest until chicken becomes the most abundant and the cheapest meat on the market."

Jozha did not exactly retreat into simple village life. He had a vision. He wanted to change things, but chose for himself an achievable and not overly ambitious goal.

"But this might be bad for the village. If you succeed, the low prices of chicken will hurt the farmer." I said to keep the conversation going.

"You mean when I succeed, not if I succeed. And chicken might be the farmers' most expensive product right now but it is also their

most inefficient product. A household has at best sixty hens and a cock or two. They wander around, feed themselves, lay their eggs wherever they wish and come home to roost. With this approach the farmer cannot meet the market demands and that is why the chickens are so expensive. Chicken-growing comes easy and chickens are a lazy farmer's excuse for not doing what he is supposed to—working on the land. No, I will not ruin the village financially. I will change my neighbor's life for the better. Who do you think, will grow the chicken feed for my enterprise? My village! And who will give them a good steady price for corn? Me!"

Jozha got quite excited. "You see, these days nobody is a true farmer. Take my brothers-in-law, the three Selec households. None of them could feed the family if they weren't also holding another steady-income job. However the sideline jobs detract them from paying full attention to farming. I will change that. Stanchich will be protected from yearly variations of corn prices. My factory will give each and every one of them a five-years contract. And guess what else? My enterprise will extend loans for farm machinery to the village."

"So you see, I am thinking of the village." said Jozha after a short pause.

He did! Jozha hit upon the chicken idea not so much to improve his own life as to raise the living standard in Stanchich. He remained a confident leader and it was great to see him in his new role.

"The one darn thing I can't do," he said with a smile," is control the weather. Farming is by nature a cyclic undertaking but every good farmer understands that and does not mind. If I take away their chicken-cane, which presently keeps their noses above the water, some farmers will have to choose. They will either improve farming techniques or opt to take city jobs. Whatever they choose, it will be for the better. It is hard to sit on two chairs. You end up underperforming on both jobs and if you are a decent person you will feel bad about it."

Jozha was a visionary and a reformer. Loath to influence things by political means, he chose to live in the village and watch whether and how his experiment changed the life in Stanchich.

After a while Mato and Franjo Selec came to the kljet. Mato brandished a *demijon* of his best vine and Franjo brought with him some of my favorite smoked cheese. There were no telephones in the village but the word about my visit got around the old oral way. Soon, one by one, old friends showed up, each bringing a selection of their best goodies.

The weather was good and we arranged the tables in front of the *kljet*. Towards the evening about twenty people joined the party. We had a great time eating good food, sipping delicious vine, exchanging war stories and singing whichever song came to mind until well into the night.

"You see, the bastard did not come again!" said Mato.

"There are plenty bastards in this world. About whom are you talking?" I wanted to know.

"Branko Tashler."

"You mean Branko Sruk, the man who married Marica Tashler?"

"Right, but since in that house he wears the skirt and she the breeches, we might as well call him Tashler."

"Maybe he did not get the word that I am here?"

"He got it alright, I made sure that he got it."

"Maybe he is busy? After all, I came unannounced."

"Oh come on Stevica, this is not the first time. Though he is supposed to have been an important Partizan organizer, he stays out of our way. He never joins veterans meetings and keeps to himself." said Mato.

"He is not supposed to have been an organizer. He was. No doubt about that!" Jozha joined the conversation.

"OK, so he was, but he is still a bastard to be so aloof." retorted Mato.

"In short, we do not like him," said Franjo Selec.

I said nothing. This was an evening for fun. We kept singing, chatting, and having a good time. But I made a mental note about the conflict and decided to visit Branko Sruk next time around.

Two weeks later on my way to the village I stopped at Tashler's store to chat with Branko. He was delighted to see me. Marica Tashler, the dragon lady, was also pleasant. Both showed me how they renovated the old premises. Everything got a facelift: their private quarters, the pub, the store and even the utility buildings in their yard. Their private rooms had large windows, the floor was covered with a new oak parquet, and the bathrooms were equipped with modern sanitation.

"Not a small thing," Branko said. "First I had to dig a septic field and then we had to chase after toilet bowls."

"You did not buy one of those exploding things?" I asked.

I referred to the fact that a local porcelain factory, which earlier made plates and tea cups, decided to capitalize on the growing market for toilet bowls and produced its own line of sanitary equipment. The shiny-white new product was very attractive but it had an Achilles heel. While somebody was sitting on them, the bowls would abruptly shatter to pieces! The catastrophe, which inevitably caused serious injuries to a person's sensitive parts, seemed not to relate to the victim's weight. It could happen at any time and to anybody.

"So you know about that," Branko laughed. "Is that what they teach you in school? No, no, these are imported Austrian bowls."

Next, Branko took me to the store that he had equipped with spacious shelves and a giant refrigerator. Branko's and Marica's pub had also been redecorated. It even had a new bathroom with a modern water-flushed toilet.

"Delighted to see how much your standard of living has improved." I said and immediately realized I had misspoken. But it was too late.

"That is not what this is all about." said Branko. "Yes, we benefit, but Marica and I are in the business of setting an example. I want the village to see that it can be done, right here in the middle of nowhere. There is no reason in the world why instead of using outhouses, my neighbors should not dig septic fields. Everybody already has or is about to get electricity. My business in wicks, kerosene and candles has been replaced by light bulbs and circuit breakers. I'd love to sell them toilet paper."

"What difference does it make to me?" continued Branko rhetorically. "Not that much. Probably we'd have fewer flies around and generally I'd be more comfortable if my neighbors were just a bit less crude. You see, I refused many good jobs in the City and made a firm decision to live here. Frankly, I do not know why. But as long as I am here, I might as well try to change things around me."

I knew Branko was not bragging about refusing good jobs. Jozha told me that Branko was indeed the highest-ranking Partizan organizer in the region. The two of them worked independently and only vaguely knew what the other one was up to. Branko was in charge of counter-intelligence. By definition his work had to be secret. Consequently, nobody in the village but Jozha knew about his activities. During the war Branko had to be aloof and after the war he continued to keep his distance from others. I wondered why.

"I do think setting an example for others is a good idea. But if you want to influence them why did you sever your relationship with the village veterans?" I blurted out.

In 1947 I was somewhat inarticulate. I meant to pose an innocent question but it came out harsh and almost accusatory. However Branko was not offended.

"Let me correct you," Branko said. "The truth of the matter is that we never had a relationship. During the war I worked alone, under strict orders to ignore others. I knew what they were doing but they did not know a thing about me. So technically I didn't sever any relationship, I failed to establish a new one after the war."

"So why did I not do a better job of relating to them after the war?" Branko continued. "First of all, for a good year after the victory I still had strict orders not to spill the beans. In the meantime all of them, except Jozha, took offense with what they considered my aloofness. When I finally could join them I quickly found out all they talked about was the wartime glory. And frankly, I'd just as soon forget the darn thing. No progress is ever made by looking backwards. Why should I partake in their silly games of one-upsmanship? And now it is too late."

Branko continued with his monologue. "Even if I wanted, I could not become a part of them. They will not accept me, no matter what

I do. And yet I like to live here. So I may as well capitalize on being different and teach them by contrast. That's why I never joined the local reunions and why I eventually dropped my membership in the league of former guerrillas.

"And by the way," said Branko after a short pause, "sanitation and cleanliness is not the only area where I will leave my mark. I will also teach them modern viniculture, whether they want it or not."

I was reminded of the marvelous Burgundy I drank during my bout with typhoid fever and of the efforts by the priest in Brckovljani to introduce new varietals to his parishioners.

"Funny," I said, "that you would attempt what old Mato Kralj always wanted to do. He failed and his trend-setting vineyard had been plowed over. What makes you believe you'll do better?"

"Because I know what I am doing. I will work through the only thing these guys truly understand—their pocket book. With the new French method of sulphuration and clarification, I get a longer-lasting and better tasting product. I offer both the new and old style wines for sale in our pub. The tally is on the wall. Already the sales are three to one in favor of the new wine."

"At the beginning, the villagers held out. In their minds the new wine was 'chemistry,' good only for ignorant city folks. How could this replace the healthy and wholesome old product, they'd ask. But gradually they realized that the new wine gave them less of a hangover and that they practically never got an upset stomach from it. To boot, I tell them how the new wine lasts for years and how it never turns sour. Finally I hit them with the price my wine commands on the market. Just about double than theirs. I know I am winning."

"Yes sir, and I am double winner," continued Branko. "Our store is selling wine-making supplies. You see, I am not a dreamer as the old priest was. I am a practical person."

"By the way, talking won't get us anywhere. Let me fetch a glass of wine from the store. Try it for yourself and you will understand what I am talking about"

When Branko returned with wine and some cheese I started to reminisce about old times and mentioned Djuka's failed sabotage of the transformer station in Bozhjakovina.

"Fools," said Branko. "I knew about their ill conceived plot but could not stop them. Working alone, I had painted myself into a corner. I could not even send word to your father in the hospital. And how could I have had faced your old man if something happened to Djuka?"

His voice trembled, his hand shook, the forehead was sweaty and there was horror in his eyes.

"You really do not like to talk about it. These things still bother you. Right?" I wondered.

"Right, and that is why I do not go to those veteran reunions. They can talk as much as they wish. Those irresponsible brutes! I'd just as soon not be reminded."

Suddenly, I understood Branko's plight. During the war he rose to the occasion, but it cost him dearly. I've come to believe that people are born with a certain amount of emotional energy. Some are blessed with a lot, others have very little, but everybody must be careful how he spends his capital. For all of us, daily living would be an unbearable routine if it were not for the rare intense moments. It does not make much difference whether it is anger, heroism, love, esthetic excitement or professional satisfaction. A person's life is worthwhile only as long as he occasionally succeeds to lift himself to a higher level.

During the war years Branko spent most of the energy he had. In peacetime he became a shadow of himself, an empty shell, a fugitive consigned to an unexciting existence. And he was unable to connect with the past. He'd rather vegetate than be reminded of past fearful moments. Fearless people, the heroes, are an uncommon breed. They draw an emotional "high," a satisfaction from their action and the elation of the moment suppresses in them all other feelings. But if an ordinary and thoughtful person is thrust into a life of heroics, he will suffer, particularly if he is such a cerebral type as Branko was. Branko knew that his own and other people's lives were on the line. He understood how brittle the arrangements were, and knowing that in an instant everything could go wrong was an immense burden to him. His wartime life was a succession of episodes he could not control. He was a well-meaning, decent, soft man, who during the war

had been forced to do a job for which he was not suited. He could not work with the same ruthless disregard for persons involved as the old time underground professionals. Branko cared about people and for that he paid dearly.

After the war, while still licking his old wounds, Branko had embarked on recovery. I was glad to see him giving winery classes and setting an example of modern living standards for others. The old Branko, a man of social conscience, was back in a modified, albeit, low-grade edition. I disagree with the village opinion. Branko was great person, an ordinary guy who once gave his best, and who just started to do good things again.

I kept visiting both with Branko and with my other friends in the village. I never attempted to stop their feud. It would not have worked. Luckily, both parties to the conflict were sufficiently civilized not to force me to choose sides. And that was all I could expect from them.

Stanchich was a lucky place. Two superb leaders returned to live in the village. Jozha and Branko were very different persons. Their motives and methods were different but both left wartime heroics behind them and looked forward to the future. Both eventually succeeded. As Jozha predicted, within a few years chicken became the cheapest meat on the table. And the villagers who preferred to work the land had a better and more secure existence than before the war. Branko's success was less dramatic. It is somewhat hard to assess his influence on Stanchich. He was either a leader or a seer. The village life changed in the direction he had predicted. After a decade, the farmers had adopted new methods of winemaking. Modern plumbing also made its way into the village but at a much slower pace and not uniformly so. To this day many villagers still use outhouses. They might be cleaner and more sophisticated but they nevertheless remain outhouses.

I enjoyed studying. We all benefited from the accelerated tempo of learning. Normally by the eighth grade a student barely remembers what he had learned years ago in the fourth grade. With our quick

tempo everything seemed fresh. I remembered what I learned previously and I could place new items in the context of the recently acquired "old knowledge."

I planned to enroll in the medical school but my plans almost came to a screeching halt. A month before high school graduation, I'd been summoned to a special meeting for good students. A member of the Croat Central Committee of the Party came to give us some good news. He had just learned that the Soviet Union granted ten fellowships for studies in top Soviet universities. Students graduating from Marshal Tito's high school would have the inside track in the selection process. Two positions were open in the Department of Philosophy at the University of Moscow. I immediately sensed the danger. I had a knack for philosophy and, sure enough, somebody recommended me for the position.

Next day I had to report to the *Agitprop* (agitation and propaganda) Division of the Communist Party of Croatia for an interview. On the way I furiously rehearsed various arguments why I should not be chosen to go to Moscow but I did not have to speak my lines. The person in charge said he had learned from others about my love of medicine and he thought I ought to stay in Zagreb. That was a heck of a surprise. Members of the Central Committee were not known for their sensitivity to other people's personal preferences. I immediately understood what was going on. My letter of characteristics must have worked its way to the Central Committee.

Thank you, thank you very much, dear Comrade secretary of the Communist Youth League in Zagreb! You saved me from cold Moscow winters, from an inevitable conflict with rigid Marxist philosophy and from a wrong career. I always wanted to be a doctor and I made the right choice. My life in medicine and science has been and remains richly rewarding.

Some of my classmates took the Russian fellowship. Unfortunately a year after they departed, Tito came to blows with Stalin and the Yugoslav Party was thrown out of the Communist international union, the Cominform. Soon the Yugoslav students in the Soviet Union faced hard choices. They could either side with the Soviets or opt to return home. On the surface the choice was not so difficult, but as soon as a student opted to return, he was automatically clas-

sified by the Soviets as anti-Stalinist. And when a student eventually returned home, the Yugoslav authorities would not trust him. Until proven otherwise, a student returning from the Soviet Union was considered as a potential double agent.

Milovan Domijan and Boris Puks from our *banca prima* went to study in the Soviet Union. Unfortunately, somebody definitely made the wrong choice when he decided to send Boris to Moscow. Highly intelligent, a brilliant mathematician, Boris did not have the right pedigree to become a trusted Party member. He voluntarily joined the guerrilla movement and was demobilized at the rank of lieutenant. But he was of German extraction and his father was a pharmacist to boot! Definitely not the right lineage! Tall with blond hair, never shy, Boris always attracted attention. He carefully cultivated an air of mystery around himself. Smarter than others, he frequently refused to answer questions. He'd just put on a whimsical smile and walk away. Occasionally Boris refused to join us for evening adventures. Not so unusual by itself but he consistently refused to elaborate. This was an odd habit in a Slavic country where adhering to normal procedures was of great social importance. We all played by the rules. If you were not able to accept an invitation you were supposed to say that you would love to come but could not for such and such reason. Boris not only refused to say what he was doing—he'd leave a distinct impression he was hiding some dark secret. He wanted, and succeeded, in being mysterious.

Boris returned from Russia even more mysterious then before. He adamantly refused to say a word about life in the Soviet Union, countering any question with a statement that as far as theoretic mathematics was concerned, the stay in Moscow was well worth it. He took up studies in Ljubljana where he met a nice Slovenian girl and hinted he was about to take the big plunge. It would be an entirely private affair. "It will be soon" he wrote in his typical secretive manner but refused to give a specific date.

Two days before his wedding Boris left for a hike in the Slovenian Alps. He never returned. It could have been a mountain climbing accident but if it was a simple hike, why did he take along his pistol, his photo album and all personal documents? Unless he had intended to descend from the Alps, straight to the wedding? But then why

would he leave his best suit behind? And what did he need the gun for? We will never know, but I cannot help thinking that what did happen had something to do with his stay in Moscow. Did somebody eliminate him at a secret meeting point? Or was he a Soviet agent who had been recalled back to Russia?

Certainly his family, unable to accept his demise, firmly believed Boris was back in Moscow. His uncle would frequently call me to report a new sighting of Boris in Moscow and ask whether I heard from him. Occasional sightings continued but nobody ever claimed to have spoken with him. It is not at all unusual to see a tall blond person in Moscow. But then again, it could have been him. Boris Puks would not have been the first or last foreigner to eventually perish in the Gulag Archipelago.

If he opted for the Soviets, he for sure acquired ruthless masters. If he was a true patriot, his refusal to criticize the Russians and his secretive behavior must have attracted the attention of the Yugoslav counterintelligence. And those guys operated under similar rules as their Soviet counterparts. There is no answer to the mystery but I am sure Boris got into big league trouble for being at the wrong place at the wrong time. The wrong place was Moscow and the wrong time, the conflict between Stalin and Tito. Was he an active participant or just a victim of perceptions? Who knows? In those times a wrong step or just being different could cost a person his life.

One thing I know for sure is that Boris is not alive. Whether he was in the East or West, whether it was politics or escaping from a wedding, Boris would have let one of us know. Over months of sitting in the first row of Tito high school in Zagreb, the four of us in the *banca prima* struck a close friendship. Yes, he would have let us know. If not for friendship's sake, then just to continue teasing. To be mysterious, you need an audience.

Milovan had no problems when he returned from Moscow. He eventually graduated from the legendary tough and selective Shipbuilding College in Zagreb. He earned high renown as chief designer in the Trogir shipyards. He also became the Adriatic champion in sailing.

The third member of *banca prima*, Vinko Guberina, graduated from the College of Engineering in Zagreb and became the director

of a large aluminum products plant in Shibenik. Serving a term as Mayor of the City, he made up for what in the high school appeared to be a lack of interest in humanities. In 1966, during his tenure as Mayor, Vinko secured money for the production of an authoritative six hundred page folio-size book to celebrate the nine hundredth anniversary of Shibenik. A committee of geographers, historians and other scholars worked on the project, but the production of the testimonial was very slow. Finally with a great help from Vinko Guberina and thanks to his persistence, the beautiful book saw the light in 1976.

I graduated from the high school in summer of 1947, and in the fall I was admitted to the medical school.

Learning Medicine

(1947-1953)

A*nno domini* 1947, my first year of medical school in Zagreb was a real zoo. In the name of historical needs and common justice, the authorities dumped close to seven hundred freshmen at the school normally geared to a class of one hundred students. It could not have happened at a worse time. A good portion of the faculty had left the country, the buildings were in disrepair, the laboratories empty, and the rickety administrative structure utterly unprepared to handle the crowd. More than half of the students were women who, with exception of a few Jewish girls, had not been displaced during the war. The men were an odd mixture of mature military officers, city draft dodgers, young war veterans and people who'd rather not talk about their past. Besides balancing the genders, the authorities also applied a "key" to mold the class according to their sense of social justice. Before the war only children of rich parents could afford medical school; now everybody from every corner of the country got a chance.

In spite of such different backgrounds the class functioned reasonably well. We would have done even better were it not for outside meddling. In 1947 intrusive Communist social engineering was at its peak. To "motivate the masses," they spoke about the goals of socialism over and over again to the point where boredom gave way to anger. To an average citizen the word socialism became a syn-

onym for incompetence, corruption, stupidity, and double standards. If you disliked somebody, you'd hope he'd eventually get some "socialist justice." A "great fighter for socialism" was the code for a bad person. "Socialistic humanism" stood for manipulative behavior and "good socialist art" meant you should not waste time to see it. To vent their anger people developed a biting dark sense of humor.

"What is the difference between socialism and capitalism?" went the question in one of the jokes.

"Well, capitalism is exploitation of a man by his fellow man. In socialism, it is the other way around."

In another joke, a man meets a friend whom he had not seen for years.

"You sure look depressed," says the friend. "What is the problem?"

"Oh I just failed the state civil service exam. They asked me what the distinction is between socialism and capitalism and for the life of me, I could not tell the difference.

"Oh, you lucky dog," replies the friend, " I got the same question three years ago, I told them what the difference was and just yesterday they released me from jail."

Most of us wanted to study hard but the Party would not leave us to our own devices. Down the pike came the directive that the class must be broken into small study groups, the so-called "*kruzhoks.*" The leadership did not bother to hide where the idea came from. "*Kruzhok*" is a Russian word for "little circle." Apparently that was the way the students were organized in the Soviet Union. Our curriculum was very demanding and we spent the whole day in classes or labs. Now the Party commanded that we also sit together in the evenings. In theory the *kruzhoks* should have been a good mix of Communists and the masses. Two flies with one swat: make the students work harder and give the Communists a chance to influence other students. Just a few days before the *kruzhok* directive came down I was assigned to the education section of the student organization. The job in the education section was by Party standards a poor assignment but it proved a blessing. The chief of the education section was an older military student. He and I took a lit-

eral view of the task; the function of the education section was to facilitate education. We wanted to focus on publishing lecture notes and on copying relevant pages from textbooks. The *kruzhok* directive was about to push us into a meaningless activity. Something had to be done.

Eventually we found our way around the directive. The *kruzhoks* were supposed to meet at night, which left very little time for commuting across town. Space was another serious limitation. As a rule, students lived in small sublet rooms barely sufficient to accommodate one person, a chair and a bed. Acknowledging these realities, the higher-ups accepted our proposal to organize the groups on a territorial basis. In exchange we promised that whenever possible, the *kruzhoks* would be a good mix of Communists with apolitical students. The principle of territorial organization right away eliminated Party members who demobilized from the Army as military students. They resided in two distant former religious seminaries. Both dormitory groups were delighted to form their own *kruzhoks*. This left only a few Communists to mix with the masses. Predictably most of them were not interested in nighttime agitation and chose to group together with similar souls. The rest of the *kruzhoks* evolved from mutual affinity or old friendships. From the lists of these voluntary groups we *post hoc* designated one member in each *kruzhok* as "progressive" and that took care of the "political education" issue.

The next directive requested that that we organize scholastic competition between study groups. It was logical; once we had a Soviet organizational structure, why not have a competition in the best Stalinist fashion? The citizens of the Soviet Union were constantly involved in some *pro forma* contest: in sports, in the work place, in cultural events or in "building socialism." Without ever saying so, these competitions were a tacit acknowledgment of human nature. Socialism was set to level the playing field and abolish competition for personal profit. The Soviets even created a new term for the process, *uravnilovka*, which loosely translates into "equalizer." According to the Communists a doctor, a janitor, a farmer, or a streetcar conductor deserved approximately the same wages. Protected from evil, the theory went, the liberated citizens would seek out what suited them best. Once happily settled in his chosen pro-

fession, each citizen would be delighted to work hard. In return, Society would implement the principle of "to everybody according to his activity and according to his needs." Theoretically if you've done your share of work and at some point needed a new house, the society would to provide it for you.

Even on the philosophical level the theory did not quite work out. Marx and Engels embraced Darwin's theory and viewed the concept that humans evolved from a series of lower species through natural selection as another confirmation of materialistic philosophy. But there was a catch to it. Survival of the fittest and natural selection are nothing but constant competitions with nature and with fellow tribesmen. Anthropologists amply documented that primitive tribes practice inequality: the unfit are discarded; stronger tribes conquer weak ones, and strong men have more wives to pass on their good genes. The competition underlying Darwin's theory of survival of the fittest created philosophical problems for the Marxists. In the mid 1920s, it got worse; every fascist or racist was in essence a social Darwinist. But the Marxists had a ready answer through the precept of dialectic materialism. According to Marx, everything in nature—inanimate objects, the cosmos, living creatures, the social structure—stems from a clash of opposites, which from time to time results in a quantum leap. The new entity arising from such a quantum leap is qualitatively different from its predecessor. Marxists proclaimed human society to be a *quantum leap* and suggested that in modern conditions natural selection ceases to operate. Socialism, born in a revolutionary confrontation of opposing forces, was another quantum leap that would redefine human relationships. A socialist society would bring out the best in people and dispose of the nasty human tendency for competing with others.

Setting aside whether or not the theory of quantum leaps was correct, the Marxists were right in the sense that a modern society, with its ethics of compassion, is antithetical to the concept of survival of fittest. But their assumption that they would succeed in removing competitiveness from human relationships proved a gross miscalculation. We all know the results: central decision-making, separation of reward from productivity, and excessive job protection resulted in a corrupt, static society of lazy, dispirited citizens.

The competitions instigated by the Soviet Communist Party were an attempt to come to grips with human nature—the need of human beings to better themselves and, alas, for an individual to feel he is better than the majority of his fellow men. In Zagreb they constantly bombarded us with news about a certain Soviet citizen, Stahanov, who could dig up more ore than any one else, about bricklayers whose buildings rose at twice the speed of others, about superb athletes and chess masters who could beat anybody in the world. Devoid of meaningful rewards, these contrived competitions failed miserably, but the leadership was hopelessly stuck with the concept. In our case the form became the content; since the *kruzhoks* competed with one another they were, by definition, good.

We kept sending glowing reports to higher authorities. We didn't have to lie; we simply failed to verify the accuracy of received reports. Only rarely, when a *kruzhok* submitted an outrageous report, did we cut the claimed effort by half in case somebody higher up was not a total fool. Fed a constant diet of competitive success, the leadership forgot that our contest was only in academics. The political goals had been effectively pushed aside and the higher-ups never inquired why the Communist students stopped spreading the gospel in the trenches.

I organized my own *kruzhok* and would have done so regardless of the Party directive. The first year of medical school was incredibly hard. Much of the material required pure repetitive memorization and you needed somebody to rehearse with. I ended up with a very compatible group of colleagues. It had nothing to do with territorial proximity. In fact one of the members, Boris, lived at the most northern point of the town, way beyond the main cemetery of Mirogoj. Each visit to his house was a small adventure. It was fun taking alternate routes through the enormous graveyard, getting lost, rediscovering paths and reading epitaphs. In the evening, just in time for the last streetcar, we'd walk together through the moonlit eerie shadows of the graveyard. No doubt we were tough guys, but somehow nobody wanted to navigate the gravestones on his own. The walk was always brisk, the conversation invariably very loud.

There is nothing special to report about Veljko's or my midtown apartments. But going for a longer ride to Niksha's freestanding

house on the East side of the town was something else. His family owned a vineyard and they always offered us some of their best wines.

In late 1948 the general atmosphere around us was quite bleak. The Yugoslav Party had just broken off with the Soviet Union over Tito's insistence on a modicum of independence. In Stalin's mind there was no place for a middle ground; every country had to chose whether it belonged to the Eastern USSR-dominated block or cast its fate with the "Imperialistic West." Tito chose to organize the "Third Block" of emerging nations and Stalin was so livid that he openly called for Tito's removal.

To cope with Stalin's threat, Tito had just played out an efficient, but cruel, charade. Every Party member had to attend an "open discussion" of the issues and at the end, one by one, each had to "declare" himself as either pro or against Stalin's position. It took about two weeks to complete this countrywide process. When the dust settled, those who were pro-Soviet were arrested and the ones who could not make up their mind, were thrown out of the Party. In our medical school the affair blew over rather lightly. A huge majority read the beans correctly and only a few got arrested. Nevertheless, it left everyone with a bitter taste. The general atmosphere was depressing.

So why not get drunk and forget it all! One evening we drank enough to become overly loud and not to disturb Niksha's parents, we took off to the empty late-night streets. We stopped at the pedestal of a monument where Boris delivered an emotional speech on behalf of students who were about to take the difficult exam we had just completed. The speech ended with a call for action in the name of "socialist justice." We must protect these honest representatives of "the people's masses" from ruthless exploitation at the hands of their professors. A piece of wire materialized out of nowhere. With a mean purpose in mind we resolutely marched towards the house of the professor of physiology. There we twisted the wire around his doorknobs to prevent the "class enemy" from leaving his house.

Everything seemed to be sheer fun. Double fun in fact—annoying the unpopular professor of physiology and giving speeches in the absurd, stupid, official lingo. By the end of the "visit" to Professor Hauptfeld's house we sobered up and should have known better. But

drunkenness has little to do with blood alcohol levels. Basically sober, we refused to come down to reality. Loose and elated, we kept finding fun in everything.

Somebody spotted a detour sign at the entry to a street, which was torn up for repairs. It was now my turn to be the chief buffoon.

"Comrades," I intoned in front of the detour. "These here signs are not in keeping with the principles of socialist equality. Is there any reason to assume the comrades in this street are more deserving, more industrious and more devoted to the causes and purposes of our great society?"

"No, absolutely no," responded the chorus, much in the style of a well-rehearsed Communist mass meeting.

"And yet citizens in this street are given an unfair headstart. Our poor comrades in the next street cannot sleep from all that diverted traffic which, against every principle of socialist evenhandedness, puts them at a disadvantage. Tomorrow morning, when they throw themselves with the usual zeal into the task of building a new society, each according to his or her job description, each in keeping with their commitment to the progress of humanity, they will find it difficult to fulfill their responsibilities. For, my dear comrades, a socialist society cannot be built by sleepy people."

"Right on, comrade." harmonized Niksha, "We all swore not to sleep until we completed building socialism, but if these citizens here were left sleepless, this would negatively affect their socialist productivity." For this Niksha got a roaring applause. The circular stupidity of his sentence was a darn good imitation of many oratorical excesses we heard during long mass meetings. We could not stop laughing.

Finally I collected myself enough to continue with my part. "And I would hope that you, my fellow students, do not think of yourselves as being above ordinary things. Therefore, you will not walk away from this gross breach of justice. Am I wrong in assuming that you are not ordinary medical students who would lose themselves in the intricacies of the human body to the point where they might forget to hone the blade of the class struggle?"

That was a good one. You couldn't attend a Communist rally without at least once hearing the metaphor about the blade of class

struggle. An absolutely useless analogy, alien to the Croatian language, and a sure sign that the speaker had nothing of interest to say.

The contest was on. The better the imitation of a typical oration, the clumsier the sentence, the louder was the applause. It was Niksha's turn. He was about six feet tall, blond, and cut an impressive figure. This time around, standing atop a heap of rubble, he was even more imposing.

"How can you, Comrade Julius, even consider that we might possibly deviate from the line of progress and sink into a self-centered solipsism, if you excuse me for the tautology." he said. "You are talking to the vanguard of socialist youth, the class-conscious few who, if proletarian modesty did not dictate against boasting, could easily call themselves the flower of our nation. No, we could not possibly ignore this sorry state of affairs. In our society everybody must get an equal chance."

And so it went. At the end of the oratory, the flower of the nation rearranged the bypass signs to direct the traffic right into the craters of the disabled street.

We moved to a safe distance to observe the results of our handiwork. It worked only too well! One after another the diverted cars got stuck in the impassable street, uselessly revving up their engines. Most frustrated drivers got out of their cars and swore at the top of their lungs to the great chagrin of alarmed tenants who, equally loudly, requested peace and quiet.

One would think we had had enough. But the worst stupidity was yet to come. Looking for trouble, we stopped across the street from the district police station. Boris decided to play on my penchant for singing and proposed that I give a serenade for "the organs of people's authority."

"Poor souls." said Boris, "While the average citizen sleeps, their uniformed comrades alertly remain on the watch. How hard it must be to keep your eyes open in the deafening silence of the night. And yet neither could they afford as individuals, nor could we permit them as a society to fall asleep. Let's cheer up these selfless heroes of our social commune. Julius—you sing the solo and we will be the chorus. However, keep in mind the refined tastes of our comrades. None of the petit bourgeois city songs, those sentimental and devoid

of content mementos of a bored middle-class existence. And no opera either. No, our comrades need to hear revolutionary songs!"

I could not resist the mood of the moment. Standing in the main street, right across from the well-lit window of the police station, I started to sing Soviet revolutionary songs! This was the evening for stupidities; in those dangerous times people got thrown in jail for lesser pro-Soviet acts.

At first there was no reaction. Then the window opened and a visibly annoyed member of the militia suggested we had better f--- off or he would throw our arsses in the slammer. This was routine swearing by somebody who suddenly woke up. But then, realizing what sort of songs I was singing, the man blew the whistle. The high-pitched rolling sound was deeply engraved in the brain of all militia men and the windows started to light up in a quick chain reaction. Soon more whistles blew from all directions and a cacophony of boots on the run, screams, cursing, authoritative commands, and pleas for order indicated the citizens in uniforms were about to act.

None of this seemed to penetrate my brain. Instead of acting in self-defense, I was busy searching the darkest recesses of my memory for forgotten inflammatory songs. By now my friends were trying to shut me up but I was out of control. The sounds from the inner court became louder. Clearly they were assembling for a decisive attack on the pro-Soviet demonstrators. I knew well what was going on but could not restrain myself. Disaster was looming. An arrest for anti-socialist provocation would get me kicked out of medical school and, very likely, land me in the concentration camp on the island of Goli Otok (Naked Island). Erected to "reeducate" people who declared themselves pro-Soviet during the "open discussion" of Tito's differences with Stalin, the camp in Goli Otok became notorious for its brutal regime. Quite a few people died there.

Finally Niksha dragged me around the corner. What a difference a little distance makes! In front of the stockade, sensing the same elation which turns some people into heroes, I was intoxicated by the tension. I savored the stress the same way a child enjoys a roller coaster. Around the corner the tension evaporated and I came back to my senses. Finally my legs connected with my brain and I began running as fast as I possibly could. Our *kruzhok* dispersed in all

four directions. When we reassembled everybody had been visibly changed. Gone was the bravado. Somewhat ashamed, each of us realized that the evening was not hilarious. Just stupid! For no good reason we'd come darn close to disaster. They set me up, I willingly played along, and in an instant, our lives could have been changed forever. In difficult times one cannot afford mistakes.

Nobody ever mentioned the incident again. It was not funny!

~

The biggest surprises in medical school were the professors. Nobody had prepared us for the encounter. Fiercely independent and uniformly eccentric, our professors were a new phenomenon to reckon with. Most of them had served on the faculty since the school's founding some thirty years before. Each became a legend. As individuals they were very different but all had the same streak of being rigid, authoritarian and unafraid. It did not matter whether you were a man or a woman, an officer of the Army, a Party dignitary or just a plain student—at the end of the year, the old professor was waiting in ambush. And what an ambush it was!

In the first year the failure rate was anywhere from thirty to forty percent. For our class the rates were bound to be even more disastrous. There were too many of us for effective classroom instruction. The exercises in overcrowded, poorly equipped laboratories were largely meaningless. But the old demanding and rigid medical school system was still in place.

The medical school in Zagreb had been established after the First World War in early 1920s and all professors in Zagreb were graduates of German and Austrian medical schools. However in the mid 1930s, German medicine lost its leading role. All Jewish professors had been removed and an agreement with Hitler's political doctrine became a selection criterion for the remaining faculty. The medicine in Austria and Germany stagnated and the focus of new medical knowledge moved to France, England, Scandinavia and the USA.

My chief and I in the student education section took it upon ourselves to advocate for changes in the school's medical curriculum.

We went about it in a reasonably organized fashion. First we spoke to younger faculty members who had some exposure to new medicine. Thereafter we convened a meeting of student representatives from medical schools in Belgrade and Ljubljana to draw up a proposal for changes. We published the proposal in the student journal *Medicinar*. That attracted everybody's attention. The Party took a neutral position. When the dean of the school asked for an explanation, the Party secretary denied the Party was behind the initiative. He was right, we did not ask for permission, but the Party quietly enjoyed our rebel-rousing. Having explained that he had nothing to do with the curriculum reform proposal the secretary invoked the student's "traditional rights of self-expression" and refused to intervene.

We decided to convene a series of class meetings to further discuss proposed curriculum changes. The sole purpose of the entire exercise was to put a chink in the armor of the old guard. They professed to have an absolute knowledge of medicine and we suggested otherwise. Needless to say, the professors were quite irritated with this challenge to their authority. We intended to talk about the reform for years to come. And then our classmate, Emanuel Reich, appeared on the scene and single-handedly derailed the reform movement.

Emanuel was famous for his short stature and an equally short temper. He was at best five feet, one inch tall. Constantly in a conflict with someone or something, he had incredibly bad luck. Some internal magnet invariably pulled him towards trouble. One day Emanuel waited for the train in Ljubljana and a stranger asked whether he'd be willing to take a small package to his uncle who was waiting at the railway station in Zagreb. Emanuel was apparently in a good mood and gladly agreed to help. Upon arrival in Zagreb, as he approached the meeting point, he was instantly arrested! It turned out that the box contained forty Swiss watches. The police must have known Emanuel was an innocent mule but, true to form, he immediately started to scream and offend the officers. How could they be so stupid to assume that he, Emanuel Reich, would smuggle watches! He had not been in Switzerland, he had no money on him, he had legitimate business in Ljubljana and they could easily check it out.

The policemen had never seen anything like it. They threw him into prison where he continued to harangue anybody in sight.

The police rounded up the whole watch-smuggling network and by the next day confirmed that Emanuel was not involved. Before they released him, the officer in charge delivered a routine lecture about being careful and not getting involved with unknown people. That did it! Emanuel took mortal offense at such a patronizing behavior, when in fact they should have offered him an apology and insisted on getting an official letter of exculpation. Nobody gets an apology from Yugoslav police. Nobody! So Emanuel sat in jail for an additional week, until it became crystal clear, even to him, that he wouldn't get his way.

Angry at the injustice, the freshly released prisoner went straight to the secretary of the Party in the medical school to rehabilitate himself. The secretary's reassurance that the Party trusted him did not suffice. Emanuel wanted action! He longed for something big and brilliant, a deed that everybody would remember for a long time.

The secretary had no burning needs and saw no barricades to attack. As he scratched his head in search of ideas, Emanuel became abusive. He wondered why a Party leader would be so complacent. Did he believe in status quo or were there some things he would like to see changed? The word "change" struck a chord in the secretary. He remembered what we were doing in the education section of the student organization and advised Emanuel to put himself at our disposal. The next day Emanuel presented himself with flair to the education section.

"I am here on the orders of the Party secretary who feels you could use my help," said Emanuel with considerable pomp. He was quite calm but knowing his reputation, I could not possibly tell him we were just fine and needed no help.

"In three days we will discuss the proposed curriculum changes in the second year's class," I explained. "Some younger professors of internal medicine are on our side, but the professors teaching the first three pre-clinical years will not budge. For them anatomy, physiology, histology and pathology are the sacred untouchable cows of medicine. The obvious imbalance—that basic sciences have three years and clinical medicine gets only two years—does not bother

them a bit. We must mobilize the students to put some pressure on the professors.

"Unfortunately," I continued, "we did not have enough time to prepare ourselves. It would be nice to know, for example, how pathology is taught in the USA and England and contrast this with our old-fashioned teaching. We have got to show the old boys that they are well behind the times. Maybe we could shame them into cooperation with us. Prepare yourself, come to the meeting and try to put some pressure on the professors."

"No problem," said Emanuel with glee in his eyes. He jumped from the chair and dashed off ready to do battle. On the day of the meeting I'd almost forgotten about Emanuel, but he arrived early, chose a good position on the first bench, and when I came, waved at me.

"Did you prepare yourself?" I asked.

"But of course. You know my situation. I will not miss this opportunity to exonerate myself. Just watch me!"

He literally trembled with excitement. I should have known what that meant. What transpired was an unmitigated disaster. I finished my introductory talk and before the next speaker could present the outline of the proposed curriculum, Emanuel stood on the bench and started to orate. He said very little about the proposed curriculum and only vaguely mentioned modern teaching in England. Having disposed with this formality, Emanuel launched an attack on the professors. And what an attack it was!

Standing on the bench did not fully compensate for his very short stature. Undeterred by the fact that the back row could barely see his head Emanuel unleashed a horrendous stream of character assassinations. It was an equal opportunity performance. The students could not believe their ears as Emanuel recited who was sleeping with whom, who was corrupt, who did not keep regular working hours, who was politically suspect and who had lost his marbles. The audience first took Emanuel's ranting for a big joke and kept egging him on to reveal more dirt. But as the speech went on, Emanuel's anger started to rub off on others.

Sensing that the masses were behind him, Emanuel could not stop. His voice became louder, the accusations became more outra-

geous and the genuinely indignant audience roared its disapproval of the professors.

"How could we ever become good doctors with so profoundly incompetent teachers?" asked Emanuel.

"We can't!" came the response.

"Can such jokers be our role models?"

"No!"

"Should we teach them a lesson instead of acting as timid sheep?"

"Yes, yes!" Emanuel succeeded in establishing the typical rhythm for Communistic mass-meetings where the speaker throws out slogans and the chorus responds. But this wasn't the usual perfunctory and reflexive response, Emanuel's audience acted with conviction.

Guided by his infallible internal magnet for trouble, Emanuel was now ready for the punch-line.

"We cannot let these fools spoil our education. Let's go on strike and not return to classes unless all professors have been dismissed. Are you ready to strike?" Emanuel screamed at the top of his lungs.

All hell broke loose. The participants were more than willing to join a general strike.

In an attempt to endear himself to the Party, Emanuel had again succeeded in rubbing the authorities the wrong way! The leadership of Yugoslavia could not stand any spontaneous expressions. The "masses" had to be led by the Party and they viewed acceptance of "dictates from citizens" as the ultimate weakness. The new Yugoslav constitution spoke about freedom of assembly and the right to strike, but that didn't mean a thing. It was a historic throwback to Marx's times, when socialists used constitutional rights to promulgate the revolution and to create workers' unions. Not putting these central tenets into the Constitution was as impossible as it would be to take *Genesis* out of the Bible. Not too many believed it but it got to stay there.

Something had to be done in a hurry! Not only was Emanuel on his way to another arrest, he could have pulled me with him. The same Party secretary who'd unloaded him on me would blame me, rather than take the responsibility.

I yelled at Emanuel to sit down. He did, but not before, all pleased with himself, he gave me a nasty gaze as if saying "OK! You are jealous and want to take credit for my excellent job. Go ahead, I will let you have your moment."

I jumped on the long table in front of the huge blackboard and from that strategic position tried to out-shout the unruly crowd. After a while they let me talk. I insisted that a strike without a larger agenda would be meaningless. Calling for dismissal of professors, besides not giving them due process, was unrealistic. They had tenure but even if we were successful in forcing them into retirement, where would replacements come from? Developing new teachers, I suggested, was a long-term proposition. Talking about the new curriculum was the first important step towards an educational reform.

The audience was now listening. They had probably figured out the potential political cost of a strike, as well as how much havoc a strike would play with their timely graduation. I continued to talk about the new curriculum while others kept passing leaflets with the proposed reform package. I then asked the rhetorical question whether they would like to continue with the meeting. There was no response and I closed the meeting.

To his credit, Emanuel understood how close he came to new trouble and left without protest. But the damage was done. Next day the Party secretary offered his apologies to the Dean and issued an order for us to cease and desist.

In spite of occasional incidents, by the end of the second year we made our adjustments to the double nuisance of the Party and the old professors. For one thing, the professors had pruned away close to forty percent of the student body. Those remaining were a motivated and capable lot. At the same time the local leadership of the Party had undergone a transition. Professional politicos moved to other schools and the remaining leaders were more interested in passing exams than in politics.

Building the Highway

(1948)

Whereas the atmosphere in the medical school improved, the Party in did not entirely change its ways. During summer vacation periods, the Communists exerted immense pressure on the youth to join various building projects. In the summer of 1948, the campaign was particularly ambitious; the youth would build, all in one year, 280 miles of a new highway from Zagreb all the way to Belgrade! The Croatian word for "voluntarily" is *dobrovoljno*, which roughly translates into "goodwilling." Soon a new word *dobromorno* started to circulate. The term *morno*, which sounds vaguely similar to *voljno*, derives from *must do* and it described well the less than voluntary nature of the participation. The secretary of the Party at the university summoned me to his offices and skillfully used my good grades as well as the "successes" in the education section to explain why I was the logical choice to lead the effort. On the spot he appointed me as the commander of the medical school brigade. The campaign had already enlisted hundred twenty "volunteers." The fact that my name was not on the list did not bother the secretary a bit. I was made a volunteer.

The secretary handed me the preliminary roster of the Sixth Zagreb Brigade. None of the top medical school Party brass had volunteered! The military students were exempted and the majority of others needed to make up time they had lost in unproductive meetings during the school year. Like a fool, I'd taken all my exams early.

There was no reasonable way to refuse but I extracted two concessions. With the exception of the political commissar I'd be able to select my staff and I would not be involved in the recruitment. If the comrades could not physically work on the highway, let them at least complete the job of corralling the youth.

The secretary was clever. Obviously he reached to the bottom of the barrel to find a former Partizan for a commander and was not about to spoil the prospect by asking why I did not want to get involved with the recruitment. He may have sensed I was sick and tired of Party machinations. After they applied every conceivable pressure to complete the enlistment, the executives congratulated themselves with elaborate ceremonies. They did not care as much about the highway as they cherished the power to prevail. Achieving what they had set out to achieve was the major achievement. If it sounded good, it must be good! That they had gotten themselves a bunch of resentful, teeth-grinding, foot-dragging participants did not matter. During the war there was a purpose to activities and everybody was a true volunteer. The peacetime efforts were a mockery. Unwilling to give up its 'leadership of the masses', the Party sought to recreate the war. Everything, including sporting activities, was structured along military lines. Not a volunteer group of medical students but the Sixth Zagreb Brigade, which consisted of three companies, further divided into platoons!

Obviously it had to be done but how it would be done was up to me. With plenty of help from others we turned a potentially difficult experience into a memorable vacation.

We took the train to Ruma, a village about twenty five miles from Belgrade, where trucks waited to take us on a lengthy ride over tortuous paths to complete what was, as the crow flies, a four-mile distance to the camp. Like a huge tree, the main road out of the village kept dividing into ever-smaller branches. The final barely passable dendrites eventually turned into two-track wheel imprints leading to individual farming plots. In one of them, amid endless corn and wheat fields, was our camp. The camp was quite comfortable. It consisted of five barracks: four dormitories, one with a mess hall, a meeting room and a few offices. We had electricity and running

water from a well. You could even take a cold shower. The bunk beds had *slamaricas* instead of mattresses. These straw-filled, bed-size bags made of rough sackcloth are at first quite comfortable. Under the weight of the body, the straw eventually hardens, but if you shake the *slamarica* every morning you can soften your lair. The latrines were the only inconvenience in the camp but who could possibly expect a sewer at a work camp?

Each camp also had a PA system for announcements and music but ours was inoperative. Nobody cared to fix the PA system. Normally this would be the domain of the political commissar, but in an about-face, the Party decided not to appoint commissars. Instead, the position was classified as the "delegate for socio-cultural affairs." Not unlike nowadays in the USA where the phrase "revenue enhancement" stands for taxes. Whether by design or because the new organizational structure had not yet taken root, our "delegate" was so non-assertive that I cannot remember his name or face. At my age it is prudent to accept memory failures as facts of life. I do, however, recall that he did not kick up a fuss when I suggested that instead of repairing the PA system we organize the cultural and political work on a "one on one basis." Everybody was familiar with the art of double talk and knew what the euphemism stood for. Accepting work "on an individual basis" was tantamount to approving a resolution against organized political activity. Nobody objected.

I also argued that we must secure reasonably comfortable conditions for our volunteers. It may escape the reader that this was a radical and unconventional position. A commander was supposed to care only about political education and the productivity of his brigade. Therefore, I painted my plea for comfort as a part of the larger campaign for better productivity. Talking about people's comfort was antithetical to Party thinking. The Yugoslav leaders went to the same well from which Mao drew ideas for the Cultural Revolution. The more Spartan the conditions, the higher their educational value! As far as they were concerned, the youth ought to be shaken out of its petit bourgeois comfort and "forged in the flames of revolution"—yet another inane slogan from the October Revolution. Somebody should write a study about Communist slogans. How

could such a stupid idea and such a crude allegory become commonplace? "Forging in the flames of the revolution," my foot! What revolution, what flames?

Having disposed of the political work, I proceeded to organize the leadership of the brigade. I appointed as quartermaster an old Partizan who'd had a similar responsibility during the war. He threw himself at the work with abandon. It did not take him long to figure out where the stores were, who was in charge and how to beat the red tape. We had plenty of good food, excellent work clothes and shoes. If anything was needed, the quartermaster waved his magic wand and the goods were delivered the next day. He also had a good sense of humor. One day, beaming with pleasure, he informed me he had located a new high quality PA system.

I was petrified. Without the PA system, the "cultural delegate" limited himself to rehearsals for an evening show and had no means to organize larger activities. Furthermore a brigade of high school students from Uzhice also moved into the camp. Nice kids from the border of Bosnia and Serbia, but I hated the thought of being subjected to their musical tastes—not to mention their commander, who loved to summon the whole brigade for a daily something. Every day they'd line up in proper military fashion to hear him yelling instructions at the top of his voice. It was as exhausting for him as it was boring for them. Now imagine the length of their "review of troops" and the amount of nonsense if the commander had the use of a microphone.

I did not know the quartermaster all that well. As I searched for the right words to deflect the danger, he started to laugh. "You'd be a terrible poker player; your face is an open book. Do not worry," he said cryptically. "I will take care of it." It could have meant he'd have the PA delivered tomorrow or that he would get rid of it. I was still puzzled. Finally he broke the ice.

"Oh, come on! I have my priorities right. I first placed a large order for earplugs. When they come we can discuss the PA system further." Good! He was in on the game and we could discuss the issue openly. Things were not as simple as I thought. The quartermaster didn't find the PA system, it had been forced on him. Furthermore if we did not order one, the Uzhice Brigade would have

ordered it and when the amplifier arrived they would control it. A horrible thought!

Milivoj, the quartermaster, was quite sure of himself. "Do not worry; I have my ways," he said. It turned out he was equally brilliant in refusing as in acquiring supplies. First he misinformed his opposite number in the Uzhice Brigade where to send their requisition for the PA system. Thereafter he informed the superiors that the camp had submitted two requisitions. He suggested that such redundancy made no sense and that the authorities should decide who'd be in charge of the system. He then wrote two pages of justification why the system should be entrusted to us. To buy some time, the *higher echelons* requested the Uzhice Brigade to send its justification. Eventually the commander of the region appointed a commission to resolve the problem and predictably the commission urged the two brigades to work it out. All of a sudden my brigade developed a terrific interest in the PA system. We turned out quite uncooperative and, frankly, not very polite. Finally, the chief of the section gave me a stern lecture to the tune that we were not the senior partners in the camp and people from Uzhice should be treated as equals. I promised to cooperate and one week before we left the camp, after a few meetings regarding ground rules, the PA system had been activated.

Stuck in the middle of the cornfield with nothing else to do we were quite prepared for hard work. If we only could find it! The cement pavement next to our camp had already been completed. We were supposed to grade the terrain and work on the water drainage. Nobody seemed to have a master plan. We kept filling up ditches, which had just been dug up by other brigades, only to dig up new ones, roughly parallel to previous canals. We patrolled the graded sides to fill in furrows from yesterday's rain. As soon as we completed the job, the rain fell again and we had to start anew. The women in the brigade kept sweeping the highway with long brooms. As soon as somebody stepped onto the pavement and deposited a new chunk of dirt, the broom detail went back to work. Nothing is as irritating as senseless work. Our strip of highway was in the middle of nowhere. Isolated from both sides by unfinished bridges and without access roads, the ten miles strip had no function whatsoever. What was the use of cleaning it? But that is what we were supposed

to do. Under these circumstances the position of the scheduling clerk and the brigade statistician were crucially important. The scheduling clerk carefully rotated people around and distributed the jobs fairly. He negotiated with the section chief for special assignments and frequently landed jobs in distant locations. Anything to break the monotony!

Milosh, a serious former Partizan, a good five years older than the rest, became our statistician. Upon his productivity reports depended the evaluation of the brigade. We were supposed to be locked in fierce competition with others and a simple reporting of hours at work could not suffice. Extraordinary productivity had to be shown to earn an official commendation from the section commander or, even better, have the commander in chief proclaim us a "striker" (*udarna*) brigade. But how do you quantify intrinsically unproductive work? What do you say about cleaning the highway with brooms? That you moved such and such amount of dirt or that you rendered X square meters of the surface sparklingly clean? And what about patching up little rivulets on the graded sides of the highway?

Lunatic propositions call for crazy solutions. Milosh proved a veritable magician. With a straight face to everybody, including me, he argued that it ought to be possible to compare light work with heavy physical activities. To 'bring objectivity into the process' he developed a complicated and totally arbitrary formula to assess the caloric expenditure of each job. He then reported both the caloric expenditure and also the amount of dirt moved to cover or dig up ditches. The authorities could choose whichever method they liked; on both accounts our brigade showed an incredibly deep commitment to long working hours and an unmatched productivity. It worked like a charm. By the end of the first week we got our first commendation. Three more commendations followed and eventually we got the designation of a "striker" brigade—a remarkable achievement in the face of meager work assignments! No wonder we were genuinely elated and felt it our patriotic duty to celebrate each of these commendations at the campfire.

Right after dinner, weather permitting; we piled up some used construction lumber for a campfire. One could stargaze in splendid

isolation, sing with others or partake in small talk around the fire. On weekdays we extinguished the flame at ten o' clock; on weekends the party regularly extended well beyond midnight. Thanks to the quartermaster, we never ran out of morsels to pass around; melons, corn on the cob, grilled sausages, shish kebab and the like. I never questioned how he got them. Officially we were not permitted to solicit from the villagers or touch the produce in the fields. By and large everybody stuck to the rules. Everybody but a certain Tomisha S. who one day came loaded with bacon, ham and sausages. Everything would have been fine if he had just kept quiet. But that was not his style. Claiming he'd done it for the common benefit, Tomisha distributed the goods to everybody. This was too large a violation and I had to deal with it. When reminded that we were not permitted to visit villages and that solicitation had been strictly forbidden, Tomisha responded in style.

"I never set foot in the village proper. I just took a walk and happened to run into this farmer who loves the youth. What a patriot that man was! He could barely wait to reward us for partaking in the reconstruction of our fatherland. And when he spotted the foreign student at my side, he was overcome with kindness."

"What foreign student?"

"An innocent little joke," Tomisha said. "The farmer was returning from the field with a wagon full of melons. A friend of mine whose name I swore to protect, agreed to pretend he was an Englishman who'd never seen a melon. He took the huge round object, looked at it from all angles, knocked on it, smelled it, turned it around but to no avail; he just could not figure out what one does with a melon. When he pulled a can opener out of his pocket acting as if the melon were a gigantic can, the farmer roared with laughter."

Tomisha continued his web of lies explaining how the farmer felt guilty for laughing aloud and soon returned with presents for the foreign student.

"You see," Tomisha said with a straight face, "this was given to a foreign student. Foreigners are not obliged to abide by the rules."

Everybody knew Tomisha was lying and he knew we knew, but nothing could stop him. Tomisha was a psychopath who mixed real-

ity with fantasies and who, as he spun a story, lost the thread until he himself finally did not know the truth. However he was not stupid. There was a purpose to this confabulation. The funnier his stories, the more we laughed, the less likely it was that I would get to the heart of the problem. And the core was serious indeed.

Tomisha had gone to the village, proclaimed himself a fifth-year medical student about to receive his MD diploma, and with the help of drinking buddies he succeeded in setting up a consultation room in the local pub for "treating" gullible patients. When confronted, Tomisha did not bat an eyelash. He simply turned another page in his book of stories, this time about the true and imaginary adventures of his "practice." I did what I had to do to restrain this dangerous man. Luckily he was a coward. A threat of ill-defined future measures was sufficient to keep him under control. In reality, had he decided to misbehave, we could not have done a thing to him. I am sure Tomisha parlayed our warnings into new stories of great personal danger.

We were not mature enough to report the incident to the medical school. He was unable to pass through the rigid system in Zagreb, but eventually lied and charmed his way to a diploma from another school.

By the end of our stay we quite enjoyed our compulsory vacation in the camp near Ruma. For the last weekend we scheduled the mother of all celebrations. The brigade had just gotten its fourth commendation. There was to be a gala dinner before we started the campfire. The quartermaster outdid himself; we had a lamb on the spit and for dessert the volunteers prepared *ushtipci*. When properly done these fritters can be as delicious as their cousins in New Orleans, the beignets.

The quartermaster got the right flour and located an absolutely gigantic frying pan. The monster must have been one meter in diameter! A good *ushtipak* hides under the crunchy shell—soft, airy, well-cooked dough. But if things go wrong, the grease-laden product turns heavy and chewy. Various recipes were discussed and candi-

dates for a chef proposed. Overall there was consensus on only one topic. The oil, everybody agreed, must be super hot. Jovica P. badly wanted to be the main cook. This was surprising. A straight Party man, he initially objected to the lack of discipline. But inside, he must have known how stupid it was to send a group of students to do meaningless labor. By and by Jovica came around. His candidacy for the position of chef was the final proof of his conversion. He came down from the pedestal of Party propriety to become Jovica, the friendly cook. How could I refuse! He got the job.

Somebody woke me up from my afternoon nap. "Fire, fire," he screamed. I wouldn't fall for that cheap trick. As soon as I jumped, somebody would drench me with water. When the noise increased and people started to run around, I realized this was not a joke. The superheated oil in Jovica's frying pan had exploded into a giant Olympic torch. By the time I got there, black smoke billowed through all kitchen windows. In an instant the fire spread from the kitchen to the adjacent administrative barrack. Conceding the loss of that barrack, we set out to protect other buildings. The water pressure from the well was negligible and it would not have done any good to sprinkle a few drops on the raging fire. We formed a chain to pass water-filled pails from the pond in two directions: to the next building, which by that time had also caught fire, and to keep our dormitory wet. With the prevailing wind it was only a matter of time, before one of the big sparks hit the dormitory too.

By nighttime the fire had run its course. Two buildings had been lost and one was badly damaged but our personal comfort was not greatly affected; we could use the space of the Uzhice Brigade, which had already left the camp. Totally exhausted from fighting the fire, we sat on the ground in an eerie silence, our eyes hypnotically drawn from the beautiful night skies towards the remaining embers of the giant bonfires. After a while I snapped out of the mesmerizing trance. A bunch of buildings could not possibly be written off without a formal inquiry. I summoned the inner circle to prepare for the investigation. All agreed that legally we could not be found negligent. We were volunteers and the fire was accidental. Nevertheless an inquiry in a Communist country was serious business. If we were found at fault the consequences could range from annoying to disastrous. At

worst somebody could decide to turn the fire at the camp near Ruma into a countrywide example of negligence to "socialist property" with dire personal consequences. You never know. A neighbor of my family's in Zagreb worked in a large department store. When the annual inventory found minor discrepancies he viewed them as an ordinary business problem and set out to rectify the situation. The poor fellow should have immediately defended himself. Within weeks the press portrayed the story as a major scandal. He was arrested, found guilty, sentenced to death, and summarily executed.

We decided to go on the attack. As soon as the officials arrive we would press charges about inadequate safety at the camp. First and foremost, the kitchen was not a freestanding building, as the safety code required. It was a disaster waiting to happen. Second, the camp had no firefighting equipment nor did we ever have a fire drill. Obviously the higher-ups did not have contingency plans either; throughout the fire, which could be seen from far away, nobody came to our help. At that point we would extol the bravery of the brigade and relate how everybody bemoaned the absence of firefighting equipment. Finally we'd inform the visitors that the "brigadiers" were asking us hard safety-related questions and requested that the commission meet with the entire brigade.

This was not so much a line of defense as it was the truth, but in those times of obedience to higher authorities our stance was a radical departure from usual practices. Instead of being asked, we'd ask the questions. But first we had to resolve the problem of Jovica P. Under the stress the poor fellow reverted to the standard mode of self-criticism, which the Party taught him so well.

"As soon as the commission arrives," he said, "I will stand up, take responsibility, and let the chips fall where they may. After all I had no experience with cooking and should never have volunteered for the job."

Overcome with guilt, he sat in an corner and every once in a while loudly proclaimed. "Comrades, I will sell my oxen and cows to compensate the state for the loss."

Jovica may have been cunning in his stupid ways. His self-criticism would create a positive impression with the commission. "A real comrade!" they would say, and right away start looking for bet-

ter targets. Why was Jovica permitted to go to the kitchen? Who came up with the stupid idea to make *ushtipci*? Why did we see fit to celebrate in such a loose way? Would it not have been better to summarize our achievements and go over our productivity figures? Was this possibly a "good riddance" celebration? If Jovica gave them an opening, the commission would have had a field day. We'd be too busy defending ourselves to ask any probing question about the higher-ups. And if we ever said something negative, Jovica's example would be thrown right at us. Why couldn't we own up to our responsibilities as he did?

Plain and simple we had to neutralize Jovica. But how? We tried to talk some sense to him but he wouldn't budge. He conceded that the designers of the camp may have not followed all safety rules, but it was he, Jovica, who lit the match. Again and again he kept reciting his new mantra." Comrades, I will sell my oxen and cows and compensate the state for the loss."

In a perverse way he was enjoying the newfound martyrdom and no matter what you told him, Jovica responded with the offer of oxen and cows. What do you do with a would-be martyr? You promise him an audience! First the senior staff of the brigade would meet with the commission and Jovica would address them later in front of the whole brigade. There in front of everybody he could make his generous offer of cow and oxen. At least we got a jump-start on Jovica.

The commander of the region arrived alone the next morning. A commission to take stock of the damage and to file a formal report was on its way. Before I could say a thing, the statistician and the quartermaster launched a ferocious and clever attack, suggesting that somebody higher up must be responsible. They wanted to know whether other camps had a similar design flaw and if so who was responsible for erecting them. Was there a fire emergency organization in other regions and who was responsible for the fire prevention in the chief of staff's office? We were lucky not to have injuries, but what if we had a large number of burns? Were there any provisions for field hospitals or emergency evacuation?

The commander was not prepared for such open criticism. Seeing us ready to raise questions with his superiors, he conceded that there may have been some problems, congratulated us on our brav-

ery and requested to tour the ruins. When the commission arrived, he held an executive session. In an hour we were presented with a signed document that characterized the fire as accidental, summarized the extent of the damage and complimented the brigade's exemplary behavior under difficult circumstances. The commander politely refused to address the brigade, promised unspecified measures to strengthen the safety of the camp, shook hands and left. Jovica lost his audience but everybody else was happy.

To this day I am proud of the way we handled the inquiry. It was a clear victory over the authorities, a rare occurrence in post-war Yugoslavia. I also have fond memories of the brigade's thunderous reaction to the announcement that we had been exonerated. It was a great, unsolicited vote of confidence to the leadership.

The next morning we decorated the trucks with flags and banners and took the completed portion of the highway on our way to a remote railway station. Everybody on the truck was in a festive mood and to our surprise the brigades still laboring along the route appeared to know we were coming. Each working group met us with great ovations and some laughter. No wonder; a smart aleck on the first truck deployed a large banner introducing us as "The Sixth Zagrebian, four-times-commended, one-time-striker, and one-time-burned brigade." The last irreverent act of a group of nonconformists!

⁂

In spite of deficiencies, the Belgrade-Zagreb highway was completed in one year and, surprisingly, it functioned well for years to come. The youth, cynical and not always very willing, gave a real gift to the nation. In a single swoop the country had been upgraded to an entirely different functional level. The monopoly of the inefficient, slow railways had been broken. All of a sudden trucks, busses and private cars started to make sense. Earlier Zagreb had only twenty kilometers of hard surface roads to the east, a similar distance to the west and nothing in the south-north direction. Before the completion of long highway, a trip to the countryside was a major adventure. The new highway brought everything within reach. A few years after

the highway had been completed, a network of paved secondary roads started to spread throughout the countryside. New attractive *Pullmans* replaced the old, rickety, road-beaten busses. Private cars started to proliferate. Before I graduated, the University Hospital found it necessary to improvise a few parking lots. This, more than anything else, was an open admission how things had changed in the medical school. Three years earlier there was not a single private car in sight. Professors and students alike took the streetcar to the nearest station and willingly negotiated the fifteen minutes of uphill walk to the hospital. A car in those times was viewed as a luxury and a rare a privilege. Only high Party functionaries were driven in official limousines, a situation well described in a popular riddle:

Question: "What is a Mercedes?"

Answer: "A Mercedes is a vehicle by which our nation travels through its representatives."

There was no way of stopping the proliferation of private cars. Soon aggressive jockeying for parking space replaced the fifteen-minute leisurely walk from the streetcar station. Within two years we had veritable jams in front of the hospital. A new way of living, sometimes mistaken for civilization, was knocking on the doors.

Everything around us started to change. In my third year of medical school, the Party began to release its grip and, with occasional exceptions, left us to our own devices. Liberated from nonsensical activities, the education section of the student organization could finally do some good. My *kruzhok* reconstituted itself into a nucleus of the editorial board of the journal *Medicinar* and I became its editor. The main purpose of the journal was to provide a forum for student research reports. The word research must be taken with a grain of salt but the principle was important and sound. The *Medicinar* fostered rudimentary research; we learned to synthesize the literature, to statistically analyze outcomes garnered from patient's charts, and to systematically approach a problem.

Publishing the journal was quite an adventure. For each issue we had to seek sponsorship from various sources: the medical school, the university, the youth organizations, Ministry of Health, advertisers and the like. Next the purchase of the paper, which was in short supply, had to be approved by the Ministry of Culture. Then came

negotiations with the printers to beat down the price and to get us in line for publishing. You might cajole the foreman into giving you priority only to find out tomorrow that they had run out of paper. When there was enough paper, somebody from high up would invariably bump us off the schedule. After printing, we had to get in line for page cutting and binding. Here too, the outcome much depended on our powers of persuasion.

We worked long hours without complaint. It was a labor of love, a volunteer work in the best sense of the word. Students around the *Medicinar* were the most bright, dynamic, enthusiastic group of individuals with whom I ever worked. The human mind, as it dwells on the past, tends to remember the good and forget the bad but I stand by the description of my colleagues in the *Medicinar*. Many of them went on to develop exceptional careers. L. R. became a professor of physiology in Boston, R.V. became a professor of gastroenterology at the University of Virginia, I. B. another gastroenterologist, teaches in an upstate New York medical school, M. V. a physiologist is member of the Royal Academy of Sciences in Canada, and Z.Sh. became a world-class diabetologist. From my *Kruzhok* Niksha Pokrajac is professor of physiology in Zagreb, Veljko Novak is a renowned endocrinologist in Rijeka, Boris Hranilovich became chief surgeon in the traumatology hospital in Zagreb, and I teach medicine and physiology at the University of Michigan. None of us had an easy time. Those who succeeded in emigrating, which was a feat in its own right, had to start from scratch and prove themselves to peers who knew nothing about their previous achievements. Those who remained in Croatia prevailed as non—Communists in a Communist environment. Apparently the inner drive which sustained us during our studies in Zagreb served us well later in life. Not bad for a group of youngsters who, undeterred by a grim reality and isolated from the rest of the world, did not give up striving for excellence.

The longer I was in school, the easier it was to study. In the fourth and fifth year we were finally ready to use what we had learned by

rote in the previous three years. Our group was particularly lucky to connect with Dr. J. Matovinovich who'd just returned from a two—year fellowship at Harvard University. Under his guidance we could practice real medicine years before becoming qualified physicians. We took daily notes, examined patients, ordered tests, drew blood, gave intravenous injections and presented patients progress at afternoon rounds. We managed to fulfill our ward responsibilities without missing regular classes. Everything had to be completed early in the morning or late in the afternoon. I loved every moment of this demanding advanced medical clerkship.

During that period I had one of the most emotional experiences of my entire medical career.

Slavko Kolar, the Croat novelist who created the little haven for us in Stanchich, survived the war. After the war we visited Kolar to thank him, but this marvelous man stopped Father in his first sentence.

"I did what I could and I am sure that whenever you could, you also helped others. Please don't embarrass me. Let's just have a nice dinner," he said.

However, I got a chance to help Mr. Kolar. Sick with terminal cancer, Slavko Kolar was admitted to my room in the University Hospital in Zagreb. At the end of their lives many people fall apart. Not Slavko Kolar! This dignified man maintained his poise and never lost his great sense of humor. After the war he had fallen into a conflict with the writer's union of Croatia. To Kolar, the whole situation was quite funny, a carryover of an old confrontation with Miroslav Krlezha. Great people are not necessarily nice people. Krlezha was an undisputed giant of Croatian letters, but not a pleasant companion to people around him. In his young fireball days before the Second World War, Krlezha was invited to the Pen Club where he delivered himself of a tirade punctuated by references to sweeping winds of reform, the red tide and the "proletariat" poised to shake the putrid inertia of old times. In his rhetorical fervor Krlezha occasionally banged the club's piano with his fists and, stunned by reverberations, paused for an instant, before embarking on another crescendo. Kolar, having had his fill, suggested during such a pause that, if he was

unwilling to spare listeners ears, Krlezha ought to at least go easy on the piano. Krlezha never forgot this bit of humor.

Krlezha was first at the extreme left, then, half recognizing the Communist excesses, moved politically to a more tolerant stance and succeeded, in spite of his Communist background, to sit out the war in Zagreb tucked away in a private sanitarium. Somebody higher up in the Ustashe movement must have appreciated Krlezha's literary contributions. Tito also admired Krlezha and protected him from vengeful comrades who could not forget the fact that Krlezha did not contribute to the resistance movement. In a few years, his star rising, Krlezha began to dominate the literary scene of post-war Croatia including the writers union. Kolar was not about to kow-tow to this talented survivalist. One thing lead to another, and Krlezha, "leaning over the same old piano," had Kolar expelled from the writers union.

When they heard about Kolar's terminal disease, the members of the writers union sent out peace feelers. Cowards, who should have stood by Kolar, now wanted to appease their guilt feelings.

Kolar rejected such peace offerings out of hand. With his keen sense of irony he sent a message to the league of novelists, "Stay true to tradition; rehabilitation only after death!" A clear reference to Stalinist practices of killing many a revolutionary and exculpating them many years later.

In his final days, Kolar set out to settle personal affairs. Once, having received a weekend pass, he returned to the hospital totally exhausted. He winked me to a bedside chat. He had just paid for the cemetery plot and had seen his tombstone. It read simply: "Slavko Kolar."

"I had as much fun seeing my name on that stone as I had when I saw it on the covers of my first book. It is a good name and I wish it to stay that way." whispered Uncle Slavko. "I made sure that the state does not pay for my funeral. That way they will not be able to put some self-serving garbage on the grave stone."

Kolar took a good five minutes to regain his breath and looking straight into my eyes he said, "Don't let them make any speeches at my grave. You know how it is: "*pokapat smo navek znali gospodski.*"

He referred to a poem by Krlezha about a poet who, spurned in real life and having contracted tuberculosis, was buried with great pomp amid a sea of crocodile tears.

We always knew how to bury in style

On the open grave,
oh dear departing friend
As lapis our tears are burning and

To our pain there is no end.
Oh God, to your sky, stars and meteors
we send
Another fallen talent . . . ."

Krlezha masterfully caught in the poem the pompous self-serving catharsis of a public burial. And Kolar did not want any of it, particularly if it were to come from the ranks of Krlezha's sycophants.

How right he was! The officialdom and the union showed up in numbers at the funeral. His nephew and I politely rejected all requests for eulogies. Nevertheless somebody, sheet of paper in hands, tried to assert himself. We restrained him physically. We could not tolerate falsehoods at the funeral of such a great and brave man.

Time went by in a hurry and after five years, right on schedule, I was poised to graduate. But before graduation there was another matter to attend to. I got strongly attracted to a beautiful, sophisticated and elegant divorcee who had a 5 years old daughter from her first marriage. Mara and I got married a few months before my graduation. The turbulent external circumstances which soon ensued caused a few early fractures, the passage of time widened them, and seventeen years later, we agreed to get a divorce.

The medical school preserved all pomp and circumstance of the graduation ceremony. The solemn procedure, entirely in Latin, took place in the *Aula* (auditorium) of the University. Adorned with the

golden insignia of the school the dean or his representative, ceremoniously handed out diplomas. All of this was exciting enough, but my promotion was even more engrossing. That year my father became the associate dean of the medical school, and not entirely by chance, the school delegated him to bestow the diplomas on the graduating class of 1953. My class selected me as its representative and I dutifully recited to Father the Latin formula that "having completed all the courses we respectfully request the Lord promoter to confer on us the title of Doctor Medicine with all the rights and privileges associated with such a title." It was one of the best moments in my life. Father and I were in seventh heaven.

The Tragedy

(1953-1954)

Though we lived together in a large centrally located apartment, Mother, Father and I had little time to interact. Mother tried to recreate regular dinners, which were the focal point of our family life before the war. But times had changed. Before the war we lived a structured life and getting together for dinner was a sacred ritual. But in the bustle of post-war Zagreb, each of us had different evening obligations, and it was near impossible to keep a steady schedule. Furthermore, Mother's personal life had radically changed. Before the war she disliked her role as a professional mother and wife. After she returned "from the forest," Mother acquired a new status of an independent health-care professional and soon realized that maintaining family togetherness and a full employment could not be reconciled. At best we succeeded to get together two to three times a week for dinner. And when we met, instead of discussing school, books and arts as we did in Vrapche, the dinner talk was all about work-related issues or politics.

Mother's wartime expertise in surgery and physical rehabilitation landed her the job as head nurse in the Department of Orthopedics at the University hospital in Zagreb. With her uncompromising style, Mother "shaped up" the personnel and ran the orthopedic wards with military precision. She proved to be an excellent teacher and trained a number of first-rate surgical nurses. Mother loved her work and became a much happier person.

Father became the Chief of Staff in the modern University Hospital "Rebro," a good four miles away from Mother's hospital. Besides his organizational work in the Rebro hospital, he was preoccupied with the three hundred odd severe cases of Kozara Disease, which continued to linger in Yugoslav hospitals. These patients turned the hospital visiting hours into nightmares. As soon as the visitors arrived, as if they were acting on a cue, all patients with Kozara Disease developed severe attacks. Violently acting out their wartime experience and convulsing in front of the visitors, they broke windows, turned over the furniture, destroyed chairs, and left the hospital in shambles. The hospital personnel didn't know what to do. Furthermore, led by the worst and most assertive individuals, groups of patients occasionally escaped the hospital and terrorized the neighborhood. By the evening, as if nothing had happened, they would sheepishly return for dinner in the hospital. Something had to be done.

The Chief of Medical Services of the Yugoslav Army received two completely different suggestions. My father pleaded for firmness. Under no circumstances should the troublemaker benefit from his histrionics. The condition should be looked upon as a weakness, not as a proof of a particularly difficult or heroic past. The patients should be institutionalized only in regular psychiatric wards where they would participate in special rehabilitation programs. However, they would neither get extra privileges, nor qualify for medical retirement.

The other proposal originated with Stephi Betleheim who trained under Sigmund Freud in Vienna. He firmly stuck to Freud's ideas and viewed the disease as a response to sexual repression during the war. Whereas the manifestations might be similar, he argued, every patient had a different personal experience, which rendered him susceptible to stress. Betleheim suggested that the Army organize special hospitals in pleasant surroundings. There each patient would be individually analyzed and receive full pension until his case was resolved. Suppressive therapy, Betleheim suggested, might get the patients back on their feet, but if they were not properly psychoanalyzed, the problem would return in a much more serious form.

Eventually the army medical service endorsed Father's approach. Patients were treated with dignity but to each of them the disease was

described as an inappropriate reaction to the war, which they must overcome. The major focus of the therapy was on relaxation techniques, vocational rehabilitation, and job placement. Patients soon realized that, no matter how severe their symptoms were, they wouldn't earn permanent medical retirement. Every request for pension was turned down with a standard explanation that "due to changing circumstances" the disease "has been abolished by the orders of the chief of the Staff of the Yugoslav Army." Only two avenues were left to a patient, either join the rehabilitation course to learn how to control the symptoms or be classified as a psychiatric case. And nobody wanted the label of a lunatic!

After a while the attacks started to recede and in few years the Kozara Disease practically disappeared. It is hard to tell whether Father's approach contributed to the decline. Most likely patients realized that their show time had run out. Audiences were shrinking. Bored by the spectacle and trying to forget the war, the average citizen had more important things to do than gawk at a yet another relic of past hard times.

Father did not draw much satisfaction from his battle against the Kozara Disease. He dreamed of returning to his old post in Vrapche and in 1948 he got his chance. At the end of the war the Ustashe-appointed boss of the hospital in Vrapche escaped to Germany. Dr. Gostl, the lonely bachelor who once tried to teach me appreciation of Bruckner's music, had been appointed as temporary director. Gostl, a desperately shy and indecisive man, hated his new job. He urged Father to return to Vrapche as the hospital's permanent director. Father, who before the war advocated radical reforms of psychiatric hospitals, saw Gostl's proposal as a unique opportunity to make a difference, and gladly accepted the offer.

The hospital in Vrapche occasionally had spectacular results with advanced methods of electro convulsion and intravenous insulin in acute depression. But the psychiatrists in the 1940s and 50s could do very little for chronic delusions in schizophrenics. If the initial treatment failed, patients were assigned to a chronic ward with standing orders for heavy sedatives to control agitation, and if that failed, a strait-jacket was always on standby. My father disliked this state of affairs. He firmly believed that the hospital ought to make life

bearable to people who were out of touch with reality. He was convinced that even the most disconnected psychiatric patient could sense whether he was being treated well or brutalized.

His point was well proven during the occupation, when the Nazis came to Vrapche with trucks to deport the most deprived chronic patients. The officer in charge made no bones about his intentions. The patients were a burden to the society and would be eliminated. Though they appeared lost behind their private curtains of delusions, the unfortunate patients had an instinctive sense of foreboding. They screamed and kicked as if saying, "Leave me alone, I am happy where I am. I do not wish to go elsewhere." Most likely they were just responding to the brutal change in their routines. But that was exactly the point. There was an order to their lives and it meant something to them.

Father wanted to give every chronic psychiatric patient a chance to lead a meaningful life. In the old hospital he spent considerable time making the patients productive, instilling in them a sense of achievement and giving them an occasional break from monotony. Work and entertainment were the cornerstones of his approach and as the director, Father expected to expand these activities. He wanted to institute a program of regular re-examination of all chronic patients and develop a system for their advancement. Those showing some promise would be considered for another round of treatment. If a patient remained stable but had learned to socialize, he'd be rewarded with an occasional pass for out-of-hospital trips. Once a patient learned some simple skills he would be trained to master more complex tasks as well as to learn the basics about money and economics. Finally, Father wanted to develop a teaching program for foster-care adoption and hoped to start discharging chronic patients to "halfway houses." Eventually the hospital in Vrapche would organize a network of villages skilled in handling stable, productive mental patients along the lines of the Scandinavian model.

Of course all this called for major reorganization. New physicians, psychologists and educators would be recruited. Regular reviews of the health status of each individual chronic patient would be instituted. Furthermore, Father envisioned regular conferences

to discuss recent medical literature and to organize research in the hospital. Full of idealistic energy, Father described his vision in a letter to the personnel.

In retrospect, Father should have known better. His letter did not sit well with a small group of hospital employees who during the war joined the Partizans, and upon armistice, returned to the hospital not to work, but to claim wages. During the war they commanded a considerable respect among other combatants and it was difficult for them to step back into the civilian role of a small cog in a large psychiatric hospital. Yet they were not fit for better jobs. Going back to school was unappealing to these barely literate middle-aged men. Under the guise of political reeducation, and with considerable help from the district Party leadership, the former Partizan employees organized themselves into a meddling, overbearing group bent on running all aspects of the hospital's life.

The hospital personnel in Vrapche were highly inbred. Employees kept signing up relatives for open jobs until an extended family grew into a large and powerful clan. Before the war much time was spent in skirmishes between various clans. After the war, the district Party leadership headed by Jurica Draushnik, a local son and a ruthless political operator, acted with dispatch to include the hospital jobs into its system of political patronage. Recognizing the threat to their hegemony, old families united to fight the Party.

A few days before Father took up the post in Vrapche, a certain Comrade Kavedzich, the foreman of the hospital's tailoring workshop and presently the secretary of the Party in the hospital, paid a visit to Father. He came to discuss the results of an "in-depth analysis" of the local situation. The Party was very happy with the way things were going. There was no real need for changes. Father would do better to stay on as director of the University Hospital in Zagreb, where he could have a much larger impact.

Plain and simply, the Party did not want him but Father expected to prevail. On the foundations of the old institution, with or without the help of the Party, he'd transform Vrapche into a new modern psychiatric hospital. Sadly, Father failed to understand the new reality. After the war the hospital became split into us, the forty odd party

members—former Partizans versus them, the majority of the personnel. The *us* must have known that the real *them*, the few people who truly cooperated with the Nazis, had run away. However, as far as the former guerrillas were concerned, the large apolitical majority of hospital workers could not be trusted. The Party was set to reeducate "misled masses," whether they wished it or not! In this scheme of things there was little place for patient care. Ideological purity was the order of the day and Father had nothing to contribute to that. The battle lines were drawn. Even today I do not know who was at fault. Sometimes I think Father should have understood the situation and should not have returned to the hospital. But return he did.

Soon after Father assumed his new post, the veterans realized that Partizan solidarity notwithstanding, Father would let the chips fall where they might. Once the old employees saw that Father was not taking orders from the Party, there was no way of stopping them. They ruthlessly challenged the Party at every step. Any time a conflict arose, the old employees painted it as a clash of political operatives with the hard-working loyal personnel and sought Father's protection. I am sure most conflicts were exaggerated. It was a constant tug of war. "You can't get us," the old personnel signaled to the Party leadership. "What is the use of all your political grandstanding when you have no actual influence?"

Father lost a great deal of time in adjudicating conflicts, all the while not realizing what was really going on. He felt it his noble duty to protect the workers, but failed to see that many conflicts were contrived only to humiliate the ever more frustrated political leadership.

After he took the new job in Vrapche, I saw Father even less frequently than before. Distance sometimes helps to understand people. Had I seen him daily I might not have noticed subtle changes but at those rare dinners when we got together, Father looked increasingly withdrawn and tired. He normally tended to keep things to himself, but the struggle in Vrapche was getting to him; the goings-on in the hospital became regular topics during our dinners. Mother's emotional outcries and her expressions of disgust at Father's opponent were of little help. Something else was needed and I itched to organize an open battle with Father's enemies. In my opinion, if he wanted to succeed, Father should have requested that a few key "opposi-

tion" leaders in the hospital be reassigned to outside jobs. However, whenever I came up with a specific proposal to challenge this and that or to look for support among our wartime friends, Father was unusually passive. He'd pass all my ideas off with a reference to his belief that ultimately, the only thing that counted, was that he was right. Once he even used the cliché that "justice would prevail."

I just about blew my top.

"C'mon, Tata," I said. "How could you believe in justice. You experienced none in the old Yugoslavia. You were one on the most talented and best-trained psychiatrists in the country and yet they kept you on ice. And as far as justice in the new regime goes, you ought to remember Mr. Dorich."

Mr Dorich, who had been executed on trumped up charges of "economic crimes against the state," lived one floor above us. He too had clashed with the Party leadership in his store and it cost him his life.

"But I am not Mr. Dorich!" said Father. This was not an answer; it was a plea to be let alone.

Had I known better, instead of urging him to action, I would have looked up a psychiatrist. Father was getting depressed.

With the passage of time, the conflict in Vrapche grew deeper. The Party kept proposing an ever-increasing list of new job to accommodate friends of Kavedzhich and his gang. Frequently they did not even pretend that the jobs were needed. They would show Father a curriculum vitae of some reliable and deserving local party member requesting that Father create a job for him. Father routinely refused such requests, which was exactly what the local Party cell hoped for. They knew that Father's refusal to accept the Party's dictum would not sit well with Jurica Draushnik, the local political bigwig. He was the region's deputy in the parliament and the hospital was the largest employer in his area. Draushnik could ill afford to lose the largest political patronage in his district. To regain the initiative, Draushnik conspired with Kavedzich and the Party cell in the hospital to replace the hospital's entire administrative staff with their own people. So started a relentless campaign to malign the administrators. They were called incompetent, accused of defrauding, stealing from the hospital stores, taking bribes for appointments, living

on hospital supplies and so on. It is amazing how effective such a harangue can be if the perpetrators are ruthless and spare no time. Kavedzich, the tailor, left to take up a political job in the district, but not before he appointed his wife, an inventory clerk, as the Party secretary in the hospital. Now the Kavedzich duo had both inside and outside bases for the campaign. The wife regularly came up with new accusations, while the sympathetic husband, professing horror at the new accusations, kept appointing new outside investigators. As soon as one investigative body finished its report, the other was on its way. In all there were six investigations; by the county, labor unions, Ministry of Health, Ministry of Labor, county health authorities and the City Council of Health in Zagreb. None could find fraud. The three health-authority-based commissions found substantial progress in patient care and expressed their confidence in the medical leadership. Even the worst examiner appointed by the county could not come up with specifics but suggested that the associate director be removed for lack of proper "inter-human relationships." Each commission recognized that there were two groups in the hospital, that the accusations stemmed from infighting between them, and that both sides had lost objectivity. However none of the commissions suggested a remedy.

Shameless and mean, Kavedzich and his group kept reheating old accusations and fabricating new ones. Regardless that they were discredited in previous hearings, the same witnesses again showed up to repeat the same old story.It was difficult to deal with such an amoral and determined enemy. Jurishich, the assistant hospital director got the message and left. My father fell victim to his own rigid sense of duty. Like the captain in a sinking ship story, he would be the last to bail out. And there was no end in sight.

Having succeeded in shooting at the kneecap level, the Party now readied itself for a salvo at the head. In the Party's view, Jurishich's resignation was a proof of guilt. When he resigned the hospital Party cell organized a steady stream of new commissions to investigate Father's alleged misdeeds.

After the fourth commission, Father felt he'd done enough and started to ask for protection. Everybody was very sympathetic, but nobody offered to stop the harangue. Father was in essence sent back

to fight a battle without ammunition. There is only so much a person can take.

At that point I realized Father was in real trouble. He was too proud to step down under pressure. After a few conferences with Father's friends I thought we had found a good way to divert his attention from Vrapche. The school of medicine in Zagreb had been asked to organize a new medical school in Rijeka on the Adriatic coast. The dean in Zagreb offered Father the job of Associate Dean for the development of the fledgling seaside medical school. The new job was exciting. Father would have considerable latitude in setting up the curriculum and selecting the new faculty. And he could choose whether he wanted to commute or move to Rijeka.

Father refused the offer out of hand and assured the dean that under normal circumstances he'd love to take the job, but he could not take another responsibility until he resolved the mess in Vrapche.

The conflict in Vrapche boiled over immediately after the local elections. There were two lists of candidates for the hospital's self-management council—one by the Party and another by the alliance of clans. District-wide Draushnik was the only candidate for the parliament. The voters could register their dissatisfaction with the single candidate by dropping the ballot into a "black box." A particularly depraved communist technique: You had a choice but you could not elect anybody other than the Party candidate. It is known as the *paradise technique*. When God presented Eve to Adam he said," There she is. Now you choose."

In the hospital the election results were radically different from any other poling unit in the district. The Party candidates routinely recorded a ninety five percent victory against their nonexistent opponents but in the hospital sixty five percent of votes went into the black box. And to add insult to injury, Party's slate for the self-management-council lost by a margin of four to one.

The single most glaring perversion of communism is its insistence on formal solutions, which are never sincerely implemented. Workers' councils in Yugoslavia were another case in point. People in these councils were supposed to run enterprises and make economic decisions. But the decisions were not implemented if the Party disagreed. Totally anesthetized by their own double standards, the

Yugoslav leaders never contemplated that the workers might actually act independently. But unpleasant surprises were in store. People started to assert themselves and the Party could not take it.

Draushnik was profoundly embarrassed by the election results in Vrapche. His grip on the district was slipping. A few days after the elections, he convened a public meeting to "analyze the situation" in the hospital and to embarrass Father. Draushnik organized the meeting outside of the hospital walls but Father decided to attend. In Father's mind the election results in the hospital proved that he had a strong majority support, the latest commission exonerated him again, and he expected to prevail. I was concerned and convinced Father to let me attend the meeting.

Draushnik did his homework. A group of local ruffians booed and applauded on signal, the silent majority remained silent, the same disgruntled employees brazenly repeated old assertions, and journalists came to duly record the accusations. No matter that all previous commissions found no wrongdoing and that the courts consistently rejected the insinuations!

Anytime Father stood up, he was booed. I frequently got up to defend him but it was an uphill battle. My only help, and a pleasant surprise, came from Branko Bucalo, a journalist and a colleague who I occasionally met in various youth forums. He came to the meeting in line with his duties, had no personal obligations to us, but could not tolerate the gross injustice. He and I fought for hours, but to no avail. The meeting was a vehicle to get all the accusations into the press. There was nothing we could do about it. It was a setup, a moral lynching, and a terrible, disheartening experience.

I am afraid I have nothing good to say about the "silent majority" in the hospital. They comfortably hid behind Father's back and equally comfortably abandoned him when he needed support. The silence at the public meeting, at the staged drama, when he was accused and nobody had the guts to defend him, was the hardest thing to take. In spite of his stereotypic middle-European intellectual leftist leanings, deep down Father was an aristocrat. Somewhat aloof, uncompromising, firmly believing that everybody should do his job, no matter what it was. He went to great lengths to be fair to the last janitor, but he was not a populist. He stayed clear of mass meetings,

kept in touch only with a few similar souls, and did not try to endear himself to anybody. It was not his style. As far as Father was concerned, the fight in and around the hospital was a byproduct of his directorial position. It came with the turf. It was up to him to provide a good working environment, assure good patient care and keep politics out of the hospital. That horrible evening he must have felt that others were not doing their share, that it all was futile.

Leaving the meeting, Father was composed but somewhat withdrawn. I was planning future moves. "Let's talk about it later," he said. "Right now I want to thank you. Never in my life will I forget what you have done for me."

Father defending himself at the fatal conference in Vrapche.

Next morning in the hospital, he closed the door to his office, wrote a number of concise farewell letters, put the pistol in his mouth and, in the style of an Austrian officer whose honor was at stake, pulled the trigger. "They extinguished the flame in me," he said in one and "I am tired," in another letter. As simple as that!

The very same morning when Father pulled the trigger, I was in the office of the copy editor of the leading newspaper in Zagreb haggling with him about the wording of his description of the meeting in Vrapche. The article detailed all accusations against Father and gave no space to our side. A telephone call came through. It was uncle Branko Gostl from Vrapche. He could not quite get himself to tell it straight. "Take a taxi and come to the hospital, something tragic has happened," he said. I pretty much knew what to expect, but on my way to Vrapche I kept inventing various less tragic scenarios. When

the taxi arrived in Vrapche one look through the window took away the last hope. At the main entrance to the hospital a group of employees, including some crying women in black attire, waited to express their condolences.

The scene in Father's office was eerily serene. The body had been tidied up, the stains were removed and Father's corpse sat in the armchair as if he had an afternoon nap.

Mother arrived minutes later. She was overcome with grief. Nobody can come up with right words for such a horrible event. But in her pain, for reasons that I will never fully comprehend, Mother kept screaming about Father's knowledge of anatomy. How only a person that masters the anatomy as well as he did could shoot himself in such a precise fashion. I presume she tried to convince herself that Father had died instantly. Branko Gostl managed to restrain Mother from hugging the body, the back of Father's head had been practically blown off by the exiting bullet.

In me the sadness soon gave way to anger. Anger beyond description at that political turncoat, Jurica Draushnik.

Before the war Draushnik was a small entrepreneur, owner of a flourmill and an avid local politician. He used to parade around in the green semi uniform of the virulently anti-Serbian Croat Peasant party. During the first few weeks of the German occupation, he still wore his green regalia. He had good reason for celebration: the Germans broke the Serbian yoke and an "Independent State of Croatia" was about to be founded. Unfortunately for him, the true Croat Nazis had little use for the former Peasant party and as soon as the elite Ustashe returned from exile, Draushnik disappeared from sight. It was not in his style to lie low unless there was a good reason. I suspect he had personal enemies among the repatriates. Whatever made him, as the peasant would say, "smaller than the poppy seed," eventually also led to his complete disappearance. He resurfaced in the resistance movement. Once with the Partizans, Draushnik acquired a special status as one of the few non-communist professional politicians in the movement. This perceived political importance served him well after the war. Though he had long since joined the Communist party, Draushnik helped the communists to maintain the illu-

sion that the new regime represented a democratic alliance of diverse antifascist political factions.

As soon as Mother half-calmed down, I placed a call to Draushnik. I thought of poetic justice. No doubt Draushnik would be shocked when he heard from the victim's son.

How ludicrous and romantic to think that a village bully, who thrived on controlling every aspect of life in Vrapche, would ever feel ashamed!

"I do not care what he did to himself," said the brute, "Don't expect me to go soft. I have seen many deaths. Furthermore, your father was not such an important person as you make him out to be."

What then transpired cannot be recorded. I started by saying that Father's standing was irrelevant and an honest person should feel responsible even if he did accidentally run over a dog. At the end it all deteriorated into a long helpless string of curses peppered with unrealistic threats.

Getting nowhere, I slammed down the receiver. There were some other urgent practical matters to attend. First I had to convince the newspaper editor to publish the full report. This was quite a switch. Earlier I'd fought with him, sentence by sentence, to mollify his description of the meeting. Now I wanted everything published in its roughest form for people to see how dirty the campaign was and what pushed my father to suicide. Unfortunately Draushnik was not stupid. In the name of "good taste," he suppressed the story.

But Draushnik was quite worried. In 1948, Tito started to change the public face of the Party. Whereas the communists remained in full control, a sense of order started to evolve. Travel to foreign countries was liberalized and economic emigration had been permitted. An ordinary citizen could go to court, challenge the authorities and, as long as the stakes were small, win. But liberalization is a funny thing, as world leaders from the Shah to Gorbachev have learned. Once the grip is just a bit less tight, people do not stop to express their thanks. They push for more. The same thing happened in Yugoslavia in 1953. Milovan Djilas, an old time communist, and Tito's personal friend, started the challenge from inside. In the beginning Tito had no idea how far Djilas would go and permit-

ted his friend to express some dissent. Both were long-time comrades accustomed to carefully planned political moves. Tito needed Djilas as an antidote to the pro-Stalin faction and permitted him to organize a semblance of a progressive wing within the Party. A little bit of democracy could not hurt. Or so Tito thought. But in his latest book, *New Class,* Djilas declared an open war against both Russian and Yugoslav communism!

Father's tragedy became a test case in the conflict between the feuding party factions. The pro-Djilas papers in Zagreb wrote in great detail about forces at play, whereas the conservative stalwarts floated myriad variations on the old "aberration of the system" theme. For me the conflict was strictly personal; the larger issues did not matter. In simple terms, I wanted Draushnik's head. He was responsible. Whether an aberration or an inevitable consequence of a corrupt system, he was the perpetrator and he should suffer the consequences.

Our home became headquarters of a political action, something unheard of before Djilas changed the ways of the Party. We wanted to remove Draushnik from his influential Party post and force him to resign from the parliament. A group of Party members from the medical school carried the brunt of our offensive. As former Partizan physicians they had a leg to stand on. Tactically they distanced themselves from the Djilas-versus-Party conflict and spoke only about specifics in Vrapche. They requested an audience with Dr. Vladimir Bakarich, the secretary of the Communist party of Croatia, a fellow intellectual and a chronically ill person. He was the high priest of communism in Croatia and was known for his interest in theoretic concepts and his dislike of dealing with details. Nevertheless, some members of the delegation who handled Bakarich's frequent medical problems, expected to prevail upon him.

It did not work. Bakarich politely complained about the very difficult and complex times. He suggested that it would be much better if comrades had focused on other problems than attacking a member of the Party executive. When a whole organization of intellectuals makes requests, a false impression might be created. Their activism might be seen as an attempt to set their own political agenda, that they are out to prove that physicians are invulnerable and that they

should be exempted from daily cares of socialist reality. Whereas he personally does not share such a distorted view of the physicians' action, Bakarich bemoaned the fact that he might not be able to offer them any protection should others decide to attack them. Furthermore Bakarich stated that he did not feel well and could not possibly increase his workload with this added task. However, he'd like to return to the problem at a later date.

Little did the delegation know what Bakarich's postponement of further action meant! In a fortnight the political winds changed and in a 180-degree turn, Bakarich wrote a "cease and desist" article against the physician's movement.

In the meantime, the public campaign to force Draushnik to resign from the Parliament developed a momentum of its own. Its cornerstone was a petition by prominent physicians. Mild in tone, the petition simply asked for public discussion but everybody knew that such a discussion would have been the end of Draushnik. After a while he would be sufficiently humiliated to resign.

The physicians' petition carried its weight and forced the editor of the official Party newspaper to get off the fence. In addition to the physicians' petition, he also published Father's letter, which he had received ten days earlier. Here is the text of the article from the national edition of *Borba,*

Why did Dr. Dezider Julius commit suicide?

On December 24. 1953, Dr. Dezider Julius, Director of the mental hospital in Vrapche committed suicide.

The day before the suicide of Dr. Julius, a public meeting was held in Vrapche by the local Communist party organization at which there was very strong criticism of the work and attitudes of the Director of the mental hospital, Dr. Dezider Julius.

After the meeting, just before his death, Dr. Julius wrote a letter to the editor of Borba *which included the following:*

"Comrade Editor,

During my lifetime, I never have asked for space in your paper. Thus allow me the exception now. Will you please put in your paper that I have been the victim of a well-planned slander campaign. When I decided to take this step, I was not afraid of the con-

sequences of this campaign. It would be easy to repudiate the unfounded accusation. No, it was not that! I just could not keep fighting unscrupulous people. I am tired. This should also be a reminder to honest and conscientious journalists not to use unreliable and untruthful information just for the sake of sensationalism, but to be careful and objective."

The cause of Dr. Julius' death is still unclear. An investigation is under way.

In connection with the death of Dr. Julius 147, physicians from the People's Republic of Croatia also have sent a letter to the editor of Borba, *which we publish in full.*

Following is the Physicians letter concerning the death of Professor Dr.Dezider Julius:

"On the 24th of December, Professor Dr.Dezider Julius met his tragic death. His death disrupted a very fruitful career and the manifold activities which Professor Dr. Dezider Julius was carrying out while alive. His work was for the benefit of our socialist society and the international reputation of our country. Among his positions Professor Dr. Julius was a long-time member of the Executive Board of the Physicians Association of Croatia and the Vice-President of its Neuropsychiatric Section; Vice-President of the International Congress of Psychiatry; Vice-President of the International Association of Mental Hygiene; professor and past Associate Dean of the Medical School, University of Zagreb; director of the mental hospital in Vrapche; Lecturer at the Law School, University of Zagreb and councilman of the second district of the Township of Zagreb.

Just before his tragic death Professor Dr. D. Julius was accused in public. After his death the public was left disoriented and uninformed about the true facts of the case. There are even some who think that his death proves that these accusations were true.

This is not the first time that some individuals in the hospital have accused the management of the mental hospital in Vrapche, where Dr. Julius was the director. Because of such accusations, the Council for Public Health and Social Welfare formed another investigating commission over a year ago. Their conclusion was that all the accusations against Dr. Julius were unfounded and untrue.

It is our opinion that there should be a public discussion of this case. The irresponsible method of accusations should be publicly

condemned, especially in the case of Professor Dr. Julius, because it is not the first time. This kind of irresponsible public "criticism," whose goal is to discredit a man's work in spite of the established facts, should be disavowed as not in the best interest of our community. With full trust in the work and accomplishments of Dr. Julius, the undersigned believe in the need for quick action which will inform the public about the true facts in Dr. Julius' case and also to give him the well deserved public approval for his work."

Follow 147 signatures.

A mild letter, but sufficient to aggravate Bakarich. He did not want an investigation within the Party and a public debate, but didn't quite know how to stop the whole thing. These were difficult times. Tito appeared to tolerate such excesses. What if Djilas succeeded in winning? Bakarich was biding his time.

My brother Djuka had returned from America, where he was the corespondent to the Belgrade newspaper *Politika*. Bakarich knew him and invited us both for a chat. After platitudes about Father and formal condolences, he got to the point.

"We cannot set a precedent," said Dr. Bakarich," whereby a group of intellectuals can mount a campaign to remove a leader of proletarian background. This is not to say that Draushnik is without fault and that he will not eventually be removed. Just wait a few years. He will slowly fade away. In the meantime, believe me, any time your paths cross, he will, from sheer shame, pass to the other side of the street. I understand how you feel, but there are certain political realities, which cannot be overlooked. Stop the agitation and let me do it my own way."

It was nice of him to take the time and he probably did his best. But there was also the implied threat. Draushnik has been promoted to the exalted position of a "proletarian." Actually he was a middle-class businessman, but not having a University degree was sufficient to not brand him as an intellectual. Ergo, by Bakarich's logic of the moment, he became a proletarian. In the inner circles of the Party, Bakarich, a lawyer and an intellectual, labored under a stigma. How else was he to prove his emancipation from a bourgeois background but by consistently siding with "exploited masses." By classifying him as a proletarian, Bakarich had promoted Draushnik to an

untouchable status. Furthermore, Bakarich branded our activities as "agitation." Agitation is, by definition, a political act. All our future activities would be considered hostile acts against the Party. If you grew up in former Yugoslavia, understanding the context of a word became second nature, a mark of social intelligence. I got the hint, but would not stop. Events were out of control.

The atmosphere during those intensive weeks after Father's death was very similar to what we experienced at the beginning of the war. Again, you could easily find out who was who. Just as before, some cowards didn't dare to show up. Others, overtaken by the emotion of the moment, visited and pledged help only to wake up next morning in a cold sweat. Challenging the government was a serious business. Roughly half of the visitors who showed initial inclination later quietly distanced themselves from any concrete action. As far as I was concerned this was fine. They had good intentions, and that was all that counted.

But, just the same as during the war, there were also pleasant surprises. Help came from people we barely knew. My "Angel Protector," was a case in point. We'd met three years earlier in a summer camp as volunteers to build the dam for a new hydroelectric power station. I was more or less forced to go there but the Angel, a high-ranking member of the Central Committee of the Party, volunteered freely. As a true idealist Angel joined the guerrilla movement immediately after the German occupation. Literate and highly intelligent, he made his mark first as a political commissar of a brigade, later of a division and finally as *Agitprop* Chief of a region. Presently he was the chief for ideological activities in the Central Party Committee in Zagreb. Not unlike Father, he had an exaggerated sense of fairness. Since he urged the youth to work instead of vacationing, he felt he ought to set an example. So there he was, a decade older than the rest of us, working hard and seeking no privileges. But when evening fell, he had no time for childish campfire activities. And that is how we became friends. With me he could at least share war stories and talk about the future. The Angel was not happy with running the ideology machine. Before he joined the guerillas he had completed the first year of medical school. If he were to resume medical studies, he could shift from general politics to healthcare issues. The Party would not

give him full leave, but his present job was not all that difficult. Could he possibly master both tasks? He'd have to study at a slower pace than other students and that bothered this proud man.

During those evening conversations we came up with a plan. If he decided to enroll, and if he needed help, I'd work with him in the evenings. It would help me refresh my knowledge and give him an opportunity to rehearse with somebody. As it turned out, this was not necessary. He worked very hard and passed all the theoretical exams with ease. Later, during the clinical years, the Party gave him a paid leave of absence and he was on his way to a diploma.

The Angel was one of the first visitors after Father's death. I spoke with him about our plans to impeach Draushnik. He listened with sympathy but he knew the score.

"Most likely you will not succeed," he said, "but I understand why you have to do it. There is a great deal of sympathy for you and I think everybody will understand your actions. You will be protected, but be careful not to ruin other people's lives. And watch who joins you. Everybody has his own agenda."

This old communist operative did not give me the Johan Sebastian Bach routine. He did not play a variation on the aberration-which-must-be-ignored fugue. He just gave me honest advice and a realistic assessment of the situation. He came to help his young friend and protect him both from dangerous company and from self-destruction.

"I must stay out of the fray," he continued, "but I will be very well informed. You are playing a dangerous game and, frankly, you are likely to get burned."

"I am ready for it. It is a cause well worth getting burned for!" I protested with youthful abandon.

"Right. Get burned. But I do not want to see you consumed by the flame. You will not hear from me unless it is absolutely necessary. To the extent that I can, I will help. But if I call you, it will not be to give you advice. It will be a directive!" In the Party jargon, a "directive" was an order, which had to be executed without further question.

The Party pretended as if nothing had happened but the pro-Djilas group kept the pressure on. Their newspaper *Naprijed* published a series of thoughtful articles suggesting that Dr. Julius was the victim of a system which must be reformed.

In the meantime, Bakarich continued playing a political stick-and-carrot game. The carrot was Draushnik's well-publicized disappearance from the scene. Suddenly the Army felt an urgent need to retrain him in the school for higher officers in Belgrade. In line with Soviet practices, such a development signaled the fall from power. First a person would disappear from public sight. He might later reappear in a lesser position or permanently end up on the sidelines.

Eventually, Angel Protector's warning proved correct. "Watch who joins you; everybody has his own agenda." he said. The increasingly strident opposition around Djilas kept using Father's tragedy for their purposes. There was little I could do about it.

And the star of my unsolicited ally, Djilas, was in a sharp descent. The Angel called. He had arranged for me to read a manuscript Bakarich had submitted to the editor of *Vijesnik* in Zagreb. Bakarich, a clever politician, was on his way to the session of the Yugoslav Central Committee in Belgrade, which would determine Djilas' fate. He prepared the piece to put himself into a good light should Djilas lose. Angel was ninety five percent sure that the article would be published. Reading it would give me an idea what was coming down the pike.

It was quite an article and if it got published my fate was sealed. About twelve hours later Bakarich developed a good feel for the political winds, left the session in progress, called the editor, and had the paper published half a day before the final vote in the Central Committee. Under the guise of discussing the Julius case, he took an anti-Djilas stance a day before anybody else.

The article took up two newspaper pages. Bakarich wrote in a typical communist style, rooted in German philosophy and Stalin's paranoia. Marx had adopted Kant's and Hegel's style of lengthy multiple interpolated sentences and Stalin made sure that nothing was ever stated straight. One had to read such a text first to parse its grammatical composition and then, once again, to hopefully unravel the hidden meaning. All those elements were in Bakarich's text—and

then some. He liberally used parentheses either to mollify a previous tough statement or to hit, in passing, another target. And the paper was cleverly composed to paint Bakarich all at once as a benevolent liberal and a staunch guardian of ideological purity. When he praised my father, a disclaimer immediately followed; when he lashed out against communist intellectuals, he'd in the same breath indicate that he speaks about a "vocal minority" and so on. It is impossible to translate Bakarich's "style." His very long sentences were idiosyncratic and the thinking was convoluted.

First, Bakarich paid perfunctory respects to Father "because it appears that this is requested of us." Thereafter, Bakarich described Father as a good specialist who could not understand the social context of the struggle in Vrapche. Julius might have taken some events personally but, in fact, the conflict in his hospital was a battle between the *old* and the *new*. Father, the social illiterate, wanted to improve the hospital but deep down he was fighting for old privileges. Ditto for the communists from the medical school, who tried to defend my father. Knowing it or not, they too were fighting for old privileges. These same communists favored keeping nuns in the University Hospital when the Party attempted to "protect these nuns" against "slave labor" by returning them back to their monasteries. This proved, so Bakarich said, that doctors would rather keep old privileges than deal with "a modern work-force."

Having disposed of the physicians as a privileged class, Bakarich took a swipe at the legal system, which repeatedly ruled against the Party interests. The judges also failed to understand the modern society.

After that he, undertook to comment on elections in Vrapche and to explain the difference between the *new* and *old* democracy. Here I must quote a few of his most obfuscating passages:

> *"The 'democracy' in Vrapche did not go that route. It was fighting for the 'majority.' This is a classic position of the kind of democracy which our country strives to liquidate (and that is why ours is called a socialist democracy). In our democracy, the governance is not elected and should not be elected on the principle 'who will govern' but should be elected to permit a maximal participation of all. Instead, in Vrapche people's mouths have been shut by voting*

and by majority. The overall results are an unhealthy situation and the suicide of comrade Julius."

In case the reader did not get it right, in another part Bakarich came again back to the issues of democracy:

"Under the guise of humanism and democracy they, (the Julius group) asked for protection of old "working relationships" in the hospital. They sought the protection of formal democracy in its dirtiest form of "democratic" concealment of autocratic obstinacy."

I am not making this up! This is how most of the article sounded. The new democracy means, *forget the majority*, democracy is what the Party tells you.

Bakarich ended his strange piece by perversely blaming the communists from the medical school for preventing him from giving a proper recognition to Father.

"A quiet recognition of his life strivings was properly due, but forced public clarification of these issues leads us to anything but giving the recognition, and the public campaign threatens to reduce everything to unsolvable local issues which, if aired, would only cause the dirt to fly in all directions. Those who might be interested in the details of the life of the deceased (that is, washing out small spots that have been thrown at him) may well pursue it but this is not a task for us. We think that he does not need it. To the opposite, we think that the deceased Comrade Julius needs to be washed of the intent of the largest part of the campaign. . . . Contrary to his present defenders, Julius did not try to cover up areas where he was not in the right but he did try to protect himself where thought he was in his right. And whereas he thought a campaign was organized against him, he did not see it as an effort with criminal intentions. He, in fact, was not only honorable, but also reasonable. And it is a pity that somebody did not explain in time to him what was the matter, that he should not consider as small, those things that in reality are essential. Had this been done, the tragedy could have been avoided and our cause would have gotten somebody who could have liquidated the discussion in Vrapche and could have continued his (not small) life's work.

> *The ones that wish to give him recognition and to prevent (in his honor) such case from arising again should put their weight behind efforts to solve the problems through which we have lost him. That will be the best monument to him, a monument to an honorable fighter and a revolutionary who unfortunately died from a stray bullet."*

To this date, these last lines make my blood boil. If Bakarich just had time to explain things to him, Father would have magically understood the error of his ways. Forget that Father sought help and counsel from the Party and that he never got any. And his brave deed, his appeal for justice, had been converted into a meaningless act. A "stray bullet" of the revolution!

Studded with ambivalence and Delphic inscrutability, Bakarich produced another showpiece of communist penmanship. Under the superficial softness and past the condescending passages, the paper was loaded with such malevolence that it brought the movement against Draushnik to a grinding halt. Everybody knew what the article really meant. Julius died from a stray bullet. Nothing we can do about that. However, those who may continue to analyze the case or dare to make further public requests would be dealt with.

The doors were closing. But Bakarich was not about to lose his credit among the intellectuals. Having gotten his way, he started to backtrack. Rough times were ahead: people would lose their jobs, some would get arrested, and he wished to distance himself from such unpleasant things. A few weeks after publication of the article, he invited a group of prominent physicians to assure them that the fact that they signed the published petition would not be considered a counterrevolutionary act. In fact he was sympathetic and wished more could be done, but the times were just not right. Upon rereading his speech in the parliament, he thought it was a bit too harsh. Nor should his article be misunderstood. He was not anti-intellectual but wanted to stop them before they went too far. He wished everybody to know that if the "workers" decided to rebel, he might not be able to protect the intellectuals. Furthermore, as physicians they should understand that he was under a great deal of stress. Under such circumstances, one makes mistakes.

A master politician! But Bakarich may have this time been sincere. A repression was in full swing and some of his bloodthirsty comrades considered Bakarich's stance as much too soft.

The situation was sufficiently tense for the Angel to call and order me out of town.

"Leave tomorrow morning. Go to Bosnia. They need physicians. I've got two job interviews lined up for you. If the one in Gorazhde looks at all good, stay there. It is far enough."

"But I am on call tomorrow" I protested.

"It has been all arranged. I spoke with Professor Hahn. He won't mind. And with your mother's help, we will pack up your things and

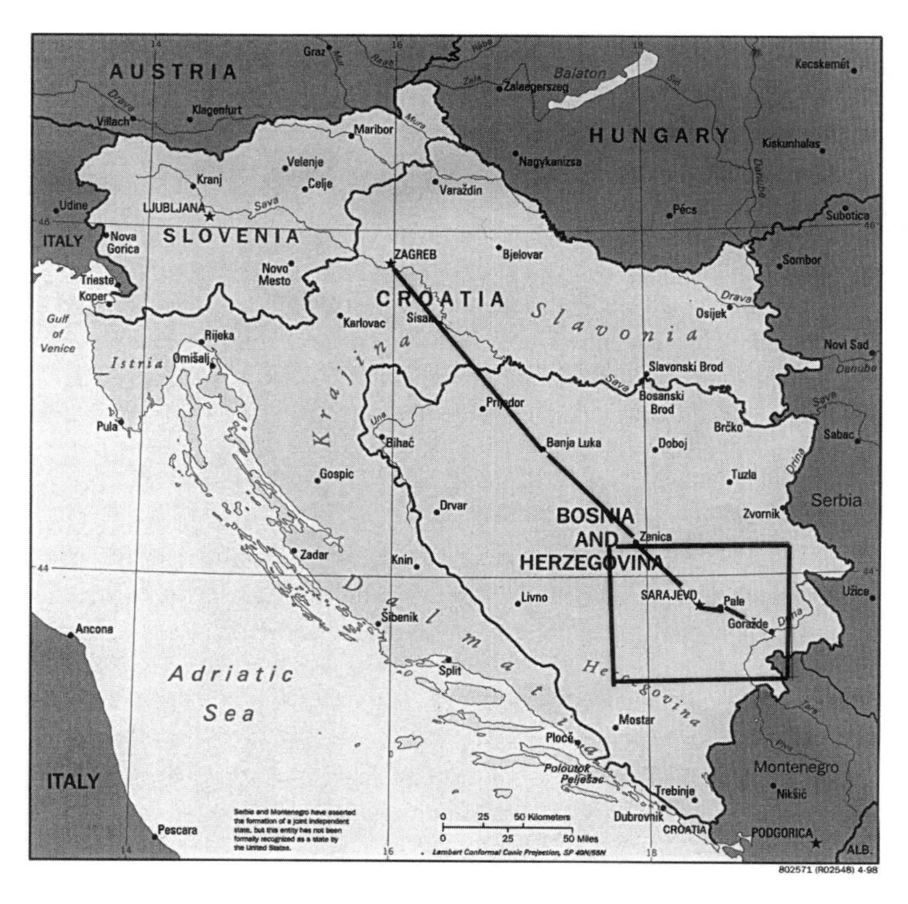

send them after you." Angel was very well organized and left nothing to chance.

"Are they really after me?" I asked

"No need to go into detail. In my judgment, you should not wait a day longer. You know the rabbit story?"

I knew the rabbit story.

A Yugoslav rabbit was seen running across the border to Italy. "Why are you running so fast?" asked the Italian rabbit.

"They are killing all the bears in Yugoslavia!"

"But you are not a bear!"

"No, but they might shoot me before I have a chance to explain."

Things were getting out of control and I could have easily been lumped together with the true (and soon to be jailed) opposition.

The next morning I took the first train to Bosnia.

Exiled to Gorazhde

(1954-1956)

Courtesy of slow railways, it took twenty-four hours to reach Gorazhde. After a good night's sleep in a nice hotel in Sarajevo I took the early morning narrow-gauge train to Gorazhde. Fresh and ready for the interview, I first took a good look at the Drina River.

The view well justified Drina's celebrated status as the most beautiful river in the country. Its crystal clean waters deceived the senses: the colored pebbles shining from ten feet under the surface left the false impression that the river might be shallow. A hundred yards wide, loudly bouncing off the piers of the wooden bridges, the powerful and rapid river entered a forbidding canyon about a mile downstream. Upstream there was just enough space for a handful of white Mosques contrasting against the dark roofs of a rather large village, a few orchards and an occasional arable plot. The mountain slopes gently descended upon the river valley all the way from the very distant Zelengora Mountain, where a decade earlier the Partizans had fought their bloodiest battle with the German Army.

So fierce was the conflict that twelve years later one could still find sobering mementos of the past war: Together with boulders and driftwood, human skulls ended up at the bottom of steep ravines. Looking towards the mountains I wondered what power brought sixty thousand people together to fight in this most unusual place. From a military standpoint it could not be less interesting. There were no roads, no local sources of food; no industry and the area did not appear worth fighting for. In fact, Zelengora is right in the middle of nowhere. Whether it was the genius of German generals, planning ever-shrinking encirclements until they steered the Partizans to a mountain wedged between two rivers, or Tito's instinct to consolidate deep inside the country, this was where they met.

And what drew Ivan Goran Kovachich to his death at the foot of the mountain? His poetry fitted the times. Kovachich's major poem *Jama* (*The Pit*) was a gory, inspired description of one of those things that happen with some regularity in the Balkans, when ordinary people facing extraordinary circumstance, lose themselves in a fit of convulsive rage. In a horrifying crescendo the poem tells of

The old wooden bridge over Drina in 1940.

people strung on a wire pierced through their earlobes, their eyeballs dug out, each member of the terrible chain counting the violent jerks of the wire to judge the distance from the butcher's knife at the end of the pit. It was not the poetry but the man that I admired. Neither a Serbian nor a Jew, the young teacher didn't have to get involved. Yet a deep inner sense of commitment made him face frostbite, hunger, and finally death in the wilderness.

During the German offensive, Goran Kovachich got separated from his unit and sought shelter in a notorious village under the mountain. The days after a big conflict were full of sheer misery. Thriving on rumors and hoping that salvation hid behind the next mountain, small bands of displaced soldiers, lost civilians, the sick and the wounded moved about aimlessly. If such a group chanced upon the village, the sentries turned them away. Intruding strangers were at best trouble and frequently a direct threat. So, very early, the

village declared its own rules. Strangers should stay out, lest they risk being shot on sight. It worked, this perverted Bosnian version of active neutrality. Everybody avoided the place. Exceptionally, if it was absolutely necessary, a larger unit dared to pass through. If the village sentries spotted the advancing column, all able-bodied men withdrew into the forest, the food was hidden and the village elders were left behind to negotiate. Nobody had a real interest in holding on to twenty odd houses under the hostile mountain. After a few hours the troops would withdraw leaving the village to its own ways, to its freedom from political organizers, from small territorial guerrilla units and above all, from the aftermath of a nearby battle.

Unaware of the danger Goran Kovachich entered the village. He was arrested, robbed and executed. How come the villagers could not recognize who was in front of them? A peasant can tell a good man just as he can spot a thoroughbred in the herd. And his deep admiration for quality usually prevails. A friend of mine grew up in a village which was not given to killing, but otherwise was every bit as ruthless. Anybody passing through the hamlet had to pay his way. No money, no food. One day a little hungry man came and offered his golden pocket watch for some food. My friend went to fetch his father to negotiate the price. When they returned there were tears in the man's eyes. He did not sob, spoke clearly and drove a hard bargain, but tears kept rolling down his cheeks. After a while my friend's father, who had before turned away many a weeping woman, returned the watch and invited the strange man to dinner. Because, as he said, some things are just not done. The watch meant a lot to the man. To take it from him would be a "sin of the soul." Anyone committing such a sin becomes a person without a soul, a *bezdushnik*, the lowest of all the human beings.

How come the villagers did not recognize the poet's obvious quality and let him go? Did they already lose their soul? And if so, what would such a brutal person look like today, a decade after the war? There must be hundreds of them walking around hiding their dark secrets. That pleasant neighbor of yours could be one of

them. For in peacetime, I knew only too well, you could not tell a decent man from a bastard.

A glance at my watch put an end to my musings on the wooden bridge over the Drina. It was time to meet with the village leaders.

Scanning the unusual faces in the room, I remembered the words of Slobodan Grgac, a perennial medical student who gave me a few tips about Bosnia. "Don't be impatient. They will go through a centuries-old ritual. First they will inquire about your health, the health of your family and about your trip. After some coffee, the conversation will move from personal to general small talk about the weather, the farming prospects and the like. It may seem a waste of time to you but it is not to them. If it takes five cups of coffee, so be it, but they will not speak until they have sized you up. When they choose to speak, listen carefully. If specifics are not mentioned, forget it. They will not turn you down outright. That is not done. Rather, the chat will continue about the good water in the village and the fresh air in the mountains. For hours if needed. Finally even the most insensitive visitor gets the message."

I will never understand why Grgac did not finish his studies. He was intelligent and had fantastic powers of observation. All his predictions were right on target.

The Mayor of Gorazhde, a slim soft-spoken Serbian, met me at the door and instantly fired the first part of the formula. "How are you?" with an air of true concern for my well being. It was quite different from those formal, hurried urban questions. It called for an answer. I obliged by telling that one could not feel any way but well in such a beautiful part of the world.

That was fine, but Slobodan had not coached me well enough. He forgot to tell me about the pace. My answer elicited sympathetic nods and about two minutes of dead silence. Then, Mustafa, a burly Moslem who was the secretary of Health, uttered the second most solemn question. "How is your health, are you feeling well?"

Funny thing to ask a doctor, I thought, while giving him every assurance about my health. Obviously relieved to find me in such splendid shape, the secretary lapsed into a few minutes of silence. Then it was the Party secretary's turn to ask about my travel.

Quite embarrassed by those long pauses, I was about to launch into a blow-by-blow description of the lengthy trip from Zagreb. The excruciating wait in Sarajevo, the marvelous new railway station and how I almost missed the narrow gauge train to Gorazhde. But I was learning fast and willingly joined in the silence. Anything beyond a leisurely exchange of meaningless words would rob my hosts of time to observe and think.

Eventually I found the ritual quite relaxing. It left me with plenty of time for my own watching. The next question, about my mother's health was perplexing. One usually does not ask an adult about his parents. When they failed to ask about my father, I realized that they knew about his death, and the political circumstances surrounding it. Was this a polite way to express sympathy for a widow or was I made to understand that they were well informed?

As the coffee kept pouring I had ample opportunity to observe my hosts. The Mayor, in his late fifties, was genuinely comfortable. He did not fidget in the chair and his hands moved only to accompany the words. The relaxed face might have left the impression of disconnected boredom were it not for his bright eyes, which remained shamelessly trained on me, whether I talked or listened. He was sizing me up.

Zdravko, the Mayor, and Mustafa, his secretary of Health, were quite a duo; a thinker and an entertainer. The secretary was excellent at small talk, jokes and superficial warmth; whatever it took to give the Mayor enough time to think. The Party secretary was bored beyond hope. Duty-bound to partake, he couldn't have cared less about the proceedings. After a while he lapsed into the catatonia of a professional committeeman. The body was there, but the mind had gone. There was an empty face if I had ever seen one. This is not to say that he was devoid of feelings. He was the high priest of public ethics and, as I learned later, an apparent breech of propriety could move him to brisk action. However, practical matters such as

whether the village will have a good or bad doctor, were none of his concerns.

All of a sudden, the Mayor broke off the silence. "Why don't you, Mustafa, stop kidding and wasting our doctor's time."

What an operator! I felt sorry for poor Mustafa, who'd done what he had to and was now being blamed. Mustafa, however, was not the least embarrassed. With ease he succinctly outlined the community's need for a few new physicians. The salary was very good. They had a nice modern apartment for me. And, of course, I could have a private practice if I so desired.

The pace of the interview dramatically changed. After spending hours in preliminaries, as far as the leaders of Gorazhde were concerned, the whole matter could be settled in a few minutes. The salary was sensational and they expected me to jump at the opportunity. Instead, I started to inquire about their overall views of healthcare needs of the community.

Boy, did I make a mistake! Such conceptual talk was beyond the scope of these sincere, but simple village leaders. Mustafa instantly got up to order yet another round of coffee, a clear sign we were back to small talk. How handy that oriental etiquette! Mustafa would chit-chat, I would politely smile, and Zdravko would meditate until he was ready to give an answer.

I made the wrong move and there was no way out. We would have to drink as many cups of coffee as it took for the Mayor to come up with some reply. I expected a nice blend of generalities about peoples' right to good health and the leadership's sacred duty to meet the people's needs. What took him so long? As a politician he should be able to come up with a few good ones. But the Mayor was not an ordinary politician. "It's like this," he finally said. "We buy ourselves the best doctor we can, and he tells us what to do."

He did not need all that time to compose such a simple answer. He needed the break to decide whether to level with me. I was pleased with his confidence and kept searching for the right words of appreciation, but Zdravko ended the session.

"Mustafa will show you around and arrange for a visit to your future apartment. We would also like you to see our new Home of

Culture. It has just been completed and we are quite proud of it," he said.

"Let me also see the hospital," I insisted.

"Sure, but do not judge us by what you find there. Look at the Home of Culture. Two years ago it was just an apple orchard." Then with the ease of a born leader, he got up and escorted us to the door. That was it—no room for more questions.

~

The Home of Culture was an impressive modern building with a 400-seat auditorium, a movie screen, and a stage. It also had other facilities, including a library and a chess room. The theater was used for movies, mass meetings and, when a traveling troupe ventured into the village, for live performances.

A stage show always drew large audiences, no matter what the content. Live performance fit well into the rich Bosnian oral tradition. Listening to songs and stories is the mainstay of the village social life during the winter. No wonder a large audience turned up one unusual evening to be treated to the spectacle of a Greek violinist and his French bed mate accompanist playing Mendelsohn and Paganini. The man was obviously drunk, but that turned out to be an asset. His red cheeks made the public accept without laughter those odd gyrations of the body that city folks consider as part and parcel of a violin performance. In fact the listeners went all out for the performer and gave him big applause. After all, the guy stuck to his guns in spite of shljivovica, the famous local plum brandy. How was he to know the powers of the deceptive local potion? Once at peace with the man's odd behavior, the listeners settled back in their chairs and willingly absorbed the strange sounds. The pyrotechnics of Paganini were akin to what a local Gypsy would do for a good tip, and the strange slow movements, on the whole were quite soothing.

Despite the good personnel and a gorgeous terrace overlooking the river, the restaurant in the Home of Culture never made it. In their wisdom the locals were not ready to mix culture with digestion. Also they liked a good drink with their meals. And just as one would

not drink in a church, this temple of politics and arts was not conducive to relaxation. There were many better places to eat.

Mustafa took me to the popular shack on the riverside, the restaurant with a magic ping-pong ball. There was a small fountain in the garden and, weather permitting, the owner would place the little plastic ball atop the single straight jet. You'd quietly sip brandy, munch on goodies from the grill, and with total abandon watch the bouncing ball as it rode atop the jet, tumbled down into the basket until the stream picked it up for yet another turn of the endless cycle. What a gorgeous totally empty feeling! Eyes so fixed on the little object and the ever-changing droplets, that not a single thought crosses one's mind. That ingenious, hypnotic, helpful ping-pong ball! Anywhere else it would not be much of an entertainment, but as a part of the Bosnian slow motion lifestyle, the ball had magic powers. In Bosnia, it is perfectly proper to go to public places with the express purpose of passing the time. No need to pretend. If you are in the ball-gazing mood, nobody will interrupt.

During the lunch with Mustafa, I was much too tense to watch the ball. I wanted information. Yes, it was true that previous physicians had not lasted long and left. No, he did not know why. Maybe they did not feel at home. Sure, we would visit the hospital, but what was the hurry? "You have seen sick people before and will see many more in your life," said Mustafa, visibly overcome by the postprandial inertia.

Finally we were on our way to the hospital, a barrack with a central corridor and few rooms on each side. The large entrance room served as a central reception, minor surgical theater, and the physician's office. There was no obvious pattern to the furniture in this all-purpose room. There was a desk here and a cupboard there and the examining table was under the window for everybody to see. Not much privacy if you needed an exam.

All that hesitation and delay had me well prepared. I'd expected much worse. The place was reasonably clean. Two Army-trained male nurses took care of the patients. There was running water, but the hospital had no electricity.

"Why is electricity so important?" wondered Mustafa. "The power is frequently down and kerosene is much more reliable."

That one was hard to handle. How do you explain something as self-evident as the need for electricity? I gave a lengthy lecture on sterilization equipment, X-rays and the like, only to find Mustafa totally unimpressed. The more I argued, the less convinced he seemed to be. Finally Mustafa shrugged his shoulders and with the look of an exasperated victim gave in. Surely there was no real need for all that, but if this was the price to keep me happy, let it be.

Two years ago the electricity had come to the edge of the village and immediately became the "in" thing. Everybody wanted it. In the absence of a master plan, the power lines ran the path of loudest and most influential demanders. For Mustafa, the hospital was just another case in point and he followed an established procedure. First reject, then procrastinate and if everything else fails, yield. The merit of the request was never a consideration. As a newcomer I did not understand the process and must have shown my feelings since Mustafa immediately shifted to his "no problem" mode. From then on, every request was met with an appeasing smile and a cheerful, "Sure doctor. No problem. We will do as you wish." It worked like a charm. First I stopped asking for small items and soon desisted from requesting anything. Clearly Mustafa wanted to get it over with but was neither in the mood nor in the position to deliver on all his promises. I would have to concentrate on major items and discuss them with the Mayor. The small stuff would have to fall in line later.

When you think about it, Mustafa's way was ingenious. Instead of a hard bargain, just keep agreeing until it became so absurd that even a thick skull like I got the message. Mustafa's "no problem" modus operandi became later an inside joke. In advance of some serious meeting I would call him up and ask for a decision. "And none of that 'no problem' business of yours."

"Sure doctor," he would deadpan, "just come down and we will talk about it. No problem."

Finally it was time to take leave from Mustafa. The hotel was predictably called "Victory," as were so many enterprises all over Yu-

goslavia. One should not blame genuinely brave people for a bit of overindulgence. After all they had won a very difficult battle.

The restaurant was clean. You could easily tell the locals from the business-suit-type visitors. There were four of us city types oddly isolated at our respective tables. But the waiter appeared to be even more out of place than we were. You would not exactly expect to find a multilingual waiter in Gorazhde. But there he was, chatting in fluent German with the portly gentleman at the next table. He turned around and with crisp, purposeful movements came to wait on me. A real pro! He had that special aura that separates men from boys among the waiters. He was elegant, polite and rather aloof. Only a seasoned waiter can instantly let you understand that while being attentive, he really does not want to hear much from you. He suggested the best dishes and brought them with decorum befitting a top-flight restaurant. It was all so oddly out of place and the waiter enjoyed every moment of it.

After serving me, the waiter moved to a table of locals who, warmed up by the brandy, loudly discussed the so-so performance of the village soccer team. Approaching the lively company our waiter totally changed his stance. The smooth, elegant walk gave way to a wide based, duck-like swaying, the straight back was now slouched, the white towel previously hanging on the forearm was now in his back pocket. His demeanor, however, did not change. He was not chummy with the local folks and he carried his duties with the same reserved efficiency. No, he was not putting on an act for me and going back to his old ways. There was an act for everybody, commensurate to his or her backgrounds. Always just a step ahead, showing his professionalism to the extent it was possible. His city style would have made him the laughing stock of the local clientele. So he did the best he could and when the opportunity presented itself, upgraded his performance. There was much to learn from this accomplished professional. The snootiness he could keep for himself. However, the message that you can keep standards without making yourself ridiculous was not lost on me.

The waiter came to my table to straighten the cover: "So what is a guy like me doing in a place like this? Right?"

"Right. You seem to be able to read my thoughts." I responded.

"I make a living. During the summer I am in the Hotel Excelsior in Dubrovnik and in the low season I come here. The money is much better than in a larger city." And then, as an afterthought, he added, "Just as some physicians leave the town for want of money." He was not going to lose his superiority, not this seasoned waiter.

I was not a bit surprised that he knew who I was. And he knew the others as well. The German gentlemen finished his dinner. The rest of us strangers proceeded at about the same pace. When the dessert time came, Shandor, the grand master of restaurant etiquette, rounded us up with the outmost ease. "Why don't you gentlemen have your dessert together?" Without further ado he pulled together the chairs, introduced us by our professions and took orders. This was a smart business move. Individually we were ready to go, but now there was a chance that we might strike up a conversation and order some drinks-which was exactly what happened.

The elderly gentleman was a high school inspector from Sarajevo, an average face on an average frame. The younger man was a physician who a few months ago came from Sarajevo to work in Gorazhde. He had an interesting elongated face with fine lips, a rather prominent hawkish nose, and a pair of intense dark eyes. There was a trace of melancholy about this relaxed and elegant man. We later became best friends but that evening everybody was careful and noncommittal. To keep the conversation going, I told him about my weird experience during the interview with the Mayor. He just grinned, "I am from Sarajevo and know well enough how business is transacted in these parts of the world." Did he ever! As it later turned out, Mehmed Mutevelich known to his friends as 'Meshek', was a descendant of a 500-years long line of Moslem *Begs* in Sarajevo. *Begs* are akin to dukes, the highest level of hereditary Turkish nobility. A mausoleum erected in 1540 for the progenitor of my colleague's family, Murat beg Tardich, is still intact in the yard of the main Mosque in Sarajevo. However, during the dinner, the young doctor from Sarajevo was reserved and would speak up only when the conversation was about to stop.

The evening progressed slowly. The elderly gentleman, hearing I considered moving to Gorazhde, shook his head. He just could not

understand it. Not for the life of his family would he ever agree to come. And if the quality of the local hospital was anything similar to that of the local high school, good luck to me. The high school was cause for great concern to the inspector. Just as they were now hotly interested in developing the health service, a few years earlier, the local officials went around dangling money to attract teachers to their newly built high school. Naturally, the money attracted all sorts of problematic people. A defrocked Orthodox priest taught French. "It is a religious experience, a true miracle," mused the inspector. "The pupils love him and work very hard. They seem to appreciate his questions and he understands their answers, but which language they speak is a mystery. It is not Serbian, and it doesn't even resemble French."

It was meant to be funny, that description of the struggling school in the backlands, but I was not laughing. I remembered my own official school inspections. The teachers and nervous pupils were edgy and even the janitors looked concerned. Just the thought of an inspector visiting the class used to send shivers up the students spine, and here he was poking fun at the poor kids.

The conversation became somewhat frosty and soon the inspector left. It was late, but I hesitated. Finally Shandor came to the table and spoke in a low voice of studied confidence. "Don't worry, doctor. The sheets may be somewhat gray, but the hotel is quite clean. No bedbugs, no lice." The man was a genius. How could he read my thoughts so accurately?

We got up to leave. Meshek's hotel room was next to mine. "Come on," he said, "if you worry about such things you should not come to Bosnia. The waiter is a bloody cynic but he is not lying. Relax and have a good night."

~

The room was OK, somewhat Spartan, but here and there was a decent piece of furniture. I immediately started to look for lice. As I searched through the bed and found nothing, some old pictures kept coming to mind. It is remarkable how your perspective changes with time. Sitting on the edge of the bed in Gorazhde, only nine years after

the war, I found myself longing for those "book reading" sessions in Trnavac when all of us got together to chat while looking for lice. Just as I got pleasantly drowsy, somebody knocked on the door. Half awake and half confused by memories, I didn't respond right away. The person in the corridor now began to bang and scream. It was the local midwife. She had a case of neglected transverse position. Could the doctor help her?

Neglected transverse position? Neglected transverse position! Good lord, my first night in the town and already somebody wanted me to attend the worst life-threatening condition in obstetrics.

To understand my state of mind the reader must know something about the powerful, petulant, querulous, intimidating teacher of obstetrics in my medical school. Professor Durst had a uniquely perverse teaching technique: he taught by fear. After outlining a pathologic condition, the old man would launch into a long story about the worst-case scenario. Everything could end up with a stillborn or damaged child. The danger to the mother was immense and it would all come to haunt the incompetent physician. The doctor was damned. If he refused to help, he was liable, and if he intervened, there was an overwhelming chance of disaster. The cumulative effect of Durst's lectures was devastating. One could laugh off a single "I knew a physician" story, all of them ending up in some calamity, but by the end of the semester, the students were paralyzed and scared of the thought of ever having attending a pregnant woman.

Now, the neglected transverse position was Durst's favorite scare story. Instead of coming down head first, the baby is caught in a horizontal position, and as the labor progresses the fetus is wedged in the birth canal. The shoulder goes first, the head presses against the chest and there is no chance whatsoever of a successful delivery. If it is caught early, the child can be turned around, or a Cesarean section performed. But *neglected* meant that the arm was born and protruded from the vagina. You can't push the hand back; this would inevitably cause an intractable blood-born infection, and in Bosnia, very likely tetanus. Nor can you deliver the baby. The solution at that time was to sacrifice the baby for the Mother's sake by using the Braun's hook, a medieval-looking instrument that today rightly belongs in obstetric museums.

The maternity house, Gorazhde 2002. During the recent war, similarly to Sarajevo, Gorazhde was surrounded and bombarded by Serbs. The small house received many direct hits.

I was simply frozen in my hotel room. After a while the banging moved down the corridor to the other doctor's door. He also chose not to answer and the midwife dashed away cursing. I sneaked out and knocked on his door.

"Come in. Scared stiff, weren't you?" He smiled, not in the least embarrassed by his own failure to respond.

"You are not much better yourself," I retorted.

"Sure I am. In fact I am quite good at obstetrics. Just did not feel like answering. Why should I, if you did not?

I was flabbergasted. There I stood trembling from fear and he, all smiles, seemed perfectly at ease.

"So if you are so good, why the hell don't you help the woman?" I protested.

"Sure, let's go," he said, putting on a coat.

The maternity house was just a few minutes away. Meshek transformed into a wizard. Not an unnecessary word was said, not a movement wasted. With cold expert proficiency he took care of the job in half an hour. Just as we were taught in medical school, the baby had no chance of surviving. We were both deeply saddened by the abominable archaic obstetric surgery. The fact that Meshek saved the mother's life was no consolation. They taught us when and how to do the surgery, but they never explained how we would feel. For a good hour we sat in the delivery room, motionless, depressed, unable to say a word.

I was in awe of the man's competence and to reestablish the balance, quite ineptly, steered the conversation towards my good knowledge of Internal Medicine. He should consult me, and I would ask for help when it comes to Obstetrics and Gynecology. He affected excitement, called it an excellent deal, and we shook hands over it. But there it was again, that twinkle in his eye. It later turned out that he had a superb grasp of general medicine.

The day was breaking and eventually we dragged ourselves towards the hotel. Our trusty waiter was already in the restaurant and offered to serve us some tea.

Knowing I had shirked my duty and that Meshek did a whale of a job, I felt rather inadequate and childishly bragged about my superb class standing. "What do you know," he said, "this dump may get itself two top-of-the-class young doctors. It does not make sense, but I guess both of us must have some good reason to pitch our tents next to the Drina River."

I knew my reasons and wondered what his were.

The waiter was back with two trays, each with a pot and a cup to serve us our teas. I have never tasted anything as disgusting in my life! Meshek took a sip and his face lit up with a whimsical smile.

"I thought you would not like it," announced the waiter, " I can bring you some good coffee. It will be a pleasure to return the tea to the cook."

"If you knew we would not like it, why in the world did you make us order it? What is this anyhow? It sure is not tea," I complained.

"You see, our cook finds the imported tea too expensive and produces a caramel sugar solution instead. He perfected it to where the color is right on target. Unfortunately the taste is not." The waiter then proceeded to tell us of his constant struggle to get tea on the menu. He hoped to score a point if we were to return the order. Frequent complaints might force the cook to change his ways.

From that day on the three of us played out a well choreographed conspiratorial farce by ordering and returning the tea. It took us three months to win. Besides building a new hospital, the introduction of proper tea was my most important civic contribution to Gorazhde.

Of course it took single-minded commitment to keep the tea going in this fortress of Turkish coffee. The entire village used Janja's coffee-only parlor. Thousands of deals were closed and tons of gossip exchanged across the austere tables of the widows one-room establishment. Telephones were hard to come by in Gorazhde, but Janja's parlor had one. If somebody were not in his office you'd call Janja's. If he wasn't there, she knew where he was. If she became evasive, you knew that she knew, but you were not supposed to know. The person was either with your enemy or having another go at it with his mistress.

I had an appointment with Mustafa, the secretary of Health, at noon and Meshek also had a lot of time on his hands. There was no use going to bed and instead, we kept ordering coffees, one after another.

Eventually our waiter excused himself. "You know I am not a doctor," he said, "and nobody's life will be threatened if I stop serving breakfast. I am off to my bed. You two have a good day."

Having somewhat recovered from the aftermath of Meshek's obstetric surgery, we moved to the riverside restaurant with the ping-pong ball. As we sat there sipping more coffee, out of the river came a perfectly dressed fisherman, waders, fly rod and all, ordered a coffee and sat next to us. With all this gear on him he had to be a Party official with access to one of the exclusive "diplomatic stores."

The two of us glanced at the man with passing curiosity, exchanging meaningful looks as if to say: "What is a such a top banana doing in Gorazhde?" The man pulled his chair closer. "Didn't you know there are also comrade fishermen in addition to comrade hunters?" he said with a benevolent smile.

He broke us up. It was a great "in" joke. Branko Chopich, a well-known humorist, had just published "Election of Comrade Hector," a terrific parody about a hunting club consisting of hunters and comrade hunters. The comrade hunters were well dressed and loaded with latest equipment. They would let off a few rounds before the plain hunters even got their aim set. But, somehow the plain hunters always bagged the bird. During the election for the club's officers, a comrade hunter proposed a slate which included Comrade Hector. "Who is Hector?" asked a plain hunter indignantly. As it turned out, Hector was a comrade's dog. "I am not voting for a dog," said the plain hunter only to be elbowed by the comrade hunter next to him: "It may appear like a dog to you," whispers the comrade "but he must be mighty important if the leadership demands that you vote for him." The story will not enter into anthologies of Yugoslav humor, but it was a welcome spoof of the absurd Yugoslav pseudo-elections.

The man from the river pointed at his basket-full of trout." See! This comrade fisherman does not return empty-handed." It was all so sudden and disarming that we let down our guard. By laughing, we admitted reading the story, which was not very smart. It had been printed in a copy of Djilas' recently banned dissident paper. But what do you do when somebody just walks out of the river and catches you off guard?

"Come on, don't worry," continued the fisherman," First of all, I am not a small-time informer and second, it looks like you two doctors and I will be stuck in this dump for a while. May as well be friendly."

Meshek was visibly uncomfortable and fell silent but I spoke up.

"So you know who we are. Not such a big trick; by now the whole village must know who we are. But what are you doing besides fishing? You don't belong here. The closest diplomatic mag-

Gorazhde 2002. The former hospital building still stands tall between new high-rises.

azine is as far as Belgrade." It was worth a try. At least the guy would know that I too could put two and two together.

"Just as I thought—a smart Alec," replied the fisherman. "However you are right on target. I am from Belgrade, my name is Brana, and I work for UDBA."

He was playing tit for tat. You were not supposed to know who works for UDBA, the secret security service. This was the second stunner in just a few minutes. The game was on. Who could outsmart whom.

"Is that what you folks do? Walk on water? Aren't you supposed to be submerged and peek out through a periscope at mortals? Why would you surface for us?"

"Aha, but this is a visibility mission," he replied "But don't ask me for details right now. I will tell you more about my job if you

decide to stay in Gorazhde. One needs somebody to talk to. In the meantime, let me buy you a round of shljivovica."

Shljivovica serves the same purpose as coffee. The light variety he ordered was aptly called *brbljacha*, the chatting brandy. Meshek was now ready to pick up the cue. "Since you are so well informed you should know that an Allah-fearing Moslem like me should not drink," he said, downing the whole glass in a swift move.

"Good Moslem, my foot. If you were one, you would not be dating that Orthodox girl."

"Boy, was he ever well informed! It must be true since he'd stated it so categorically. If he expected to surprise Meshek, he was wrong. With a perfectly straight face and as if he were accustomed to strangers who know about his personal life, Meshek retorted, "You are wrong. I am not dating her; she is dating me. I am the catch, my dear fisherman."

So that is how you do it! Be calm and pass it off with a small joke. As if saying, "OK. I got your point but you are not upsetting me." True to form, Meshek lounged into a cheerful, sometime humorous, discussion of local shlivovica and how to 'bake' it just right. After a while we parted ways. I was off to the Social Security office to hear their views on the organization of health service. Or so I thought.

The Director of Social Security was a bland scribe very proud of the good financial balance of his enterprise. There were two factories in the area and a substantial pool of employees in various offices. Plenty of money kept coming in every month, and very little was spent. Just recently, he boasted, his office had lent a substantial sum to the local soccer club.

"Of course you have a surplus with a hospital that has no electricity and a practically nonexistent health service," I thought. He kept on and on about the good financial state, and with each word I was getting angrier. There he was in a comfortable modern office, and on the other hill was the sadly neglected so called hospital. I restrained myself and politely suggested that a modern health service might be rather expensive. He nodded in agreement, but you could see that my words flew right past him. As far as he was concerned there would always be money around and he expected to remain the

patron of local sports. I had no patience for this unenlightened paper pusher. The chemistry was wrong.

"You do not seem to know or care what sort of a health service you have. It costs money. If I take the job, you will soon be in debt," I said.

"Who says that we don't know about healthcare facilities?" he said somewhat defensively, "Come here, let me show you the blueprints for the new hospital. We will build it right in the Russian stockade if and when the Army permits it."

The stockade had been built at the end of the ninetieth century by the Austrian Army after the Austro-Hungarian Empire annexed Bosnia. After it had been incorporated into the Viennese Empire, Gorazhde acquired strategic importance as the southernmost outpost on the border of the Ottoman Empire. However after the First World War the newly formed Yugoslavia had no use for the albatross on the River Drina. Eventually the King of Yugoslavia decided to "lend" the stockade to the "white" Russian emigrants. At that time, fleeing from the communist revolution, a large number of Russian nobility and Czarist generals emigrated to Europe. These emigrants were not well received by the Yugoslav citizens. Back in Russia some of them were very important people and during the Soviet revolution most had their share of life threatening dramas.

Naturally, they loved to talk about the past but the average Yugoslav was neither able to share nor willing to discriminate. Who cared whether the person was true nobility or an impostor!

Thriving on the past, unable to assimilate into life's mainstream, many Russian *émigrés* became caricatures of themselves. There was something incongruous in a former general picking up your luggage in a hotel, all the while insisting on the proper decorum. The reminder of the past importance was irritating, the pomp under reduced circumstances hilarious. Thus one day a Zagreb newspaper featured a drawing of a lap dog on an old lady's leash telling another dog: "You know, back in Russia I was actually a Saint Bernard!"

The Russian stockade in 2002. The building now serves as the local school. Note the ruins of the restaurant on the river shore.

However, as a token of royal solidarity, the King of Yugoslavia felt a "moral obligation" to help the followers of the dethroned Russian emperor. After the king offered the useless stockade to the Russian émigrés, a few of them got together, recruited some young people and formed a military academy in Gorazhde.

Deep in the godforsaken countryside, the Czarist generals were no problem to Belgrade. The academy flourished for a decade and then started a fast downslide. Finally, the king was stuck with a large empty building. Eventually the Kingdom of Yugoslavia sent a small cavalry garrison to occupy the stockade. I suspect it was the ultimate punishment for stray personnel. Go to Gorazhde and be forgotten.

After the Second World War, the fortunes of Gorazhde changed for the better. Having won the war and based on his own bitter experience, Marshal Tito developed a new military doctrine. If the country were ever attacked again, the Pannonian Plains around Sava and Danube would be scorched and the Army would withdraw to Bosnia. A smaller state in the hills of Bosnia could be defended endlessly. Orders went out to build a logistic support base in the "core" defense area. Factories started to mushroom in the most unbelievable places, big storage depots were dug into the mountainside, and army units were stationed all around the area. Gorazhde got special attention as, in its wisdom, the government located an ammunition factory on the periphery of the village. Of course locating the factory in a place that had neither industrial tradition nor trained work force was total nonsense. Try to hire illiterate workers to handle explosives and see what happens! We called it the "flying factory." Every month there was a major explosion. To protect this important enterprise, about 200 soldiers were stationed in the stockade in Gorazhde.

~

We went to see the building. The inside was off limits for civilians, but the outside was in excellent shape. It certainly was the nicest and largest edifice in the village. Three stories high, with solid thick walls, overlooking Drina, the stockade could easily accommodate 300 soldiers.

"Isn't it nice?" the man from Social Security said. "If we just could get the army to leave."

I knew exactly what was on his mind, "We have this nice plan to show to higher authorities and fools like you. But nobody seriously expects the Army to leave the stockade."

It was a setup! The Director of Social Security never expected to dislodge the Army and in the meantime had a good excuse not to invest in the existing hospital. As far as he could see, the director would remain the powerful community banker and benefactor.

Meshek, who that morning had an appointment with the secretary of Health, arrived at the scene to have a look for himself. The

director continued to talk about the great resources he had stashed away.

Soon Meshek became as annoyed as I was. While I desperately searched for a way to stop this waste of time, Meshek, all smiles, broke into the middle of the director's sentence. "Sure, sure. I see. So the water took a bath in the well." Having said that, Meshek announced that we both must leave, and shook hands with the director.

"The water took a bath in the well? What was that nonsense supposed to mean?" I asked.

"It means just that: nonsense. Glad you got it. So did the director," Meshek said. "It refers to redundant, meaningless conversation. Yet the director cannot complain. I never said he talked nonsense. It could mean anything, including that I was unable to concentrate."

Clearly, I needed a lot of training in this ornate, oblique but effective Bosnian art of interpersonal communication.

Meshek informed me he and the Secretary of Health agreed on the new organizational scheme of health services in Gorazhde: "You will be the director and I your trusty coworker."

"Wait a moment. I have not yet accepted the position of director. In fact, after talking to this bastard I might just decide not to. It is much to early to talk about who will be director." I protested.

"Oh, but you will. No matter what you think, you will. The Mermaid says so."

"You mean the guy that came out of the water?"

"Right. And what the Mermaid says happened, is happening or will happen. And that is the truth," announced Meshek matter-of-factly. He was not being oriental or fatalistic. During that short encounter both of us realized that the predictions of the self-assured, shrewd fisherman were likely to be correct. Sometimes, while you agonize over a decision an objective outsider can safely predict what you will do. In Yugoslavia this is even easier, as the other guy may be privy to information not available to you.

As it turned out, the Mermaid was one step ahead of me. I called home and found a message from the Angel Protector. It was laconic: Take the job and stay put.

I had no reason to doubt Angel's judgment. Things must have gotten really hot in Zagreb.

For a moment I wondered whether Brana the Mermaid and my Angel had communicated. I suspect they did not. Brana probably knew the general situation, the alignment of forces in Zagreb and must have figured out that I would have to accept the position in Gorazhde, unless I wanted to become a martyr—which I didn't.

Meshek was right: What the Mermaid says, happens!

The Fisherman Goes Hunting

(1955)

After a few days Meshek and I settled into daily routines. What the Mermaid says—goes. He predicted he might want to talk to us and, sure enough, almost every morning he'd join our "tea ceremony" and order himself a "Serbian tea," a cup of diluted warm shljivovica. Brana was in his early forties, round-faced, and his thick dark brown hair had started to recede. There was nothing remarkable in the appearance of this man and he could have been any of the thousands of clerks from Belgrade, were it not for his compartmentalized behavior. If he arrived at the restaurant before us, we were sure to find him in a corner of the dining room, his back against the wall. If he came after we already took a table, he'd move his chair to give himself the best view of the entire restaurant. He was genuinely engaged in our conversations. He responded quickly, his face was lively and expressed the mood of the moment, but his eyes perpetually scanned the room. There were two independent parts to his body: the relaxed torso for everybody to see and the nervous, feet tapping under the table. And both parts were genuine. He never missed a line, he fully concentrated on all aspects of our conversation but I have no doubt that, had he felt threatened by some newcomer, Brana would have been the first to draw his gun.

"OK, Mermaid," I said one morning "what are you doing here?"

"I was afraid you'd never ask. I am in charge of the counterinsurgency operation. Have to mop up the remnants of Draza Mihajlovich's Chetniks. There are ten of them all together and hanging in tough. This is, mind you, ten years after the end of the war and long after the capture of their leader. Politically and militarily they are insignificant."

"Sure," said Meshek at his stinging best, "that's why you are here. Spend some time fishing and on the side, chase a neat little gang of nomads."

"I did not say they are insignificant all together. The words were 'politically and militarily.' Politically they barely have followers. Militarily how can ten people be significant? For the last three years they've been wandering through the forest, touching nobody, doing no harm. However two months ago an Army officer visited his village way up in the mountains. They killed him. Stupid clowns! If they hadn't done it, I'd happily be in Belgrade leisurely doing whatever I usually do."

"Aha," Brana interrupted his own train of thought, "don't ask what I do in Belgrade. Let's just say that I have a nice office, an important jurisdiction. And a darn good-looking secretary," he added after a short pause.

"After that murder all of a sudden, they became important," Brana continued. "The Army kicked up a hell of a fuss and threatened to go out in full force to chase them. Boy, what a fiasco that would be!"

"Come on, don't you trust our heroic national defense forces?" I affected the official Party jargon. "I feel obliged to defend the honor of our arms. After all I am . . ."

"A reserve lieutenant," interrupted the uncanny mind reader." By the way, did you check recently? Are you sure you still are on the roster?" There was malice in his voice, and for a short moment, he gave me a cold menacing look.

I got up to leave. It was my fault. One should not start needling unless one is willing to pay the price. However, too much happened in the last six months and I was just not ready to handle this display of ill will.

Brana jumped up and grabbed me by the shoulders. "That was wrong. I should not have done it. I've had to do a few dirty things in my life, but I am not an insensitive swine. Furthermore, I like you. You see," he continued all the while holding my shoulders, "I am a reserve colonel and it means a lot to me. You were a fellow traveler; I am the real thing. I criticized but you were poking fun at the Army. Please sit down."

We sat down and for a while there was a tense silence. Meshek saved the day. "OK boys," he said, "so the wolf ate the donkey. We had better have a good drink." What was done could not be changed. The wolf had eaten the donkey and we may as well forget it. Shljivovica materialized out of nowhere, thanks to the omnipresent and alert waiter. We gulped it down.

"Seriously, Brana, why shouldn't the Army do it? After all, one of theirs got killed," inquired Meshek.

"It is not only whether they should, which they should not, but whether they can, and I guarantee they can't. The Army should not do it for two reasons. First it would elevate the guerrillas to a status of a military force, and secondly the Army should stay out of internal matters. Beware of the day when generals start to call the shots. But, more importantly, they are plain not capable of doing it. It can not be handled by conventional warfare. What if they capture the guerrillas? Will they treat them as prisoners of war, according to the Geneva Convention? These people are common criminals and should be handled accordingly." Brana spoke with unusual forcefulness, attesting to the effect of the second shot of brandy.

"You will not abide by the Geneva Convention?" asked Meshek

"You bet your sweet diploma I won't. You can't fight insurgents by the rule book. Remember how the Germans failed with us. If the Army had to do it, they would repeat all the mistakes the Germans did. No, it is up to me to do it." He pounded on the table. He was agitated far beyond a few glasses of brandy. It must have taken quite a battle to prevail over the Army and Brana was still smarting. I could almost see it. Endless meetings in smoke-filled rooms make you sleepy, but you must listen very carefully. Just in case that somewhere in all that verbiage there is a warning, or a meaningful sen-

tence. Then you politely respond, circumlocuting your way through the necessary patriotic phrases, all the way looking for an indirect, but perfectly clear way to let them know that you got their message and don't like it a bit. Later in the corridor you corner the right person and tell it to him straight. Then for days you wait to learn whether you prevailed and if you didn't, whether you went too far. If you end up on the losing side, you may lose also your job. Brana was probably still not in the clear. It was too small a job for a top person. Somebody must have sent him the last curve ball. "If he so badly wants it, let him personally take care of it." And now Brana commanded the operation in Gorazde and he had nobody but himself to blame if things did not work out. Brana was no less in exile than myself.

Realizing this, I comfortably joined the conversation. "You said 'I have to do it.' You are not about to do it all on your own, are you?"

"No, but almost alone. I have 150 militiamen and some other assets. It will be perfectly adequate. You doctors think biology is the only science. Well, police work is scientific too. Just watch me. It may look to you like a tough proposition finding 10 people in thousands of square miles of mountains and forest, but it will be done. Within four months we will catch at least half of them. And through all this I will continue fishing. You will not see me charging on a horse. The time for heroics is gone."

"Sounds like a pretty difficult proposition to me," I said. "It's like looking for needle in a hay stack. I doubt it can be done."

"Let me make a bet with you," said Brana. But he immediately retracted the offer. "No, we can't bet. Doctors should not participate in this sort of thing. You are not to bet on whether people will or will not survive." The question of ethics had not yet crossed my mind, and Brana was first to recognize the potential conflict. He was a very smart man.

"And one thing more," continued the policeman, "Our jobs are opposite by nature, and though I am not without appreciation for medicine, during the next few months we will play by my rules. Should you ever be called to attend somebody we have hurt, we will

grill you without mercy until you cough up the information. So do not accept any calls outside of the village limits. You see," he added with a broad smile, "I am making your practice much simpler. No house calls." There was no doubt in my mind that, superficial politeness aside, our companion would do just what he said. Professionally and without emotion, he would grill you until you told him where the patient was.

"Since we can't bet, let me do it the other way. Halfway through the campaign I will invite you to a fish dinner. I spoke with Huso, the professional, and he has a few big *mladicas* (brown trouts) lined up. When we get our fifth guy I will invite some friends and we will have ourselves a big party. If I fail to do so within four months, you can call me an ineffective boaster."

"You may be able to keep your end of the promise," I said, "but how can you be so sure that Huso will catch the big fish right on schedule?"

"But he will," insisted Brana. "The man is a genius. He will go out on the river with a simple rod and within a few hours catch the big fish. Absolutely no problem."

Whether Huso was a genius could be debated, but he was a superb fisherman indeed. He was a child of nature. Unmarried, illiterate, he made the big river his home. Occasionally he'd sell a fish, but that was really not his trade, just a by-product of the relationship with the river. He was permanently out on the banks, either patrolling up and down or for hours sitting at one point and gazing at the water. There was more to it than idle fascination. He was studying the wildlife above and below the surface.

Total fascination with the river and the endless time at his disposal made Huso a superb expert. To a casual observer the fish and game appeared to be on constant move. In fact their habits were remarkably monotonous. The older, larger, ones would stake out their territory, be it forest or river, and rarely move away. Huso patiently studied the large brown trout in their private pools: when they broke water, what they fed on and how frequently they struck.

Now, when I say a large one, I mean it. A large *mladica* can be in the eighty-pound range. Huso was so good at his hobby that the

villagers believed he'd already caught the big fish and had them tied to the bottom at various secret places.

Maybe Brana had no reason to worry about the fish, but I wondered, external confidence notwithstanding, how would he accomplish his police objectives? On the surface, besides daily fishing, he did not seem to do a thing. At one of our breakfasts he looked tired. "Had a sleepless night," he said. "Sometimes it is hard to see the next step. But I cannot afford to get discouraged. After all, I must show you what I can do." Then, after a short pause he added, "Frankly, I also like to keep my skin intact." That was the first and only admission that he had a large personal stake in the whole enterprise. Even so, he appeared relaxed and unconcerned.

The first month of apparent inactivity was probably the most important in Brana's campaign. He made himself visible. Secrecy would serve no purpose. He needed information and was ready to pay. The river became his office. Informants wanting to meet him could pretend to fish, wash their animals or whatever. And you did not have to make an appointment. Like Huso, Brana was there every morning. In due course, he knew his river well and could tell the visitor from the regulars.

You had to hand it to him. The man was brave and made a point of always being alone. One of those faces in the bushes could have been a rebel with a gun. But that was all part of the package, and the price he had to pay. Brana had to show that he could do what he pleased in the rebel's territory.

Much of the information passed along the riverbanks was small gossip, but nothing was unimportant to the Mermaid. He painstakingly assembled a profile of each of his opponents. Who is a macho, who was a glutton, who was greedy and who liked to drink. Above all, who had a relative or a girlfriend in which village.

One morning Brana announced that his job was cut by one tenth. No, they had not caught one of the Chetniks, the man had died a natural death. "I've seen his grave," he said. "Of course it could be any-

body's grave, but you can't fool me. It was him, all right." That was an obvious invitation for questions, so we obliged. "Well, first of all he was not seen for ten months. We knew he was in bad health. The guerrillas were making all sorts of excuses why he was not seen. It is not in their interest to show attrition."

"So if he is sick," I argued academically, "why couldn't they have faked his death and sent him under some false name to a hospital? Nobody would know. And as for the body, those are not hard to come by in this part of the world. They could have led you to the wrong grave."

"Yeah," he said, "if it were not for the shells. I found six empty shells quite close to the grave. Had to look for them. Figured they would fire a final salvo in honor of their comrade." Brana was not an amateur!

In the first two months Brana also offered full amnesty, coupled with a rich reward, if the defector brought important information. But the two months passed without results.

"I never expected it to work," Brana said. "First of all, they do not trust us, and second, in their own minds, they are heroes. Surrender would be a miserable finale to seventeen years of gallant service for a cause," explained Brana. "I was simply organizing their social life. Had they dispersed before I completed my homework, it would be almost impossible to do the job. After I offered the amnesty, they had to stay together. Anybody leaving the camp could be heading for surrender." Devious, but it obviously worked. Weary of each other, forced to forgo their usual pleasures in villages, the tired fighters were stuck in their camp.

This forced isolation became the main ingredient in turning a girlfriend into an informant. Brana, the cunning master of psychological intrigue, added a few finer touches. For a whole month a troop of militiamen kept a conspicuous twenty-four hour watch of the girlfriend's house. Then one day, without obvious reason, the militia left. Even the regular outpost in the next village was abandoned. The official explanation, that manpower was needed for hot pursuit elsewhere, just did not wash. Far from being overextended, in larger villages dozens of militiamen leisurely strolled around.

This unexplained withdrawal became the hottest conversation topic. What could it mean? The rebel commander concluded it was a trap and proclaimed the village off-limits.

Soon the militiamen withdrawn from the village appeared in another one. The surveillance of the new village was less conspicuous. They camped in the forest, patrolled the access and came down the mountain slopes only to buy food.

About that time Brana confided to one of the riverside visitors that Radakovich, the girl's boyfriend, had a new romance going. They knew in which village, but not which house. Could the informer find out the name of the newest recipient of Radakovic's attention?

The village was rampant with rumors. It had to be one of the three widows. Soon Zora became the prime candidate. The more she protested, the more she became suspicious. Why did she occasionally send her son to his grandparents and then, ostensibly on her way to visit him, spend hour upon unaccounted hour in the forest? Picking berries for the kid! Who should believe such transparent nonsense? Why did she always keep to herself and shied away from communal activities. Particularly conspicuous was her absence from the last *komushanje*—a splendid affair. For sure she must have entertained somebody in her bedroom, while the village was looking the other way!

There was absolutely nothing to it. Brana chose the village with three widows to plant the rumor, and everything else took care of itself.

After the village decided who it was, everybody had something suspicious to report. Unusual people have been seen coming or leaving the house at dusk. Apparently the lights in the house went on and off at unusual hours. Finally the word got out that two militiamen were permanently stationed in Zora's attic, laying ambush for the incoming lover.

It worked. After two months, maddened by Radakovich's failure to show up, blindly jealous and seeking revenge, the real girlfriend offered to cooperate with the police. Brana, the mind reader, got his first big breakthrough. But he was not in a hurry to capitalize on it. Not until the rest of his plans were completed.

"You educated folks like to stick together," said Brana one morning. "For your personal fun, I am bringing in some real scientists. Not exactly to open a University on the river banks. That is not in line with my duties. But I have become an employer of academia. I need skilled help and for a large pile of cash, you good people are always ready to sell your souls."

By then I learned not to respond to Brana's provocations. "Oh yeah?" I yawned. Lack of interest was the best catalyst. So we learned that he hired two University professors from Belgrade. One, a speleologist, would do a survey of caves. The militia would then locate the entrances but refrain from entering.

The other professor, a cartographer, would draw maps of access routes, and mark the exact location of the cave. He was also given a number of collaborators and asked to map out every source of water, be this a village well, a roadside spigot, a watering hole in the field, or a spring in the forest. Of equal interest were those isolated mountain houses, which, on the border of forest and open fields, stand witness to the ability of Bosnians to eke out a living against formidable odds. Small paths and rarely traveled back-roads, overgrown by vegetation, were also mapped. However, sometimes a path was too dangerous to follow and the professor made a mark to that effect. It was up to others to decide whether it was worth pursuing the rarely used trail.

We met the cartographer, an elderly gentleman with the proper academic air about him, and the scruffy younger speleologist. The old man's task seemed straightforward, but how do you find caves?

The younger professor was obsessed with caves and could not stop talking about them. Certain configurations of the terrain are conducive to discoveries. Follow the dry bed of a mountain creek and you may end up in the cave from which it used to flow. Watch for sudden dips of the mountain slope. However the best information lives in local history. When the going gets tough people seek refuge in caves. The harder the times, the longer the stay, the more likely the event would be described in one of the songs. In the fifties, songs were still the main mode of mass communication and entertainment. Old stories were told and retold in the typical chanting monotone.

The speleologist was first and foremost a connoisseur of folklore. He knew almost all the classic tales and was rather good at singing

them. He'd go to a village get-together and start chanting songs of past hard times. Others would join and eventually a "run for your life" cave would pop up in somebody's song. The speleologist could not directly ask for the location. However, comparing songs in different villages gave him a pretty good general idea where the cave might be. To his chagrin he could not engage in his true hobby; to go out and find himself a new cave. Brana was not about to show his hand.

After the two scientists left, an undistinguished group of small bureaucrats descended upon Gorazde. Next day they were dispatched to distant villages. There they'd stay a few weeks compiling a detailed registry of all large animals. Each household had to declare every horse, cow, pig, and sheep. If an animal was sold or slaughtered, this had to be reported. The militia constantly crosschecked the actual stock against the registry.

This was quite effective. While using the amnesty to keep them together, Brana was cutting off the guerrilla's food supplies. You need a large animal to feed nine active men. Of course they could supplant themselves by hunting and receiving smaller shipments from sympathizers, but the bulk food was cut off.

"You don't seriously think they will die from hunger? There are enough wild vegetables and mushrooms to keep them going at least until the winter," I opined over one of our breakfasts.

"Right," retorted Brana, "but that is not the point. You have to understand these people. After almost two decades in the forest, food and booze are the most important parts of their lives. A great evening around the campfire, eating to the hilt, drinking and reminiscing about past exploits is what keeps them going. You might say, I am out to spoil their quality of life. See, we have not yet fired a single shot, and already they are feeling the pressure."

"I guess there is a risk that they may disperse in search of food," Brana continued, "but I figure they'll stay together as long as they can. Earlier they used to take small vacations in villages and reconvene at a prearranged date. If they disperse this time, they will never reconvene again. And they know it. I am keeping them together and making their life as miserable as possible. I bet that without an adoring audience, separated from their girls, they are by now pretty

unhappy. So the food becomes even more important to them. Instead of sympathizers delivering the livestock, they have to steal it themselves. My people in the field log in every instance when an animal disappears without a trace. What was an unaccounted pig here and a lamb there became a clear pattern. They are not as mobile as I thought. The needle is always in the same haystack.

"No, my dear doctor," said Brana after a pause, "I am not out to starve them, I am recording their movements."

~

The preparations took about three months. When Brana eventually struck, the end was swift and brutal. It was also the end of our intense, interesting, but totally unrealistic companionship. After all, Brana was a policeman and a defender of the regime and I was a politically suspect, presumably humanitarian physician. Some conflicts in life are sadly predictable and you may as well not have illusions. Unfortunately, in spite of bitter experiences in life, I was, and still am, hopelessly romantic and when the predicted conflict evolves, I manage to get disappointed.

In the final phase Brana started to deploy the militia. Houses of friends and sympathizers were under constant open surveillance. There were sentries at wells, bridges or footpaths over creeks. With all this in place, Brana first ordered raids on all known caves. In a few days they came upon a deep cave with two entrances. Nobody was in it, but a row of straw beds, fairly recent newspapers, a substantial amount of conserved food and hot coals under the ashes told the story. The guerrillas were robbed of their most recent main base.

After that, the emphasis changed. While half of the militia remained stationed at lookouts, the other half combed the terrain. They'd walk in long chains, ten feet away one from the other, crisscrossing the forests, mountain meadows and open fields. Occasionally after screening one area, they'd jump on trucks and start at some distant point. At other times, they'd turn right around and scan the same area again. Sometimes two chains started separately and converged one on other. Sometimes they started back to back, and moved in opposite directions. The unpredictability was the essence

of the method. It was harassment, simple and pure. After keeping them together, Brana was now equally determined to disperse the guerrillas.

Suddenly forced to act as individuals, the guerrillas lost confidence and became easy prey. The first one was shot crossing a creek. Three decided on a mini-raid and challenged two sentries at a relative's house. The two militiamen withdrew, waited for reinforcement and then gave chase. However, they left a few sharpshooters inside the house. One of the guerrillas hid in the forest and when the posse disappeared, returned toward the house. He was shot on sight.

The biggest success came all in one day. With her approval, two sharpshooters were secretly stationed at Radakovich's girlfriend's attic. When the famous fighter finally came to visit, the twosome in the attic froze in fear. Seeing no action, the girl was sure they were waiting to shoot them both in bed. She fended off the advances as long as she could. When there was no more excuse, fearing for her own life, the girl shot the lover as he was busy undressing her. Two other fellows waiting in the forest came forward and surrendered.

Radakovic was a true hero and an acknowledged leader. This led Brana to organize a despicable macabre show. The body was placed on an oxcart and displayed in every village. It arrived in Gorazde on market day and the police had it displayed in the middle of the village square. I dashed to intervene. Not in my town! I was the health inspector and had legal rights to put a stop to this horror. On the way I made up my little speech to the effect that corpses could not be displayed together with produce at the market. Danger of infection!

I should have listened to Meshek and ignored the whole affair. During the war and later as a physician, I have grown accustomed to corpses, but was not ready for the one in the market place. Long unkempt hair, tattered clothing, bare and swollen feet, bloated stomach, a gaping hole in the head. Flies swarmed all over competing for the chance to land on the protruding brain. The face was frozen in a pitiful grimace of anguish, the open mouth full of yellow, decaying teeth. It was horrible!

People encircled the oxcart, but kept their distance. Only an occasional child would dash, touch the corpse, and with that bit of bravado accomplished, run back.

I went after the lieutenant in charge. "You have to remove the body instantly. It is a danger to public health and shows a shameful disrespect for human life. As the county sanitary inspector, I have the right and power to stop this."

The officer looked at me in absolute disbelief. "With all due respect to your position and wisdom, may I point out that I am getting my orders from other quarters. I suggest that you discuss the matter with Comrade Brana. He is in the command trailer around the corner," he said in a proper military lingo.

I dashed around the corner to challenge Brana. He was not a bit surprised by my visit.

"I thought it might bother you," said Brana in his relaxed fashion, "but you do not seriously believe that I will yield. I am the power here, and in fact you have no legal standing. You may be in charge of quality of meat, but not that kind of meat." With these unbelievably crude words all the patina of civility disappeared from Brana's face. There he was at his policeman's worst—mean, powerful and menacing.

It is hard to tell what did it, but I completely snapped. In retrospect, I would like to believe that it was an issue of ethics and that I reacted to the indecency of it all. Brana had pushed me to a point where, no matter what the consequences might have been, I had to stand up for my values. However, more likely, the reason was in my immediate past, in the similarity to Father's head wound and in the sudden realization that Brana symbolized the forces that destroyed my father. Whatever the reason, I lost control and threw myself at Brana to hit him.

They did not exactly knock me out, but the next thing I remember is sitting in a chair held from both sides by a strongman, Brana calmly in front of me. All the malice was gone from his face. He appeared tired and sad. "Look, Doctor, I can see where this means a lot to you, but for Christ's sake, control yourself! Guys around me are not exactly famous for their sensitivity. You attacked their senior officer and almost got yourself killed. What good would that do to anybody? I told you long ago that I could not abide by the Geneva Convention. Not with that kind of enemy, and not in my line of work. I do what I have to. Sometimes it's not fun at all. I will say this

only once so you understand. Had I not shown the body, nobody would have believed that we killed him. He was very brave and immortal as far as local followers are concerned. The fame outgrew the man. They had to see what a miserable existence it was. I had to punch the balloon."

I was tired, deeply unhappy and unable to speak. Not drawing a reaction, Brana ordered the men to let go of me and continued to talk. "I think I understand you. Things cannot be changed, but I may be able to do something for you. To help you go on living. You may not see it my way now or ever, but I am doing you a favor."

And with this off his chest he ordered me arrested, handcuffed and via the village square taken to the local jail.

The reception in the jail was friendly. The jailers held me in the front office and poured coffee at will. The man in charge kept repeating that I was only temporarily detained, not arrested. After a few hours he drove me back to the hospital.

Again, the Mermaid was right. He could not ignore an open challenge to his authority. But the highly symbolic handcuffing was for my own benefit. "To let me go on living," as Brana said. By and large we are all trained to accept reality. I was reaching for the impossible in a totalitarian society. Any doubts about whether I had done enough, or could have done more, were cleared with that arrest. Furthermore, parading me handcuffed through the village did marvels for my local standing. I became an instant hero, a guy who stood up for his beliefs. I will never know for sure, but I believe that was the favor Brana had in mind.

The next day, his job half-accomplished, Brana left the village and I never saw him again. He failed to give his big party—out of disgust with the whole affair, or so I prefer to think. For all I know, the big fish is still swimming in the Drina.

Brana's second-in-command completed the operation and at the end eight guerrillas were apprehended or slain. The last survivor disappeared into thin air. He continued to live in the forest, occasionally coming down to visit his girl friend, a bright, lonely teacher. Everything was forgotten and he moved freely until one day, four years later, he hitched a ride with a trucker. A policeman stopped the truck to berate the driver for accepting passengers in the cab. Safety

rules required the driver to be alone. Usually such an infraction lead to off-loading of the passenger, and that was the end of it. But this hitchhiker got into a heated argument with the patrolman. When asked to show his ID papers, the passenger pulled a handgun and killed the policeman. He then ordered the stunned driver to fetch the police from the town. "I am Jovo Sinchich. Tell them to come and get me." When they came he opened submachine gunfire, killed another policeman, and then charged through the open field until he was mowed down. It was a suicide. A last senseless, glorious stand of an unemployed hero!

The Mountain Interlude

(1955)

Little did the Social Security secretary know that his safe plan to build the hospital in the Russian stockade, if and when the Army moved out, would backfire. Against his expectations, things all of a sudden lined up. First, upriver the village of Focha was about to build a new hospital and that jolted the good people of Gorazhde. The two towns were in constant competition. If one could have a hospital, why should the other not have one? Second, Mitar Bakich, the war hero and regional deputy in the Yugoslav Parliament, was very sick. He became a patient of Professor Hahn, the chief of medicine in Zagreb, an old family friend and my mentor. Hahn told Bakich about the talented young doctor who went to serve in Gorazhde. This, Hahn suggested, would be an ideal opportunity to improve the health services in the area. Bakich remembered the Russian stockade plan, lined up a few allies and got the ball rolling.

We didn't think much of the rumors until, without fanfare and practically overnight, the garrison left the stockade and the cold fall weather notwithstanding, moved into it's summer camp. Just like that. A few days later the building was officially transferred to the county. Soon an excited bank clerk told us that a large sum of money had come from Belgrade and upon the Mayor's signature would be transferred to the hospital account. However two weeks passed by and nothing happened. An empty building, money in the bank, but

none transferred to the hospital. What was going on? After six months in Gorazhde I had an idea how things worked and should have kept quiet. Instead I asked for an appointment with the Mayor. He'd be delighted to see me but rather than me coming to his office, he'd come to Janja's coffee house. There we could transact the business. Any Bosnian would have understood that subtle hint. Not me. I thought it was an excellent sign; we'd talk informally in pleasant surroundings. Naturally, Janja's coffee parlor was full of customers. The otherwise reserved Mayor turned sociable. He was out to learn everything he could about people's health, their family, and business fortunes. The weather was also very much on his mind. He introduced me to strangers and those I already knew he'd enthusiastically wave to our table. "Join our good doctor. Isn't it great to have him! Quite a lad! And you should see him play soccer. As good as a pro!"

It hit me after about an hour. We would not transact any business at Janja's. It could have been done had the Mayor chosen a distant table. Bosnians are polite and would not think of imposing. But the Mayor willingly encouraged interruptions.

"Let's talk about the new hospital," I insisted.

"That's what is wrong with you city folks. Always in a hurry! Have another coffee."

"I am not in a hurry for myself, but a whole bunch of patients are waiting in the clinic," I explained.

The Mayor was not impressed. "You know," he said," six months ago we had no physicians. Imagine how long they would wait if we had not hired you. So what's a little additional time for them?"

You will never win against a skillful Bosnian. According to the protocol I should have given up, but there was no way of stopping a city fool like myself. So I kept pressing to find out whether the money had arrived.

"Of course," came the answer, "the money is in the bank. No sweat. Have a brandy."

"When will you transfer it?"

"Transfer? What is the hurry? The money is in the bank and the Army out of the stockade. Great going. I wish the weather were as

good as your hospital's future. They say it will rain tomorrow. And you know what that means. A bit closer to the flood line," mused the Mayor.

"For crying out loud! Will you or will you not transfer the money?"

"Well, Doctor," said the Mayor in utter disbelief, "if you are pushing me so hard; the answer is no. No, I will not transfer the money, not just yet."

"But why?"

"Things are not done that way. I like to stroll through the village and when I get to the market I call out: Good morning my old square; good morning to all your four sides."

Another ornate Bosnian expression. Before releasing the money, the Mayor wanted to cover all bases. But why? It was a simple transaction. Why not complete it? Did he have real reasons, or was this force of habit, the generic Bosnian indecision?

"Are we in some sort of trouble?" I inquired.

"No, no," he assured me. "Just had no time to stroll around. You never know what you may hear on the village square. You are right, after all. Maybe those patients should not wait any longer. Let me walk you to the hospital." And that was that.

At the hospital door we shook hands. "Who knows?" said the Mayor." Maybe I am wrong. The weather might be better tomorrow. Let's hope!" He was not talking about the climate. Something was bothering him and I wondered what.

The answer came from the living exception to Darwin's law of natural selection, the village pharmacist named Franjo. Meshek and I called him "Exception" and the nickname stuck. Franjo did not follow Darwin's tenet of the survival of the fittest. Tall, skinny, and excessively polite, Exception looked naive and vulnerable. In terms of his IQ and mental quickness Franjo was utterly unimpressive. But he had a unique social skill, which Darwin failed to describe: the ability to quickly identify the center of power in any new situation. And that made him a veritable virtuoso survivalist. During the war Gorazhde changed hands at least thirty times. Not only did Franjo survive all those changes, but he also succeeded turning the experi-

ence into a profitable business. Never was his shop closed, nor were his supplies confiscated. In times of danger he acted with aplomb. Within an hour of the new masters' arrival, thermos bottle in hand, Exception would introduce himself to the commanding officer, offer him some coffee and tender an invitation for dinner. Next, he'd find somebody from the medical corps. Soon enough they would agree on a mutually useful swap of medical supplies. Franjo was somewhat of a hoarder. At the outset of the war, he stashed away large amounts of just about everything. He was now parlaying these supplies into a profitable business. After a while, through exchanges, his pharmacy had a good average of German, Italian and later, via the Partizans, English stock.

Everybody realized the advantages of having this little Switzerland in a Bosnian war. In fact, Franjo facilitated indirect trading between the warring parties. Through all this he became richer. He'd trade lesser drugs for food. The most desired items: sulfonamides, tetanus antiserum, typhoid vaccine, were sold for gold. Both the Serbian and Moslem cultures cherish precious metals and quite a few coins were in circulation. There would have been more had Franjo not kept burying them at secret locations.

I expected to learn many interesting things from this capable man, but got practically nothing. Not that he hesitated to talk about the war. Just the opposite, he enjoyed reminiscing and told numerous anecdotes. But he had nothing of substance to offer. Trying to make it from today to tomorrow, Franjo had no time for generalizations. He barely knew what the war was about, who stood for what. All he cared was to identify the power and be on its good side.

Closest to a piece of philosophic wisdom was Franjo's reverence for authority. "It is better to have the devil in charge than nobody," Franjo would say. Not infrequently one master withdrew and the other had not yet arrived. According to Franjo, these were the toughest times in Gorazhde. Neighbors would settle scores, the streets were not safe and if somebody had it in his mind to rob you, to whom were you to complain? During a period of lawlessness robbery need not be a straight break-in. In the absence of legal authority, a caller may come to your door and politely inform you how much he

cherishes your bicycle. Will you take a chance of not offering it to him as a present?

Those days in-between two administrations were a real nightmare The pharmacist, whose survival depended on association with power had no time, to build relationships with ordinary people. They did not hate him, nor did he harm them, but that lack of human bond was potentially disastrous. Franjo knew it. In those interregnums he stayed inside the house and quietly prayed for somebody, any authority, to show up.

During the war information was Franjo's lifeline and he paid solid gold for it. In the dangerous gambit of survival it was less important to know who was coming, than to figure out who was in charge. Why waste your time with a general if his captain was running the show? After the war Franjo saw no reason to change his ways. He had a pathological obsession with gossip. Just in case! If anybody, he should know why the Mayor stonewalled the hospital project.

Good relationships with doctors were important to Franjo and I took him up on his standing invitation to dinner. Over the soup he laid it all out:

"A major reorganization is afoot. The counties of Gorazhde, Focha, and Chajniche will merge into a single large county. Our Mayor will keep his job, but the leader of the new county will go to a big shot, a Serb from Sarajevo, who was firmly committed to Focha. Rajko Gagovich, that was his name, was the main driving force behind the hospital-building project in Focha. He wanted the county seat to be in Focha. However, geographically Focha was furthermost from all other points in the new county. Logic prevailed and because of its central location, Gorazhde had been chosen for the county seat of the new county. To slow things down, Rajko immediately requested that the Russian stockade be used for the new county building. A masterful stroke! It would have delayed his transfer from Sarajevo and it could have stopped the building of the hospital in Gorazhde. In the meantime the Mayor was slowing the hospital project so as not to look that he worked against his designated boss. However the Mayor's heart was in the right place.

"Don't worry. The Mayor may look simple, but he is capable. Eventually you will get your money." So predicted Franjo.

A battle of wits was shaping up around the hospital project. One day Mitar Bakich, the deputy, showed up with a retinue of journalists, toured the stockade, and officially opened the construction. Thereafter, the Mayor stopped procrastinating. To Rajko, who knew the score only too well, the Mayor could now claim that he had done his best to stop the hospital, but was overruled by higher authority. Comrade Rajko would have to run the county from a smaller building, no fault of the Mayor. It was all a well-choreographed charade, a win by centuries-old rules, with a face-saving-gesture to the loser.

Even now it is hard to comprehend what was going on. Why did two hospitals in neighboring villages assume such a disproportionate significance? Both were needed. I got together with my opposite number in Focha. We both recommended that each hospital have Surgery, Pediatrics, General Medicine and Obstetrics. Other specialties could be distributed between the two centers. It came to naught. One side wanted to stop the other and nobody was interested in a countywide health service. To counteract Mitar Bakich's blessing, Focha secured sponsorship from the veteran's organization. During the epic fifth offensive, Partizans had a hospital in Focha. The new one quickly became a memorial to the war hospital. The dedication was widely reported in newspapers.

Each community had the other over the barrel and the medical personnel were drawn into the conflict. In spite of it all I enjoyed the experience. Everything became a challenge. The hospital construction was tortuous. Sometimes it almost completely stopped; on other occasions it jumped by leaps and bounds. Depending on who had the upper hand at a given moment. Nothing was spared, and everybody got involved in the act.

As soon as Rajko arrived, he had me in his office. "You ought to know," he said, "had I come just three weeks earlier, your hospital construction would have never started. You'd be where you belong; in that little clinic on the hill. We do not need a white elephant here."

"In that case, it was mighty nice of you not to come earlier," I retorted. Not a brilliant response, but perfectly appropriate for a bully.

The new man was intelligent, quick, and extremely inpatient. Small and rotund, this former teacher spoke fast and his hands punctuated every word. If he was forced to listen, his feet were in constant motion. The tempo depended on whether he truly listened or followed his own thoughts. A fast machine gun tapping meant he was waiting for a chance to interrupt. If Rajko disliked what you had to say, it was best not to look at him. There was murder in those eyes.

I could see anger build in Rajko. There was no point in pushing my luck further. "Look," I continued, "we both seem to be stuck in a place somebody else chose for us."

"So you are well-informed. And it is also true that we both are transients. You will eventually return to Zagreb, and I for sure will not grow old in Gorazhde. That is where the comparison stops. To you this is all sport. A game. But even in a temporary situation I take things seriously. So do not expect any of that 'nothing personal' nonsense from me. It is very personal. If you are in my way I will hate you. I do not jump over obstacles; I crush them."

No doubt he was telling the truth. Free-floating hostility was all over the man.

Of course he was right. The new hospital did not mean that much to me. But there was no way back. Never yield under threat. Resistance is the only thing a bully appreciates. If you ever show weakness, he will pile humiliation upon humiliation on you until he breaks you spirit. After that, having you in his pocket, he will move to new more exciting targets. Had I ventured one conciliatory word, he'd right away press for a public statement against the hospital, or extract a private promise of cooperation. And the only reward for such a cooperation would be his utter scorn. There was no choice. We were on a collision course.

To keep the spectacle going, I professed a profound commitment to the new hospital project. I was not looking for trouble, but there was no other way; each of us had to play his role.

All of a sudden Rajko changed his tune. "We do have a lot in common. You and your buddy will do what you must and so will I,"

he said, "Frankly, nobody will win. I may need your professional help in the future. Also talking to illiterate clerks gets on my nerves. Maybe we should commiserate over some dinners." Rajko stopped for a second, but then quickly added, "This is not a truce. Nothing has changed. If you are in my way and if I can, rest assured, I will walk over you."

Thus started a weird relationship, always intense, sometimes pleasant, sometimes confrontational, and much too frequently confessional. Rajko wished he could control his temper. He'd press us for tranquilizers and sleeping pills. The more he confided, the more resentful he became. I urged him not to consult me, but when he was in a mood to ask for help, nothing could stop him.

It was all so predictable. The next day after he'd asked for help he'd be sour and unpleasant. One morning he was at his level worst and I blew my top. "Last night I spent two hours listening to you. This morning instead of thanks, I get your mad-dog act. What the hell is going on?"

"My dear fellow, you are acting like an offended prima donna," said Rajko with gusto. "If you expect thanks, you are in the wrong profession. Even the Bosnian peasant knows the truth, but I guess they failed to teach it in medical school. Nobody likes dependence. Thankfulness amounts to an unbearable bondage. My uncle constantly fought his neighbor. After each skirmish he would say 'I do not know why he hates me so much, I have never done him any good."

There was a lot of truth in this Bosnian wisecrack. Faced with generosity, people frequently rationalize their way out of the bondage. You were nice to them because you had to be. It made you feel good. You acted for your and not for their sake. That is the standard western reaction, but an occasional Bosnian will go a step further and hate you for doing him some good.

"OK. So you don't owe me a thing. But for Christ's sake if it puts you in such a terrible state of mind, why are you coming to see me? Stay away. You don't need me."

"But I do need you," protested Rajko. "I like to be loved and I love to hate!"

What do you do with such a complex person, who draws you

into his private problems and makes them your own misery? I was caught. If he insisted on seeing me, there was absolutely no way of escaping. And, just as he said, he wanted my compassion but was delighted with his hatred for it. Elsewhere, a man like Rajko would be constantly stretched on an analyst's sofa seeking to find the root of his problems. In Gorazhde, he enjoyed acting out and had no need to ponder why he behaved the way he did.

~

The fight around the hospital sometimes took unusual turns. One morning Rajko requested that I attend an important person in a remote mountain village. I thought he ought to bring him down to the hospital where we could take better care of the patient.

Rajko was adamant. "This man needs to see that we care. If it were anything else, an Army helicopter could easily take him to Sarajevo. But he has Kozara Disease. The appearance of care and not the availability of cure is what counts for this man."

"You want me to mount a donkey and ride a whole day to minister to a hysterical village bigwig?"

"I would," Rajko interrupted, "but seeing how important you have become, I've secured you a jeep and a personal driver. However, go you must. I promised the old hero I'd get him a doctor. I am sure you can handle the guy. By the way, the Militia was unable to disarm him." There was a great deal of delight in Rajko's malicious eyes.

I could see it in my mind—a berserk man, screaming, frothing at the mouth and letting off an occasional round to keep the militia at bay. Everybody half-scared, half-compassionate, waiting for the grand finale, usually a convulsion and collapse.

I had seen plenty of such attacks in Italy, and later, after the war, in Zagreb. But this was 1955, ten years after the end of the war, and by that time the epidemic of hysteria was over. However, time flows slower in Bosnia, and up in the mountains, somebody was still doing his wartime thing. Trust Rajko to find me the last existing case!

We came upon the village after three solid hours of driving. The man had already suffered two convulsions but nobody dared to dis-

arm him while he was unconscious. He was back in his house, swearing and yelling but not having a real fit. As I circled around the house looking for the right approach I came to the lunatic's attention.

"Are you the fucking doctor Rajko has sent my way?" screamed the man. "You can't help me. Nobody can. The bloody Germans did it. Destroyed my nerves. Kill the bastards. Bam bam bam."

"Where are they? I hate Nazis. Let's get them together." I responded in a fit of zany inspiration.

"You must have fallen off a pear tree," came the stunned answer. "There are no Germans around. It is in my mind. Only I can see them."

"Well if they are only in your mind and not for real, why are you banging around with real ammunition? You may hurt somebody."

"But I haven't shot anybody yet. Not in peacetime. I just scare the spirits away."

At least we were talking! I continued to follow my hunches. "I hear you were a really good shot during the war and there was a ransom on your head. I bet you were good at ambushes. Let's move on and lay one."

Out we went, sneaking through the village and crawling through the field. Quite a sight! I guess that in standard psychiatric terms you would call it role-playing. After a while, exhausted, we sat under a tree. He handed me the gun. I kept asking about his past deeds while quietly pulling out the firing pin. I turned picky about the details. Was he sure this was in such and such village? Which German division was it? Which offensive?

"Don't you believe me?" he barked, ready to throw himself into another fit.

"Of course I do, but I wonder whether your memory is affected. After all, your brain is not working right. If you see Germans where there are none, maybe the recollection is gone too."

"It is not my brain; it is my nerves."

"Oh yeah? Which nerve. Show it to me." And with this I started a physical exam under the old oak tree. "Raise your arm, move your head, turn around. Up. Down." The stream of commands caught him by surprise. He became obedient and I grew more demanding. I could barely hold back from ordering him to do something silly. The

temptation to show full command over this lunatic was overwhelming. Power corrupts. No doubt about it.

We finally went into the man's house where I gave him some strong sedatives to swallow. For the next few hours I had him talk about his past. One by one, neighbors filed in. Once again there was a room full of listeners and my patient took advantage of it.

Poor, miserable, war hero! All he needed was an audience to hear for the thousandth time the accounts of his past exploits.

In the midst of all this the driver came to talk to me.

"I have bad news for you, Doc," he said, "The water pump on the jeep has sprung a leak."

"People told me you are a pretty good mechanic. Can't you somehow glue the darn thing together?"

"No way, Doc. But I got an idea. Tomorrow morning I will fetch a horse ride to Chajniche. The lumber company in Chajniche has two jeeps." He said.

"But doesn't that mean that they will either lend you one of their jeeps or let you take out the pump from a jeep? In both cases they would be out of one jeep. Why should they cooperate?" I asked.

"If they refuse to cooperate I could easily call Comrade Rajko and he'd order them to do what was right. I will be back by noon, for sure," said the driver. "In the meantime, why don't you just relax. It will take me a few minutes to figure out which is the best place in the village to stay overnight."

He left the room and after a while returned in the company of the local teacher. The teacher, a man in his late twenties offered me the bed in his guestroom and his kitchen floor for the driver.

"That is perfectly OK," said the driver. " A person in my profession must be ready for anything. It will be great to have a roof over my head, and with a blanket under me, I will be comfortable. With this jeep of mine I've many time been in tougher spots than this."

When I woke up the driver had already gone. He'd left a note. We should expect him late in the afternoon. Funny. Yesterday he said he'd be back by noon.

I went with the teacher to examine the school children. They were healthy and clean. No lice. Than I looked up my patient. Yesterday I'd promised to take him back to Gorazhde but did not have

the foggiest idea what to do when we arrived there. Now I got more than an idea. A plot was hatching. Rajko had made the patient my problem; I'd repay him in kind. After all, a large part of the patient's problem was related to his social and political status. While other veterans had been given high positions, my patient was relegated to useless retirement in his village.

I steered the conversation to sensitive topics and immediately hit gold. Rajko and my patient had fought in the same brigade. He was the commanding officer, and Rajko his political commissar. The two of them got along just fine. After the war, Rajko's star shot up and he never turned back to inquire what happened with his old buddy. It was about time for him to cash in on the old friendship, I suggested, and my patient had no objections. But in order to help, I had to be first quite sure that he was fully cured. Neither he nor I could afford the embarrassment of him having an attack in Gorazhde.

"Am I cured?" inquired my new friend.

"No, you are not, but I will teach you how to prevent an attack. The real cure will come when you regain self-respect by doing something useful."

With this opener I immediately launched into teaching the German autogenic training relaxation technique. Whenever he felt tense, the patient should sit down, close his eyes, and concentrate on his left hand. Make it feel heavy.

He was a fast learner and within half an hour claimed to be able to relax both arms. We then discussed his future. He might have to go to school or get practical training in some specialized field. He agreed, and professed to understand that this meant starting from the bottom of the heap. During vocational training he was to work hard and seek no exceptions. In return, Rajko, who must arrange all this, should guarantee him a good career after the training. In the meantime he was never to talk about the past since it upset him so much. Even a hint of an attack might destroy his prospect for a career.

"Sounds good to me," said the patient. "Let's talk about it tonight. I will throw a big party."

"I don't think I have time for a party," I responded, "I count on being in Gorazhde tonight and you are supposed to come with me."

"Well, if you are really keen," said my patient, "let's get a pair of

horses and start right away. You will not make it by car. The driver has orders to keep producing engine malfunctions. Rajko wants you out of sight for a few days. I am just trying to make it more comfortable for you, but if you really want to outfox the Commissar, I will help you. We can make it on horses."

I wondered what that was all about. Should I fight? What for? Whatever Rajko wanted to do in my absence was probably unpleasant. I decided to stay on in the village and spare myself a confrontation. I, too, was learning fast.

~

The party was a grand event. Our host informed everybody of his cure and hinted at leaving the village. That helped a great deal. Those who feared another attack were now free to join. Soon thereafter the number of guests doubled. There was plenty of food and shljivovica. In addition, our host also organized somewhat of a formal program. First the teacher recited a few poems. Then the singing started.

I love singing. Nothing matches the catharsis of rendering aloud and in good company a simple melodic song. I had a whale of a good time and by midnight was completely hoarse.

Later a few storytellers covered everything from jokes, to war anecdotes to old-fashioned horror stories. Finally a *guslar* took to the old single-string instrument and started to chant heroic poems. I have respect for oral tradition, but the chanting monotone of a *guslar* is not exactly my cup of tea. It drove me to the most distant corner.

From my protected vantage-point, I could see the host. He was pleasant, and restrained. Most importantly he did not boast or seek to be the center of attention. Maybe he could be saved. That would be really nice. Salvageable heros are a rare commodity!

By and large heroes are not what the newspapers make them out to be. Their incomparable deeds are a matter of public record but little is ever said about their fate after the war. My host was the typical, run-of-the-mill hero. An ordinary person who knew nothing about his potential until circumstances brought it out. At first such people surprise themselves. Soon they bask in other people's admiration and the newly acquired fame completely transforms their lives. The excite-

ment of their deeds and other people's admiration blot out the previous gray existence. The new hero needs new deeds almost as badly as an addict needs his daily fix. And akin to an addict, he needs to escalate. In an ongoing crescendo one deed begets another. Of course, that's why there are more dead than living heroes. After the war the few who survived were struck by a devastating low. What was there left to do? Lacking inner drive, the former hero hoped for some new stimulus to bring back that lost part of him, which he and everybody else admired. But the uneventful life after the war drags on at a snail's pace and nothing happens to prevent the inevitable slide towards oblivion. Knowing what he had been, the former hero can't stand the old ordinary fellow inside his skin.

Even the highest recognition cannot replace the lack of tension. With time it gets worse. The audiences thin out, the circle of admirers narrows, and the reality of civilian life relentlessly sets in. Once you run in the highest gear it is hard to cope with normal speed. There is a need to do something new—live a better existence than the one before the war. As the hero fails to find it, he becomes a disillusioned, tragic and sometimes insufferable person.

As the party advanced I was growing more confident that I could help this former hero. He'd already started to adjust. All I had to do was to show him a way out. Frankly, had I gotten stuck in his village under the mountain, I too would have gone mad.

My host seemed to have connected with his old self. My visit gave him an opportunity to exert some leadership. He threw himself with abandon into the dual roles: as the director of the counter-play against Rajko, and the chief of the protocol of the village honoring an important visitor.

"Don't go back to Gorazhde," said my patient. "Stay as long as it takes. They wanted you out of the way. Let them now pay for it. In time they will have to fetch you. Leave it to me. I know how to talk to the driver. He will continue to play the defective car game. He had to take the pump out to convince you the car was defective. But you know how repairs go. The air could have leaked into the lines, a thread could have warn off on a rusty nut, a washer on the pump might have rusted through. Once you start messing with an old car you can easily run into real troubles. I am sure the driver will play

along. He doesn't mind staying; there are many pretty girls in the village."

~

The extra days under the mountain were sheer joy. Under the patient's leadership the whole village treated me as a guest, and nobody asked me for professional help.

I went on my own for some mountain climbing and mushroom picking. But the word got out that I loved hunting. True enough. In the past, my only quarry had been a rabbit or a bird, but the villagers had other ideas. We were to go after mountain goats. For years they'd been observing an old fellow who had lost his position as the leader of the flock and had to live all by himself. Like other solitary goats, he had a limited territory and his habits were very predictable. In that regard animals are like people. Loss of companionship breeds further isolation and life turns in to a monotonous routine.

"You will see the old boy for sure," said my host, "but he is very shy and it will be very hard to come close to him."

"If his habits are so well-known," I wondered aloud, "why has somebody not already taken a shot at him?"

"If you want to know the truth, we were saving this one for an important leader from Belgrade," said the self-appointed master of village hospitality. "You should not think we do not know which side of the bread is buttered. This might be a small village, but we know how to cultivate friends. It helps when it comes to such things as getting a new road or a good teacher." After a short pause, almost as an afterthought, he added, "In fact, we have been saving him for Comrade Rankovich."

That was a surprise. Rankovich, the minister of internal affairs, was Tito's designated heir. Was he kidding me? Would the omnipotent leader come to such a godforsaken hamlet?

As if he had the ability to read my thoughts, my much-improved patient chimed in. "It was all set for last year," he said. "I know Rankovich from the Partizans. He loves to hunt, but hates to return empty-handed. The previous year he spent a week in the hotel at the Maglich Mountain but did not as much as see a goat.

You know how things are up here," continued my friend, "the word gets around pretty quickly. I contacted the chief forester of the area and told him about our goat. It was too late for Rankovich to come over, but an appointment was set for the past year. We even got a letter to that effect. However, when the time came, he did not show up. The Comrade was too busy we were told. The heck he was!" continued my friend. "He had other things to worry about than hunting. And frankly, I do not think he will have another chance to hunt."

I was stunned. This isolated village kept up very well with most current political developments. Not so long ago in Gorazhde, in one of his characteristic asides, Brana the policeman turned fisherman, told us about the impending changes in the leadership. We were sworn to silence. Nothing was reported about the possible conflict in the newspapers. In fact, the readers were fed the regular diet of sycophantic reports about Rankovich's activities. Only a few months later did the story become public. How did the village get wind of the new alignment in Belgrade? I will never know.

Anyhow, Rankovich's downfall was my gain. The village had decided to blow its political capital on me!

I could not refuse the offer. Next morning they gave me gun, a rucksack full of goodies and with a few selected experts at my side, we were off to hunt. After a healthy walk into the mountains we spotted the old boy. He was gorgeous and to this day I am sorry to have shot him. The old goat had a favorite peak from which he'd proudly look around. We could not get closer to him and I had to take a chance to shoot at a distance of over 800 feet. My first shot broke the goat's spine and the paralyzed animal tumbled down the hill. It was a terrible sight. The goat dragged himself by his front legs through the deep snow. Somebody rushed off to finish the job.

Amid wild cheers and congratulations, I was on the verge of tears. Out of best intentions the villagers had caused me to kill. And I was not ready; I'd seen too much of it not so long ago.

It was now my patient's turn to become the psychotherapist. Instinctively he understood my attack of guilt. He dispatched a group to remove the dead animal to an out-of-sight glen. There they skinned the animal and cut up the meat. The head was preserved

and, according to tradition, after a few weeks, I received a gift of the mounted head of the unfortunate animal.

While the others were busy with the goat, I sat down with the rest of the hunting party. Understanding the mood of the moment, they quietly worked their way through the assortment of sausages, cheese and other delicacies. Instead of offering them to me, each of them put aside a portion of his goodies. Only once did my patient interrupt this funerary atmosphere.

"Here you are, Doctor," he said, "When you feel like eating—here is a nice little pile for you."

Slowly my behavior affected the others and we all fell into a morose silence. However, even in the deepest Bosnian mountain, you are not alone. The distant camps of lumberjacks and sheep herdsmen somehow manage to spice up their boring existence by a quick exchange of news. And the shooting of a mountain goat was important news indeed!

The hunting rules, to which everybody adhered, were rather strict. The hunter could keep his trophy, but the meat belonged to the region's forestry department, which had the right to sell it off on the spot. You would be wrong to think that, deep in the forest, nobody will show up to buy meat. According to local tradition, eating the meat of the vivacious, jumping mountain goat confers these youthful qualities on the consumer. Within an hour, delegations from three distant camps arrived at the scene. I had to snap out of my nasty mood, accept congratulations and start to socialize. One of the groups brought a selection of sheep cheeses, ranging from a one-day-old one to very well-aged varieties. By and by, as custom required, a small feast of good food and brandy interrupted the monotony of mountain life.

I had to hand it to my hosts. Their respectful non-interference followed by delicious food and good drinks was every bit as effective a psychotherapy as any doctor could have offered.

Fully recovered from the attack of remorse, I stayed a whole week in the village. First we reported that the car had truly become defective. They dispatched another one, but before it arrived, the teacher and I went higher up into the mountain to survey children's

literacy and give them free physical exams. Next day I developed a "fever." It took a few days before I was "in shape to be transported." Finally, when we ran out of excuses, my war hero and I, both much improved, drove back to Gorazhde. Back to reality.

We arrived at nightfall and drove straight to Rajko's apartment. He greeted his old Comrade with genuine warmth. I immediately launched a dissertation about the need to both create an educational opportunity and find a good job for my patient but Rajko stopped me short.

"Right," said Rajko. "Knowing you are a bleeding heart, I thought you might come up with such a proposal. And guess what? I've got it all lined up."

He then turned to the patient. "Marko, I've got a room reserved for you in the hotel. And there is a job waiting for you in Gorazhde, but first you must go for some practical training in Sarajevo. Come to my office tomorrow and we will discuss details."

That was it. Rajko did not wish to hear a lecture from me. In fairness, Rajko had a sincere interest in his Comrades well being. Later, on many occasions, in between his fits of anger, Rajko found time to give me a progress report. Marko was doing very well. To everybody's surprise, he studied hard and was catching on with ease.

It turned out that Rajko wanted me out of Gorazhde only for a day or two, long enough to bring in a group of technical experts to reconsider the feasibility of our hospital building plans. The commission completed its work in a day and, as far as Rajko was concerned, the next day I should have returned back to work. By staying longer I succeeded in beating Rajko at his own game. He needed the Jeep but could not check whether we played games or whether the car had broken down for real.

For a change, Bosnian etiquette worked in my favor. The Mayor was probably rubbing his hands in delight but could not publicly gloat. Rajko, knowing full well I had outwitted him, was not about to show irritation. Nobody ever questioned my prolonged absence and the whole affair was roundly ignored. And Rajko's ploy with the commission failed. They found no faults with the existing plans and after a few days the hospital construction resumed without further technical impediments.

The Tower of Babel

(1955–1956)

Mustafa, the secretary of Health, started as a procrastinator but eventually became our strong supporter. Though he initially professed not to understand why the health clinic needed electricity, he got us connected to the network in less than a month. By local standards this was quite an achievement. Besides securing electricity and giving us a generous budget, he steered every purchase order to the right place. In the early 1950s nothing could be taken for granted. Shops were practically empty and if a merchant accepted your order he was unable to predict when the goods would arrive. Under those conditions only a fool would place an order and hope for the best. In this seller's market one had to use VIP for everything. In Croatian the term VIP (*veza i poznanstvo*) stands for "connections and acquaintances." Mustafa, who was a virtuoso of the VIP system, sent the purchase order for hospital supplies to, of all places, the local lumber company.

The head of the *Stakorina* company was Salman, a man in his early fifties and a genius in disguise. He dressed like the locals, had the same crude manners and spoke with the typical local drawl, but under that facade was a shrewd businessman. He did not wish to look different but different he was. A decade after the end of the Second World War, Salman had succeeded in parlaying a few outdated and rusty sawmills into a sizeable, well-functioning enterprise. Noth-

ing could stop this resourceful man. His timber was high up in the mountains, the connecting roads were terrible, and the lumber had to be first transferred from trucks onto the narrow-gauge railway and then reloaded onto the normal train. Nevertheless, Salman was trading with far away foreign countries. This in spite of the fact, that neither he nor anybody around him spoke any foreign languages. Salman, who understood the basic rules of foreign trade, had trustworthy advisors in Sarajevo and never came out on the short end of a deal.

I thought this lumber specialist would not wish to bother with purchasing hospital equipment, but to my surprise, he did not hesitate at all. In three months the clinic received sufficient equipment to furnish a few neat examination rooms, a small surgery suite and an X-ray facility. This was by no means a small feat. First Salman had to find a foreign fellow lumber dealer who had to locate a medical supplier, read through catalogues and place the order. Next, Salman tackled the financial issues. His enterprise generated foreign currency, but all of it was directly deposited into special "hard currency" accounts from where he could not withdraw funds without the approval of high authorities. Salman got around the problem through bartering. His opposite number in Germany received a reduced invoice for the delivered lumber with the understanding that the difference would be used to purchase medical equipment. Next, Salman secured an import license through a company authorized to import general goods. The company got a nice commission for doing nothing; they never saw the merchandise and had no responsibilities for shipping or storing. But that's how business was done those days. At the end of the complex transaction, Mustafa used local currency from his health care budget to settle the bill with Salman.

Soon after we received the hospital supplies, I went to thank Salman for his extraordinary effort. The wall of his office was covered with framed certificates and plaques of appreciation. One of the exhibits caught my eye. The certificate praised the lumber company *Stakorina* for giving money to plant 1000 trees in Israel. Next to it was a smaller certificate acknowledging Salman's personal contribution of 100 trees towards reforestation in Israel.

Salman caught me looking at the certificates.

"A lowly citizen of Gorazhde planting trees in Israel. Funny, isn't it?" he said. "But, you see, I like trees—I truly do. They are things of beauty, no matter where they grow. The more of them the merrier."

"But what about the politics of it?" I inquired, alluding to his Moslem roots and at the less than cordial relationship between Yugoslavia and Israel.

This slightly indiscreet line of questioning did not perturb Salman. In fact, he was enjoying himself. As his eyes lit up, the ever-present generic business smile changed in to the naughty grin of a child who just got away with a mischief.

"I know you would not mind," he said, "but when other less friendly characters ask, I explain it as the cost of business."

At that point, visibly enjoying his response, Salman roared with laughter. By stating that I would not mind, he let me know he knew I was Jewish. Why not? After all, I was the first to allude to religion.

"The facts of the matter are true. I had to repay a real business debt," said the director of *Stakorina* with glee.

It was my turn. "What sort of a debt?" I asked, "Would it perhaps be related to one of those walnut stumps in the ground?"

"Yes indeed, it was related to one of those walnut stumps in the ground," said Salman, repeating my sentence on purpose with a good imitation of my haughty city accent.

Salman was well-known for unorthodox business practices and his dealings with walnut stumps had become part of local lore. In the lumber business the huge stumps of walnut trees were worth their weight in gold. Close to the roots, the wood has a particularly intricate pattern of inner markings. Properly finished walnut stumps yield light brown, shiny and very hard wood for elegant gunstocks. And Salman knew the sites of hundreds of stumps, each of them at least a yard wide! He shamelessly used the stumps to drum up his business. Though he never intended to sell a single stump, he took prospective customers on a tour of stumps; fresh air, drinks and snacks included. At the right moment Salman would promise to "throw in" a few stumps if the visitor ordered a sufficiently large shipment of regular lumber.

"Gratis, mind you," he would say, "as a token of my appreciation for giving us your business."

And in that lay the hook. The stumps were never a part of the official deal and no paper trail was left.

When they got the shipment without the promised walnut stumps, most of the customers were too timid to ask. They had received some excellent high-grade lumber and wanted more of it. So what if the walnut stumps did not materialize? Very few were upset by a small lie from the lips of the charming Bosnian entrepreneur who invented a new variation on the old bait and switch theme.

For the minority who insisted, Salman had a wide variety of delaying tactics, all the while waiting for the stubborn foreigner to get the message. There were broken chainsaws, labor disputes, and difficulties in obtaining the proper export license for a gift.

If the truth did not set in, and the fool continued to insist, Salman was ready for the *coup de grace*. With a wide happy grin and not a trace of embarrassment he would say, "I promised and if you really have to know, I lied." It amounted to a swift shock treatment. He spoke with such finality and appeared so shamelessly happy, that even the most insensitive person recognized he had reached the end of the walnut stump road. Keeping your word is a millennium-old ethical construct, but if somebody does not abide by it, there is really nothing you can do.

So why then, when he reached the end of the line, did Salman choose to compensate the merchant from Israel? I prefer to think that from the beginning he wanted to donate trees to Israel. Salman loved trees and his company practiced conservation. They did not strip cut; every fallen tree bore the state forester's mark of approval, and they regularly planted new trees on the barren slopes of Bosnian mountains. But his action in Israel went beyond the love of trees. Salman, a Moslem, grew up in Sarajevo where the Jewish and Moslem communities used to live in harmony. I am convinced that the gift of trees was Salman's way to commemorate some old friend. But I could not ask—I had already nosed around too much. And had I asked, Salman would not have told me the truth. You do not share your inner thoughts with a stranger. Not in Gorazhde!

The customer from Israel already learned the truth on his first

return visit. “I did not wait for him to ask,” said Salman. “I figured he was not of the forgetting variety. I explained I could not secure an export license but was delighted, instead, to plant trees in his homeland.”

“You should have seen his face,” continued Salman. “The little bastard was not at all pleased, but I left him no way out.” And as he finished the story, Salman’s face was again full of joy. The joy of a double victory—over the official Yugoslav aloofness to Israel and over the not-so-pleasant Israeli merchant.

It was time to leave, and as he escorted me to the door Salman said: “I am so proud of it, that I hung the diploma on the wall.”

What was he proud off? Exactly what did he mean? Well, your guess is as good as mine. However I do know that a gift to Israel was highly unusual. Furthermore the memento on the wall amounted to a declaration that when he wanted to, Salman could be different from others. He had a few good reasons to be proud.

The little clinic on the hill had a staff of three physicians and four physician’s assistants. Meshek and I worked alongside of Dr. Edhem Plevljakovich, a graduate of the medical school in Zagreb. He was born to a Moslem family in Gorazhde and a few years after graduation, returned home to practice medicine. Two physician assistants, both local men, had learned their trade as Army medics and it showed. Both were disciplined and worked hard. A well-qualified female nurse helped in the clinic and a capable midwife worked in the maternity home under strict supervision of the retired midwife Johanna. Johanna, after four decades in Gorazhde still spoke her native German better than Serbo-Croatian. Never thinking of charging her patients, she retired as poor as a church mouse and became a charity case of sorts. She was given food and shelter in the maternity home. Her hands were too weak to conduct a birth, but her brain was excellent, and when it came to obstetrics, she knew it all. She was a valuable advisor to all of us and by living in the maternity home, Johanna kept setting the highest Germanic standards of cleanliness.

The quality of care in Gorazhde was improving by leaps and bounds. Our laboratory started to produce reliable readings of blood cell counts, urine tests and a few basic biochemical tests. If more complex analyses were required, the blood was sent to Sarajevo. We also established a good contact with the University Hospital in Sarajevo and could at any time call for advice. After a while, we organized weekly visits from specialists from Sarajevo who examined complex cases and suggested appropriate treatments.

My personal development as a physician was also helpful. I saw one-third of all patients in Gorazhde. I started with a very good knowledge of medical facts, but had no practical experience. My ability to diagnose a disease and choose the correct treatment improved a great deal. I soon learned how to work fast and was able to see up to eighty patients per day. The examining rooms were divided into three functional units; one for taking temperatures, a second for physical exam behind a screen, and a third for dressing and undressing. Patients had very little privacy but that is the way it was.

To keep this merry-go-round turning, one had to separate the important from the trivial, the urgent from less acute problems.

Next I had to learn setting priorities. In medical school nobody ever taught us such issues. If anything, the teaching was opposite to what goes on in real life. In the medical school much was said, and for good reason, about compassion for the patients. But in real life, a physician must also be effective. The humane thing, and when possible, the right thing, is to attend to the needs of a slowly dying patient. But if other serious potentially salvageable cases are waiting, the physician must see them first.

After a few months I got it down pat. Febrile patients were sent for a blood test and waited until I could pay more attention. Cases with diarrhea gave a stool sample and if it contained mucus or blood, antibiotics were prescribed. People with chronic diseases or suspected malignancies were sent to visiting specialists or to the University Hospital in Sarajevo.

The most frequent complaint, stomach pain, was definitely low on the priority list. As if they had rehearsed the same scenario, all patients described exactly the same symptom. They would place the

finger on exactly the same spot above the navel and speak of a sharp pain, which got aggravated by eating.

People in Gorazhde loved spicy food and drank large amounts of the harsh local plum brandy. No wonder many of them developed gastritis. If a quick physical exam did not point to other causes, I prescribed antacids and recited a list of foods the patient should avoid, but my dietary recommendations fell on deaf ears. Politely, but sincerely, my patients begged to disagree. They saw no connection between their eating habits and their bellyache. It did not help to point out that a few minutes earlier they provided me with an excellent description of food-induced pain. As far as the patients were concerned, they could have caught a cold to the stomach, their stomach might have moved out of place or, possibly, they'd exercised too much. No matter what I said, what they ate could not possibly be important.

When it comes to personal health, local beliefs count and rational explanations rarely prevail. I learned this the hard way from the hospital bookkeeper. He came in with abdominal pain and explained that he had fallen asleep in a field and while he slept, a snake descended into his stomach. He requested in no uncertain terms that I remove the vile serpent from his innards.

I could not believe my ears. How could a reasonably literate person, who spent years working around doctors, believe such nonsense?

Like a fool, I started arguing with him.

"Look, how in the world could a snake get into your body?" I said.

"Nothing wakes me up when I sleep," said the victim of the imaginary zoological assault, "and I always sleep with a wide open mouth. Snakes love to descend into open holes. And that is where they thrive; in deep holes."

I was in trouble. A pseudo logical explanation that has a ring of truth to it, is hard to fight. By a sleight of imagination the bookkeeper converted his stomach into a snake pit. As always, we were not alone in the clinic. A chorus of other patients joined in the discussion, all of them bent on explaining to me the facts of life. They personally had the same problem or knew somebody who had been invaded by

a snake. Fortunately, they told me, the local herb doctor had a cure for it. He usually prepared a pail of warm goat's milk to which he added special herbs. The patient would lean with an open mouth over the pail, and a blanket was thrown over his head. When after a while the herb doctor removed the blanket, on the bottom of the pail, there for everybody to see, was the dead snake.

What was I to do now? Try to discredit my herbal colleague who reliably produced such excellent results? It would have been written off as professional jealousy. I should have simply referred the patient to the medicine man, but I was too young and too stubborn.

In what I thought was a flash of brilliance, I proposed to conduct a scientific experiment. We kept in the clinic a rubber tube for gastric lavage. It was a brute of a tube, roughly the same shape and diameter as a sizable snake. Brandishing the "snake," I dared my patient to let me push the tube down his throat, as gently as I could.

The scene was as disgusting as it was silly. Surrounded by about ten patients I administered the tube, which instantly induced gagging and vomiting.

"You see," I said triumphantly, "the snake could not possibly get into your stomach without you noticing it."

"But Doctor, anything can happen while one is asleep. Your profession regularly puts people to sleep and performs surgery on them," mumbled the patient through the gauze with which he was wiping his mouth.

"I must say he's got a point," chimed in my well-educated male nurse.

This was it! I lost the argument. Never again did I try to challenge the herbal doctors. In fact, later, when I understood how useful they could be, I started to cooperate with many practitioners of what is nowadays euphemistically called "alternative medicine."

I found the herbalists and other paramedical personnel well suited for management of psychosomatic diseases. Psychosomatic problems are the bane of modern medicine and we are not trained to resolve them. By the end of the ninetieth century, when medicine began to emerge as a real science, the knowledge of underlying "organic" pathologic processes increased and the hope grew that

soon all causes of all ailments would be resolved. What could not be found with a microscope or with other laboratory methods was either considered not to exist or called a "functional" disease. When Freud developed a general theory of functional diseases, these disorders became the domain of psychiatrists or psychologists. The organic-minded physicians were delighted with the new division of labor and with gusto sent to the psychiatrists their own worst failures. Eventually organic physicians succeeded in convincing themselves that functional diseases are annoying but never deadly and, therefore, could be more or less ignored. What started in the nineteenth, accelerated in the twentieth century, and presently organic diseases are at the core of our training. We view ourselves as detectives whose task is to sort out clues for a definitive diagnosis. If tests yield no results, we are not likely to help the patient. Intellectually we may understand that there are psychosomatic diseases, but we do not know what to do with them. We might refer the patient to a psychiatrist but nowadays, they are also better trained to deal with true mental symptoms than with patients psychosomatic symptoms.

Whereas we were bound to be objective, our *alternative medicine* colleagues around Gorazhde freely used the power of suggestion as a medical tool. It did not matter that they had to cheat a bit. If helping a patient called for a dead snake in a pail of goat's milk, so be it!

It would be unfair to say that all herbalists around Gorazhde were charlatans. Just like the diploma carrying physicians, the faith healers were either generalists or specialists. The generalists would take whoever came and do whatever it took, but the specialists understood the bounds of their knowledge and what they did was done well.

I was particularly impressed with the local specialist for jaundice. He worked only with one herb. His father passed onto him the secret herb and taught him how to sort out various types of jaundice. He knew that patients with obstruction of the hepatic ducts had a greenish-yellow tinged jaundice and did not hesitate to send them to a regular doctor. But the man definitely had something to offer to patients with infectious hepatitis. We could only suggest bed rest, give vitamins and explain that after about three weeks, the condition would

slowly subside. But patients who visited the herbalist got rid of the jaundice within days.

Convinced that the herbalist had excellent results, I decided to look into the matter. Unfortunately, I used what one could only call a well-balanced approach, I was both sincere and stupid. First I expressed my respect for herbal medicine by reciting a long list of widely used modern drugs of herbal origin. I spoke about ephedrine, digitalis, strophantine, morphine and about the newest discovery, reserpine. Some clever fellow thought that the plant Rauwolfia Serpentina, whose root had been used as a sedative in India, might be able to decrease people's blood pressure. Proper trials had been organized and indeed, the drug proved to be effective. A few years later the active compound, reserpine, had been isolated, synthesized, put on the market and in the early fifties became one of the first effective drugs for lowering blood pressure.

In my mind the story of reserpine should have been sufficient to motivate the Bosnian jaundice healer to match the feat of his Indian counterpart and give me the magic root for further development. Most physicians viewed the lay healers as meddlesome, unscientific and downright dangerous practitioners. I fully expected the herbalist to recognize that I was different and, since I was such a nice fellow, to jump at this unique opportunity to help humankind. It never crossed my mind that the man had nothing to gain from the transaction and that I asked him to betray his family tradition and risk losing his livelihood.

After he missed a few appointments, it became quite clear that the herbalist was not about to reveal the source of his wonder potion. Bosnian etiquette required that I quietly give up. Had I forced him, the unwilling man would have had to resort to some face-saving maneuver, but he would never cough up the secret.

Frequently one can win by not persisting. My chance came when the herbalist's son fell sick with pneumonia. The poor twelve year-old had high fever and was short of breath. The diagnosis was quite obvious. The boy's face had started to turn blue. Under such dire circumstances, the practitioners of alternative medicine readily acknowledged the superiority of classical medicine. These were the

magic years when hardly any bacteria were resistant to antibiotics. Within a day from the first injection of penicillin the boy had no fever, on the second day his breathing returned to normal, and on the third day he was ready to go home. The success was so smashing that the thankful father spontaneously offered to hand me his herbal roots when I left Gorazhde. He only asked that I keep him informed of the results.

I have done plenty of research in my life and we had some good results but I never felt so close to a major discovery as I did leaving Gorazhde with a shoe box full of roots. Unfortunately, I soon learned an important lesson about human rigidity. When I handed the roots to the chairman of the department of pharmacology in Zagreb, he gave me a look as if I'd just landed from Mars. The learned professor had no time to waste on such nonsense, no matter how appealing my story might have been. Crestfallen, I stored the shoebox in my basement. When I left for America, thanks to the USA Department of Agriculture, I could not take the box with me. Ten years later, when I returned for the first time to Zagreb, I found that some compulsive cleaner had thrown out the box.

In 1956, the Party had already switched from using the police to control society, to ruling through the control of employment. This new method of supervision was equally effective. Party members or well-connected individuals would get the plum jobs, the average population could count on average jobs and dissidents would find all doors closed.

The health secretary in Gorazhde was no exception. He loved his hiring privileges and never consulted me. If a physician applied for the job, Mustafa would first close the deal and then proudly introduce my new co-worker. All around us, people with similar attitudes but less talented than Mustafa, were busy assembling their healthcare teams. In those days most physicians opting to work in Bosnia had some problems. Some took refuge from political pressure, others were not competent enough to get a better job and the

rest expected to make quick money through sign-on bonuses and good salaries.

One could predict the results of this process in which incompetent people had to select employees from suspect pool of candidates. The health care of Gorazhde and its surroundings fell into the hands of a motley crew.

One afternoon, just as soon as I managed to doze off for my usual "beauty" nap, somebody decided to wake me up. He was yelling and banging on the door with both fists.

"Come on, open the door, I know you are in there. I have to talk to you," yelled the insistent visitor. It was a high-pitched male voice, a voice I vaguely remembered but could not quite make out. Half asleep, I dragged myself to the door. As soon as I took a peek through the half open door I became wide-awake. What a surprise! It was Emanuel Reich, all five feet of him, in his usual angry and abusive mood; his curly dark hair seemed to stand on end and those fiery eyes were full of ill-intent. The very same disaster-prone Emanuel with whom, a few years earlier, I had clashed over his inopportune call for a students' general strike.

"How could you do this to an old friend," he screamed trembling with anger, " I had to wait on your doorstep like a beggar."

"Hey, man," I said, "how was I to know who was out there?"

Emanuel's magic was already working-he had me on the defense. He pushed himself into the room, comfortably sat on my chair and continued to talk somewhat less loudly.

"I have just accepted a job as the physician in the *Pobjeda* factory. They told me you are making oodles of money in Gorazhde. Since I intend to work in this riverside dump, I thought I'd join you in the clinic to see how you do it."

"Come on!" I protested. "I can't have another doctor with me. My patients are entitled to privacy."

"Oh yes, you can!" said Emanuel. "This is Bosnia. Privacy, my foot! Your patients have no idea about such an esoteric concept."

There was no way to stop Emanuel when he was in one of his moods and I admitted defeat by changing the topic.

"The job in the factory has not yet been advertised," I said. "In

fact, the previous physician is still on sick leave. How could they offer you his job?"

"Well, I am not in habit of waiting for advertisements and as far as the job is concerned, if the other guy ever returns, the factory will have two physicians. It's as simple as that," retorted Emanuel.

"So why are you in such a hurry to move to Gorazhde?" I wondered.

"Well, I do have my reasons and I do not mind telling you," said Emanuel as a prelude to a lengthy monologue.

It turned out that Emanuel had gotten into a conflict with the whole leadership of the town of Tuzla and was unceremoniously kicked out. I didn't have to ask for details, I'd seen it before. Emanuel was highly intelligent and witty but had absolutely no control over his behavior. Sooner or later he'd blow up for no good reason. In Zagreb, he was assigned to take the fifth year student surgical internship in a large city hospital. After a week or so, he felt inspired to criticize the technical proficiency of the chief surgeon. The surgeon, a giant of a man, was so provoked that he grabbed Emanuel by the back of the collar and dragged him through the hospital to the entrance stairway. There he delivered a soccer-type and anatomically correct kick, which propelled poor Emanuel from the top of the stairs to the street.

Emanuel somehow managed to look at these incessant conflicts and defeats with a sense of self-critical humor. He finished the current story about Tuzla as if it all were a great joke. But the truth of the matter was that he had to seek a new job and was told the ammunition factory in Gorazhde had an open position. When I inquired how he learned about the yet-to-be-opened position, he changed the topic.

"You know, I got married and have a beautiful daughter," he said proudly.

I was pleased with the good news. In spite of his madness Emanuel had a great sense of family. He was Jewish; all the adults in his family had perished and only he and two cousins survived. At age twenty two, he became the head of the household. The three cousins lived in an apartment and by all accounts, Emanuel ran the family affairs with devotion and love. The modest stipends they had as vic-

tims of Fascism were well below what they needed. Nevertheless, Emanuel succeeded in finishing medical school and somehow provided sustenance for all of them. His two cousins graduated in time from the university and one of them became a levelheaded, compassionate physician.

It was sad to see that responsibility for his new family had not changed Emanuel's ways. He let himself get kicked out of Tuzla and badly needed a job. Unfortunately, of all places, he'd ended at my doorstep in Gorazhde! I knew he'd cause me all kinds of problems but I could not stand in his way. As Emanuel continued to tell the story, I mentally rehearsed what I might say if Zhika, the director of the factory, called on me to evaluate the new candidate. Luckily it was not necessary. Emanuel was crazy but not stupid. He had married the daughter of the vice-president of the Republic of Bosnia! He had the job locked up before he came for an interview. Obviously his father-in-law did all the explaining.

As we returned to complete the afternoon shift at the clinic, Emanuel gave me a good demonstration of things to come. He loudly contested every diagnosis, and argued over every prescription. No, he had not changed a bit!

Though he crashed into my room, woke me up and insinuated himself into my clinic, I was pleased that he considered himself a friend. I was never comfortable with what I had to do to him when he called for a general strike in the medical school. At that time I succeeded in shutting him down and he had been, more or less, kicked out of the class meeting. Obviously, Emanuel thought it over and with passage of time realized that I saved him from being arrested. In his crazy way Emanuel was now showing that he liked me.

"I will be moving to Gorazhde in a few weeks," he said. "Let's have dinner at the riverbank restaurant. I have seen them preparing the fire for a lamb on the spit. It should be ready by now."

~

We went to the restaurant with the ping-pong ball fountain. In spite of its fame for the best lamb on the spit, on that particular day, the

restaurant was practically empty. The owner gave us a table with a great view of the river and the mountain. The day was remarkably clear and the sun had just started to set behind the mountain. The quick, restless waters of the Drina started to reflect an ever-changing mixture of silvery and orange hues. Beneath us, a flock of wild pigeons landed on the riverbank, each bird looking for the right stone on which to perch and soak up the last of the sun's rays.

The beauty of nature becalmed the ever-jittery Emanuel. For the first time I saw him relaxed. Instead of fixing his fiery gaze on me, Emanuel trained his dreamy eyes on the distant mountain. A new person was in front of me: a drained, tired, aged and deeply saddened Emanuel. The new Emanuel was not a psychopath who, bereft of empathy for others, goes from conflict to conflict without any emotions. Emanuel paid a physical and emotional price for his conflicts. Looking at him I realized that Emanuel had never matured. Having lost both his parents during the war, the aging Emanuel continued to act like the attention-seeking, insecure teenager he once was.

There is no dusk in Gorazhde. Once the sun dips behind the mountain the sky above you might still be blue but the night instantly overtakes the village and the river valley. Emanuel remained silent and as the darkness fell on us, I too started to feel detached and began to sink into the twilight between sadness and depression.

Just then, the restaurant owner brought food to our table. The great scent of freshly broiled lamb, potatoes and shljivovica put an end to the morose atmosphere. During the dinner Emanuel sought information about his predecessor in the *Pobjeda* factory, what sort of a health problem did he have and whether he might eventually return to claim his old post.

"Plain and simply; he will never return to Gorazhde," I said reassuringly. "He is as weird and as sick as they come."

"Yeah, I heard something about him being a bit of an addict."

"A bit of an addict? You must be kidding," I said and proceeded to tell him the story of his predecessor.

Dr. Ozrenovich's behavior was weird from the first day on. Though he had not been introduced to anyone in our clinic, he showed up with a patient in tow and demanded immediate access to the X-ray room. The nurse in charge suggested he ought to wait until she found me. When I came he was already in the X-ray room and, the "do not disturb" sign notwithstanding, I opened the door. As I groped my way through the dark room a deep, raspy voice said:

"Oh, you must be Doctor Julius. I am Dr. Ozrenovich. The factory *Pobjeda* hired me as their industrial health physician. I intended to introduce myself but this is a gynecologic emergency. My patient has abdominal pain and she is infertile."

I had sufficiently adjusted to darkness to see that the doctor kept the X-ray screen low over the patient's pelvis.

"I think her infertility is due to blocked Fallopian tubes and I wanted to take a look," resounded the baritone.

Who was he kidding? The Fallopian tubes cannot be visualized with a simple X-ray and we had no means to use contrast radiology.

I waited a few minute to cool off and politely inquired what he had found with the examination but got no response. The good Dr. Ozrenovich was fast asleep! Not dozing off but in a deep and lasting state of profound sopor.

I led the surprised patient out of the dark room and apologized for the inconvenience. The confused woman wanted to know whether I had seen anything abnormal during the X-Ray. Resisting the urge to tell her that the only abnormal thing in the room was her doctor, I promised she'd receive a follow-up from Dr. Ozrenovich.

By the end of the afternoon the man was still sleeping. He woke up late in the evening and left the clinic not saying a word to anybody.

Soon thereafter, stories about the new doctor's odd behavior spread like wildfire. Out on the street, like an out-of-control steamroller, the six feet tall, two hundred pound man took no notice of others and forced everybody to give way. His posture was peculiar; his head was bent down as if he were watching every step, his upper torso was fixed in a stiff, unchanging, vertical position while his big legs moved forward in scissor-like small steps. This was strange

enough but on occasion, as if he were stung by a swarm of bees, the huge man would suddenly jump. The long jump was inelegant but rather effective. It was quite a sight to observe the way he propelled his large body over surprisingly long distances. His upper body remained frozen in the peculiar walking stance but the arms and legs, akin to a drowning man, kept frantically moving in every direction. Once he landed, he'd proceed with his solitary perambulation as if nothing had happened.

I suspected that Doctor Ozrenovich might be an addict, but it fell upon Franjo, the pharmacist, to enlighten me. Franjo usually invited me to dinner when he needed to talk to me. He always pretended there was no particular purpose to the invitation but he invariably succeeded to steer the dinner conversation in the desired direction. However, this time Franjo came out with the flat truth as soon as I took off my coat.

"Doctor Julius," he said, "I need some help from you and if I do not get it, I will not be able to discharge my responsibilities as the town's pharmacist."

"Do you have a health problem?" I inquired.

"No, no. I have a supply problem. If something is not done within a week I will not be able to fill prescriptions for morphine or any other analgesics. In the last month Dr. Ozrenovich has ordered delivery of as much morphine as all of Gorazhde uses in three years. Apparently he decided to stockpile a large amount of morphine in the clinic. Dr. Ozrenovich seems to feel that the factory clinic needs enough morphine to cover about half of the staff in case of a massive explosion. This amounts to single doses of morphine. I had only twenty on hand and had to back-order the rest."

"What about the German engineering marvel?" I asked.

Franjo knew what I was talking about. The German architects had designed the *Pobjeda* factory to minimize accidents. The explosives were mixed in small separate pavilions, each having three concrete walls; the fourth wall was made of thin metal sheets. These weaker walls, each facing an earth embankment, were oriented away from adjacent buildings. In case of an accident, the weak wall would divert the force of the blast in the most innocuous direction and pre-

vent a chain reaction of explosions. It worked quite well. The factory had many small explosions and occasionally some people lost their lives, but there never was a major calamity.

"Well, I could not broach that subject with the doctor," responded Franjo ever so carefully. "He is the expert and if he judges he ought to have that much at hand, who am I to stand in his way?"

Franjo was looking for a response and I nodded in agreement. Morphine is indeed needed to minimize pain and prevent shock. It is up to the physician to decide what reserves he needs at hand.

"Now you can understand why I sent a request for a second shipment of about the same amount of morphine," Franjo continued. "As it happens the second half of the first shipment fell on the clinic's floor and many ampoules were broken."

Franjo stopped for a moment to see my reaction and continued, as a lawyer would, to develop his argument.

"It was a bit odd," he said, "but such things do happen. He did show me the broken ampoules. Of course he could have drained the content before he broke the glass, but I would never think of making such a direct accusation. What do you say, Doctor?"

Franjo wanted me to make a more affirmative statement than he was ready to make. But I had already learned how to cope with the roundabout ways of Bosnia. If he did not wish to make a direct allegation, why should I be more explicit?

"I agree it looks rather odd but, yes, things can happen." I responded in kind. "His public behavior is peculiar but before we jump to conclusions we ought to consider whether he could have some unusual neurological disease which caused him to drop the shipment of morphine. On the other hand his behavior might reflect excessive use of morphine."

I could not believe my own ears. In Zagreb I would have said straight: "The man is an addict." But I had fallen in to the Bosnian habit of circumlocution. Why would I have otherwise offered fake alternative diagnoses?

Franjo understood the game much better than I and proceeded to get me ensnared in the web of his problems.

"I agree with you that we should not jump to conclusion. However, I share your concern that the use of drugs may be the primary cause of his behavior," said Franjo with a smile.

This is how it is done! You draw the other guy into discussion and make him produce the statements you all along wanted to make. According to Franjo, it was I and not he, who first expressed concern that the doctor might be an addict.

Having accomplished his tactical goal, Franjo was now ready to continue with the rest of the story. "I ordered the third lot of morphine and got quite an excited telephone call from my supplier who told me outright that he wouldn't approve any further shipments to my pharmacy. Even that would not be so bad had I been able to get some cooperation out of Dr. Ozrenovich. However, when I asked him to let me keep a part of the shipment in the pharmacy, he blew his top. He insisted that I hand him over the whole shipment and, unfortunately, I capitulated."

Franjo was now ready to come out with his real agenda. "Will you, Doctor Julius, please help me recover some of the supplies? I know I made a mistake but we cannot leave the town without essential medical supplies. As a senior medical officer in the town, would you go with me to talk with Dr. Ozrenovich?"

It was a logical request and after a while Franjo and I worked out a plan to talk to Dr. Ozrenovich in the presence of the factory director who was personally responsible for the hiring and firing of physicians in the factory. I knew Zhika would not shy away from the responsibility. As a colonel of the Yugoslav Army, he ran the nominally civilian factory with military precision. The very next day the director summoned Dr. Ozrenovich and us to his offices.

I expected a violent confrontation during which Dr. Ozrenovich would deny the accusations and grudgingly agree to release some morphine for general use. Surprisingly, Dr. Ozrenovich immediately admitted his addiction to morphine. It turned out he was former water-polo player. Once during a game a sudden and very severe pain struck him in the back. The orthopedic consultant diagnosed a slipped disk with nerve compression and recommended immediate

surgery. The first and two subsequent surgeries failed to relieve his pain. Not knowing what else to do, the surgeons freely gave him morphine. Only when he was discharged did Ozrenovich realize he had become addicted. He was concerned about the addiction and took the job in Gorazhde to stay for a while out of the limelight and to slowly rid himself of the problem. He'd broken open all those ampoules to dilute the contents into a weaker solution, which he intended to use to wean himself from narcotics.

Zhika, who was not known for his compassion, proved to be patient and quite enlightened. He refused all Ozrenovich's pleas for more time but did offer him four months leave of absence if he signed up for immediate treatment in a psychiatric ward. The next day Zhika assigned two guards to take Dr. Ozrenovich to a hospital in Belgrade. As a matter of course I started receiving follow-up letters from Belgrade. It turned out they knew Ozrenovich very well. He was hopelessly addicted, the recent hospitalization being his tenth admission for the same problem. There was very little hope that this hospitalization would be any more successful than previous ones. Each time, a similar scenario evolved. After keeping him free of morphine for a few weeks, the hospital had no legal right to keep the patient incarcerated. He'd make promises never to resume taking drugs but after a few months he'd be back again.

When I finished my story about Dr. Ozrenovich, Emanuel asked for a few details and during the rest of the evening he was in excellent form. He was witty, made clever observations, told good jokes and volunteered a few funny self-deprecating anecdotes. Had I not known him, he could have fooled me, but I knew this was just a lull before the storm. I did not know what, but there was no doubt that something would happen.

As it turned out, Emanuel initially visited most of his craziness upon the factory. First he decided to endear himself to the workers. The Yugoslav social security system envisioned all kinds of privileges for the patient but there was very little money to pay for them.

Emanuel started to mete out long leaves of absence, "rehabilitation" visits to sanitariums on the seaside, and courses of hydrotherapy in various spas. Soon the rate of absenteeism in the factory doubled and Emanuel found himself in trouble with the leadership. Emanuel served ex-officio on the governing board of the factory. He initially refused to change his ways but as every week the situation got worse, he had to accept the responsibility. And he accepted it in a typical Emanuel fashion.

Overnight, the previously generous doctor became extremely stingy. Even the most deserving patients could not get a leave of absence. This would be bad enough by itself, but guided by his magnet for trouble, he prefaced each rejection with a small lecture about sagging factory productivity and how he and the factory management had decided to put things in order. In a way, the little sermon was designed to put some of the blame on the factory leadership, but Emanuel delivered his speech with the conviction of a true convert. And when it came to giving speeches, precious few people could match his oratorical flair.

The workers were not fooled by Emanuel's orations; for them he was an unprincipled weakling and turncoat. Again, as so many times in the past, Emanuel found a way to get himself into trouble with just about everybody. The factory management realized it must distance itself from the doctor and his zany speeches. The Party cleverly painted the situation as a temporary response to market forces and kept holding out the prospect of a quick return to normalcy. This worked to a certain degree, but the embittered workers demanded Emanuel's head. To delay the action the management played the "fairness" card. After all, this was the doctor's first mistake and everybody deserved a chance. In reality the board knew that Emanuel was too well connected for a summary dismissal but they were also genuinely ambivalent about this intelligent, witty and irreverent madman. Once during a board session, somebody asked him whether he was not afraid of the workers and he quickly responded that "he could run faster" than them. What do you do with someone who is so out of touch with reality?

Emanuel stayed on and continued to entertain the manage-

ment with his outrageous excesses and with his quirky sense of humor. Once, when the board discussed ways to convert the factory to manufacture non-military products, Emanuel jumped into the discussion.

"Inasmuch as you are looking for something that explodes but can be used for peaceful purposes," he said, "why don't you start making condoms?"

Zhika, the director, did not want to hurt this witty madman who, incidentally, was quite a capable physician. Eventually, to pacify everybody, he instituted an appeals process whereby the workers could challenge Emanuel's decisions regarding leaves of absence. Of course, I was selected as the arbitrator. I could have been on a collision course with Emanuel but to my surprise, only a few people complained and in general Emanuel accepted my decisions.

~

Within a year of my arrival, the structural work of turning the old Russian stockade into a hospital had been completed. However, the more complex installations of plumbing, heating and the like were moving at a slower and more unpredictable pace.

As a reward for my good works, the Mayor of Gorazhde offered me an apartment in a soon-to-be-completed house on the main street. This would permit my wife to join me and I accepted with pleasure. With Franjo's pharmacy directly across, Janja's coffee room two hundred paces to the left and the market place less than five minutes away, one could not have asked for a better location. Or so I thought.

Unfortunately, I overlooked a huge problem. A public broadcast loudspeaker had been neatly placed right under my window. The very first night I learned the bitter truth. Before sunrise, the system started to welcome the "working masses" with "inspirational" patriotic songs and the noise did not stop until the system completed serenading the last homebound hero of socialist labor.

Something had to be done and I immediately lodged a complaint with the ever-helpful Mustafa. When he did not respond in his usual "no problem" fashion, I knew I was in trouble.

"Technically this may be rather difficult," said Mustafa.

"Come on Mustafa, you know better than that," I fired back. "Give me a ladder and a screwdriver and I'll take the darn thing down in about ten minutes."

"I would never presume to challenge your technical skills," replied Mustafa, "but I was referring to different kinds of technical problems."

Mustafa looked ill at ease and I realized that to help me, he would have to cross paths with the Party secretary. The Party relied heavily on public broadcast systems in its mission to "lead the masses." I remembered how difficult it was to delay the installation of the loudspeaker at our camp when we were "building" the Zagreb-Belgrade highway. The Party secretary in Gorazhde could have easily portrayed my request to remove the loudspeaker as the desire of a spoiled petit bourgeois to interfere with the "rights of the masses."

"Is it really that much of a problem?" I asked Mustafa in a voice of a defeated person.

Mustafa's reply had none of the usual Bosnian ambiguity. "I am afraid it is and there is not much I can do."

And as I was leaving the room he added, "Thank you, Doctor."

I knew exactly what the 'thank you' was for. Mustafa appreciated that I did not force him into a conflict. For the first time we acted as friends who need only a few words to understand one another.

I also grasped the other implications of the situation. If it was so difficult to remove the loudspeaker, it must have been placed in front of our building on purpose. The house was built to accommodate teachers, engineers and other professionals. The Party secretary disliked intellectuals and if he had to yield the building to such "non-proletarian elements," he at least would expose them to some "re-education."

Everything pointed to the Party secretary's. Surprisingly, as soon as I concluded that he was behind the nuisance under the window, I cooled down. After all, the secretary was not after me personally. He moved against all the undesirable intellectuals in the building, and I could leave it to others to take some action. I hated the prospect of yet another confrontation with the dour secretary.

A few months before the placement of the loudspeaker I had

been invited to the Party offices where, after the obligatory coffee, the secretary seemed to be stuck in an endless monologue about the weather. After a while I had enough.

"Did you invite me to share your thoughts on the weather, or do you have something else on your mind?" I said. "Why don't you just tell me what this is all about?"

Fishing for words, the secretary seemed genuinely uncomfortable. "Well, it is kind of personal," he finally said, "and I do not know where to start."

"I usually start at the beginning," I fired back, and immediately realized this was wrong. There never was a good time to poke fun at the secretary but it was particularly inappropriate at the moment when, for the first time, he showed some human traits. He was visibly uncomfortable about the business he had to transact with me.

"Fine," I continued, "I meant to say that you shouldn't worry. Just tell me what is on your mind and we can take it from there."

But the secretary was unable to come to the point, "As you know," he said somewhat sheepishly, "a man's personal appearance is his calling card. You city folks care about such things but so do the citizens of this little town on the Drina."

What in the world was he talking about?

"I most certainly have a high respect for the way people are dressed and groomed in Gorazhde. They may look different than people in Zagreb," I responded, "but I realize they have high standards." I was stunned by my own response. I felt that some automatic part of my brain managed the conversation, while the stunned thinking part came to a full stop. To organize a response, the brain needs information, and I didn't have the foggiest idea what were we talking about.

Finally the secretary came out straight. "We are not talking about the townspeople, but about you," he intoned in a voice tinged with indignation.

Now, that was a stunner! Reflexively I took a look at my clothing. Everything was fine. I may not have looked like a fashion magazine model but the jacket fitted well and the clean pants were an eloquent testimony to my skillful navigation around mud puddles.

Having not a clue, I took refuge in Bosnian etiquette and quietly I took another long sip of coffee. There ensued what novelists describe as a "poignant pause." Only this was a Bosnian drawn-out, seemingly endless, pause. The secretary drank more coffee, inspected his fingertips, all the while studiously avoiding eye contact. Obviously I had not understood his fine hints and he had to search for better words.

"All right," he said, "I am asking you to shave off your beard and you had better do it today."

So it was the beard, my new pride and glory! I'd grown it more or less accidentally after a long layover in a distant village where I delivered a baby.

"C'mon." I responded rather quickly, "You must have a thousand other things to do than to worry about my beard. And incidentally, why are your mustaches fine and my beard is not?" I thought this was quite a logical and witty reply, but it did not move the secretary.

"I do not worry about things that do not concern me," he said, "and yes, mustaches are fine; the beard is not. Shave it off!"

"Why?" I wanted to know. "I didn't think that passing an esthetic judgment was in your job description."

"You are right," came the answer "and it is not an esthetic judgment. In fact it is not a judgment at all, it is a political decision."

"What?" I could not believe my ears. "What politics?"

"Go home and think about it."

And with these words, the secretary ushered me out of his office.

Eventually the fishing policeman volunteered to tell me the facts of life. As usual, he knew everything about the incident.

"You look downtrodden," said Brana. "I know where you are coming from and why you are irritated."

It was no use to ask how he knew. It was his business to know everything.

"He ordered you to shave your beard," Brana continued, "and though I do not share the secretary's dim view, he is in fact, on solid grounds. You know darn well that all Chetniks wear a beard. Your beard could be seen as a political act. I am in charge of chasing the

Chetniks out of here and I will accomplish the task whether you have a beard or not, but to the secretary, this is an entirely different matter."

Feeling that I was about to protest, the mind-reading Brana continued his monologue. "Yes, I know it is not logical," he conceded. "You are Jewish and could not possibly sympathize with Chetniks. Even the secretary knows it. But he finds it simpler to order you to cut the beard than to waste time telling others that your little beard is innocent."

Brana was smiling in his half secretive and half benign way but the message was very clear. He used the word "ordered" and not "asked." Knowing what that meant, I shaved off my beard the next day. The general principle, that in volatile times you ought to watch what you are doing was not new to me. The specifics were, however, novel. Never before had it crossed my mind that my personal appearance might matter to others. Another lesson learned.

To his credit, the secretary refrained from boasting about his victory. It was all part of doing business. He gave orders, I followed, and that was all that was to it. However, we both remembered the unpleasant incident and whenever possible avoided each other's company.

The mere thought that, to resolve the "loudspeaker issue" I'd have to face this cold and relentless person, slowed me down. I wasn't happy but I kept my temper under control. It was better to wait and see whether somebody else in the house complained. And complain they did, to each other, but nobody took specific action.

Help sometimes comes from unexpected quarters. In this case it came from the local incarnation of Dr. Jekyll/Mr. Hyde, Rajko, the county executive. The topic of loudspeakers came up during a lunch break at Janja's coffeehouse. A good portion of the political elite was there and I joined Rajko's table. As is my habit with unpleasant things, I turned my suffering into comedy. I said something to the effect that I rarely see a sunrise and that, the beauty notwithstanding, I'd just as soon sleep a few hours longer. Everybody smiled and Rajko responded in kind. "I am glad that, in spite of your changed circumstances, your productivity has not decreased," he pronounced. Rajko

was a good politician. His words were polite, conciliatory but non-committal. After a while we went our different ways.

An hour later Rajko rang me up at the hospital.

"Do you know who is behind this?" he said.

"I think I do."

"Don't tell me, I am sure you are right," continued Rajko not permitting me to mention the secretary. "Come to my office and we will talk it over."

When we met, Rajko was in a jovial mood and indicated he'd like to teach the secretary a lesson in public relations. Together we cooked up a simple plot. The secretary and his wife left to Sarajevo, he for a conference and she for leisure. We would capitalize on their absence and secretly, overnight, install a loudspeaker on the utility pole in front of secretary's house. Rajko knew where to get hold of a speaker and one of my reliable patients was an electrician.

"You will not leave me to my own devices if the secretary gets vindictive?" I said.

Rajko's face lit up in a pleasant smile. "He can't, if we pass it on as a practical joke. The secretary has no sense of humor but he can't risk looking sour. If he rose to our bait, there would be no end to new practical jokes."

Rajko could see I was not quite convinced and added. "All right, if you really need reassurance, there is also another reason for him not to react. Nothing in this place goes unnoticed. He will know I was involved and he will not risk a conflict with me."

"Couldn't you not just order him outright to cease and desist?"

"I could," he said, "but he would most likely appeal to higher authorities. The affair would linger for a while and then turn into an open conflict. I would win and he would have to go. All for a small thing! It's not worth it. This way it is much more fun."

I could see his point, but it still struck me as odd: "Why would you all of a sudden want to help me?"

"I am helping myself," Rajko volunteered. "First, the music and the repeated messages are a matter of the past. It did us some good when nobody had a radio and we needed to pass a quick message or two. Now there are other, better, ways to communicate. Second, the

secretary is using the public announcement system as an excuse for inactivity. He probably knows as well as I that it doesn't work, but can't come up with a better idea. I want him to think about new ways."

"So you are a progressive, forwarding-looking prankster," I suggested.

"Right on, right on! And what are you, Doc?"

"A volunteer co-conspirator."

"Glad you got the point," said Rajko with glee. "For a change lets us both be involved in this little affair. You could say we are on the way to becoming temporary allies."

"You mean real and loyal allies?"

"Yes, but the accent was on the word *temporary*," said Rajko.

The plan succeeded beyond our expectations. The electrician did a superb job. Early in the morning, when most people were asleep, he installed the loudspeaker but didn't activate it. Nobody paid attention to the mute loudspeaker on the utility pole across from the secretary's house. Next evening the secretary returned home and the electrician activated the speaker. After a few hours of sleep, the secretary woke up to the tune of a loud early-morning march. He took a look through the window, reached for his shotgun and with two well-aimed blasts, blew away the source of the noise. And, as Rajko had predicted, he never uttered a word about the incident.

The word about the prank and how the secretary had made short work of the loudspeaker spread throughout the town like wildfire. The secretary knew that everybody knew, but publicly, in true Bosnian style, everybody ignored the incident. Having shown his hand, the secretary couldn't justify the placement of loudspeakers in front of other people's residences. After a week or so, all tenants of the house, but me, signed a petition asking the Mayor of the city to move the loudspeaker to a "better position." The next day it was gone!

The loudspeaker affair equalized the score; both the Party secretary and I had won a round. He made me cut off the beard; I forced him to remove the loudspeaker in front of my apartment house. I understood this could not last forever. Eventually the secretary would have to reassert his authority. He did not have to wait too

long: Only a month after the loudspeaker clash, I gave him a new target.

With the approval of the Secretary of Health, I opened a private practice in my new apartment. The office hours were from 4:00 to 6:00 P.M. This, I thought, would give me time to finish the work in the hospital, take an afternoon nap and be ready for another round of doctoring. Unfortunately, most of patients had only vague ideas about time. This was a boon to the health service clinic where it seemed not to matter whether a patient waited a few minutes or five hours. A Bosnian is never in a hurry. If a day is set aside for a visit to the doctor, that was it, a whole day. The downside to this life style was a total absence of any sense of time. By and large the villagers recognized only four major portions of a day; the morning, noon, afternoon and the evening. In this system of timing, the finer points in between the four major categories of day were of little concern. What worked to my advantage in the public clinic, became a real drag in private practice. To put it simply, and I am not joking, most of villagers outside the town could not tell when it was four o'clock. I usually returned home at 2 P.M. and most of the time the corridor was already full of waiting patients. Working my way towards the apartment door I'd explain that I need two hours for lunch and a bit of rest and that the office would open exactly at four o'clock. This was always met with strong encouragement. "By all means," somebody would say. "We understand. Take your rest and we will quietly wait." Easier said than done. I could never fully relax knowing that a crowd was waiting outside my doors. It was no use giving out numbers and suggesting that the patient could attend to other business and then return. As far as they were concerned, there was no other business for that day. But even if they accepted the suggestion, it would not work. On the few occasions when nobody waited in front of the apartment door, as soon as I dozed off for a nap, somebody would ring the bell to inquire whether I had already started seeing patients. Most of these folks simply had no idea about time.

I was making reasonable money in private practice but the thought that some people could not afford my services made me uncomfortable. Finally I decided to set up a free clinic, once a week.

To assure that everybody had access, the free clinic coincided with the weekly market day, when the place teemed with people from outlying villages and everybody could easily find transportation to Gorazhde. Greatly pleased with myself, I amended the sign outside of the apartment building to the effect that on Wednesdays the clinic would be free "for the poor." That sign gave me more trouble than it was worth.

I was summoned to the Mayor's office. Talking on behalf of the Party secretary, he asked me to remove the free-for-the-poor practice sign.

"Oh, not again," I said. "What in the world is wrong with the man? Here I am trying to do a decent and socially responsible deed and he objects."

"You really do not understand what the problem is?" asked Zdravko. "It's rather simple. Don't you know that in our just society we have no poor people?"

"Gee, really, and what is that office a few doors down the corridor?" I said, "Every day your Social Welfare Department metes out all sorts of money to poor people."

"Aha!" smiled Zdravko, "There is your problem. You see, the office is not called the 'Department for the Poor' and the money is given to *socially* endangered individuals, not to the *poor* ones." By now the Mayor could not keep a straight face. He was roaring with laughter, knowing how silly the demand was.

"All right, what do I do?" I asked laughing along. "Do I stop having a free clinic, do I take the sign of the wall, or do I just ignore your request?"

"No you cannot ignore it," responded the Mayor. "How would I look in the eyes of the secretary? Why don't we just simply agree that you will remove the words 'for the poor' from your sign? It is not much to ask."

"Just so the secretary has another little victory!" I complained.

"No, not really," responded the Mayor. "The request is over a minor issue and if I were in charge of the Party I would ignore your sign. But if you really wish to help the needy, removing the designation of 'poor' may help your purpose. You see, most poor people are too proud to admit that they need help."

That made sense and, in fact, was well in line with my experience on free days. I could not have thought in my wildest dreams that some well-to-do citizens of Gorazhde would show up on free days. But that is exactly what happened. The richest man in the town, the do-it-all mechanic, plumber and wholesaler, regularly came to my office on the free day. Finally when he showed up just a few days after he landed the lucrative contract to install central heating for the new hospital, I could not take it anymore.

"Aren't you concerned that you might be taking the place of other needy persons?"

"Oh come on, Doctor," he said, "it does not make any difference to your bottom line who shows up on the free day. Your idea to serve the poor will never work. The real poor are illiterate and don't know how to avail themselves of the opportunity. Furthermore, they will never fill your prescriptions."

Stopping for a second to see my reaction, the self-centered cynic resumed talking. "Only somebody like me can appreciate your expertise. The destitute man will conclude that your free services must be inferior. Otherwise, why would you offer them without charge?"

I asked a straight question and got a straight answer. This, more than anything, convinced me to 'cave in' to the party secretary's demand. Next day I quietly covered up the *free for the poor* designation on my office sign. The secretary was right for the wrong reasons, but the fact that I yielded gave him a two to one victory, and he didn't bother me again.

The Easy Slalom to Zagreb

(Fall 1956)

About a year and a half after I left for Gorazhde good news from Zagreb started to trickle in. Mother was quite optimistic about the political situation. After the public discussion of Father's case came to a full stop, the angry reaction against the people who blamed the Party for his death, quickly subsided. Only two employees of the pro-Djilas newspaper had been arrested but no specific charges were pressed and after a few months of "investigative imprisonment" they were released. The ever-careful politician Vlado Bakarich, even extended an olive branch to the dissenting Party members at the medical school. He invited two of the most influential rebels, both young associate professors, to partake in a discussion of ways to maintain "party unity" in the new ideological battle against followers of Milovan Djilas. Bakarich genuinely needed advice from the best and the brightest. The political situation was quite delicate. Djilas was thrown out of the Party and removed from all official positions, but much of his critique against Stalin's "primitive version of communism" was quite welcome.

To differentiate itself from Stalinism, the Yugoslav Party introduced "workers' self-government councils" into every enterprise. Theoretically, These councils were the first step towards a future par-

ticipatory democracy. Congratulating itself on this innovation, the Party kept a stranglehold on all aspects of life. As far as the Yugoslav leaders were concerned, the "withering of the state" and full participatory democracy would begin on somebody else's watch.

But Djilas understood only too well the fallacy of the Yugoslav doctrine. In his writing he predicted that the self-appointed "leaders of the masses" would never give up their power. Under the guise of fighting for a classless society, these bureaucrats would continue to "exploit the masses" with the same zeal as their nominal enemies—the capitalists. Bakarich needed all the intellectuals he could get to counter Djilas' prediction and somehow implement the illogical doctrine of democracy within a totalitarian system. The fact that Bakarich sought out the same people he criticized a year ago was a very good sign.

Soon, even more encouraging news came from Zagreb. Kavedzich, the tailor-turned politician whom Bakarich defended in his obtuse newspaper editorial, had lost the battle. In spite of the lament in Bakariche's article about how the legal system had failed to uphold Kavedzich's rights, the courts reaffirmed their original decision and refused to reinstate Kavedzich to his old job in Vrapche. In a normal society one would celebrate this as a triumph of justice but in fact, Kavedzich's failure meant only that Bakarich had refused to intervene. Having published his plea for Party unity, Bakarich achieved his primary objective-to endear himself to Tito. The fate of Comrade Kavedzich was of no consequence and in due course Bakarich withdrew further support for his *protégé* of convenience.

Soon thereafter, the Angel protector sent me an "all is clear" letter. Things had improved and he thought that in "a half a year or so." I could easily return to Zagreb.

Good old Angel! Circumspect and careful as he was, he must have done a lot of footwork before he could write such an optimistic letter. One way or another he had to get Bakarich's approval. I never asked Angel how he pulled it off, but I got a pretty good picture a few weeks later when my mother called to complain. In the last few years she'd drawn some consolation from the fact that Representative Draushnik, the man responsible for Father's death, had been consistently kept out of the public eye. All of a sudden, Mother reported,

he was appointed to the plum position of director in a large import-export company in Zagreb. I immediately grasped that to help me, Angel had had to trade some horses. The Party must have decided to let bygones be bygones and agreed to rehabilitate all sides in the conflict. My invitation to return to Zagreb was part of a well-choreographed public demonstration of Communist "fairness." But in true Orwellian style, the Party had decided that Draushnik was "more equal" than others and had to be rehabilitated first.

When he inquired about my situation, Angel probably got from Bakarich a typical Delphic pronouncement to the tune that it might not be a bad idea to encourage my return to Zagreb "at some point." Angel then decided on his own that "a half a year or so" after Draushnik's reinstallation was about the right interval. As far as Bakarich was concerned, justice had been done. By giving him a job in "the economic sector," Bakarich removed Draushnik from political power. That the villain got a job with an excellent chance for personal enrichment did not matter. In Bakarich's eyes, Draushnik had been sufficiently punished. To a Communist there is nothing worse than a fall from political power. And in their game of relativistic justice I got the better part of the deal. Draushnik lost a perk whereas upon my return to Zagreb, I could continue my professional career. There are weird rules in weird societies. Under circumstances prevailing in Zagreb in 1956, a rehabilitation of the villain and the victim alike was the best deal one could hope for.

By the winter of 1956, everything had been worked out. Professor Hahn offered me a fellowship in internal medicine at the university hospital in Zagreb. We agreed I should stay in Gorazde until autumn to inaugurate the new hospital. Mitar Bakich, who secured support for the remodeling of the old stockade, was very sick. Dr. Hahn hoped I'd complete the job while his patient was still alive. Staying a bit longer was not a problem. I could easily endure small inconveniences as long as I knew that, while slaloming through obstacles, I was on my way to a friendly finish line.

In the coming months Rajko Gagovich was a bit less vitriolic but the game was still on. Rajko continued sabotaging the hospital, but his moves were more tricks of an incurable prankster than evil plots of a true enemy. At one point Rajko summoned a team of health

technicians to condemn the sewage "system" which discharged the waste from the stockade directly into the river. It had not been a problem when soldiers inhabited the stockade but the county now argued, with some logic, that the waste from a hospital might be a much more serious matter. That stopped construction for fifteen days, after which the Ministry of Health came to a Solomonic solution. The hospital construction could proceed until the Institute for Public Health in Sarajevo drew up a waste disposal plan. By then we had adjusted to the stop-and-go in the construction. Why be concerned about one more interruption?

However, the sewage issue developed a life of its own. After a month I received a rather stern letter requesting data about the "volume of effluent" from the hospital and the "volume of the recipient" into which the sewage was emptied. There was also a request that we take a water sample for bacterial count 100 meters above and 100, 500, and 1000 meters below the drainage area. Though it would be somewhat difficult to judge what exactly constituted 1000 meters along the tortuous river's bank, I could send them some water samples. But how in the world could I measure how much water flowed in the River Drina and guess the amount of sewage discharged into the water? For one thing, even if I had a way of measuring, the building was empty, and there was no sewage to assess.

I went to complain to the mayor.

"So what is your problem?" he wanted to know. "Give them some numbers. They will file your report and you will never hear about it again. But if you don't respond they will be on your case until the end of time."

"Look Zdravko," I said defensively, "I must take this seriously. These are my professional colleagues and they expect some real data from me."

"Oh, for sure they do," said the Mayor bending down to inspect one his drawers, "but they do not necessarily expect the data to be correct."

Zdravko found what he was looking for. "This is for your education," he said handing me a nicely bound file. "This is my report to the Department of Natural Resources about the number of rab-

bits in the forest. No sweat! We responded right away and if they don't believe what we said, they are welcome to count the rabbits themselves."

In all fairness, the Mayor had somewhat of a system to count the rabbits. He asked each mailman to jot down how many rabbits he had encountered on the route. However his piece of common sense that impossible questions generate improbable answers has never been lost on me. Every once in a while I remember this Bosnian wisdom as I send yet another 'rabbit letter' on its way.

In spite of obstacles, the remodeling of the stockade had progressed to a point of no return. Rajko kept inventing delays and I took most his maneuvers in stride. But on one occasion Rajko succeeded in offending me.

At the beginning, Rajko's phone call sounded innocent enough. "Now that the building is almost finished," he said, "I am getting just a bit concerned about organizational issues. Some time ago you indicated that an overlap in services between future hospitals in Focha and Gorazde might be a good idea. I thought this might be the right time to talk about the division of super-specialty services between the two hospitals."

"But the other hospital is nowhere near completion!" I protested more out of habit than conviction. Long ago I had established the operational principle that nothing should be accepted from Rajko without objections.

"Come on, you ought know better than that. Maybe your exalted health profession does not practice what we simple-minded executives call planning. You have got to anticipate instead of reacting to events, my dear comrade," replied Rajko.

"I guess you've got a point," I admitted.

"A point? It is not a point; it is the only proper way to run an organizational entity!" said Rajko. "Come to think of it, Doctor, you are talented in matters of diagnosis but that does not mean you know how to run an organization," he added with a solid dose of vinegar.

I'd given him an opening for abuse and it made no sense to argue. After all, in organizational issues, he was a pro and I was a novice.

"Had you thought through the whole organizational scheme of the hospital?" inquired Rajko, feigning concern.

"Somewhere in your office there ought to be a rather complete document about that. I submitted it almost a year ago. You see, I can be a planner too." I said, feeling I'd found a way out of the corner. But once Rajko got going, nothing could stop him.

"Oh, *that* plan? I read it some time ago and vaguely remember not being overwhelmed. I thought of it as, at best, a starting point for further discussion. Unfortunately I don't have time to get personally involved," continued Rajko after a short pause, "but I will ask for an objective outside review."

"Sure, you should do just that," I responded with a very poor Slavic imitation of the British stiff upper lip. But Rajko was not done.

"We need an expert opinion but we do not need a formal panel. Incidentally, when I said outside expertise I did not mean to go all the way to Sarajevo," said Rajko. "It would take too much time."

What a rascal! All this time he'd tried to slow things down and now, all of a sudden, he was in a hurry.

I decided not to respond. After quite a long pause, Rajko pulled the ace out of his sleeve.

"I thought I would ask Djoka Janjich to do the job," he said triumphantly.

"Djoka Janjich? You must be joking!"

"No, I am not. In fact he already accepted the assignment."

I slammed down the receiver.

Djoka Janjich was a legendary physician from Focha but there were two sides to his legend. People in and around Focha venerated him for his presumed diagnostic skills, but I knew him for what he was—a survivalist, an opportunist and a medical charlatan of the worst kind. He'd finished medical school in Belgrade just before the German occupation of Yugoslavia. When the Germans quickly destroyed the Yugoslav Army, he joined the Chetnik resistance move-

ment, led by General Drazha Mihajlovich. Together with Mihajlovic, Janjich roamed the forests of Bosnia and Montenegro for four years. Though he had just come out of medical school and had no practical training, Janjich acted as a doctor and in due time became General Mihajlovich's personal physician. At the end of the war, both he and General Mihajlovic were arrested by Tito's victorious partizans. General Mihajlovich "committed suicide" in a Belgrade prison and Janjich was sent to serve a long prison sentence in Focha.

Janjich had an electrifying personality and soon endeared himself to the prison warden by taking care of his and his family's true or imaginary symptoms. The warden could not stop bragging about Janjich's healing powers. Soon the good doctor's services were available to the entire personnel of the jail. Thereafter, selected "reliable" persons from the outside community could come to the jail to be examined by Janjich. As his fame increased, Janjich eventually obtained a permit to open a private practice in Focha. He'd leave the prison every second day and returned by the evening. A year later, he could take leave every day, including holidays. Soon he was paroled to live in the community but could not leave Focha. A few years later, Janjich had full freedom to move and charge for his services. For all intents and purposes his sentence had been commuted.

During the war Janjich acquired some practical experience, but in medicine personal experience can be very deceptive. Particularly when the "experience" is garnered by an uncritical mind. If a person writes off all deaths as inevitable and remembers only successes, whether they were spontaneous improvements or real cures, he will deceive himself.

Janjich evolved into the most self-deceiving, self-adulating, stubborn-as-a-mule, know-nothing practicing physician I ever met in my life. He occasionally ventured to Gorazde to provide "second opinions" and suggest alternative remedies for some of my well-to-do patients. He gave advice with a great deal of authority and with the conviction of a person who could not possibly be wrong. Most of his patients were orthodox Serbs and even if they were politically opposed to Chetniks, as Serbs they were fascinated by General Miha-

jlovich's exploits. The well-advertised fact that he had been the general's personal physician gave Dr. Janjich an even a bigger aura of infallibility.

I generally tolerated Janjich's unsolicited advice but on one occasion I came to blows with him. Janjich had a fascination with blood. According to him, most patients either needed a transfusion or had to be bled to "purify the blood." The patient over whom we clashed had cirrhosis of the liver and just a day before Janjich's visit suffered massive bleeding from esophageal varicosities. Such bleeds are frequently a prelude to death from cardiovascular shock. Fortunately, the bleeding stopped and while still in coma, the patient's vital signs stabilized, color returned to his face and generally he was doing a bit better. As soon as Janjich came into the room he ordered me to draw half a liter of blood from the patient. I could not believe my ears. It was just plain dangerous to withdraw another large amount of blood from a patient who'd barely stopped bleeding. Not to mention that the whole idea of blood withdrawal, even if the patient were stable, made absolutely no medical sense. In terms of professional knowledge, Janjich not only failed to keep up with modern medicine, he was a few centuries behind the times! A council of physicians who kept bleeding him probably killed George Washington and, even then, one of the physicians vigorously objected.

To buy some time I pointed to two chairs in the other room and offered to give Janjich a full account of the patient's medical history.

"Oh, I do not believe in secrecy. You can give me all details right here in front of everybody," said Janjich with a smirk, "but from what the family told me on the phone, I believe I am quite familiar with the case."

"Are you aware that yesterday the patient had a massive bleed and was on the verge of a cardiovascular collapse?" I asked. "I am afraid he cannot tolerate another bleed." Purposefully I did not question Janjich's rationale for blood withdrawal and expressed concerns only about the cardiovascular consequences of a new hemorrhage. But Janjich was visibly offended.

"I did not propose to withdraw the blood quickly. If it is done with proper caution, the patient can take it. Difficult conditions call

for dramatic measures but, unfortunately, young and less experienced physicians are sometimes frozen with fear. Believe me, I know what I am doing," said this confident ignoramus.

Seeing me stunned and speechless, Janjich continued to give me a lesson.

"You see," he explained, "our patient's body attempted to do the right thing and rid itself of the bad blood. Unfortunately the body only knows how to start but has no clues when to stop the bleed. By a slow bleed we will complete what the body intended to do in the first place."

The man uttered this absolute nonsense with the air of a great teacher speaking to a retarded pupil. "I do not hesitate to do what needs to be done," he added, "but I detect that you might be a bit afraid. I don't blame you. It takes years of medical practice to strike the right balance between a patient's desperate need and a physician's natural reluctance."

The bastard said this on purpose in front of the entire family! He was the brave experienced super doctor and I a reluctant young apprentice.

"Yes, Dr Janjich," I said, "I am indeed too scared to perform the venipuncture. If you wish, please feel free to do it yourself. I will send a nurse with the necessary equipment."

As I walked out, I could hear him shouting. "It will not be necessary. I brought my own tools."

Roaming around on his motorcycle, this modern version of Dracula left behind him a trail of blood and a large number of thoroughly impressed customers! There is something dramatic about drawing blood and for a long time, people remembered both the act and the pseudo-logical rationale Janjich provided for the treatment.

Having completed his deed, Janjich triumphantly returned to Focha. The next day the patient became moribund. The distraught family called Dr. Janjich but he reassured them that a deepening of the coma was to be expected and that things must get worse before they get better. The family could not take it anymore and decided to transfer the patient to Sarajevo. He died a few hours after admission to the hospital.

Having learned that the patient died, Janjich blamed me. Instead of providing the ambulance, I should have told the family that a patient in such a delicate condition could not be transported to Sarajevo. Janjich suggested to the grieving family that young physicians have no patience and that they would rather ship the patient to die on somebody else's watch than take personal responsibility.

What a nasty callous man! He convinced the patient's relatives that I had lost my nerve and did send the patient to a sure death! The family never spoke to me again.

And now, of all people, Rajko chose Dr Janjich, to advise him on the organization of the new hospital in Gorazde. This was truly a low blow and I expected the worst. Surprisingly the dreaded visit went without a hitch. Janjich made it very clear he did not care about organizational issues. Buildings do not make hospitals, he opined; it all depended on who would work there. He gave some vague advice about how to chose the right personnel. Discussing the division of expertise between the hospitals in Focha and Gorazde, Janjich felt that both towns should have full service hospitals. Thirty kilometers, he suggested, was quite a distance for people whose main modes of transportation were their own feet or horse-pulled wagons.

Janjich was downright pleasant. He indicated he'd strongly support the existing plans for the development of both the Gorazhde and Focha hospitals, shook hands and after barely an hour, returned to Focha.

That evening I had a meal with Brana, the fishing policeman. We loved to tease one another and I thought I had a good opening.

"Brana, you are always looking for Chetniks and rarely find them." I said, "Guess what, I just spent an hour speaking with one of them."

You could never surprise Brana. "I know who you mean, but Janjich does not count. He is an ornament, a monument to our magnanimity and fairness. What other regime would be so trusting?" Brana accompanied his word "magnanimity" and "fairness" with finger signs for quotation marks. Clearly Brana was not pleased with the situation.

"But truly," he added, "I do not mind him. He is no trouble. The man always does what he is told and he is too much of a coward to resume contacts with his wartime colleagues."

I then told Brana how surprised I was that Janjich, whom Rajko had sent to give me trouble, turned out to be such a benevolent visitor. I speculated aloud on whether he'd wanted to make up for the trouble he created around the patient with the cirrhosis of the liver.

"Julius, you innocent child," laughed Brana. "You are an incurable romantic. After what he went through I doubt whether Janjich could have any feelings, but even if for some reason he felt guilty, he could not afford to show remorse. How do you think he survived? He did what he was told. He was nice because somebody else, more powerful than Rajko, told him how to behave."

"Do you know who it was?" I asked.

"No, I know nothing about specifics, but I understand people's behavior."

No doubt about it, Brana was a master psychologist. I could dream as much as I wanted but in reality such a thing as benevolent conversion of the great healer from Focha couldn't possibly exist. Too bad! It felt rather good, for a moment.

We started well in advance with preparations for the transfer to the renovated stockade. We held meetings to distribute the office space, organize working teams and to hire new personnel. Many hours were spent in group-sessions with the personnel discussing cleanliness in the new hospital and the need for a new, kinder, attitude towards visitors. Much was said about keeping the corridors clear of people and how to politely shepherd patients' families into waiting rooms.

The new building was large and we had to develop means for visitor orientation. I took charge of ordering signs. The local Serbs used the Cyrillic alphabet but everybody else was accustomed to Roman letters. I bit the bullet and ordered all signs in the Roman alphabet. Surprisingly, nobody objected.

We could not depend only on signs—the literacy rate in the county was well below hundred percent. We emphasized that if a visitors asked for directions, or appeared lost, the employees ought to drop what they were doing and escort him to their destination.

Most clinic employees lived in villages. They routinely fertilized the fields with animal waste. Frequently they cleaned stables and men occasionally slaughtered domestic animals. The danger of infection, particularly with the dreaded spores of tetanus, was very real. We instituted some preventative measures against infection. Before entering the hospital-proper, all employees would change to hospital robes including shoes, skirts or pants, and thoroughly wash their hands. Such organizational changes would be of little consequence had we not also attempted to change the personnel's attitudes. While the building site still teemed with workers, we organized regular dress rehearsals. I invited Mother from Zagreb to organize the surgical theatre. She did a splendid job. She demonstrated proper sterilization procedures; taught how to dispose of used materials, how to keep inventories and how to re-order materiel. She loved the role-playing rehearsals. The fact that during the war Mother had been the director of a Partizan hospital held her in high stead in Gorazde. She gave loud orders and never accepted a negative answer. Normally in Bosnia the men would not accept an order from a woman, but she was an equal opportunity screamer and had no problems breaking the gender barrier. Her technique bordered on abuse but nobody ever complained. Mother's repeated drills proved very successful. When we moved into the new hospital, the surgical team functioned with the automatic precision of a well-tuned Swiss watch.

I took responsibility for training employees in patient registration, laboratory management, admission procedures, and cleaning of the hospital. Things went quite well until the day when I announced, with considerable glee, that modern toilet bowls had been installed in the new hospital. I said something to the effect how much better this was than outdoor privies or squatting over a ceramic hole in the ground in some public toilet. I could feel the audience was not with me. I cracked a few jokes but nobody laughed. Not knowing how else to get their attention I rhapsodized about the shining bowls, the lack of odor and the clean toilet seats. That did it!

After some whispering and nudging by others, a male nurse asked to talk.

"Excuse me, Doctor, for interrupting you," he said, "but it is hard to believe that you agreed to order those toilet bowls. I would much prefer to use a "squatter" in a public toilet than one of these modern contraptions. Yes, the squatters stink and if the previous guy was not a good marksman, you may have to step around a "mine" but, by golly, nobody asks you to sit with your naked bottom on the same place where someone else's ass has been. They may shine, but believe me, those seats are dirty."

The audience gave him huge applause.

I was stunned. Where I'd come from, modern toilets were a fact of life and their advantages were quite obvious. But how was I to explain this to a person with a different frame of reference? I hate the stench and am so inured, that if a public toilet does not reek and passes my visual inspection, I go through perfunctory cleaning motions and then comfortably use the seat.

Admittedly, the man had a point. In absolute terms there is no particular advantage to toilet bowls over the water-flushed "squatters." My preference for toilet bowls was just that, a preference. I protected my nose; my opponent guarded his glutei. I preferred comfortable sitting; he opted for acrobatic squatting. It was all a matter of habit and when you think about it, as long as it reaches the destination, it does not matter which way the excrement floats into the sewage. To this day squatters are widely used in Italy and whenever I am forced to use one, I laugh about the surrealistic discussion in Gorazde. Not to mention that each time, I come away with a renewed appreciation for the isometric strength and coordination required to accomplish the deed. More power to those who like the squatters!

I should add that, back in Gorazde, the discussion was not only about preferences but also had unstated religious overtones. Cleansing is very important to Moslems. One has to wash one's feet prior to entering a mosque and hygienic rules also guide sexual intercourse. If a Moslem wanted to give you a hint about his private exploits he'd say he "washed himself" last night.

To counter my opponent I assured the audience that the toilets would be cleaned twice a day and solemnly promised that a bottle of

disinfectant fluid with a supply of rags would be placed next to each seat. I then extolled the powers of modern disinfectants but was quickly running out of steam. Luckily, sensing my discomfort, my opponent professed to have been swayed by the antiseptic argument. But his eyes and his monotonic apology spoke volumes. He was doing me a favor but deep down, he had not changed his mind.

After the public incident, I convened an official "task force" for the proper usage of the hospital's new toilets. The group developed written guidelines for the personnel as well as a short "how to" text which would read to every admitted patient. We implemented these measures but when the hospital opened for business, some of the personnel and most of the patients did not accept the novelty. The toilets turned into an unmitigated disaster as people stood on the seats and from that awkward position attempted to complete their squatting act. Not too many virtuosos hit the target! The poor cleaning women had a horrible task.

The situation started to improve ever so slightly just before I left. The personnel could not avoid using toilets and they gradually realized that utilizing them in a manner for which they had been designed, was more practical. And reading the "bible" to every admitted patient also seemed to help. However, the battle was not won and I never learned whether we eventually prevailed.

As it wiggles through the mountains, the River Drina provides a stable mild climate to the narrow tract of flat land around its course. The forefathers of Gorazde chose the right spot when they settled next to a bend in the river. The mountain slopes around Gorazde were somewhat less forbidding than in other places and the spot benefited from a natural air-conditioning. In summer, the cold river provides relief from the heat and in the winter the water is warmer than the icy air around it. My last winter in Gorazde was quite tolerable, but around us the bad weather had a devastating effect. The roads and railways in all directions, including to Sarajevo, were snowed in. We were bottled up. The tough winter around us was both a relief and a burden. The workload decreased as the less sick people opted to tough it out at

home. But patients who made it to the clinic were quite sick. One late afternoon, after a horse dragged her for four hours on a makeshift sled, a very sick teenage girl arrived at the clinic. She initially had some fever and felt very weak but soon her parents realized she had trouble breathing and could barely talk. They were right to undertake the difficult trek; the girl needed quick help. The back of her throat as well as her tonsils were badly swollen and covered by leathery bluish sheets, which obstructed the airways. Her lips were blue, her pulse was weak and her heart rate was very fast.

A sample from her throat quickly confirmed the diagnosis of diphtheria. The girl was in very bad shape and the worse the patients are the more antitoxin they need. We gave her the whole supply on hand and hoped nobody else with the same diagnosis would show up before we could restock. At first I decided to sweat it out and wait a few days for the antitoxin to take hold. Unfortunately, the girl was getting worse by the hour. There were no two ways about it-she needed a tracheotomy or she would die of suffocation. I'd never before performed a tracheotomy, nor had I ever watched someone else doing it.

First I phoned to seek advice from Professor Herbinger in Sarajevo. He agreed that I must do the tracheotomy and led me through a few finer points of the procedure. I then spoke to patient's parents. As is frequently the case in Bosnia, they were very fatalistic. They knew the child might not make it through the surgery, but could not understand why I had to ask for their permission to operate.

"Don't ask me, just do what you think is right. I cannot judge what my girl needs, but I am pretty sure if you do nothing, she will die. We would not have embarked on the trip had we not thought she was seriously sick," said the father with an infallible logic.

I proceeded to describe possible complications of surgery and the overall seriousness of the underlying diphtheria. Again, the parents were calm and unperturbed. Only once, when I mentioned that the girl might end up with a large scar on her throat, did the mother squirm just for a minute before she regained composure.

I told the personnel I would meet them in the surgical suite in about half an hour. They thought I needed some peace and quiet to relax, but I actually needed time to read up on tracheotomy.

A few minutes after I started reading, there was a commotion in the corridor. A male nurse was telling somebody that I could not be disturbed. It did not help. The door of the room opened and there stood Emanuel Reich in his most bellicose pose.

"What a primadonna!" he barked. "His majesty takes an afternoon nap and appoints a pretorian guard of slow-witted peasants to protect him. You sold them a bunch of goods and the poor bastards act as if they are guarding a national treasure. They trembled in horror when a mere mortal, another doctor, threatened to interrupt your solitude."

I just looked at him.

"This is socialism, my comrade, and we are all equal," continued Emanuel in somewhat lower voice, "By not working during regular hours you are corrupting others, which we both know is an unforgivable sin. You are misleading the masses and your bad example might undermine the basic fabric of our society. Don't you know that physicians are at the forefront of the battle for socialism? We have to be vigilant, enthusiastic and work tirelessly for the Fatherland."

Emanuel had a sense of humor and his own parroting of the official lingo cheered him up. He sank into a chair and started to laugh like a maniac.

"Boy, you shift gears faster than anybody I know," I said. "Just as I was working up some anger you turned into a charmer. You poor helpless slave of your emotions! I never know which Emanuel I am talking to, but frankly today both of you—the angry and the jovial one—are not welcome. I have other things to do."

As soon as he'd entered the room Emanuel realized that, rather than sleeping, I was actually reading a book. But he had preprogrammed himself to become angry and could not stop. The little ditty he delivered in the official jargon was his way to calm down and an indirect admission that he was wrong. And now a third Emanuel was sitting in front of me, the nosy one.

"Okay," he said, "why are you reading the textbook of surgery. What is going on?"

I informed him about the girl with diphtheria and my plans to perform a tracheotomy. Recalling that Emanuel loved surgery, on

the spur of the moment, I offered him to assist me with the procedure.

Emanuel jumped from his chair as if a wasp had bitten him. He even let out a shriek. "Oh sure, now I see what you are up to," he yelled. "You want to have a tracheotomy under your belt and just in case it does not go right, I will be there to share the blame. Well, I am not your fool."

I should have known better. Each time in the past when I tried to be nice to him, Emanuel either found a way to offend me or got me into some trouble. Now, instead of preparing for surgery, I wasted time to deal with his senseless accusations.

"You dropped in on me uninvited," I said. "I gave you a chance to join me as a matter of courtesy but, of course, wild as you are, you don't even have a concept of what courtesy is. Get the hell out of here and come back in one of those rare moments when you are a near-normal human being."

Once again Emanuel had succeeded; I was getting mad. But it was naive to think that one single offensive sentence would rid me of my tormentor. He was now curious.

"Okay," he said, "maybe I was a bit too excited. What I wanted to say is that the odds are against you; you are more likely to hurt than to help the girl. Tracheotomy is a dangerous surgery. You know the chief surgeon in the Holy Spirit Hospital in Zagreb—the one that I had little disagreement with?"

"You mean the guy who played soccer with your behind as he was kicking you out of the hospital?"

"Yes, that very man," Emanuel said calmly. "And he used to weasel his way out of performing tracheotomies if he possibly could. Early in his career he cut somebody's recurrent laryngeal nerve. This left the poor man who loved to sing with a permanent raspy, whispering, voice. If a famous surgeon approaches each tracheotomy with trepidation, what can an amateur like you do?"

Emanuel sure knew how to build one's confidence. But I would not be deterred and planned to read up on the anatomy of the recurrent nerve as soon as I got rid of the gatecrasher. However, Emanuel continued the monologue.

"But who says she really needs a tracheotomy? I bet you are over-

reacting. You told me she is cyanotic, but that might be due to poor circulation. You know that the myocardium is the most frequent target for the diphtheria toxins. Maybe she is just in congestive heart failure and you could afford to wait until the antitoxin takes hold."

"Go see for yourself, and then tell me whether she needs the surgery or not," I said in desperation and turned to the textbook of anatomy. As students we'd spent many long nights poring over that book and it took me only a minute to find the right illustration. But Emanuel returned before I could take a good look at the drawings.

"It did not take you long. What is your verdict?"

"This girl will die within a few hours," Emanuel pronounced solemnly, "but she is too far gone for an intervention. Let her die, let her die."

Emanuel was near tears and said something I would have never expected from him.

"I am scared, Stevo. Let her die!"

"You mean let her suffocate? Let her die fighting for each last breath?"

Ashamed of his confession and irritated by my reply, Emanuel again lost control. "I am leaving," he screamed on the way to the door and as he disappeared into the corridor, I could hear, loud and clear, the rest of his rambling. "Yes, let her die, let her suffocate, and yes, let her fight for her breath."

Emanuel was spewing these horrible words right in front of the girl's parents in the corridor. But before I could say anything, Emanuel was back on my doorstep.

"Watch for the *arteria thyreoidea ima*," he barked, "It sometimes takes an unusual course and passes right in front of the trachea. If you cut it, the blood will squirt all over your face. It is a large vessel and the patient can bleed out in ten minutes. You will not be able to stop it alone. You might stick your finger in the wound to halt the bleeding but I doubt you could hold it there forever. If it happens, call on somebody else for help, not me. You created the problem and I do not want any part of it."

And with these mean words, Emanuel made his final exit.

I went to reassure the parents but it was not necessary. The girl's father waved me to the side. "Do not worry, Doctor," he said,

"Everybody knows the small doctor is a big fool. Please go ahead and do what is needed. You should not be distracted his words. The man is missing a plank in his head."

I had not heard that expression for a while. It fitted Emanuel perfectly. His brain indeed missed a plank—a plank called inhibition. I thanked the father and went to the surgery room smiling.

In his nasty way, Emanuel was rather helpful. The textbooks I perused barely mentioned the complications which Emanuel so vividly evoked. His harassment made me very careful. I thoroughly infiltrated the entire area with local anesthetic and made the first cut through the skin. Thereafter I utilized only blunt instruments to carefully work my way towards the trachea. It took time but by working that way I diminished chances of cutting through a blood vessel. In fact, one would have to be rather crass to cut a larger artery—they pulsate. Exploring with my finger I felt nothing beating in synch with the heartbeat. I was also very careful not to inadvertently cut some hidden nerve. After a while I succeeded in moving the excess tissue out of the way. Once the trachea came in sight, I took the scalpel again and made the cut. As soon as I pierced the windpipe a powerful blow of air came out hissing. The girl could now exhale with reasonable ease but each time she inhaled, the surrounding soft tissues collapsed into the hole. This impediment would disappear as soon as I placed the cannula into the windpipe. In theory it should have been easy to slip the curved metal tube into the trachea, but I had an awful time. The pipe was quite large and when I tried to push it in, the girl coughed and wiggled. I tried many times and started to lose hope but then, by sheer chance, the tube elegantly slid into the windpipe.

It was magic! Soon the girl's breathing normalized, a healthy color returned to her previously cyanotic lips, her heart rate was normal and the pulse was strong.

I became a hero of the moment. Everybody congratulated and cheered. However, the girl was not out of danger. It was too early to tell whether the serum would fully protect her heart and kidneys from bacterial toxins. But her elated parents did not care for my warnings.

"Doctor, you saved my girl's life. It takes great knowledge and courage to do what you did and I thank you from the bottom of my

heart," said the father, "but there are things that a parent knows better than a doctor. I know she will be fine. Do not worry about the poison in her blood, I just know she will be all right. Please have a rest. And may Allah help you helping many more people."

It was one of the nicest thanks I ever heard. I went to bed with a great sense of accomplishment and relief.

As her father predicted, the girl started to improve rather quickly. Within three days, her electrocardiogram, chest X-rays and urine exams were normal. The only remaining problem was the cannula in her windpipe. The tube could not stay in place endlessly, but I found no reference in my textbooks as to what one does with the cannula after tracheotomy. I called the ear-nose-throat department in Sarajevo and got to talk to a young hotshot faculty member. I wanted to know when was the right time to take the cannula out.

"Well you should take it out every second day, clean it and then reposition the device," the man said.

"I had a great deal of trouble inserting the cannula during the tracheotomy," I admitted, " and it never occurred to me to remove it."

"My goodness! How long ago did you perform the tracheotomy?"

"Ten days ago. Sorry I had not called you before but I had my hands full just keeping her alive," I said quite defensively. "To be frank, I am still not comfortable with removing the device. What could be the complications of keeping the cannula in place for a while longer."

"Obstruction, infection and necrosis of the cartilage," the guy shot back with the ease of a person who learns everything by rote.

"There are no signs of obstruction, and I see no pus," I responded. "But what are the signs of necrosis?"

"Necrosis is associated with discomfort and possibly with an enlargement of the hole," said the wise guy. "And as to how long after the surgery it can occur, I do not know. We frequently reposition the cannula in order to avoid the complication and I have never seen a case."

Fine, I thought, after all it is a rare complication. But the guy would not let me off the hook.

"It is not that much of a problem to remove the tube," he said. "My nurses do it routinely"

Bastard! That was a fat bit of help!

"Well, let me give you a piece of news," I said in anger, "Your nurse is in Sarajevo, the roads are snowed in and I cannot bring her here to help me. So what should I do?"

The man realized he had overdone it.

"What I meant to say is that after a while the patient tolerates the procedure much better. There is no bleeding, the patient is not short of breath and when you push it in, the tube seems to magically find its way." he said soothingly. "Believe me, you will have no trouble."

That was a bit better. I needed reassurance rather than academic pontification. I thanked and promised to call back if needed.

I removed the tube and when I closed the hole with a finger, the girl was able to breathe without any problem. I did not put the tube back and packed the girl's wound with gauze. The snow finally melted and a few days later we sent her to Sarajevo for further management.

Unfortunately, Emanuel would not let me rest on my laurels.

"If you could do it, so can I. I want to perform the next tracheotomy." he insisted on the phone.

The crazy guy! After he'd done his best to discourage me he was now green with envy. Instead of apologizing, he wanted to get even.

"This is the first case we ever had and I don't see another one coming anytime soon," I said. "I will call on you if a similar patient shows up and the roads are snowed in. Under normal circumstances we send such patients to Sarajevo."

"That is the same as saying it will never happen," screamed Emanuel. "I do not care how, but you had better find me a patient. Create the circumstances."

"You are asking me to find some guinea pig just for your fun?" I wondered.

Generally Emanuel was not an immoral man but, again, he could not contain his craziness.

"That is exactly what I am asking you to do," he barked into the receiver.

"And what will happen if I do not find a victim for you?"

"I will never speak to you again."

"That is fine with me. If you change your mind, do not hesitate to call on me. No questions will be asked," I replied and hung up.

I expected he would soon get over it but, as it turned out, Emanuel never again spoke with me. Seven days after our conversation, the Party secretary in Gorazhde gave Emanuel a 24-hour ultimatum to get out of town. The pretext for his expulsion from Gorazde was a well-publicized conflict between him and a police officer, but Emanuel's marital troubles were the real reason. The Party secretary could not act as rudely as he did without a tacit approval of Emanuel's very influential father-in-law.

For those of us who knew him, Emanuel was a legend of sorts and news about him continued to flow. The gossip was never malicious and without being judgmental, we continued to receive a steady stream of "did you hear?" Emanuel stories. Apparently Emanuel's highly placed father-in-law had actually orchestrated his son-in-law's exile from the country. It was not easy to get out of Yugoslavia in those days. The Yugoslav Party still considered itself part of the worldwide Communist movement and viewed defections to the West as failures of the regime. And yet, apparently without too much trouble, Emanuel found himself in Italy. The story has it that he immediately had a huge blowout with the Italian police, and they tried to deport him to Yugoslavia, but the border police refused to take him back. Who knows? It would be a good story even if it were not true. But the fact is that Emanuel ended up practicing medicine in the USA.

About thirty years after we'd parted ways in Gorazde, I got some news about Emanuel, of all places, in Acapulco in Mexico. During the break in a symposium I was attending there, I decided to soak up some Mexican sun. Next to me at the pool was a physician renowned for her excellent laboratory work. Let's call her Dr. X. The inevitable question about my accent popped up, as it always does when people do not know me well. By that time I had already learned not to be irritated by such a line of questioning, which in Europe would be considered quite impolite. It is not nice to point out to a foreigner that he has not yet fully mastered the language. It is much better to

congratulate him on how well he speaks English and in due course you might find out from whence he came. Anyhow, I told the lady I was from Zagreb. She wanted to know whether I ever met a certain Dr. Reich. I sure had! She then proceeded to tell me how she hired Emanuel's daughter as a laboratory assistant.

That was a surprise but not because of the improbable coincidence. I have long ago learned that in life, one way or another, you meet the same people again or at least hear about them. The surprise was that Emanuel's daughter also came to the USA. Was he permitted to take the child with him to Italy? Did he bring her to the USA later? What about the girl's mother? Did she change her mind and came to the States?

But I did not have a chance to ask those questions. Dr. X, my pool acquaintance, hated her lab assistant passionately! Apparently before she could be even remotely useful to her boss, the new assistant started to reorganize the records of previous experiments in the laboratory. Within a few days Dr. X realized she could not find most of her old data. She ordered the new technician to stop moving the records around and, instead, start learning the technical aspects of her job. But Emanuel's daughter responded with an angry letter accusing her boss of sloppy work and in essence, questioning her scientific integrity. She was fired on the spot!

What genes will do! The country was different—but the story was almost identical to the famous encounter between Emanuel and the chief surgeon in Zagreb. Only Doctor X was either more polite or did not know how to play soccer. Emanuel's daughter got away without a kick to her behind.

~

By early spring the old stockade had been almost entirely renovated and in the summer we were poised to move into the new building. The actual transfer to the hospital was quite anticlimactic. I'd gone to the building so many times, and the personnel had gone through so many dress rehearsals that, when the time came, we felt more tired than triumphant.

The official opening did nothing to improve our mood. Some big

shots came from Sarajevo and delegations from surrounding communities showed up on time but the whole ceremony was notably subdued. Nobody seemed genuinely happy and my nemesis Rajko Gagovich, did not even try to hide his feelings. He walked through the entire hospital pretending to read a newspaper!

I called Rajko the next day to give him a piece of my mind.

"Why didn't you just stay at home?" I wondered. "You could have pretended to be sick or something. Instead, you ruined the whole event. How could you be so childish?"

"And how could you be so stupid?" fired Rajko right back. "You are a transient in Gorazde. With a ticket to Zagreb in your pocket you can play games but for me this is a deadly serious affair. Most of your visitors came just to annoy me, rub it in, as it were. Had I stayed home, they would have enthusiastically praised you and your hospital and there would be no end to celebrations. Now they know where I stand. There is plenty of fighting spirit left in me and this is not the end of the battle."

"How can an intelligent person like you be so dense?" Rajko continued after a pause. "You've lived for two years in this community and you still do not know what is up and what is down. You think that mending people is all that there is to it. The good Saint Stevo! He hands out alms and is above pesky little local frays."

Rajko was famous for his outbursts, but he sounded angrier than ever before. "So I am stupid," I said. "You are a leader and educator. Teach me! And I mean it! What did I miss? You said I do not know what this is all about and you are right."

But Rajko would not be mollified.

"So his holiness is still riding the clouds," he said. "Just keep floating. One day you might understand. But for the time being, let me tell you that at the end I will get my way."

There was no use in continuing the conversation and we both hung up. Rajko's predictions proved correct; he got his way. About three years after I left Gorazhde, the new hospital in Focha had been completed and Rajko acted with dispatch to downgrade the hospital in Gorazhde. He increased the salaries in Focha, attracted permanent specialists to the new hospital, and provided them with generous housing. While he was smart enough to recognize the power of eco-

nomic incentives, Rajko also continued wielding rough political power. Dr. Plevljakovich, a local man devoted to his town, was summarily and without explanation fired as the director and a layman had been appointed to the post. Eventually Plevljakovich left the town and the hospital fell into an irreversible tailspin.

~

I am still very proud of the job we did in Gorazhde. Within a period of two years, the health service in the area made a remarkable progress. We had well-trained personnel, a functioning surgical suite, a high-standard diagnostic laboratory, and we started to provide good quality modern healthcare. Instead of sending complex patients to Sarajevo, we brought a team of specialists to visit Gorazhde once every week. In the beginning the specialists mainly triaged the patients. They gave therapeutic advice for easier cases and the more complex ones, they'd select for treatment or further diagnostic evaluation in Sarajevo. As they developed more confidence in our hospital, the specialists started to perform invasive diagnostic procedures and routine surgeries in Gorazhde.

We also organized a network of satellite clinics in the vicinity of Gorazhde. In my mind our most hard-earned and impressive achievement was the fact that the new hospital was remarkably clean. This required a thorough change of our personnel's, patients, and visitors attitudes—something that is not easily done. How many times have you, dear reader, made an earnest promise to improve some aspect of your behavior only to find out that you keep repeating the same misdeeds over and over again?

It is therefore not surprising that, while people of Gorazhde started to alter their behavior inside the hospital, their general attitudes did not change. Had I understood that fact-of-life, I would have saved myself a bitter disappointment. I knew that Rajko would not give me a farewell party and I expected that other authorities, including the Mayor of Gorazhde, would have to follow Rajko's suit. I was also aware that Bosnians, particularly the Moslems, tend to be reserved and rarely express emotions. But deep inside I had hoped that people would meet me in private, shake my hand, give me a pat

on the shoulder, and wish me well. Nothing of the sort happened! Absolutely nothing! As far as the good citizens of Gorazhde were concerned, I was just another carpetbagger. I might have worked a bit harder and cared a bit more than others, but I was nevertheless a transient. It did not make that much difference that others of my ilk came to Gorazhde to make money, whereas I went there for political reasons. I'd done my turn and that was all that was to it! It was a bitter pill to swallow but I eventually came to terms with reality. And then just about when I was ready to depart, a single expression of gratitude came from somebody I never considered a friend.

One afternoon I went to Janja's coffeehouse and sat next to Salman, the director of the sawmill and the renowned shady dealer in oak stumps.

"I was told," he said, "that people walk past you as if you were a Turkish cemetery."

I laughed. Salman used the witty local expression for being ignored. After they have paid proper respect at the funeral, the Bosnians rarely visit graves.

"Do not take it personally," Salman continued, "that is how things are here. But I am sure the Mayor's office will find some practical way to express their appreciation."

"I don't think so. They are running out of time. And, believe me, the leadership is keeping quite a distance from me. I have not met our noble Secretary of Health or his honor the Mayor for about two weeks."

" I am surprised. Didn't they at least offer some help with moving you back to Zagreb."

"No, not at all."

"Maybe they intended to, and had not gotten around to it."

"I very much doubt that. Nothing happens around here by chance."

"Bastards. Political trash! That's what they are. Let me tell you, Sonny—I will take care of it." Salman stood up and walked to the door. He was too mad to shake hands with me.

"This is for everybody to hear," he yelled from the door, "As a token of appreciation for his work in this community, the industrial

Farewell from the hospital. The author is in the middle.

enterprise *Stakorina* will underwrite the cost of moving Dr. Julius back to Zagreb!"

There were at least ten patrons in Janja's coffee house. All of them as one kept looking into coffee cups pretending not to have heard what Salman said. He turned towards them and yelled at the top of his lungs. "You can tell this to anybody you want. If our leadership does not like it, they can call me up. I will be in my office."

I ran after Salman and caught up with him on the street. "I do not want you to get into any trouble. I came here on a train and I will leave that way again."

"No, you will not." Salman was still fuming. "And as far as me getting into trouble, do not worry. This old Moslem gets angry only when he can afford it. All three of them Rajko, Zdravko and Mustafa can kiss my . . . !" The first compiler of the Serbo-Croat vocabulary, Vuk Karadzhich, had recorded close to thirty synonyms for the end of the rectum, and Salman used the most vulgar one.

I was flabbergasted with Salman's open contempt for Rajko. "Nobody in this place dares to talk so candidly about the big boss. You must be much more powerful than I thought."

"Foxy would be a better term," Salman sneered. "For one thing, Mustafa and Zdravko owe me one. I got them all that equipment for your clinic. Remember?"

I remembered very well how Salman arranged to purchase medical supplies for the hospital through one his foreign customers.

"But what about Rajko? Couldn't he question the legitimacy of your gift? Moving me to Zagreb will cost your enterprise a pretty penny. Rajko could hang this around your neck."

"For one thing, it is not a gift. The town of Gorazhde still owes us a bundle of money for the purchase of medical equipment. I will send them a bill and subtract the amount from their debt. So you see, they will still end up paying your trip."

We had reached Salman's office building. Holding the doorknob Salman said. "And second, Kid, do not worry about Rajko. He will not ask any questions. I can't tell you why. Just take it from me—he will not ask questions."

The old fox must have had a few things on Rajko.

"Come tomorrow morning and we will arrange details." Salman said.

This time around we shook hands.

The next day, as soon as I entered the office, Salman took over the conversation. "First of all, forget your city manners and don't even think of thanking me. Your work here deserves recognition, but that is not why I am doing this."

The water in the coffeepot had boiled over and Salman arose to "bake" us coffee. He returned with two demitasses.

"Boy, this is really a fine coffee," I said.

"Yeah, yeah, yeah. If you forbid a city boy to express his thanks, he will find something else nice to say." He sounded irritated. Was he getting mad at me for inadvertently pulling him into a conflict?

I tried to defuse the situation.

"Look, Salman, when I told you I am ready to leave Gorazhde by train, I meant it. You seem to be upset with me. Be straight. If I am causing you undue trouble, just say so and let's forget the darn idea about your enterprise moving me back to Zagreb."

"No, I am not like a soccer player who misses the goal and then curses the ball. I am not unhappy with my promise to you. To the

contrary I welcome the opportunity. You see, only once in a while do I get the chance to do the right thing. And when I choose to do so, I feel good."

"Like when you forked out money for reforestation in Israel?" I asked.

"Yes! You have no idea how many times I've been ribbed for it. Each time somebody appears stunned that a Moslem from Bosnia would support Jews in Israel, I just laugh. And when the guy leaves, I proudly dust off the diploma on the wall."

"But helping me is not as important a cause as sending money to Israel!"

"Oh, yes, it is. It is! And, by the way, I just realized why something about you irritated me a few minutes ago. You always interrupt me, young man! Now drink your coffee and let me do the talking."

Fighting the urge to apologize, I poured myself more coffee, leaned back in the chair and kept quiet.

"I am not doing this for you. When that mad dog Rajko came to Gorazhde, everything changed. The place has lost the last vestige of civility. Yes, local folks don't like to show emotions but they used to know what was right. Normally an official would have organized a dinner. The topic of your departure would never come up, nobody would give speeches, but you'd understand that the meal was in your honor."

"You see," continued Salman, "people from Bosnia, be they Serbs or Moslems, might appear rough, but they do have feelings. Departures are by nature sad and nobody wishes to be reminded. In the house of a hanged man, you do not talk about the rope!

Remember I asked you yesterday if people were treating you as a Turkish cemetery. And I told you that you should not take it personally. In this part of the world there is enough sorrow around and nobody wishes to be reminded. Wasn't there a poet who said that each time you say goodbye to someone, a little part in you dies?"

This was a surprise. I viewed Salman as an intelligent, competent but uneducated person. I never expected hearing from him a literary qoute.

Salman continued with the monologue. "And I told you not to take the superficial insensitivity of the locals to your departure as a personal insult. I know how they normally behave in Gorazhde and I would not expect them to throw flowers at you. But this community has an obligation to you-an obligation, which the leadership understands only too well. Unfortunately Rajko, once a small teacher from Focha-now a big shot in Gorazhde, broke their spirit. He made your departure into a 'who-is-with-and-who-against-me' issue. The Mayor should have not caved in. There ought to be some norms of civilized behavior even at these distant, God-forsaken shores of the Drina River."

Salman took a breath and helped himself to another coffee. As ordered, I remained silent.

After a while he looked at me and said. "Thank you for permitting me to give you a little lecture about Bosnia. Now you know that I am doing this for myself and not for you. Unfortunately what I am about to do is only a gesture. Nothing will change in Gorazhde. Rajko got the Mayor to capitulate and that is the beginning of his end. Once you give in to a bully, you've lost it all. From now on Rajko will toy with him. The fact that our Mayor is as much of a Serb as Rajko is does not help. You see, Zdravko, who was born here, loves Gorazhde so much that he sometimes forgets this is a predominantly Moslem place. Rajko will force him to work against the interests of Gorazhde and eventually the Mayor won't be able to take it. In a few weeks he will have no choice but to resign."

Salman had an errand to do, excused himself, and asked me to wait. He'd be back in ten minutes. That gave me time to wonder about this extraordinary man. Since I first set my eyes on him, I had realized that behind his façade of a 'local boy' resided a shrewd and unusual persona. Salman was abiding by a dual moral code. He saw no problems with his own, slightly shady, business practices, but there were certain thresholds beyond which nobody ought to pass. And as far as I was concerned, this practitioner of relativistic morality was a much better person than many a rigid moralist I had met in my life.

But I never expected him to be so open with me. He was the first and only person in Gorazhde to allude to the wider context of the

conflict in Gorazhde. Back in the 1950's Tito declared "brotherhood and unity" between all Yugoslav factions. Mentioning anything even distantly relating to the possible discord between religious or ethnic groups was the greatest of all taboos.

Until then, I viewed the events in Gorazhde as a clash of personalities and a frivolous competition between two neighboring villages. Even my good friend and professional colleague Meshek never commented on the background of the battle between Gorazhde and Focha. Not because he did not trust me. Meshek, a Moslem who dated and later married a Serbian woman trained himself to ignore the rift. By the choice of his life partner, he made a sufficient statement about his views. Many of his friends in Sarajevo were Serbs. Their friendship defied the local sectarians who, thriving on the old cultural conflict, preached ethnic intolerance. Whether out of good intention or because he put his head in sand, Meshek left me clueless about the reality in Gorazhde.

About three decades after I left Gorazhde, when the horrible fratricidal war in Bosnia broke out, I finally understood the context and the passions of the rivalry between the Gorazde and Focha hospitals. Rajko was a Serb and his roots were in Focha. To me his actions in Gorazde were the mere antics of a local boy wishing to do something good for his town. Focha had one of the oldest and most venerated mosques, but the town, which abuts on Montenegro, had a large Serbian population. In Gorazde the population was predominantly Moslem. Unfortunately the skirmishes around the hospitals in Gorazde and Focha were a prelude to the future war between Serbs and Moslems in Bosnia.

When it broke out in 1992, the terrible war vividly illustrated the deep rift between Gorazde and Focha. During the war, the Serb forces occupied most of the territory of Bosnia. Only a small parcel of land in Gorazde and the area around Sarajevo remained out of their control. Gorazde was never overrun by Serbs but remained completely encircled and isolated throughout the war.

Focha became the headquarters to Serb military and paramilitary forces. The local Moslems sought protection in the local hospital. However the hospital was not what it used to be. As early as one month before the Serbian military takeover of Focha, the Serbian

staff of the hospital began transferring medical supplies to a clinic in nearby Velechevo, which they were setting up exclusively for Serbs. Soon thereafter the Serb paramilitary forces took over the hospital in Focha. Nobody was permitted to leave the hospital and the new masters took all people of military age to detention centers. The first group of detainees included seven Moslem male nurses and four physicians. After a while they disappeared from the detention centers and to this day they have not been seen again. According to the Human Rights Watch report, the backyard of the hospital in Focha was used for executions and became a makeshift graveyard.

I am glad I was as "stupid" as Rajko said, and failed to understand the depth of passions in Gorazde. It would have been much harder to work. At least I did not lose hour upon hour contemplating the wider implications of every move I made. Sometimes, but not very often, it is a blessing to be ignorant.

"I've said enough about what goes on in this godforsaken place," said Salman, returning and offering me another coffee. "When you look down from the mountain on Gorazhde the beautiful view is breathtaking, but when you descend into the village, it is the stench that takes your breath away. In the past that unique mixture of dung, sweat, brandy, the meat on the spit, and the fresh wind, was a good stench. The way the place stinks now, from inside, is unbearable. It will suffocate us all."

I was amazed with this unexpected burst of eloquence and found no words to respond.

"All is fine," said Salman after a pause. "I will send the truck early tomorrow morning. You don't have that much to haul; load the truck up by noon. The driver will depart first and we will later take my car to Sarajevo. Next morning I will attend my conference and the sedan's driver will take you to Zagreb. He will drive fast enough to overtake the truck and help you to unload it in Zagreb."

"Hey, that is great! I did not expect to be driven all the way to Zagreb."

"Don't let it go to your head, Doctor. And don't brag about it. This little extra courtesy will remain our secret. Rajko could level at me one of those 'using the official car for private purposes ' charges and that would not sit well."

"Won't say anything to anybody. Thank you ever so much," I said.

"No thank you! Go and get packed!"

I did as told, packed late into the night and had just a few hours of sleep before the truck driver knocked on my door.

"Well, Doctor," said the driver, "it is a pleasure to be of service to you. I did not forget what you did for my sick son and because of that, I will give it to you straight. The truck will not leave today. I have orders to load it up and then make it defective."

I did not even have to ask who gave the order. This was Rajko's style. But Rajko had trained me well. Instead of getting mad or offended, I was all business. I couldn't refuse to load the truck and thereby let Rajko know that the driver coughed up the secret. And then the unthinkable happened. Rajko came to say goodbye!

What a nerve! But, for the driver's sake, I could not give him a piece of my mind.

"So, nobody came to see you off," said Rajko shamelessly, "After everything you have done for this community, nobody found it in his heart to thank you. That's how it is in these geographic latitudes."

"I thought you told them not to come."

"Sure. But they didn't have to listen to me. I say all sorts of things. What could I have done if they did not take my hints? Put them in jail for wishing you well? No, my dear doctor, they could have come but these good-weather friends of yours are thankless cowards. That's who they are."

There was some logic to what Rajko said.

"It fell upon Salman, the only straight and gutsy guy in this town and me, the neurotic admirer of yours, to say farewell. You were in my way but I will miss you. Do you realize that the two us are the best-educated and very likely smartest guys in the town? It won't be fun with everybody clicking his heels but worst of all, nobody will

ever challenge my verbal skills. You were the only one with whom I transacted business in other than simple abridged sentences. No more teasing, word plays, and clever comebacks. And having gotten my way, I will rot in this place until I become as much of a simpleton as they are."

Rajko got me off stride. Just when he was about to play one of his nasty "broken car" tricks on me, I felt compassion for him. Something inside me was reaching out to this difficult and complicated man.

"It is not all that bad. Salman is a smart cookie and he can be quite eloquent," I said.

"Yes," Rajko said," Salman is a lucky man of nature and a clever enough person to find the right job. He loves his trees and everything outdoors so much that he gets quite poetical talking about it. But try to strike a conversation with him on any other matter, and he will sit mute in front of you with his eyes endlessly trained at his coffee cup. Nevertheless I do appreciate his talents. Why else do you think he got away with challenging me publicly?"

Rajko stretched his hand my way.

"I will miss you, Stevo," he said, for the first time calling me by my name. "And tell the driver that I have changed my mind."

I was pleased, but did not trust him. It could have been a trick to check whether the driver told me the truth.

"About what did you change your mind?"

"If you don't yet know, tell the driver that I told him to tell you what his orders were and that those orders are now rescinded."

Rajko's hand was still outstretched in my direction and I shook it firmly.

"In a few years, I will send you an invitation to visit Gorazhde as the guest of the county, "Rajko yelled on his way out.

"Oh, yeah? Just make sure it is not on the day when you open the new hospital in Focha."

"Why not? What is it to you? Wouldn't you come?"

"Probably not!"

We were back to our old tricks.

Salman stopped the car to enjoy the panoramic view of Gorazhde from the top of the Jabuka Mountain. Underneath, the Russian stockade towered over other buildings and dominated the view. To the left of the huge building I spotted the small roof of the old clinic where I worked prior to the renovation of the stockade. My thoughts wandered to the early days in Gorazhde and the circumstances that brought me there. I remembered Father and his tragedy. All of a sudden, I was struck by a thought I had never entertained before. Looking at the stockade I realized how remarkably similar were my father's and my own life. Like father, like son! We both left the city for political reasons; we both started our career in a remote village; we both landed in a village that had a military stockade and we both transformed an old stockade into a modern hospital.

A decade after he completed the construction of the hospital in Kovin, Father built yet another hospital in Stanchich. Would I follow suit? Was I destined to build yet another hospital?

And would I . . . ?

No I would not! There on the top of the Jabuka Mountain, I promised myself not to repeat Father's mistake. I would not permit anybody to annoy me to the point of losing judgment. Father had lost all sense of proportion. What to others seemed to be an insignificant episode became to Father a monumental overreaching issue. A battle he had to win or else! I would never overestimate the importance of a situation. Some true matters of honor may be worth dying for. But in Vrapche, people around my father entrapped him in his own sense of honor and manipulated him for their personal benefit. If I ever faced similar circumstances, I'd do what I suggested to Father he should do. I'd rather run away than fight a battle which I could not possibly win.

Salman tapped me on the shoulder, interrupting my thoughts.

"It is beautiful down there, isn't it?"

A magic bluish haze of open-fire smoke, probably from grills, lingered around the banks of the silvery, shining Drina River. The sun, still providing light to some parts of the valley, had started to hide behind a reddish curtain and a lone eagle, floated majestically above the river, as if he had only leisure and not prey on his mind.

"It's a fantastic view. I love Gorazhde and I will come back to visit." I said.

"Beautiful it might be, but you will never come back."

"Why wouldn't I? Rajko invited me to come back."

"You should not fall for it. Just because for a second he appeared human, you should not forget what a swine the man is. I, for one, will never forgive him for destroying the Gorazhde I once knew."

Salman did not mince words and he was right. After a few years, when the invitation came, I was too busy to respond.

I did not feel slighted then or later, but the truth of the matter is that I had no urge to return. Maybe Salman understood better than I could, what made me tick.

I am afraid I will never again visit Gorazhde, that solitary, forlorn, and beautiful cradle of my medical career.

Epilogue

Upon my return to Zagreb everything became easy. Rajko, my nemesis in Gorazhde, wrote a surprisingly positive letter of recommendation to the hospital and possibly also to the Party. Nobody seemed to discriminate against me. I greatly enjoyed my new work and got on very well with fellow residents in internal medicine. There would be enough material to write yet another book about these happy times, but I doubt I will ever get to it. Let's just say that we entertained ourselves by working hard, studying in earnest, playing practical tricks one on another, and cracking political jokes.

I managed to convince a bookstore in Zagreb to order for me (at an exorbitant price) two American textbooks of medicine: the Cecil's and Harrison's. Both were loaded with valuable facts and I used the books to complement the practical teaching from the staff. I spent the rest of my savings from Gorazhde on practicing English conversation with an excellent tutor.

The political regime in Zagreb had mellowed and Professor Hahn had a good enough standing to encourage visits by foreign experts. Eventually Professor Hahn thought my English was good enough to anoint me as the department's official translator. The more contact I had with visitors, the more I understood the difference between good clinical medicine and research-based medicine. Our instructors could teach us only qualitative medicine based on their personal experiences. In contrast, the Americans could quote

good studies and back up everything they recommended with numbers. The foreign visitors to our department were more interested in the causes and mechanisms of diseases than in their clinical signs. And they did not care to make bedside guesses—they compiled the diagnosis almost exclusively from laboratory findings. Though they could not match the intuition of some of our clinical virtuosos, their painstaking method of assembling laboratory clues into a cogent and objective pattern was most impressive.

By and by, I developed a true interest in the research aspects of medicine. When I completed the board exams in internal medicine, Professor Hahn appointed me as senior instructor in medicine. I thought the new position would give me good opportunities for research but in reality I could do very little. Research was time-consuming, very expensive, and required good logistic support. I could steal away some time but most of it I lost in trying to find research supplies and cajoling others to cooperate. Everything was unpredictable. Foreign medical journals arrived sporadically and to different libraries. Drugs for treatment were sometimes available and sometimes not. Similarly fickle were the supplies of chemicals for laboratory tests. Even the provisions of paper for recording electrocardiograms or X-ray films oscillated.

The less research I could do, the more interested I became in various research topics. I'd dream up all sorts of schemes as to what I would like to investigate, if only I could. Eventually it became an obsession.

I decided to study for the American Foreign Graduate Exam and passed it with excellent marks. It took a lot of explaining to the authorities why I had taken an exam in the "enemy's den"—the U.S, Embassy in Zagreb. I think I was sincere when I told everybody willing to listen, that I wished to study research methods in the USA and would return to foster proper research back home. And then, through an unusual set of circumstances, I got a chance to work a full year in the Department of Medicine at the University of Michigan. But I came on the special exchange visitor visa which was designed to prevent "brain drain" from underdeveloped countries to the USA. The U.S. Government guaranteed that I would return home, and return I did.

Funny things started to happen upon my return to Zagreb. I had already acquired the status of a medical starlet, sought by patients, and destined for a successful academic career. All doors were open but the better the things got, the less satisfied I became. Within a year or so I could not take it any more. I had to get out of there no matter how! I confided to a few wartime friends and they began looking for ways to help me. Eventually a friend we dubbed the "double internist"—doctor of internal medicine in the department of internal affairs (police)—struck gold. He sent my way a rather neurotic secret policeman who had mild hypertension.

At that time I got myself in trouble with the city police in Zagreb. They noticed that after my return from the USA, I had been visited by foreigners. I explained to the man in the city police that these were my personal friends, but he was not impressed. He suggested rather sternly that I "refrain from contacts with foreign elements." I bitterly complained to my patient. He organized an interview with the top man in the Department of Internal Affairs of Croatia. The well-mannered and sophisticated top-level police official apologized for the unwarranted overly ambitious action of his "lower organs." He explained that the Zagreb police had no suspicions about me and that they only wished to "decrease their work load" by attempting to scare people into having fewer foreign visitors.

"Doctor, if you could find a way to have fewer patients, you would do the same. Wouldn't you?" he said, and I could not argue with his logic.

He then suggested that I had his fullest confidence and that I should feel free to exercise my "citizens rights of free association" with anybody I wished.

Right then I got the best idea of my life!

"How can I be sure that these are not just soothing words?" I asked.

"You've got my word of honor!"

"That is good enough for me. I am glad to have your confidence. I presume that means I am also free to travel to other countries?"

"Yes!"

I took a short pause and, as if it were an afterthought, popped the important question:

"Could I have a standing exit visa in my passport?"

And that is how I got out of the country again.

A word of honor is very important in Croatia. I think the officer knew I would not return but he lived up to his word.

Upon reflection, I still do not fully understand why I became possessed by an irresistible urge to leave the country. I felt rather strongly that I wanted to do research, but it could not have been only that. It must have had something to do with my father's death, with the disappointment in my former comrades, with a search for stability in an unpredictable world, and with my inner penchant for adventure.

It all worked out beautifully. I returned to the University of Michigan in 1964. Over a period of thirty-seven years this great institution of learning permitted me to grow and treated me with the same respect it afforded to others. I never regretted the decision to leave Croatia and, in a clear break from Marxist doctrine, I profoundly enjoyed the opportunity to compete with others. I am now a loyal and devoted Michigan Wolverine.

There is a happy end to my personal story. In Ann Arbor I met a very attractive, witty and highly intelligent British lady. This time around things worked out very well. Susan and I married in 1971 and in due course had first a boy and later a girl. It was, and still is, a good marriage. Susan took care of our children and gave me unlimited freedom to pursue my scientific interests. It is absolutely true: "Behind every successful man, there is a strong and supporting woman."

~

Mother never recovered from Father's death. She worked for another ten years as the head nurse in the Orthopedic Department at the University Hospital in Zagreb. After she retired, Mother lived a comfortable life in our large apartment in Zagreb, had a circle of friends, but remained deeply unhappy. She could not get over the fact that both Djuka and I lived in foreign countries. And yet she could not join us. In Zagreb everybody knew her and she had everyone's respect. Whenever she visited one of us, Mother bitterly realized how

ill suited she was for a new life. Without the built-in respect that she had in Zagreb, without people jumping up off their chairs when she entered the room, and without a common thread to anybody but her children, she'd become insecure. In Zagreb she was somebody. In Ann Arbor or Mexico City, she quickly became just another old lady. Disappointed, she'd sadly return to her life in Zagreb.

Mother would frequently call me about this or that kind of health problem. I'd arrange some tests, but none of her suspicions were ever confirmed. It became a way of life. Each time we spoke or a letter arrived; I'd brace myself for a new stream of bad news. She was not making it up. Life dealt her a very bad hand and she needed support. Unfortunately, neither Djuka nor I, found a good way of alleviating her internal pain.

Mother was in good health; she was mobile and had a clear mind to the last day. Her lifelong smoking caught up with her when she was seventy years old. She died within hours of a massive heart attack. Djuka and I managed to return to bury her next to Father in Zagreb. A large group of people, mostly the same ones who witnessed Father's funeral, came to see her off. I was overcome by the heart-wrenching remembrance of Father's tragedy and a sudden realization of what the separation from her sons meant to my lonely and deeply unhappy mother. Only when she died did both of us manage to pay her a simultaneous visit! Some things in life are beyond anybody's control, but no matter how many times I repeat that hard fact, it still bothers me to think of Mother's fate.

Mother always tried to improve communications between Djuka and me. She'd pass on news about our families and urge us to write one another. Having lost the intermediary, Djuka and I began communicating directly. Occasionally, we'd take trips together and a few times we organized common vacations for both our families. But we never became very close. Or so I thought.

Behaviorally and professionally, Djuka and I developed in different directions. I thought of Djuka as a dogmatic, strong-headed, rough sort of a guy. In Djuka's eyes, my emigration to the USA was

an act of treason. I had turned my back on the country and comrades who had saved our skins.

Djuka was a very capable person. He became a reporter and leading foreign policy commentator for the Belgrade newspaper *Politika*. The paper sent him to various posts around the world. He soon learned, the hard way, the cardinal rule of his trade: to separate personal preferences from reality. As he followed Adlai Stevenson on the campaign trail, Djuka sent back reports full of admiration for the candidate. That was in itself a transgression of journalistic objectivity. But then a few days before the elections, Djuka predicted a Stevenson victory! Never again did he make a similar mistake.

He was also incredibly brave. When everybody wanted to leave Budapest, he sneaked through the Russian lines to report about the Hungarian revolution. Without any recommendation, on the spur of the moment, he went into the warring Sudan to interview the rebel leader. After Tito's death, when Yugoslavia started to disintegrate, he had the guts to tell Slobodan Miloshevich where his nationalism would lead the entire country.

But these braveries pale in comparison with Djuka's greatest achievement—his transformation from a Yugoslavian into a Mexican journalist. Unexpectedly, in 1978, Djuka faced a serious threat to his career. After the Second World War the Yugoslav government decided to credit each year of service with the Partizans as two years towards retirement. Before we ever were employed, Djuka and I had accumulated five years towards a Yugoslav pension. Unfortunately for Djuka three decades later, some Yugoslav social engineer decided, in essence correctly, that the wartime leadership must make room for new faces. A law of mandatory retirement was enacted for everybody with thirty-five years of service, regardless of his chronological age. At fifty-two years of age, in his journalistic prime, when his hard work had started to pay off, Djuka was sent to the sidelines.

Djuka decided to stay on in Mexico City as a freelance journalist. I knew he was resourceful and would find some way to supplement his meager Yugoslav pension. I figured he'd send an occasional piece to Yugoslavia or to Germany where he had excellent professional connections. Not so! Djuka became a foreign news editor and regular columnist for Mexico's most widely circulated newspaper,

the *Excelsior*. As a child Djuka spoke Serbo-Croatian, German and Hungarian. English and French came later. Spanish and Portuguese he had learned in his forties. One can be a reasonably good doctor in another country with only passable language skills. But could Djuka pass muster in journalism, where the local language is the primary tool? Amazingly, Djuka composed his article in the rich, ornate Spanish language straight into the typewriter, with no correction; just as if he were writing in his mother tongue.

Djuka came to Ann Arbor in 1990 to seek treatment for his malignant melanoma. The Mexican doctor told him he had "a few spots on the lung." Could be bad, but then who knows; there may be a chance of help in the highly reputed American hospital in Ann Arbor. By the time he reached Ann Arbor, Djuka was extremely short of breath. This highly intelligent and extremely brave man had always been an activist. For him there was a solution to everything. Djuka viewed his bout with melanoma as just another brush with death that he would somehow overcome. He faded fast but did not give up. And then he met the American oncologist who I had asked to be as gentle to Djuka as possible. The words were kind, but the content had its usual in-your-face finality. The doctor told Djuka he had only a few weeks to go, that he might not return alive to Mexico and that he had better use the remaining time to straighten his personal affairs.

Djuka was furious. He had not come all the way to Ann Arbor to hear this. It fell on me to backpedal and tell little lies. Brother Djuka died as he had wished: with the hope that he might beat this nasty obstacle. I did for him what Father had done for me when I had the typhoid. A little deception couldn't hurt.

During those days, Djuka was a great and concerned uncle to my children, a good brother-in-law and a loving brother. And I understood that, differences not withstanding, we were always close. We just never quite found a way to express ourselves. Not until it was too late!

Djuka died in 1991 in Ann Arbor, Michigan, and was buried with honors in Mexico City. The president of Mexico, Mr. Salinas, took a personal one-page ad in the *Excelsior* to acknowledge Djuka's contributions to Mexican journalism. The mayor of Mexico City,

Mr. Camachio, organized the funeral. When we arrived with the body, the former President Echeveria met us at the airport.

Whereas Mexican papers teemed with long articles, his paper in Belgrade, *Politika*, found space only for one short paragraph on its fourth page. What he had told Slobodan Miloshevich was not forgotten. After so many years of excellent service, Djuka became a *persona non grata* in the country he loved so much. A good lesson in the relative values of patriotism!

The South Slavs

(A Historical Primer)

The events described in this book happened in the territory of former Yugoslavia, a country created in 1918 at the end of World War I. After they defeated the Germans and the Austro-Hungarian Empire, the victorious Allies carved out of the Austro-Hungarian territory just enough land to accommodate the Southern Slavs who for centuries craved independence. The new country had very little chance of success.

The area of former Yugoslavia is a classical example of how geography affects people's lives. A huge natural barrier, the Carpathians and the Balkan Mountains divide central from eastern Europe. To avoid climbing through forbidding mountains, a traveler must follow the course of the Danube which, flowing to the east, works its way through the mountains to reach the Black Sea. Having negotiated its way through the narrows of *Djerdap*, the "Iron Gate," the Danube flows through wide-open plains of Romania and Moldavia. From there to the northeast there are no mountains to impede progress through the Ukraine and Russia until the Ural Mountains—an approximate distance, as the crow flies, of a good two thousand miles. The Danube's tributaries are also the natural roads to the Middle East. The River Morava comes straight from the south and if one follows its course up-streams past the watershed, the river Vardar leads to the Aegean Sea. Bear to the east and you will end up at Istanbul, the door to the Middle East.

These river roads invited traders, soldiers and adventurers. One of the first travelers may have been Jason. According to one version Jason, in search of the Golden Fleece, boarded the "Argo" in Greece, turned north up the Adriatic Sea, and got shipwrecked at the Istrian Peninsula, where he came upon the daughter of the King of Colchis, Medea. She joined him in the search for the Golden Fleece. From Istria they followed the river Lim to the bottom of mountains, passed over them and came upon the territory of present-time Slovenia. There they found the Sava River, which flows straight east. The argonauts followed the Sava to the Danube and from there navigated the majestic Danube all the way to the Black Sea. Having reached the Black Sea, they were well on the way back to Greece.

Various forays along these well-traveled roads between the East and West kept repeating themselves with great regularity. History is full of stories about hordes of people in a hurry to get somewhere, stopping in the Balkans and in the Panonian Plains just long enough to loot, burn and rape. From the east came Ghengis Khan, Attilla the

Hun, the Vandals, the Celts, the Ottomans; and from the west, the Romans, the Crusaders, the Austrian Empire, Napoleon and Hitler. Each of these incursions was a relatively short episode in the never-ending confrontation between the east and the west.

In the sixth century the southern Slavic tribes were overcome by the same unexplainable *wanderlust* that, between the fifth and fourteenth centuries, moved large tribes, sometimes hundreds of thousand people strong, to look for greener pastures. The Slavs took off from the area around the Dnjepr River in the Russo-Ukrainian plains and after a long trek to the west, settled in the plains around the Sava, Drava, and Danube rivers and their tributaries. Eventually, they climbed over the Dinara mountain complex to the Adriatic seaside and became solidly rooted in an area, which in the twentieth Century became Yugoslavia.

Unfortunately, the South Slavs chose to settle in a territory rife with religious conflicts. After the decline of the Roman Empire, Christianity evolved around two independent and bitterly competing centers: Rome on the west and the Byzantium Empire (Constantinople) in the east. From the west, the Roman-Catholic influence took hold among Slavs in Dalmatia, Croatia, and Slovenia. The territories to the southeast of the Roman Catholic sphere of influence (Montenegro, Macedonia and Serbia) accepted the authority of the Byzantium. In the seventh century two residents of the Byzantine Empire, the brothers Cyril and Methodius earned sainthood for spreading Christianity among the Slavs to the north-east of Constaninople.

They started from scratch. Cyril invented a new alphabet and the brothers spread literacy, and proselytized the new religion. Organizationally, the Orthodox (Eastern rite) Christian church offered a number of advantages. The elaborate mesmerizing liturgy was in the once common, but now obsolete, old Slavic language. Whereas their Catholic brethren to the West chanted and prayed in Latin, which they could not comprehend, the Serbs, Bulgarians and Russians had the privilege of half-understanding the content of the liturgy. There was a purpose to this rite in the local tongue and to the new alphabet. The suspicious eastern Slavs got themselves a strictly National Church and the weird alphabet minimized communications with the outside world. Various regimes came and went, but the Orthodox

Church remained. To this day the church is the primary keeper of local history and a fierce defender of nationhood. When the Germans attacked the USSR, differences were put aside and the presumably agnostic commissars looked the other way, while the Orthodox priests ceremoniously blessed the weapons. Nowadays the Serbian Orthodox Church is on the forefront of the conflict with Croats, Bosnians and the Kosovars.

The most recent major intrusion from the east, by the Ottoman Empire, lasted from the fourteenth to the nineteenth century. At the crest of its power, in the sixteenth century, the Ottoman Empire reached up north to Budapest and Vienna. Eventually, the overstretched Empire started to recede. Prince Eugene of Savoy, an unemployed military officer and a minor French nobleman, led the Austrian troops in the "final" battle for Belgrade in 1717. The battle in 1717 was only one of many sieges that befell Belgrade because of its unfortunate strategic importance. Located at the confluence of the Sava and Danube rivers, Belgrade stood in the way of just about anyone wishing to move to and from Central Europe. Those pushing south or north through the Pannonian plains along the Danube as well as those following the Sava in the east-west direction eventually had to conquer Belgrade.

When the dust settled, Prince Eugene defeated the Turks, occupied Belgrade and "liberated" the lands of present-day Croatia as well as all of northern Serbia.

Though the Ottoman Empire eventually collapsed, the Turks left behind a new element to the South Slav equation—the Moslem religion. In Serbia and Montenegro, the Turks did not bother to convert the Orthodox Christians to Islam. In fact, the Ottoman Empire cleverly ruled the occupied territories through preexisting local institutions. Churches and the local nobility were entrusted with collection of the taxes and as long as the correct dues came on time, the authorities in Istanbul did not care what else went on. However, in Bosnia the situation was quite different. In the tenth century, long before the Turkish invasion, most Bosnians joined the Bogomil (Cathari) Christian sect. This unusual sect viewed the world as a conflict between the spiritual and the material. The devil created all material things,

including the use of wine. Since the evil beverage could not be used for the Holy Communion, the Bogumils separated themselves from mainstream Christians. More importantly, the Bogumils also viewed all forms of arms as devil's work. This theoretically laudable medieval commitment to nonviolence had its practical down side. When the Turks came, the religion did not permit the Bogumils to take up arms. In due course, they were assimilated and converted to Islam. So much for pacifism!

Eventually the Southern Slavs became what they are now-a group of people of the same ethnic stock speaking nearly the same language but sharply divided by three religions. There is much more to religious division than praying in a different way to the same God. Hand in hand with religion comes the judgment between right and wrong and the intolerance which the practitioners of a "right" religion show towards other worshippers. By religion, culturally and politically the Serbs are oriented to the east and south, whereas the Slovenes and Croats consider themselves western Europeans. The Bosnians maintain a loose cultural affinity to the Middle East, but politically and economically, they are Europe-oriented. The Bosnians had no interest in joining the Serbo-Croat fray but their crazy and violent brethren would not let them alone.

That would have been bad enough, but throughout their history the Serbs, Croatians and Bosnians had very little chance to govern themselves. As they strove to leave their roots in the fertile valleys around the Danube and its tributaries, other powers constantly subjugated the Slavs. Only in the Midle Ages did the Serbs succeed in establishing a kingdom, but after a few royal generations everything was lost to Turkey. Croats had similar luck. Their kingdom fell to the Hungarian conqueror. Even the Bosnians had established a short-lived kingdom.

These old Kingdoms never amounted to more than a feudal folly. However, the memories of past glories did not fade and these medieval states became rallying points for generations of fervent Nationalists who, calling on the past, continued to plot strategies for future independence. By the end of the nineteenth century national theaters, academies of arts and sciences, printing houses and news-

papers in the national language became commonplace in Sarajevo, Belgrade and Zagreb. Soon the battle for language, fueled by the strong nationalistic content of arts and letters, became openly political. And where art and politics meet, politics takes over, usually with disastrous consequences!

The Serbs got the earliest chance of independence. From 1912 to 1913, they joined Bulgarians, Montenegrins and Greeks in the Balkan Wars. After they solidly beat the Turks, the winning combatants divided the liberated lands. Serbia had won sufficient territory to proclaim a new kingdom.

The nascent little kingdom did not sit well with the Austro-Hungarian Empire. As far as they were concerned, what the Ottoman Empire had lost should have become Austrian. However, Vienna failed to assert control over the Kingdom of Serbia and instead of going east, the Empire spread straight south to Bosnia. In 1914 the heir to the Austrian throne traveled to Sarajevo for an official visit to the newly annexed territory of Bosnia. A small group of Serb conspirators took note of the visit and assassinated Prince Franz Ferdinand and his wife. The sad affair gave Austria a pretext to settle the score with Serbia. Predictably, the conflict boiled over into a larger war and Serbia joined the anti-Austro-German Alliance. After the dust of the First World War settled, the Austro-German Alliance lost and, together with its Allies, the small Serbian kingdom won the war.

The intellectual leaders always appreciated the commonality among the European Slavs. In the nineteenth century, the strongly nationalistic catholic bishop Strossmaier, founded the Academy of Sciences in the Croatian capital of Zagreb and, in a tribute to the dream that the South Slavs might one day live together, named it the Yugoslav Academy of Science. (*Yug* means south in Slavic languages). In 1848 the intellectuals convened the first Pan-Slavic Congress in Prague. One of the major agenda topics was the feasibility of creating Yugoslavia as a common state for the South Slavs. Unfortunately, while paying lip service to unity, these same intellectuals continued to lead strongly chauvinistic local movements.

When after the First World War the Allies began to carve up the defeated Austro—Hungarian Empire, the triumphant Kingdom of

Serbia resurrected the old idea of a State of South Slavs. During the meeting in Rapallo, the invited Croat, Slovene, and Bosnian leaders were not enthusiastic about the idea of a new state but they had a lesser standing than the victorious Serbs. In due course, the Allies mandated the formation of a state called "Kingdom of Serbs, Croats and Slovenians," with the Serbian king at the helm. The king proceeded to consolidate his power in no uncertain terms. He soon renamed the new entity into the Kingdom of Yugoslavia, with Belgrade as its capital. The king's regime imposed a new constitution, which gave him and the Serb political leaders near dictatorial powers. The Serbian repression against Croat Nationalists was quite brutal. In 1928, during the plenary session of the Yugoslav parliament, three Croat deputies were shot to death. As far as the Croats were concerned, nothing had really changed. They had just acquired a new ruler and the state of Yugoslavia was equally as bad as Austria and Hungary. There is no right or wrong in these matters. Perceptions count. The hatred between the Serbs and Croats became palpable. Not having outside enemies at hand, the Slavs turned against one another. In due course, in 1934, the Croat Nationalists killed the king of Yugoslavia during his visit to France.

There is such a thing as collective inheritance-not in the strict Jungian sense, but in the fact that previous generations have a way of passing on their dreams and their unsettled scores. Old yearnings work their way into the daily reality of the new generation. What might have been a specific conflict, a reasonable grievance for the father, becomes an ill defined, but acutely felt, intolerance in the son. In his irrational hatred of Serbians, a Croat (and vice versa) is mostly unaware of the historical background. And yet what went on after the German occupation in 1941 was just a replay of the old history of the Balkans. Just another facet of a never-ending struggle between the East, Middle East and the West! Busy blaming and killing each other, firmly believing they were right, guided by a sense of deep personal stakes, and quoting specific instances of injustice to their

own group, the South Slavs faithfully carried out somebody else's bidding.[1]

When the Second World War broke out the inhabitants of Yugoslavia were ready for a fratricidal internal conflict. The Germans had strategic reasons to occupy Yugoslavia. The Italians were about to lose their battle against the Greeks and the German army could not invade Russia before it secured its flank against a possible invasion of Allied troops from Africa. But the Croats felt so aggrieved by the Serb—dominated Kingdom of Yugoslavia, that they viewed the invading foreigners as liberators from the Serbian yoke. In 1941, having forgotten that only a half-century ago Croatia sought to free itself from the Austrian joke and, not realizing what would befall them, the citizens of Zagreb lined the streets to shower incoming German soldiers with flowers.

The Germans were brutal but not stupid. They had a clearly defined policy for the newly occupied territory of Yugoslavia. Germany needed troops for the evolving "Eastern Front" in Russia and its military planners hated the thought of maintaining thousands of soldiers to keep order in former Yugoslavia. Fully aware of nationalistic divisions among Southern Slavs, the Germans organized their occupation to reflect the emotional fracture-lines of former Yugo-

---

1 The recent fratricidal disintegration of former Yugoslavia is just another case in point. Calling on old injustices, but never openly stating what was on his mind, Slobodan Miloshevich fought for expansion of the Serb sphere of influence. One would not expect this to happen in the twentieth century, but it is true that Miloshevich assumed his status as national leader when he gave a rousing speech to commemorate the battle of Kosovo Polje. Evoking the fact that six hundred years ago the Turks defeated the Serbs in the Field of Kosovo, Miloshevich promised to reestablish Serbian "historical rights." To an outsider the speech in Kosovo Polje sounded feeble minded. One should celebrate victories and not defeats. Nevertheless, Miloshevich's call on the emotions buried in the collective national memory resonated very well with the majority of Serbs. To avenge the heroic deaths of his ancestors, many a twentieth -century Serb was ready to put his life on the line. All for the sake of old glory! It would take a better historian than me to explain how such a nonsense becomes a deadly force. And who were the Serbs' strongest supporters in the most recent bloodbath on the Balkans? The offshoots of the old Byzantium; the Orthodox Churches of Greece and Russia!

slavia. They relegated Slovenia together with the Dalmatian Coast to Italy, and installed nationalistic puppet governments in Serbia and Croatia. The Germans faithfully executed the *divide et impera et tu Austria nube* "divide and rule and you, Austria, flourish," slogan of the old Austro-Hungarian kingdom. By keeping the Slavs at each other's throats, they hoped to maintain only a skeleton occupation force in former Yugoslavia.

In Croatia the Germans installed to power a group of rabid Nationalists who the Kingdom of Yugoslavia had earlier exiled to Italy. These Croat Nationalists, the *Ustashe*, loosely translated into 'those that rebelled," organized the Independent State of Croatia. The new regime turned out to be far more brutal than anything the SS troops or the infamous Gestapo could have imagined. The Germans did everything methodically and in cold blood. The Ustashe were passionate in their borderless hatred. After their elite troops took over military responsibilities from the Germans, the Ustashe proceeded to secure "internal order." The Internal Affairs Department of the Independent State of Croatia assembled a murderous police force and overhauled the legal system. They appointed new judges to every existing court but gave them very narrow jurisdictions. For dealing with "matters of state," and that included everything from evading the draft to suspicion of political activities, the Ustashe established a special court marshals called the "Prijeki Sud." (*Sud* is a court and the word *prijek* means 'short, brief, hasty or sudden.') Short indeed! The chance of being acquitted, or even sentenced to jail by a Prijeki Sud was near zero. The procedure lasted less than an hour and the verdict was invariably a death sentence. Firing squads carried out the execution the very next morning. A few lawyers who dared to represent the defendants mysteriously disappeared, never to be seen again. But the Martial Court was not the worst that could befall an individual. If the Ustashe thought that somebody harbored useful information, they took things into their own hands. They'd torture the accused and if the victim survived torture, regardless of whether he had provided information or not, they'd execute him without judicial formalities.

And then there were concentration camps, those horrible places where people faced extinction, not for an individual crime, but be-

cause they belonged to an undesirable group! The Ustashe entrusted these camps to totally dehumanized, brutal psychopaths. Any one of these sadists could in the course of a working day murder over twenty persons. They could have done even more but, to save ammunition, they preferred to use knives or sledgehammers.

The Independent State of Croatia also had its army; a group of benign and disinterested conscripts called the *Domobrani* (translated: "home protectors"). These conscripts had no other interest but to survive and return to their farms. The well armed but inert Domobrani eventually became a huge liability to the Independent State of Croatia.

Having transferred the local policing responsibilities to the Ustashe, the Germans had hoped to move their troops from Croatia to the Eastern Front against the USSR. However, as the Germans soon learned, nothing was simple in former Yugoslavia and the plan did not work out. The alliance of Germans, Ustashe and Domobrani met with growing guerilla resistance in Croatia. The resistance came from two different sources: the Chetniks and the Partizans."

In Croat provinces with a large Serb population, particularly in the province of Lika, the oppressed Serbs had the option of joining paramilitary troops loyal to the King of Yugoslavia, the Chetniks. Initially, the Chetniks took up arms to avenge the loss of the country to Germans but, lead by officers of the defeated Yugoslav army, they also fought for Serbian super nationalism, the Orthodox Church, and the Monarchy. As the war progressed, the Chetniks shifted from fighting the Germans to doing battle with the Communist Partizans. The Chetniks rightly perceived the Communists are antimonarchists enemies of the old regime. By the end of the war the Chetniks dropped any anti-fascist pretense and openly fought alongside the Germans and Italians. Furthermore, in Croatia they were not only against Ustashe but also pretty much against all Croats. And in Bosnia the Moslems became the Chetniks favorite target. The Chetniks were every bit as brutal as the Ustashe. Burning, looting, raping, and cutting peoples' throats, was a Chetnik's signature.

As Chetnik activities waned, the Germans and the Ustashe faced an ever-increasing threat from a new group of players in Yugoslav

intrigues: the Partizans. The Nazis had great difficulties in handling the Partizan's good organization and their well-defined ideology. The Communist party had been outlawed in the Yugoslavia but its members worked in secret cells. The Yugoslav police constantly battled those cells and the Communists were unable to spread their ideology. Whereas the average Yugoslav citizen had no idea that they even existed, the small band of Yugoslav Communists systematically prepared themselves for a confrontation with the Germans. When the Yugoslav army disintegrated under the German onslaught, the Communist turned their illegal cells into an infrastructure for collection of arms from fleeing soldiers and from unguarded storehouses. Soon the Communists had enough military equipment to assemble a few "Partizan" fighting units. By taking on the Germans, the Yugoslav Communists provided support for the Soviet Union but at the war's end they hoped to acquire political legitimacy and power.

To quickly emerge from deep secrecy and establish themselves in the public eye, the Yugoslav Communists successfully played the Pan-Slavic card. A Serb or a Croat cannot speak to a Russian, Czech or Pole but the languages are close enough for a Slav to feel a kinship with other Slavs. Czarist Russia cleverly parlayed this affinity among Slavs into a Pan Slavic political movement. When the Communist teachings of Marx and Engels, both Germans, took root in Russia, Stalin used the Pan-Slavic sentiment to foster communism in all Slavic countries. The Serbian Communists called on the natural affinity of the Serbs and Montenegrins towards Russia to promote communism in their region. However, the Yugoslav Communist were less successful in extend their base to Croatia and Slovenia. Hoping to widen its appeal, before the Second World War the Yugoslav Communist Party chose a Croat, Josip Broz Tito, as its leader. Tito understood both the local nationalistic feelings and the Slavic historical hatred against foreign invaders. His Partizans welcomed all prospective fighters, irrespective of ethnicity or religion. This strategy of fostering a wide-based antifascist coalition worked well. By taking a supra-nationalist stance the Communists continued to operate within the framework of Yugoslavia, while blaming the king and capitalism for previous Yugoslav problems. Tito promised that un-

der his leadership, Yugoslavia would become a socialist federation of states, of Slovenia, Serbia, Croatia, Bosnia, Macedonia and Montenegro. The Communist card played very well. A year after the invasion the Partizans evolved into a fighting force, which the Germans had to reckon with. By 1943, having well distanced themselves from the old regime, the Communists openly took on the mantle of the Yugoslav state. They organized a convention in the Bosnian town of Jajce, wrote a new federal Constitution and officially reconstituted the Partizans into the "Peoples Liberation army of Yugoslavia." By the war's end, Tito's army tied up to ten German divisions in a constant war of attrition. In Croatia Tito had a clever policy of differentiating between the Ustashe and their official army, the Domobrani. Anytime they met the Partizans, loath to fight, the Domobrani would turn their heads the other way. Tito eventually turned the Domobrans into semi-allies. The Partizans had strict orders to treat the surrendering Domobrans with respect and not to try recruiting them into the Partizan movement. Born in a Croat village, Tito knew that the Domobrans would not fight for anybody. When a Domobran surrendered, he was disarmed, stripped of his uniform, given a blanket and sent home in underwear. Not having anything to lose, the Domobrans repeatedly surrendered and eventually became an important source of weapons to the Partizans. Needles to say, if the Ustashe were caught, the Partizans did not show them any mercy. As the Ustashe's cruelty became more evident, the number of people willing to join them decreased. Remaining a small elite force, the Ustashe badly needed the cooperation of Domobrans for larger military actions. But, towards the end of the war, not willing to fight and not afraid of surrendering, the Domobrans became so undependable, that the Ustashe spent more time supervising them than fighting the enemy.

Tito's platform proved eminently effective. The new Yugoslav army grew by leaps and bounds and by the war's end, the Communists were poised to take over the country. But in early 1945 Tito also had

the luck to obtain timely information about the extraordinary meeting of Allied leaders in the Crimean resort of Yalta. At the conference in Yalta, Churchill, Stalin and Roosevelt had defined the shape of postwar Europe. Nobody knows who told Tito of the top-secret meeting in Yalta, but the information passed on to him was accurate. Having reached an agreement that postwar Eastern Europe would be the Soviet "zone of interest," and that Greece, the cradle of modern democracy, would remain under the influence of the West, the negotiators could not quite agree what to do with Yugoslavia. Whether by design or because everybody was too tired to negotiate further, it was decided that the Soviets and the West would have an equal influence in Yugoslavia. Once again Yugoslavia proved to be what it always was: the crossroads of the East and the West and a territory in which neither East nor the West could establish a durable supremacy.

There is a difference between a finding and a discovery. When the Scottish bacteriologist Alexander Fleming (later, Sir Alexander) noted that a yeast infection inhibited the growth of a bacterial culture that was a simple finding. But by understanding the potential of that finding, Fleming turned the initial observation into the discovery of modern day's antibiotics. Similarly, Tito understood the wider potential of the meaning of the single bit of information from Yalta, and translated it into a strategic discovery.

Stalin thought that by ceding some influence in Yugoslavia to the West, he had de facto won a diplomatic victory in Yalta. Tito was an old-time Communist and Stalin expected him to tow the Soviet party line. But Tito had other ideas. He saw in the Yalta conference a historic opportunity for a true independence of the South Slavs. Whereas the world had been formally divided into Eastern and Western blocks, Yugoslavia had been left in limbo. And Tito decided to stay in that middle ground between two giant camps. Under his leadership, the new Yugoslavia would not be neutral but "not aligned." That apparent semantic finesse of differentiating "non-aligned" from "neutral" actually had a substantive political meaning. He would neither accept the western economic model of capitalism, nor would he be a Soviet sycophant. But he would not stay neutral, Tito was

conceited enough to appoint himself the censor of both systems. Politically he would seek to unite the underdeveloped and developing nations into a nonaligned "third block."

Tito's new attitude towards the Soviets grew out of bitter personal experience. Stalin leeched on to Lenin's egocentric idea that the whole world owes a debt of gratitude to the Russian Communist party for establishing the first Communist country in the world. In 1919 Lenin founded the "Comintern" to wrestle away the international socialist movement from the "bourgeois" social democrats. When Stalin brutally eliminated all competitors and took over Lenin's business, he proceeded to run the Comintern in his unique paranoiac, iron-handed way. In Stalin's mind, every Communist in the world had the primary and sacred responsibility to support the Soviet Union. Just as Soviet Communists did, the Comintern accepted the doctrine of "democratic centralism." Technically the doctrine meant that once a decision had been made through a democratic debate, every Party member had to implement it. In practice all semblance of democratic discussion disappeared and the principle of "centralism" was transformed into utter, mindless, obedience of every Communist to decisions from above. And just as in the Soviet Union, Stalin ruled the Comintern by terror. Heads started to roll in the Comintern with the same regularity and with the same capricious lack of reason as in the Soviet Union. Many a Yugoslav Communist was invited for consultation to the Soviet Union never to be heard of again. Tito wanted none of that! But his ambitions to become the leader of nonaligned nations called for more than just a proclamation of independence from the Soviet and the Western blocks. He had to set Yugoslavia on a different political and economic course from both blocks. And that was not a small order!

The general public saw the first flash of Tito's independence when he succeeded in convincing the Soviets not to occupy Yugoslavia. He insisted that the Yugoslavs should alone rid themselves of the Germans. Tito argued that if the Soviet army invaded Yugoslavia, the British and American forces would implement the Yalta agreement and invade from the west. But Tito understood that on their way to Budapest, Vienna and Prague, the Soviets would have to use old historical routes along the course of Danube. Eventually the

Soviet army agreed to pass through Serbia but never to permanently post military units in Yugoslavia.

The History will judge some of Tito's political designs as failures, partial failures or successes. But his first maneuver in the gambit of separation from Stalin—the successful negotiations to keep the Soviet army out of Yugoslavia—was a brilliant move of historic proportion. As a result, nobody in Bosnia, Montenegro, Croatia and Slovenia has ever seen a Soviet soldier. And many a Serb, having encountered his idols in their unpleasant flesh, had second thoughts about Slavic unity and about the Soviet Mother of Socialism. Just by passing through, the Soviet soldiers became hugely unpopular. They were neither harbingers of a new culture nor the paragons of socialist propriety. The Russians were as rough and nasty as any other occupying force.

Soon Tito started to implement his solution to the nationalistic issue of former Yugoslavia. The Constitution of the new "Federal People's Republic of Yugoslavia" mandated that Yugoslavia would be a federation of six republics: Bosnia, Croatia, Macedonia, Montenegro, Serbia and Slovenia. Each republic had its parliament and a Government. Having in the meantime legally or illegally executed or arrested the worst local Fascists and Nationalists, Tito declared a general amnesty. Next the Communist proclaimed the leading principle of the new Yugoslavia would be "brotherhood and unity." After they had been at each other's throats, the Serbs and Croats, the Catholics, Orthodox and Moslems, had better start living in harmonious bliss! This was patently unfeasible; people could not overnight forget the differences that had lead them to a bloody conflict. By officially proclaiming the new era of South Slavic brotherly love, the Communists forbade all expressions of nationalism. They figured that giving each nationality its statehood would eventually heal the wounds. And it might have worked had they really meant what they said. But they did not! Tito was first and foremost an old-school Communist. He permitted things to change on the fringes but the new Yugoslavia would operate under a well-centralized one-party political system. Tito requested of the Communist leadership in the new "independent" republics to work first and foremost on behalf of Yugoslav national unity. It was a farce, the local leaders could not

work on local issue nor could they in the new era of brotherhood and unity talk about the political or economic interests of their Republics. When a few Croat Communists inquired what Belgrade did with the substantial money generated by Croat industry and tourism, they were branded sectarian Nationalists and instantly removed from leadership positions.

In many ways, Tito had no choice but to centralize. The country had been ravaged in the war and he needed to build a modern infrastructure for the entire country. He might have hoped to eventually give more independence to various nations of Yugoslavia. But he should have not pretended that establishing the pro-forma Republics was a solution to the religious and nationalistic conflicts within Yugoslavia. Nobody was appeased. On the contrary, by prematurely forming the republics, Tito planted the seeds of future disintegration of Yugoslavia. Nothing is worse than showing something to somebody and then not letting him have it. Particularly when the "somebody" is a politician and the "something" is independent power. After Tito's death, in each republic there was a political elite ready to play the national independence card. It is not by chance that when Slovenia, Croatia and Macedonia seceded from Yugoslavia, local Communists became presidents of these new states. And, never forgetting that Tito was a Croat, resenting his support for Bosnian and Macedonian statehoods, and furious at Tito's "treachery" of giving a formal autonomy to Kosovo, the Serb Communists began their fight for a Serb-dominated centralized Yugoslavia!

Realizing that the one-party system in his Socialist People's Republic of Yugoslavia looked and smelled like the Soviet Union, Tito felt a need to distance himself from Stalin's communism. A group of intellectuals around Tito got busy defining the political base for the new Yugoslav variety of communism and providing a new economic model for the nonaligned nations. The new Yugoslav-type socialism would be rooted in the works of young Karl Marx. Apparently the father of communism was more thoughtful and flexible at the outset than later, when he got embroiled in the revolutionary anti capitalist struggle. Young Marx preached revolution but gave some thought to the conflict between the Communist-lead "dictatorship of the proletariat" and the need for a wider-based participatory democ-

racy. The young Marx foresaw an ever-increasing participation of workers in the affairs of their enterprises, which in turn, would slowly provide a balance to the political leadership. Eventually in this utopian mode, the need for a political state would disappear. Marx called it the "withering of the state." How a revolutionary who saw the whole world as a conflict of opposite forces and viewed all changes as "quantum leaps" came to propose such a meek evolutionary theory, is beyond me.

Anyhow, the cornerstone of the new political regime in Yugoslavia was the concept of "workers' self-government." Each working unit, be it an enterprise, a factory, hospital, restaurant or a graveyard had to elect a "worker's council." Whereas the director and his administration would run the daily affairs of the enterprise, these councils would be responsible for the overall success of the enterprise. But, of course, the party would appoint the director and the leadership of the factory!

Knowing that nobody in the foreseeable future would challenge the Party dominance, and deeply satisfied that they had planted the seeds of future democracy, the Yugoslav Communist set out to develop a new socialist economic model. Whereas the Yugoslav State invested the initial capital, the success of an enterprise depended entirely on its performance in the open market. And, just as in a capitalist society, an entity could succeed or fail. This was hugely different from the Soviet model. In the Soviet Union the planning was a way of setting a network of government enterprises based on what the planners thought was appropriate. If the five years plan called for tractors and somebody forgot to produce electric heaters, you'd be cold for the next five years.[2] Because the government considered them important, factories couldn't fail. And because the Soviet was a "fair society," market forces could not determine the prices. They were planned and supervised centrally.

Having set their tripartite agenda—non-alliance with blocks, workers self-government and the state-owned-market-ruled econ-

2 That is why Soviet soldiers in Europe stole every wristwatch in sight. There were none in the Soviet Union. The same for cameras!

omy, Yugoslav Communists were ready to enjoy supervising their sociopolitical experiment. But it was not as simple as that. Stalin was mad as hell!

Sore that he hadn't occupied the country and thereby had lost the chance to physically control the events, Stalin decided to put "moral pressure" on the upstarts in Yugoslavia. During the Second World War, to endear himself to western allies, Stalin liquidated the Comintern. One of his first moves was to reestablish his leadership of the international Communist movement by forming a new, on-the-face-of-it, more benign international forum called the "Cominform." An informative forum for exchange of ideas with Uncle Joe? Sure!

The pressure from the Cominform was enormous and eventually Tito faced an ultimatum to change his ways or else! Knowing that the Soviet Union was not about to start a third World War, Tito called Stalin's bluff and opted for "else." But not before he settled internal affairs in Yugoslavia. Tito used the official letter from the Cominform as a tool to clean his house. The letter was read at special meetings of every Party cell. The cells engaged in a "democratic" discussion of issues raised by the Cominform. At the end of the meeting every member had to declare whether he/she supported Tito's or the Cominform's positions. This would help the Party in deciding which way it ought to proceed. And help it did! Tito won a large majority and those supporting the Soviet position were either ejected from the Party or arrested and sent to a special concentration camp on the island of Goli Otok. That, probably, was the only way to handle the Soviet pressure but it was not funny. Some people died in the concentration camp, others repented and were released after a few months. Those still holding onto their beliefs faced formal indictment for "activities against the State" in regular courts. The sentences ranged from two to fifteen years of jail.

Having overnight eliminated the opposition, Tito proceeded to build his alternative path to communism. The introduction of a market-oriented economy forced the Party to slowly, and rather reluctantly, release its grip on the populace. In the sixties the regime started to open the borders and permitted economic immigration. This was probably the single most important economic move. Instead of jealously hanging onto their people, and contrary to the

Eastern Block countries, the Yugoslav party learned the beauty of exporting its unemployment to Europe. The steady stream of hard currency sent home by expatriates greatly accelerated the economic recovery.

Whereas the Communists still maintained a one-party political system serious debates about internal policies started to develop within the Communist party. Unfortunately my family was caught by the whirlwind surrounding one of these debates.

And that is about the time when this book ends!

ACT ONE

[MUSIC NO. 01 "ROAD TO HELL"]

*(**COMPANY** and **BAND** assemble at an aboveground gathering place. **HERMES** holds court.)*

HERMES. *(To **COMPANY**.)*
Alright?

COMPANY.
Alright!

HERMES. *(To audience.)*
Alright?

AUDIENCE.
Alright!

HERMES. *(To **BAND**.)*
Alright!
Mmmm...

COMPANY.
Mmmm...

HERMES. *(Like a train.)*
Mm-mmm

COMPANY.
Mm-mmm

HERMES.
Chucka chucka chucka chucka chucka chucka chucka chucka

COMPANY.

Chucka chucka chucka chucka chucka chucka chucka chucka

HERMES.

Once upon a time there was a railroad line

COMPANY.

Mmmm...

HERMES.

Don't ask where, brother, don't ask when

COMPANY.

Mmmm...

HERMES.

It was the road to hell
It was hard times
It was a world of gods...
And men

COMPANY.

Mmm-mmm-mmm

HERMES.

It's an old song

COMPANY.

It's an old song!

HERMES.

It's an old tale from way back when
It's an old song

COMPANY.

It's an old song!

HERMES.

And we're gonna sing it again
Gods and men, alright?

We got some gods in the house tonight!
See on the road to hell there was a railroad line

COMPANY.
Mmmm...

HERMES.
And there was three old women all dressed the same

COMPANY.
Mmmm...

HERMES.
And they was always singing in the back of your mind
Everybody meet the Fates!

(**FATES** *acknowledge audience.)*

COMPANY.
Mmm-mmm-mmm

HERMES.
And on the road to hell there was a railroad line

COMPANY.
Mmmm...

HERMES.
And a lady stepping off a train

COMPANY.
Mmmm...

HERMES.
With a suitcase full of summertime
Persephone, by name!

(**PERSEPHONE** *acknowledges audience.)*

COMPANY.
Mmm-mmm-mmm

HERMES.

And if you ride that train

COMPANY.

Ride that train!

HERMES.

If you ride that train

COMPANY.

You ride that train!

HERMES.

If you ride that train to the end of the line

COMPANY.

Mmmm...

HERMES.

Where the sun don't shine and it's always shady

COMPANY.

Mmmm...

HERMES.

It's there you'll find the king of the mine
Almighty Mister Hades!

(**HADES** *acknowledges audience.)*

COMPANY.

Mmm-mmm-mmm

HERMES.

We got any other gods?
Oh yeah, almost forgot...
On the road to hell there was a railroad station

COMPANY.

Mmmm...

HERMES.

And a man with feathers on his feet

COMPANY.

Mmmm...

HERMES.

Who could help you to your final destination
Mister Hermes, that's me!

(**HERMES** *acknowledges audience.)*

COMPANY.

Mmm-mmm-mmm

HERMES.

See someone's got to tell the tale
Whether or not it turns out well
Maybe it will turn out this time
On the road to hell, on the railroad line
It's a sad song

COMPANY.

It's a sad song!

HERMES.

It's a sad tale; it's a tragedy
It's a sad song

COMPANY.

It's a sad song!

HERMES.

We're gonna sing it anyway
Now not everyone gets to be a god
And don't forget that times are hard
Hard times in the world of men
Lemme introduce you to a few of them
You can tip your hats and your wallets
Brothers and sisters, boys and girls
To the hardest-working Chorus
In the gods' almighty world!

(**WORKERS** *acknowledge audience.)*

HERMES.

And working just as hard for you
Let's see what *this* crew can do!

(**HERMES** *indicates* **BAND.** *Instrumental break.* **COMPANY** *applause.)*

Alright, alright...
Alright!
On the road to hell there was a railroad line
And a poor boy working on a song

ORPHEUS.

La la la la la la...

HERMES.

His mama was a friend of mine
And this boy was a muse's son
On the railroad line on the road to hell
You might say the boy was "touched"

ORPHEUS.

La la la la la la...

HERMES.

Cos he was touched by the gods themselves
Give it up for Orpheus!

(**ORPHEUS** *misses the cue.)*

Orpheus!

(**ORPHEUS** *acknowledges audience.)*

There was one more soul on this road
Girl, come on in from the cold!
On the railroad line on the road to hell

COMPANY.
Mmmm...

HERMES.
There was a young girl looking for something to eat

COMPANY.
Mmmm...

HERMES.
And brother, thus begins the tale
Of Orpheus...and Eurydice!

*(**ORPHEUS** and **EURYDICE** see each other for the first time.)*

COMPANY.
Mmm-mmm-mmm

HERMES.
It's a love song

COMPANY.
It's a love song!

HERMES.
It's a tale of a love from long ago
It's a sad song

COMPANY.
It's a sad song!

HERMES.
But we're gonna sing it even so
It's an old song

COMPANY.
It's an old song!

HERMES.
It's an old tale from way back when

HERMES.

And we're gonna sing
We're gonna sing
We're gonna sing it again!

[MUSIC NO. 02 "ANY WAY THE WIND BLOWS"]

FATES.

Oooooh
Oooooh
Oooooh
Oooooh

HERMES.

Eurydice was a hungry young girl
A runaway from everywhere she'd ever been
She was no stranger to the world
No stranger to the wind

*(**EURYDICE** wears an overcoat and carries a backpack with her few possessions, among them a hurricane candle.)*

EURYDICE. *(To herself and audience.)*

Weather ain't the way it was before
Ain't no spring or fall at all anymore
It's either blazing hot or freezing cold
Any way the wind blows

FATES.

And there ain't a thing that you can do
When the weather takes a turn on you
'Cept for hurry up and hit the road
Any way the wind blows
Wind comes up, ooooh

EURYDICE.

Do you hear that sound?

FATES.
Wind comes up, ooooh

EURYDICE.
Move to another town
Ain't nobody gonna stick around

EURYDICE & FATES.
When the dark clouds roll
Any way the wind blows

FATES.
Oooooh
Oooooh
Oooooh
Oooooh

HERMES.
You met the Fates, remember them?

EURYDICE. *(To* **COMPANY** *and audience.)*
Anybody got a match?

HERMES. *(Offering a match.)*
Always singing in the back of your mind...

EURYDICE. *(To* **HERMES.***)*
Give me that...

HERMES.
Wherever it was this young girl went

*(***EURYDICE** *lights her candle.)*

The Fates were close behind

*(***FATES** *blow it out.)*

EURYDICE.
People turn on you just like the wind
Everybody is a fair-weather friend

EURYDICE.

In the end you're better off alone
Any way the wind blows

(**EURYDICE** *re-lights her candle.)*

FATES.

When your body aches to lay it down
When you're hungry and there ain't enough to go around
Ain't no length to which a girl won't go
Any way the wind blows
Wind comes up, ooooh

EURYDICE.

And sometimes you think

FATES.

Wind comes up, ooooh

EURYDICE.

You would do anything
Just to fill your belly full of food
Find a bed that you could fall into
Where the weather wouldn't follow you
Wherever you go
Any way the wind blows

FATES.

Ooooh
Ooooh
Ooooh
Ooooh

HERMES.

Now Orpheus was the son of a muse
And you know how those muses are
Sometimes they abandon you

And this poor boy, he wore his heart
Out on his sleeve
You might say he was naïve
To the ways of the world
But he had a way with words
And a rhythm and a rhyme
And he sang just like a bird up on a line
And it ain't because I'm kind
But his mama was a friend of mine
And I liked to hear him sing
And his way of seeing things
So I took him underneath my wing
And that is where he stayed
Until one day...

[MUSIC NO. 03 "COME HOME WITH ME"]

*(***ORPHEUS** *approaches* **EURYDICE. HERMES** *intercepts him.)*

You wanna talk to her?

ORPHEUS.

Yes

HERMES.

Go on...
Orpheus –

ORPHEUS.

Yes?

HERMES.

Don't come on too strong

ORPHEUS & CHORUS.

Come home with me!

EURYDICE.
Who are you?

ORPHEUS & CHORUS.
The man who's gonna marry you

ORPHEUS.
I'm Orpheus!

EURYDICE. *(To* **HERMES.***)*
Is he always like this?

HERMES.
Yes

EURYDICE. *(To* **ORPHEUS.***)*
I'm Eurydice

ORPHEUS & CHORUS.
Your name is like a melody...

EURYDICE.
A singer? Is that what you are?

ORPHEUS.
I also play the lyre

EURYDICE.
Ooh, a liar, and a player too!
I've met too many men like you

ORPHEUS.
Oh no – I'm not like that

HERMES.
He's not like any man you've met
Tell her what you're working on!

ORPHEUS & CHORUS.
I'm working on a song
It isn't finished yet

But when it's done, and when I sing it
Spring will come again

EURYDICE.
Come again?

ORPHEUS.
Spring will come

EURYDICE.
When?
I haven't seen a spring or fall
Since – I can't recall

ORPHEUS.
That's what I'm working on

ORPHEUS & CHORUS.
A song to fix what's wrong
Take what's broken, make it whole
A song so beautiful
It brings the world back into tune
Back into time
And all the flowers will bloom

ORPHEUS.
When you become my wife

EURYDICE. *(To* **HERMES.***)*
Oh, he's crazy!
Why would I become his wife?

HERMES.
Maybe...
Because he'll make you feel alive

EURYDICE.
Alive...that's worth a lot
(To **ORPHEUS.***)* What else you got?

[MUSIC NO. 04 "WEDDING SONG"]

EURYDICE.

Lover, tell me if you can
Who's gonna buy the wedding bands?
Times being what they are
Hard and getting harder all the time

ORPHEUS.

Lover, when I sing my song
All the rivers'll sing along
And they're gonna break their banks for us
And with their gold be generous
All a-flashing in the pan
All to fashion for your hand
The river's gonna give us the wedding bands

EURYDICE.

Lover, tell me if you're able
Who's gonna lay the wedding table?
Times being what they are
Dark and getting darker all the time

ORPHEUS.

Lover, when I sing my song
All the trees gonna sing along
And they're gonna bend their branches down
To lay their fruit upon the ground
The almond and the apple
And the sugar from the maple
The trees gonna lay the wedding table

EURYDICE.

So when you sing your song
The one you're working on
Spring will come again?

ORPHEUS.
Yes

EURYDICE.
Why don't you sing it then?

ORPHEUS.
It isn't finished

EURYDICE.
Sing it!
You wanna take me home?

ORPHEUS.
Yes

EURYDICE.
Sing the song

ORPHEUS.
La la la la la la la
La la la la la la

COMPANY.
La la la la la la

ORPHEUS.
La la la la la la

ORPHEUS & COMPANY.
La la la la la la la...

(Magic. The melody spontaneously produces a flower, surprising them both. **ORPHEUS** *gives it to* **EURYDICE.***)*

EURYDICE.
How'd you do that?

ORPHEUS.
I don't know
The song's not finished, though

EURYDICE.
Even so, it can do this?

ORPHEUS.
I know

EURYDICE.
You have to finish it!
Lover, tell me when we're wed
Who's gonna make the wedding bed?
Times being what they are
Hard and getting harder all the time

ORPHEUS.
Lover, when I sing my song
All the birds gonna sing along
And they'll come flying from all around
To lay their feathers on the ground
And we'll lie down in eiderdown
A pillow 'neath our heads
The birds gonna make the wedding bed

EURYDICE.
And the trees gonna lay the wedding table

ORPHEUS.
And the river's gonna give us the wedding bands

ORPHEUS & EURYDICE.
Mmmmm...

[MUSIC NO. 05 "EPIC I"]

HERMES. *(To* **ORPHEUS.***)*
Where'd you get that melody?

ORPHEUS.
I don't know – it came to me
As if I'd known it all along

HERMES.
You have
It's an old song
A song of love from long ago
Long time since I heard it, though

ORPHEUS.
You've heard that melody before?

HERMES.
Sure...

ORPHEUS.
Tell me more

HERMES.
Remember that tale I told you once?
About the gods?

ORPHEUS.
Which ones?

HERMES.
Hades and Persephone
Remember how it used to be
Their love that made the world go round?

ORPHEUS.
Yeah, I remember now
But that was long ago

HERMES.
Tell it again, though...

(**ORPHEUS** *accompanies himself.*)

ORPHEUS.
King of shadows, king of shades
Hades was king of the underworld
But he fell in love with a beautiful lady

ORPHEUS.

Who walked up above in her mother's green field
He fell in love with Persephone
Who was gathering flowers in the light of the sun
And he took her home to become his queen
Where the sun never shone on anyone...

(**ORPHEUS** *pauses.*)

HERMES.

Go on...

ORPHEUS.

The lady loved him and the kingdom they shared
But without her above, not one flower would grow
So King Hades agreed that for half of each year
She would stay with him there in the world down below
But the other half she could walk in the sun
And the sun in turn burned twice as bright
Which is where the seasons come from
And with them the cycle
Of the seed and the sickle
The lives of the people
And the birds in their flight...

HERMES.

Singing...

ORPHEUS.

La la la la la la la

HERMES.

Down below and up above

ORPHEUS.

La la la la la la la

HERMES.

In harmony and rhythm

ORPHEUS.
La la la la la la la

HERMES.
The gods sang a song of love

ORPHEUS.
La la la la la la

HERMES.
And the world sang it with them
But that was long ago
Before we were on this road...

[MUSIC NO. 06 "LIVIN' IT UP ON TOP"]

And on the road to hell there was a lot of waiting

COMPANY.
Mmmm...
Waiting...

HERMES.
Everybody waiting on a train

COMPANY.
Mmmm...
Waiting on the lady with the...

HERMES.
Waiting on that train to bring that lady

COMPANY.
Mmmm...
Lady...

HERMES.
With the suitcase back again
She's never early, always late

COMPANY.
Waiting... Waiting...

HERMES.

These days she never stays for long
But good things come to those who wait

COMPANY.

Mmmm...

(**HERMES** *blows a train whistle.* **PERSEPHONE** *arrives aboveground.)*

HERMES.

Here she comes!

PERSEPHONE.

Well it's like he said, I'm an outdoor girl

HERMES.

And you're late again!

PERSEPHONE.

Married to the king of the underworld

HERMES.

She forgot a little thing called "spring"!

PERSEPHONE.

Are you wondering where I been?

WORKERS. *(Variously.)*

Yeah!
Where you been?
I'm wondering

PERSEPHONE.

Been to hell and back again
But like my mama always said:
Brother, when you're down, you're down
And when you're up, you're up
If you ain't six feet underground
You're living it up on top!

Let's not talk about hard times!
Pour the wine!
It's summertime!
And right now we're livin' it

COMPANY.
How are we livin' it?

PERSEPHONE.
Livin' it – livin' it up
Brother right here we're livin' it

COMPANY.
Where are we livin' it?

PERSEPHONE.
Livin' it up on top!
Who makes the summer sun shine bright?
That's right! Persephone!
Who makes the fruit of the vine get ripe?

COMPANY.
Persephone!

PERSEPHONE.
That's me!
Who makes the flowers bloom again
In spite of her man?

COMPANY.
You do!

PERSEPHONE.
Who is doing the best she can?
Persephone, that's who

(To **EURYDICE.***)* Now some may say the weather ain't the way it used to be
But let me tell you something that my mama said to me:
You take what you can get

PERSEPHONE.

And you make the most of it
So right now we're livin' it

COMPANY.

How are we livin' it?

PERSEPHONE.

Livin' it – livin' it up
Brother right here we're livin' it

COMPANY.

Where are we livin' it?

PERSEPHONE.

Livin' it up on top!

HERMES.

It was summertime on the road to hell!

FATES.

Mmmm...

HERMES.

There was a girl who had always run away

FATES.

Mmmm...

HERMES.

You might say that it was in spite of herself

FATES. *(Like "tsk-tsk-tsk.")*

Mmm-mmm-mmm

HERMES.

That this young girl decided to stay
There was a poor boy with a lyre!

PERSEPHONE.

Who says times are hard?

HERMES.

The flowers bloomed, the fruit got ripe
And brother, for a moment there...

PERSEPHONE.

Anybody want a drink?

HERMES.

The world came back to life!

*(**WORKERS** dance. Wine is poured and cups are passed around.)*

PERSEPHONE.

Up on top we ain't got much, but we're

COMPANY.

Livin' it – livin' it up

PERSEPHONE.

Just enough to fill our cups

COMPANY.

Livin' it up on top!

PERSEPHONE.

Brother, pass that bottle around, cos we're

COMPANY.

Livin' it – livin' it up

HERMES. *(Indicates **ORPHEUS.**)*

Let the poet bless this round!

ORPHEUS.

To the patroness of all of this: Persephone!

HERMES.

Hear, hear!

WORKERS. *(Variously.)*

Hear, hear!

ORPHEUS.

Who has finally returned to us
With wine enough to share
Asking nothing in return
'Cept that we should live and learn
To live as brothers in this life
And to trust she will provide

WORKERS.

Alright!

ORPHEUS.

And if no one takes too much
There will always be enough
She will always fill our cups

PERSEPHONE.

I will!

ORPHEUS.

And we will always raise 'em up

(**ORPHEUS** *raises his cup.* **COMPANY** *raises cups and acknowledges audience.)*

To the world we dream about!
And the one we live in now...

(**COMPANY** *drinks.)*

Cos right now we're livin' it

COMPANY.

How are we livin' it?

ORPHEUS.

Livin it' – livin' it up
Brother right here we're livin' it

COMPANY.

Where are we livin' it?

ORPHEUS.

Listen here, I'll tell you where we're livin' it
Up on top!

COMPANY.

Up on top!

ORPHEUS.

Livin' it up and we ain't gonna stop!
Livin' it, livin' it

COMPANY

Livin' it, livin' it

ORPHEUS.

How are we livin' it?

COMPANY.

Where are we livin' it?

ORPHEUS.

Livin' it, livin' it

COMPANY.

Livin' it, livin' it
Livin' it up on top!

[MUSIC NO. 07 "ALL I'VE EVER KNOWN INTRO" / MUSIC NO. 08 "ALL I'VE EVER KNOWN"]

HERMES.

Orpheus was a poor boy
But he had a gift to give
He could make you see how the world could be
In spite of the way that it is
And Eurydice was a young girl
But she'd seen how the world was
When she fell, she fell in spite of herself
In love with Orpheus

EURYDICE.

I was alone so long
I didn't even know that I was lonely
Out in the cold so long
I didn't even know that I was cold
Turn my collar to the wind
This is how it's always been

All I've ever known is how to hold my own
All I've ever known is how to hold my own
But now I wanna hold you, too

You take me in your arms
And suddenly there's sunlight all around me
Everything bright and warm
And shining like it never did before
And for a moment I forget
Just how dark and cold it gets

All I've ever known is how to hold my own
All I've ever known is how to hold my own
But now I wanna hold you

Now I wanna hold you
Hold you close
I don't wanna ever have to let you go
Now I wanna hold you
Hold you tight
I don't wanna go back to the lonely life

ORPHEUS.

I don't know how or why
Or who am I that I should get to hold you
But when I saw you all alone against the sky
It's like I'd known you all along
I knew you before we met

And I don't even know you yet
All I know's you're someone I have always known

ORPHEUS & EURYDICE.
All I know's you're someone I have always known
And I don't even know you
Now I wanna hold you
Hold you close
I don't wanna ever have to let you go

EURYDICE.
Suddenly there's sunlight, bright and warm

ORPHEUS.
Suddenly I'm holding the world in my arms

(**ORPHEUS** *and* **EURYDICE** *make love.)*

EURYDICE.
Say that you'll hold me forever
Say that the wind won't change on us
Say that we'll stay with each other
And it will always be like this

ORPHEUS.
I'm gonna hold you forever
The wind will never change on us
Long as we stay with each other

ORPHEUS & EURYDICE.
Then it will always be like this

[MUSIC NO. 09 "WAY DOWN HADESTOWN"]

(**HERMES** *blows the train whistle.)*

HERMES.
On the road to hell there was a railroad track

COMPANY.
Mmmm...

PERSEPHONE. *(Hungover.)*
Oh, come on!

HERMES.
There was a train coming up from way down below

COMPANY.
Mmmm...

PERSEPHONE.
That was not six months!

FATES. *(To* **PERSEPHONE.***)*
Better go get your suitcase packed
Guess it's time to go...

HERMES.
She's gonna ride that train

COMPANY.
Ride that train!

HERMES.
She's gonna ride that train

COMPANY.
She'll ride that train!

HERMES.
She's gonna ride that train to the end of the line

COMPANY.
Mmmm...

HERMES.
Cos the king of the mine is a-comin' to call

COMPANY.
Mmmm...

HERMES.
Did you ever wonder what it's like?
On the underside

COMPANY.
Way down under

HERMES.
On the yonder side

COMPANY.
Way down yonder

HERMES.
On the other side of his wall?

Follow that dollar for a long way down
Far away from the poorhouse door
You either get to hell or to Hadestown
Ain't no difference anymore
Way down Hadestown
Way down under the ground!

Hound dog howl and the whistle blow
Train come a-rollin' clickety-clack
Everybody tryna get a ticket to go
But those who go, they don't come back
They're going

HERMES & COMPANY.
Way down Hadestown
Way down under the ground

PERSEPHONE.
Winter's nigh and summer's o'er
Hear that high and lonesome sound
Of my husband coming for
To bring me home to Hadestown

COMPANY.
Way down Hadestown
Way down under the ground!

PERSEPHONE.

Down there it's a buncha stiffs!
Brother, I'll be bored to death
Gonna have to import some stuff
Just to entertain myself
Give me morphine in a tin!
Give me a crate of the fruit of the vine
Takes a lot of medicine
To make it through the wintertime

COMPANY.

Way down Hadestown
Way down under the ground!

FATES.

Every little penny in the wishing well
Every little nickel on the drum

WORKERS.

On the drum!

FATES.

All them shiny little heads and tails
Where do you think they come from?

WORKERS.

They come from

COMPANY.

Way down Hadestown
Way down under the ground!

HERMES.

Everybody hungry, everybody tired
Everybody slaves by the sweat of his brow
The wage is nothing and the work is hard
It's a graveyard in Hadestown

COMPANY.
Way down Hadestown
Way down under the ground!

HERMES.
Mister Hades is a mean old boss

PERSEPHONE.
With a silver whistle and a golden scale

COMPANY.
An eye for an eye!

HERMES.
And he weighs the cost

COMPANY.
A lie for a lie!

HERMES.
And your soul for sale!

COMPANY.
Sold!

PERSEPHONE.
To the king on the chromium throne

COMPANY.
Thrown!

PERSEPHONE.
To the bottom of a sing-sing cell

HERMES.
Where the little wheel squeal and the big wheel groan

PERSEPHONE.
And you better forget about your wishing well

COMPANY.
Way down Hadestown
Way down under the ground!

(**HERMES** *blows the train whistle.* **HADES** *arrives aboveground.)*

HERMES.
On the road to hell there was a railroad car

COMPANY.
Mmmm...

HERMES.
And the car door opened and a man stepped out

COMPANY.
Mmmm...

HERMES.
Everybody looked and everybody saw
It was the same man they'd been singin' about

PERSEPHONE.
You're early

HADES.
I missed you

FATES.
Mister Hades is a mighty king
Must be making some mighty big deals
Seems like he owns everything

EURYDICE.
Kinda makes you wonder how it feels...

(**HADES** *eyes* **EURYDICE. ORPHEUS** *steps between them.)*

HERMES.
All aboard!
A one, a two, a one-two-three-four!

COMPANY.
Way down Hadestown

Way down under the ground!
Way down Hadestown
Way down under the ground!
Way down under the ground!
Way down under the...ground!

*(***HADES** *and* **PERSEPHONE** *descend to the underworld.)*

[MUSIC NO. 10 "A GATHERING STORM"]

(Sudden cold. **WORKERS** *leave.)*

FATES.
Ooooh
Ooooh
Ooooh
Ooooh

HERMES.
With Persephone gone, the cold came on

ORPHEUS.
He came too soon
He came for her too soon
It's not supposed to be like this

EURYDICE.
Well, till someone brings the world back into tune
This is how it is

HERMES.
Orpheus had a gift to give

EURYDICE.
Hey – where you going?

HERMES.
Touched by the gods is what he was

ORPHEUS.
I have to finish the song

EURYDICE.
Finish it quick
The wind is changing
There's a storm coming on

FATES.
Wind comes up, ooooh

EURYDICE.
We need food

FATES.
Wind comes up, ooooh

EURYDICE.
We need firewood

HERMES.
Orpheus and Eurydice

EURYDICE.
Did you hear me, Orpheus?

HERMES.
Poor boy working on a song

EURYDICE.
Orpheus!

(**ORPHEUS** *is working on his song and doesn't hear* **EURYDICE.**)

HERMES.
Young girl looking for something to eat

EURYDICE.
Okay
Finish it

HERMES.

Under a gathering storm...

(**EURYDICE** *leaves.*)

[MUSIC NO. 11 "EPIC II"]

(**ORPHEUS** *accompanies himself.*)

ORPHEUS.

King of silver, king of gold
And everything glittering under the ground
Hades is king of oil and coal
And the riches that flow where those rivers are found
But for half of the year, with Persephone gone
His loneliness moves in him, crude and black
He thinks of his wife in the arms of the sun
And jealousy fuels him
And feeds him, and fills him
With doubt that she'll ever come
Dread that she'll never come
Doubt that his lover will ever come back

King of mortar, king of bricks
The River Styx is a river of stones
And Hades lays them high and thick
With a million hands that are not his own
With a million hands he builds a wall
Around all of the riches he digs from the earth
The pickaxe flashes, the hammer falls
And crashing and pounding
His rivers surround him
And drown out the sound
Of the song he once heard
La la la la la la la...

[MUSIC NO. 12 "CHANT"]

(Split scene: **ORPHEUS, EURYDICE, FATES,** *and* **HERMES** *aboveground;* **HADES, PERSEPHONE,** *and* **WORKERS** *in the underworld.)*

WORKERS & FATES.

Oh, keep your head, keep your head low (kkh!)
Oh, you gotta keep your head low (kkh!)
If you wanna keep your head (huh! kkh!)
Oh you gotta keep your head low
Keep your head, keep your head low (kkh!)
Oh, you gotta keep your head low (kkh!)
If you wanna keep your head (huh! kkh!)
Oh, you gotta keep your head

PERSEPHONE.

In the coldest time of year
Why is it so hot down here?
Hotter than a crucible
It ain't right and it ain't natural

HADES.

Lover, you were gone so long
Lover, I was lonesome
So I built a foundry
In the ground beneath your feet
Here I fashioned things of steel
Oil drums and automobiles
And then I kept that furnace fed
With the fossils of the dead
Lover, when you feel that fire
Think of it as my desire
Think of it as my desire for you

ORPHEUS.

La la, la la, la la la la la

La la, la la, la la la la la
Laaaaaaa, la la la la la
Laaaaaaa, la la la la la
La, la, la la la la la la
La la la la la la
La la la la la la

WORKERS & FATES.
Oh, keep your head, keep your head low (kkh!)
Oh, you gotta keep your head low (kkh!)
If you wanna keep your head (huh! kkh!)
Oh you gotta keep your head low
Keep your head, keep your head low (kkh!)
Oh, you gotta keep your head low (kkh!)
If you wanna keep your head

ORPHEUS.
La la la la la la la

EURYDICE. *(To* **HERMES.***)*
Is it finished?

ORPHEUS.
La la la la la la la

HERMES. *(To* **EURYDICE.***)*
Not yet

ORPHEUS.
La la la la la la la

EURYDICE. *(To* **HERMES.***)*
Is he always like this?

ORPHEUS.
La la la la la la

*(***EURYDICE** *is pursued by* **FATES.***)*

EURYDICE. *(To herself and audience.)*
Looking high and looking low
For the food and firewood I know
We need to find and I am
Keeping one eye on the sky and
Trying to trust
That the song he's working on is gonna
Shelter us
From the wind, the wind, the wind

WORKERS & FATES.
Aooh! Kkh!
Aooh! Huh! Kkh!

PERSEPHONE.
In the darkest time of year
Why is it so bright down here?
Brighter than a carnival
It ain't right and it ain't natural

HADES.
Lover, you were gone so long
Lover, I was lonesome
So I laid a power grid
In the ground on which you stood
And wasn't it electrifying?
When I made the neon shine
Silver screen, cathode ray
Brighter than the light of day
Lover, when you see that glare
Think of it as my despair
Think of it as my despair for you

ORPHEUS.
They can't find the tune

HERMES.
Orpheus...

ORPHEUS.
They can't feel the rhythm

HERMES.
Orpheus!

ORPHEUS.
King Hades is deafened
By a river of stone

HERMES.
Poor boy working on a song

ORPHEUS.
And lady Persephone's blinded
By a river of wine
Living in an oblivion

HERMES.
He did not see the storm coming on

FATES.
Ooooh...

ORPHEUS.
His black gold flows
In the world down below
And her dark clouds roll
In the one up above

HERMES.
Look up!

WORKERS.
Keep your head low...

ORPHEUS.
And that is the reason we're on this road

ORPHEUS.

And the seasons are wrong
And the wind is so strong
That's why times are so hard
It's because of the gods
The gods have forgotten the song of their love!

Singing la la la la la la la
La la la la la la la
La la la la la la la
La la la la la la

WORKERS & FATES.

Oh, keep your head, keep your head low (kkh!)
Oh, you gotta keep your head low (kkh!)
If you wanna keep your head (huh! kkh!)
Oh you gotta keep your head low
Keep your head, keep your head low (kkh!)
Oh, you gotta keep your head low (kkh!)
If you wanna keep your head

EURYDICE. *(Again pursued by* **FATES.***)*

Looking low and looking high

FATES.

There is no food left to find
It's hard enough to feed yourself
Let alone somebody else

EURYDICE.

I'm trying to believe
That the song he's working on is gonna
Harbor me
From the wind, the wind, the wind

FATES. *(Surrounding* **EURYDICE.***)*

Ooooh, Ooooh, Ooooh, Ooooh
Ooooh, Ooooh, Ooooh, Ooooh

HERMES.
Eurydice was a hungry young girl

*(**FATES** take **EURYDICE**'s backpack.)*

EURYDICE. *(To **FATES**.)*
Give that back!

HERMES.
She was no stranger to the wind

*(**FATES** take **EURYDICE**'s overcoat.)*

EURYDICE.
It's everything we have!

HERMES.
But she had not seen nothing

EURYDICE.
Orpheus!

HERMES.
Like the mighty storm she got caught in

EURYDICE.
Orpheus!
Shelter us!

HERMES.
Only took a minute

EURYDICE.
Harbor me!

HERMES.
But the wrath of the gods was in it

PERSEPHONE.
Every year it's getting worse
Hadestown, hell on earth!
Did you think I'd be impressed

PERSEPHONE.

With this neon necropolis?
Lover, what have you become?
Coal cars and oil drums
Warehouse walls and factory floors
I don't know you anymore
And in the meantime up above
The harvest dies and people starve
Oceans rise and overflow
It ain't right and it ain't natural

HADES.

Lover, everything I do
I do it for the love of you
If you don't even want my love
I'll give it to someone who does
Someone grateful for her fate
Someone who appreciates
The comforts of a gilded cage
And doesn't try to fly away
The moment Mother Nature calls
Someone who could love these walls
That hold her close and keep her safe
And think of them as my embrace

WORKERS & FATES.

Oh, keep your head, keep your head

ORPHEUS.

Singing la la la la la la la

EURYDICE.

Shelter us!

HADES.

Think of them as my embrace

WORKERS.
Oh, keep your head, keep your head

ORPHEUS.
La la la la la la

EURYDICE.
Harbor me!

(**HADES** *appears aboveground.)*

HADES. *(To* **EURYDICE.***)*
Think of them as my embrace...of you

[MUSIC NO. 13 "HEY, LITTLE SONGBIRD"]

(To **EURYDICE.***)* Hey, little songbird, give me a song
I'm a busy man and I can't stay long
I've got clients to call, I've got orders to fill
I've got walls to build, I've got riots to quell
And they're giving me hell back in Hades

Hey, little songbird, cat got your tongue?
Always a pity for one so pretty and young
When poverty comes to clip your wings
And knock the wind right out of your lungs
Hey, nobody sings on empty

EURYDICE.
Strange is the call of this strange man
I wanna fly down and feed at his hand
I want a nice soft place to land
I want to lie down forever

HADES.
Hey, little songbird, you got something fine
You'd shine like a diamond down in the mine
And the choice is yours, if you're willing to choose

HADES.

Seeing as you've got nothing to lose
And I could use a canary

EURYDICE.

Suddenly nothing is as it was
Where are you now, Orpheus?
Wasn't it gonna be the two of us?
Weren't we birds of a feather?

HADES.

Hey, little songbird, let me guess
He's some kind of poet, and he's penniless
Give him your hand, he'll give you his hand-to-mouth
He'll write you a poem when the power is out
Hey, why not fly south for the winter?

Hey, little songbird, look all around you
See how the vipers and vultures surround you
And they'll take you down, they'll pick you clean
If you stick around such a desperate scene
See, people get mean when the chips are down...

[MUSIC NO. 14 "WHEN THE CHIPS ARE DOWN INTRO"]

*(**HADES** gives **EURYDICE** two coins. "Rattlesnake" sound.)*

HERMES.

Songbird versus rattlesnake...

FATES.

Mmm...

EURYDICE.

What is it?

HERMES .

Eurydice was a hungry young girl...

FATES.
Mmm...

HADES.
Your ticket

HERMES.
And Hades gave her a choice to make

FATES.
Mmm-mmm-mmm

HERMES.
A ticket to the underworld

[MUSIC NO. 15 "WHEN THE CHIPS ARE DOWN"]

FATES.
Life ain't easy, life ain't fair
A girl's gotta fight for a rightful share
What you gonna do when the chips are down?
Now that the chips are down
What you gonna do when the chips are down?
Now that the chips are down

Help yourself, to hell with the rest
Even the one who loves you best
What you gonna do when the chips are down?
Now that the chips are down
What you gonna do when the chips are down?
Now that the chips are down

EURYDICE.
Oh, my aching heart...

FATES.
What you gonna do when the chips are down?
Now that the chips are down

FATES.

Take if you can, give if you must
Ain't nobody but yourself to trust
What you gonna do when the chips are down?
Now that the chips are down
What you gonna do when the chips are down?
Now that the chips are down

Aim for the heart, shoot to kill
If you don't do it then the other one will
What you gonna do when the chips are down?
Now that the chips are down
What you gonna do when the chips are down?
Now that the chips are down

And the first shall be first
And the last shall be last
Cast your eyes to heaven
You get a knife in the back!
Nobody's righteous
Nobody's proud
Nobody's innocent
Now that the chips are down

Now that the, now that the
Now that the, now that the
Now that the chips are down!

[MUSIC NO. 16 "GONE, I'M GONE"]

EURYDICE. *(To herself and audience.)*

Orpheus, my heart is yours
Always was, and will be
It's my gut I can't ignore
Orpheus, I'm hungry
Oh, my heart it aches to stay

But the flesh will have its way
Oh, the way is dark and long
I'm already gone...

(**EURYDICE** *gives the coins to* **HERMES.**)

I'm gone

(**HERMES** *blows the train whistle.* **EURYDICE** *descends to the underworld.*)

FATES. *(To audience.)*
Go ahead and lay the blame
Talk of virtue, talk of sin
Wouldn't you have done the same?
In her shoes, in her skin
You can have your principles
When you've got a bellyful
But hunger has a way with you
There's no telling what you're gonna do
When the chips are down
Now that the chips are down
What you gonna do when the chips are down?
Now that the chips are down

[MUSIC NO. 17 "WAIT FOR ME INTRO"]

(**ORPHEUS** *reappears.*)

ORPHEUS.
Mr. Hermes?

HERMES.
Hey, the big artiste!
Ain't you working on your masterpiece?

ORPHEUS.
Where's Eurydice?

HERMES.

Brother, what do you care?
You'll find another muse somewhere

ORPHEUS.

Where is she?

HERMES.

Why you wanna know?

ORPHEUS.

Wherever she is is where I'll go

HERMES.

And what if I said she's down below?

ORPHEUS.

Down below?

HERMES.

Down below
Six feet under the ground below
She called your name before she went
But I guess you weren't listening

ORPHEUS.

No!

HERMES.

So
Just how far would you go for her?

ORPHEUS.

To the end of time
To the end of the earth

HERMES.

You got a ticket?

ORPHEUS.

No

HERMES.

Yeah, I didn't think so
'Course, there is another way, but –
Nah, I ain't supposed to say

ORPHEUS.

Another way?

HERMES.

Around the back
But that ain't easy walkin', jack
It ain't for the sensitive of soul
So do ya really wanna go?

ORPHEUS.

With all my heart

HERMES.

With all your heart?
Well, that's a start

[MUSIC NO. 18 "WAIT FOR ME"]

(**ORPHEUS** *begins his journey.*)

How to get to Hadestown
You'll have to take the long way down
Through the underground under cover of night
Laying low, staying out of sight
Ain't no compass, brother, ain't no map
Just a telephone wire and a railroad track
Keep on walking and don't look back
Till you get to the bottomland

ORPHEUS.

Wait for me, I'm coming
Wait, I'm coming with you
Wait for me, I'm coming too
I'm coming too

HERMES.

River Styx is high and wide
Cinderbricks and razorwire
Walls of iron and concrete
Hound dogs howlin' round the gate
Those dogs'll lay down and play dead
If you got the bones, if you got the bread
But if all you got is your own two legs
Just be glad you got 'em

ORPHEUS & COMPANY.

Wait for me, I'm coming
Wait, I'm coming with you
Wait for me, I'm coming too
I'm coming too

FATES. *(To* **ORPHEUS.***)*

Who are you?
Where do you think you're going?
Who are you?
Why are you all alone?
Who do you think you are?
Who are you to think that you could walk a road that no one ever walked before?

ORPHEUS.

La la la la la la la

COMPANY.

La la la la la la la

ORPHEUS.

La la la la la la la

ORPHEUS & COMPANY.

La la la la la la la...

(Magic. A crack in the wall. The way opens.)

HERMES.

You're on the lam, you're on the run
Don't give your name, you don't have one
And don't look no one in the eye
That town'll try to suck you dry
They'll suck your brain, they'll suck your breath
They'll pluck the heart right out your chest
They'll truss you up in your Sunday best
And stuff your mouth with cotton

ORPHEUS & COMPANY.

Wait for me, I'm coming
Wait, I'm coming with you
Wait for me, I'm coming too
I'm coming

COMPANY.

Wait

ORPHEUS.

I'm coming, wait for me

COMPANY.

Wait

ORPHEUS & COMPANY.

I hear the walls repeating

COMPANY.

Wait

ORPHEUS & COMPANY.

The falling of my feet and
It sounds like drumming

COMPANY.

Wait

ORPHEUS & COMPANY.

And I am not alone

COMPANY.
Wait

ORPHEUS & COMPANY.
I hear the rocks and stones

COMPANY.
Wait

ORPHEUS & COMPANY.
Echoing my song

ORPHEUS.
I'm coming

COMPANY.
Coming
Coming...

*(***ORPHEUS** *journeys into darkness.)*

[MUSIC NO. 19 "WHY WE BUILD THE WALL"]

(In the underworld.)

HADES.
Why do we build the wall?
My children, my children
Why do we build the wall?

COMPANY.
Why do we build the wall?
We build the wall to keep us free
That's why we build the wall
We build the wall to keep us free

HADES.
How does the wall keep us free?
My children, my children
How does the wall keep us free?

COMPANY.

How does the wall keep us free?
The wall keeps out the enemy
And we build the wall to keep us free
That's why we build the wall
We build the wall to keep us free

HADES.

Who do we call the enemy?
My children, my children?
Who do we call the enemy?

COMPANY.

Who do we call the enemy?
The enemy is poverty
And the wall keeps out the enemy
And we build the wall to keep us free
That's why we build the wall
We build the wall to keep us free

HADES.

Because we have and they have not
My children, my children
Because they want what we have got

COMPANY.

Because we have and they have not
Because they want what we have got
The enemy is poverty
And the wall keeps out the enemy
And we build the wall to keep us free
That's why we build the wall
We build the wall to keep us free

(**EURYDICE** *arrives in the underworld.)*

HADES.

What do we have that they should want?
My children, my children
What do we have that they should want?

COMPANY.

What do we have that they should want?
We have a wall to work upon
We have work and they have none

HADES.

And our work is never done
My children, my children
And the war is never won

HADES & COMPANY.

The enemy is poverty
And the wall keeps out the enemy
And we build the wall to keep us free
That's why we build the wall
We build the wall to keep us free

COMPANY.

We build the wall to keep us free

[MUSIC NO. 20 "WHY WE BUILD THE WALL OUTRO"]

HERMES.

Then Hades told Eurydice:

HADES.

There are papers to be signed
Step into my office

HERMES.

And he closed the door behind
Now a lot can happen behind closed doors
That's for sure, brother, that's a fact

But a lot can happen on the factory floor
When the foreman turns his back

(**EURYDICE** *disappears behind closed doors with* **HADES**.)

PERSEPHONE. *(To audience.)*
Anybody want a drink?

ACT TWO

[MUSIC NO. 21 "OUR LADY OF THE UNDERGROUND" (AN ENTR'ACTE)]

PERSEPHONE. *(To* **BAND** *and audience.)*
Step into *my* office...!
I don't know about you, boys...

But if you're like me then hanging around
This old manhole is bringing you down
Six feet under getting under your skin
Cabin fever is a-setting in
You're stir-crazy! Stuck in a rut!
You could use a little pick-me-up
I can give you what it is you crave
A little something from the good old days
Hey, I got the wind right here in a jar
I got the rain on tap at the bar
I got sunshine up on the shelf
Allow me to introduce myself

Brother, what's my name? My name is

HERMES (& BAND).
Our Lady of the Underground!

PERSEPHONE.
Brother what's my name?

HERMES (& BAND).
Our Lady of Ways!
Our Lady of Means!

PERSEPHONE.

Brother, what's my name? My name is

HERMES (& BAND).

Our Lady of the Upside Down!

PERSEPHONE.

Wanna know my name? I'll tell you my name:
Persephone!

Come here, brother, let me guess
It's the little things you miss
Spring flowers, autumn leaves
Ask me, brother, and you shall receive
Or maybe these just ain't enough
Maybe you're looking for some stronger stuff
I got a sight for the sorest eye
When was the last time you saw the sky?

Wipe away your tears, brother
Brother I know how you feel
I can see you're blinded
By the sadness of it all
Look a little closer and
Everything will be revealed
Look a little closer...
There's a crack in the wall!

(Trombone solo. **PERSEPHONE** *introduces* **BAND** *members.* **BAND** *members acknowledge audience.)*

Ladies and gentlemen, *[Trombonist]* on the trombone!
[Cellist] on the cello! *[Violinist]* on the violin!
[Drummer] on the drums! *[Bassist]* on the bass!
[Guitarist] on the guitar! And *[Pianist]* on the keys!

You want stars? I got a skyful

Put a quarter in the slot, you'll get an eyeful
You want the moon? Yeah, I got her too
She's right here waiting in my pay-per-view

How long's it been?
A little moonshine ain't no sin
Tell my husband to take his time
What the boss don't know, the boss won't mind...

[MUSIC NO. 22 "WAY DOWN HADESTOWN REPRISE"]

*(***FATES*** pull a steam whistle. On the factory floor,* **WORKERS** *work.* **EURYDICE** *reappears from behind closed doors.)*

FATES.
The deal is signed?

EURYDICE.
Yes

FATES.
'Bout time
Get on the line

EURYDICE.
I did what I had to do

FATES.
That's what they did, too

*(***EURYDICE*** joins* **WORKERS** *on the factory floor.)*

HERMES.
Now in Hadestown there was a lotta souls

WORKERS.
Oh, keep your head, keep your head

HERMES.
Working on a wall with all their might

WORKERS.
Huh! Kkh! Oh you gotta keep your head

HERMES.
Ya see, they kept their heads down low

WORKERS.
Huh! Kkh! If you wanna keep your head

HERMES.
You couldn't quite see their faces right...
But you could hear them singing

WORKERS.
Oh, keep your head, keep your head

HERMES.
Swinging their hammers in the cold hard ground
You could hear the sound of the pickaxe ringing

WORKERS.
Huh! Kkh! If you wanna keep your

HERMES.
And they called it

HERMES & WORKERS.
"Freedom"

EURYDICE. *(To* **WORKERS.***)*
I'm Eurydice
(To **FATES.***)* Doesn't anybody hear me?

FATES.
They can hear
But they don't care
No one has a name down here

Mister Hades set you free
To work yourself into the ground
Free to spend eternity
In the factory
And the warehouse
Where the whistles scream
And the foremen shout
And you're punchin' in
And punchin' in
And punchin' in
And you can't punch out

And you're way down Hadestown
Way down Hadestown
Way down Hadestown
Way down under the ground

WORKERS.

Oh, keep your head, keep your head
Low, oh you gotta keep your head
Low, if you wanna keep your head
Oh, keep your head low

EURYDICE.

Why won't anybody look at me?

FATES.

They can look
But they don't see
You see?
It's easier that way
Your eyes will look like that someday

Down in the river of oblivion
You kissed your little life goodbye
And Hades laid his hands on ya

FATES.

And gave you everlasting life
And everlasting overtime
In the mine
In the mill
In the machinery
Your place on the assembly line
Replaces all your memories

Way down Hadestown
Way down Hadestown
Way down Hadestown
Way down under the ground

WORKERS.

Oh, keep your head, keep your head
Low, oh you gotta keep your head
Low, if you wanna keep your head
Oh, keep your head low

EURYDICE.

What do you mean I'll look like that?

FATES.

That's what it looks like to forget

EURYDICE.

Forget what?

FATES.

Who you are
And everything that came before

EURYDICE.

I have to go

FATES.

Go where?

EURYDICE.
Go back

FATES.
Oh – and where is that?

(**EURYDICE** *can't remember.*)

So – what was your name again?
You've already forgotten...

HERMES.
Ya see, it's like I said before
A lot can happen behind closed doors
Eurydice was a hungry young girl
But she wasn't hungry anymore
What she was instead, was dead
Dead to the world anyway
Ya see, she went behind those doors
And signed her life away

FATES.
Saw that wheel up in the sky
Heard the big bell tolling
A lot of souls have gotta die
To keep the rust belt rolling
A lot of spirits gotta break
To make the underworld go round
Way down Hadestown

FATES, WORKERS & HERMES.
Way down under the ground

[MUSIC NO. 23 "FLOWERS"]

EURYDICE. *(To herself and audience.)*
What I wanted was to fall asleep
Close my eyes and disappear

EURYDICE.

Like a petal on a stream
A feather on the air
Lily white and poppy red
I trembled when he laid me out
You won't feel a thing, he said
When you go down
Nothing gonna wake you now

Dreams are sweet until they're not
Men are kind until they aren't
Flowers bloom until they rot
And fall apart
Is anybody listening?
I open my mouth and nothing comes out
Nothing
Nothing gonna wake me now

Flowers, I remember fields
Of flowers, soft beneath my heels
Walking in the sun
I remember someone
Someone by my side
Turned his face to mine
And then I turned away
Into the shade

You, the one I left behind
If you ever walk this way
Come and find me
Lying in the bed I made

[MUSIC NO. 24 "COME HOME WITH ME REPRISE"]

*(**ORPHEUS** arrives in the underworld.)*

ORPHEUS.
Come home with me!

EURYDICE.
It's you!

ORPHEUS.
It's me

EURYDICE.
Orpheus

ORPHEUS.
Eurydice

EURYDICE.
I called your name before –

ORPHEUS.
I know

EURYDICE.
You heard?

ORPHEUS.
No – Mister Hermes told me so
Whatever happened, I'm to blame

EURYDICE.
No –

ORPHEUS.
You called my name

EURYDICE.
You came
But how'd you get here? On the train?

ORPHEUS.
No, I walked! A long way...

EURYDICE.
And how'd you get beyond the wall?

ORPHEUS.

I sang a song so beautiful
The stones wept and they let me in
And I can sing us home again

EURYDICE.

No, you can't

ORPHEUS.

Yes, I can

EURYDICE.

No – you don't understand

[MUSIC NO. 25 "PAPERS INTRO" / MUSIC NO. 26 "PAPERS INSTRUMENTAL"]

*(**HADES** appears.)*

HADES.

Young man!
I don't think we've met before
You're not from around here, son
I don't know who the hell you are
But I can tell you don't belong
These are working people, son
Law-abiding citizens
Go back to where you came from
You're on the wrong side of the fence

PERSEPHONE.

Hades, I know this boy

HADES.

One of the unemployed

PERSEPHONE.

His *name* is Orpheus

HADES.
You stay out of this

HERMES.
Orpheus was a poor boy...

HADES.
Did ya hear me, son?

HERMES.
You might say he was naïve

HADES.
You better run!

HERMES.
But this poor boy raised up his voice
With his heart out on his sleeve

EURYDICE.
No!
Orpheus, you should go

ORPHEUS.
I'm not going back alone
I came to take her home

HADES.
Who the hell you think you are?
Who the hell you think you're talking to?
She couldn't go anywhere
Even if she wanted to
You're not from around here, son
If you were, then you would know
That everything and everyone
In Hadestown, I own!

But I
Only buy

HADES.
What others choose to sell
Oh
You didn't know?
She signed the deal herself
And now she –

ORPHEUS.
It isn't true

HADES.
Belongs to me

ORPHEUS.
It isn't true
What he said
Eurydice –

EURYDICE.
– I did
I do

HADES.
As for you...
Everybody gather round!
Everybody look and see!
What becomes of trespassers
With no respect for property!

*(***HADES** *gestures to* **WORKERS. WORKERS** *chase, surround, and beat* **ORPHEUS. HADES** *disappears behind closed doors.* **WORKERS** *turn away.)*

[MUSIC NO. 27 "NOTHING CHANGES"]

FATES. *(Surrounding* **ORPHEUS.***)*
Why the struggle, why the strain?
Why make trouble, why make scenes?

Why go against the grain?
Why swim upstream?
It ain't, it ain't, it ain't no use
You're bound, you're bound, you're bound to lose
What's done, what's done, what's done is done
That's the way the river runs
So why get wet? Why break a sweat?
Why waste your precious breath?
Why beat your handsome brow?
Nothing changes
Nothing changes
Nothing changes anyhow

[MUSIC NO. 28 "IF IT'S TRUE"]

(**WORKERS** *return to the factory floor.* **PERSEPHONE** *witnesses.)*

ORPHEUS.

If it's true what they say
If there's nothing to be done
If it's true that it's too late
And the girl I love is gone
If it's true what they say
Is this how the world is?
To be beaten and betrayed
And then be told that nothing changes
It'll always be like this

If it's true what they say
I'll be on my way

WORKERS.

Huh!

HERMES.

And the boy turned to go

WORKERS.
Huh!

HERMES.
Cos he thought no one could hear

WORKERS.
Huh!

HERMES.
But everybody knows
That walls have ears

WORKERS.
Huh!

HERMES.
And the workers heard him

WORKERS.
Kkh!
If it's true what they say
Huh!

HERMES.
With their hammers swingin'

WORKERS.
Kkh!
What's the purpose of a man?
Huh!

HERMES.
And they quit their workin'

WORKERS.
Kkh!
Just to turn his eyes away?
Huh!

HERMES.
When they heard him singin'

WORKERS.
Kkh!
Just to throw up both his hands?

HERMES.
No hammers swingin'

WORKERS.
What's the use of his backbone?

HERMES.
No pickaxe ring

WORKERS.
If he never stands upright

HERMES.
And they stood and listened

WORKERS.
If he turns his back on everyone

HERMES.
To the poor boy sing

WORKERS.
That he could have stood beside

ORPHEUS.
If it's true what they say
I'll be on my way
But who are they to say
What the truth is anyway?

Cos the ones who tell the lies
Are the solemnest to swear
And the ones who load the dice
Always say the toss is fair
And the ones who deal the cards
Are the ones who take the tricks
With their hands over their hearts

ORPHEUS.

While we play the game they fix
And the ones who speak the word
Always say it is the last
And no answer will be heard
To the question no one asks

So I'm asking if it's true
I'm asking me and you, and you, and you

I believe our answer matters
More than anything they say

WORKERS.

We stand and listen, listen

ORPHEUS.

I believe if there is still a will then there is still a way

WORKERS.

We're standin' with him

ORPHEUS.

I believe there is a way
I believe in us together
More than anyone alone

WORKERS.

We're standin' near him, near him

ORPHEUS.

I believe that with each other we are stronger than we know

WORKERS.

We hear him

ORPHEUS.

I believe we're stronger than they know
I believe that we are many
I believe that they are few

WORKERS.
We're standin', standin', standin'

ORPHEUS.
And it isn't for the few to tell the many what is true

WORKERS.
We understand him

ORPHEUS.
So I ask you
If it's true what they say
I'll be on my way
Tell me what to do
Is it true?
Is it true what they say?

[MUSIC NO. 29 "HOW LONG?"]

(Behind closed doors, **PERSEPHONE** *approaches* **HADES.***)*

PERSEPHONE.
What are you afraid of?

HADES.
What?

PERSEPHONE.
He's just a boy in love

HADES.
Have a drink, why don't you?

PERSEPHONE.
No
I've had enough
He loves that girl, Hades

HADES.
Well, that's too bad

PERSEPHONE.

He has the kind of love for her
That you and I once had

HADES.

The girl means nothing to me

PERSEPHONE.

I know
But she means everything to him

HADES.

So?

PERSEPHONE.

Let her go

Hades, my husband, Hades, my light
Hades, my darkness
If you had heard how he sang tonight
You'd pity poor Orpheus
All of his sorrow won't fit in his chest
It just burns like a fire in the pit of his chest
And his heart is a bird on a spit in his chest
How long, how long, how long?

HADES.

How long? Just as long as Hades is king
Nothing comes of wishing on stars
And nothing comes of the songs people sing
However sorry they are
Give them a piece and they'll take it all
Show them the crack and they'll tear down the wall
Lend them an ear and the kingdom will fall
The kingdom will fall for a song

PERSEPHONE.

What does he care for the logic of kings?
The laws of your underworld?

It is only for love that he sings!
He sings for the love of a girl

HADES.

You and your pity don't fit in my bed
You just burn like a fire in the pit of my bed
And I turn like a bird on a spit in my bed
How long, how long, how long?

PERSEPHONE.

How long? Just as long as I am your wife
It's true the earth must die
But then the earth comes back to life
And the sun must go on rising

PERSEPHONE & HADES.

And how does the sun even fit in the sky?
It just burns like a fire in the pit of the sky
And the earth is a bird on a spit in the sky
How long, how long, how long?

[MUSIC NO. 30 "CHANT REPRISE"]

(Split scene: **HADES** *and* **PERSEPHONE** *behind closed doors;* **HERMES, ORPHEUS, EURYDICE,** *and* **WORKERS** *on the factory floor.)*

HERMES.

Now everybody knows that walls have ears

ORPHEUS.

Is it true?

WORKERS.

Is it true?

HADES.

What's that noise?

HERMES.

And the walls had heard what the boy was sayin'

ORPHEUS.
Is it true?

WORKERS.
Is it true?

HADES.
It's the boy!

HERMES.
A million tons of stone and steel

ORPHEUS.
Is it true?

WORKERS.
Is it true?

HERMES.
Echoed his refrain...

*(***HADES** *and* **PERSEPHONE** *join* **WORKERS** *on the factory floor.* **HADES** *pulls the steam whistle.* **WORKERS** *work.)*

WORKERS.
Oh, keep your head, keep your head low (Kkh!)
Oh, you gotta keep your head low (Kkh!)
If you wanna keep your head (Huh! Kkh!)
Oh, you gotta (keep your head)

Why do we turn away when our brother is bleeding?
Oh, keep your head
Why do we build a wall and then call it freedom?
Oh, keep your head
If we're free, tell me why
I can't look in my brother's eye
Keep your head!

HADES. *(To* **ORPHEUS.***)*

Young man! Got to hand it to ya
Guess you don't scare easy, do ya?
Are you brave, or stupid, son?
Doesn't matter which one
Cos it seems your song made quite
A strong impression on my wife
But it takes more than singin' songs
To keep a woman in your arms
Take it from a man no longer young
If you want to hold a woman, son
Hang a chain around her throat
Made of many karat gold
Shackle her from wrist-to-wrist
With sterling silver bracelets
Fill her pockets full of stones
Precious ones, diamonds
Bind her with a golden band
Take it from an old man

ORPHEUS.

If I raised my voice

WORKERS.

If I raised, if I raised, if I raised my –
Keep your head low

EURYDICE.

If I raised my head

WORKERS.

If I raised, if I raised, if I raised my –
Keep your head low

EURYDICE.

Could I change my fate?

WORKERS.

Could I change? Could I change? Could I change my –
Keep your head low

ORPHEUS.

If I raised my voice could I

WORKERS.

Keep your head low

ORPHEUS & EURYDICE.

Could I change the way it is?

WORKERS.

Why do we turn away 'stead of standin' with him?
Oh, keep your head
Why are we digging our own graves for a livin'?
Oh, keep your head
If we're free, tell me why
We can't even stand upright
If we're free, tell me when
We can stand with our fellow man
Keep your head!

HADES.

Young man! I was young once too
Sang a song of love like you
Son, I too was left behind
Turned on one too many times
Now I sing a different song
One I can depend upon
A simple tune, a steady beat
The music of machinery
You hear that heavy metal sound?
The symphony of Hadestown
And in this symphony of mine
Are power chords and power lines

Young man! You can strum your lyre
I have strung the world in wire!
Young man! You can sing your ditty
I conduct the electric city!

I'll tell you what, young man
Since my wife is such a fan
And since I'm gonna count to three
And put you out of your misery

HADES & COMPANY.

One!

HADES.

Give me one more song
One more song before I send you

HADES & COMPANY.

Two!

HADES.

To the great beyond
Where nobody can hear you singing

HADES & COMPANY.

Three!

HADES.

Sing a song for me
Make me laugh, make me weep
Make the king feel young again...
Sing! For an old man

[MUSIC NO. 31 "EPIC III"]

(**ORPHEUS** *accompanies himself.*)

ORPHEUS.

King of shadows, king of shades
Hades was king of the underworld

HADES. *(Amused.)*
Oh, it's about me...

*(**ORPHEUS** pauses.)*

HERMES.
Go on...

ORPHEUS.
But he fell in love with a beautiful lady
Who walked up above in her mother's green field
He fell in love with Persephone
Who was gathering flowers in the light of the sun
And I know how it was because he was like me
A man in love with a woman

Singing la la la la la la la
La la la la la la la

HADES.
Where'd you get that melody?

ORPHEUS.
La la la la la la la

PERSEPHONE.
Let him finish, Hades

ORPHEUS.
La la la la la la

You didn't know how, and you didn't know why
But you knew that you wanted to take her home
You saw her alone there against the sky
It was like she was someone you'd always known
It was like you were holding the world when you held her
Like yours were the arms that the whole world was in
And there were no words for the way that you felt
So you opened your mouth and you started to sing
La la la la la la la...

COMPANY.
La la la la la la la

ORPHEUS.
La la la la la la la

ORPHEUS & COMPANY.
La la la la la la...

(Choral section. **ORPHEUS** *leads* **COMPANY.** **HADES** *is overwhelmed.)*

ORPHEUS.
And what has become of the heart of that man?
Now that the man is king
What has become of the heart of that man?
Now that he has everything
The more he has, the more he holds
The greater the weight of the world on his shoulders
See how he labors beneath that load
Afraid to look up, afraid to let go
So he keeps his head low, he keeps his back bending
He's grown so afraid that he'll lose what he owns
But what he doesn't know is that what he's defending
Is already gone

Where is the treasure inside of your chest?
Where is your pleasure? Where is your youth?
Where is the man with his arms outstretched
To the woman he loves with nothing to lose?
Singing la la la la la la la

HADES. *(Softly.)*
La la la la la la la

ORPHEUS.
La la la la la la la

HADES & PERSEPHONE.

La la la la la la la...

(Magic. The melody spontaneously produces a flower, surprising them both. **HADES** *gives it to* **PERSEPHONE.***)*

[MUSIC NO. 32 "EPIC III INSTRUMENTAL"]

HERMES.

Orpheus was a poor boy
But he had a gift to give
This poor boy brought the world
Back into tune, is what he did
And Hades and Persephone
They took each other's hands
And brother you know what *they* did?
They danced...

ORPHEUS.

La la la, la la
La la la la la la
La la la la la la...

*(***ORPHEUS** *sings.* **HADES** *and* **PERSEPHONE** *dance, then embrace.)*

[MUSIC NO. 33 "PROMISES"]

*(***HADES** *and* **PERSEPHONE** *hold their embrace.* **EURYDICE** *approaches* **ORPHEUS.***)*

EURYDICE.

Orpheus...

ORPHEUS.

Yes?

EURYDICE.

You finished it...

ORPHEUS.

Yes
Now what do I do?

EURYDICE.

You take me home with you
Let's go
Let's go right now

ORPHEUS.

Okay, let's go – how?

EURYDICE.

We'll walk – you know the way
We'll just go back the way you came

ORPHEUS.

It's a long road – it's a long walk
Back into the cold and dark
Are you sure you want to go?

EURYDICE.

Take me home

ORPHEUS.

I have no ring for your finger
I have no banquet table to lay
I have no bed of feathers
Whatever promises I made
I can't promise you fair sky above
Can't promise you kind road below
But I'll walk beside you love
Any way the wind blows

EURYDICE.

I don't need gold, don't need silver
Just bread when I'm hungry, fire when I'm cold
Don't need a ring for my finger

EURYDICE.
Just need a steady hand to hold
Don't promise me fair sky above
Don't promise me kind road below
Just walk beside me love
Any way the wind blows

ORPHEUS. *(Indicating* **HADES.***)*
What about him?

EURYDICE.
He'll let us go
Look at him – he can't say no

ORPHEUS. *(Indicating* **WORKERS.***)*
What about them?

EURYDICE.
We'll show the way
If we can do it, so can they

EURYDICE & ORPHEUS.
I don't know where this road will end
But I'll walk it with you hand in hand
I can't promise you fair sky above
Can't promise you kind road below
But I'll walk beside you love
Any way the wind blows

ORPHEUS.
And do you let me walk with you?

EURYDICE.
I do

ORPHEUS.
I do

ORPHEUS & EURYDICE.
I do

EURYDICE.
And keep on walking come what will?

ORPHEUS.
I will

EURYDICE.
I will

ORPHEUS, EURYDICE & WORKERS.
We will

[MUSIC NO. 34 "WORD TO THE WISE"]

(**ORPHEUS** *approaches* **HADES.**)

HERMES.
And so the poor boy asked the king

ORPHEUS.
Can we go?

HERMES.
And this is how he answered him

HADES.
I don't know

FATES. (*Surrounding* **HADES.**)
Gotta think quick
Gotta save face
Caught 'tween a rock and a hard place
What you gonna do?
What you gonna do?
What you gonna do?
What you gonna do now?

If you tell 'em no, oh, you're a heartless man
And you're gonna have a martyr on your hands
If you let 'em go, oh, you're a spineless king
And you're never gonna get 'em in line again

FATES.

Damned if you don't
Damned if you do
Whole damn-nation's watching you
What you gonna do?
What you gonna do?
What you gonna do?
What you gonna do now?

Here's a little tip
Word to the wise
Here's a little snippet of advice
Men are fools
Men are frail
Give them the rope and they'll hang themselves

[MUSIC NO. 35 "HIS KISS, THE RIOT"]

HADES. *(To himself and audience.)*

The devil take this Orpheus
And his belladonna kiss
Beautiful, poisonous
Lovely! Deadly!

Dangerous, this jack of hearts
With his kiss, the riot starts

All my children came here poor
Clamoring for bed and board
Now what do they clamor for?
Freedom! Freedom
Have I made myself their lord
Just to fall upon the sword
Of some pauper's minor chord
Who will lead them?

Who lays all the best-laid plans?
Who makes work for idle hands?

(*To* **HERMES.**) Only one thing to be done
Let them go, but let there be some
Term to be agreed upon
Some...condition
Orpheus, the undersigned
Shall not turn to look behind
She's out of sight!
And he's out of his mind

Every coward seems courageous
In the safety of the crowd
Bravery can be contagious
When the band is playing loud
Nothing makes a man so bold
As a woman's smile and a hand to hold
But all alone his blood runs thin
And doubt comes
Doubt comes in

[MUSIC NO. 36 "WAIT FOR ME REPRISE INTRO"]

ORPHEUS. (*To* **HERMES.**)
What is it?

HERMES.
Well, the good news is
He said that you can go

EURYDICE.
He did?

ORPHEUS & WORKERS.
He did?

HERMES.
He did...
There's bad news, though

EURYDICE.
What is it?

HERMES.
You can walk...
But it won't be like you planned

ORPHEUS.
What do you mean?

EURYDICE.
Why not?

HERMES.
Well, you won't be hand in hand
You won't be arm in arm
Side by side, and all of that
He said you have to walk in front
And she has to walk in back

ORPHEUS.
Why?

HERMES.
And if you turn around
To make sure she's coming too
Then she goes back to Hadestown
And ain't nothing you can do

EURYDICE.
But why?

HERMES.
Why build walls?
Make folks walk single file?
Divide and conquer's what it's called

ORPHEUS.
It's a trap?

HERMES.

It's a trial
Do you trust each other?
Do you trust yourselves?

ORPHEUS & EURYDICE.

We do

HERMES.

Well, listen brother
If you wanna walk outta hell
You're gonna have to prove it
Before gods and men
Can you do that?

ORPHEUS & EURYDICE.

We can

HERMES.

Alright…time to go

ORPHEUS.

Mister Hermes!

HERMES.

Yes?

ORPHEUS.

It's not a trick?

HERMES.

No –
It's a test

[MUSIC NO. 37 "WAIT FOR ME REPRISE"]

The meanest dog you'll ever meet
He ain't the hound dog in the street
He bares some teeth and tears some skin
But brother, that's the worst of him

HERMES.

The dog you really got to dread
Is the one that howls inside your head
It's him whose howling drives men mad
And a mind to its undoing

EURYDICE & ORPHEUS.

Wait for me, I'm coming
Wait, I'm coming with you
Wait for me, I'm coming too
I'm coming too

WORKERS.

Show the way so we can see
Show the way the world could be
If you can do it so can she
If she can do it so can we
Show the way the world could be
Show the way so we believe
We will follow where you lead
We will follow if you
Show the way

PERSEPHONE.

You think they'll make it?

HADES.

I don't know

WORKERS.

Show the way

PERSEPHONE.

Hades, you let them go

WORKERS.

Show the way

HADES.
I let them try

PERSEPHONE.
And how 'bout you and I?

WORKERS.
Show the way

PERSEPHONE.
Are we gonna try again?

WORKERS.
Show the way

HADES.
It's time for spring
We'll try again next fall

PERSEPHONE.
Wait for me

HADES.
I will

EURYDICE, PERSEPHONE, FATES & WORKERS.
Wait for me, I'm coming
Wait, I'm coming with you
Wait for me, I'm coming too
I'm coming too

FATES. *(To* **ORPHEUS.***)*
Who are you?
Who do you think you are?
Who are you?
Who are you to lead her?
Who are you to lead them?
Who are you to think that you can
Hold your head up higher than your fellow man?

HERMES.

You got a lonesome road to walk
And it ain't along the railroad track
And it ain't along the blacktop tar
You've walked a hundred times before
I'll tell you where the real road lies
Between your ears, behind your eyes
That is the path to paradise
Likewise the road to ruin

COMPANY.

Wait for me, I'm coming
Wait, I'm coming with you
Wait for me, I'm coming too

COMPANY. *(Except* **ORPHEUS.***)*

Wait for me, I'm coming
Wait, I'm coming with you
Wait for me, I'm coming too, I'm coming

WORKERS, HERMES & PERSEPHONE.

Show the way

EURYDICE.

I'm coming, wait for me

WORKERS, HERMES & PERSEPHONE.

Show the way

EURYDICE.

I hear the walls repeating

WORKERS, HERMES & PERSEPHONE.

Show the way

EURYDICE.

The falling of my feet and
It sounds like drumming

WORKERS, HERMES & PERSEPHONE.
Show the way

EURYDICE.
And we are not alone

WORKERS, HERMES & PERSEPHONE.
Show the way

EURYDICE.
I hear the rocks and stones

WORKERS, HERMES & PERSEPHONE.
Show the way

EURYDICE.
Echoing our song
I'm coming

WORKERS.
Coming, coming...

[MUSIC NO. 38 "DOUBT COMES IN"]

*(***ORPHEUS*** and ***EURYDICE*** journey into darkness, single file.)*

ORPHEUS.
La la la la la la la
La la la la la la...

FATES. *(Surrounding* **ORPHEUS.***)*
Doubt comes in
The wind is changing
Doubt comes in
How cold it's blowing
Doubt comes in
And meets a stranger
Walking on a road alone

FATES.

Where is she?
Where is she now?
Doubt comes in

ORPHEUS.

Who am I?
Where do I think I'm going?

FATES.

Doubt comes in

ORPHEUS.

Who am I?
Why am I all alone?

FATES.

Doubt comes in

ORPHEUS.

Who do I think I am?
Who am I to think that she would follow me into the cold and dark again?

FATES.

Where is she?
Where is she now?

EURYDICE.

Orpheus
Are you listening?

WORKERS.

Are you listening?

EURYDICE.

I am right here

WORKERS.

We are all right here

EURYDICE.

And I will be till the end

WORKERS.

Will be till the end

EURYDICE.

And the coldest night

WORKERS.

Coldest night

EURYDICE.

Of the coldest year

WORKERS.

Coldest year

EURYDICE & WORKERS.

Comes right before the spring

ORPHEUS.

La la la la la la la
La la la la la la...

Who am I?
Who am I against him?
Who am I?
Why would he let me win?
Why would he let her go?
Who am I to think that he wouldn't deceive me
Just to make me leave alone?

FATES.

Doubt comes in
The wind is changing

ORPHEUS.

Is this a trap that's being laid for me?

FATES.

Doubt comes in
How dark it's grown

ORPHEUS.

Is this a trick that's being played on me?

FATES.

Doubt comes in and meets a stranger

ORPHEUS.

I used to see the way the world could be

FATES.

Walking on a road alone

ORPHEUS.

But now the way it is is all I see, and

ORPHEUS & FATES.

Where is she?
Where is she now?

EURYDICE.

Orpheus
You are not alone

WORKERS.

You are not alone

EURYDICE.

I am right behind you

WORKERS.

We are all behind you

EURYDICE.

And I have been all along

WORKERS.

Have been all along

EURYDICE.
And the darkest hour

WORKERS.
Darkest hour

EURYDICE.
Of the darkest night

WORKERS.
Darkest night

EURYDICE.
Comes right before the –

(The aboveground world comes into view. **ORPHEUS** *pauses...then he turns.)*

ORPHEUS.
It's you

EURYDICE.
It's me
Orpheus

ORPHEUS.
Eurydice

*(***EURYDICE** *descends to the underworld.)*

[MUSIC NO. 39 "ROAD TO HELL REPRISE"]

HERMES.
Alright...
It's an old song
It's an old tale from way back when
It's an old song
And that is how it ends

That's how it goes
Don't ask why brother, don't ask how

HERMES.

He could have come so close
The song was written long ago
And that is how it goes

It's a sad song
It's a sad tale; it's a tragedy
It's a sad song
But we sing it anyway

Cos here's the thing
To know how it ends
And still begin
To sing it again
As if it might turn out this time
I learned that from a friend of mine

COMPANY.

Mmm...

(**COMPANY** *reassembles at the aboveground gathering place.)*

HERMES.

See, Orpheus was a poor boy

(**EURYDICE** *appears, with overcoat, backpack, and candle, as in the beginning.)*

EURYDICE. *(To* **COMPANY** *and audience.)*

Anybody got a match?

HERMES. *(Offering a match.)*

But he had a gift to give

EURYDICE. *(To* **HERMES.***)*

Give me that

(**EURYDICE** *lights her candle.)*

HERMES.

He could make you see how the world could be
In spite of the way that it is
Can you see it?

COMPANY.

Mmm...

HERMES.

Can you hear it?

COMPANY.

Mmm...

HERMES.

Can you feel it like a train?
Is it comin'?
Is it comin' this way?
On a sunny day there was a railroad car

COMPANY.

Mmm...

HERMES.

And a lady stepping off a train

COMPANY.

Mmm...

HERMES.

Everybody looked and everybody saw

COMPANY.

Mmm...

HERMES.

That spring had come again
With a love song

PERSEPHONE.

With a love song

WORKERS & FATES.
With a love song

HERMES.
With a tale of a love from long ago
It's a sad song

EURYDICE.
It's a sad song

PERSEPHONE.
It's a sad song

HERMES.
But we keep singing even so
It's an old song

PERSEPHONE & EURYDICE.
It's an old song

COMPANY.
It's an old song

HERMES.
It's an old tale from way back when
And we're gonna sing it again and again
We're gonna sing
We're gonna sing

COMPANY.
It's a love song

EURYDICE.
It's a love song

HERMES.
It's a love song

PERSEPHONE.
It's a love song

COMPANY.

It's a tale of love from long ago
It's a sad song

EURYDICE.

It's a sad song

HERMES & PERSEPHONE.

It's a sad song

HERMES.

But we keep singing even so
It's an old song

EURYDICE & PERSEPHONE.

It's an old song

HERMES.

It's an old, old, old tale from way back when
And we're gonna sing it

COMPANY.

Again and again

HERMES.

We're gonna sing it again

*(***ORPHEUS** *appears, as in the beginning.* **EURYDICE** *and* **ORPHEUS** *see each other, as if for the first time.)*

End of Play

(Curtain call.)

[MUSIC NO. 40 "WE RAISE OUR CUPS" (AN ENCORE)]

(Wine is poured and cups are passed around.)

PERSEPHONE.

Pour the wine and raise a cup
Drink up, brothers, you know how
And spill a drop for Orpheus
Wherever he is now

PERSEPHONE & EURYDICE.

Some birds sing when the sun shines bright
Our praise is not for them

PERSEPHONE.

But the ones who sing in the dead of night
We raise our cups to them

PERSEPHONE & EURYDICE.

Wherever he is wandering
Alone upon the earth
Let all our singing follow him

PERSEPHONE.

And bring him comfort

COMPANY.

Some flowers bloom

PERSEPHONE & EURYDICE.

Where the green grass grows

COMPANY.

Our praise is not for them

PERSEPHONE & EURYDICE.

But the ones who bloom in the bitter snow

COMPANY.

We raise our cups to them
We raise our cups and drink them up

PERSEPHONE.

We raise them high and drink them dry

COMPANY.

To Orpheus, and all of us

PERSEPHONE.

Goodnight, brothers, goodnight

*(***COMPANY** *raises cups and acknowledges audience, encouraging them to do the same.* **COMPANY** *drinks.)*

CPSIA information can be obtained
at www.ICGtesting.com
Printed in the USA
BVHW041317241221
624596BV00026B/2271